Oracle SQL*Plus
The Definitive Guide

Other Oracle resources from O'Reilly

Related titles

Mastering Oracle SQL

Optimizing Oracle
 Performance

Oracle SQL*Plus Pocket
 Reference

SQL Pocket Guide

SQL Tuning

Oracle Regular Expressions
 Pocket Reference

Oracle Essentials

Oracle in a Nutshell

Oracle SQL Tuning Pocket
 Reference

Oracle SQL*Loader: The
 Definitive Guide

SQL in a Nutshell

Learning Oracle PL/SQL

Oracle PL/SQL Programming

**Oracle Books
Resource Center**

oracle.oreilly.com is a complete catalog of O'Reilly's books on Oracle and related technologies, including sample chapters and code examples.

oreillynet.com is the essential portal for developers interested in open and emerging technologies, including new platforms, programming languages, and operating systems.

Conferences

O'Reilly brings diverse innovators together to nurture the ideas that spark revolutionary industries. We specialize in documenting the latest tools and systems, translating the innovator's knowledge into useful skills for those in the trenches. Visit *conferences.oreilly.com* for our upcoming events.

Safari Bookshelf (*safari.oreilly.com*) is the premier online reference library for programmers and IT professionals. Conduct searches across more than 1,000 books. Subscribers can zero in on answers to time-critical questions in a matter of seconds. Read the books on your Bookshelf from cover to cover or simply flip to the page you need. Try it today with a free trial.

SECOND EDITION

Oracle SQL*Plus

The Definitive Guide

Jonathan Gennick

O'REILLY®

Beijing · Cambridge · Farnham · Köln · Paris · Sebastopol · Taipei · Tokyo

Oracle SQL*Plus: The Definitive Guide, Second Edition
by Jonathan Gennick

Copyright © 2005, 1999 O'Reilly Media, Inc. All rights reserved.
Printed in the United States of America.

Published by O'Reilly Media, Inc., 1005 Gravenstein Highway North, Sebastopol, CA 95472.

O'Reilly books may be purchased for educational, business, or sales promotional use. Online editions are also available for most titles (*safari.oreilly.com*). For more information, contact our corporate/institutional sales department: (800) 998-9938 or *corporate@oreilly.com*.

Editor:	Deborah Russell
Production Editor:	Matt Hutchinson
Production Services:	GEX, Inc.
Cover Designer:	Edie Freedman
Interior Designer:	David Futato

Printing History:

March 1999:	First Edition.
November 2004:	Second Edition.

 This book uses RepKover,™ a durable and flexible lay-flat binding.

ISBN: 0-596-00746-9

[M]

*I dedicate this book to my wife Donna, who,
in spite of all my crazy dreams and ambitions,
continues to stand with me.*

Table of Contents

Preface

Every day, computer professionals the world over wake up, travel to the office, sit down in front of a computer, and begin another day working with the database called Oracle. Programmers write queries and store procedures. Database administrators monitor performance, make database changes, and perform other maintenance tasks. Operations people may need to back up or recover a database. Analysts may need to explore the structure of a database to answer the question, "What's out there?" Testers may work on developing and loading test data. A wide variety of people perform a wide variety of tasks, yet the vast majority of them are likely to have one thing in common: SQL*Plus.

SQL*Plus is the command-line interface to the Oracle database. It's a client-server application that allows you to enter and execute SQL statements and PL/SQL blocks. One of the most common uses for SQL*Plus is as an ad hoc query tool. You type in a SELECT statement, execute it, and see what results come back from the database. Programmers do this all the time when developing queries and when experimenting with Oracle's built-in functions. Database administrators sometimes issue queries against Oracle's data dictionary tables to see what objects are available in the database. SQL*Plus is also frequently used as a tool for loading stored code, such as a stored procedure, into the database.

One important capability of SQL*Plus is its ability to format and paginate query results. You can enter a SELECT statement, execute it, and have the results formatted so you can print them and produce a credible-looking report. SQL*Plus implements a full range of formatting commands allowing you to add page headers and footers to your reports. There are also commands that allow you to format the data displayed in the report. You can control column headings, number formats, and column widths.

Another important capability of SQL*Plus—and one you should take advantage of if you don't already—is its ability to run predefined SQL script files. A script file is analogous to a DOS BAT file, and is simply a text file that contains commands to execute. These commands may be SQL statements, PL/SQL code blocks, or

SQL*Plus commands. Scripts may be used to automate frequently performed tasks. One of the easiest things to do is to write a script to generate a report. You do this by placing all the formatting commands and the SELECT query for the report into the script file. Then whenever you want the report, you simply execute the script. In addition to producing printed reports, scripts can automate routine tasks such as creating a new user or displaying data on the screen. You might, for example, write a script to display constraint definitions for a table or perhaps to list the system privileges granted to one of your users.

A sometimes overlooked capability of SQL*Plus is its use as a data extraction tool. If you have been around Oracle for a while, you are no doubt familiar with SQL*Loader. SQL*Loader is Oracle's general-purpose data load utility. Using it, you can read data from a flat file and load it into one or more database tables. The strange thing is that Oracle does not have a corresponding SQL*Unloader utility. When people want to extract data from Oracle into a flat file, such as a comma-delimited file, they often get frustrated when looking for a utility to do the job. SQL*Plus, it turns out, is a viable choice for the task. It's a relatively simple matter to spool the results of a query to a file. It doesn't take much extra work to format that output so that it is comma- or tab-delimited.

Finally, SQL*Plus gives you a reliable way to propagate database structure changes when you need to make the same change to more than one database. If you have a table change that needs to be made on several similar databases, you can write a SQL*Plus script to do the job. This script can easily be executed against each database, saving you the trouble of making the same change several times over. This is a great convenience if you deal with clients in a variety of locations, because you can send the script out to each client for them to execute against their own databases.

To many people, SQL*Plus, with its command-line interface, must seem increasingly like an anachronism. Graphical user interfaces (GUIs) are prevalent everywhere, and often it seems as if computer users have forgotten how to do anything but point and click with a mouse. You might ask, then, "Why bother to learn SQL*Plus? Why bother with an ancient command-line utility?" These are fair questions.

I have come to lean heavily on SQL*Plus because it is always there, and it always works. Back when I used to work as a consultant, I frequently visited clients and worked with databases on a variety of platforms. One thing I could always count on, no matter where I went, was that SQL*Plus would be available. Not only was SQL*Plus available on the database administrator's PC, it was often available on user PCs as well. No matter which machine I used at a client site, I could almost always count on this venerable utility being available, and because I knew it well, I could immediately be productive.

Scripting and batch processing are two important reasons I use SQL*Plus these days. Following proper procedures is important, and SQL*Plus allows me, for example, to encapsulate the commands necessary to add a new database user into one script, so each time I create a new user, the creation process is done consistently.

Finally, one more reason I use SQL*Plus is speed. I type very fast and with reasonable accuracy. Wonderful as many of the modern GUI applications are, I can often perform a task more quickly using SQL*Plus. This is not always true, but it is true often enough, especially when you consider the time it takes to load and start a GUI interface such as Oracle Enterprise Manager versus the time it takes to load and start SQL*Plus.

Why I Wrote This Book

My motivation for writing this book stems from my early experiences learning about the Oracle database. Oracle's documentation tends to be narrowly focused, each manual discussing only those things strictly related to the product being written about, and the manual for SQL*Plus is no exception. Oracle's manual will tell you about SQL*Plus but only about SQL*Plus. There is little information on how to use SQL*Plus in conjunction with other Oracle products such as PL/SQL or SQL*Loader. There is also little information on using SQL*Plus to perform common tasks like viewing a constraint definition or extracting data.

I remember clearly the difficulties I had working with three manuals spread out in front of me: the SQL manual, the SQL*Plus manual, and the PL/SQL manual. I remember the frustration of frequently picking up the wrong manual because I didn't understand fully the relationship between these three products. Was DESCRIBE a SQL statement? How could I use a SQL*Plus variable in a PL/SQL script?

Even when I knew that something could be done with SQL*Plus, I frequently didn't find clear direction in the Oracle manuals. The first time I wrote a script to extract data to a file, I spent quite a bit of time flipping back and forth in the manual and experimenting with various commands before I finally got the results I wanted. Things became even more complicated when I began to write scripts and batch jobs with SQL*Plus. Suddenly I found myself wanting to branch, and even to loop, from a SQL*Plus script. SQL*Plus doesn't officially provide this functionality, but there are some tricks you can put to good use.

Finally, this is the book I want to give my clients and coworkers when they ask me how-to questions. Next time I'm asked how to get data out of Oracle and into a comma-delimited file, I'll just refer them to Chapter 9. When I'm asked about formatting a report, I'll refer them to Chapter 5, and when I'm asked how to write an IF statement in SQL*Plus, I'll refer them to Chapter 11. Each of these chapters presents a solution to its respective problem and leads you step by step through the process of implementing that solution.

Objectives of This Book

The single, driving objective of this book is to help you squeeze every last possible ounce of productivity and usefulness out of SQL*Plus. If you read this book cover to cover, at the end you will have learned the following:

- How to methodically perform common tasks such as generating a report and extracting data to a flat file
- How to enter and edit commands in the SQL*Plus environment, with and without an external editor
- How to write simple scripts using SQL*Plus
- How to use the basic building blocks of SQL to write queries and other statements
- How to prompt for user input and use that input in SQL statements, PL/SQL blocks, and SQL*Plus commands
- How to stretch the limits of what you can do in a SQL*Plus script by implementing pseudo-IF statements and by using one script to generate another
- How the Product User Profile, an Oracle security feature, works with SQL*Plus
- How to customize your SQL*Plus environment
- How you can use SQL*Plus to view the definitions for database objects such as views, tables, constraints, triggers, indexes, and synonyms
- How to use SQL*Plus as a tuning aid to maximize the performance of your SQL queries

An additional objective of this book is to serve as a ready reference you can pull out when faced with a common task. If you need to generate a report, open to the chapter on reports and follow the steps. Need to extract data? Open to the chapter on data extraction, and again follow the steps. Every effort has been made to organize the information topically, so all the information you need to accomplish a specific task is in one chapter. Where feasible, step-by-step instructions are provided so you don't need to wade through a lot of theory to accomplish something.

What's New in the Second Edition?

The first edition of this book was published in March 1999. At the time, I didn't think that SQL*Plus would ever change much. After all, it was a mature product, and certainly, I thought, Oracle would focus its creative energies elsewhere. I was wrong. It was that same year, at OracleWorld 1999, I believe, when I first learned about the new SET MARKUP command and the impending addition of HTML output to the SQL*Plus repertoire. And as if that wasn't surprise enough, those HTML capabilities were the prelude to a full-blown, three-tier, browser-based version of my favorite and most used command-line utility that we now know as *i*SQL*Plus. So, the first thing I did when revising this book was to add coverage for these and other new developments that have taken place over the years:

- Following the chapter on interacting with command-line SQL*Plus, you'll find the new Chapter 3 covering the use of the new, browser-based iSQL*Plus.

- It turns out that you can use the HTML capabilities represented by SET MARKUP to generate some impressive-looking web pages, and thus SQL*Plus is one tool that you can use to develop database-backed web reports. Chapter 6 shows you how.

One of the strengths of this book is that it uses SQL*Plus as an excuse to range over a wide swath of Oracle functionality, perhaps making the book a reasonably good introduction to Oracle as opposed to just SQL*Plus. For example, Chapter 9, after showing you how to extract data, goes on to introduce you to the equally venerable SQL*Loader utility. Some of the Oracle functionality that I cover has been updated and enhanced, leading me to likewise update this book's coverage:

- To Chapter 9, I've added an introduction to the external table feature introduced in Oracle9i Database. External tables provide you with SELECT statement access to external data, greatly increasing your options for transforming such data during a load.

- Chapter 12, which covers the use of EXPLAIN PLAN to show execution plans for SQL statements, has been updated to reflect all the hints supported by Oracle Database 10g. This chapter also shows the use of the new DBMS_XPLAN package introduced in Oracle9i Database Release 2. That package makes it easier than ever before to generate a well-formatted display of an execution plan.

Finally, I've been privileged to receive many reader comments and suggestions over the years that have led to many improvements and changes throughout the book. These range from the minor (but oh so useful!) information, such as K. Vainstein's suggestion in Chapter 10 for using PROMPT to remind users of command-line arguments, to the addition of an entirely new chapter, consisting of a lightning tutorial on SQL.

I'm pleased with the way this second edition has turned out, and I hope you will be too. I've tried to keep all the good from the first edition while adding new content in response to reader suggestions and Oracle's product enhancements. While doing all that work, I've had two of the pickiest and most careful Oracle people that I know, Tom Kyte and Gregor Theis, looking over my shoulder and pointing out mistakes, suggesting ways that I could say things better and more clearly, and even offering up for inclusion a few useful techniques that I hadn't thought of. You hold the result in your hands, and all of us who have been involved hope you are well satisfied with the value between the two covers.

Which Platform and Version?

SQL*Plus changes frequently. Each new version brings with it new commands, and new options to use with old commands. Most of the examples in this book use SQL*Plus 10.1. However, you should be able to apply the information in this book to any reasonably current version of the product. If you have any doubts about whether or not a command will work with the specific version of SQL*Plus you are using, check the *SQL*Plus User's Guide and Reference* manual for that version.

Structure of This Book

This book is divided into fourteen chapters and two appendixes. Many chapters are task-oriented and show you how you can use SQL*Plus to perform common tasks such as printing a report, or extracting data to a file. The appendixes contain reference material, such as a list of all SQL*Plus commands.

Chapter 1, *Introduction to SQL*Plus*, goes into more detail about what SQL*Plus really is and why you should master it. It gives you a taste of the many different tasks SQL*Plus can be used for. A short history of SQL*Plus is included, as well as a description of the database used for many of the examples in this book, particularly the reporting examples.

Chapter 2, *Command-Line SQL*Plus*, shows you how to start command-line SQL*Plus, and how to enter, execute, and edit commands. This is basic information you need to know.

Chapter 3, *Browser-Based SQL*Plus*, is all new, and shows you the basics of interacting with *i*SQL*Plus, a three-tier application you access through any standard web browser. Now you can access SQL*Plus from anywhere, without having to first install Oracle software on your client.

Chapter 4, *A Lightning SQL Tutorial*, is another new chapter, and one that you'll want to read if SQL is new to you. It provides a swift and fast-paced introduction to the basic SQL statements used in retrieving, modifying, and deleting data in a database. Once you've been introduced to the core statements, the chapter goes on to cover key points about transactions, walks you through the treacherous territory of the null value (which isn't a value at all), and explains common operations such as table joins and union queries.

Chapter 5, *Generating Reports with SQL*Plus*, introduces the reporting features of SQL*Plus, and presents a step-by-step method for creating a report that has worked well for me.

Chapter 6, *Creating HTML Reports*, is an exciting new chapter, or at least it was for me to write. This chapter shows some of the incredible things you can do using SET MARKUP to invoke SQL*Plus's ability to generate HTML output. As I researched and wrote this chapter, I was pleasantly surprised at the great-looking web reports that I could produce using SQL*Plus. It was great fun watching my old friend SQL*Plus generate such good-looking HTML.

Chapter 7, *Advanced Reports*, picks up where Chapter 5 leaves off, and shows you how to use the more advanced reporting features of SQL*Plus to generate totals and subtotals, generate grand totals, place the date and other values into page headers, format object columns, and produce summary reports that show only totals, subtotals, and the like, but no detail. You'll see an interesting way in which you can use SQL's UNION operator to combine the results from several queries into one report.

Chapter 8, *Writing SQL*Plus Scripts*, explains the basic scripting capabilities of SQL*Plus. Primarily, this chapter shows how SQL*Plus substitution variables work, and how you can use them to your advantage. In addition, it covers the subject of getting input from a user, and shows you how to control the output the user sees as the script is executed.

Chapter 9, *Extracting and Loading Data*, shows how you can use SQL*Plus to extract data from an Oracle database and place it into a text file suitable for loading into another program such as a spreadsheet. This text file may be delimited—by commas, for example—or may consist of fixed-width columns. You'll also learn how to use SQL*Loader to reload the data. The chapter ends with an example showing the use of the relatively new external table feature introduced in Oracle9i Database.

Chapter 10, *Exploring Your Database*, shows how you can query Oracle's data dictionary tables to see the structure of commonly used database objects, such as tables and indexes.

Chapter 11, *Advanced Scripting*, builds on Chapter 8, but covers some advanced, and sometimes unusual, scripting techniques. This chapter introduces bind variables, and explains how they differ from user variables. This chapter also shows some creative techniques you can use to add some limited branching, and even some looping, to your SQL*Plus scripts.

Chapter 12, *Tuning and Timing*, presents the SQL*Plus features that support the tuning of SQL statements. Also covered in this chapter is Oracle's EXPLAIN PLAN statement, which gives you a look at the execution strategy that the Oracle optimizer will use for any given SQL statement.

Chapter 13, *The Product User Profile*, introduces a security feature that a database administrator can use to limit what a user can do with SQL*Plus. The product user profile allows you to turn off specific SQL statements and SQL*Plus commands for one user or a group of users. It can be used to limit a user's access to certain roles while connected via SQL*Plus.

Chapter 14, *Customizing Your SQL*Plus Environment*, shows a number of ways in which you may customize your SQL*Plus environment. The site and user profiles are explained, as well as several environment settings that affect SQL*Plus's behavior.

Appendix A, *SQL*Plus Command Reference*, contains syntax diagrams for all SQL*Plus commands.

Appendix B, *SQL*Plus Format Elements*, describes the various format elements that may be used to build up format strings to be used with commands, such as COLUMN and ACCEPT, that format output or accept user input.

Obtaining the Scripts and Sample Data

Many examples from the book, as well as SQL*Plus scripts to load the data used for the examples, can be downloaded from O'Reilly's web site at *http://www.oreilly.com/catalog/orsqlplus2*.

To load the data, download the file named *SQLPlusData.zip*, unzip the files, and follow the instructions provided in Chapter 1.

What About Those Names?

To add interest to the book and because I'm half Ukrainian, I've used the names of notable Ukrainian literary and historical figures for the employee names in my example data. Thanks to Professor Myron Hlynka, University of Windsor, Windsor, Canada for his kindness in providing the following, very brief biographical sketches of the people whose names I used:

Marusia Bohuslavka
> A legendary Ukrainian heroine of the 16th or 17th century. Like Roxolana Lisovsky (see later in this section), Marusia was captured by the Turks and added to the harem of a Turkish lord. A famous Kozak duma (epic poem) of the period tells the story of how Marusia rises to such a level that her Turkish master leaves her with the keys to his castle (and dungeon). She uses the opportunity to free a group of Ukrainian kozaks who had been in captivity there for 30 years. Strangely, she does not flee with them but remains with her harem, as this has become the only life she is now comfortable with. Marusia symbolizes those who leave Ukraine but still have a strong connection to the land of their ancestry.

Pavlo Chubynsky (1839–1884)
> Born in Boryspil, Ukraine. He was a geographer and ethnographer who collected information on folk customs and folk music in Ukraine. He wrote a book of poetry entitled *Sopilka* ("Ukrainian wooden flute"). He is best known for writing the lyrics to the current Ukrainian national anthem, "Shche ne vmerla Ukraina" ("Ukraine is Not Yet Dead"). This strange negative title reflects the fact

that Ukraine has often been under foreign rule; in Chubynsky's time, Ukraine was divided among Russia, Austria, and Romania.

Marusia Churai (1625–1650)

A singer and composer of Ukrainian songs. A historical novel in verse, *Marusia Churai,* by Lina Kostenko (1979), tells the story of Marusia who died during the Ukrainian struggle for independence from Polish rule. Among the songs she composed is "Oy ne khody, Hrytsiu" ("Don't go to the party, Hrytz"). This song (with its story about a poisoning by a betrayed lover) was turned into a novel *V Nedilyu rano zillya kopala* ("On Sunday morning, she gathered herbs") by Olha Kobylianska, 1909. Further, the song had completely different English lyrics written by Jack Lawrence (who learned the music from his Ukrainian born mother). The English language version of the song was "Yes, My Darling Daughter." Singer Dinah Shore sold over a million copies of this song in 1940.

Mykhailo Hrushevsky (1866–1934)

A scholar and politician, he was arrested by the Russian government in 1914 for his outspoken pro-Ukrainian positions. He was released in 1917. In 1918, he became President of the short-lived Ukrainian National Republic. In 1919, he left Ukraine, but returned in 1924 with the hope that the new Soviet government would allow more Ukrainian autonomy. However, in 1929, the Soviet authorities limited his work and, in 1929, he was exiled from Ukraine to Moscow. He died in 1934, one year after Stalin's famine genocide in Ukraine. Hrushevsky's 10-volume *History of Ukraine* is the standard on which all other major Ukrainian histories are based. An abridged English language version was published in the United States in 1941.

Hryhory Kytasty (1907–1984)

Born in the Poltava province of Ukraine. Kytasty was a performer on the bandura, a conductor, and a composer. (The bandura is the multistringed national instrument of Ukraine.) In 1935, Kytasty became the concert master of the Ukrainian State Bandurist Capella, and in 1941, he was drafted into the Red Army. Captured by the Nazis, he escaped to form and direct the Shevchenko Ukrainian Bandurist Capella in Kyiv. This group was captured and interned by the Nazis. In 1949, after World War II, having escaped from the Communists, Kytasty and many of the members of the group settled in Detroit and formed the Ukrainian Bandurist Chorus, with Kytasty as conductor. This marvelous choir and bandura ensemble continues to amaze audiences across North America and Europe, long after the death of its founder.

Mykola Leontovych (1877–1921)

A Ukrainian composer, arranger and conductor. In 1918, he moved to Kyiv where his arrangements caught the attention of Oleksander Koshetz, who directed the Ukrainian National Choir. One of the works that Koshetz's choir performed on its world tour was Leontovych's arrangement of a Ukrainian New Year's carol called "Shchedryk." Peter Wilhousky, an American, heard the choir and obtained a copy of the score. He wrote a new set of English lyrics and titled the piece "Carol of the Bells." Under this name, the song has become one of the most popular Christmas carols in the world. "Hark, how the bells, sweet silver bells...."

Roxolana Lisovsky (1505–1558)

A Ukrainian girl captured by Tatars. She was purchased as a slave and added to the harem of Sultan Suleyman (the Magnificent) of the Ottoman Empire (Turkey), 1494–1566, who ruled as Sultan from 1520. This was at the height of the power of the Ottoman empire. Roxolana persuaded the Sultan to marry her and she acquired great power. Her Turkish name was Hurrem. One comment on her influence was "The slave girl enslaved Suleyman." One of the sons of Suleyman and Roxolana was Selim II, who became the next Sultan (one of the worst). Their only daughter, Mihrimah, was born in 1522. She became one of the most powerful princesses in the history of the Ottoman empire. Roxolana is the subject of a 1991 opera by composer Denys Sichynsky.

Ivan Mazepa (more often spelled Mazeppa) (1638–1709)

The hetman (chief) of the Ukrainian kozaks from 1687 until his death. In his youth, he served as a page of Jan Casimir in Poland. A famous legend tells the story of how Mazepa had an affair with a Polish noblewoman and how her husband got revenge by tying Mazepa to a wild Ukrainian horse that was sent into the steppes of Ukraine. Mazepa was supposed to perish but he was rescued by Ukrainian kozaks and eventually became their leader. This legend was the subject of a poem by Byron and a symphonic poem by Liszt. Mazepa was the subject of a book by Pushkin and an opera by Tchaikovsky. In 1709, when the Ukraine was under Russian rule, Mazepa joined forces with Charles XII of Sweden to secure Ukraine's independence. At the famous Battle of Poltava, Tsar Peter I defeated Charles and Mazepa, leaving much of the Ukraine under Russian control for most of the next 300 years.

Taras Shevchenko (1814–1861)

Born a serf in central Ukraine. In 1830, his owner, Engelhardt, moved with his serfs to St. Petersburg, Russia. There Shevchenko's talent as an artist was discovered and in 1838, generous artists and writers raised enough money to purchase his freedom. In 1840, Shevchenko's first collection of poetry, *The Kobzar*, was published in the Ukrainian language. This work was immensely successful among the Ukrainian people, who had not been able to boast of a literary figure of his stature. His poetry encompassed many different styles: historical epics, lyrical poetry, philosophical musings, and political commentary. Speaking of the many nationalities held forcibly in the Russian empire, he wrote, "Each, in his own language, holds his tongue." Shevchenko's political poetry got him in trouble with the tsarist government. As a result, he was arrested in 1847 and did not see Ukraine again until 1859, two years before his death. His fame and importance to Ukrainian literature is so immense that even outside Ukraine there are major statues erected in his honor, in cities as diverse as St. Petersburg, Buenos Aires, Winnipeg, and Washington.

Igor Sikorsky (1889–1972)

Born in Kyiv, Ukraine at a time when Eastern Ukraine was part of Russia, and Western Ukraine was part of Austria, he began studies at the Kyiv Polytechnic Institute in 1907. He built his first (unsuccessful) helicopter in 1909. During and prior to World War I, Sikorsky designed and flew planes in Russia. He helped develop the world's first multiengine aircraft. After coming to the United States in 1919, he continued working on fixed wing aircrafts. Other people had developed helicopters prior to Sikorsky; however, none of their designs led to commercial development. In 1939, Sikorsky successfully designed and flew what was to be the world's first practical helicopter. The successful Sikorsky Aircraft Corporation in the United States stands as a legacy to his achievements. He was honored with a United States postage stamp in 1988 and a Ukrainian postage stamp in 1998.

Lesia Ukrainka (1871–1913)

The pseudonym of Ukrainian poetess Larysa Kosach. She is considered one of the three major early pillars of Ukrainian literature, along with Taras Shevchenko and Ivan Franko. Tuberculosis affected her most of her life, so she spent many years outside of Ukraine seeking medical aid. Her poetry often showed her yearning for Ukraine. Some of her lyric poetry appears in the collection *Na Krylakh Pisen'* ("On the Wings of Song"), 1892. Her most famous work was "Lisova Pisnya" ("Forest Song"), 1912.

Mykhailo Verbytsky (1815–1870)

Born in the Ukrainian region of Halychyna. He was a composer, conductor, and priest. His most famous composition is the music for the Ukrainian national anthem "Shche ne vmerla Ukraina" ("Ukraine is Not Yet Dead") with words by Chubynsky. He arranged church and choral music, and composed overtures, operetta music, and other musical works.

Pavlo Virsky (1905–1975)

A Ukrainian dancer and choreographer. In 1937, he helped found the State Dance Ensemble of Ukraine. From 1955 to 1975 he was the artistic director. The ensemble was renamed the Virsky Ukrainian National Dance Company in 1977, two years after Virsky's death. Since 1980, the artistic director has been Myroslav Vantukh. The company of 90 performers has toured the world many times. At the end of its first performance in New York City in 1958 (during the Cold War era), the company received a 25-minute standing ovation. The company has been called one of the ten best dance companies in the world. The concluding dance is usually the colorful, fiery, athletic Ukrainian Hopak.

Conventions Used in This Book

The following conventions are used in this book:

Italic
> Used for filenames, directory names, URLs, and occasional emphasis.

`Constant width`
> Used for code examples, and used in text for table names, view names, and other user-defined names of database objects.

`Constant width bold`
> Used in examples that show interaction between SQL*Plus and a user. Commands typed by the user are shown in bold, but output from SQL*Plus is shown in normal text.

`Constant width italic`
> In some code examples, and in many syntax diagrams, indicates an element (e.g., a filename) you supply.

UPPERCASE
> Generally indicates SQL and SQL*Plus keywords.

lowercase
> In code examples, generally indicates user-defined items such as variables, parameters, etc.

--
> In code examples, a double hyphen begins a single-line comment, which extends to the end of a line.

/* and */
> In code examples, these characters delimit a multiline comment, which can extend from one line to another.

.
> In code examples and related discussions, a dot qualifies a reference by separating an object name from a component name. In this book, dot notation is most often used in fully qualified column names, which you will see written as `table_name.column_name`. The dot separates the table name from the column name.

[ ]
> In syntax descriptions, square brackets enclose optional items.

{ }
> In syntax descriptions, curly brackets enclose a set of items from which you must choose only one.

|
> In syntax descriptions, a vertical bar separates the items enclosed in square or curly brackets, as in {VARCHAR2 | DATE | NUMBER}.

::=
> In syntax descriptions, indicates an expansion of a syntax element.

Indicates a tip, suggestion, or general note. For example, I'll tell you if you need to use a particular SQL*Plus version, or if an operation requires certain privileges.

 Indicates a warning or caution. For example, I'll tell you if SQL*Plus does not behave as you'd expect, or if a particular operation has a negative impact on performance.

Using Code Examples

This book is here to help you get your job done. In general, you may use the code in this book in your programs and documentation. You do not need to contact us for permission unless you're reproducing a significant portion of the code. For example, writing a program that uses several chunks of code from this book does not require permission. Selling or distributing a CD-ROM of examples from O'Reilly books *does* require permission. Answering a question by citing this book and quoting example code does not require permission. Incorporating a significant amount of example code from this book into your product's documentation *does* require permission.

We appreciate, but do not require, attribution. An attribution usually includes the title, author, publisher, and ISBN. For example: *"Oracle SQL*Plus: The Definitive Guide*, Second Edition, by Jonathan Gennick. Copyright 2005 O'Reilly Media, Inc., 0-596-00746-9."

If you feel your use of code examples falls outside fair use or the permission given above, feel free to contact us at *permissions@oreilly.com*.

Comments and Questions

Please address comments and questions concerning this book to the publisher:

O'Reilly Media, Inc.
1005 Gravenstein Highway North
Sebastopol, CA 95472
(800) 998-9938 (in the United States or Canada)
(707) 829-0515 (international or local)
(707) 829-0104 (fax)

We have a web page for this book, where we list errata, examples, and any additional information. You can access this page at:

http://www.oreilly.com/catalog/orsqlplus2

To comment or ask technical questions about this book, send email to:

bookquestions@oreilly.com

For more information about our books, conferences, Resource Centers, and the O'Reilly Network, see our web site at:

http://www.oreilly.com

Acknowledgments from the First Edition

The first book that I ever wrote consumed so much energy that I promised myself, and my family, that I would never write another. That promise lasted about two months, when I became consumed with the idea of writing the book you are now reading. I owe a lot to my wife Donna, who understands my drive to write, and who bears a lot more of the load than she should have to while I hole up in my office and work. This book has been my excuse for avoiding just about every household chore imaginable, yet Donna has been very supportive during the endeavor.

My children have contributed to the development of this book. If nothing else, they burst into my office on a daily basis to distract me and to remind me that there are more important things in life than typing on a computer all day. They have also contributed time that I might otherwise have spent with them. My three-year-old son Jeff has grown up watching me write, and must think that all daddies come with a laptop computer attached. To my daughter Jenny, I want to say that I have enjoyed all our late-night excursions together to the local bookstore. I'm glad to see that you have developed the same love for books that I have. You may not always believe it, but you are my pride and joy. I see a lot of myself in you, and I'm glad you ended up as my daughter.

My profound thanks also go out to John-Paul Navarro and David Dreyer, who read each chapter as I wrote it. David Dreyer is an independent consultant residing near Detroit, Michigan, and specializes in PowerBuilder and Oracle development. Dave is one of the most cerebral programmers that I know. Always calm and thoughtful, Dave has added a great deal to this book with his insightful comments. John-Paul Navarro is a systems administrator for Argonne National Laboratories in Argonne, Illinois. John-Paul and I go way back both as friends and colleagues, and I have no end of respect for his technical abilities. He was always willing to discuss technical issues that came up during the writing of this book, and for that I am in his debt.

Thanks to Alison Holloway, product manager for SQL*Plus. "Home" for Alison, and SQL*Plus, too, in case you ever wondered, is in Melbourne, Australia. Alison helped dig up background information and history on SQL*Plus. She provided information on new features being added to SQL*Plus for the upcoming Oracle8*i* release, and also provided me with an early look at the documentation. In addition to all her other help, Alison did a technical review of the entire book after it was written.

Kirk Bradley, Ken Jacobs, Jay Rossiter, and Richard Rendell, all of Oracle Corporation, provided the historical information about SQL*Plus in Chapter 1. It's always nice to know something of the tools one works with besides just the raw technical details of how they are used. SQL*Plus has been around a long time, and Kirk, Ken, Jay, and Richard have provided some interesting historical tidbits.

A number of technical reviewers read and commented on the final manuscript. These include David Kaufman of TUSC, Dave Kreines, Eric Givler, Alison Holloway, and John-Paul Navarro. I am grateful to each of these people for giving me an unbiased view of the manuscript, pointing out errors, and providing suggestions on ways to improve the clarity of the text. This book is the better for their efforts.

Howard Vanderstow and Paul Cheney, both database administrators with the State of Michigan's Office of Technology Resources, provided some welcome assistance in generating the examples for the HELP command in Chapter 2. They helped me research the location and structure of the database table containing the help text used by SQL*Plus.

I owe a great debt to Brian Gill, who encouraged me when I had the initial idea for this book. Without him, this project might never have gotten off the ground. Thanks to my agent, David Rogelberg of Studio B, who helped me keep up with the business end of this project, and who manages that wonderfully interesting email list that serves so well to distract me from my real work.

Several O'Reilly people contributed to this book in various ways. To Debby Russell of O'Reilly, the editor of this book, I say: "thanks for all the red ink!" Debby is a great editor to work with. She had a lot of good ideas for organizing this book. She was very understanding when I fell behind schedule. She was very encouraging, always drawing attention to things I did well.

Edie Freedman designed the cover, and is responsible for that wonderful looking moving leaf insect on the front. Steve Abrams helped in various ways during the development of the book. Many thanks! Rob Romano did a great job with the figures. Ellie Maden pulled everything together and saw this book through the production process.

Second Edition Acknowledgments

Many hands helped prepare this revision of *Oracle SQL*Plus: The Definitive Guide*. To begin, I want to thank my editor, Debby Russell, for her continuing faith in me over the years, and for her support of my many writing projects despite my occasionally hare-brained ideas. Editors have as much to do with good books as authors, and my editor is simply one of the best.

Special thanks go out to Tom Kyte and Gregor Theis for their diligent efforts in reviewing the second edition chapters as I revised and wrote them. Tom and Gregor are excellent Oracle technologists. Their comments and suggestions helped me a great deal to improve the text.

Thanks, too, to Alison Hollaway, Oracle's Product Manager for SQL*Plus, and to Christopher Jones, who is one of the SQL*Plus developers. Alison and Chris read draft chapters and answered many questions relating to the behavior of SQL*Plus.

Arup Nanda, Don Bales, Dick Goulet, Peter Linsley, Ken Jacobs, Srinivasan Vasan, and Jeff Thomas were gracious enough to answer questions I had about SQL*Plus, or about their use of specific SQL*Plus features, such as SET MARKUP.

Lex de Haan, a member of the Dutch national body of the ANSI/ISO standardization committee for the SQL Language, took the time to read and comment on the Lightning SQL Tutorial that you find in Chapter 4. Lex is an Oak Table (*www.oaktable.net*) member and stands among the best SQL experts whom it is my privilege to know.

You can thank Matt Williams, my neighbor and aspiring artist down the street, for the three-headed null monster that you find in Chapter 4. His sketch captures well the pitfalls and perils that nulls and their associated three-valued logic bring to the writing of SQL. Thanks Matt. I'll think of your monster from now on every time I write an IS NULL predicate.

I can't thank Myron Hlynka of Windsor, Canada, enough for his help in choosing the list of Ukrainian historical and literary figures from which I drew names for my example data for this book. Myron went well beyond the call of duty. He helped me choose the names of interesting and significant Ukrainians and contributed the biographical sketches in the section "What About Those Names?". Myron maintains an extensive list of famous Ukrainians, which you can find at *http://www2.uwindsor.ca/~hlynka/ukfam.html*.

Not all names came from Myron! Young Andrew Hlynka, Myron's son, is the one who thought to mention Igor Sikorsky. I have fond memories of watching helicopters as a kid, as they airlifted heavy equipment into a factory near my home. Thanks, Andrew!

As with the first edition, I'm greatly indebted to my immediate family members, especially my wife Donna. Without Donna's steadfast support I wouldn't be published at all, I'm sure. Proverbs 12:4 is surely right in saying that "An excellent wife is the crown of her husband." And don't let me forget the kids! Jenny and Jeff tolerate many evenings without me, but, just as important, give me a reason to get away from the computer once in awhile. Thanks, to all of you. I'm blessed to have such a good family.

Lastly, I want to thank all the many readers of the first edition. Because of you, this book was successful, and its success was one of the watershed events that led me down the path of becoming a part-time writer, something that has made a huge difference in my life, and for which I'm ever grateful. I very much enjoy all the reader emails you've sent over the years, from those asking questions related to the book to those offering suggestions for future editions. Keep those emails coming, and thanks for reading.

CHAPTER 1

Introduction to SQL*Plus

SQL*Plus is the command-line interface to the Oracle database. It exists to let you enter and execute ad hoc SQL statements and PL/SQL code blocks, and, if you're a database administrator (DBA), to issue database administration commands such as STARTUP and SHUTDOWN. This chapter explains what SQL*Plus is, how it relates to the Oracle database, and why you should master it. At the end of the chapter, I'll introduce you to the sample data used for many of the examples in this book. You can load the data and follow along as you read.

What Is SQL*Plus?

SQL*Plus is essentially an interactive query tool with some scripting capabilities. You can enter a SQL statement, such as a SELECT query, and view the results. You can execute *data definition language* (DDL) statements to create tables and other objects. DBAs can use SQL*Plus to start up, shut down, and otherwise administer a database. You can even enter and execute PL/SQL code.

SQL*Plus is primarily a command-line application, but, despite its lack of "flash," it is a workhorse tool used daily by database administrators, developers, and yes, even end users. As a DBA, it is my tool of choice for managing the databases under my care. I use it to peek under the hood—to explore the physical implementation of my database, and to create and manage users, tables, and tablespaces. In my role as a developer, SQL*Plus is the first tool that I fire up when I need to develop a query. In spite of all the fancy, GUI-based SQL generators contained in products such as PowerBuilder, Clear Access, and Crystal Reports, I still find it quicker and easier to build up and test a complex query in SQL*Plus before transferring it to whatever development tool I am using.

Uses for SQL*Plus

Originally developed simply as a way to enter queries and see results, SQL*Plus has been enhanced with scripting and formatting capabilities and can be used for many different purposes. The basic functionality is simple. With SQL*Plus, you can do the following:

- Issue a SELECT query and view the results.
- Insert, update, and delete data from database tables.
- Submit PL/SQL blocks to the Oracle server for execution.
- Issue DDL statements, such as those used to create, alter, or drop database objects (e.g., tables, indexes, and users), as well as any other types of SQL statements that Oracle supports.
- Execute SQL*Plus script files.
- Write output to a file.
- Execute procedures and functions that are stored in a database.

While these operations may not seem significant, they are the building blocks you can use to perform various useful functions.

Consider the ability to enter a SELECT statement and view the results. Example 1-1 shows how to do this using SQL*Plus.

*Example 1-1. Executing a query in SQL*Plus*

```
SQL> SELECT employee_id, employee_name, employee_billing_rate
  2    FROM employee;

EMPLOYEE_ID EMPLOYEE_NAME                               EMPLOYEE_BILLING_RATE
----------- ------------------------------------------- ---------------------
        101 Marusia Churai                                                169
        102 Mykhailo Hrushevsky                                           135
        104 Pavlo Virsky                                                   99
        105 Mykola Leontovych                                             121
        107 Lesia Ukrainka                                                 45
        108 Pavlo Chubynsky                                               220
        110 Ivan Mazepa                                                    84
        111 Taras Shevchenko                                              100
        112 Igor Sikorsky                                                  70
        113 Mykhailo Verbytsky                                            300
```

Combine this capability with SQL*Plus's formatting abilities and you can turn these results into a credible-looking report, such as that shown in Example 1-2, complete with page titles, page numbers, column titles, and nicely formatted output.

*Example 1-2. A SQL*Plus formatted report*

```
Employee Listing                  Page   1

                            Billing
     Emp ID Name               Rate
---------- -------------------- --------
       101 Marusia Churai      $169.00
       102 Mykhailo Hrushevsky $135.00
       104 Pavlo Virsky         $99.00
       105 Mykola Leontovych   $121.00
       107 Lesia Ukrainka       $45.00
       108 Pavlo Chubynsky     $220.00
       110 Ivan Mazepa          $84.00
       111 Taras Shevchenko    $100.00
       112 Igor Sikorsky        $70.00
       113 Mykhailo Verbytsky  $300.00
```

Another twist on the same theme is to format the output as a list of comma-separated values, such as that shown in Example 1-3.

*Example 1-3. Comma-separated values from SQL*Plus*

```
101,"Marusia Churai",169
102,"Mykhailo Hrushevsky",135
104,"Pavlo Virsky",99
105,"Mykola Leontovych",121
107,"Lesia Ukrainka",45
108,"Pavlo Chubynsky",220
110,"Ivan Mazepa",84
111,"Taras Shevchenko",100
112,"Igor Sikorsky",70
113,"Mykhailo Verbytsky",300
```

Using the SQL*Plus SPOOL command, which you'll read more about in Chapter 5, you can write this output to a *.csv* file easily readable by most, if not all, spreadsheet programs. In fact, if you are running Microsoft Windows with Microsoft Office installed, simply double-clicking on a *.csv* file will open that file in Microsoft Excel, where you can further manipulate the data.

Beginning with SQL*Plus in Oracle8*i* Database, you can use the SET MARKUP HTML command to generate HMTL output, such as that shown in Example 1-4.

*Example 1-4. A SQL*Plus report formatted in HTML*

```
<html>
<head>
<meta http-equiv="Content-Type" content="text/html; charset=US-ASCII">
<meta name="generator" content="SQL*Plus 10.1.0">
<style type='text/css'> body {font:10pt Arial,Helvetica,sans-serif; color:black;
 background:White;}
...
<tr>
```

Example 1-4. A SQL*Plus report formatted in HTML (continued)

```
<td align="right">
      101
</td>
<td>
Marusia Churai
</td>
<td align="right">
 $169.00
</td>
</tr>
<tr>
<td align="right">
      102
</td>
<td>
Mykhailo Hrushevsky
</td>
...
```

By writing such HTML output to a file, you can easily generate ad hoc reports for users to view from a corporate intranet. One DBA whom I spoke with regularly refreshes the phone list on his departmental intranet using this mechanism. Figure 1-1 shows the output in Example 1-4 as you would see it rendered in a browser.

It's a small leap from executing only queries to executing any other SQL statement. In fact, SQL*Plus will let you execute any valid SQL statement and is frequently used during database maintenance tasks. For example, you can create a new user with the following statement:

```
CREATE USER sql_dude IDENTIFIED BY some_password;
```

Of course, it's rare that you would issue such a simple statement, or just one statement, when you add a new user. Usually, you also want to assign a default tablespace and often a quota on that tablespace. You may also want to grant the privilege needed to connect to the database. Whenever you have a task that requires a sequence of statements to be executed, you can simplify things by taking advantage of SQL*Plus's scripting capabilities. The statements in Example 1-5, when placed in a script file, allow you to add a new user with just one command.

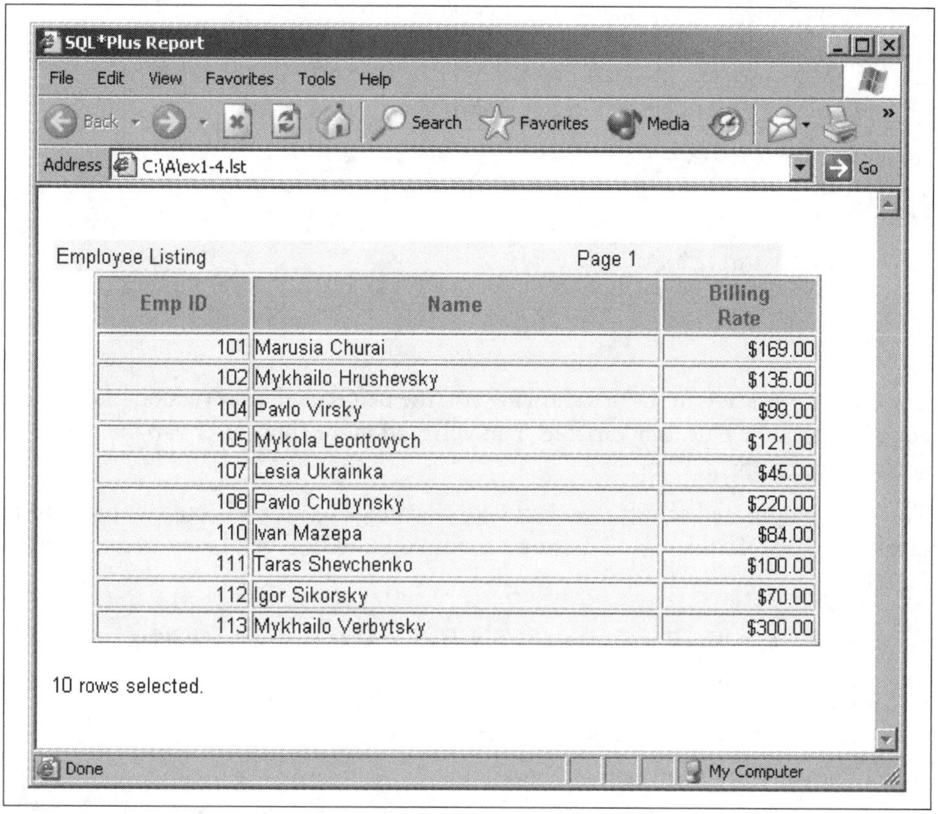

Emp ID	Name	Billing Rate
101	Marusia Churai	$169.00
102	Mykhailo Hrushevsky	$135.00
104	Pavlo Virsky	$99.00
105	Mykola Leontovych	$121.00
107	Lesia Ukrainka	$45.00
108	Pavlo Chubynsky	$220.00
110	Ivan Mazepa	$84.00
111	Taras Shevchenko	$100.00
112	Igor Sikorsky	$70.00
113	Mykhailo Verbytsky	$300.00

*Figure 1-1. A SQL*Plus-generated HTML report rendered in a browser*

Example 1-5. Script to create a new database user

```
CREATE USER &&1 IDENTIFIED BY &&2
   DEFAULT TABLESPACE users
   TEMPORARY TABLESPACE temp
   QUOTA &&3.M ON users;

GRANT CONNECT TO &&1;
```

The `&&1`, `&&2`, and `&&3` in Example 1-5 are SQL*Plus user variables marking the locations at which to insert parameters that you pass to the script. Assuming that you give the name *create_user.sql* to the file shown in Example 1-5, and assuming that you are the DBA, you can issue the following command from SQL*Plus whenever you need to add a user to your database:

```
@create_user username password quota
```

Example 1-6 shows how this works, by creating a user named `sql_dude` with a password of yooper and a quota of 10 megabytes.

Example 1-6. Running a script to create a new database user

```
SQL> @ex1-5 sql_dude yooper 10
old    1: CREATE USER &&1 IDENTIFIED BY &&2
new    1: CREATE USER sql_dude IDENTIFIED BY yooper
old    4:    QUOTA &&3.M ON users
new    4:    QUOTA 10M ON users

User created.

old    1: GRANT CONNECT TO &&1
new    1: GRANT CONNECT TO sql_dude

Grant succeeded.
```

The output you see is SQL*Plus showing you the before and after version of each line containing a SQL*Plus user variable. You will read more about user variables and the subject of scripting in Chapter 8.

To write complicated scripts, you can take advantage of Oracle's built-in procedural language, PL/SQL. Example 1-7 shows a simple PL/SQL block being executed from SQL*Plus.

*Example 1-7. "Hello World" written as a PL/SQL block and executed from SQL*Plus*

```
SQL> SET SERVEROUTPUT ON
SQL> BEGIN
  2    DBMS_OUTPUT.PUT_LINE('Hello World!');
  3  END;
  4  /
Hello World!
```

You've just seen several examples of what can be done using SQL*Plus to generate simple text reports, perform database administration tasks, extract data, generate HTML reports, run automated scripts, and otherwise make your life easier. Subsequent chapters delve deeply into each of these areas and more.

SQL*Plus's Relation to SQL, PL/SQL, and the Oracle Database

SQL*Plus is often used in conjunction with two other products, both of which have the letters "SQL" in their names. The first is SQL itself. Without a doubt, the most common use of SQL*Plus is to submit SQL statements to the database for execution. The second product is Oracle's PL/SQL procedural language. Table 1-1 provides a short summary of each of these three products.

Table 1-1. The three SQLs: SQL, PL/SQL, and SQL*Plus

Product	Description
SQL	SQL is an ANSI and ISO standard language used to insert, delete, update, and retrieve data from relational databases. SQL is also used to manage relational databases.
PL/SQL	PL/SQL is a proprietary procedural language developed by Oracle as an extension to SQL, for use in coding business rules and other procedural logic at the database level. Like SQL, PL/SQL executes inside the database engine.
SQL*Plus	SQL*Plus is an Oracle-developed tool that allows you to interactively enter and execute SQL commands and PL/SQL blocks.

Because these three products all have "SQL" as part of their names, people occasionally get confused about the relationships among them and about which statements get executed where. SQL*Plus does have its own set of commands that it recognizes and executes (for example, SET SERVEROUTPUT ON from Example 1-7), but any SQL statements and PL/SQL blocks are sent to the database server for execution. Figure 1-2 illustrates this relationship.

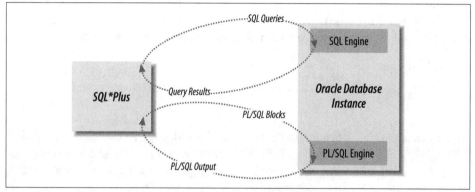

Figure 1-2. Relationships among SQL*Plus, SQL, and PL/SQL

Think of SQL*Plus as kind of a middleman, standing between you and Oracle and helping you to communicate with your database. You type in a SQL query, SQL*Plus takes it and sends it to the database, the database returns the results to SQL*Plus, and SQL*Plus displays those results in a format you can understand.

History of SQL*Plus

SQL*Plus has been around for a long time, pretty much since the beginning of Oracle. In fact, the original author was Bruce Scott. Any DBA will recognize the name Scott. It lives on, immortalized as the owner of a set of example tables that used to be installed with every version of Oracle and that you still can install even today. The original purpose of SQL*Plus can be summed up in the succinct words of Kirk Bradley, another early author of SQL*Plus, who told me, "We needed a way to enter statements into the database and get results."

Kirk's reason is still arguably the major reason most people use SQL*Plus today, more than 15 years after it was originally written. SQL*Plus certainly satisfies a compelling and enduring need.

The original name of the product was not SQL*Plus. The original name was UFI, which stands for *User Friendly Interface*. This name has its roots in one of the first relational database systems ever developed, IBM's System R, the product of a research effort by IBM. Some of IBM's documents referred to the command-line interface as the UFI, and that name was adopted by Oracle for its interactive SQL utility.

One of the more interesting uses Oracle had for UFI was as a tool to produce its documentation. The SQL*Plus DOCUMENT command, now considered obsolete, was used for this purpose. Script files were created that contained the manual text, interspersed with the SQL statements needed for the examples. The DOCUMENT command was used to set off the manual text so it would just be copied to the output file. When these scripts were run, the text was copied, the SQL statements were executed, and the result was documentation complete with examples.

UFI was used extensively in Oracle's internal testing and QA efforts. Even today, SQL*Plus still plays a significant role in Oracle's testing.

SQL*Plus maintains a fascinating relic from the old days in the form of the SET TRIMOUT, SET TRIMSPOOL, and SET TAB commands. These commands control the printing of trailing spaces and the use of tabs to format columnar output. To understand why these commands even exist, you have to realize that when SQL*Plus first made its appearance, people thought that a dialup speed of 1200 bits per second (bps) was fast. In those days you could get your results much faster by avoiding the need to transmit large numbers of space characters across a dialup connection.

If you had a lot of whitespace in your report, you spent a lot of time watching spaces print across your screen. In that environment, trimming spaces and using tabs to format columns provided a huge gain in throughput. Today, with our 10-megabit-per-second (10 Mbps) LAN connections and our 56-KB modems, we hardly give this a thought.

While TRIMSPOOL can be considered a relic from the standpoint of interacting with SQL*Plus via an interactive session, it's helpful to trim trailing spaces from the kinds of large files you might create when using SQL*Plus to extract data, as described in Chapter 9. Example 9-8 uses TRIMSPOOL for just this reason.

During the mid-1980s, Oracle experimented with efforts to add procedural capabilities to UFI. The result of this effort was AUFI, which stood for *Advanced User Friendly Interface*. AUFI implemented such things as IF statements and looping constructs, and was demonstrated publicly at an International Oracle User Group meeting in 1986 by Ken Jacobs, who is now Oracle's Vice President, Product Strategy, Oracle Server Technologies.

In spite of the public demos, whether or not to release AUFI as a shipping product was the subject of some debate within Oracle. Layering a procedural language on top of the existing UFI command set was proving difficult. It was made more difficult by the need to maintain full, backward compatibility so existing scripts written by Oracle's clients would not suddenly break when those clients upgraded. Because of these issues, the code to support the procedural enhancements became complex and somewhat unreliable. The issues of reliability and complexity led to Oracle's ultimate decision to kill the product, so AUFI never shipped. With the later advent of PL/SQL, procedural logic was supported within the database, and efforts to support a procedural scripting language were then seen as unnecessary. The name AUFI lives on in the name of the temporary file created when you use the SQL*Plus EDIT command. That file is named *afiedt.buf*. Even today, AFI is the prefix used for all the source code.

With the release of Oracle 5.0 in 1985, the name of the interactive query utility was changed from UFI to SQL*Plus. Most changes since then have been evolutionary. Each new release brings with it a few new commands and new options on existing commands. Some commands have been made obsolete, but many of these obsolete commands are still supported for purposes of backward compatibility.

Only a couple of truly significant changes to SQL*Plus have occurred over the years. In 1988, with the release of Oracle8*i* Database, Server Manager's STARTUP, SHUTDOWN, and RECOVER commands were implemented in SQL*Plus, which was designated the primary, command-line interface into the Oracle database. Server Manager was deprecated, and by the time Oracle9*i* Database came along, Server Manager no longer existed.

By far the most significant and visible change to SQL*Plus in recent years has been the introduction of *i*SQL*Plus, a three-tier application that gives you access to SQL*Plus functionality via any standard web browser.

As a prelude to *i*SQL*Plus, it was first necessary to give SQL*Plus the ability to generate output in HTML form. This took place in Release 8.1.7, which introduced the SET MARKUP command. Chapter 6 describes this wonderful, new functionality, which you can use to generate HTML reports from command-line SQL*Plus.

*i*SQL*Plus was first released in 2001 as a Windows-only application (part of Oracle9*i* Database Release 1). *i*SQL*Plus was expanded to most other operating systems in

2002 with the release of Oracle9*i* Database Release 2. Beginning with the release of Oracle Database 10*g*, *i*SQL*Plus is supported across all platforms.

Why Master SQL*Plus?

SQL*Plus is a universal constant in the Oracle world. Every installation I have ever seen has this tool installed. For that reason alone, it is worth learning. This is especially true if you are a consultant and move around a lot. The last thing you want is to be at a client site needing to look up something mundane, such as an index definition, and not be able to do it because you're not familiar with the client's tools. SQL*Plus is always there.

If you are a DBA, SQL*Plus is undoubtedly a tool you already use on a daily basis. Anything you use that often is worth learning and learning well. You probably use SQL*Plus to query Oracle's data dictionary tables in order to understand the structure of your database. SQL*Plus can be used to automate that task. Sometimes it's difficult to remember the specific data dictionary tables you need to join together in order to get the information you want. With SQL*Plus, you can figure this out once and encapsulate that query into a script. Next time you need the same information, you won't have all the stress of remembering how to get it, and you won't have to waste time rereading the manuals in order to relearn how to get it.

SQL*Plus is useful for automating routine DBA tasks. For example, you can write scripts to help you create new users (as in Example 1-5), report on database free space or the lack thereof, perform nightly maintenance tasks, and the list goes on. Anything you do to the database on a routine basis, SQL*Plus can help you automate it.

If you are a developer, you can use SQL*Plus to build up queries, develop ad hoc reports, and explore the data in your database. You can use SQL*Plus to create and debug stored procedures, stored functions, packages, and object types. If you have queries that aren't performing well, you may be able to find out why by using Oracle's EXPLAIN PLAN statement from SQL*Plus. EXPLAIN PLAN will tell you the execution strategy chosen by the optimizer for the query. Chapter 12 discusses EXPLAIN PLAN in more detail.

Many modern development tools provide GUI-based query generators. These typically let you drag and drop tables into your query and then draw lines between fields joining those tables together. This drag-and-drop functionality may be great for a simple query that joins a few tables, but I find that it quickly becomes cumbersome as the query grows in complexity. It's not unusual, when developing reports, to have queries that are many pages in length. Sometimes these queries consist of several SELECT statements unioned together, each query having one or more subqueries. When developing one of those mega-queries, I'll take SQL*Plus and a good editor over a GUI query tool any day of the week. Why? Because with an editor I can keep bits and pieces of the query lying around. Using copy and paste, I can pull out a sub-query and execute it independently without losing track of the larger query I am building. I can easily comment out part of a WHERE clause when debugging a query and then uncomment it later. A good text editor lets you manipulate query text in powerful ways that GUI interfaces do not.

Almost anything that you want to do with an Oracle database can be done using SQL*Plus. You can write scripts to automate routine maintenance tasks, report on the state of your database, or generate ad hoc reports for end users. You can execute queries to explore your database, and you can use SQL*Plus to create and manage any schema or database object. Because of its universal availability, you will be able to perform these functions anywhere you go. If you manage an Oracle database or develop software to run against an Oracle database, you will improve your productivity by mastering this tool.

Creating and Loading the Sample Tables

Many of the examples in this book, particularly the reporting examples, have been developed against an example database for an employee time-tracking system. It's a fairly simplistic database, containing only three tables, but it's enough to illustrate everything I talk about in this book. You may or may not wish to create this database for yourself. Creating the database will allow you to try all the examples in this book exactly as they are shown. If you choose not to create and load the sample database, at least familiarize yourself with the data model. Glance at the sample data, which are reproduced later in this section. If you have looked at the model and at the data, you shouldn't have any trouble following and understanding the examples in this book.

 Every numbered example in this book is provided in a set of example scripts that you can download from the catalog page for this book at *http://oreilly.com/catalog/orsqlplus2*. Example 1-1 is in the file named *ex1-1.sql*, Example 1-2 is in the file named *ex1-2.sql*, and so forth.

The Data Model

Figure 1-3 shows an Entity Relationship Diagram (ERD) for the sample database.

As you can see from the ERD, there are only three entities: EMPLOYEE, PROJECT, and PROJECT_HOURS. Table 1-2 gives a brief description of each entity.

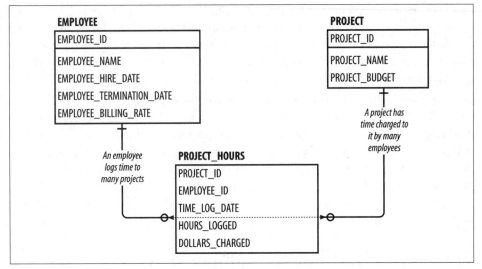

Figure 1-3. The sample database

Table 1-2. Entity descriptions

Entity name	Description
EMPLOYEE	Contains one record for each employee. This record contains the employee's name, hire date, termination date, and billing rate. The primary key is an arbitrary employee ID number. The termination date for current employees is set to NULL.
PROJECT	Contains one record for each project that an employee may work on. Contains the project name and budget. The primary key is an arbitrary project ID number.
PROJECT_HOURS	Each time an employee logs time to a project, a record is generated in this table. The record contains the number of hours charged against the project as well as the total dollar amount charged. The dollar amount charged is calculated at the time the record is created because an employee's billing rate may fluctuate over time. The primary key is a combination key made up of an employee ID, a project ID, and the date.

The number of employees and projects is fairly small. However, a large amount of data in the PROJECT_HOURS table allow for the generation of multiple-page reports, which are needed to demonstrate pagination, page headings, page footings, and summarization.

The Tables

This section shows the column descriptions, including column datatypes and lengths, for each of the three example tables. This is the same information you would get using SQL*Plus's DESCRIBE command.

EMPLOYEE table

```
Name                            Null?     Type
------------------------------- --------  -------------
EMPLOYEE_ID                     NOT NULL  NUMBER
EMPLOYEE_NAME                             VARCHAR2(40)
EMPLOYEE_HIRE_DATE                        DATE
EMPLOYEE_TERMINATION_DATE                 DATE
EMPLOYEE_BILLING_RATE                     NUMBER(5,2)
```

PROJECT table

```
Name                            Null?     Type
------------------------------- --------  -------------
PROJECT_ID                      NOT NULL  NUMBER(4)
PROJECT_NAME                              VARCHAR2(40)
PROJECT_BUDGET                            NUMBER(9,2)
```

PROJECT_HOURS table

```
Name                            Null?     Type
------------------------------- --------  -----------
PROJECT_ID                      NOT NULL  NUMBER(4)
EMPLOYEE_ID                     NOT NULL  NUMBER
TIME_LOG_DATE                   NOT NULL  DATE
HOURS_LOGGED                              NUMBER(5,2)
DOLLARS_CHARGED                           NUMBER(8,2)
```

The Data

This section shows the data contained in the three example tables.

EMPLOYEE table

```
    ID Name                   Hire Date    Term Date    Billing Rate
------ ---------------------- -----------  -----------  ------------
   101 Marusia Churai         15-Nov-1961                     169.00
   102 Mykhailo Hrushevsky    16-Sep-1964  05-May-2004        135.00
   104 Pavlo Virsky           29-Dec-1987  01-Apr-2004         99.00
   105 Mykola Leontovych      15-Jun-2004                     121.00
   107 Lesia Ukrainka         02-Jan-2004                      45.00
   108 Pavlo Chubynsky        01-Mar-1994  15-Nov-2004        220.00
   110 Ivan Mazepa            04-Apr-2004  30-Sep-2004         84.00
   111 Taras Shevchenko       23-Aug-1976                     100.00
   112 Igor Sikorsky          15-Nov-1961  04-Apr-2004         70.00
   113 Mykhailo Verbytsky     03-Mar-2004  31-Oct-2004        300.00
```

PROJECT table

```
    ID Project Name                           Budget
------ -------------------------------------- -------------
  1001 Corporate Web Site                      1,912,000.00
  1002 Enterprise Resource Planning System     9,999,999.00
```

```
      1003 Accounting System Implementation        897,000.00
      1004 Data Warehouse Maintenance              294,000.00
      1005 VPN Implementation                      415,000.00
```

PROJECT_HOURS table

The PROJECT_HOURS table contains the following information, repeated for each employee:

```
Proj ID Emp ID Log Date    Hours Charged Amt Charged
------- ------ ----------- ------------- -----------
   1001    101 01-Jan-2004          1.00      169.00
   1003    101 01-Jan-2004          3.00      507.00
   1005    101 01-Jan-2004          5.00      845.00
   1002    101 01-Feb-2004          7.00    1,183.00
   1004    101 01-Feb-2004          1.00      169.00
   1001    101 01-Mar-2004          3.00      507.00
   1003    101 01-Mar-2004          5.00      845.00
   1005    101 01-Mar-2004          7.00    1,183.00
   1002    101 01-Apr-2004          1.00      169.00
   1004    101 01-Apr-2004          3.00      507.00
   1001    101 01-May-2004          5.00      845.00
   1003    101 01-May-2004          7.00    1,183.00
   1005    101 01-May-2004          1.00      169.00
   1002    101 01-Jun-2004          3.00      507.00
   1004    101 01-Jun-2004          5.00      845.00
   1001    101 01-Jul-2004          7.00    1,183.00
   1003    101 01-Jul-2004          1.00      169.00
   1005    101 01-Jul-2004          3.00      507.00
   1002    101 01-Aug-2004          5.00      845.00
   1004    101 01-Aug-2004          7.00    1,183.00
   1001    101 01-Sep-2004          1.00      169.00
   1003    101 01-Sep-2004          3.00      507.00
   1005    101 01-Sep-2004          5.00      845.00
   1002    101 01-Oct-2004          7.00    1,183.00
   1004    101 01-Oct-2004          1.00      169.00
   1001    101 01-Nov-2004          3.00      507.00
   1003    101 01-Nov-2004          5.00      845.00
   1005    101 01-Nov-2004          7.00    1,183.00
   1002    101 01-Dec-2004          1.00      169.00
   1004    101 01-Dec-2004          3.00      507.00
```

The detail is the same for each employee. They all work the same hours on all projects. There are enough PROJECT_HOURS records to produce some reasonable summary reports, as you will see in Chapters 5 through 7.

Loading the Sample Data

In order to load the sample data you will need an Oracle username and password. If you are accessing a remote database (often the case for people using Windows), you will also need a net service name. You must have the necessary privileges and quotas to create tables in the database you are using. Specifically, you must have the following system privileges:

- CREATE SESSION
- ALTER SESSION
- CREATE TABLE
- CREATE VIEW
- CREATE TRIGGER
- CREATE PROCEDURE
- CREATE SYNONYM
- CREATE SEQUENCE
- CREATE TYPE (Oracle8 and higher)

Your DBA can help you with any of these items. Once you have a username and password and have been granted the necessary privileges, you can create the sample tables and data by following these four steps:

1. Download and unzip (or untar) the script files.
2. Start SQL*Plus.
3. Log into your Oracle database.
4. Run the *bld_db.sql* script file.

If you are new to SQL*Plus and are completely uncertain how to start it in your particular environment, you should first read the section "Starting Windows SQL*Plus" in Chapter 2. Once you know how to start SQL*Plus, you can come back here and run the script to create the sample tables and fill them with data.

Step 1: Download and unzip the script files

The SQL scripts to create the tables and data used for the examples in this book can be downloaded from O'Reilly's web site:

> *http://www.oreilly.com/catalog/orsqlplus2*

Download either *SQLPlusData.zip* or *SQLPlusData.tar.gz*, depending on whether you prefer to work with zip files (Windows) or tar files (Linux/Unix). Extract the contents of the file that you download into a directory on your hard disk.

 You can extract the script files into any directory you wish, but if you're a Windows user you may want to avoid using a directory with spaces in its name, or with spaces in any of the parent directory names. Some releases of SQL*Plus throw errors when confronted with path and filenames containing spaces.

Running bld_db.sql from iSQL*Plus

If you're running *i*SQL*Plus, or a recent release of SQL*Plus, you're in for a real treat. You may not need to download any scripts at all to create the example data. From any release of *i*SQL*Plus (assuming that you have Internet access), you can execute scripts directly from a web site, or from an FTP site, simply by giving a URL rather than a filename. Use the following command to invoke the example data script over the Internet:

```
@http://gennick.com/sqlplus/bld_db
```

Once you have invoked the script, you can follow the remaining instructions in "Step 4: Run the bld_db.sql script file" for responding to the prompts.

In addition to *i*SQL*Plus, you can invoke scripts directly over the Internet from all versions of SQL*Plus in Oracle Database 10*g* and Oracle9*i* Database Release 2, and from the Windows version of SQL*Plus in Oracle9*i* Database Release 1. This is a much handier feature than you might initially think.

Step 2: Start SQL*Plus

SQL*Plus has three variations: command-line, Windows GUI, and *i*SQL*Plus. Unless you know a bit about SQL*Plus already and know how to connect to *i*SQL*Plus in your environment, you'll find it easiest to use command-line SQL*Plus to load the example data. For Windows users, this means opening a command-prompt window, which I know is something not often done under Windows.

Once you have a command prompt, navigate to the directory into which you unpacked the example scripts. Make that directory your current working directory. For example, under Linux:

```
oracle@gennick02:~> cd sqlplus/ExampleData
oracle@gennick02:~/sqlplus/ExampleData>
```

or under Windows:

```
C:\Documents and Settings\JonathanGennick>cd c:\sqlplus\ExampleData

C:\sqlplus\ExampleData>
```

Next, invoke SQL*Plus using one of the following forms:

```
sqlplus username
sqlplus username@net_service_name
```

Use the first form if you're running SQL*Plus on the same computer as the Oracle instance. Use the second form if you're accessing Oracle over a network connection.

Prior to the Oracle8*i* Database release, the name of the SQL*Plus executable under Windows varied from one release to the next and followed the pattern *plus80* (Oracle8), *plus73* (Oracle7.3), etc. Thankfully, Oracle has recovered from this bit of insanity.

Step 3: Log into your Oracle database

After starting SQL*Plus, you'll be prompted for a password. Enter the password corresponding to your username, and you should be connected to your database:

```
oracle@gennick02:~/sqlplus/ExampleScripts> sqlplus sql_dude

SQL*Plus: Release 10.1.0.2.0 - Production on Fri Apr 9 19:13:44 2004

Copyright (c) 1982, 2004, Oracle.  All rights reserved.

Enter password:

Connected to:
Oracle Database 10g Enterprise Edition Release 10.1.0.2.0 - Production
With the Partitioning, OLAP and Data Mining options

SQL>
```

After you enter your password, you should see a message beginning with "Connected to:", after which you should land at the SQL> prompt. If you have trouble logging in, ask your DBA for help. If you are the DBA, then it's "Physician, heal thyself!"

You may know that SQL*Plus allows you to enter your password on the command line. Avoid doing that. Many Linux and Unix systems make your command line visible to *all* users on the system. Don't give your password away by typing it on the command line. Let SQL*Plus prompt you for it instead.

Step 4: Run the bld_db.sql script file

The final step is to run the *bld_db.sql* script file, which is one of the files in the ZIP archive you downloaded in step 1. To do that, simply use the @ command as shown below:

```
SQL> @bld_db
```

Ideally, your current working directory will be the directory containing the file. If that's not the case, you'll need to specify the full directory path to the script:

```
SQL> @c:\sqlplus\ExampleData\bld_db
```

After you type one of these commands and press Enter, you'll be prompted to confirm your intention to create and populate the example tables:

```
SQL> @bld_db

This script creates the tables and sample data needed
to run the examples in the SQL*Plus book.

Do you wish to continue (Y/N)? Y
```

Respond by entering Y or N and pressing Enter again. In this example, I've responded in the affirmative with Y.

 If you make any mistakes in input while running the *bld_db.sql* script, the script will simply end. You'll get a message telling you to rerun the script and answer correctly. SQL*Plus is incapable of repeatedly asking you to retry bad input. A graceful exit is the most you can hope for.

Next, you'll be asked whether you wish to drop the tables before creating them:

```
You have the option of dropping the sample
tables before creating them. This is useful
if you have previously created the sample
tables, and are recreating them in order to
reload the original data.

Do you wish to DROP the tables first (Y/N)? N
```

This option to first drop the sample tables is convenient if you have loaded them before and wish to reload them quickly. If this is your first time running this script, you should answer this question with N. If you have loaded the tables previously, and you know that they exist now, then you should answer with Y.

Now you can just sit back and watch while the script creates the example tables and populates them with data. You'll see progress messages such as these:

```
Creating employee table...

Creating project table...

Creating project_hours table...

Creating projects...

Creating Employees...

Creating employee time log entries for 2004...


Thank-you for loading the sample data!
Please press ENTER.
```

The entire load process should take less than a minute. When the load is complete, you will be asked to press Enter one final time. Be sure to do that! Then you can use the EXIT command to leave SQL*Plus and return to your operating system command prompt:

```
SQL> exit
Disconnected from Oracle Database 10g Enterprise Edition Release 10.1.0.2.0 -
Production
With the Partitioning, OLAP and Data Mining options
oracle@gennick02:~/sqlplus/ExampleData>
```

Now that you have loaded the sample data, you can proceed with the book and try out the examples as you go. Enjoy!

CHAPTER 2

Command-Line SQL*Plus

SQL*Plus comes in three flavors. It can be a command-line program that you execute from your operating-system prompt. Under Microsoft Windows, SQL*Plus can also be a command-line application wrapped inside a rudimentary, graphical user interface (GUI). I refer to that as *Windows SQL*Plus*, and it's only slightly different from standard, command-line SQL*Plus. Finally, beginning with Oracle9*i* Database, SQL*Plus can be a three-tier application, known as *i*SQL*Plus, that you access through a web browser.

This chapter shows you how to interact with the two command-line versions. You'll learn how to start them, how to enter and execute commands, and how to take advantage of the built-in line-editing features. *i*SQL*Plus is different enough to be covered separately in Chapter 3.

Starting Command-Line SQL*Plus

You'd think that starting SQL*Plus and connecting to a database would be a simple affair to explain, but it isn't. There are many permutations available for entering your username and password, and for specifying the target database. You've seen a couple of them already in Chapter 1. I won't cover every possibility in this section, only those permutations that are most useful.

Connecting to a Default Database

Perhaps the simplest way to start SQL*Plus is to issue the *sqlplus* command and let SQL*Plus prompt you for your username and password:

```
oracle@gennick02:~> sqlplus

SQL*Plus: Release 10.1.0.2.0 - Production on Wed Apr 21 20:17:47 2004

Copyright (c) 1982, 2004, Oracle.  All rights reserved.
```

```
Enter user-name: gennick
Enter password:

Connected to:
Oracle Database 10g Enterprise Edition Release 10.1.0.2.0 - Production
With the Partitioning, OLAP and Data Mining options

SQL>
```

This approach works well if you're connecting to a default database, usually running on the same machine that you are logged into. SQL*Plus does not echo your password to the display, protecting you from those who would steal your password by looking over your shoulder as you type.

 Prior to Oracle8i Database, SQL*Plus executables under Windows were named *plus80* (Oracle8), *plus73* (Oracle7.3), *plus72* (Oracle7.2), and *plus71* (Oracle7.1).

Choosing Your Default Database

On Linux and Unix, when you're running SQL*Plus on the same machine that is the database server, you'll often use the *oraenv* utility to specify the (local) database to which you want to connect. For example, to set your default database to the db01 instance, specify the following:

```
oracle@gennick02:~> . oraenv
ORACLE_SID = [prod] ? db01
```

You specify the database, which must be local to your machine, by typing its system identifier (SID) in response to the prompt. This example shows the Oracle SID being changed from prod to db01. Subsequent invocations of SQL*Plus and other Oracle utilities will connect to db01.

Connecting to a Remote Database

To connect to a remote database, you must supply a *connect string* as part of your login. The connect string specifies the target database to which you wish to connect, and can take on several forms. Commonly, your DBA will configure what is called a *net service name* for you to use in connecting to a remote database. However, SQL*Plus won't prompt for this net service name. How then, do you enter it?

One way to enter a connect string is type it after your username, separating the two values with an at sign (@) character:

```
C:\Documents and Settings\JonathanGennick>sqlplus

SQL*Plus: Release 10.1.0.2.0 - Production on Wed Apr 21 20:28:21 2004
```

```
Copyright (c) 1982, 2004, Oracle.  All rights reserved.

Enter user-name: gennick@db01
Enter password:

Connected to:
Oracle Database 10g Enterprise Edition Release 10.1.0.2.0 - Production
With the Partitioning, OLAP and Data Mining options

SQL>
```

In this example, db01 is the net service name defined by my DBA. It happens to be defined in a file known as *tnsnames.ora*, and its definition looks like this:

```
DB01 =
  (DESCRIPTION =
    (ADDRESS_LIST =
      (ADDRESS = (PROTOCOL = TCP)(HOST = gennick02.gennick.com)(PORT = 1521))
    )
    (CONNECT_DATA =
      (SERVICE_NAME = db01.gennick.com)
    )
  )
```

If for some reason you don't have a net service name defined, aren't able to define one, and desperately need to connect to a remote database anyway, and you happen to know all the relevant connection information, you can provide your connection details in the *tnsnames.ora* format:

```
C:\Documents and Settings\JonathanGennick>sqlplus

SQL*Plus: Release 10.1.0.2.0 - Production on Wed Apr 21 20:38:58 2004

Copyright (c) 1982, 2004, Oracle.  All rights reserved.

Enter user-name: gennick@(DESCRIPTION = (ADDRESS_LIST = (ADDRESS = (PROTOCOL =
CP)(HOST = gennick02.gennick.com)(PORT = 1521)))(CONNECT_DATA = (SERVICE_NAME =
db01.gennick.com)))
Enter password:

Connected to:
Oracle Database 10g Enterprise Edition Release 10.1.0.2.0 - Production
With the Partitioning, OLAP and Data Mining options

SQL>
```

The connect string in this example is (DESCRIPTION...db01.gennick.com))). Truly, you would need to be desperate, and a bit of an Oracle networking wizard, to remember and use such convoluted syntax. However, bear in mind that the *tnsnames.ora* syntax was never really designed for interactive use.

Fortunately, for those of us who are challenged by the task of matching up so many parentheses, SQL*Plus in Oracle Database 10g recognizes a much simpler syntax, at least for TCP/IP connections. This syntax is called the *easy connection identifier*. Here is the general format of this simplified connect string:

```
//host:port/service
```

You should be able to use this syntax as follows:

```
C:\Documents and Settings\JonathanGennick>sqlplus

SQL*Plus: Release 10.1.0.2.0 - Production on Wed Apr 21 20:38:58 2004

Copyright (c) 1982, 2004, Oracle.  All rights reserved.

Enter user-name: gennick@//gennick02.gennick.com:1521/db01.gennick.com
...
```

Unfortunately, in Oracle Database 10*g* Release 1 there is a bug that prevents this syntax from working. One workaround is to append the connect string after your password. If you could see your password when typing, that workaround would look like this:

```
C:\Documents and Settings\JonathanGennick>sqlplus

SQL*Plus: Release 10.1.0.2.0 - Production on Wed Apr 21 20:50:35 2004

Copyright (c) 1982, 2004, Oracle.  All rights reserved.

Enter user-name: gennick
Enter password: secret@//gennick02.gennick.com:1521/db01.gennick.com

Connected to:
Oracle Database 10g Enterprise Edition Release 10.1.0.2.0 - Production
With the Partitioning, OLAP and Data Mining options

SQL>
```

SQL*Plus does not echo characters typed in response to the password prompt, making this workaround rather difficult to manage. One workaround for *that* issue is to first invoke SQL*Plus without logging in, which you do by specifying the /NOLOG option, and then issuing a CONNECT command with all the necessary login and connection information:

```
C:\>sqlplus /nolog

SQL*Plus: Release 10.1.0.2.0 - Production on Mon Aug 9 18:52:01 2004

Copyright (c) 1982, 2004, Oracle.  All rights reserved.

SQL> CONNECT gennick/secret@//gennick02.gennick.com:1521/db01.gennick.com
Connected.
SQL>
```

Of the previous two alternatives, this last approach is best on Unix and Linux systems because it ensures that your password is not visible to anyone executing a *ps* command (which displays commands and arguments used to start running programs).

Read more about CONNECT later, in the section "Some Basic SQL*Plus Commands."

Using the /NOLOG Option

Using the /NOLOG command-line option, you can start SQL*Plus without connecting to any database at all. If you're a DBA, you'll use that option often, as it's a common way to connect using the SYSDBA and SYSOPER roles. For example:

```
oracle@gennick02:~> sqlplus /nolog

SQL*Plus: Release 10.1.0.2.0 - Production on Thu Apr 22 20:52:10 2004

Copyright (c) 1982, 2004, Oracle.  All rights reserved.

SQL> connect system as sysdba
Enter password:
Connected.
SQL>
```

This example uses /NOLOG to start SQL*Plus without making a database connection. A CONNECT command is then issued to connect as the SYSTEM user in the SYSDBA role. Once connected, this user can perform administrative tasks such as shutting down or recovering the database.

Specifying Login Details on the Command Line

I've always found it easiest to type my login information on the SQL*Plus command line, thus avoiding the entire prompt/response process. I want to get to that SQL> prompt just as fast as I can. To that end, you can specify your username and password on the command line as follows:

```
oracle@gennick02:~> sqlplus gennick/secret

SQL*Plus: Release 10.1.0.2.0 - Production on Wed Apr 21 21:13:47 2004

Copyright (c) 1982, 2004, Oracle.  All rights reserved.


Connected to:
Oracle Database 10g Enterprise Edition Release 10.1.0.2.0 - Production
With the Partitioning, OLAP and Data Mining options

SQL>
```

This is nice. But nothing good comes without its price. You must be aware of two problems when providing login details on the command line. One rather obvious problem is that your login information—username and password in this example—are visible to onlookers until you scroll that information off the screen. (Be aware, too, of the ability to scroll back, and of the possibility under Unix/Linux that your commands may be recorded in a shell history file.) Another, less obvious problem is that some Unix and Linux systems make your entire command line, password and all, visible to any system user who happens to issue a *ps* command. The following example comes from a Solaris system (thanks Tom!). The first command reported is the *ps* command that is executing, while the second is an invocation of SQL*Plus clearly showing the username and password of scott/tigertkyte.

```
scott@ORA817DEV> !ps -auxww | grep sqlplus
tkyte    22046  0.3  0.1 1512 1264 pts/1    S 13:23:05  0:00 -usr/bin/csh -c ps
-auxww | grep sqlplus
tkyte    22035  0.2  0.4 9824 5952 pts/1    S 13:22:57  0:00 sqlplus scott/tigertkyte
         22054  0.0  0.1  984  768 pts/1    S 13:23:05  0:00 grep sqlplus
```

To play it safe, you can provide just your username on the command line, and let SQL*Plus prompt you for your password. That way, your password is never displayed, nor will it show up in any *ps* process listing or shell history file:

```
oracle@gennick02:~> sqlplus gennick

SQL*Plus: Release 10.1.0.2.0 - Production on Wed Apr 21 21:24:45 2004

Copyright (c) 1982, 2004, Oracle.  All rights reserved.

Enter password:

Connected to:
Oracle Database 10g Enterprise Edition Release 10.1.0.2.0 - Production
With the Partitioning, OLAP and Data Mining options

SQL>
```

If you're connecting to a remote database, you can specify username, password, and connect string, all on the command line, as follows:

```
sqlplus gennick/secret@db01
```

Better perhaps, specify only your username and connect string, leaving SQL*Plus to prompt for your password:

```
sqlplus gennick@db01
```

This approach even works when using the rather complex *tnsnames.ora* format:

```
sqlplus gennick@(DESCRIPTION = (ADDRESS_LIST = (ADDRESS = (PROTOCOL = TCP)(HOST =
gennick02.gennick.com)(PORT = 1521)))(CONNECT_DATA = (SERVICE_NAME = db01.gennick.
com)))
```

Remember that easy connection identifier syntax from the previous section? Unfortunately, to use it on the command line, you must also specify the password on the command line. The following will not work:

```
sqlplus gennick@//gennick02.gennick.com:1521/db01.gennick.com
```

However, the following *will* work:

```
sqlplus gennick/secret@//gennick02.gennick.com:1521/db01.gennick.com
```

This command works because the password, secret in this example, is given on the command line as part of the *sqlplus* command. That shouldn't be necessary, and with any luck Oracle will fix the problem in a future release.

Connecting as SYSDBA

Using /NOLOG isn't the only way to connect in the SYSDBA or SYSOPER roles. (See the earlier sidebar "Using the /NOLOG Option.") You can specify those roles from the command line by enclosing your connection information within quotes:

```
oracle@gennick02:~> sqlplus "/ AS SYSDBA"

SQL*Plus: Release 10.1.0.2.0 - Production on Mon Aug 9 20:19:52 2004

Copyright (c) 1982, 2004, Oracle.  All rights reserved.


Connected to:
Oracle Database 10g Enterprise Edition Release 10.1.0.2.0 - Production
With the Partitioning, OLAP and Data Mining options

SQL>
```

In SQL*Plus 10.1 and higher, it is no longer necessary to enclose / AS SYSDBA within quotes.

A potentially useful program to hide Unix command-line arguments can be found at *http://www.orafaq.com/scripts/c_src/hide.txt.*

Starting Windows SQL*Plus

To start the Windows GUI version of SQL*Plus, first find the icon. Figure 2-1 shows SQL*Plus for Oracle Database 10*g* in the Windows Start menu. It looks like a blue disk drive topped with a yellow plus sign.

You'll find the SQL*Plus icon in a program group under the Start menu. The path varies slightly from one release of Oracle to the next but will usually be something along the lines of Start → All Programs → Oracle → Application Development →

SQL Plus

Figure 2-1. The SQL*Plus icon

SQL*Plus. Figure 2-2 shows the Windows Start menu expanded to show the SQL*Plus icon.

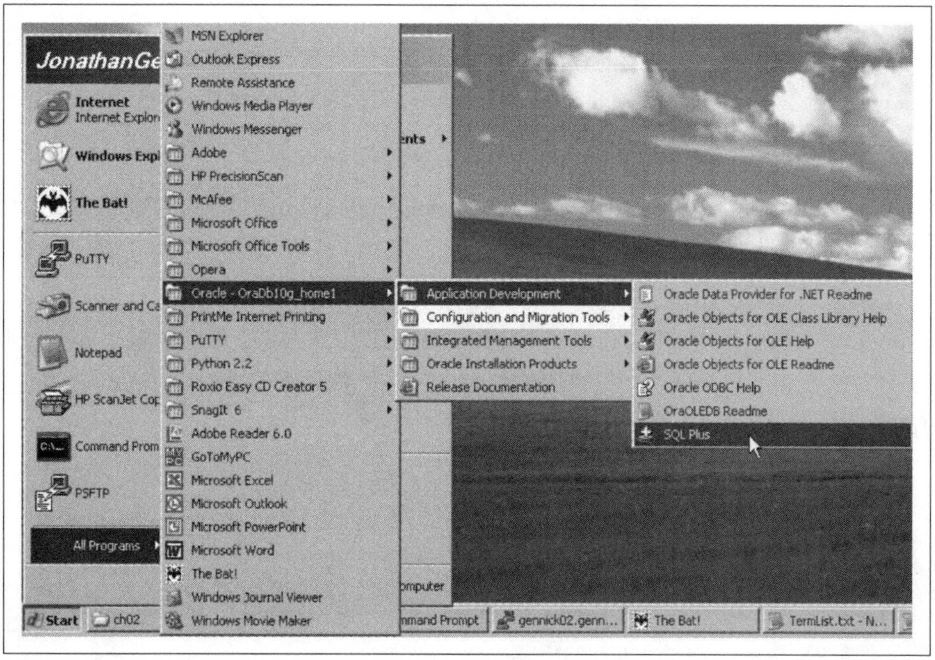

Figure 2-2. Start menu expanded to show the SQL*Plus icon

After starting SQL*Plus, you'll see the dialog box shown in Figure 2-3. To log into your database, simply enter your database username, password, and host string into the dialog box and click OK.

The example in Figure 2-3 uses the net service name db01. You may use the *tnsnames.ora* and easy connection identifier formats (Oracle Database 10g only) for the connect string.

> Make sure to enter the correct information in the logon dialog box. If you make a mistake, SQL*Plus will reprompt you for your username and password but not for the connect string. This is annoying when you are connecting to a remote database.

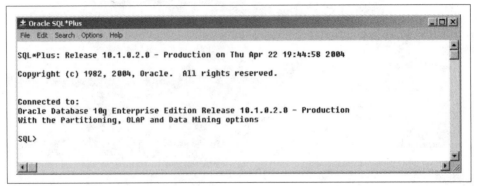

Figure 2-3. SQL*Plus logon dialog box

After you have successfully logged into your database, the SQL*Plus screen will look much like that shown in Figure 2-4.

Figure 2-4. The Windows SQL*Plus GUI

At first glance, the Windows version of SQL*Plus doesn't seem to add much to the command-line version because it implements only a simple, scrolling window into which you type commands. But there are some advantages to using the Windows GUI. The GUI version implements copy and paste using the standard Ctrl-c/Ctrl-v key combinations, allows you to easily size the window any way you want (think large), and implements a scroll-back buffer so that you don't need to worry too much about query results scrolling by before you can read them. Once you get used to using SQL*Plus with a 1000-line scroll-back buffer and a large, vertical window size, you won't want to go back to the default, 25×80 character command-prompt window environment.

Newer versions of Windows implement scroll-back from command-prompt windows, so that's not such a great advantage anymore.

Missing the Product User Profile

SQL*Plus implements a security feature known as the product user profile. Sometimes DBAs neglect to create the tables and views that support this feature. Consequently, SQL*Plus users will occasionally see an error message such as the following when connecting to a database:

```
Error accessing PRODUCT_USER_PROFILE
Warning:  Product user profile information not loaded!
You may need to run PUPBLD.SQL as SYSTEM
```

Alarming as it sounds, this message is nothing to worry about. Nothing is wrong with your database, and all SQL*Plus commands will work as normal. This message is telling you only that the product user profile security feature has not been implemented at your site or, more specifically, that you do not have SELECT access to the PRODUCT_PROFILE table owned by SYSTEM. Chapter 13 describes this feature in detail, and also shows how your DBA can easily create the necessary tables to make this message go away. If you don't know your DBA, or you can't persuade him to create the profile table, don't worry about it. Just ignore the message, and do whatever you need to do.

Some Basic SQL*Plus Commands

Now that you know how to start SQL*Plus, it's time to learn a few basic commands. This section shows you how to exit SQL*Plus, how to change your database password, how to get help, how to view a database table definition, how to switch your database connection to another database, and more.

 All SQL*Plus commands are case-insensitive; you may enter them using either lowercase or uppercase. In this book, commands are shown uppercase to make them stand out better in the text and examples. In practice, you're more likely to enter ad hoc commands in lowercase, and that's perfectly fine.

Filenames may or may not be case-sensitive, depending on your operating system. For example, under Windows, filenames are not case-sensitive, but under Unix, they are.

EXIT

A good place to start, because you've just seen how to start SQL*Plus, is with the EXIT command. EXIT terminates your SQL*Plus session and closes the SQL*Plus window (GUI version) or returns you to the operating system prompt. Used in its simplest form, the EXIT command looks like this:

```
SQL> EXIT
Disconnected from Oracle Database 10g Enterprise Edition Release 10.1.0.2.0 -
Production
With the Partitioning, OLAP and Data Mining options
oracle@gennick02:~>
```

Some optional arguments to the EXIT command may be used to return success or failure values to the operating system. These are useful when running scripts in batch mode and are described fully in Chapter 11.

 EXIT should really be thought of as two commands: COMMIT and EXIT. Any pending transaction will be committed, or made permanent, when you issue an EXIT command to leave SQL*Plus. Don't make the mistake of thinking that to EXIT is to ROLLBACK.

PASSWORD

Use the PASSWORD command to change your database password. You may abbreviate the command to PASSWD.

 The PASSWORD command was introduced beginning with SQL*Plus Version 8. In prior versions, you needed to use the ALTER USER command to change a password. To change other people's passwords, you need the ALTER USER system privilege.

Here is an example showing how the PASSWORD command is used:

```
SQL> PASSWORD
Changing password for GENNICK
Old password: *******
New password: *******
Retype new password: *******
Password changed
```

If you are a DBA, you can change passwords for other users:

```
SQL> PASSWORD gennick
Changing password for gennick
New password:
...
```

If you are running a version of SQL*Plus prior to Version 8 (and I surely hope you are not running anything that old), the PASSWORD command will not be available. Instead, use the ALTER USER command to change your password. Here's how:

```
SQL> ALTER USER gennick IDENTIFIED BY secret;

User altered.
```

As you can see, you'll have to provide a username even when you are changing your own password. You'll have to live with your password's being displayed visibly on the screen. The PASSWORD command, on the other hand, has the advantage of not showing your new password.

HELP

Use the HELP command to get help on SQL*Plus commands.

 Prior to Oracle8i Database, HELP also gave help on SQL and PL/SQL statements. In Oracle8i, SQL and PL/SQL syntax became so complex that the SQL*Plus developers refocused the HELP system on only SQL*Plus commands.

Here's an example of how HELP INDEX (or HELP MENU prior to Oracle8i Database) can be used to get a list of help topics:

```
SQL> HELP INDEX

Enter Help [topic] for help.

 @            COPY        PAUSE        SHUTDOWN
 @@           DEFINE      PRINT        SPOOL
 /            DEL         PROMPT       SQLPLUS
 ACCEPT       DESCRIBE    QUIT         START
 ...
```

After identifying a topic of interest, you can get further help by using that topic name as an argument to the HELP command. Here is the information HELP returns about the DESCRIBE command:

```
SQL> HELP DESCRIBE

DESCRIBE
--------

 Lists the column definitions for a table, view, or synonym,
 or the specifications for a function or procedure.

DESC[RIBE] [schema.]object[@connect_identifier]
```

Help is not available on all implementations. Early Windows versions (in Oracle8*i* Database and earlier) of SQL*Plus don't implement the feature, and issuing the HELP command will yield nothing more than the dialog shown in Figure 2-5.

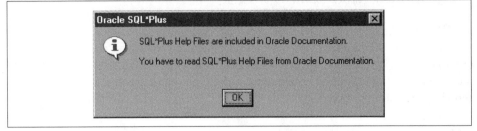

Figure 2-5. The "No Help" dialog

SQL*Plus reads help text from a database table named HELP, owned by the user SYSTEM. You will get a "HELP not accessible" message if that table does not exist or if SQL*Plus cannot select from it because of some other problem:

```
SQL> HELP
HELP not accessible.
```

Entering HELP without an argument will get you help on using HELP itself.

 SQL*Plus help text comes from the database and not from SQL*Plus. If you connect to a database using a version of SQL*Plus not matching the database version, there's a chance that any help text that you see may not match up with the capabilities of the version of SQL*Plus you are using.

DESCRIBE

The DESCRIBE command lists the column definitions for a database table. You can use it to view procedure, function, package, and object definitions. If you have created and loaded the sample tables described in Chapter 1, you can use the DESCRIBE command to view their column definitions. The following example uses DESCRIBE to list the columns in the employee table:

```
SQL> DESCRIBE employee
 Name                                      Null?    Type
 ----------------------------------------- -------- ---------------------------
 EMPLOYEE_ID                               NOT NULL NUMBER
 EMPLOYEE_NAME                                      VARCHAR2(40)
 EMPLOYEE_HIRE_DATE                                 DATE
 EMPLOYEE_TERMINATION_DATE                          DATE
 EMPLOYEE_BILLING_RATE                              NUMBER(5,2)
```

As you can see, the command lists three things for each column in the table:

- The column's name
- The column's datatype, and length if applicable
- Whether the column is allowed to be null

See Chapter 10 for more information about DESCRIBE, including examples of its use against procedures, functions, packages, synonyms, and object types.

CONNECT

Use CONNECT to log into your database as a different user or to log into a completely different database. This command is useful if you develop against, or manage, more than one database because you can quickly switch between them when you need to. A developer or DBA can commonly have multiple usernames on one database, with each being used for a different purpose. A DBA might log in as SYSTEM to create users and manage tablespaces but might choose to log in with a less privileged username when running reports.

The simplest way to use the CONNECT command is to use it by itself, with no arguments, as shown here:

```
SQL> CONNECT
Enter user-name: gennick
Enter password:
Connected.
SQL>
```

In this example, SQL*Plus prompted for a username and a password. SQL*Plus did not prompt for a connect string (and won't), so using this method allows you only to connect to your default database.

Another form of the CONNECT command allows you to specify the username, password, and connect string all on one line:

```
SQL> CONNECT gennick/secret
Connected.
SQL>
```

If you are security conscious (you should be) and happen to have someone looking over your shoulder, you may omit the password and let SQL*Plus prompt you for it. The advantage here is that the password won't be echoed to the display:

```
SQL> CONNECT gennick
Enter password:
Connected.
SQL>
```

The Windows version of SQL*Plus will echo asterisks to the display when you type your password. Command-line versions of SQL*Plus echo nothing at all.

In at least one version of SQL*Plus, Version 8.0.4, there is a bug that prevents the CONNECT *username* technique from working. You can enter CONNECT with the username as an argument, then enter the password when prompted, but SQL*Plus won't pass the correct information to the database.

As you might expect, you can pass a connect string to CONNECT. You'll need to do that any time you connect (or reconnect) to a database other than your local, default database:

```
SQL> CONNECT gennick@db01
Enter password:
Connected.
SQL>
```

Go ahead and try the CONNECT command a few times, trying the variations shown above. If you have only one username you can use, try reconnecting as yourself just to get the hang of it.

DISCONNECT

The DISCONNECT command is one I rarely use. It's the analog of the CONNECT command, and disconnects you from the Oracle database while leaving you in SQL*Plus. Here's an example:

```
SQL> DISCONNECT
Disconnected from Oracle Database 10g Enterprise Edition Release 10.1.0.2.0 -
Production
With the Partitioning, OLAP and Data Mining options
SQL>
```

Any pending transactions are committed before you are disconnected from Oracle. At this point you have three choices:

- Reconnect to Oracle using the CONNECT command.
- Exit SQL*Plus.
- Execute SQL*Plus commands that do not require a database connection. The SET command, for example, does not require you to be connected.

DISCONNECT is useful if you want to leave a SQL*Plus session open for a long period of time but do not wish to tie up a database connection.

HOST

The HOST command lets you temporarily drop out of SQL*Plus to your operating system command prompt but without disconnecting your database connection:

```
SQL> HOST
oracle@gennick02:~/sqlplus/ExampleData> ls
```

```
bld_db.lst      bld_db1y.sql  bld_db2y.sql  bld_tab.sql
bld_db1n.sql  bld_db2n.sql  bld_ins.sql    build_db.sql
oracle@gennick02:~/sqlplus/ExampleData> mv build_db.sql bld_db.sql
oracle@gennick02:~/sqlplus/ExampleData> exit
exit

SQL>
```

I've found HOST to be a *very* handy command. Many times, I've begun a SQL*Plus session only to realize I needed to execute one or more operating system commands. Rather than exit SQL*Plus and lose my connection and any settings I've made and rather than open a second command-prompt window, I can use the HOST command to drop out of SQL*Plus, execute whatever commands I need, and then exit my operating system shell (usually via an *exit* command) to return to where I was in SQL*Plus.

 As a shorthand for typing HOST, you can type a dollar sign ($) under Windows, or an exclamation point (!) under Unix/Linux:

```
SQL> !
oracle@gennick02:~/sqlplus/ExampleData> ls
bld_db.lst  bld_db1n.sql  bld_db2n.sql  bld_ins.sql
bld_db.sql  bld_db1y.sql  bld_db2y.sql  bld_tab.sql
oracle@gennick02:~/sqlplus/ExampleData>
```

The dollar sign also happens to be the shortcut character under VMS.

Running SQL Queries

Using SQL*Plus, you can execute any SQL query or statement that you desire. This includes data manipulation language (DML) statements such as INSERT, UPDATE, DELETE, MERGE, and SELECT. This also includes data definition language (DDL) statements such as CREATE TABLE, CREATE INDEX, CREATE USER, and so on. Essentially, you can execute any statement listed in the *Oracle SQL Reference* manual.

Example 2-1 shows a simple SELECT statement against the project table.

Example 2-1. A simple SELECT statement

```
SQL> SELECT * /* All columns */
  2    FROM project;

PROJECT_ID PROJECT_NAME                            PROJECT_BUDGET
---------- --------------------------------------- --------------
      1001 Corporate Web Site                             1912000
      1002 Enterprise Resource Planning System            9999999
      1003 Accounting System Implementation                897000
      1004 Data Warehouse Maintenance                      294000
      1005 VPN Implementation                              415000
```

Look again at the query shown in the example. Notice that the statement spans more than one line. Notice that it contains an embedded comment and that it ends with a semicolon. All of these things are important because they illustrate the following rules for entering SQL statements:

- SQL statements may span multiple lines.
- Line breaks may occur anywhere SQL allows whitespace, but blank lines are not normally allowed.
- Comments, delimited by /*...*/, may be embedded anywhere whitespace is allowed. A comment entered this way may span multiple lines.
- Comments denoted by a leading dash (-) may be added anywhere in a line and mark the remainder of that line as a comment.
- SQL statements must be terminated in one of three ways:
  - The statement may end with a trailing semicolon.
  - The statement may end with a forward slash character, but the forward slash must be on a line by itself and it must be in column one of that line.
  - The statement may end with a blank line, in which case it will be stored in the *SQL buffer* rather than be executed immediately.

Pay close attention to the three ways to terminate an SQL statement. You have to worry about this because statements can span multiple lines, and when you press ENTER for a new line, SQL*Plus needs some way of knowing whether you are done with the statement or whether you just want to continue it on another line. Until you enter a semicolon, a forward slash, or a blank line, SQL*Plus assumes that you are continuing your statement from one line to the next.

 From Oracle8*i* Database onward, you can issue the command SET SQL-BLANK-LINES ON to allow blank lines within SELECT statements. This is useful when running scripts originally designed to be run by the now obsolete Server Manager utility.

I usually recommend terminating SQL statements with semicolons, because I think that's the simplest and cleanest-looking method. The SELECT statement in Example 2-1 shows a semicolon at the end of the line, but if you forget and hit ENTER too quickly, you can also put it on the next line by itself, as shown in Example 2-2.

Example 2-2. The terminating semicolon on a line by itself

```
SQL> INSERT INTO project
  2     /* All columns */
  3  (project_id, project_name, project_budget)
```

Example 2-2. The terminating semicolon on a line by itself (continued)

```
 4  VALUES (1006,'Mainframe Upgrade',456789)
 5  ;

1 row created.
```

You can also use the forward slash (/) character to terminate a SQL statement, but it must be on a line by itself and must be the first and only character on that line. Example 2-3 demonstrates this usage.

Example 2-3. A statement terminated by a forward slash

```
SQL> UPDATE project
  2      SET project_budget = 1000000
  3  WHERE project_id = 1006
  4  /

1 row updated.
```

You will read more about the forward slash character later in this chapter because it's used to execute the SQL statement, or PL/SQL block, currently in the SQL buffer.

The final option for terminating an SQL statement is to simply press Enter on a blank line. This is shown in Example 2-4. There is a catch to this method, though.

Example 2-4. A statement terminated by a blank line

```
SQL> DELETE
  2  FROM project
  3  WHERE project_id = 1006
  4
SQL>
```

Look carefully at Example 2-4. Nothing happened. You typed in the DELETE statement, pressed Enter on a blank line, got back another SQL> prompt, but SQL*Plus said nothing about deleting the row that you just asked to delete. Why not? Because when you terminate an SQL query with a blank line, SQL*Plus stores that statement in an internal buffer but does not execute it. You'll read more about this later in this chapter in the section "The SQL Buffer." For now, though, if you haven't entered any other statements after the DELETE statement shown above, just type a forward slash on a line by itself and press Enter:

```
SQL> /

1 row deleted.
```

The DELETE has been executed and the row deleted. The forward slash tells SQL*Plus to execute the SQL statement most recently entered.

If you have been following along with SQL*Plus, and entering the examples while reading this section, you've probably noticed a couple of things. First, it's a pain when you make a mistake. Second, it's even worse when that mistake is on a previous line. If you were using the GUI version of SQL*Plus, you may have even tried to arrow up to correct a mistyped line. Well, don't waste your time because you can't do that. However, SQL*Plus does have some built-in line-editing capabilities, and it can call the text editor of your choice. You'll read about these options in just a bit, after the next section on executing PL/SQL blocks.

Executing Unrecognized SQL Statements

Under "Running SQL Queries," I stated that SQL*Plus may be used to execute any SQL statement. That's sort of true. You do need to have a version of SQL*Plus recent enough to "know" about whatever SQL statement you are attempting to execute. For example, SQL*Plus 8.1.7 does not recognize MERGE:

```
SQL> MERGE INTO project dest

SP2-0734: unknown command beginning "merge into..." - rest of line ignored.
```

SQL*Plus looks only at the first word of the statement before returning the error shown in this example. MERGE was introduced in Oracle9i Database, and no previously existing statements began with that keyword. New ALTER statements don't cause the same problem because ALTER *something* has been around forever.

If you find that you must execute an unrecognized SQL statement from an older version of SQL*Plus, and if that statement does not return any kind of result set that SQL*Plus would otherwise try to display, you likely can execute the statement from a PL/SQL block. For example:

```
BEGIN
   MERGE INTO project dest
   USING (SELECT * FROM project) source
   ON (dest.project_id = source.project_id)
   WHEN MATCHED THEN UPDATE
      SET dest.project_name = source.project_name;
END;
/
```

See the section "Working with PL/SQL" for information on executing PL/SQL from SQL*Plus.

Working with PL/SQL

PL/SQL is a programming language developed by Oracle as an extension to SQL to allow procedural logic to be implemented at the database level. PL/SQL is used to write stored procedures, stored functions, and triggers and, beginning with Oracle8, to define object types. It can also be used to simply write a block of procedural code for the database to execute. SQL*Plus was originally one of the only front ends that could be used to send PL/SQL code to the database, and even today it is still one of the most widely used.

This section explains the mechanics of entering and executing PL/SQL code with SQL*Plus. You'll learn what PL/SQL mode is, and you'll learn the differences between entering a PL/SQL block and a SQL query.

If you are unfamiliar with PL/SQL, you may want to pick up a copy of Steven Feuerstein and Bill Pribyl's book, *Oracle PL/SQL Programming*, Third Edition (O'Reilly). PL/SQL opens up a world of possibilities. You'll want to take advantage of it if you are doing serious work with Oracle.

What Is a PL/SQL Block?

The PL/SQL *block* is the fundamental unit of PL/SQL programming. The term block refers to a program unit that contains some or all of the following elements:

- Variable and subprogram declarations
- Procedural code, which may include nested PL/SQL blocks
- An error handler

Example 2-5 shows a reasonably simple, but complete, PL/SQL block.

Example 2-5. "Hello World!" written in PL/SQL

```
DECLARE
    X    VARCHAR2(12) := 'Hello World!';
BEGIN
    DBMS_OUTPUT.PUT_LINE(X);
EXCEPTION
WHEN OTHERS THEN
    DBMS_OUTPUT.PUT_LINE('An error occurred.');
END;
```

This code contains all the elements of a PL/SQL block and is one implementation of the traditional "Hello World!" program. Using SQL*Plus, you can send it to the database for execution.

Executing a PL/SQL Block

To execute a PL/SQL block, you type it into SQL*Plus and terminate it with a forward slash. The forward slash tells SQL*Plus that you are done entering the block and to send it to the database for execution. Example 2-6 shows how it would look to enter and execute the block from Example 2-5.

Example 2-6. Executing a PL/SQL block

```
SQL> DECLARE
  2      X    VARCHAR2(12) := 'Hello World!';
  3  BEGIN
  4      DBMS_OUTPUT.PUT_LINE(X);
  5  EXCEPTION
  6  WHEN OTHERS THEN
  7      DBMS_OUTPUT.PUT_LINE('An error occurred.');
  8  END;
  9  /

PL/SQL procedure successfully completed.
```

Where's the output?

You may be wondering why there was no output from the code block in Example 2-6. After all, the code does contain a call to the PUT_LINE procedure that sure looks as if it ought to display something.

In fact, the code did generate some output. You just didn't see it. Remember from Chapter 1 that SQL*Plus itself does not execute PL/SQL code. It simply sends that code to the database server, which executes the code for you. The Oracle database server doesn't have any way to display the output for you to see. Instead, any output from PL/SQL code is buffered by the server for later retrieval by the application that executed it, in this case SQL*Plus.

By default, SQL*Plus doesn't retrieve PL/SQL output from the server. You have to tell it to retrieve the output if you want to see it. Here is the command:

```
SET SERVEROUTPUT ON
```

If you enter this command, followed by the same PL/SQL block that you entered earlier, your output will look like that shown in Example 2-7.

Example 2-7. Enabling the display of DBMS_OUTPUT

```
SQL> SET SERVEROUTPUT ON
SQL> DECLARE
  2      X    VARCHAR2(12) := 'Hello World!';
  3  BEGIN
  4      DBMS_OUTPUT.PUT_LINE(X);
  5  EXCEPTION
  6  WHEN OTHERS THEN
  7      DBMS_OUTPUT.PUT_LINE('An error occurred.');
  8  END;
  9  /
Hello World!

PL/SQL procedure successfully completed.
```

This time around, you do see the output from the block. The SERVEROUTPUT setting "sticks" for the duration of your SQL*Plus session, so you don't have to keep turning it on each time you execute another block. There are some other parameters to the SET SERVEROUTPUT command that affect formatting and the output buffer size. The:SIZE parameter lets you increase the buffer size from the default of 2,000 bytes, something you should do if you expect to display a lot of information from PL/SQL. The FORMAT parameter lets you control whether, and how, long lines of output are wrapped when they are displayed. The following example shows how you can turn server output on, allow for a maximum of 1,000,000 bytes to be displayed, and word-wrap any long lines.

```
SET SERVEROUTPUT ON SIZE 1000000 FORMAT WORD_WRAPPED
```

Prior to Version 8 of SQL*Plus, the SIZE and FORMAT parameters did not exist. To increase the buffer size, you had to make a call to DBMS_OUTPUT.ENABLE. Example 2-8, in the section "Executing a Single PL/SQL Statement," shows how that's done.

Rules for entering PL/SQL blocks

When you begin entering a PL/SQL block, SQL*Plus switches to what is called *PL/SQL mode*. It knows to do this by watching for the keywords BEGIN and DECLARE, either of which may start a PL/SQL block. Once in PL/SQL mode, you can pretty much type anything you please. SQL*Plus simply buffers everything you type until you terminate PL/SQL mode by typing one of the termination characters—a forward slash or a period on a line by itself. Parsing and syntax checking of your PL/SQL code is done by the database server, not by SQL*Plus> and doesn't happen until after you have completely entered and terminated the block.

The following SQL statements put you into PL/SQL mode: CREATE PROCEDURE, CREATE FUNCTION, CREATE TRIGGER, CREATE PACKAGE, CREATE PACKAGE BODY, CREATE TYPE, CREATE TYPE BODY, and the CREATE OR REPLACE versions of each of these. That's because these statements allow you to define stored objects based on PL/SQL code.

The rules for entering a PL/SQL block are as follows:

- The first word of a PL/SQL block must be BEGIN, DECLARE, CREATE PROCEDURE, CREATE FUNCTION, CREATE TRIGGER, CREATE PACKAGE, CREATE TYPE, or CREATE TYPE BODY. Lowercase is acceptable; PL/SQL is not case-sensitive.
- PL/SQL blocks may span multiple lines.
- Line breaks may occur anywhere you can legally enter whitespace.
- Comments, delimited by /*...*/, may be embedded anywhere whitespace is allowed. These commands may span multiple lines.
- A double hyphen (--) makes everything after it on the same line a comment.

- Blank lines are allowed in a PL/SQL block.
- Entry of a PL/SQL block must be terminated in one of two ways:
  — Using the forward slash character. The forward slash must be on a line by itself, and must be in column one of that line. Using a forward slash tells SQL*Plus to execute the block you have just entered.
  — Using a period. The period must be on a line by itself, and in the first position. Using a period causes the statement to be stored in the SQL buffer rather than be executed immediately.

Because blank lines are allowed within a block of code, they can't be used to terminate a block. That's where the period comes into play. Just as you can enter a SQL statement into the buffer without executing it, so you also need a way to enter a PL/SQL block into the buffer without executing it. Because a blank line can't be used for that purpose, as it can be with an SQL statement, Oracle decided to allow the period on a line by itself to serve this function.

Likewise, because a PL/SQL block may be made up of many statements, each of which itself ends with a semicolon, that character cannot reliably be used as a termination character. So, to enter and execute a block, you are left with only the forward slash.

Executing a Single PL/SQL Statement

If you wish to execute a single PL/SQL statement, you can use the SQL*Plus EXECUTE command rather than write an entire block. The syntax for EXECUTE is:

```
EXECUTE plsql_statement
```

EXECUTE is most helpful when you want to make a quick call to a PL/SQL function. Example 2-8 shows EXECUTE being used to make a call to DBMS_OUTPUT. ENABLE, in order to allow more than the default 2000 bytes of PL/SQL output to be displayed.

Example 2-8. EXECUTE allows you to execute a single PL/SQL statement

```
SQL> EXECUTE DBMS_OUTPUT.ENABLE(10000)

PL/SQL procedure successfully completed.
```

The value of 10,000 in this example tells Oracle to allow for up to 10,000 bytes of output to be displayed by the DBMS_OUTPUT.PUT_LINE procedure. The EXECUTE command is nothing more than an SQL*Plus shortcut. SQL*Plus takes whatever text you type after EXECUTE, adds a semicolon to the end, wraps the keywords BEGIN and END around it, and sends it to Oracle as just another PL/SQL block.

The SQL Buffer

SQL*Plus keeps a copy of the most recently entered SQL statement or PL/SQL block in an internal memory area known as the *SQL buffer*, often referred to as the *buffer*. Command-line SQL*Plus needs a place to store your statement or block until you are finished entering it. SQL*Plus provides you with the ability to edit the statement in the buffer. This can be a real convenience if you make a mistake halfway through typing a long, multiline query.

> SQL*Plus buffers SQL statements and PL/SQL blocks, but not SQL*Plus commands. For example, the DESCRIBE command would not be buffered but a SELECT statement would be. To help make the distinction, think in terms of where the command is executed. If you enter something to be executed by the database server, then it is buffered. If it's a command local to SQL*Plus, then it is not buffered.

SQL*Plus provides two ways to edit the statement currently in the buffer. The first method is to use the set of line-editing commands built into SQL*Plus. The second method is to use the EDIT command to invoke an operating system-specific text editor, such as Notepad in the Windows environment, or *vi* under Unix.

> If you are editing a statement in the buffer, be sure you don't forget yourself and execute any other SQL statement. Even a simple SQL statement like COMMIT will overwrite the buffer. Commands to SQL*Plus, such as the editing commands, do not affect the buffer.

There are some other useful things you can do with the buffer. If you have several similar SQL statements to execute, using the buffer can save you the effort of completely typing out each one. You may be able to enter the first statement, execute it, make a minor change, execute the new statement, and so on, until you are done. SQL*Plus also allows you to save and load the buffer to and from a text file, allowing you to store frequently executed statements for later use.

Line Editing

The concept of line-editing goes way back to the days when all many people had to work with were *dumb terminals* that didn't allow full-screen editing, and connection speeds were so slow that full-screen editing would have been very painful anyway. A good line editor will allow you to work productively at connection speeds as low as 300 bits per second. While working at that speed isn't much of a concern today, it accurately reflects the environment at the time SQL*Plus was first conceived.

The line-editing process in SQL*Plus follows these steps:

1. Enter a SQL statement or PL/SQL block, which SQL*Plus stores in the buffer.
2. List the contents of the buffer to the screen.
3. Enter SQL*Plus commands telling SQL*Plus to make changes to the statement or block in the buffer.
4. List the buffer again.
5. If you like what you see, execute the statement or block; otherwise, you go back to step 3 and make some more changes.

I can remember that in my younger days my fellow programmers and I always took great pride in the number of line-editing changes we could make and visualize in our heads before we had to break down and list our code again.

The Current Line

When working with the line editor in SQL*Plus, you must understand the concept of the *current line*. The current line is the one that you have most recently "touched." When you are entering a statement, the most recently entered line is the current line.

The statement shown in Example 2-9 is six lines long. Line 7 doesn't count and is not added to the buffer because that's where the blank line is used to terminate entry of the statement. In this case, the last line "touched" happens to be the last line entered, so line 6 is the current line.

Example 2-9. Line 5 is the current line

```
SQL> SELECT employee_name, project_name
  2  FROM employee JOIN project_hours
  3         ON employee.employee_id = project_hours.employee_id
  4      JOIN project
  5         ON project_hours.project_id = project.project_id
  6  GROUP BY employee_name, project_name
  7
SQL>
```

Most line-editing commands, by default, operate on the current line. Some commands, such as LIST and DEL, allow you to specify a line number. When you specify a line number for an editing command, the command is executed, and that line then becomes the new current line. You'll see how this works as you read through the examples that follow.

Line-Editing Commands

SQL*Plus implements a number of useful line-editing commands, some of which have several variations. Most of these commands may be abbreviated to one letter.

Table 2-1 describes each of these commands and shows the abbreviations and variations for each one.

*Table 2-1. SQL*Plus line-editing commands*

Command	Abbreviation	Variations	Description
APPEND	A	A *text*	Appends text to the end of the current line.
CHANGE	C	C /*from*/*to*/	Scans the current line for the string *from*, and replaces the first occurrence of *from* with *to*.
		C /*delete*/	Deletes the first occurrence of *delete* from the current line. Think of this as changing *delete* to an empty string.
DEL	None	DEL	Deletes the current line.
		DEL *linenum*	Deletes line number *linenum* from the buffer.
		DEL *start end*	Deletes lines *start* through *end* from the buffer.
INPUT	I	I	Allows you to add one or more lines of text to the buffer. These lines are inserted into the buffer immediately following the current line.
		I *text*	Adds just one line to the buffer, consisting of *text*, which is inserted immediately following the current line.
LIST	L	L	Displays the entire buffer on the screen for you to see.
		L *linenum*	Lists a specific line number and makes that line current.
		L *start end*	Displays the specified range of lines, making the last line of that range current.
linenum	None	None	Lists that line number, making the line current.
CLEAR BUFFER	CL BUFF	CL BUFF	Clears the buffer. This deletes all the lines in one shot.

Notice that two of the commands, LIST and DEL, allow you to specify a line number or a range of line numbers. For these two commands, there are two special keywords you can use in place of a number. These keywords are * and LAST, and have the following meanings:

*
   An asterisk always refers to the current line.

LAST
   The keyword LAST refers to the last line in the buffer.

You will see examples of how these elements are used as you read more about each of the commands.

Getting a statement into the buffer

To put a SQL statement into the buffer, enter the statement and terminate it with a blank line, as shown in Example 2-10.

Example 2-10. Entering a SQL statement into the buffer

```
SQL> SELECT *
  2  FROM project
  3
SQL>
```

The statement is inserted into the buffer one line at a time as you enter it. Pressing Enter on a blank line tells SQL*Plus to leave the statement in the buffer without transmitting it to the server. PL/SQL blocks are entered the same way except that you terminate them by entering a period on the last line. Example 2-11 shows one of the shortest PL/SQL block you can write.

Example 2-11. A very short PL/SQL block

```
SQL> BEGIN
  2      NULL;
  3  END;
  4  .
SQL>
```

Terminating the block with a period tells SQL*Plus not to send it to the database, but to keep it in the buffer.

LIST

The LIST command shows you the current contents of the buffer. It is fundamental to the use of the other line-editing commands. Use LIST to view your SQL statement as it currently exists to see if any changes need to be made. Use LIST after making changes to be sure that they were made correctly.

Look at Example 2-12, which shows a SQL statement being entered into SQL*Plus, and then shows the LIST command being used to display it again.

Example 2-12. Listing the buffer

```
SQL> SELECT employee_name, time_log_name, project_name
  2  FROM employee JOIN
  3          ON employee.employee_num = time_log.employee_num
  4      JOIN project
  5          ON time_log.project_id = project.project_num
  6  HAVING employee_num = project_name
  7  GROUP BY employee_name, project_name
  8
SQL> LIST
  1  SELECT employee_name, time_log_name, project_name
  2  FROM employee JOIN
  3          ON employee.employee_num = time_log.employee_num
  4      JOIN project
  5          ON time_log.project_id = project.project_num
  6  HAVING employee_num = project_name
  7* GROUP BY employee_name, project_name
```

Notice the asterisk marking line 7. The asterisk indicates the current line, which LIST always sets to be the last line displayed. You can display just the current line by using LIST *, as in the following example:

```
SQL> LIST *
  7* GROUP BY employee_name, project_name
```

You can display one specific line by specifying the line number as an argument to the LIST command. The next example shows how to list line 3:

```
SQL> LIST 3
  3*          ON employee.employee_num = time_log.employee_num
```

Notice the asterisk. By listing line 3 you have made it the current line for editing purposes.

The keyword LAST may be used to display the last line in the buffer:

```
SQL> LIST LAST
  7* GROUP BY employee_name, project_name
```

You may specify a range of lines to be displayed. Do this by specifying the starting and ending lines as arguments to the LIST command. Either or both of these arguments may be the keyword LAST or *. Following are several different ways to display a range of lines using LIST:

```
SQL> LIST 1 3     List lines 1 through 3
  1  SELECT employee_name, time_log_name, project_name
  2  FROM employee JOIN
  3*          ON employee.employee_num = time_log.employee_num

SQL> LIST * LAST     List everything beginning from the current line
  3          ON employee.employee_num = time_log.employee_num
  4       JOIN project
  5          ON time_log.project_id = project.project_num
  6  HAVING employee_num = project_name
  7* GROUP BY employee_name, project_name

SQL> LIST 4 *     List from line 4 through 7 (the current line)
  4       JOIN project
  5          ON time_log.project_id = project.project_num
  6  HAVING employee_num = project_name
  7* GROUP BY employee_name, project_name

SQL> LIST * *     A one-line range, same effect as LIST *
  7* GROUP BY employee_name, project_name

SQL> LIST LAST LAST     A one-line range, same as LIST LAST
  7* GROUP BY employee_name, project_name
```

As a shortcut to using the LIST command, if you are only interested in one line, you can list it by entering the line number and then pressing Enter. This won't work for a range of lines, but it will work for just one. Here's an example:

```
SQL> 3
  3*          ON employee.employee_num = time_log.employee_num
```

On a seven-line statement, you might wonder why you would ever bother to list just one line or a range of lines. Remember, line speeds were slow when SQL*Plus was first developed. In addition, SQL statements and PL/SQL blocks are often much longer than seven lines. Listing a range allows you to focus on one area at a time while you fix it.

Keep the SQL statement from Example 2-12 in the buffer (or at least in mind) as you read about the rest of the line-editing commands. It has several mistakes that we'll fix using the other commands.

APPEND

Use the APPEND command to add text onto the end of a line. It works on the current line, so you must first decide which line you want to change and then make that line current. Use the LIST command to review the SQL statement currently in the buffer:

```
SQL> LIST
  1  SELECT employee_name, time_log_name, project_name
  2  FROM employee JOIN
  3          ON employee.employee_num = time_log.employee_num
  4      JOIN project
  5          ON time_log.project_id = project.project_num
  6  HAVING employee_num = project_name
  7* GROUP BY employee_name, project_name
```

I intended this SELECT statement to join all three sample tables, but if you look at line 2, you will see that I forgot to include the project_hours table. This can be corrected by first making line 2 the current line and then using the APPEND command to add the third table to the join. The first step is to LIST line 2 in order to make it current:

```
SQL> L 2
  2* FROM employee JOIN
```

Now that line 2 is the current line, the APPEND command may be used to add project_hours to the join:

```
SQL> A  project_hours
  2* FROM employee JOIN project_hours
```

It's a bit difficult to see from the example, but two spaces follow the A (for APPEND) command. The first space separates the command from the text you wish to append. SQL syntax requires a space following the keyword JOIN, so my text to append consisted of a space followed by the table name. Now the SELECT statement in the buffer joins all three tables.

CHANGE

The CHANGE command searches the current line for a specified string and replaces that string with another. CHANGE replaces only the first occurrence it finds, so if you need to change multiple occurrences of a string in the same line, you will need to execute the same CHANGE command several times. CHANGE may also be used to simply delete text from a line.

List the contents of the buffer again. Your output should match that shown below:

```
SQL> LIST
  1  SELECT employee_name, time_log_name, project_name
  2  FROM employee JOIN project_hours
  3          ON employee.employee_num = time_log.employee_num
  4      JOIN project
  5          ON time_log.project_id = project.project_num
  6  HAVING employee_num = project_name
  7* GROUP BY employee_name, project_name
```

Line 1 references a column that does not exist. A little later you will see how to remove that column reference with the CHANGE command. Next, the two ON clauses contain four mistakes: the table name time_log is used twice instead of project_hours, and employee_num is used twice when it really should be employee_id. The CHANGE command can be used to fix these problems. To start with, here's how to change time_log to project_hours:

```
SQL> L 3
  3*          ON employee.employee_num = time_log.employee_num
SQL> C /time_log/project_hours/
  3*          ON employee.employee_num = project_hours.employee_num
SQL> L 5
  5*          ON time_log.project_id = project.project_num
SQL> c /time_log/project_hours/
  5*          ON project_hours.project_id = project.project_num
```

In this example, the LIST command is first used to make line 3 the current line. Then the CHANGE command, abbreviated to C, is used to change the table name. After the edit is complete, the line is automatically redisplayed so you can see the effects of the change. The process is repeated to make the same change to line 5. You can change only one line at a time.

Next, the employee_num field name needs to be corrected. It should be employee_id. Although the two occurrences of employee_num are in the same line, CHANGE will have to be executed twice. The following example shows this:

```
SQL> L 3
  3*          ON employee.employee_num = project_hours.employee_num
SQL> c /employee_num/employee_id/
  3*          ON employee.employee_id = project_hours.employee_num
SQL> c /employee_num/employee_id/
  3*          ON employee.employee_id = project_hours.employee_id
```

Notice that the CHANGE command searched the current line from left to right. The leftmost occurrence of employee_num was the first to be changed. Notice also that the CHANGE command had to be retyped each time. SQL*Plus does not have any command-recall capability.

While SQL*Plus itself has no command-recall capabilities, your operating system shell may. Run command-line SQL*Plus from a Windows XP command-prompt window, and you'll be able to use the up and down arrows to move back and forth through your recently entered commands.

Now that line 3 is fixed up, take another look at line 1. This time, omit the L command, and just type the line number in order to list the line:

```
SQL> 1
  1* SELECT employee_name, time_log_name, project_name
```

Line 1 contains a bad column name, which needs to be deleted. A variation of the CHANGE command, where you don't supply any replacement text, can be used to do this. The following example shows how:

```
SQL> C /time_log_name, //
  1* SELECT employee_name, project_name
```

At first glance, the use of the CHANGE command to delete text may not seem very intuitive. Think in terms of searching for a string, in this case for "time_log_name, " and replacing it with nothing.

With the CHANGE command, you can use delimiters other than the forward slash character. You simply need to be consistent within the command. SQL*Plus interprets the first non-space character following the CHANGE command as the delimiter character. The following commands, for example, are all equivalent:

```
C /FRUB/FROM/
C *FRUB*FROM*
C XFRUBXFROMX
```

The only time you would ever need to use a delimiter other than / is if you need to include a / as part of the text to be searched for or replaced. You have the option of leaving off the trailing delimiter as long as you aren't trying to include trailing spaces in your substitution string. The following two commands are equivalent:

```
C /FRUB/FROM/
C /FRUB/FROM
```

However, if your substitution strings contain spaces, you do need to include the trailing delimiter. The following two commands will *not* produce equivalent results:

```
C / FRUB / FROM /
C / FRUB / FROM
```

It's probably easiest to be in the habit of including the trailing delimiter all the time. You'll make fewer mistakes that way.

DEL

Use the DEL command to erase one or more lines from the buffer. Used by itself, DEL erases the current line. You may specify a line, or a range of lines, as an argument to the DEL command. Unlike the other line-editing commands, DEL cannot be abbreviated. This is perhaps a safety measure to keep you from accidentally deleting a line.

 Be careful that you do not spell out the command as DELETE instead of DEL. SQL*Plus will interpret DELETE as a new SQL statement, and will place it in the buffer in place of the statement that you are editing. You will then have lost your statement.

If you have been following along through all the line-editing examples, use the L command to list the buffer. You should see the following output:

```
SQL> L
  1  SELECT employee_name, project_name
  2  FROM employee JOIN project_hours
  3         ON employee.employee_id = project_hours.employee_id
  4      JOIN project
  5         ON project_hours.project_id = project.project_num
  6  HAVING employee_num = project_name
  7* GROUP BY employee_name, project_name
```

Line 6, with its HAVING clause, is completely spurious. It can be erased by specifying the DEL command as follows:

```
SQL> DEL 6
SQL> L *
  6* GROUP BY employee_name, project_name
```

SQL*Plus doesn't echo anything back at you, but line 6 has been erased. Notice that L * was used following the delete to list the current line, which is now line 6. Why line 6? Because 6 was the number of the line most recently touched by an editing command. In this case, the original line 6 was erased, what was line 7 became line 6, and the new line 6 became current.

The DEL command may be used to erase a range of lines. As with LIST, the keywords LAST and * may be used to specify the last line in the buffer and the current line, respectively. The following example shows how to erase lines 4 through the current line, which is line 6:

```
SQL> DEL 4 *
SQL> L *
  3*         ON employee.employee_id = project_hours.employee_id
```

Because line 6 was current, the DEL command just shows erased lines 4 through 6. The new current line would ordinarily still be line 4 because that was the last number line touched (erased) but, in this case, because only three lines are left in the buffer, the last line becomes current.

INPUT

The INPUT command is used to insert one or more lines of text into the buffer. The INPUT command with a text argument allows you to insert only one line, which is placed into the buffer following the current line. The INPUT command with no arguments puts you into a multiline input mode where you can type as many lines as desired, ending with a blank line. These lines are inserted into the buffer following the current line.

List the buffer again. You can see that we have done serious damage to our SELECT statement by our most recent, and evidently careless, deletion:

```
SQL> L
  1  SELECT employee_name, project_name
  2  FROM employee JOIN project_hours
  3*        ON employee.employee_id = project_hours.employee_id
```

The original intent was to list each employee together with all projects to which the employee actually charged hours. To do that, the join to project and the GROUP BY clause need to be put back in. The following example shows how to insert the GROUP BY clause by using the INSERT command with a text argument:

```
SQL> L    Make line 3 current, in order to insert after it
  1  SELECT employee_name, project_name
  2  FROM employee JOIN project_hours
  3*        ON employee.employee_id = project_hours.employee_id
SQL> I GROUP BY employee_name, project_name
SQL> L
  1  SELECT employee_name, project_name
  2  FROM employee JOIN project_hours
  3         ON employee.employee_id = project_hours.employee_id
  4* GROUP BY employee_name, project_name
```

An easier alternative, when you have several lines to insert, would be to use the INPUT command with no arguments. This places you into *input mode*, in which you can type as many lines as you like. Pressing a blank line exits input mode, and terminates the entry. Here's how to put back the join to the project table using this method:

```
SQL> L 3
  3*        ON employee.employee_id = project_hours.employee_id
SQL> I
  4i     JOIN project
  5i        ON project_hours.project_id = project.project_id
  6i
SQL> L
  1  SELECT employee_name, project_name
  2  FROM employee JOIN project_hours
  3         ON employee.employee_id = project_hours.employee_id
  4      JOIN project
  5        ON project_hours.project_id = project.project_id
  6* GROUP BY employee_name, project_name
```

The LIST command was used to make line 3 current, so that new lines will be inserted after it. Then the I (for INPUT) command was used by itself to enter input mode, and the two lines defining the join to project were entered into the buffer. The prompt included an "i" following the line number to remind you that you were inserting lines into an existing statement.

If you are picky about formatting, use the second form of the INPUT command shown above. That will let you enter leading spaces to make things line up nicely. INPUT *text* will trim off leading spaces before text is inserted.

To add lines at the end of a buffer, first do a LIST or a LIST LAST to make the last line current. Then use the INPUT command to put yourself into input mode. Any lines you type will be appended onto the end of the buffer.

To add a line to the beginning of the buffer, prior to the first line, add it as line 0:

```
SQL> SELECT * FROM dually
  2
SQL> L
  1* SELECT * FROM dually
SQL> 0 WITH dually AS (SELECT * FROM dual)
SQL> L
  1  WITH dually AS (SELECT * FROM dual)
  2* SELECT * FROM dually
```

Retyping a line

Using the line editor, you can completely replace a line in the buffer by entering the desired line number followed by a new version of the line. Following is our now executable statement:

```
SQL> L
  1  SELECT employee_name, project_name
  2  FROM employee JOIN project_hours
  3        ON employee.employee_id = project_hours.employee_id
  4        JOIN project
  5        ON project_hours.project_id = project.project_id
  6* GROUP BY employee_name, project_name
```

Suppose that for reasons of aesthetics, or perhaps to follow your site's coding standards, you wish to make the JOIN keyword flush-left. You can do that by retyping the entire line in one go, as follows:

```
SQL> 4 JOIN project
SQL> l
  1  SELECT employee_name, project_name
  2  FROM employee JOIN project_hours
  3        ON employee.employee_id = project_hours.employee_id
  4  JOIN project
  5        ON project_hours.project_id = project.project_id
  6* GROUP BY employee_name, project_name
```

Notice that line 4 has been replaced by the text that was typed after the numeral 4 on the first line of this example. You can replace any line in this way. If you want to preserve the indenting, you can insert extra spaces following the line number.

Executing the Statement in the Buffer

Once you get a statement into the buffer and have edited it the way you want it, the next step is to execute that statement. You can do that using one of the following two methods:

- Type a forward slash on a line by itself, then press Enter.
- Use the RUN command, which you may abbreviate to R.

The only difference between using / and RUN is that the RUN command lists the contents of the buffer before executing it, and the / command simply executes the command without re-listing it. Assume that you have the SQL statement shown next in the buffer, which you will if you have followed through all the examples in this chapter:

```
SQL> L
  1  SELECT employee_name, project_name
  2  FROM employee JOIN project_hours
  3        ON employee.employee_id = project_hours.employee_id
  4  JOIN project
  5        ON project_hours.project_id = project.project_id
  6* GROUP BY employee_name, project_name
```

Here is how you would execute it using the / command:

```
SQL> /

EMPLOYEE_NAME                     PROJECT_NAME
-----------------------------     ---------------------------------------
Ivan Mazepa                       Corporate Web Site
Ivan Mazepa                       VPN Implementation
Ivan Mazepa                       Data Warehouse Maintenance
...
```

Now, here is how you would execute it using the RUN command, which in the following example is abbreviated to R:

```
SQL> R
  1  SELECT employee_name, project_name
  2  FROM employee JOIN project_hours
  3        ON employee.employee_id = project_hours.employee_id
  4  JOIN project
  5        ON project_hours.project_id = project.project_id
  6* GROUP BY employee_name, project_name
```

```
EMPLOYEE_NAME                    PROJECT_NAME
----------------------------     ------------------------------------------
Ivan Mazepa                      Corporate Web Site
Ivan Mazepa                      VPN Implementation
Ivan Mazepa                      Data Warehouse Maintenance
...
```

This time, the SQL statement in the buffer was first displayed on the screen, and then executed. I almost always use the forward slash to execute commands, but RUN is useful if you are printing an ad hoc report, or sending the query results to a file, and wish to have a copy of the SQL statement included for future reference.

If Your Statement Has an Error

If a SQL statement fails to execute, SQL*Plus does three things:

- Makes the line triggering the error current
- Displays that line for you to edit
- Displays the error message returned by Oracle

Look at the following example of a SQL SELECT statement with an invalid column name:

```
SQL> SELECT employee_name
  2  FROM project;
SELECT employee_name
       *
ERROR at line 1:
ORA-00904: "EMPLOYEE_NAME": invalid identifier
```

SQL*Plus displays the error returned by Oracle, which tells you that your column name is bad. The offending line is displayed, and an asterisk points to the incorrect column name. You can quickly edit that line, change employee_name to project_name, and re-execute the command as follows:

```
SQL> c /employee_name/project_name/
  1* SELECT project_name
SQL> /

PROJECT_NAME
------------------------------------------
Corporate Web Site
Enterprise Resource Planning System
Accounting System Implementation
Data Warehouse Maintenance
VPN Implementation
```

This feature is convenient if you have entered a long command and have made one or two small mistakes.

When debugging SQL statements (or PL/SQL blocks), don't get too hung up on where Oracle thinks the error is. When SQL*Plus displays an error line with an asterisk under it, that asterisk is pointing to where Oracle was "looking" when the problem was detected. Depending on the nature of the error, you may need to look elsewhere in your statement. Getting the table name wrong, for example, may lead to spurious invalid column errors. The error in the example just shown could also have been corrected by changing the table name from employee to project. Know what results you are after, and be prepared to look beyond the specific error message that you get from Oracle.

If you want to create a stored object, such as a stored procedure, you will need to use the SHOW ERRORS command to see where any errors lie. Example 2-13 demonstrates this.

Example 2-13. Using SHOW ERRORS when stored procedure creation fails

```
SQL> CREATE PROCEDURE wont_work AS
  2  BEGIN
  3     bad_statement;
  4  END;
  5  /

Warning: Procedure created with compilation errors.

SQL> SHOW ERRORS
Errors for PROCEDURE WONT_WORK:

LINE/COL ERROR
-------- -----------------------------------------------------------------
3/4      PL/SQL: Statement ignored
3/4      PLS-00201: identifier 'BAD_STATEMENT' must be declared
```

The reason for this difference is that when you compile code for a stored object, such as a procedure or function, Oracle parses all the code and reports all the errors it finds. This is convenient because if you have a large code block, you certainly don't want to have to find and correct errors one at a time:

Doing It Again

Three other things are worth knowing about the RUN (or /) command:

- Unless an error occurs, the current line is not changed.
- Executing a statement does not remove it from the buffer.
- Executing a SQL*Plus command leaves the buffer intact.

These three features make it easy to rerun an SQL statement either as it stands or with minor changes. Take a look at Example 2-14, which displays the name for employee number 107.

Example 2-14. Retrieving an employee's name

```
SQL> SELECT employee_name
  2  FROM employee
  3  WHERE employee_id = 107;

EMPLOYEE_NAME
-----------------------------
Lesia Ukrainka
```

A quick change to line 3 will let you see the name for employee ID 110:

```
SQL> 3
  3* WHERE employee_id = 107
SQL> c /107/110/
  3* WHERE employee_id = 110
SQL> /

EMPLOYEE_NAME
-----------------------------
Ivan Mazepa
```

At this point, line 3 is still current. Because no error occurred, SQL*Plus had no reason to change the current line, so it's even easier to look at the name for employee number 111:

```
SQL> c /110/111/
  3* WHERE employee_id = 111
SQL> /

EMPLOYEE_NAME
-----------------------------
Taras Shevchenko
```

Sometimes it makes sense to execute the same statement again without making any changes to it. A SELECT statement that queried one of the V$ tables, perhaps V$SESSION, to get a list of current users, would be a good example of this. INSERT statements are often repeatedly executed to generate small amounts of test data.

As I mentioned earlier, Windows XP supports command-recall. Press F7 from the Windows XP command prompt, or from the command-line SQL*Plus prompt while running under Windows, and you should see a list of commands that you have previously typed. Use the up/down arrows to select one, and press Enter to execute it again. Press Esc to dismiss the command-recall dialog.

This technique does *not* work from the Windows GUI version of SQL*Plus, but only from the Windows command-line version.

Saving and Retrieving the Buffer

SQL*Plus allows you to save the contents of the buffer to a file and to read that file back again. If you have built up a long and complicated SQL statement, you can save it for later reuse and save yourself the bother of figuring it all out again. Two commands, SAVE and GET, are provided for this purpose.

SAVE

Example 2-15 shows the SAVE command being used to save the contents of a long SQL query to a file. First, the query is entered into the buffer without being executed; then the SAVE command is used to write the buffer to a file.

Example 2-15. Writing the current buffer contents to a file

```
SQL> SELECT employee_name, project_name
  2 FROM employee JOIN project_hours
  3     ON employee.employee_id = project_hours.employee_id
  4 JOIN project
  5     ON project_hours.project_id = project.project_id
  6 AND employee_billing_rate IN (
  7         SELECT MAX(employee_billing_rate)
  8         FROM employee)
  9 GROUP BY employee_name, project_name
 10
SQL> SAVE highest_billed_emp_projects
Created file highest_billed_emp_projects.sql
```

The SAVE command in Example 2-15 creates a *new* file, with the default extension of *.sql*, and writes the contents of the buffer to that file. After writing the buffer contents, SQL*Plus writes a trailing forward slash on a line by itself, so the resulting output file looks like this:

```
SELECT employee_name, project_name
FROM employee JOIN project_hours
    ON employee.employee_id = project_hours.employee_id
JOIN project
    ON project_hours.project_id = project.project_id
AND employee_billing_rate IN (
        SELECT MAX(employee_billing_rate)
        FROM employee)
GROUP BY employee_name, project_name
/
```

SQL*Plus will not automatically replace an existing file. Had the file already existed, SQL*Plus would have reported an error. You must use the REPLACE option to overwrite an existing file:

```
SAVE C:\A\HIGHEST_BILLED_EMP_PROJECTS REPLACE
```

You can use the APPEND option to add the contents of the buffer onto the end of an existing file. If you append multiple statements to a file, you won't be able to load that file back into the buffer and execute those commands. However, you will be able to execute the file using the START command.

> Use descriptive filenames when saving your SQL statements. You want the filename to jog your memory later when you need to retrieve that statement. The query shown in Example 2-15 returns a list of projects worked on by the employee (or employees) with the highest billing rate; thus, the filename of *highest_billed_emp_projects* seems appropriate. The length of a filename is governed by what your operating system allows.

GET

The GET command is the opposite of SAVE. It retrieves the contents of a file to the buffer. The file extension defaults to *.sql*. For example, to retrieve the statement saved earlier in Example 2-15, specify the following:

```
SQL> GET highest_billed_emp_projects
  1  SELECT employee_name, project_name
  2  FROM employee JOIN project_hours
  3      ON employee.employee_id = project_hours.employee_id
  4  JOIN project
  5      ON project_hours.project_id = project.project_id
  6  AND employee_billing_rate IN (
  7        SELECT MAX(employee_billing_rate)
  8        FROM employee)
  9* GROUP BY employee_name, project_name
```

The GET command automatically displays the contents of the retrieved file for you to see. This allows you to confirm that you have loaded the correct statement. You can use the NOLIST option, as in GET highest_billed_emp_projects NOLIST if you don't want that behavior. Once the statement has been loaded into the buffer, you may execute it using RUN or /, or you may use any of the editing commands to change it.

> The GET command will load *any* text file into the buffer, whether that file contains a valid statement or a PL/SQL block. This might be a useful thing to know if you are ever really hard up for an editor. Any file you write back out will include a trailing forward slash.

Although SQL*Plus will let you load any text file into the buffer, be aware that you cannot execute the buffer unless it contains exactly *one* SQL statement or *one* PL/SQL block. To be safe, the text file should terminate the statement (or block) with a forward slash on a line by itself. See the previous section on the SAVE command for an example of this.

Executing Unrecognized SQL Statements Redux!

That SQL*Plus lets you GET any arbitrary text into the buffer, which presents another solution to the problem of executing a SQL statement not recognized by your version of SQL*Plus. This time, consider a SELECT statement beginning with a WITH clause, which SQL*Plus 8.1.7 does not recognize:

```
SQL> WITH dually AS (SELECT * FROM dual)

SP2-0734: unknown command beginning "with dually..." - rest of line ignored.
```

Suppose that you want, nay need, to execute this statement. Executing it from within PL/SQL doesn't work because PL/SQL doesn't handle statements that return a result set in the manner that this one does.

A solution is to place the statement within a text file, and GET that file. Say you place the following statement into a file named *dually.sql*:

```
WITH dually AS (SELECT * FROM dual)
SELECT * FROM dually
/
```

You can now GET and execute that statement:

```
SQL> GET dually
  1  WITH dually AS (SELECT * FROM dual)
  2* SELECT * FROM dually
  3  /

D
-
X
```

This technique works because, while SQL*Plus tests the first keyword from any statement you enter interactively, it doesn't do so for any file that you read into the buffer. GET bypasses the mechanism whereby SQL*Plus attempts to determine whether a given statement is valid.

Thanks to Tom Kyte for suggesting this fascinating use of GET.

The EDIT Command

You don't like line-editing? SQL*Plus does not have a built-in full-screen editor, but it does have the EDIT command. The SQL*Plus EDIT command allows you to invoke the text editor of your choice to use in editing SQL statements and PL/SQL blocks.

Choosing Your Editor

Although you issue the EDIT command, SQL*Plus invokes the editor named in a SQL*Plus user variable named _EDITOR. You can view the current editor choice by issuing the command DEFINE _EDITOR, as follows:

```
SQL> DEFINE _EDITOR
DEFINE _EDITOR          = "ed" (CHAR)
```

If you don't like the default choice (and I'm reasonably certain you won't), you can change the editor, but only for the duration of your current session, using another variation of the DEFINE command:

```
DEFINE _editor = "vi"
```

Now, SQL*Plus will invoke the *vi* editor in response to the EDIT command.

If you're using the Windows version of SQL*Plus, you can change the value of EDITOR from the GUI, using Edit → EditorDefine → Editor, as shown in Figures 2-6 and 2-7. The default editor choice under Windows is Notepad.

Figure 2-6. The Define Editor menu option

To make an editor choice permanent, you can place a DEFINE _EDITOR command in either your global or local login file. SQL*Plus login files are executed whenever SQL*Plus starts, or, beginning with Oracle Database 10g, whenever you connect to a database. See Chapter 14 for more information on login files and other aspects of SQL*Plus configuration.

> Neither the command nor the user variable name is case-sensitive, so define _editor will work just as well as DEFINE _EDITOR.

Invoking the Editor

You invoke the editor with the EDIT command, which may be abbreviated ED. SQL*Plus then invokes your external editor to let you edit the statement currently

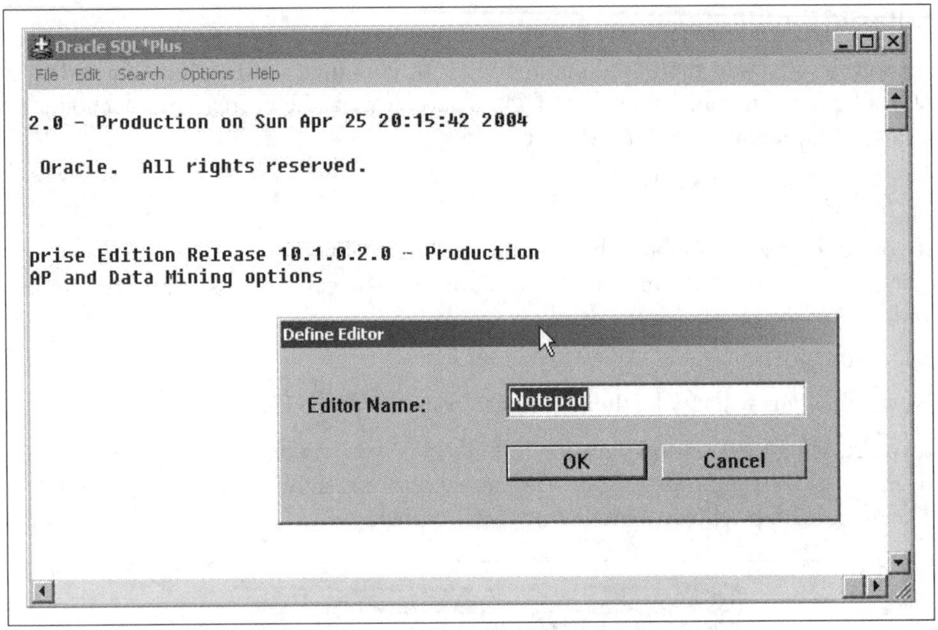

Figure 2-7. Specifying the executable to invoke in response to the EDIT command

contained in the buffer. Example 2-16 shows a query being entered and the editor being invoked.

Example 2-16. Invoking an external editor

```
SQL> SELECT project_name
  2  FROM project
  3  WHERE project_id IN (
  4      SELECT DISTINCT project_id
  5      FROM project_hours)
  6
SQL> EDIT
Wrote file afiedt.buf
```

When you execute the EDIT command, the contents of the buffer are written to a file named *afiedt.buf*, and your editor is invoked. The filename *afiedt.buf* is passed as the first argument in the editor's invocation (e.g., *vi afiedt.buf*, or *Notepad afiedt.buf*). Figure 2-8 shows what your screen would now look like on a Windows system.

The filename *afiedt.buf* is simply a work file used by SQL*Plus to hold your command while it is being edited. The name is a throwback to the very early days of SQL*Plus when it was briefly known as AFI, which stood for Advanced Friendly Interface.

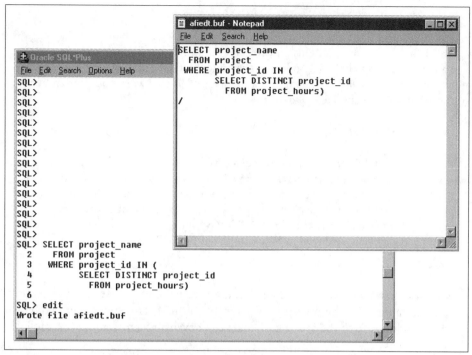

Figure 2-8. Results of the EDIT command under Windows

SQL*Plus will not invoke the editor if the buffer is empty; instead, you will see the following message:

```
SQL> edit
SP2-0107: Nothing to save.
```

If you have an empty buffer and wish to enter a new query, you must type something, perhaps just the first line, into SQL*Plus before using the EDIT command.

Beware Editing Conflicts!

There is the potential for conflict if you and another user happen to be sharing the same current working directory, and you both invoke an external editor to edit the contents of your SQL buffer. After all, only one *afiedt.buf* file can be in a directory.

The following editing sequence was generated on a Windows system with SQL*Plus set to use Windows Notepad as the external editor:

```
SQL> select * from project
  2
SQL> edit
Wrote file afiedt.buf

  1* select * from employee
```

Beware of ed!

The default editor for SQL*Plus on Unix and Linux systems is, unfortunately, not *vi*. Rather, it is *ed*, which is a line-oriented text editor along the lines of SQL*Plus's built-in editing functionality. You'll know you've dropped into *ed* when you issue an EDIT command with results like the following:

```
SQL> edit
Wrote file afiedt.buf
21
```

Press Enter at this point, and the only feedback you'll get is a question mark (?). It's not at all obvious how to exit *ed* and return to SQL*Plus. If you don't happen to know how to use *ed*, you might feel trapped in an editor that you can't get out of. When that happens, just press Ctrl-D. That key sequence will exit the *ed* editor and return you to SQL*Plus, from which you can define EDITOR to point to *vi*, or any other editor you're comfortable with, as described in "Choosing Your Editor."

The original statement was *not* changed in the external editor. The result statement, which only appears to be an edited version of the first, is a statement I edited in another window. I used the following sequence of events to generate this example:

1. Opened SQL*Plus window #1, entered select * from project.

2. Opened SQL*Plus window #2, entered select * from employee.

3. Issued EDIT command from window #1. The file *afiedt.buf* now contains select * from project.

4. Issued EDIT command from window #2. The file *afiedt.buf* now contains select * from employee.

5. Closed window #2's Notepad instance. No change to *afiedt.buf*. SQL*Plus in window #2 reads back the same statement that it wrote out.

6. Closed window #1's Notepad instance. SQL*Plus in window #1 reads back the statement written out from window #2.

Of course, on Windows you usually have only one user per system, so this scenario is unlikely. However, it's common to have many concurrent users on Linux and Unix systems, so the possibility of this scenario is something you should remember.

 The Linux/Unix *vim* editor will detect the conflict I've just described, through the existence of a swap file that *vim* attempts to create based on the name of the file you are editing. However, the *vim* editor can't determine whether two users are trying to edit the same file, or whether the swap file is left over from a previous editing session that crashed.

Editing Specific Files

Another use for the EDIT command is to edit an existing text file. You can edit any text file you like whether it contains a query or not. The following EDIT command, for example, lets you edit your Unix profile:

```
EDIT .profile
```

When you edit a file in this way, the contents of the file are *not* loaded into the buffer. This is just a convenient way for you to edit a file without having to exit SQL*Plus first.

This technique will not work for files without extensions, as SQL*Plus will always attempt to add *.sql* to any filename you supply to the EDIT command that does not already have a period in the name.

Formatting Your Command

Take another look at Figure 2-8. Pay attention to the way in which the SQL statement is terminated. No trailing semicolon exists, and the statement is terminated by a forward slash on a line by itself. You can include or omit the trailing forward slash, but do not attempt to terminate a SQL statement with a semicolon when editing the SQL buffer using an external editor.

When you type a SQL statement directly into SQL*Plus and terminate it with a semicolon, SQL*Plus strips off that semicolon, which is not properly part of SQL syntax. However, if you include a terminating semicolon while editing a SQL statement with an external editor, that semicolon gets loaded into the SQL buffer as part of the statement, and the result will be an invalid character error when you go to execute the statement.

Although SQL statements do not require a trailing semicolon, a PL/SQL block does because the trailing semicolon is part of the PL/SQL syntax but not part of the SQL syntax.

Here are some rules to follow when editing the SQL buffer with an external text editor:

- Do not end SQL statements with a semicolon.
- End PL/SQL blocks with a semicolon.
- Optionally, terminate the file with a forward slash on a line by itself.
- Include only one SQL statement or PL/SQL block.

Getting Back to SQL*Plus

Once you are finished editing your statement, you need to exit the editor in order to return to SQL*Plus. If you are using Notepad under Windows, you do this by going to the File menu and choosing Exit.

 Be sure to save the file before leaving the editor. To make SQL*Plus see your changes, they must be written back to the work file. Most editors, including Notepad, will remind you to save your changes before you exit, but *vi* will not. You should explicitly save your changes unless you want to throw them away.

When you exit the editor, control returns to SQL*Plus. The contents of the work file are loaded into the buffer and displayed on the screen for you to see. You may then execute your revised statement by using either the RUN or / command.

 The work file (*afiedt.buf*) is not deleted. Its contents remain undisturbed until your next use of the EDIT command.

Executing a Script

Most of this chapter has focused on what you need to know to enter a command directly into SQL*Plus and have it executed. Another option available to you is to have SQL*Plus execute a *script*, which is simply a text file that contains one or more statements to execute. When SQL*Plus executes a script, the commands or statements in the file are executed just as if you had typed them in directly from the keyboard. A script file can contain any combination of valid SQL*Plus commands, SQL statements, or PL/SQL blocks.

Let's say you have a file named *ex2-17.sql*, and it contains the following SQL*Plus commands:

```
SET ECHO ON
DESCRIBE employee
DESCRIBE project
DESCRIBE project_hours
```

You can execute this file using the @ command, as shown in Example 2-17. Type an @ character, follow it by the path to the script you wish to execute, and press Enter.

*Example 2-17. Executing a SQL*Plus script*

```
SQL> @$HOME/sqlplus/ExampleScripts/ex2-17
SQL> DESCRIBE employee
 Name                                      Null?    Type
 ----------------------------------------- -------- ----------------------------
 EMPLOYEE_ID                               NOT NULL NUMBER
```

*Example 2-17. Executing a SQL*Plus script (continued)*

```
EMPLOYEE_NAME                                    VARCHAR2(40)
EMPLOYEE_HIRE_DATE                               DATE
EMPLOYEE_TERMINATION_DATE                        DATE
EMPLOYEE_BILLING_RATE                            NUMBER(5,2)

SQL> DESCRIBE project
Name                                   Null?    Type
-------------------------------------- -------- ---------------------------
PROJECT_ID                             NOT NULL NUMBER(4)
PROJECT_NAME                                    VARCHAR2(40)
PROJECT_BUDGET                                  NUMBER(9,2)

SQL> DESCRIBE project_hours
Name                                   Null?    Type
-------------------------------------- -------- ---------------------------
PROJECT_ID                             NOT NULL NUMBER(4)
EMPLOYEE_ID                            NOT NULL NUMBER
TIME_LOG_DATE                          NOT NULL DATE
HOURS_LOGGED                                    NUMBER(5,2)
DOLLARS_CHARGED                                 NUMBER(8,2)
```

The @ command in Example 2-17 specifies the full path to the script. If the script happens to be in your current working directory, you can omit the path. By default, SQL*Plus doesn't display commands, statements, and blocks as it executes them from the script. The SET ECHO ON command in *ex2-17.sql* changes this behavior and is the reason why you see the three DESCRIBE commands in the output from the script. Otherwise, you'd see only the output from those commands.

You can do a lot with scripts. They are handy for running reports, extracting data, creating new database users, and performing any other complex task that you need to repeat on a periodic basis. Much of this book centers on the concept of writing SQL*Plus scripts to automate these types of routine tasks. You will begin to see scripts used beginning in Chapter 5 where you will learn how to write scripts to take advantage of SQL*Plus's reporting functionality. Chapters 8 and 11 delve into the subject of scripting even more deeply.

The Working Directory

Whenever you work with files in SQL*Plus, you must understand the concept of a working directory. The *working directory* is simply the directory that is used whenever you specify a filename without also including a path. The working directory is where SQL*Plus writes temporary files, such as the *afiedt.buf* file created when you invoke the EDIT command.

If you work under an operating system like Unix, you will be familiar with the concept of a current working directory. You will likely need to know how to move between directories, and will be familiar with commands such as *pwd* that tell you what your current directory is. The working directory simply happens to be whatever directory you are in when you invoke SQL*Plus.

Users of the Microsoft Windows operating system tend to be a bit insulated from the concept of a current directory. SQL*Plus is often invoked under Windows by clicking an icon, and the user often does not think of himself as being "in" any particular directory when this is done. Nonetheless, some directory will be current when you run SQL*Plus under Windows. Take a look at Figure 2-9. It shows the properties for the SQL*Plus menu item under Windows XP.

Notice the *Start in* setting shown in Figure 2-9. It's set to the *c:\oracle\product\10.1.1.0\ Db_1\BIN* directory, the same directory in which the executable sits. The implication is that whenever you run SQL*Plus under Windows and use the @ command to execute a file, and you don't specify a path, SQL*Plus will look in Oracle's *BIN* directory. Likewise, the SAVE and GET commands will write and read from the *BIN* directory, at least by default. And when you use the EDIT command, the temporary file *afiedt.buf* will be created in the *BIN* directory.

 It's best, if you are using SQL*Plus under Windows, to specify a path when you save a query to a file. If you save a file and later can't seem to find it, the Oracle *BIN* directory is the first place you should look.

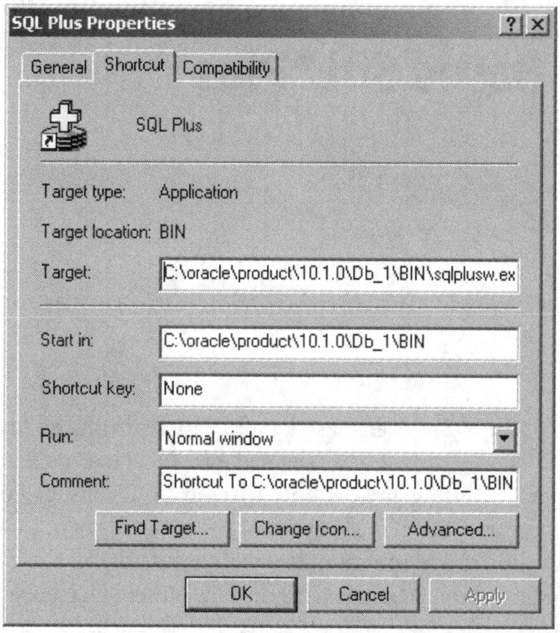

Figure 2-9. The SQL*Plus shortcut properties under Windows XP

You can change the default directory if you like. One way would be to edit the short-cut properties and change the *Start in* setting to some other directory. Sometimes, I'll create a second copy of the SQL*Plus shortcut, for a specific project, pointing the *Start in* directory to my project directory. Then I can easily start the Windows GUI version of SQL*Plus and begin editing or executing my scripts.

CHAPTER 3

Browser-Based SQL*Plus

The new three-tier, web browser–based *i*SQL*Plus introduced in 2001 as part of Oracle9*i* Database shook up the staid world of SQL*Plus, and certainly surprised many Oracle users (including me), who expected SQL*Plus to continue on as the simple, client-server application it always had been. Since then, Oracle has made virtually all of its administrative functionality web-accessible in the form of the newer, web-based Oracle Enterprise Manager interface in Oracle Database 10*g*.

In Oracle9*i* Database, *i*SQL*Plus ran under Oracle's HTTP Server, which was a version of the Apache web server connected to your Oracle database. In Oracle Database 10*g*, *i*SQL*Plus runs as a Java 2 Enterprise Edition (J2EE) application server using Oracle Containers for Java (OC4J) as the server engine. In Oracle9*i* Database, *i*SQL*Plus was installed separately from the database along with the HTTP Server. In Oracle Database 10*g*, *i*SQL*Plus is installed by default with the database on the database server.

Using *i*SQL*Plus means that you can connect to your database from any machine on your network without the need to first install Oracle's client software. That's a real convenience, even for those of us who prefer the older, two-tier, command-line SQL*Plus.

Starting iSQL*Plus

Starting *i*SQL*Plus and connecting to a database is relatively easy. The most difficult part is to remember the URL to type into your web browser.

Starting the iSQL*Plus Server

If you're the DBA, you may need to worry about starting the *i*SQL*Plus server. The concept is similar to starting an Oracle Net listener. The *i*SQL*Plus server is what clients running web browsers connect to when they enter the *i*SQL*Plus URL into their web browsers. Figure 3-1 illustrates.

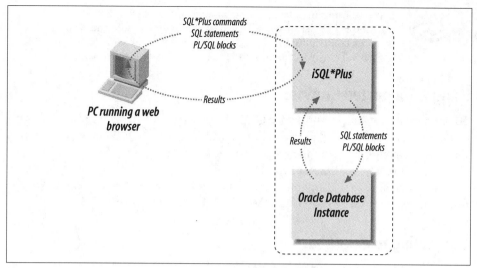

*Figure 3-1. iSQL*Plus architecture*

To start the *i*SQL*Plus server in Oracle Database 10*g* on a Unix or Linux system, log in as the Oracle software owner and issue the *isqlplusctl start* command:

```
oracle@gennick02:~> isqlplusctl start
iSQL*Plus 10.1.0.2.0
Copyright (c) 2004 Oracle.  All rights reserved.
Starting iSQL*Plus ...
iSQL*Plus started.
```

Once you've started *i*SQL*Plus on your server, clients will be able to freely connect and use *i*SQL*Plus via their web browsers. You can use the *isqlplusctl stop* command to shut down the *i*SQL*Plus server, although you'll normally want to leave *i*SQL*Plus running for as long as your database is open.

To start Oracle Database 10*g*'s *i*SQL*Plus server under Windows, go to the Services control panel, look for the Oracle service with a name ending in "iSQL*Plus", and start that service.

> You can also use *isqlplusctl start* to start the *i*SQL*Plus server under Windows. Issue the command from the Windows command prompt. You *may* need to leave open the command-prompt window from which you issue the command, but I did not find that to be the case when running Oracle Database 10*g* under Windows XP. You may want to investigate the use of the Windows *start* command, as in *start isqlplusctl start*.

In Oracle9*i* Database, *i*SQL*Plus starts and stops along with the HTTP Server. Under Unix, use the commands *apachectl start* and *apachectl stop*. Under Windows, use *Apache –k start* and *Apache –k shutdown*.

If you're using the Oracle9i Database version of iSQL*Plus, and you start the HTTP Server while logged in as the Oracle software owner, then any user connecting through iSQL*Plus will be able to connect as SYSDBA. Thus, you should start HTTP Server as some other user.

Using a Supported Browser

To connect to a database through iSQL*Plus, you need to be using a web browser that supports HTML 4.0 Transitional or higher. Oracle's iSQL*Plus documentation specifically mentions Netscape Navigator 4.7 or later, and Microsoft Internet Explorer 5.0 or later. These are the browsers Oracle officially supports. However, you should be able to use any reasonably current browser. I've had good luck using the Opera web browser Version 7.23, Mozilla 1.4, and Konqueror 3.0.3.

Connecting to a Database

You start iSQL*Plus in your web browser by entering a URL. In Oracle Database 10g, the default URL takes the following form:

```
http://server.domain.com:5560/isqlplus
```

Thus, to connect to iSQL*Plus running on the database server named *gennick01. gennick.com*, you would enter the following URL:

```
http://gennick01.gennick.com:5560/isqlplus
```

5560 is the default port number used by iSQL*Plus in Oracle Database 10g. Your DBA may have changed that port number. If you have doubts about the URL, ask your DBA. If you *are* the DBA, see the sidebar "Which Port to Use?."

Upon entering the correct URL, your browser will display the iSQL*Plus login page shown in Figure 3-2, which has been filled out to connect to a database through the net service name db01. From here, you have two choices:

- You can enter only a username and password to connect to the default database. Be aware that this default database is the one specified for iSQL*Plus on the server. If you have specified a default database at the client level, that has no effect here.

- You can also enter a *connect identifier*, usually a net service name, to connect to some other database. If you use a net service name, that net service name is resolved on the iSQL*Plus server, not on your local machine.

 The term *connect identifier* is synonymous with *connect string*. Oracle uses *connect string* in some of its documentation but uses *connect identifier* on the iSQL*Plus login page.

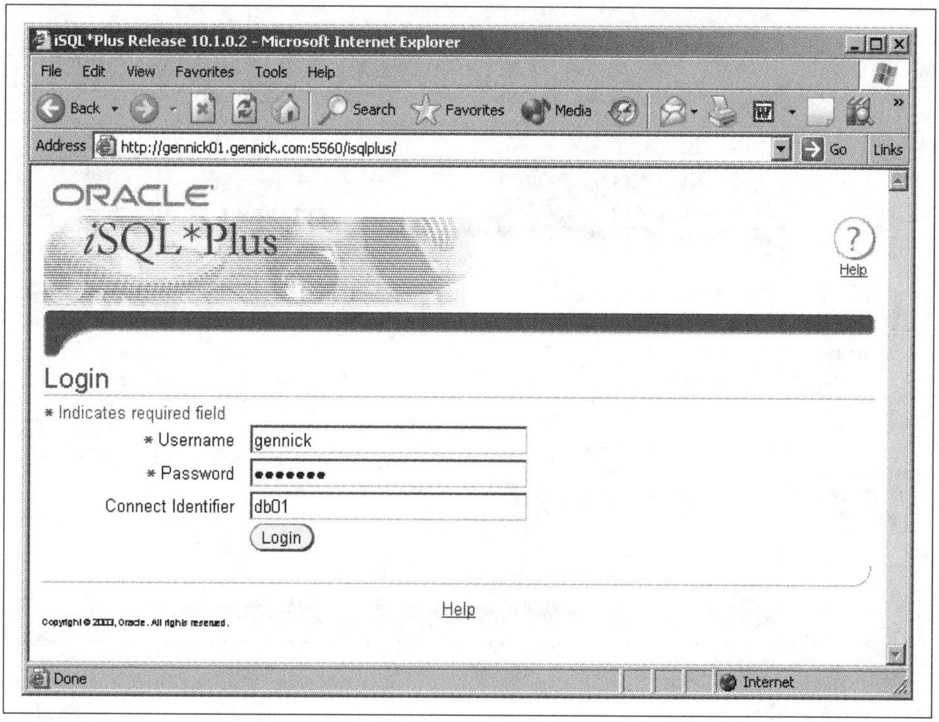

*Figure 3-2. The iSQL*Plus login page*

After entering your login information, click the Login button. You'll be logged in to your database and presented with the *i*SQL*Plus Workspace page shown in Figure 3-3.

Several things are worth noticing about this page:

- The biggest element on the page—you can't miss it—is the text box into which you type SQL statements, SQL*Plus commands, and PL/SQL blocks.

- Just above and to the right of the text box is a recap of your login information, minus the password.

- There is a Logout button that you might mistake as being part of the page header. To log out, click the round icon with the key at the upper right of the page.

For the most part, operation of *i*SQL*Plus is fairly simple. Type a command, statement, or block into the text box and click the Execute button.

Connecting as an Administrator

In Oracle Database 10*g*, you can use a special URL to connect to *i*SQL*Plus in the SYSDBA or SYSOPER administrative roles. You can then proceed to use *i*SQL*Plus for administrative tasks such as starting and stopping your database.

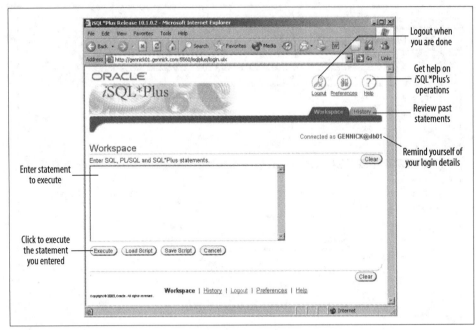

Figure 3-3. The iSQL*Plus Workspace

Which Port to Use?

As I mentioned, the hardest part of using *i*SQL*Plus might be remembering, or figuring out, the correct URL and which port to use. The following information might be helpful:

- In the beginning, in Oracle9*i* Database Release 1, the default port was 80, and you connected using a URL in the form *http://server.domain.com/isqlplus*.

- Oracle9*i* Database Release 2 changed the default port to 5560, and you used a URL such as *http://server.domain.com:5560/isqlplus*.

- Using Oracle9*i* Database, you can determine the currently used port number by looking in *$ORACLE_HOME/Apache/bin/conf/httpd.conf* (Unix/Linux) or *%ORACLE_HOME%\Apache\Apache\conf\httpd.conf* (Windows).

- Using Oracle Database 10*g*, you can determine the currently used port number by looking in *$ORACLE_HOME/oc4j/j2ee/isqlplus/config/http-web-site.xml*.

- Using Oracle Database 10*g*, if you (or your DBA) specify a non-default port number during installation, that port number will be recorded along with several other important port numbers in *$ORACLE_HOME/install/portlist.ini*.

When you connect to *i*SQL*Plus as a DBA, you must authenticate twice, as in the following process:

1. Enter a special URL that brings up an *i*SQL*Plus DBA login dialog.

2. Enter a username and password to identify yourself to *i*SQL*Plus as a DBA. This username/password has meaning only to *i*SQL*Plus and is unrelated to your database username/password.

3. *i*SQL*Plus takes you to a special version of the login page that includes a pull-down menu for choosing between SYSDBA and SYSOPER.

4. Authenticate to your database using your database username/password.

Before you can use *i*SQL*Plus as SYSDBA or SYSOPER, you must create a special username and password to use in the first step. This username and password is tied to the specific instance of *i*SQL*Plus to which you connect. Thus, if you connect to *i*SQL*Plus on *gennick01.gennick.com* to reach a database on *gennick02.gennick.com*, you must have an *i*SQL*Plus DBA password on *gennick01.gennick.com*.

Creating iSQL*Plus DBA users

To authenticate you as a DBA, *i*SQL*Plus uses a Java Authentication and Authorization Service (JAAS) provider named *Java AuthoriZatioN*, which Oracle calls JAZN. You must create a username/password within JAZN in order to use *i*SQL*Plus as SYSDBA or SYSOPER.

 You can store *i*SQL*Plus DBA usernames and passwords within the Oracle Internet Directory. For details on doing that, refer to the chapter "Configuring SQL*Plus" in the *Oracle SQL*Plus User's Guide and Reference* (Oracle Corporation).

To create a JAZN user for *i*SQL*Plus, use the JAZN shell. Follow these steps:

1. Log into your database server as the Oracle software owner, or as a user having the DBA role.

2. Create a JAVA_HOME environment variable:

   ```
   oracle@gennick02:~> export JAVA_HOME=$ORACLE_HOME/jdk
   ```

3. You *must* invoke the JAZN utility from the correct directory. If you fail to do so, this process will also fail. Set your current working directory as follows:

   ```
   oracle@gennick02:~> cd $ORACLE_HOME/oc4j/j2ee/isqlplus/application-deployments/
   isqlplus
   ```

4. Invoke the JAZN shell for the "iSQL*Plus DBA" realm as the *admin* user using the following, rather horrendous command. Type it as one, long line. Type it

exactly as shown, but supply your own password if you've changed it from the default of welcome:

```
oracle@gennick02:/oracle10g/product/10gr1/oc4j/j2ee/isqlplus/application-
deployments/isqlplus> $JAVA_HOME/bin/java -Djava.security.properties=$ORACLE_
HOME/sqlplus/admin/iplus/provider -jar $ORACLE_HOME/oc4j/j2ee/home/jazn.jar -user
"iSQL*Plus DBA/admin" -password welcome -shell
```

5. Issue an *adduser* command to create a new, *iSQL**Plus DBA user. The following example creates a user named dude with a password of secret:

```
JAZN:> adduser "iSQL*Plus DBA" dude secret
```

6. Grant the *webDba* role to the user you just created:

```
JAZN:> grantrole webDba "iSQL*Plus DBA" dude
```

7. If this is your first time using the JAZN shell, change the *admin* password to something other than the default. The following example changes the *admin* password from welcome to secret:

```
JAZN:> setpasswd "iSQL*Plus DBA" admin welcome secret
```

8. Exit the JAZN utility:

```
JAZN:> exit
```

In order for *iSQL**Plus to see the new JAZN user you've created, you'll need to bounce *iSQL**Plus by issuing the command *isqlplusctl stop* followed by *isqlplusctl start*.

Authenticating to iSQL*Plus as a DBA

To access the DBA login page, append */dba* to the URL you normally use to invoke iSQL*Plus. For example, if you normally use:

```
http://gennick02.gennick.com:5560/isqlplus
```

then to log in as a DBA, you would use:

```
http://gennick02.gennick.com:5560/isqlplus/dba
```

Entering the DBA URL should result in the login dialog shown in Figure 3-4.

Enter the username and password you created from the JAZN shell, and you should be taken to the login page shown in Figure 3-5. This login page will have an additional field, a pull-down menu from which you can choose to connect as SYSDBA or SYSOPER.

Upon logging in to your database as SYSDBA or SYSOPER, you'll be taken to the same *iSQL**Plus workspace page shown in Figure 3-3. The difference is that you will be able to execute commands such as STARTUP and SHUTDOWN.

Figure 3-4. Authenticating to iSQL*Plus as a DBA

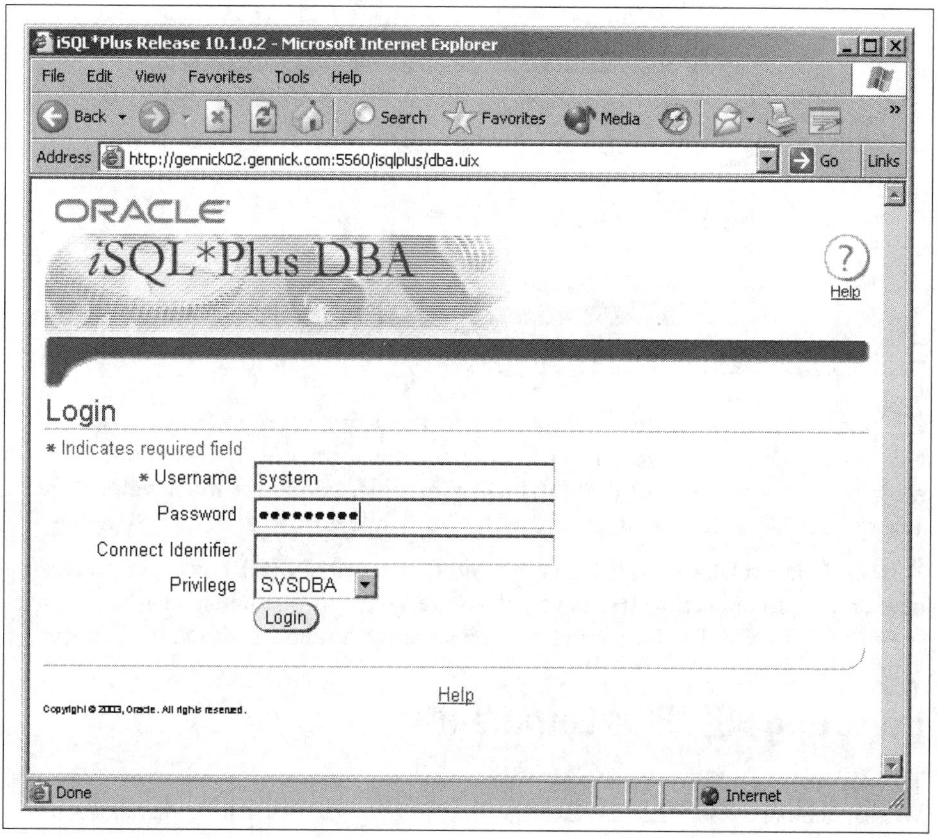

Figure 3-5. Logging in to Oracle as SYSDBA

Upon logging out of an *i*SQL*Plus DBA session, be sure to close your browser, unless you plan to immediately connect again in either the SYSDBA or SYSOPER role. Once you authenticate to *i*SQL*Plus as a DBA (as in Figure 3-4), you remain recognized as a DBA, and you retain the ability to choose SYSDBA and SYSOPER as long as your browser remains open.

Ending a Session

Figure 3-6 illustrates two ways to end an *i*SQL*Plus session. You can click the Logout button in the upper right of the page, or you can issue the SQL*Plus DISCONNECT command.

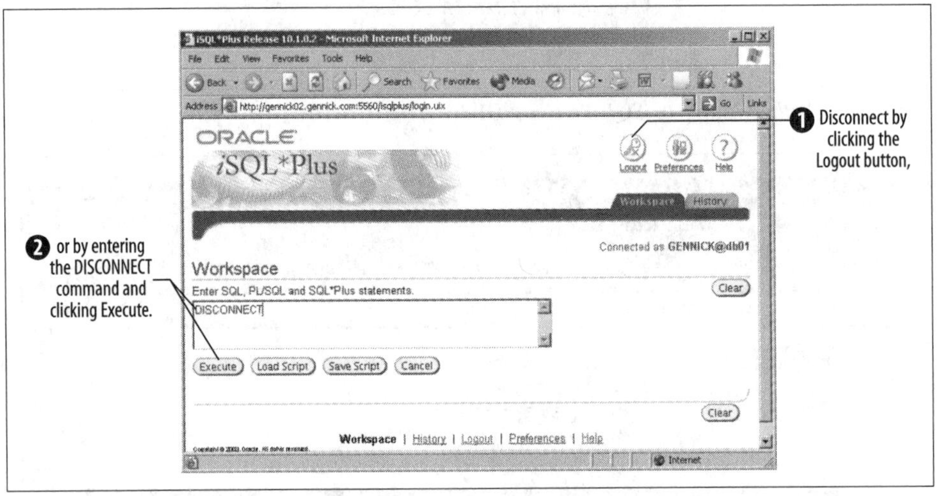

*Figure 3-6. Disconnecting from an iSQL*Plus session*

Clicking the Logout button returns you to the login page. Issuing the DISCON-NECT command leaves you in a position to enter further SQL*Plus commands but neither SQL statements nor PL/SQL blocks. Frankly, I don't see much value in being able to issue SQL*Plus commands in *i*SQL*Plus while not connected to a database.

You can follow a DISCONNECT command with a CONNECT command to create a new database connection. However, if you're going to do that, you might as well enter the CONNECT command to begin with and skip the DISCONNECT step.

Executing SQL*Plus Commands

To execute a SQL*Plus command, type it into the large text box on the *i*SQL*Plus Workspace page and click the Execute button. Any results will be displayed below the button. Figure 3-7 illustrates by using DESCRIBE to show the structure of the project table.

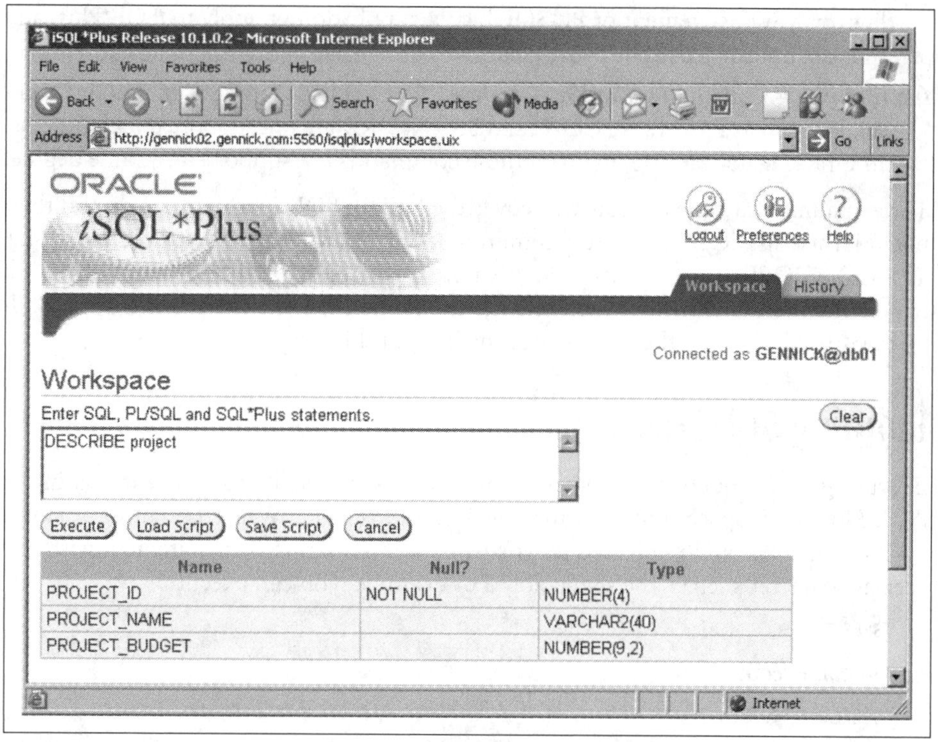

Figure 3-7. Issuing a SQL*Plus command in iSQL*Plus

Some SQL*Plus commands are not supported for use in *i*SQL*Plus. The following are some guiding principles to help you remember which commands are and aren't supported:

You have no access to files on the iSQL*Plus server. *i*SQL*Plus runs on a server. In the interests of security, you are not given any access to files on that server. You can't use commands such as SPOOL and SAVE to write files, nor can you use commands such as GET, START, and @ to read or execute files.

You have no access to the server command prompt. Similarly, you are not allowed to execute programs or operating system commands that run on the server. Thus, you can't issue SQL*Plus commands such as HOST or EDIT.

Line editing is not supported from iSQL*Plus. The entire suite of line-editing commands described in Chapter 2 is not supported from *i*SQL*Plus. The one exception is the LIST command, which will still list the current contents of the buffer. Line editing makes little sense when you can more easily edit by clicking and typing anywhere in the text box.

Many SQL*Plus concepts simply do not apply to iSQL*Plus. Commands such as SET SQLCONTINUE, which sets the prompt used for the second and subsequent lines of a SQL statement or PL/SQL block, simply do not apply to *i*SQL*Plus, and thus are not supported by *i*SQL*Plus.

Interactivity is limited in Oracle9*i* Database.   In Oracle9*i* Database, interactive commands such as PAUSE, ACCEPT, and PASSWORD are not supported in *i*SQL*Plus. In Oracle Database 10*g*, many of these commands are supported to some degree.

These guiding principles adequately cover the bulk of SQL*Plus commands and their potential use in *i*SQL*Plus. Yet a certain amount of arbitrariness does remain. SET TERMOUT OFF is a good example. It's not supported in *i*SQL*Plus, yet I can think of no good reason why not. If you're in doubt about a specific command's applicability to *i*SQL*Plus, check the reference at the back of this book.

Running SQL Queries

Executing a SQL query or statement is as simple as typing it into the text box in the *i*SQL*Plus Workspace and pressing the Execute button. When executing a single SQL statement, you do not need to worry about terminating your statement with any special character such as the semicolon. For example, you can execute:

```
SELECT * FROM dual;
```

or you can execute:

```
SELECT * FROM dual
```

Any output from SQL statements that you execute will be displayed below the Execute button.

Paging Through Results

When a SQL statement brings back a large number of rows, *i*SQL*Plus displays results a page at a time. The number of rows displayed per "page" is determined by the PAGESIZE setting and defaults to 24. *i*SQL*Plus places a page break in between successive queries. Figure 3-8 shows two queries executed with one click of the Execute button. You can see that *i*SQL*Plus has displayed the result of the first query and has followed that result with a Next Page button. Click that button to see the next page with the result from the second query.

One thing worth noticing about Figure 3-8 is that the first of the two statements was terminated with a semicolon. When executing multiple SQL statements in one go, you must terminate all but the final one.

 Use SET PAGESIZE *n* to specify a page size other than the default of 24 rows. Use SET PAGESIZE 0 to turn off pagination entirely, causing all rows returned by a query to be displayed in one potentially very long page.

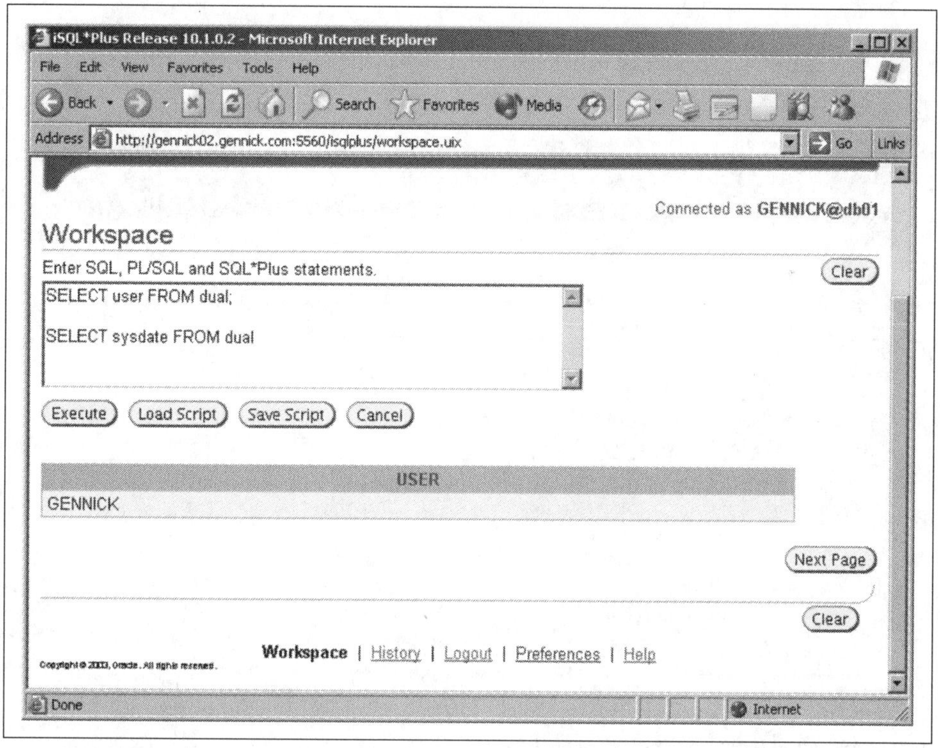

Figure 3-8. Paging through query results

Getting Output as Plain Text

By default, *i*SQL*Plus displays query results in the form of an HTML table, as shown in Figure 3-9. While visually pleasing, such a table may get in the way when you want to copy and paste query results into a text document. If you'd rather see query output as preformatted HTML, issue the following command:

```
SET MARKUP HTML PREFORMAT ON
```

Output from queries executed after issuing this SET MARKUP command will be formatted using the HTML <pre> and </pre> tags, as shown in Figure 3-10. Use the command SET MARKUP HTML PREFORMAT OFF to go back to using HTML tables.

For those who are strongly GUI-oriented, *i*SQL*Plus provides a Script Formatting preferences page from which you can toggle the PREFORMAT setting using a radio button. Click on the Preferences button next to the Logout button, look on the left side of the resulting page under the heading System Configuration, click on Script Formatting, and scroll way down to the Preformatted Output radio buttons. Choose whichever option you prefer, scroll to the bottom of the page, and click the Apply button. Click the Workspace tab to return to the workspace page.

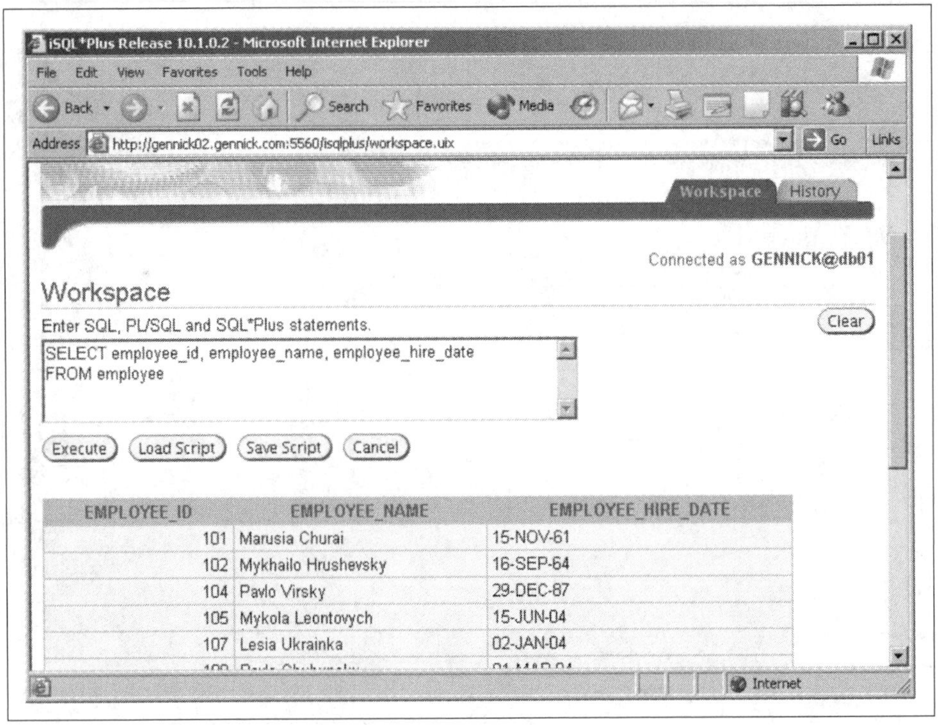

![iSQL*Plus Release 10.1.0.2 window showing a Workspace tab with a SQL query and results table]

Figure 3-9. Displaying results as an HTML table

 Any change you make to the PREFORMAT option is good only for the duration of your *iSQL*Plus session. Chapter 14 talks more about customizing your SQL*Plus environment and shows some ways to make such customizations permanent or, in the case of *iSQL*Plus, at least easy to repeat.

Working with PL/SQL

There's not much to say about executing PL/SQL blocks via *iSQL*Plus. You execute those in much the same way as you execute statements. You do not need to include the forward slash that command-line SQL*Plus requires following a PL/SQL block, but you do need to be sure to include the semicolon following PL/SQL's END keyword. As in command-line SQL*Plus, you'll want to SET SERVEROUTPUT ON if your PL/SQL block uses DBMS_OUTPUT to return results. Figure 3-11 demonstrates.

Figure 3-11 was created using *iSQL*Plus from Oracle Database 10g with the default setting of PREFORMAT OFF. Because the output is not the result of a query, it's not in the form of an HTML table. Examine the HTML source, and you'll see that <br> tags separate the three lines of output. Interestingly, if you SET MARKUP HTML PREFORMAT ON, *iSQL*Plus correctly omits the <br> tags and incorrectly omits

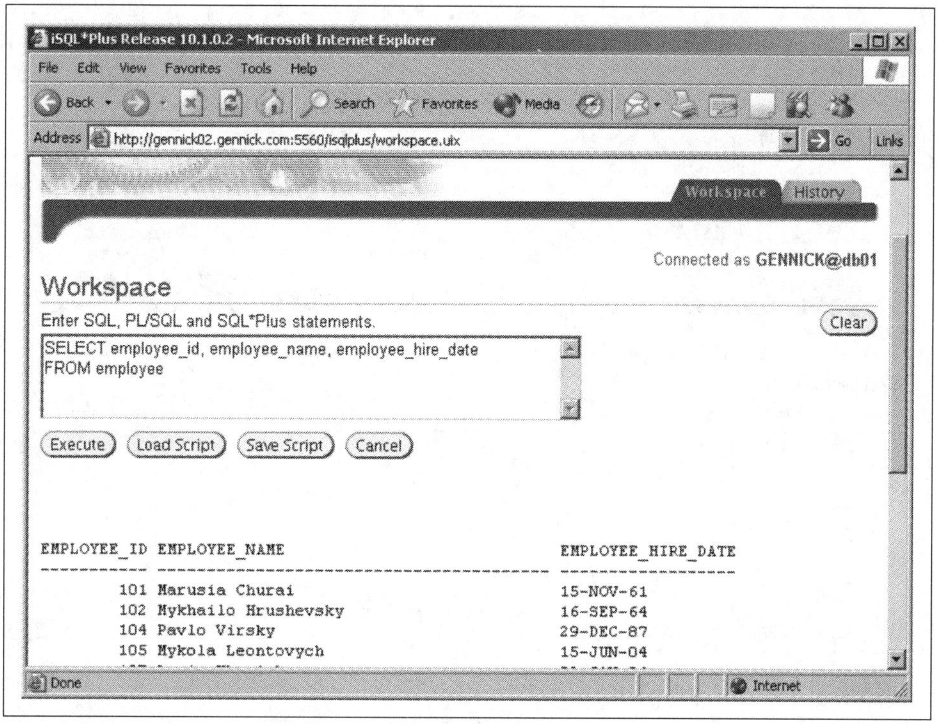

Figure 3-10. Displaying results as preformatted text

wrapping the output in `<pre>` and `</pre>` tags. Thus, with PREFORMAT ON, the results from executing the block in Figure 3-11 would all run together on one line:

```
Line 1 Line 2 Line 3 PL/SQL procedure successfully completed.
```

No doubt this behavior is a bug. It is present in Oracle Database 10*g* Release 1, but I hope it will be fixed in a later release. In the meantime, if you encounter difficulty with line breaks in your DBMS_OUTPUT results, you may find that a SET MARKUP HTML PREFORMAT OFF command fixes the problem.

Executing Scripts

*i*SQL*Plus provides you with two mechanisms for running SQL*Plus scripts. Which you use depends largely on where the script is located. One method is optimized for running scripts off a web server (or FTP server) over the Internet. The other method, slightly more cumbersome, allows you to run scripts from your workstation's hard drive.

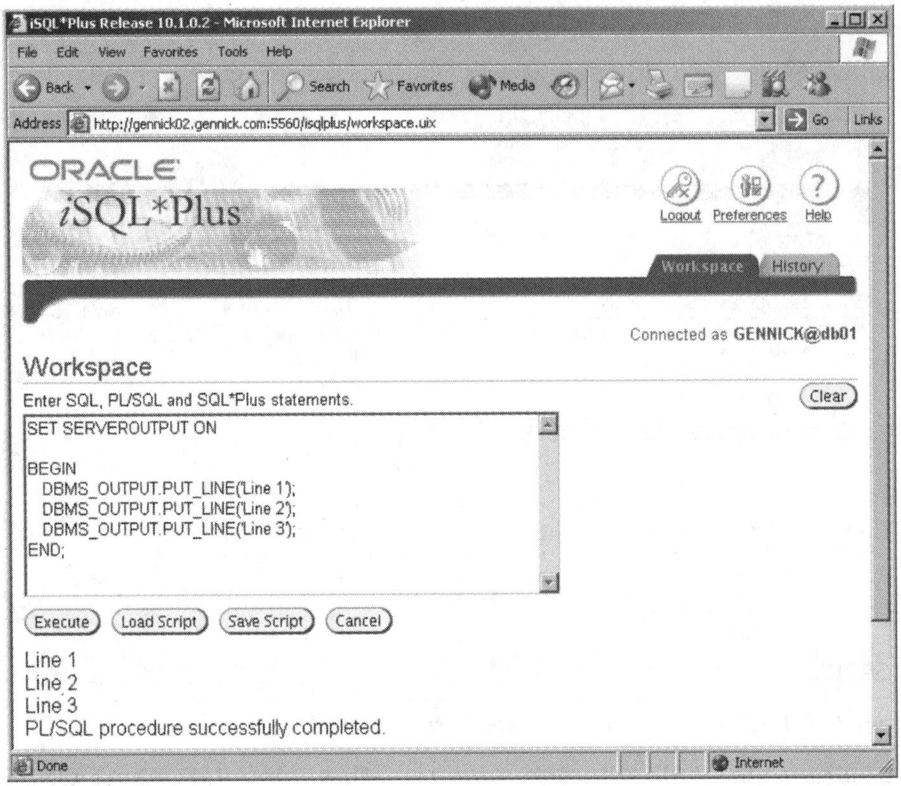

Figure 3-11. Executing a PL/SQL block

Using the @ Command

In Chapter 2, you saw how to use the @ command to execute a script file containing SQL*Plus commands, SQL statements, and PL/SQL blocks. You can use the @ command in *i*SQL*Plus but only to execute scripts over the Internet. For example, suppose that you had the following commands in a file named *login.sql* that was accessible from a web server:

```
SET ECHO ON
SET MARKUP HTML PREFORMAT ON
SET PAGESIZE 20
```

You could easily invoke this file to configure your environment each time you logged in to *i*SQL*Plus. You would use an @ command similar to the following:

```
@http://gennick.com/login
```

Figure 3-12 shows what it would look like to execute this script.

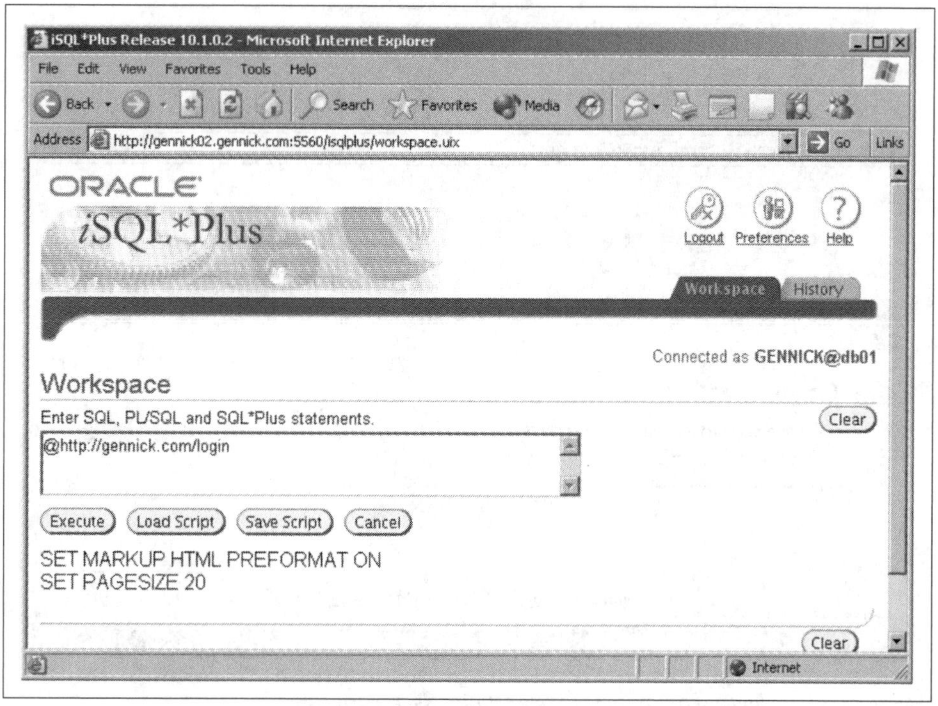

Figure 3-12. Executing a script from the Internet

You can't use the @ command to execute scripts on the server. For security reasons, you are not allowed to use *i*SQL*Plus as a mechanism for accessing files on the server. You also can't use the @ command to execute scripts located on your client PC because *i*SQL*Plus, running on the database server as it does, has no way to access files on your local disk. There is, however, a way to execute scripts stored on your local hard drive.

Using the Load Script Button

To execute a script from your local hard drive, follow these steps:

1. Click the Load Script button. You'll see the page shown in Figure 3-13.

2. Click the Browse button to open a file chooser dialog.

3. Navigate to the file you want, select it, and click the OK button. You'll be brought back to the page shown in Figure 3-13, and the File text box will be filled in with the path to the file you chose.

4. Click either Load button. The file will be loaded and placed into the text box in the Workspace page.

5. Optionally edit the script you are about to execute.

6. Click the Execute button to run the script.

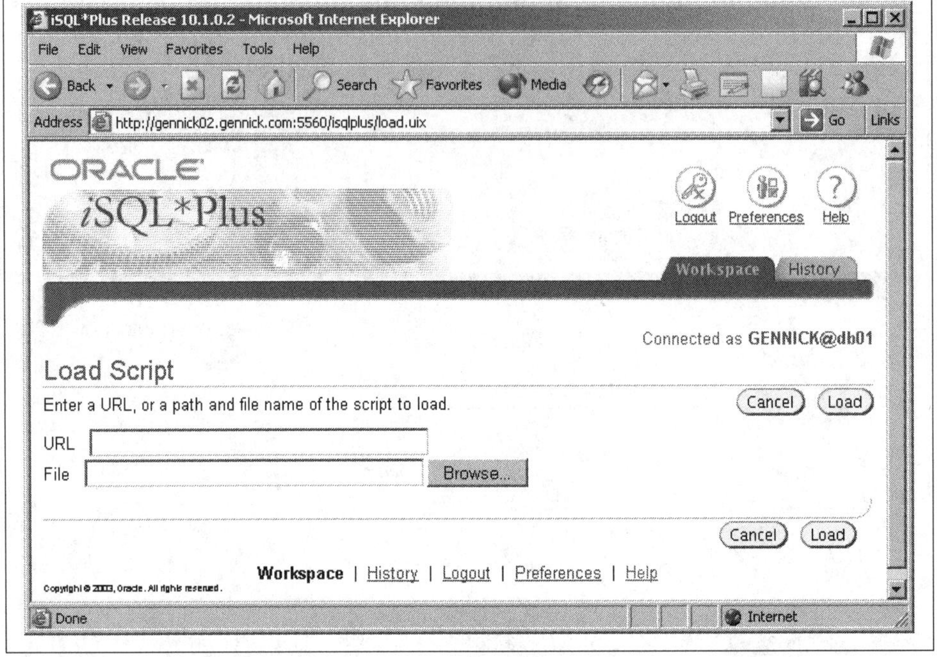

Figure 3-13. Loading a script from your workstation's hard drive

The Load Script functionality is helpful if you want to look at the contents of a SQL script that you would otherwise execute from a web server using the @ command. You can type the script's URL into the URL text box (in place of step 3), click the Load button, and *i*SQL*Plus will load the script into the Workspace text box for you to look at, edit, and possibly execute.

> *i*SQL*Plus will load just about any text file into the Workspace text box. For example, you can load the contents *http://www.oracle.com*, or of my own home page at *http://gennick.com/index.html*. However, I consistently encounter problems after loading such random text files, so my advice for now, at least until Oracle Database 10*g* Release 2 arrives, is to stick with loading files that really are SQL*Plus scripts.

iSQL*Plus Command History

Sometimes you may want to return and review what you've done. You may have executed a SQL statement five minutes ago and want to execute it again. You may wonder just what WHERE conditions you *really* had in that DELETE you just executed against a critical table. *i*SQL*Plus makes reviewing your past work easy. Click the History tab near the upper right of the page and you'll see a history listing such as what is shown in Figure 3-14.

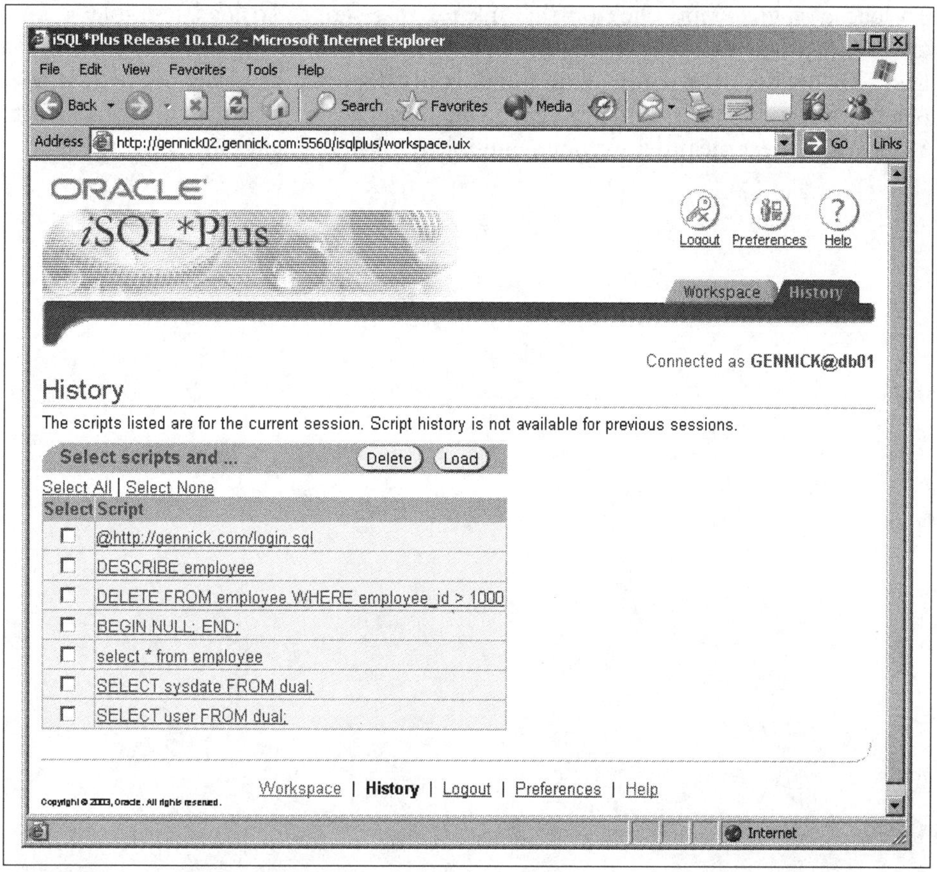

Figure 3-14. Reviewing what you've recently done

Everything in the history list is referred to as a *script*. However, in this context, a script is nothing more than the contents of the Workspace text box when you clicked the Execute button. Thus, if you execute a remote script using a command such as *@http://gennick.com/login.sql*, the script shown on the History page will be the @ command and not the contents of *login.sql*.

Scripts, or commands, are listed in reverse order of execution, with the most recently executed script at the top of the list. The most recently executed script in Figure 3-14 is the execution of *login.sql*. Prior to that was a DESCRIBE command against the employee table. Prior to that was a DELETE from employee.

You can delete scripts from the history list, although I'm not sure why you'd want to bother doing that, and you can load scripts back into the Workspace text box for review and possible re-execution. To delete scripts from the history, check the ones you want to get rid of, and then click the Delete button.

To load a single script, click on the link for that script. To load multiple scripts, check those that you wish to load and click the Load button. Usually, you'll want to load only one script. If you load multiple scripts, they will be placed in the text box, one following the other, in the order in which they were listed on the History page. You cannot affect the order in which multiple scripts are loaded.

CHAPTER 4

A Lightning SQL Tutorial

SQL is *the* language that you use to manipulate relational data. Other languages for data manipulation do exist, but SQL is the most common, and it's the reason for the "SQL" in "SQL*Plus." Because everything you do in SQL*Plus will involve SQL, it's worth digressing for a chapter to focus on learning the rudiments of the language.

Data Manipulation Statements

As manifested in Oracle, the SQL language encompasses several categories of statements: statements that work with data, other statements that define and modify the structures (such as tables and indexes) that hold data, and still other statements that control the operation of the database itself.

This chapter focuses on statements used to manipulate data:

INSERT
Places new records, or rows, into a database table.

SELECT
Retrieves previously inserted rows from a database table.

UPDATE
Modifies data in a table.

DELETE
Deletes data from a table.

MERGE
Brings a table up to date by modifying or inserting rows, as appropriate

The reason I focus on data manipulation in this chapter is that if you're just starting out with SQL, data manipulation is likely to be your first problem. You'll likely be working with tables and other database objects that have been created. Furthermore, data manipulation statements are the ones you'll need to leverage the SQL*Plus reporting capabilities I describe in the next few chapters. Other topics, such as creating database structures (e.g., tables and indexes) and controlling the operation of the database, are database administration topics that rightfully belong in other books.

Inserting Data into a Table

Use the INSERT statement to add a new row of data to a database table. The following form of INSERT should suffice for almost all your needs:

```
INSERT INTO table_name (column_list) VALUES (value_list);
```

Replace *table_name* with the name of the target table, the table to which you wish to add a new row of data. Replace *column_list* with a comma-delimited list of column names. These are the columns for which you will supply values in your *value_list*. For example, type the code from Example 4-1 into SQL*Plus to insert a new employee.

Example 4-1. Inserting a new employee

```
INSERT INTO employee (employee_id, employee_name)
   VALUES ('114','Marusia Bohuslavka');
```

This example supplies values for only two of the five employee table columns. When you insert a row and omit a value for a column, that column takes on a default value specified by your DBA when creating the table. Often, the default value for a column is no value at all, or null. I'll talk about nulls later in this chapter. They're quite important to understand.

When you insert new rows, you must supply values for the following types of columns:

* Primary key columns. These are mandatory. In the employee table, the employee_id column forms the primary key.
* Columns defined as NOT NULL that have no default value defined.

If you omit a value for one of these types of column, you'll receive an error, as in Example 4-2.

Example 4-2. Omitting a required column

```
INSERT INTO employee (employee_name) VALUES ('Hryhory Kytasty');
*
ERROR at line 1:
ORA-01400: cannot insert NULL into ("GENNICK"."EMPLOYEE"."EMPLOYEE_ID")
```

The error message here is informing you that employee_id is a mandatory column. When you receive an error such as this, supply a value for the column mentioned in the error message and retry the insert.

Retrieving Data from a Table

What good would a database be if you couldn't get information back from it? Indeed, you'll find that you spend more time using SQL to get data out of the database than you spend on any of the other data manipulation operations. The SELECT statement, often referred to as a *query*, is what you need. Example 4-3 shows a simple query that retrieves all data from a table.

Example 4-3. Retrieving all rows, all columns

```
SELECT * FROM employee;
```

The asterisk (*) in this example is shorthand for "all columns." You can enumerate the columns, as in Example 4-4.

Example 4-4. Enumerating columns in the SELECT list

```
SELECT employee_id, employee_name, employee_hire_date,
      employee_termination_date, employee_billing_rate
FROM employee;
```

In a database of any size, you aren't likely to want to retrieve all rows from a table. Rather, you'll want to define some subset of rows that you are interested in. For that, use the WHERE clause. Example 4-5 uses a WHERE clause to restrict the query's results to the row inserted in the previous section.

Example 4-5. Using a WHERE clause to constrain results

```
SELECT employee_id, employee_name
FROM employee
WHERE employee_id = 114;
```

The WHERE clause supports the same comparison operators that you'll find in just about any programming or scripting language:

=   Are two values the same?

!=, <>, ^=
: Do two values differ?

<   Is one value less than another?

<= Is one value less than or equal to another?

>   Is one value greater than another?

>= Is one value greater than or equal to another?

These are the most basic and common operators. You'll see others in this book that I'll explain as I continue. For a rigorous trip through the WHERE clause, I heartily recommend Sanjay Mishra and Alan Beaulieu's book, *Mastering Oracle SQL*, Second Edition (O'Reilly).

Beware the Asterisk!

It's OK to use the asterisk when writing ad hoc queries, but think twice before using it in any query that gets embedded into a program or a script. That's because the results from SELECT * will change in the event that you or your DBA ever add a new column to the target table, or you re-create the table using a new column order. For a SQL*Plus reporting script, such a change will likely result in nothing more catastrophic than some mangled formatting as a result of an extra and unexpected column in the report. However, operations other than simple SELECTs may fail when you suddenly add a column to a result set. When in doubt, enumerate your columns.

Multiple conditions

You can write many conditions in a WHERE clause, which you can link together using AND and OR. You can use parentheses to clarify the order of evaluation. Example 4-6 uses OR to retrieve the following two groups of employees:

- Employee number 114
- Employees with names beginning with 'Myk', but only when those employees were hired during or after 2004

Example 4-6. Using AND and OR

```
SELECT *
FROM employee
WHERE (employee_id = 114)
   OR (employee_hire_date >= TO_DATE('1-Jan-2004','dd-mon-yyyy')
       AND REGEXP_LIKE(employee_name, '^Myk.*'));
```

Parentheses ensure that the two AND conditions are collectively treated as one condition with respect to the OR operation.

The TO_DATE function converts the string '1-Jan-2004' into a true DATE value, for comparison to the hire dates. The call to REGEXP_LIKE identifies those rows having names that begin with 'Myk'. The string '^Myk.*' is a regular expression.

 Regular expression support is an exciting, new feature of Oracle Database 10g. Learn more about this new feature from the *Oracle Regular Expression Pocket Reference* (O'Reilly), which I coauthored with Peter Linsley.

Negating conditions

There is also the NOT operator, which you can use to negate a condition. For example, the two queries in Example 4-7 are equivalent.

Example 4-7. Using the NOT operator

```
SELECT *
FROM employee
WHERE employee_id <> 114;

SELECT *
FROM employee
WHERE NOT employee_id = 114;
```

NOT can be handy when writing complex queries because sometimes it's easier to think in terms of those rows that you do not want in your result. You can write conditions to identify those rows you do not want, and you can use NOT to negate those conditions. Example 4-8 shows a slightly modified (NOTified?) version of the query from Example 4-6. This time, I want the statement to return all the rows not returned in Example 4-6. I could have modified each of the three comparisons individually, but that would require a fair bit of thought, and I might make a mistake. It's easier to wrap the entire original logic in parentheses and apply the NOT operator to the result.

Example 4-8. Negating complex logic

```
SELECT *
FROM employee
WHERE NOT ((employee_id = 114)
   OR (employee_hire_date >= TO_DATE('1-Jan-2004','dd-mon-yyyy')
       AND REGEXP_LIKE(employee_name, '^Myk.*')));
```

Using NOT as I've just done leaves me open to problems involving null values. This is an important topic I'll discuss later in "The Concept of Null."

Table aliases

When you're writing a query, it's often necessary to qualify column names by also specifying their table names. You do this using *dot notation*, as shown in Example 4-9. The employee. in front of each column name specifies that each column belongs to the employee table.

Example 4-9. Qualifying column names with their table names

```
SELECT employee.employee_id, employee.employee_name
FROM employee;
```

It's cumbersome to retype long table names many times over. For this reason, SQL allows you to specify alternate names, known as *table aliases*, for the tables in your query. Specify an alias by placing it immediately after its table name, thereby separating the two names by whitespace, as shown in Example 4-10.

Example 4-10. Specifying and using a table alias

```
SELECT e.employee_id, e.employee_name
FROM employee e;
```

Keep your aliases short, which is the whole idea. It's much easier to type e. than employee. in front of each column name.

You really don't need to worry about qualifying column names when selecting from only one table. Later in this chapter, you'll learn how to select from many tables at once. That's when qualifying column names becomes important. If you don't qualify column names when selecting from multiple tables, the database engine must expend extra resources sorting through which name goes with which table. That's usually a trivial performance hit, but it can add up if given enough users and statements. And woe be to you if two tables share a common column name because the database engine won't be able to determine your intent, and you'll get an error.

Column aliases

Just as you can specify aliases for tables, you can also specify aliases for columns. Many people specify column aliases just as they do table aliases, by placing the alias name immediately after the column name. Others are a bit more proper in their approach and use the AS keyword. Example 4-11 demonstrates both approaches.

Example 4-11. Specifying column aliases

```
SELECT e.employee_id emp_num, e.employee_name "Employee Name",
       e.employee_billing_rate * 0.50 discounted_rate
FROM employee e;

SELECT e.employee_id AS emp_num, e.employee_name AS "Employee Name",
       e.employee_billing_rate * 0.50 AS discounted_rate
FROM employee e;
```

Column aliases are useful for reporting, because SQL*Plus picks them up and uses them as default column titles. Having "Employee Name" at the top of a column looks much better to a user than "employee_name". Column aliases are also useful in naming expressions in your SELECT list such as the one in Example 4-11 that discounts the billing rate. Otherwise, the expression itself will be the column name. In Chapter 5, you'll see that it's much easier to define formatting for an expression column when the name is one that *you* have specified rather than one that the database has generated for you.

Updating Data with New Values

Things change. That seems to be the rule in our world today. Your data will change, too, and for that reason SQL provides the UPDATE statement. Use it to set new values

INSERT...SELECT FROM

An interesting use of SELECT is as a data source for an INSERT statement. Suppose that you want to create a project named "X Overhead" for each existing project, replacing X with that project's name. For example, for "Corporate Web Site," you'd create a new project named "Corporate Web Site Overhead." You can do that using the following INSERT statement:

```
INSERT INTO PROJECT (project_id, project_name)
    SELECT project_id+8000,
           SUBSTR(project_name,1,31) || ' Overhead'
    FROM project;
```

The nested SELECT in this statement returns a set of rows, each row consisting of a project ID and a project name. Those rows feed into the INSERT statement, which inserts those rows back into the project table. The SUBSTR (for substring) function call clips the old project names at 31 characters, to ensure enough room for adding ' Overhead'. The newly inserted projects are all numbered above 8000.

In this example, the source and target tables are the same, but that's not necessary. The SELECT is independent of the INSERT. All that's necessary is that the SELECT returns the correct number of columns corresponding in type to those listed in the INSERT statement.

for some or all columns in a row. The UPDATE in Example 4-12 changes the name and the budget for project #1005.

Example 4-12. Changing values in a single row

```
UPDATE project
   SET project_name = 'Virtual Private Network',
       project_budget = 199999.95
WHERE project_id=1005;
```

The update in Example 4-12 updates only a single row. You can be certain of that, because project_id is the primary key of the project table, so there can be at most one row with ID 1005. You can use UPDATE to change values in many rows, by writing conditions in your WHERE clause to target those rows. Example 4-13 shows budgets being cut by 30% for all projects but the corporate web site.

Example 4-13. Changing values in many rows

```
UPDATE project
   SET project_budget = project_budget * 0.70
WHERE NOT project_name = 'Corporate Web Site';
```

You'll notice that the new value for project_budget in Example 4-13 is the result of an expression; in Example 4-12, the new values are constants. When updating many rows, it rarely makes sense to apply the same value to all, so such updates should use expressions or subqueries to generate new values appropriate to each row. (See the section "Subqueries" for more information on that approach.)

When you write an update, be sure you know whether it potentially affects more than one row. If the WHERE clause does not specify a single value for the table's primary key, or for a unique key column, then the update could potentially affect many rows. When an update affects many rows, give careful thought to how you will compute new values for those rows.

 If you know for certain that you can uniquely identify a single row via a non-key field, go for it. However, you may want to issue a SELECT first just to be sure. Example 4-13 identified a project by name. Potentially, two projects can have the same name, but I knew that wasn't the case when I wrote the example. In the real world, sometimes you take advantage of what you know about your own data.

It's possible to issue an UPDATE that changes the value in a primary key, but such changes aren't often made, and you're better off avoiding them if you can. Database designers design databases in ways that minimize or eliminate the need to change primary key values. When you change the primary key of a row, you affect the referential integrity of your database. The change must be rippled through to any other rows that refer to the row you are changing. Alternately, the database must prevent you from changing a primary key value that is referenced by another row. Much depends here on how your database schema was designed. In a worst-case scenario, you might have to sort out the proper order for a whole series of updates to foreign-key columns that reference the primary-key value you wish to change.

Deleting Data from a Table

All things must come to an end, and that's true of data, too. Actually, with today's increasing hard-drive sizes, I'm not so sure that some don't plan to hold their data forever, but let's ignore that complication for now. Use the DELETE statement to get rid of rows you no longer need. Did you insert all those new projects by executing the code in the "INSERT…SELECT FROM" sidebar? Too bad. Now your boss has changed his mind. Isn't that annoying? Now it's your job to delete what you just created. Do that using the DELETE statement shown in Example 4-14.

Example 4-14. Deleting rows from a table

```
DELETE FROM project
WHERE project_id > 8000;
```

DELETE is a fairly simple statement, but be careful to craft your WHERE clause so you only delete rows that you want to delete. I often write a SELECT statement using the same WHERE conditions and check the results from that before unleashing a DELETE.

Deleting All Rows from a Table

You wouldn't think it, but deleting data can actually be an expensive proposition. There's quite a bit of database overhead involved in a large delete. If you happen to be deleting *all* table rows, and you own the table or are a DBA having the TRUNCATE ANY TABLE privilege, you can use the TRUNCATE TABLE statement to good effect:

```
TRUNCATE TABLE table_name;
```

If you plan to reload close to the same amount of data, use the following variant, which maintains the disk space currently allocated to the table:

```
TRUNCATE TABLE table_name REUSE STORAGE;
```

For a table of any size, it's far faster to erase all the rows by truncating the table than by issuing a DELETE. This is because Oracle can accomplish the entire truncation by resetting an internal pointer known as the *highwater mark*. The trade-offs are that TRUNCATE commits any transaction you might have pending, and that you can't undo a TRUNCATE TABLE statement if you discover you've made a blunder after it executes. You can, however, undo a DELETE statement if you discover your mistake before committing the transaction. Read the section on "Transactions" for more on this.

If you are at all uncertain about whether to use TRUNCATE TABLE or DELETE, then use DELETE. You generally cannot issue TRUNCATE TABLE statements from within programs, at least not as easily as you can issue DELETE statements. In SQL*Plus scripts, either is equally easy to use.

Merging Data into a Table

New in Oracle9*i* Database, and in the 2003 ANSI/ISO SQL standard, the MERGE statement solves the age-old problem of needing to update a table or insert a new row depending on whether a corresponding row already exists. Suppose that you've created those overhead projects mentioned in the "INSERT...SELECT FROM" sidebar. You'll have used the statement shown in Example 4-15.

Example 4-15. Creating overhead projects

```
INSERT INTO PROJECT (project_id, project_name)
   SELECT project_id+8000,
          SUBSTR(project_name,1,31) || ' Overhead'
   FROM project;
```

Example 4-15 creates a new set of projects from an existing set of rows. Now, let's say you're faced with the task of periodically refreshing the list of overhead projects. At the time you do a refresh, you need to account for two possibilities:

- For any new projects that have been added, you need to create new overhead projects.

- For any existing projects, you need to migrate any name changes to their respective overhead project names.

There are different ways that you can go about solving this problem. One way is to periodically issue the MERGE statement shown in Example 4-16.

Example 4-16. Bringing the list of overhead projects up to date

```
MERGE INTO project pdest
USING (SELECT project_id+8000 project_id,
             SUBSTR(project_name,1,31) || ' Overhead' project_name
       FROM project
       WHERE project_id <= 8000) psource
ON (pdest.project_id = psource.project_id)
WHEN MATCHED THEN UPDATE
   SET pdest.project_name = psource.project_name
WHEN NOT MATCHED THEN INSERT
   (project_id, project_name)
   VALUES (psource.project_id, psource.project_name);
```

Here's a step-by-step walkthrough of this MERGE statement:

1. The INTO clause identifies the target table, in this case, project. An alias of pdest is specified to make it easier to distinguish between the two occurrences of the table in the one statement.

2. The USING clause specifies a SELECT statement to use in generating rows for the merge operation. This SELECT statement's WHERE clause excludes any overhead rows, which are rows having project_id values greater than 8000. The results of this SELECT statement are identified through the alias psource.

3. Each row from the SELECT is matched to its corresponding row in pdest via the condition given in the ON clause.

4. When a match occurs, which is to say that a row in pdest has a project_id matching that of a given row in psource, an update of the project_name is triggered.

5. When no match occurs (for a given row from psource, no corresponding row in pdest can be found) a new row is inserted into pdest.

MERGE is commonly used in data warehousing environments to periodically update reporting tables from operational data. Often, the source for rows feeding into a MERGE operation will be an *external table*, a type of table corresponding to an operating system file. There's more in Chapter 9 about using external tables to load data from files.

Transactions

Like most databases, Oracle implements the concept of a *transaction*, which is a set of related statements that either *all* execute or do not execute at all. Transactions play an important role in maintaining data integrity.

Protecting Data Integrity

Example 4-17 shows one method for changing a project number from 1001 to 1006:

1. Because rows in the project_hours table must always point to valid project rows, the example begins by creating a copy of project 1001 but gives that copy the new number of 1006.

2. With project 1006 in place, it's then possible to switch the rows in project_hours to point to 1006 instead of 1001.

3. Finally, when no more rows remain that refer to project 1001, the row for that project can be deleted.

Example 4-17. Changing a project's ID number

```
--Create the new project
INSERT INTO project
   SELECT 1006, project_name, project_budget FROM project
   WHERE project_id = 1001;

--Point the time log rows in project_hours to the new project number
UPDATE project_hours
SET project_id = 1006
WHERE project_id = 1001;

--Delete the original project record
DELETE FROM project
WHERE project_id=1001;
```

You'll encounter two issues when executing a set of statements such as those shown in Example 4-16. First, it's important that all statements be executed. Imagine the mess if your connection dropped after only the first INSERT statement was executed. Until you were able to reconnect and fix the problem, your database would show two projects, 1001 and 1006, where there should only be one. The second related issue is that you really don't want other users to see any of your changes until you've made all of them. Transactions address both these issues.

To treat a set of statements as a unit, in which all or none of the statements are executed, you can wrap those statements using SET TRANSACTION and COMMIT, as shown in Example 4-18.

Example 4-18. A transaction to change a project's ID number

```
--Begin the transaction
SET TRANSACTION READ WRITE;

--Create the new project
INSERT INTO project
   SELECT 1007, project_name, project_budget FROM project
   WHERE project_id = 1002;
```

Example 4-18. A transaction to change a project's ID number (continued)

```
--Point the time log rows in project_hours to the new project number
UPDATE project_hours
SET project_id = 1007
WHERE project_id = 1002;

--Delete the original project record
DELETE FROM project
WHERE project_id=1002;

COMMIT;
```

SET TRANSACTION marks the beginning of a transaction. Any changes you make to your data following the beginning of a transaction are not made permanent until you issue a COMMIT. Furthermore, those changes are not visible to other users until you've issued a COMMIT. Thus, as you issue the statements shown in Example 4-18, other database users won't see the results of any intermediate steps. From their perspective, the project ID number change will be a single operation. All rows having 2002 as a project ID value will suddenly have 1007 as that value.

> Using SET TRANSACTION to begin a transaction is optional. A new transaction begins implicitly with the first DML statement that you execute after you make a database connection or with the first DML statement that you execute following a COMMIT or a ROLLBACK (or any DDL statement such as TRUNCATE). You need to use SET TRANSACTION only when you want transaction attributes such as READ ONLY that are not the default.

Backing Out of Unwanted Changes

A third issue, and one that I didn't mention earlier, is that you might change your mind partway through the process. Perhaps you'll start out to change project ID 1003 to 2008, issue the INSERT followed by the UPDATE, and then realize that you need to change your project ID to 1008 and not to 2008. Again, transactions come to your rescue. You can undo every change you've made in a transaction by issuing the simple ROLLBACK statement. Example 4-19 demonstrates.

Example 4-19. A transaction to change a project's ID number

```
--Begin the transaction
SET TRANSACTION READ WRITE;

--Create the new project
INSERT INTO project
    SELECT 2008, project_name, project_budget FROM project
    WHERE project_id = 1002;

--Point the time log rows in project_hours to the new project number
UPDATE project_hours
```

Example 4-19. A transaction to change a project's ID number (continued)

```
SET project_id = 2008
WHERE project_id = 1002;

--Oops! Made a mistake. Undo the changes.
ROLLBACK;
```

ROLLBACK is handy for backing out of mistakes and when testing new SQL statements. You can issue an UPDATE or DELETE statement, follow that statement with a SELECT, and if you see that the results of your UPDATE or DELETE aren't what you intended, you can issue ROLLBACK and try again. I used this technique frequently while testing the examples in this book.

You're Always Using Transactions

You may have just learned about transactions in this section, but you've been using them all along. You can't issue a SQL statement and not be in a transaction. If you omit executing a START TRANSACTION statement, Oracle will implicitly begin a read/write transaction with the first SQL statement that you do execute. Oracle will automatically commit (or roll back) transactions for you, too, under certain circumstances:

- Oracle implicitly commits any pending transaction the moment you issue a DDL statement such as CREATE TABLE or TRUNCATE TABLE.
- Oracle implicitly commits any pending transaction when you exit SQL*Plus normally, e.g., you issue the EXIT command.
- Oracle implicitly rolls back any pending transaction when your connection terminates abnormally, e.g., when your network connection is broken or when the server (or your workstation) crashes.

Open transactions consume resources, as the database must maintain the information needed to roll back and provide other users with views of data as they were before your transaction began. Unless all you're doing is querying the database, you should keep your transactions as short in time as possible.

Understanding Transaction Types

Example 4-19 specified a read/write transaction. Such a transaction is the default, and it allows you to issue statements such as UPDATE and DELETE. You can also create read-only transactions:

```
SET TRANSACTION READ ONLY;
```

Read-only transactions are particularly useful when generating reports because, in a read-only transaction, you see a consistent snapshot of the database as it was when the transaction began. Think of freezing the database at a moment in time. You can begin a report at 8:00 a.m., and even if that report takes the rest of the day to run, the data on that report will reflect 8:00 a.m. Other users are free to make their changes, but you won't see those changes and they won't show up on any report that you run until you commit (or roll back) your read-only transaction.

The Concept of Null

When writing SQL statements, you must be vigilant for possible nulls, always taking care to consider their possible effect on a WHERE clause or other SQL expression. What is a *null*? It's what you get in the absence of a specific value. Suppose that you issue the INSERT statement shown in Example 4-20 to record a new hire in your database:

```
INSERT INTO employee (employee_id, employee_name)
    VALUES (116, 'Roxolana Lisovsky');
```

Quick! What value do you have for a hire date? What about the termination date? The answer is that it depends. The employee table happens to have a default value specified for the employee_hire_date column. Because the INSERT statement doesn't specify a hire date, the hire date defaults to the current date and time. What about the termination date? There's no default for that column, so what's the value? The answer is there is no value. Because no value is supplied, employee_termination_date is said to be null. Example 4-20 uses the SET NULL command to make the null termination date obvious.

Example 4-20. Inserting a NULL value

```
INSERT INTO employee (employee_id, employee_name)
    VALUES (116, 'Roxolana Lisovsky');

SET NULL ***NULL***

SELECT employee_id, employee_name,
       employee_hire_date, employee_termination_date
FROM employee
WHERE employee_id = 116;

EMPLOYEE_ID EMPLOYEE_NAME      EMPLOYEE_HIRE_DATE EMPLOYEE_TERMINATI
----------- ------------------ ------------------ ------------------
        116 Roxolana Lisovsky  03-JUN-04          ***NULL***
```

The problem with nulls is that the theorists who originally conceived the idea of relational databases decided that the existence of nulls warranted the creation of *three-valued logic*, illustrated in Figure 4-1.

If I were to ask any person on the street where I live whether Roxolana's termination date is today, the answer I'd most likely get back would be no. People generally think in terms of something being either true or false. Roxolana's termination date is null,

Figure 4-1. The monster that is three-valued logic has bitten more than one unwary SQL developer (sketch by Matt Williams)

which is not the same as today, right? The database however, adds a new truth value, that of *unknown*. With some specific exceptions, any comparison to null yields a result of unknown. Ask the database whether Roxolana was terminated today, and the database would answer the equivalent of unknown. And unknown is neither true nor false.

 Nullity is most critical to understand. You can't be an effective SQL user without a good grounding in three-valued logic and the effects of nulls in expressions.

The three queries in Example 4-21 clearly illustrate the effect of nulls on comparison expressions. You'll notice that Roxolana appears in none of the results. The first query illustrates that null is not *not* equal to today. The second query shows that null is not equal to today. The third query shows that null is not even equal to itself.

Example 4-21. The effects of "unknown"

```
SELECT employee_name
FROM employee
WHERE employee_termination_date <> SYSDATE;

EMPLOYEE_NAME
----------------------------------------
Mykhailo Hrushevsky
Pavlo Virsky
Pavlo Chubynsky
Ivan Mazepa
Igor Sikorsky
Mykhailo Verbytsky

SELECT employee_name
FROM employee
WHERE employee_termination_date = SYSDATE;

no rows selected

SELECT employee_name
FROM employee
WHERE employee_termination_date = NULL;

no rows selected
```

If null is not equal to null, how then do you even detect its existence? How do you go about returning rows with nulls?

 I tend to refer to a specific column or expression result as *being* null. I don't usually refer to null as a value. Others, including even the authors of the ANSI/ISO SQL standard, do use the term "null value." I don't like that approach because, logically, null represents the absence of a value. The term "null value" confuses the issue. Don't get worked up over this terminology issue though. I don't. Just be aware that null and null value mean the same thing: no value at all.

Detecting Nulls

Fortunately, SQL's designers had the forethought to provide a mechanism for detecting and dealing with null values. The standard way to detect null values is to use the IS NULL predicate, as demonstrated in Example 4-22. You can use IS NOT NULL to return rows for which a given column is not null.

Example 4-22. Using IS NULL to detect nulls

```
SELECT employee_name, employee_termination_date
FROM employee
WHERE employee_termination_date IS NULL;
```

Example 4-22. Using IS NULL to detect nulls (continued)

```
EMPLOYEE_NAME          EMPLOYEE_TERMINATI
--------------------   ------------------
Marusia Churai
Mykola Leontovych
Lesia Ukrainka
Taras Shevchenko
Roxolana Lisovsky

SELECT employee_name, employee_termination_date
FROM employee
WHERE employee_termination_date IS NOT NULL;

EMPLOYEE_NAME          EMPLOYEE_TERMINATI
--------------------   ------------------
Mykhailo Hrushevsky    05-MAY-04
Pavlo Virsky           01-APR-04
Pavlo Chubynsky        15-NOV-04
Ivan Mazepa            30-SEP-04
Igor Sikorsky          04-APR-04
Mykhailo Verbytsky     31-OCT-04
```

Notice that the null termination dates in Example 4-22 are blank. This is unlike the results you saw in Example 4-20 but represents the default behavior of SQL*Plus. If you want to see nulls as something other than blanks, you will need to issue a SET NULL command to specify an alternative representation.

Nulls in Expressions

The expressions involving nulls in Examples 4-21 and 4-22 are all WHERE clause expressions. Nulls make their presence felt in other types of expressions. The general rule is that if any value in an expression is null, then the result of that expression will be null. Example 4-23 demonstrates this concept by attempting to add $100 to the hourly rate of Roxolana.

Example 4-23. Adding to NULL yields NULL

```
SELECT employee_name, employee_billing_rate,
       employee_billing_rate + 100 increased_rate
FROM employee
WHERE employee_id = 116;

EMPLOYEE_NAME          EMPLOYEE_BILLING_RATE INCREASED_RATE
--------------------   --------------------- --------------
Roxolana Lisovsky
```

In this case, null + 100 is still null. Often treating null as if it were zero can be handy. Oracle's NVL function allows you to do that. NVL takes two arguments. The first argument may be any expression or column name; the type does not matter. If the first argument is not null, then that argument will be returned. The second argument is an alternate value to be returned only when the first is null. Example 4-24 uses NVL to treat null billing rates as zero values.

Example 4-24. Using NVL to provide an alternative, non-NULL value

```
SELECT employee_name, NVL(employee_billing_rate,0) billing_rate,
       NVL(employee_billing_rate,0) + 100 increased_rate
FROM employee
WHERE employee_id IN (113, 116);
```

```
EMPLOYEE_NAME         BILLING_RATE INCREASED_RATE
--------------------- ------------ --------------
Mykhailo Verbytsky             300            400
Roxolana Lisovsky                0            100
```

If you work with nulls often, and especially if the NVL and IS NULL functionality is not meeting your needs, you'll want to get familiar with Oracle's NVL2 and DECODE functions, as well as with CASE expressions. Any good book on Oracle SQL will cover these functions and expressions.

Table Joins

It's often the case that the data you want to return from a query are spread across more than one table. Commonly this occurs as a result of master-detail relationships such as the one between the project and project_hours tables. The project table contains one row describing each project, whereas, for each project, project_hours contains many rows detailing time charged to that project. To link such master and detail data together in the results from a SELECT statement, you use a relational operation called a *join*.

Inner Joins

Imagine that you need to generate a detailed listing of time charged to each of your projects. You want that listing to include project name, the date on which work was performed, and the number of hours involved. What makes this request interesting is that you need to list two tables in your FROM clause. Project names come from the project table, while dates and hours come from the project_hours table. How do you SELECT from two tables at once? The answer is to use a JOIN clause such as the one in Example 4-25.

Example 4-25. Selecting related rows from two tables

```
SELECT p.project_name,  ph. employee_id,
       ph.time_log_date, ph.hours_logged
FROM project p JOIN project_hours ph
    ON p.project_id = ph.project_id;
```

The JOIN clause, which is a subclause of the FROM clause, is new in Oracle9i Database and specifies that data are to be drawn from not one table, but from two, in this case from the project and project_hours tables. The ON clause, subsidiary to JOIN, defines the conditions that rows of combined data must meet to be returned from the join operation. This will make more sense as you scrutinize Figures 4-2 through 4-4.

Conceptually, all joins begin as a set of all possible combinations of rows from the two tables involved. Such a set is known as a *Cartesian product*. Figure 4-2 shows the beginning of a join between a three-row project table and a four-row project_hours table.

> Databases implement all kinds of optimizations to avoid generating Cartesian products. However, understanding the conceptual process defining the join operation is critical to writing accurate SQL queries.

Each row from project has been combined with each row from project_hours. I've highlighted the JOIN clause in the query to show how much of the query has been executed so far.

Looking at Figure 4-2, you can see that not all combinations make sense. Detail from project 1004 has no business being associated with project 1002, nor does the reverse make sense. Project 1003 should have no detail at all. This is where the *join conditions* in the ON clause come into play. When you write a join, you should write join conditions to identify those rows in the Cartesian product that make sense, that you wish returned from the join operation. Rows not matching the join conditions are filtered out. Think of a sieve filtering out large gravel and passing only the sand. Figure 4-3 shows the results of evaluating the join condition in the example query.

As Figure 4-3 illustrates, the next step after forming the Cartesian product is to apply the conditions in the ON clause, using those to eliminate row combinations that make no business sense. Look at the project ID numbers in Figure 4-3's results. Each row output from the join operation corresponds to a row from project_hours. Each row contains corresponding project information (name and ID) from project. At this intermediate stage, you can think of all columns from both tables as being present in each row. Thus, each row has two copies of the project ID number, one from each table, and those two values are used (see the ON clause) to identify those row combinations that make business sense.

The join illustrated in Figure 4-3 is known as an *inner join*. In fact, you can write it using the keywords INNER JOIN instead of just JOIN. The key characteristic of an inner join is that each row of output from a join operation contains values from both tables. The choice of the term *inner join* is unfortunate because that term is not at all evocative of the results produced.

It's entirely possible to place WHERE conditions in a query containing a join and this is often done. Such WHERE conditions are evaluated after all the joins. Figure 4-4

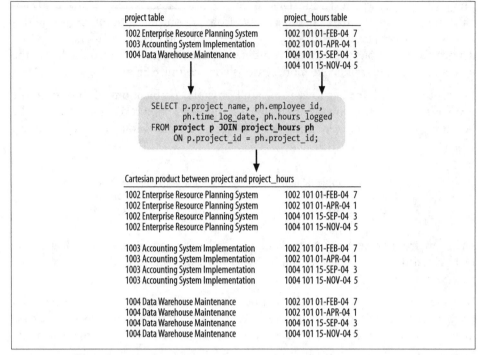

project table

1002	Enterprise Resource Planning System
1003	Accounting System Implementation
1004	Data Warehouse Maintenance

project_hours table

1002	101	01-FEB-04	7
1002	101	01-APR-04	1
1004	101	15-SEP-04	3
1004	101	15-NOV-04	5

```
SELECT p.project_name, ph.employee_id,
       ph.time_log_date, ph.hours_logged
FROM project p JOIN project_hours ph
     ON p.project_id = ph.project_id;
```

Cartesian product between project and project_hours

1002 Enterprise Resource Planning System	1002	101	01-FEB-04	7
1002 Enterprise Resource Planning System	1002	101	01-APR-04	1
1002 Enterprise Resource Planning System	1004	101	15-SEP-04	3
1002 Enterprise Resource Planning System	1004	101	15-NOV-04	5
1003 Accounting System Implementation	1002	101	01-FEB-04	7
1003 Accounting System Implementation	1002	101	01-APR-04	1
1003 Accounting System Implementation	1004	101	15-SEP-04	3
1003 Accounting System Implementation	1004	101	15-NOV-04	5
1004 Data Warehouse Maintenance	1002	101	01-FEB-04	7
1004 Data Warehouse Maintenance	1002	101	01-APR-04	1
1004 Data Warehouse Maintenance	1004	101	15-SEP-04	3
1004 Data Warehouse Maintenance	1004	101	15-NOV-04	5

Figure 4-2. All joins begin as a Cartesian product

shows the same query as Figure 4-3 but with the addition of a WHERE clause. You can see the effect of WHERE and when that clause is evaluated. You can see that the generation of columns in the SELECT list is the final operation in the query's execution.

The process I've described in this section is conceptual. It's a good way to think about joins that will help you write better queries and to write them more easily. However, this conceptual process is seldom efficient when applied in real life. Instead, databases implement many techniques to optimize joins and query executions. For example, with respect to the WHERE clause in Figure 4-4, a database's query optimizer may "decide" to evaluate that condition early, eliminating rows from project_hours for February before the join, not after it.

Don't get caught up in thinking about query optimizations when writing join queries. Think conceptually until you've written a query that yields the correct results. No matter how a database optimizes a query, especially a join query, in the end the results *must* match the conceptual model I've just described. All joins begin with a Cartesian product of all possible combinations of rows from two tables. Join conditions then eliminate unwanted rows. It's that simple.

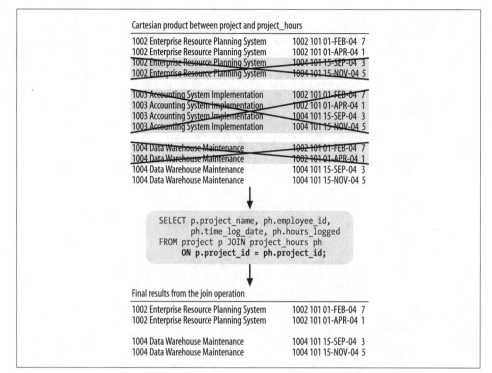

Cartesian product between project and project_hours

1002 Enterprise Resource Planning System	1002 101 01-FEB-04 7
1002 Enterprise Resource Planning System	1002 101 01-APR-04 1
~~1002 Enterprise Resource Planning System~~	~~1004 101 15-SEP-04 3~~
~~1002 Enterprise Resource Planning System~~	~~1004 101 15-NOV-04 5~~
~~1003 Accounting System Implementation~~	~~1002 101 01-FEB-04 7~~
~~1003 Accounting System Implementation~~	~~1002 101 01-APR-04 1~~
~~1003 Accounting System Implementation~~	~~1004 101 15-SEP-04 3~~
~~1003 Accounting System Implementation~~	~~1004 101 15-NOV-04 5~~
~~1004 Data Warehouse Maintenance~~	~~1002 101 01-FEB-04 7~~
~~1004 Data Warehouse Maintenance~~	~~1002 101 01-APR-04 1~~
1004 Data Warehouse Maintenance	1004 101 15-SEP-04 3
1004 Data Warehouse Maintenance	1004 101 15-NOV-04 5

```
SELECT p.project_name, ph.employee_id,
       ph.time_log_date, ph.hours_logged
FROM project p JOIN project_hours ph
  ON p.project_id = ph.project_id;
```

Final results from the join operation

1002 Enterprise Resource Planning System	1002 101 01-FEB-04 7
1002 Enterprise Resource Planning System	1002 101 01-APR-04 1
1004 Data Warehouse Maintenance	1004 101 15-SEP-04 3
1004 Data Warehouse Maintenance	1004 101 15-NOV-04 5

Figure 4-3. Join conditions pass only those row combinations that make sense, eliminating all the others

 If you're interested in the topic of join optimization, particularly for queries containing large numbers of joins, I heartily recommend and endorse Dan Tow's book, *SQL Tuning* (O'Reilly).

Outer Joins

Go back to Figure 4-3 and look at the rows feeding into and out of the ON clause evaluation. What happened to project 1003? Rows referencing that project existed in the project table, were part of the Cartesian product, but were completely eliminated by the ON clause. Why? Because the project rows for 1003 had no counterparts in the project_hours table. As a result, no rows were in the Cartesian product for project 1003 in which both project_id values matched, and thus, project 1003 completely vanished from the query's result set. This behavior is not always what you want.

To join project to project_hours using the data shown in Figure 4-3, yet preserving projects having no corresponding detail in project_hours, you need to use an *outer join*. An outer join designates one table as optional and the other as an anchor. Rows

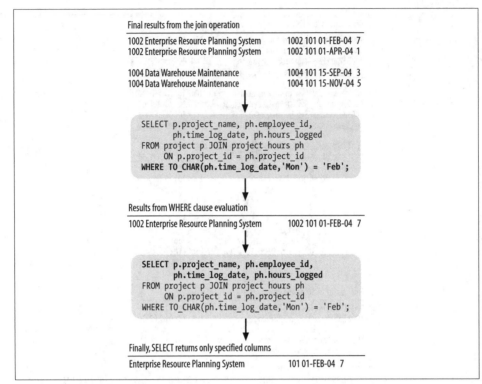

Final results from the join operation

1002 Enterprise Resource Planning System	1002 101 01-FEB-04 7
1002 Enterprise Resource Planning System	1002 101 01-APR-04 1
1004 Data Warehouse Maintenance	1004 101 15-SEP-04 3
1004 Data Warehouse Maintenance	1004 101 15-NOV-04 5

```
SELECT p.project_name, ph.employee_id,
       ph.time_log_date, ph.hours_logged
FROM project p JOIN project_hours ph
  ON p.project_id = ph.project_id
WHERE TO_CHAR(ph.time_log_date,'Mon') = 'Feb';
```

Results from WHERE clause evaluation

1002 Enterprise Resource Planning System	1002 101 01-FEB-04 7

```
SELECT p.project_name, ph.employee_id,
       ph.time_log_date, ph.hours_logged
FROM project p JOIN project_hours ph
  ON p.project_id = ph.project_id
WHERE TO_CHAR(ph.time_log_date,'Mon') = 'Feb';
```

Finally, SELECT returns only specified columns

Enterprise Resource Planning System	101 01-FEB-04 7

Figure 4-4. WHERE clause conditions are evaluated following all joins

from the anchor table in an outer join are preserved even when no corresponding detail rows exist.

Figure 4-5 shows a *left outer join*, designating the table on the left-hand side of the JOIN keyword as the anchor table. The project table is to the left, so project rows are preserved.

Look carefully at what goes on in Figure 4-5. The condition in the ON clause results in the elimination of all rows in the Cartesian product associated with the row from the project table for project 1003. This is when the outer join logic kicks in. The four combination rows for project 1003 are, in fact, removed from the join, but a new row is slipped in for project 1003 containing values *only from* the project table. Column values that would otherwise come from project_hours are set to null.

> Remember that my explanation is conceptual, a useful way of visualizing the outer join process. How the database engine implements this conceptual process may be quite different from what I've described.

Another type of join is the *right outer join*. Right and left outer joins are the same fundamental operation. The only difference lies in which side of the JOIN keyword

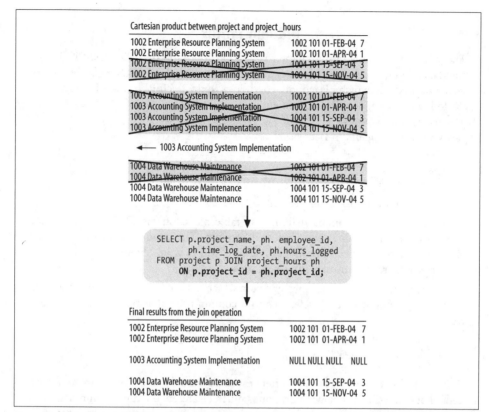

Figure 4-5. *An outer join preserving a row with no detail*

you place the anchor table. Example 4-26 shows semantically identical left and right outer joins.

Example 4-26. *Left and right outer joins are fundamentally the same operation*

```
SELECT p.project_name,  ph.time_log_date, ph.hours_logged
FROM project p LEFT OUTER JOIN project_hours ph
    ON p.project_id = ph.project_id;

SELECT p.project_name,  ph.time_log_date, ph.hours_logged
FROM project_hours ph RIGHT OUTER JOIN project p
    ON p.project_id = ph.project_id;
```

Example 4-26's first query is a left outer join: project is to the left, so project is the anchor table. The second query is a right outer join, but I've moved project to the right-hand side of the JOIN keyword, so it is still the anchor table. Both queries generate the same result.

Full Outer Joins

The final type of outer join that I want to discuss is the *full outer join*. Think of a full outer join as the combination of all three types of joins so far: inner, left, and right:

- You get all the rows that you would get from an INNER JOIN (e.g., projects and their attendant detail):

```
project p INNER JOIN project_hours ph
```

- Plus you get the *additional* rows that would result from making that inner join into a LEFT OUTER JOIN (e.g., projects without any detail):

```
project p LEFT OUTER JOIN project_hours ph
```

- Plus you further get those additional rows that would result from RIGHT OUTER JOIN, but keeping the same ordering of the tables (e.g., detail without any projects):

```
project p RIGHT OUTER JOIN project_hours ph
```

A full outer join will return at least one of each row from both tables. You would typically then have WHERE clause conditions to further filter the results.

 Oracle Database 10g introduced yet another type of join, the *partition outer join*. Read about that at *http://gennick.com/partition.html*.

Sorting Query Results

Unless you specify otherwise, query results will come back in whatever random order the database happens to retrieve them. To sort the results from a SELECT, use the ORDER BY clause as shown in Example 4-27.

Example 4-27. Sorting query results

```
SELECT e.employee_id "ID", e.employee_name "Name",
       e.employee_hire_date "Hire Date"
FROM employee e
ORDER BY EXTRACT(YEAR FROM employee_hire_date) DESC, employee_name ASC;
```

```
        ID Name                                       Hire Date
---------- ----------------------------------------   ---------
       110 Ivan Mazepa                                04-APR-04
       107 Lesia Ukrainka                             02-JAN-04
       113 Mykhailo Verbytsky                         03-MAR-04
       105 Mykola Leontovych                          15-JUN-04
       116 Roxolana Lisovsky                          03-JUN-04
       108 Pavlo Chubynsky                            01-MAR-94
       104 Pavlo Virsky                               29-DEC-87
       111 Taras Shevchenko                           23-AUG-76
       102 Mykhailo Hrushevsky                        16-SEP-64
       112 Igor Sikorsky                              15-NOV-61
       101 Marusia Churai                             15-NOV-61
```

The ORDER BY clause in Example 4-27 does the following:

EXTRACT(YEAR FROM employee_hire_date) DESC
> Sorts initially on the year in which an employee was hired, listing the most recent year first. The EXTRACT function in this case returns the four-digit year as a numeric value. The DESC keyword requests a descending sort.

employee_name ASC
> Sorts secondly by employee name. The keyword ASC requests an ascending sort.

The end result is that employees are sorted in descending order by year of hire, and within each year they are further sorted in ascending order by name. The ASC keyword is optional and is rarely used in practice.

Example 4-27 also demonstrates how column aliases may be enclosed in double quotes to allow for spaces and lowercase letters in alias names. Such names can make query results more readable.

 When you issue a query without an ORDER BY clause, it may sometimes appear that rows come back in the order in which they were originally inserted or in some order matching an index. Don't be fooled. And don't count on such behavior. Unless you write an ORDER BY clause to specify a sort order, you have no guarantee as to the order in which rows are returned.

Grouping and Summarizing

SQL allows you to divide the rows returned by a query into groups, summarize the data within each group using a special class of functions known as *aggregate functions*, and return only one row per group. For example, you can count the number of rows in a table using the COUNT function shown in Example 4-28.

Example 4-28. Summarizing data using an aggregate function

```
SELECT COUNT(*), COUNT(employee_termination_date)
FROM employee;

  COUNT(*) COUNT(EMPLOYEE_TERMINATION_DATE)
---------- --------------------------------
        11                                6
```

There's nothing in Example 4-28 to divide the data being retrieved into groups, so all 11 rows in the employee table are treated as one group. The COUNT function is an aggregate function that can count the number of values or rows in a group. COUNT is special in that you can pass it an asterisk (*) when you wish to count rows. The first use of COUNT in the example shows that the table contains 11 rows. The second use counts the number of values in the employee_termination_date column. Nulls are not counted because nulls represent the absence of value. While there are 11 employees on file, only five are currently employed; the other six have been terminated. This is the kind of business information you can obtain by summarizing your data.

The GROUP BY Clause

You'll rarely want to summarize data across an entire table. More often, you'll find yourself dividing your data into groups. For example, you might wish to group employees by the decade in which they were hired, and then ask the following question: How many employees from each decade are still employed? Example 4-29 shows how to do this.

Example 4-29. Counting the remaining employees from each decade

```
SELECT SUBSTR(TO_CHAR(employee_hire_date,'YYYY'),1,3) || '0' "decade",
       COUNT(employee_hire_date) "hired",
       COUNT(employee_hire_date) - COUNT(employee_termination_date) "remaining",
       MIN(employee_hire_date) "first hire",
       MAX(employee_hire_date) "last hire"
FROM employee
GROUP BY SUBSTR(TO_CHAR(employee_hire_date,'YYYY'),1,3) || '0';
```

```
decade           hired  remaining  first hire   last hire
-------------    -----  ---------  -----------  -----------
1960                 3          1  15-Nov-1961  16-Sep-1964
1970                 1          1  23-Aug-1976  23-Aug-1976
1980                 1          0  29-Dec-1987  29-Dec-1987
1990                 1          0  01-Mar-1994  01-Mar-1994
2000                 5          3  02-Jan-2004  15-Jun-2004
```

In addition to COUNT, the example shows the MIN and MAX functions being used to return the earliest and latest hire dates within each group, i.e., within each decade. You can see that five employees were hired in the 2000s, with all five hires occurring between January and June 2004. Two of those new hires have since left the company. By contrast, you have no attrition of people hired during the 1980s and 1990s. Perhaps you should investigate to see whether your Human Resources department is slipping in its hiring practices!

It's worth going into some detail about how GROUP BY queries execute. You should have a correct understanding of these queries. To begin, Figure 4-6 shows all the employee rows as returned by the FROM clause.

Step 1: FROM returns all employee rows	ID name	hire date	term date	rate
	101 Marusia Churai	15-Nov-1961		169
	102 Mykhailo Hrushevsky	16-Sep-1964	05-May-2004	135
	104 Pavlo Virsky	29-Dec-1987	01-Apr-2004	99
	105 Mykola Leontovych	15-Jun-2004		121
	107 Lesia Ukrainka	02-Jan-2004		45
	108 Pavlo Chubynsky	01-Mar-1994	15-Nov-2004	220
	110 Ivan Mazepa	04-Apr-2004	30-Sep-2004	84
	111 Taras Shevchenko	23-Aug-1976		100
	112 Igor Sikorsky	15-Nov-1961	04-Apr-2004	70
	113 Mykhailo Verbytsky	03-Mar-2004	31-Oct-2004	300
	116 Roxolana Lisovsky	03-Jun-2004		

Figure 4-6. The FROM operation returns all employee rows

The GROUP BY clause then divides employees into groups by decade, as shown in Figure 4-7. The TO_CHAR function returns the four-digit year of each employee's hire date as a character string. The SUBSTR function extracts the first through third digits from that string, and the || operator is used to replace the fourth digit with a zero. Thus, all years in the range 1960–1969 are transformed into the string "1960." (Appendix B provides more detail about applying TO_CHAR to dates.)

SUBSTR(TO_CHAR(employee_hire_date,'YYYY'),1,3) || '0'

	ID name	hire date	term date	rate	decade
Step 2: GROUP BY sorts rows into groups by decade	101 Marusia Churai	15-Nov-1961		169	1960
	102 Mykhailo Hrushevsky	16-Sep-1964	05-May-2004	135	1960
	112 Igor Sikorsky	15-Nov-1961	04-Apr-2004	70	1960
	104 Pavlo Virsky	29-Dec-1987	01-Apr-2004	99	1980
	105 Mykola Leontovych	15-Jun-2004		121	2000
	107 Lesia Ukrainka	02-Jan-2004		45	2000
	110 Ivan Mazepa	04-Apr-2004	30-Sep-2004	84	2000
	113 Mykhailo Verbytsky	03-Mar-2004	31-Oct-2004	300	2000
	116 Roxolana Lisovsky	03-Jun-2004			2000
	108 Pavlo Chubynsky	01-Mar-1994	15-Nov-2004	220	1990
	111 Taras Shevchenko	23-Aug-1976		100	1970

Figure 4-7. The GROUP BY operation divides rows into groups

The grouping of rows is often accomplished via a sorting operation. But as Figure 4-7 illustrates, the sort may be incomplete. Don't count on GROUP BY to sort your output. Always use ORDER BY if you want results in a specific order.

Once the rows are divided into groups, the aggregate functions are applied in order to return just one value per group. Figure 4-8 illustrates this process for just the one group of rows representing the decade 2000.

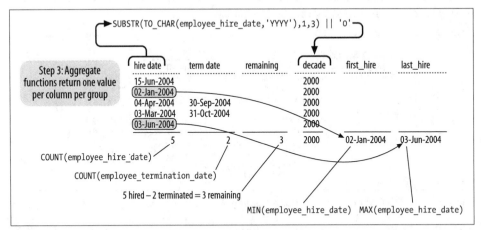

Figure 4-8. Aggregate functions are applied to return one row per group

There is one column returned by the SELECT statement in Example 4-29 to which an aggregate function has not been applied. That column is the computed column that returns the decade in which an employee was hired. Because that column is the basis by which employees are divided into groups, it makes sense to return it, so you can know to which group each summary row applies. If you omit the decade column, the results in the example will become useless. It's a good idea to identify each summary row by including the GROUP BY columns in the query results.

 All columns other than those listed in the GROUP BY clause must have an aggregate function applied to them. You cannot, for example, return individual employee IDs from the query shown in Example 4-29. You *must* apply an aggregate function to compute just one value per column, per group.

Example 4-29 uses `COUNT(employee_hire_date)` as a proxy for the number of employees hired in each decade. This is reasonable because the example database design precludes nulls in the hire date column. Things change, though, if null hire dates are a possibility. If null hire dates were to exist in the data, then those nulls would propagate throughout the decade calculation, and you'd end up with a single group having all the null hire dates. COUNT will not count null values, so the application of `COUNT(employee_hire_date)` to a group of rows with all null hire dates would result in the value zero. Furthermore, you might have termination dates in that group, so the result of `COUNT(employee_termination_date)` might be greater than zero. Among all your other output then, you might end up with an oddball result row like the following:

```
decade            hired  remaining first hir last hire
-------------     ------ --------- --------- ---------
NULL                  0        -1 NULL       NULL
```

In this case, you might be better off using COUNT(*) to count rows rather than non-null values. However, that's fixing a symptom. It might make the math look better in the results, but it does nothing to address the underlying problem of bad data. The real fix is to dig into your data and find out why you didn't record hire dates for some of your employees.

The HAVING Clause

You may not want all the summary rows returned by a GROUP BY query. You know that you can use WHERE to eliminate detail rows returned by a regular query. With summary queries, you can use the HAVING clause to eliminate summary rows. Example 4-30 shows a GROUP BY query that uses HAVING to restrict the results to only those employees having logged more than 20 hours toward projects 1001 and 1002.

Example 4-30. HAVING allows you to filter out summary rows that you do not want

```
SELECT employee_id, project_id
FROM project_hours
GROUP BY employee_id, project_id
HAVING (project_id = 1001 OR project_id=1002)
   AND SUM(hours_logged) > 20;
```

Example 4-30. HAVING allows you to filter out summary rows that you do not want (continued)

```
EMPLOYEE_ID PROJECT_ID
----------- ----------
        101       1002
        107       1002
        108       1002
        111       1002
```

Notice the use of SUM(hours_logged) to compute the total number of hours each employee has charged to each project. This expression appears only in the HAVING clause, where it is used to restrict output to only those employee/project combinations representing more than 20 hours of work. If you want to see the sum, you can put the expression in the SELECT clause as well, but you're not required to do that.

Example 4-30 is in part a good example of how *not* to use the HAVING clause. HAVING executes after all the sorting and summarizing of GROUP BY. Any condition you write in the HAVING clause should depend on summarized results. Two conditions in Example 4-30's HAVING clause do not depend on summary calculations. Those conditions should be moved to the WHERE clause, as shown in Example 4-31.

Example 4-31. Put non-summary conditions in the WHERE clause

```
SELECT employee_id, project_id
FROM project_hours
WHERE project_id = 1001 OR project_id=1002
GROUP BY employee_id, project_id
HAVING SUM(hours_logged) > 20;

EMPLOYEE_ID PROJECT_ID
----------- ----------
        101       1002
        107       1002
        108       1002
        111       1002
```

The reason you put all detail-based conditions in the WHERE clause is that the WHERE clause is evaluated prior to the grouping and summarizing operation of GROUP BY. The fewer the rows that have to be sorted, grouped, and summarized, the better your query's performance will be, and the less the load on the database server. Examples 4-30 and 4-31 produce the same results, but Example 4-31 is more efficient because it eliminates many rows earlier in the query execution process.

Subqueries

A *subquery* is a SELECT statement embedded within another SQL statement. You can use subqueries in place of column references, in place of table references, to generate values for comparison in a WHERE or HAVING condition, and to generate values for inserts and updates.

Treating Rowsets as Tables

So far in this chapter, you've selected data from tables. A SELECT statement is executed, and a set of rows comes back as the result. Imagine if you could further treat that set of rows as a table against which you issue another SELECT statement or perhaps an UPDATE or a DELETE. Using a subquery, you can do just what I've described, and that can lead to some interesting and elegant solutions to SQL problems.

One use for a subquery in the FROM clause is to aggregate data that has already been aggregated. For example, you might be faced with the following business problem:

> Find all employees who have worked on projects 1001 and 1002 during the year 2004. Sum the number of hours each of those employees has worked on each project during that year. Report the ranges. Show the lowest number of hours that any employee worked on each project during 2004, as well as the highest number of hours.

This is an interesting problem to solve because you must sum the hours for employee/project combinations using the SUM aggregate function, and you must apply MIN and MAX to your sums. Example 4-32 shows one way to approach this problem using a subquery.

Example 4-32. Aggregating aggregated data

```
SELECT phs.project_id, MIN(phs.hours), MAX(phs.hours)
FROM (SELECT employee_id, project_id, SUM(hours_logged) hours
      FROM project_hours
      WHERE project_id IN (1001, 1002)
        AND TRUNC(time_log_date,'Year') = TO_DATE('1-Jan-2004','dd-Mon-yyyy')
      GROUP BY employee_id, project_id) phs
GROUP BY project_id;

PROJECT_ID MIN(PHS.HOURS) MAX(PHS.HOURS)
---------- -------------- --------------
      1001              4             20
      1002              8             24
```

The subquery appears in the FROM clause enclosed in parentheses. The outer query treats the rows from the subquery in the same manner as it would treat rows from a table. Tables have names, and so should subqueries. Example 4-32 gives the name, or alias, phs to the subquery. The outer query uses that name to refer to the columns from the subquery. The alias hours is given to the column represented by SUM(hours_logged), making it easy to refer to that column from the outer query.

The call to TRUNC(time_log_date,'Year') converts each date to January 1st of its year. Any date in 2004 will be truncated to 1-Jan-2004. It's easy, then, to eliminate time log entries for other years.

Because subqueries in the FROM clause are treated the same as tables, it stands to reason they can take part in joins. Example 4-33 expands on Example 4-32 by adding another level of subquery and a join to the project table in order to include project names in the query output.

Example 4-33. Joining a subquery to a table

```
SELECT minmax_hours.project_id, p.project_name,
       minmax_hours.min_hours, minmax_hours.max_hours
FROM (
   SELECT phs.project_id, MIN(phs.hours) min_hours, MAX(phs.hours) max_hours
   FROM (SELECT employee_id, project_id, SUM(hours_logged) hours
         FROM project_hours
         WHERE project_id IN (1001, 1002)
           AND TRUNC(time_log_date,'Year') = TO_DATE('1-Jan-2004','dd-Mon-yyyy')
         GROUP BY employee_id, project_id) phs
   GROUP BY project_id) minmax_hours JOIN project p
     ON minmax_hours.project_id = p.project_id;

PROJECT_ID PROJECT_NAME                             MIN_HOURS  MAX_HOURS
---------- --------------------------------------- ---------- ----------
      1001 Corporate Web Site                               4         20
      1002 Enterprise Resource Planning System              8         24
```

There are different ways you can approach the join to project shown in Example 4-33. The join could occur in the innermost subquery or in the middle subquery, and either of those alternatives would eliminate the need for a third subquery. Sometimes it's a judgment call as to which approach is best. Sometimes you need to make that call based on readability or on a desire not to mess with a working query. By adding an outer SELECT statement to an already working query, I avoided the need to tamper with a SELECT statement, the middle one in Example 4-33, which I knew worked.

There's a performance issue, too, that isn't obvious in the amount of sample data used for the examples in this book. Joining to project in the innermost query would force the join to take place before any aggregation at all. Given a large enough number of rows in project_hours, a join that early would significantly increase the expenditure of I/O and CPU resources by the query, as all those detail rows would need to be joined. Having the join occur where it does in Example 4-33 means that only two rows, the two returned by the middle query, need to be joined to project.

Subqueries in the FROM clause are sometimes referred to as *inline views*, and such a subquery can be considered as a dynamically created view, for the purpose of the one query. Any subquery in the FROM clause can be replaced by an equivalent view, but then you have the problem of creating that view, which is a permanent database object.

 You can see another interesting use of inline views, this time to generate rows of data that don't already exist in the database, in the article *Creating Pivot Tables* at *http://gennick.com/pivot.html*.

Testing for Representation

You can use subqueries to see whether a row is representative of a set. The query in Example 4-32 contains the following WHERE condition:

```
WHERE project_id IN (1001, 1002)
```

This condition tests whether a row from the project_hours table is associated with project 1001 or 1002. Imagine a more complicated scenario. Imagine that you're interested in all projects having budgets of $1,000,000 or more. You don't know which projects have such large budgets. Furthermore, budgets change from time to time, and you don't want to have to modify the project ID numbers in your query each time your budgets change. Instead of hard-coding the project_id list for the IN predicate, you can generate that list using a subquery in the IN predicate, as shown in Example 4-34.

Example 4-34. A subquery generating values for an IN predicate

```
SELECT phs.project_id, MIN(phs.hours), MAX(phs.hours)
FROM (SELECT employee_id, project_id, SUM(hours_logged) hours
      FROM project_hours
      WHERE project_id IN (SELECT project_id
                           FROM project
                           WHERE project_budget >= 1000000)
        AND TRUNC(time_log_date,'Year') = TO_DATE('1-Jan-2004','dd-Mon-yyyy')
      GROUP BY employee_id, project_id) phs
GROUP BY project_id;
```

When you execute the SELECT statement shown in Example 4-34, the IN predicate's subquery is executed first to generate a list of project IDs encompassing all projects having budgets of $1,000,000 or more. Another approach to this problem is to issue a subquery for each project_hour row to see whether the associated project has the required budget. This approach is shown in Example 4-35.

Example 4-35. An EXISTS subquery checking for projects with large budgets

```
SELECT phs.project_id, MIN(phs.hours), MAX(phs.hours)
FROM (SELECT employee_id, project_id, SUM(hours_logged) hours
      FROM project_hours ph
      WHERE EXISTS (SELECT *
                    FROM project pb
                    WHERE pb.project_budget >= 1000000
                      AND pb.project_id = ph.project_id)
```

Example 4-35. An EXISTS subquery checking for projects with large budgets (continued)

```
        AND TRUNC(time_log_date,'Year') = TO_DATE('1-Jan-2004','dd-Mon-yyyy')
      GROUP BY employee_id, project_id) phs
GROUP BY project_id;
```

The subquery in Example 4-35 is known as a *correlated subquery*, meaning that the subquery references a value from the parent statement. Aliases are important when writing such subqueries. The parent query's project_hours table is aliased as ph. The subquery references the project ID from each candidate row from the main query via the reference to ph.project_id. The subquery is executed once for each row that can potentially be returned by the main query.

 Subqueries prior to Example 4-35 have all been *non-correlated*, which means that you can execute them independently of their enclosing statement. Non-correlated subqueries are executed just once per execution of their containing query. Correlated subqueries are executed once per row. Either subquery may be written using IN or EXISTS, but typically you'll find that IN subqueries are non-correlated and EXISTS subqueries are correlated.

It's pretty much impossible to provide a general rule as to when to use IN and EXISTS predicates when either can be used to solve a particular problem. Given the low number of rows in the project table as compared to the project_hours table, you might think that the SELECT in Example 4-34 would be more efficient than the one in Example 4-35. After all, the IN predicate's subquery must execute only once, and return only two values. However, in my database, with the release of Oracle that I'm running and the sample data I'm using for this book, the SELECT in Example 4-35 requires far less input/output than Example 4-34. A good practice is to test both approaches, perhaps using SET AUTOTRACE ON as described in Chapter 12, and then use the one that performs best for your particular query.

Generating Data for INSERTs and UPDATEs

Subqueries are useful in generating values for INSERT and UPDATE statements. Examples 4-36 and 4-37 show two ways of creating a reporting table of project billing data summarized by week. You might generate, and periodically refresh, such a table to make it easier for end users to check on project status using ad hoc query tools.

Example 4-36 uses a CREATE TABLE AS SELECT FROM statement, which lets you create and populate the reporting table in one step. Example 4-37 creates the reporting table separately, and then populates the table using an INSERT...SELECT FROM statement. In each case, a subquery generates the data to be inserted into the new table.

When writing NOT IN predicates, be sensitive to the possible presence of nulls in the results of your subqueries. The following query attempts to use NOT IN to return a list of all employees terminated on any date on which at least one employee hired in 2004 was terminated:

```
SELECT employee_id, employee_termination_date
FROM employee
WHERE employee_termination_date NOT IN (
    SELECT employee_termination_date
    FROM employee
    WHERE '2004' =
        TO_CHAR(
            TRUNC(employee_hire_date,'year'), 'yyyy')
);
```

Executed against the sample data for this book, this query will return no rows because the subquery returns one or more nulls. A single null prevents the NOT IN condition from ever returning true because the null is treated as an unknown. Is a given termination date not in the set? The answer is unknown because there's at least one unknown value in the set. Be very careful of this scenario when writing NOT IN subqueries. Take care that such subqueries do not return nulls.

Example 4-36. Using CREATE TABLE AS SELECT FROM

```
DROP TABLE project_time;

CREATE TABLE project_time AS
    SELECT EXTRACT (YEAR FROM time_log_date) year,
           TO_NUMBER(TO_CHAR(time_log_date,'ww')) week_number,
           p.project_id, p.project_name, SUM(ph.hours_logged) hours_logged
    FROM project p JOIN project_hours ph
        ON p.project_id = ph.project_id
    GROUP BY EXTRACT (YEAR FROM time_log_date),
             TO_NUMBER(TO_CHAR(time_log_date,'ww')),
             p.project_id, p.project_name;
```

Example 4-37. Using INSERT...SELECT FROM

```
DROP TABLE project_time;

CREATE TABLE project_time (
    year NUMBER,
    week_number NUMBER,
    project_id NUMBER(4),
    project_name VARCHAR2(40),
    hours_logged NUMBER);

INSERT INTO project_time
    SELECT EXTRACT (YEAR FROM time_log_date),
```

Example 4-37. Using INSERT...SELECT FROM (continued)

```
        TO_NUMBER(TO_CHAR(time_log_date,'ww')),
        p.project_id, p.project_name, SUM(ph.hours_logged)
  FROM project p JOIN project_hours ph
      ON p.project_id = ph.project_id
  GROUP BY EXTRACT (YEAR FROM time_log_date),
        TO_NUMBER(TO_CHAR(time_log_date,'ww')),
        p.project_id, p.project_name;
```

Having created the project_time table with its redundant project_name column, it's a given that someone, someday, will come along and change a project name on you, leaving you to sort out the resulting mess by somehow propagating the new project name to all the summary rows in project_time. That kind of update is easily done using a subquery in the SET clause of an UPDATE statement, as in Example 4-38.

Example 4-38. A subquery generating a value for an UPDATE

```
UPDATE project_time pt
SET pt.project_name = (SELECT p.project_name
                       FROM project p
                       WHERE p.project_id = pt.project_id)
WHERE pt.project_name <> (SELECT p.project_name
                          FROM project p
                          WHERE p.project_id = pt.project_id)
```

The UPDATE in Example 4-38 reads each row in the project_time table and updates those project_time rows subject to name changes.

Unions

Unions are the last major type of query I'll examine in this chapter. I find it helpful to think of unions as a way to work with two queries stacked vertically atop each other. For example, if you were interested in generating a list of all dates used in the employee table, you could issue the query in Example 4-39. The query consists of not one, but two SELECT statements. The keyword UNION is the glue that joins them together, producing one, combined column having all dates from the two original columns.

Example 4-39. Stacking two queries vertically

```
SELECT employee_hire_date emp_date
FROM employee
UNION
SELECT employee_termination_date
FROM employee;

EMP_DATE
-----------
15-Nov-1961
```

Example 4-39. Stacking two queries vertically (continued)

16-Sep-1964
23-Aug-1976
...

UNION is an additive operation, so I tend to think of it in the manner illustrated in Figure 4-9. Other so-called union operations are not additive, but I still find the vertical model helpful when writing union queries.

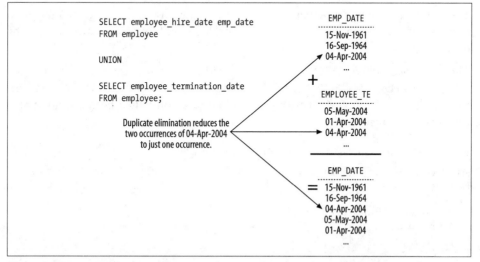

Figure 4-9. Using UNION to combine rows from two SELECT statements into one result set

The UNION operation eliminates duplicates. No matter how many times a given date appears in the employee table, the query in Example 4-39 returns that date only one time. Sometimes it's useful to "see" all occurrences. For example, you might wish to count the number of times each date occurs. Example 4-40 does this, using a UNION ALL query as a subquery that feeds a list of dates to an outer query, a GROUP BY query that counts the number of times each distinct date occurs.

Example 4-40. Preserving duplicates in a UNION operation

```
SELECT all_dates.emp_date, COUNT(*)
FROM (
   SELECT employee_hire_date emp_date
   FROM employee
   UNION ALL
   SELECT employee_termination_date
   FROM employee) all_dates
GROUP BY all_dates.emp_date
ORDER BY COUNT(*) DESC;
```

Example 4-40. Preserving duplicates in a UNION operation (continued)

```
EMP_DATE      COUNT(*)
----------- ----------
                    5
15-Nov-1961          2
04-Apr-2004          2
16-Sep-1964          1
23-Aug-1976          1
...
```

The results in Example 4-40 show that five null dates are in the employee table, two occurrences each of 15-Nov-1961 and 04-Apr-2004, and one occurrence each of the remaining dates.

There are two other UNION operations, neither of which involves the keyword UNION. You can use the INTERSECT operation to find values in common between two result sets. Example 4-41 uses it to find all dates on which both a hiring and a termination occurred.

Example 4-41. Finding rows in common between two result sets

```
SELECT employee_hire_date emp_date
FROM employee
INTERSECT
SELECT employee_termination_date
FROM employee;
```

```
EMP_DATE
-----------
04-Apr-2004
```

The last "union" operation is the MINUS, which finds values in one result set that aren't in another. Example 4-42 uses MINUS to generate a list of employees who have never logged any time against a project.

Example 4-42. Finding the difference between two result sets

```
SELECT employee_id
FROM employee
MINUS
SELECT employee_id
FROM project_hours;
```

```
EMPLOYEE_ID
-----------
        116
```

Both INTERSECT and MINUS eliminate duplicate rows from their results. INTERSECT returns at most one occurrence of any row in common between two result sets. When you use MINUS, it takes only a single row in the second result set to remove many occurrences of that same row from the first result set.

Many problems that you might solve using union queries can also be solved by other means. This doesn't mean that the UNION operations don't have their place. Sometimes they are a more efficient approach to solving a problem. Other times, they are a more succinct and clear way of stating a query.

To Learn More

I've crammed all I can manage about SQL into this one chapter. Yet SQL is a complex topic, and all I've done is to introduce you to the basic operations. If you work with Oracle—in fact, if you work with any database—you owe it to yourself to thoroughly master the use of SQL. To that end, I heartily recommend the following books, all published by O'Reilly:

Mastering Oracle SQL, Second Edition
> By Sanjay Mishra and Alan Beaulieu, this book begins where this chapter ends and plumbs the depths of what you can accomplish using Oracle's implementation of SQL. If you read only one book from this list, make it this one.

SQL Tuning
> A book by Dan Tow that teaches his unique method of diagramming SQL queries as a precursor to resolving SQL performance problems. Not only do his query diagrams help you identify the optimal or near-optimal execution plan for a query, they can also point out hidden problems in complex query logic.

SQL Pocket Guide
> A small book I wrote that can serve as a handy, portable, pocket-sized reminder of basic SQL syntax and functionality.

Generating Reports with SQL*Plus

SQL*Plus is an effective reporting tool. You can count on having SQL*Plus available in any Oracle environment, and it gets the job done well with a minimum of fuss. SQL*Plus was originally a plain-text reporting tool, but HTML support was added in Oracle8i Database Release 2. This HTML support makes SQL*Plus a handy tool for generating web reports for corporate Intranets, and I describe that support next in Chapter 6.

 iSQL*Plus is good for ad hoc query execution but not so good for polished report generation because you can't spool iSQL*Plus output to a file for later printing.

Following a Methodology

Designing a report is a development project, albeit a small one. As with any development project, it helps to have a methodology, or sequence of steps, to follow that will lead you successfully through the process of designing a report with a minimum of fuss and backtracking. For example, when designing a report, it makes no sense to worry about formatting the data until you have first decided what data to include.

This chapter presents a micro-methodology for developing reports with SQL*Plus that has worked well for me. It divides the design process for a simple report into the following steps:

1. Formulate the query.

2. Format the columns.

3. Add page headers and footers.

4. Format the page.

5. Print it.

Dividing the design process into discrete, logical steps reduces the amount and the complexity of the information you must keep in your head at any given time.

For more advanced reports, such as a master-detail report, you may want to perform additional steps:

- Add page and line breaks.
- Add totals and subtotals.

Work through report design in a methodical manner. Often the temptation is to start typing in commands. Resist this temptation.

Saving Your Work

Consider saving all the commands to produce a report in a script file. I can't remember ever producing an ad hoc report that was generated just once. Often, I don't see formatting issues until after the first printing. Other times a client will look at a report and immediately think of one or two things to add. By saving your work in a file, you will be prepared when the request for that same report, or one similar to it, comes again.

The only time I ever print a report by typing the commands interactively into SQL*Plus is when the query is simple and I don't care how the output is formatted. In such a case, if I'm in a hurry, I may simply spool off the output from a SELECT statement, print it, and live with the incorrect pagination, lack of titles, and lack of column formatting.

Saving your work in a file also protects you from simple mistakes and minor catastrophes. If you've typed 20 formatting commands into SQL*Plus and your computer locks up, you've lost your work. You'll have to restart your computer and then attempt to remember all those commands. If you are working on a long SQL query, and that query exists only in the SQL buffer, a simple thing like typing COMMIT will clobber it—something I've done many times myself. Save yourself some work by saving your work.

Designing a Simple Report

The first part of this chapter will lead you through the five steps involved in generating a simple, columnar report. This report will be complete with page headings, page footings, and column headings. In addition, you will learn about several settings, controlled by various SET commands, that are useful when printing and formatting reports.

Step 1: Formulate the Query

The first step to designing a report is to formulate the underlying SQL query. There is little point in doing anything else until you have done this. The remaining steps all involve formatting and presentation. If you haven't defined your data, there is no reason to worry about formatting.

For this chapter, let's look at developing a report that answers the following questions:

- To what projects is each employee assigned?
- How many hours have been charged to each project?
- What is the cost of those hours?

One way to satisfy these requirements would be to develop a report based on the query in Example 5-1, which summarizes the hours and dollars charged by employees to each of their projects.

Example 5-1. Summarizing hours and dollars by employee and project

```
SELECT e.employee_name,
       p.project_name,
       SUM(ph.hours_logged) ,
       SUM(ph.dollars_charged)
FROM employee e INNER JOIN project_hours ph
     ON e.employee_id = ph.employee_id
     INNER JOIN project p
     ON p.project_id = ph.project_id
GROUP BY e.employee_id, e.employee_name,
         p.project_id, p.project_name;
```

If you execute this query using SQL*Plus, here's what the output will look like:

```
EMPLOYEE_NAME
----------------------------------------
PROJECT_NAME                             SUM(PH.HOURS_LOGGED)
---------------------------------------- --------------------
SUM(PH.DOLLARS_CHARGED)
-----------------------
Marusia Churai
Corporate Web Site                                         20
                  3380

Marusia Churai
Enterprise Resource Planning System                        24
                  4056

EMPLOYEE_NAME
---------------------------------------
PROJECT_NAME                             SUM(PH.HOURS_LOGGED)
---------------------------------------- --------------------
SUM(PH.DOLLARS_CHARGED)
-----------------------
```

```
Marusia Churai
Accounting System Implementation                        24
                4056


Marusia Churai
Data Warehouse Maintenance                              20
    ...
```

Looks ugly, doesn't it? I wouldn't want to hand that to a client or my boss. It's a start though. At least now you can see what the data looks like, and you know what you have to work with.

Executing the Example Reports

You should execute the example reports in this chapter from your operating system command prompt by issuing a SQL*Plus command such as the following:

```
sqlplus username/password @scriptfile
```

For example, to execute Example 5-1, I personally use this command:

```
sqlplus gennick/secret @ex5-1.sql
```

This approach ensures that each script begins from a known state, the state in which SQL*Plus starts. Beginning with such a clean slate is important because the formatting commands you'll learn about in this chapter are cumulative and their settings stick around for the duration of your SQL*Plus session. If you run the reports in this chapter from the SQL*Plus prompt, and especially if you run them out of order, your results won't match what you see in these pages.

Step 2: Format the Columns

Now that you have the data, you can begin to work through the formatting process. Look again at the listing produced in step 1. At least three things can be done to improve the presentation of the data:

- Get each record to fit on just one line.
- Use better column headings.
- Format the numbers.

The first thing that probably leaps out at you is the need to avoid having report lines so long that they wrap around onto a second line and become difficult to read. This is often a result of SQL*Plus allowing for the maximum width in each column. Another cause is that for calculated columns, the entire calculation is used for the column heading. That can result in some long headings.

Column headings

Use the COLUMN command to format the data returned from a SELECT statement. It allows you to specify heading, width, and display formats. The following commands use COLUMN's HEADING clause to specify more readable column headings for our report:

```
COLUMN employee_name HEADING "Employee Name"
COLUMN project_name HEADING "Project Name"
COLUMN SUM(PH.HOURS_LOGGED) HEADING "Hours"
COLUMN SUM(PH.DOLLARS_CHARGED) HEADING "Dollars|Charged"
```

You can refer to the calculated columns in the query by using their calculations as their names. However, doing so is cumbersome, to say the least, and requires you to keep the two copies of the calculation in sync. There is a better way. You can give each calculated column an alias and use that alias in the COLUMN commands. To give each column an alias, the changes to the query look like the following:

```
SUM(PH.HOURS_LOGGED) hours_logged ,
SUM(PH.DOLLARS_CHARGED) dollars_charged
```

The commands to format these two columns then become:

```
COLUMN hours_logged HEADING "Hours"
COLUMN dollars_charged HEADING "Dollars|Charged"
```

The heading for the dollars_charged column has a vertical bar separating the two words. This vertical bar tells SQL*Plus to place the heading on two lines and allows you to use two rather long words without the need for an excessive column width.

> The vertical bar is the default heading separator character and may be changed with the SET HEADSEP command. See Appendix A for details.

Numeric display formats

Next, you can specify more readable display formats for the numeric columns via the FORMAT clause. COLUMN commands are cumulative, so one approach is to execute the COLUMN commands to set the headers followed by some more COLUMN commands to set the display formats:

```
COLUMN employee_name HEADING "Employee Name"
COLUMN project_name HEADING "Project Name"
COLUMN hours_logged HEADING "Hours"
COLUMN dollars_charged HEADING "Dollars|Charged"

COLUMN hours_logged FORMAT 9,999
COLUMN dollars_charged FORMAT $999,999.99
```

This cumulative approach is handy in an interactive session because you can continually refine your column formatting without having to respecify formatting that you're already happy with. In a script file, though, you're better off issuing just one

COLUMN command per column, followed by all formatting options that you wish to specify for that column. This way, all formatting for a given column is in one place:

```
COLUMN employee_name HEADING "Employee Name"
COLUMN project_name HEADING "Project Name"
COLUMN hours_logged HEADING "Hours" FORMAT 9,999
COLUMN dollars_charged HEADING "Dollars|Charged" FORMAT $999,999.99
```

Text display formats

Finally, you can use FORMAT to specify a shorter length for the employee_name and project_name columns. The database allows each of those columns to contain up to 40 characters, but a visual inspection of the output shows that the names are typically much shorter than that. The format clauses shown next make these columns each 20 characters wide:

```
COLUMN employee_name HEADING "Employee Name" FORMAT A20 WORD_WRAPPED
COLUMN project_name HEADING "Project Name" FORMAT A20 WORD_WRAPPED
```

Normally, SQL*Plus will wrap longer values onto a second line. The WORD_WRAPPED keyword keeps SQL*Plus from breaking a line in the middle of a word.

WRAPPED and TRUNCATE are alternatives to WORD_WRAPPED. WRAPPED allows a longer value to break in the middle of a word and wrap to the next line. TRUNCATE does what it says; it throws away characters longer than the format specification allows.

Report output after formatting the columns

Example 5-2 pulls together all the formatting and SQL changes discussed so far.

Example 5-2. Hours and dollars report with the columns nicely formatted

```
--Format the columns
COLUMN employee_name HEADING "Employee Name" FORMAT A20 WORD_WRAPPED
COLUMN project_name HEADING "Project Name" FORMAT A20 WORD_WRAPPED
COLUMN hours_logged HEADING "Hours" FORMAT 9,999
COLUMN dollars_charged HEADING "Dollars|Charged" FORMAT $999,999.99

--Execute the query to generate the report.
SELECT e.employee_name,
       p.project_name,
       SUM(ph.hours_logged) hours_logged,
       SUM(ph.dollars_charged) dollars_charged
FROM employee e INNER JOIN project_hours ph
     ON e.employee_id = ph.employee_id
     INNER JOIN project p
     ON p.project_id = ph.project_id
GROUP BY e.employee_id, e.employee_name,
         p.project_id, p.project_name;

EXIT
```

Here is what the output will look like:

```
Employee Name        Project Name            Hours    Charged
-------------------- ----------------------- ------ ------------
Marusia Churai       Corporate Web Site         20   $3,380.00
Marusia Churai       Enterprise Resource        24   $4,056.00
                     Planning System

Marusia Churai       Accounting System          24   $4,056.00
                     Implementation

Marusia Churai       Data Warehouse             20   $3,380.00
                     Maintenance
```

This is a great improvement over step 1. The headings are more readable. The numbers, particularly the dollar amounts, are formatted better. Most records fit on one line, and when two lines are needed, the data are wrapped in a much more readable format.

A blank line has been inserted after every record with a project name that wraps to a second line. That blank line is a *record separator*, and it's added by SQL*Plus every time a wrapped column is output as part of a report. I suppose it is added to prevent confusion because, in some circumstances, you might think that the line containing the wrapped column data represented another record in the report. I usually turn it off; this is the command:

```
SET RECSEP OFF
```

The next step is to add page headers and footers to the report.

Step 3: Add Page Headers and Footers

Page headers and footers may be added to your report through the use of the TTITLE and BTITLE commands. TTITLE and BTITLE stand for "top title" and "bottom title," respectively.

The top title

TTITLE commands typically end up being a long string of directives interspersed with text, and they often span multiple lines. Let's say you want a page header that looked like this:

```
                    The Fictional Company


I.S. Department                 Project Hours and Dollars Report
================================================================
```

This heading is composed of the company name centered on the first line, two blank lines, a fourth line containing the department name and the report title, followed by a ruling line made up of equal sign characters. You can begin to generate this heading with the following TTITLE command:

```
TTITLE CENTER "The Fictional Company"
```

The keyword CENTER is a directive telling SQL*Plus to center the text that follows. In their documentation, Oracle sometimes uses the term *printspec* to refer to such directives.

Always begin a TTITLE command with a directive such as LEFT, CENTER, or RIGHT. Failure to do this causes SQL*Plus to interpret the command as an old, now obsolete, and much less functional form of the command.

To get the two blank lines into the title, add a SKIP printspec as follows:

```
TTITLE CENTER "The Fictional Company" SKIP 3
```

SKIP 3 tells SQL*Plus to skip forward three lines. This results in two blank lines and causes the next report line to print as the third line. To generate the fourth line of the title, containing the department name and the report name, you again add on to the TTITLE command:

```
TTITLE CENTER "The Fictional Company" SKIP 3 -
       LEFT "I.S. Department" -
       RIGHT "Project Hours and Dollars Report"
```

The text "I.S. Department" will print flush left because it follows the LEFT printspec, and the report title will print flush right because it follows the RIGHT printspec. Both strings will print on the same line because there is no intervening SKIP printspec. The last thing to do is to add the final ruling line composed of equal sign characters, giving you this final version of the TTITLE command:

```
TTITLE CENTER "The Fictional Company" SKIP 3 -
       LEFT "I.S. Department" -
       RIGHT "Project Hours and Dollars Report" SKIP 1 -
       LEFT "============================================================="
```

This is actually one long command. The hyphens at the end of the first three lines are SQL*Plus command continuation characters. There are 61 equal sign characters in the last line of the title.

You must use the SKIP directive to advance to a new line. If you want to advance just one line, use SKIP 1. SQL*Plus will not automatically advance for you. If you remove the two SKIP directives from the above TTITLE command, you will end up with a one-line title consisting entirely of equal signs.

The bottom title

The BTITLE command works the same way as TTITLE, except that it defines a footer to appear at the bottom of each page of the report. As with TTITLE, you should always begin a BTITLE command with a printspec such as LEFT or RIGHT, as opposed to text or a variable name. If you want a footer composed of a ruling line and a page number, you can use the following BTITLE command:

```
BTITLE LEFT "=============================================================" -
       SKIP 1 -
       RIGHT "   Page " FORMAT 999 SQL.PNO
```

This BTITLE command introduces two features that haven't been shown in previous examples. The first is the FORMAT parameter, which in this case specifies a numeric display format to use for all subsequent numeric values. The second is the system variable SQL.PNO, which supplies the current page number. Table 5-1 lists several values, maintained automatically by SQL*Plus, that you can use in report headers and footers.

*Table 5-1. SQL*Plus system variables*

System variable	Value
SQL.PNO	Current page number
SQL.LNO	Current line number
SQL.RELEASE	Current Oracle release
SQL.SQLCODE	Error code returned by the most recent SQL query
SQL.USER	Oracle username of the user running the report

The values in Table 5-1 have meaning only to SQL*Plus and can be used only when defining headers and footers. They cannot be used in SQL statements such as INSERT or SELECT.

Setting the line width

One final point to bring up regarding page titles is that the directives RIGHT and CENTER operate with respect to the current line width. The default line width, or *linesize* as it is called in SQL*Plus, is 80 characters. So by default, a centered heading will be centered over 80 characters. A flush right heading will have its last character printed in the 80th position. This presents a slight problem because our report, using the column specifications given in step 2, is only 61 characters wide. The result will be a heading that overhangs the right edge of the report by 19 characters, and that won't appear centered over the data. You could choose to live with that, or you could add this command to the script:

```
SET LINESIZE 61
```

Setting the linesize tells SQL*Plus to format the headings within a 61-character line. It also tells SQL*Plus to wrap or truncate any lines longer than 61 characters, but the column specifications in this report prevent anything like that from occurring.

 The number of equal sign characters in the ruling line must match the linesize. Otherwise, the ruling line will be too short or too long. Either way, it will look tacky.

Report output with page titles

Example 5-3 shows our report generation script with the addition of the TTITLE, BTITLE, and SET LINESIZE commands.

Example 5-3. Hours and dollars report with page titles added

```
--Set the linesize, which must match the number of equal signs used
--for the ruling lines in the headers and footers.
SET LINESIZE 61

--Setup page headings and footings
TTITLE CENTER "The Fictional Company" SKIP 3 -
       LEFT "I.S. Department" -
       RIGHT "Project Hours and Dollars Report" SKIP 1 -
       LEFT "============================================================="

BTITLE LEFT "=============================================================" -
       SKIP 1 -
       RIGHT "Page " FORMAT 999 SQL.PNO

--Format the columns
COLUMN employee_name HEADING "Employee Name" FORMAT A20 WORD_WRAPPED
COLUMN project_name HEADING "Project Name" FORMAT A20 WORD_WRAPPED
COLUMN hours_logged HEADING "Hours" FORMAT 9,999
COLUMN dollars_charged HEADING "Dollars|Charged" FORMAT $999,999.99

--Execute the query to generate the report.
SELECT e.employee_name,
       p.project_name,
       SUM(ph.hours_logged) hours_logged,
       SUM(ph.dollars_charged) dollars_charged
FROM employee e INNER JOIN project_hours ph
    ON e.employee_id = ph.employee_id
    INNER JOIN project p
    ON p.project_id = ph.project_id
GROUP BY e.employee_id, e.employee_name,
         p.project_id, p.project_name;

EXIT
```

Executing this script will produce the following output:

```
                              The Fictional Company


   I.S. Department                  Project Hours and Dollars Report
   ==============================================================
                                                        Dollars
   Employee Name         Project Name          Hours     Charged
   -------------------   -------------------   ------   -----------
   Marusia Churai        Corporate Web Site        20    $3,380.00
   Marusia Churai        Enterprise Resource       24    $4,056.00
                         Planning System
   ==============================================================
                                                    Page     1


                              The Fictional Company


   I.S. Department                  Project Hours and Dollars Report
   ==============================================================
                                                        Dollars
   Employee Name         Project Name          Hours     Charged
   -------------------   -------------------   ------   -----------

   Marusia Churai        Accounting System         24    $4,056.00
                         Implementation
   ==============================================================
                                                    Page     2
   ...
```

Only a few things are left to clean up before you can print this report; one obvious improvement is to fix the pagination in order to get more than 14 lines per page.

Step 4: Format the Page

Most of the work to produce this report is behind you. Step 4 involves adjusting two SQL*Plus settings that control page size and pagination. These two settings are:

pagesize
> Controls the number of lines per page. SQL*Plus prints headings and advances to a new page every *pagesize* lines.

newpage
> Controls the size of the top margin, or tells SQL*Plus to use a formfeed character to advance to a new page.

The SET command is used to define values for each of these settings. The values to use depend primarily on your output device, the paper size being used, and the font size being used. Because SQL*Plus is entirely character-oriented, these settings are defined in terms of lines. The first question to ask, then, is how many lines will your printer print on one page of paper.

Ruling Lines in Page Titles

Example 5-3 shows the use of a ruling line in a page title. That particular line is composed of 61 equal-sign characters that have been painstakingly typed into the TTITLE command. Want to avoid having to count those out? Use the following incantation instead:

```
COLUMN ruling_line NEW_VALUE ruling_line
SELECT RPAD('=',61,'=') ruling_line
FROM dual;
```

Then, replace that long string of equal sign characters in TTITLE with &ruling_line:

```
TTITLE CENTER "The Fictional Company" SKIP 3 -
       LEFT "I.S. Department" -
       RIGHT "Project Hours and Dollars Report" SKIP 1 -
       LEFT &ruling_line
```

Do the same thing for BTITLE:

```
BTITLE LEFT &ruling_line -
       SKIP 1 -
       RIGHT "Page " FORMAT 999 SQL.PNO
```

The script in *ex5-3b.sql* uses this technique, which comes courtesy of Tom Kyte. If you're not familiar with substitution variables and the use of COLUMN...NEW_VALUE, you'll find a more detailed explanation of this technique in "Master/Detail Reports" later in this chapter.

How many lines on a page?

Years ago, before the advent of laser printers with their multiplicity of typefaces, typestyles, and typesizes (i.e., fonts), this was an easy question to answer. The standard vertical spacing for printing was six lines per inch, with eight lines per inch occasionally being used. Thus, an 11-inch-high page would normally contain 66 lines. Most printers were pinfeed printers taking fanfold paper, and would permit you to print right up to the perforation, allowing you to use all 66 lines if you were determined to do so.

Today's printers are much more complicated, yet most will still print six lines per inch if you send them plain ASCII text. However (and this is important), many printers today will not allow you to print right up to the top and bottom edges of the paper. This is especially true of laser printers, which almost always leave a top and bottom margin. You may have to experiment a bit with your printer to find out exactly how many lines you can print on one page.

I usually duck this issue entirely by setting PAGESIZE to a safely low setting, usually below 60 lines, and setting NEWPAGE to zero, which causes SQL*Plus to use a formfeed character to advance to a new page. My examples in this chapter use this approach.

The other issue to consider is the font size you will be using to print the report. I typically just send reports to a printer as plain ASCII text, and that usually results in the use of a 12-point, monospaced font, which prints at six lines per inch. Sometimes, however, I'll load the file containing a report into an editor, change the font size to something larger or smaller, and then print the report. If you do that, you'll need to experiment a bit to find out how many lines will fit on a page using the new font size.

Setting the pagesize

You set the pagesize with the SQL*Plus command SET PAGESIZE as follows:

```
SET PAGESIZE 55
```

This tells SQL*Plus to print 55 lines per page. Those 55 lines include the header and footer lines as well as the data. As it prints your report, SQL*Plus keeps track of how many lines have been printed on the current page. SQL*Plus knows how many lines make up the page footer. When the number of remaining lines equals the number of lines in your footer, SQL*Plus prints the footer and advances to the next page. How SQL*Plus advances the page depends on the NEWPAGE setting.

Setting the page advance

There are two methods SQL*Plus can use to advance the printer to a new page. The first method, and the one used by default, is to print exactly the right number of lines needed to fill one page. Having done that, the next line printed will start on a new page. Using this method depends on knowing how many lines you can fit on one page, and switching printers can sometimes cause your report to break. One laser printer, for example, may have a slightly larger top margin than another.

A more reliable method is to have SQL*Plus advance the page using the formfeed character. The command to do this is:

```
SET NEWPAGE 0
```

The NEWPAGE setting tells SQL*Plus how many lines to print to advance to a new page. The default value is 1. Setting NEWPAGE to 0 causes SQL*Plus to output a formfeed character when it's time to advance the page.

 If you set NEWPAGE to 0, do not set PAGESIZE to exactly match the number of lines you can physically print on your printer. Doing that may cause your output to consist of alternating detail pages and blank pages. That's because filling the physical page will itself advance your printer to a new page. The subsequent formfeed advances the page again, resulting in a skipped page. Instead, set PAGESIZE to at least one line less than what will fit on a physical page.

The examples in this chapter use a NEWPAGE setting of 0 and a PAGESIZE of 55 lines, so you can add the following three lines to the script file:

```
--Set up pagesize parameters
SET NEWPAGE 0
SET PAGESIZE 55
```

You are free to put these lines anywhere you like so long as they precede the SELECT statement that generates the report. Example 5-4 shows them added to the beginning of the script file.

Example 5-4. Hours and dollars report with pagination

```
--Setup pagesize parameters
SET NEWPAGE 0
SET PAGESIZE 55

--Set the linesize, which must match the number of equal signs used
--for the ruling lines in the headers and footers.
SET LINESIZE 61

--Set up page headings and footings
TTITLE CENTER "The Fictional Company" SKIP 3 -
       LEFT "I.S. Department" -
       RIGHT "Project Hours and Dollars Report" SKIP 1 -
       LEFT "============================================================="

BTITLE LEFT "=============================================================" -
       SKIP 1 -
       RIGHT "Page " FORMAT 999 SQL.PNO

--Format the columns
COLUMN employee_name HEADING "Employee Name" FORMAT A20 WORD_WRAPPED
COLUMN project_name HEADING "Project Name" FORMAT A20 WORD_WRAPPED
COLUMN hours_logged HEADING "Hours" FORMAT 9,999
COLUMN dollars_charged HEADING "Dollars|Charged" FORMAT $999,999.99

--Execute the query to generate the report.
SELECT e.employee_name,
       p.project_name,
       SUM(ph.hours_logged) hours_logged,
       SUM(ph.dollars_charged) dollars_charged
FROM employee e INNER JOIN project_hours ph
    ON e.employee_id = ph.employee_id
    INNER JOIN project p
    ON p.project_id = ph.project_id
GROUP BY e.employee_id, e.employee_name,
         p.project_id, p.project_name;

EXIT
```

Step 5: Print It

Run the script file one more time and look at the output on the screen. If everything looks good, you are ready to print. To print a report, you need to have SQL*Plus write the report to a file and then print that file. When people speak of writing SQL*Plus output to a file, the term *spool* is often used as a verb. You are said to be *spooling* your output to a file. The SPOOL command is used for this purpose, and you will need to use it twice, once to turn spooling on and again to turn it off.

Spooling to a file

To send report output to a file, put SPOOL commands immediately before and after the SQL query as shown here:

```
SPOOL proj_hours_dollars.lis
SELECT E.EMPLOYEE_NAME,
...
SPOOL OFF
```

The first SPOOL command tells SQL*Plus to begin echoing all output to the specified file. After this command executes, everything you see on the screen is echoed to this file. The second SPOOL command turns spooling off and closes the file.

You may wish to add two other commands to the script file before generating the report. The first is:

```
SET FEEDBACK OFF
```

Turning feedback off gets rid of the "50 rows selected" message, which you may have noticed at the end of the report when you ran earlier versions of the script. The second command you may want to add is:

```
SET TERMOUT OFF
```

This command does what it says. It turns off output to the display (terminal output) but allows the output to be written to a spool file. Your report will run several orders of magnitude faster if SQL*Plus doesn't have to deal with updating and scrolling the display, especially true if you are running the Windows GUI version of SQL*Plus. You should definitely use SET TERMOUT OFF when spooling any large report. I usually put the above two settings immediately prior to the SPOOL command. For example:

```
SET FEEDBACK OFF
SET TERMOUT OFF
SPOOL $HOME/sqlplus/reports/proj_hours_dollars.lst
SELECT E.EMPLOYEE_NAME,
...
SPOOL OFF
```

Do make sure that you set TERMOUT off prior to executing the SPOOL command to spool the output; otherwise, the SET TERMOUT OFF command will appear in your spool file.

The final script

Example 5-5 shows the script for our report after adding the SPOOL commands and the commands to turn feedback and terminal output off. Example 5-5 begins with the SET ECHO OFF command, ensuring that you aren't bothered by having to watch all the remaining commands in the script scroll by on your terminal window.

Example 5-5. Hours and dollars report to be spooled to a file for printing

```
SET ECHO OFF

--Set up pagesize parameters
SET NEWPAGE 0
SET PAGESIZE 55

--Set the linesize, which must match the number of equal signs used
--for the ruling lines in the headers and footers.
SET LINESIZE 61

--Set up page headings and footings
TTITLE CENTER "The Fictional Company" SKIP 3 -
       LEFT "I.S. Department" -
       RIGHT "Project Hours and Dollars Report" SKIP 1 -
       LEFT "============================================================="

BTITLE LEFT "=============================================================" -
       SKIP 1 -
       RIGHT "Page " FORMAT 999 SQL.PNO

--Format the columns
COLUMN employee_name HEADING "Employee Name" FORMAT A20 WORD_WRAPPED
COLUMN project_name HEADING "Project Name" FORMAT A20 WORD_WRAPPED
COLUMN hours_logged HEADING "Hours" FORMAT 9,999
COLUMN dollars_charged HEADING "Dollars|Charged" FORMAT $999,999.99

--Turn off feedback and set TERMOUT off to prevent the
--report being scrolled to the screen.
SET FEEDBACK OFF
SET TERMOUT OFF

--Execute the query to generate the report.
SPOOL proj_hours_dollars.lst
SELECT e.employee_name,
       p.project_name,
       SUM(ph.hours_logged) hours_logged,
       SUM(ph.dollars_charged) dollars_charged
FROM employee e INNER JOIN project_hours ph
    ON e.employee_id = ph.employee_id
    INNER JOIN project p
    ON p.project_id = ph.project_id
GROUP BY e.employee_id, e.employee_name,
         p.project_id, p.project_name;
```

Example 5-5. Hours and dollars report to be spooled to a file for printing (continued)

```
SPOOL OFF
EXIT
```

Executing the report

If you've stored the script for the report in a text file, you can execute that file from the SQL*Plus prompt like this:

```
SQL> @ex5-5
```

The @ character in front of a filename tells SQL*Plus to execute the commands contained in that file.

Printing the file

After you run the script, the complete report will be in the *proj_hours_dollars.lst* file. To print that file, you must use whatever print command is appropriate for your operating system. On a Windows machine, assuming that LPT1 is mapped to a printer, you can use the following DOS command:

```
COPY c:\a\proj_hours_dollars.lis LPT1:
```

A typical Unix print command would be:

```
lp proj_hours_dollars.lis
```

An alternative is to load the file into a word processor such as Microsoft Word or Lotus Word Pro. These programs will interpret formfeeds as page breaks when importing a text file, so your intended pagination will be preserved. After you've imported the file, select all the text and mark it as Courier New 12 point. Then set the top and left margins to their minimum values; for laser printers, half-inch margins usually work well. Next, set the right and bottom margins to zero. Finally, print the report.

One final option, useful with Unix and Linux but not available in any Windows version of SQL*Plus, is to use the SPOOL OUT command instead of SPOOL OFF. SPOOL OUT closes the spool file and then prints that file out to the default printer, saving you the extra step of manually printing it. For whatever reason, Oracle has chosen not to implement SPOOL OUT under Windows. It is, however, available under Unix and Linux.

Master/Detail Reports

You can add page breaks and line breaks to your reports with the BREAK command. BREAK is commonly used to suppress repeating values in report columns, which commonly occur in master/detail reports. Take a look at the script in Example 5-6, which generates a detailed listing of all the time charged to each project by each employee.

Running SQL*Plus Reports from Shell Scripts

In production settings, you want to generate SQL*Plus reports from shell scripts that you schedule via *cron* or some other scheduling system. It's not a safe practice to embed passwords in shell scripts, so how then do you safely invoke SQL*Plus from them? One approach is to use operating system authenticated users, which authenticate to Oracle by virtue of being logged into the operating system.

For example, you can create an Oracle user such as *ops$reports* to correspond to the Unix user named *reports*. Any shell script that you schedule to run as the Unix *reports* user may then invoke SQL*Plus without having to specify a username and password, and the database will implicitly log the SQL*Plus session in as the *ops$reports* user. You request such an implicit login by using the forward slash (/) where you would otherwise specify a username and password:

```
sqlplus / @ex5-1
```

The advantage of this technique is that it enables you to invoke SQL*Plus to run scripts without having to compromise security by embedding login information in script files where others may see it. Do be careful, though, to control access to the associated Unix login. In this case, you would need to protect the password for the Unix *reports* user, as anyone logging on as *reports* would have implicit access to the database via *ops$reports*.

Example 5-6. Detailed listing of time charged to projects

```
SET ECHO OFF

--Set up pagesize parameters
SET NEWPAGE 0
SET PAGESIZE 55

--Set the linesize, which must match the number of equals signs used
--for the ruling lines in the headers and footers.
SET LINESIZE 76

--Set up page headings and footings
TTITLE CENTER "The Fictional Company" SKIP 3 -
       LEFT "I.S. Department" -
       RIGHT "Project Hours and Dollars Detail" SKIP 1 -
       LEFT "========================================" -
            "===================================" -
       SKIP 2

BTITLE LEFT "========================================" -
            "===================================" -
       SKIP 1 -
       RIGHT "Page " FORMAT 999 SQL.PNO

—Format the columns
COLUMN employee_id HEADING "Emp ID" FORMAT 9999
```

Example 5-6. Detailed listing of time charged to projects (continued)

```
COLUMN employee_name HEADING "Employee Name" FORMAT A16 WORD_WRAPPED
COLUMN project_id HEADING "Proj ID" FORMAT 9999
COLUMN project_name HEADING "Project Name" FORMAT A12 WORD_WRAPPED
COLUMN time_log_date HEADING "Date" FORMAT A11
COLUMN hours_logged HEADING "Hours" FORMAT 9,999
COLUMN dollars_charged HEADING "Dollars|Charged" FORMAT $999,999.99

--Execute the query to generate the report.
SELECT e.employee_id,
       e.employee_name,
       p.project_id,
       p.project_name,
       TO_CHAR(ph.time_log_date,'dd-Mon-yyyy') time_log_date,
       ph.hours_logged,
       ph.dollars_charged
  FROM employee e INNER JOIN project_hours ph
       ON e.employee_id = ph.employee_id
       INNER JOIN project p
       ON p.project_id = ph.project_id
ORDER BY e.employee_id, p.project_id, ph.time_log_date;

EXIT
```

The query in Example 5-6 introduces the use of Oracle's built-in TO_DATE function to convert datetime values such as time_log_date to character strings you and I can read. You'll see examples of date conversion scattered throughout this book, and Appendix B goes into detail about the various format elements that provide control over how datetime values are formatted.

When you execute this script, here's what the output will look like:

```
                              The Fictional Company


   I.S. Department                           Project Hours and Dollars Detail
   ============================================================================

                                                                       Dollars
   Emp ID Employee Name    Proj ID Project Name Date          Hours    Charged
   ------ ---------------- ------- ------------ -----------   ------ -----------
      101 Marusia Churai      1001 Corporate    01-Jan-2004       1     $169.00
                                   Web Site

      101 Marusia Churai      1001 Corporate    01-Mar-2004       3     $507.00
                                   Web Site

      101 Marusia Churai      1001 Corporate    01-May-2004       5     $845.00
                                   Web Site
   ...
      102 Mykhailo            1001 Corporate    01-May-2004       5     $675.00
          Hrushevsky               Web Site
```

```
102 Mykhailo          1002 Enterprise   01-Feb-2004     7      $945.00
    Hrushevsky             Resource
                          Planning
                          System
...
```

The first four columns repeat the same values for each employee/project combination. This clutters the output and makes the report a bit difficult to follow because you may not see when a value actually changes. The following sections show how to suppress duplicate values in a column, making the report less repetitious. You will also see how to add page and line breaks to improve readability. Finally, you will learn how to turn this report into a master/detail report that shows the employee information in the page header with the detail listed below it.

> BREAK lets you specify actions to take whenever a column's value changes. Page breaks, line breaks, and printing of the value (i.e., duplicate suppression) are some examples of the actions you can ask for.

Suppressing Duplicate Column Values

To eliminate repeating values in a report column, use the BREAK command to specify the NODUPLICATES action for that column. For example, to eliminate duplicate values in the employee_id and project_id columns, you can issue the following command:

```
BREAK ON employee_id NODUPLICATES ON employee_name NODUPLICATES
    ON project_id NODUPLICATES ON project_name NODUPLICATES
```

NODUPLICATES is the default action for BREAK and is almost never specified explicitly. Instead, the command just shown is usually simplified:

```
BREAK ON employee_id ON employee_name ON project_id ON project_name
```

Be sure to sort or group your report by the same columns that you specify in the BREAK command, and in the same order. The script in Example 5-6 sorts on employee_id followed by project_id followed by time_log_date. The BREAK command just shown corresponds to the first two of those. Because employee_id drives the value of employee_name, there is no need to ORDER BY employee_name (likewise with project_id and project_name).

It's fine for the ORDER BY clause to be more granular than the BREAK command, but the converse is not OK. If you do not sort your data to correspond to your BREAK command, you will probably be unhappy with the results.

> SQL*Plus allows only one break setting to be in effect at any given time. Unlike the case with COLUMN, multiple BREAK commands do not build on each other, but rather each subsequent BREAK replaces the previous setting. However, any number of ON clauses may be used to accommodate breaks on more than one column.

Adding the BREAK command shown earlier to the report script from Example 5-6 makes the output look like the following:

```
                         The Fictional Company


I.S. Department                         Project Hours and Dollars Detail
========================================================================

                                                              Dollars
Emp ID Employee Name    Proj ID Project Name Date       Hours Charged
------ ---------------- ------- ------------ ----------- ----- ----------
   101 Marusia Churai      1001 Corporate    01-Jan-2004     1    $169.00
                                Web Site

                                             01-Mar-2004     3    $507.00
                                             01-May-2004     5    $845.00
...
   102 Mykhailo            1001 Corporate    01-Jan-2004     1    $135.00
       Hrushevsky               Web Site

                                             01-Mar-2004     3    $405.00
...
```

This is an improvement over the previous report version. You can now spot changes in the employee and project columns.

Page and Line Breaks

To aid readability, you might wish to start a new page when the employee name changes and to leave one or two blank lines between the detail for each project. Having each employee start on a new page has the benefit of allowing you to give each employee his own section of the report. Perhaps you want each employee to check the hours he has reported. You can accomplish both these objectives via the SKIP action of the BREAK command.

Adding a page break

To have each employee's data start on a new page, add SKIP PAGE to the list of actions to be performed each time the employee changes. The resulting BREAK command looks like this:

```
BREAK ON employee_id SKIP PAGE NODUPLICATES -
      ON employee_name NODUPLICATES -
      ON project_id NODUPLICATES -
      ON project_name NODUPLICATES
```

Because the employee_id and employee_name columns change simultaneously, the page break could have been defined on either column. In this case, I chose employee_id because it is the primary key for the table and can be depended on to be unique for each employee.

Adding a line break

To add two blank lines between projects, use the SKIP 2 action. SKIP allows you to advance a specified number of lines each time a column's value changes. It takes one numeric argument specifying the number of lines to advance. Here's how the BREAK command looks with page and line breaks specified:

```
BREAK ON employee_id SKIP PAGE NODUPLICATES -
      ON employee_name NODUPLICATES -
      ON project_id SKIP 2 NODUPLICATES -
      ON project_name NODUPLICATES
```

Report output with page and line breaks

Example 5-7 shows the report script, with a BREAK command that generates a page break for each new employee and skips two lines between projects.

Example 5-7. Detailed time listing, with page and line breaks

```
SET ECHO OFF

--Set up pagesize parameters
SET NEWPAGE 0
SET PAGESIZE 55

--Set the linesize, which must match the number of equals signs used
--for the ruling lines in the headers and footers.
SET LINESIZE 76

--Don't repeat column values, page break for new employees,
--skip a line when projects change.
BREAK ON employee_id SKIP PAGE NODUPLICATES -
      ON employee_name NODUPLICATES -
      ON project_id SKIP 2 NODUPLICATES -
      ON project_name NODUPLICATES

--Set up page headings and footings
TTITLE CENTER "The Fictional Company" SKIP 3 -
       LEFT "I.S. Department" -
       RIGHT "Project Hours and Dollars Detail" SKIP 1 -
       LEFT "==========================================" -
            "=====================================" -
       SKIP 2

BTITLE LEFT "==========================================" -
            "=====================================" -
       SKIP 1 -
       RIGHT "Page " FORMAT 999 SQL.PNO

--Format the columns
COLUMN employee_id HEADING "Emp ID" FORMAT 9999
COLUMN employee_name HEADING "Employee Name" FORMAT A16 WORD_WRAPPED
COLUMN project_id HEADING "Proj ID" FORMAT 9999
```

Example 5-7. Detailed time listing, with page and line breaks (continued)

```
COLUMN project_name HEADING "Project Name" FORMAT A12 WORD_WRAPPED
COLUMN time_log_date HEADING "Date" FORMAT A11
COLUMN hours_logged HEADING "Hours" FORMAT 9,999
COLUMN dollars_charged HEADING "Dollars|Charged" FORMAT $999,999.99

--Execute the query to generate the report.
SELECT e.employee_id,
       e.employee_name,
       p.project_id,
       p.project_name,
       TO_CHAR(ph.time_log_date,'dd-Mon-yyyy') time_log_date,
       ph.hours_logged,
       ph.dollars_charged
  FROM employee e INNER JOIN project_hours ph
       ON e.employee_id = ph.employee_id
       INNER JOIN project p
       ON p.project_id = ph.project_id
ORDER BY e.employee_id, p.project_id, ph.time_log_date;

EXIT
```

When you run the report, the output will look like this:

```
                       The Fictional Company


I.S. Department                      Project Hours and Dollars Detail
=========================================================================

                                                              Dollars
Emp ID Employee Name   Proj ID Project Name Date       Hours  Charged
------ ---------------- ------- ------------ ----------- ------ ------------
   101 Marusia Churai      1001 Corporate    01-Jan-2004     1     $169.00
                                Web Site

                                             01-Mar-2004     3     $507.00
                                             01-May-2004     5     $845.00
                                             01-Jul-2004     7   $1,183.00
                                             01-Sep-2004     1     $169.00
                                             01-Nov-2004     3     $507.00


                                1002 Enterprise   01-Feb-2004     7   $1,183.00
                                     Resource
                                     Planning
                                     System
   ...
                       The Fictional Company


I.S. Department                      Project Hours and Dollars Detail
=========================================================================
```

Emp ID	Employee Name	Proj ID	Project Name	Date	Hours	Dollars Charged
102	Mykhailo Hrushevsky	1001	Corporate Web Site	01-Jan-2004	1	$135.00
				01-Mar-2004	3	$405.00
				01-May-2004	5	$675.00

...

Each change in employee starts a new page, and two blank lines follow each project.

> Sometimes, column breaks and page breaks coincide. When that happens, SQL*Plus performs both sets of break actions, which can result in some pages that start with leading blank lines. In this example, if a project and a page break occur simultaneously, SQL*Plus first advances to a new page, then prints the two blank lines required for a project break. SQL*Plus has not been designed to recognize that, because of the page break, the two blank lines from the project break are not needed.

When using BREAK to create page breaks and line breaks, you should ensure that the column order in your BREAK command matches the sort order (or grouping) used for the query. Suppose you took the BREAK command just used and turned it around like this:

```
BREAK ON project_id SKIP 2 NODUPLICATES -
      ON project_name NODUPLICATES -
      ON employee_id SKIP PAGE NODUPLICATES -
      ON employee_name NODUPLICATES
```

You would find that every change in each project resulted in a skip to a new page. Why? Because when SQL*Plus executes a break action for a given column, it first executes the break actions for all columns to the right of it in the list. It does this because column breaks are used to trigger the printing of totals and subtotals, which you'll read about in Chapter 7. Given this particular BREAK command, if you were totaling up hours by project and employee and the project changed, it would be important to print the total hours for the final employee on the previous project before printing data for the new project.

Master/Detail Formatting

With column breaks on the employee and project columns, the Project Hours and Dollars Detail report contains quite a bit of whitespace. This is particularly true under the Employee Name column because that value changes so infrequently. This report is a good candidate for conversion to a master/detail style of report.

A master/detail report is one that displays the value of one record in a heading and then lists the detail from related records below that heading. The record shown in the heading is referred to as the *master*, and the records shown below that heading are referred to as *detail* records.

Three additional steps are needed to convert this report from a plain, columnar report to the master/detail style of report:

1. Retrieve the employee name and ID into substitution variables.
2. Modify the page heading to print the value of those variables.
3. Revise the report width and the width of the remaining fields.

Substitution variables are text variables that can be used to hold values retrieved from the database or to hold values entered by a user. Substitution variables allow you to include report data as part of a page header or footer, which is just what we are going to do here. Chapter 8 talks about using these variables to facilitate user interaction with your SQL*Plus scripts.

Retrieve the employee information into substitution variables

Use the COLUMN command to get the value of the employee name and ID columns into substitution variables. Instead of specifying a display format for those columns, use the NEW_VALUE and NOPRINT clauses:

```
COLUMN employee_id NEW_VALUE emp_id_var NOPRINT
COLUMN employee_name NEW_VALUE emp_name_var NOPRINT
```

The NEW_VALUE clause tells SQL*Plus to update a user variable with the new contents of the column each time a row is returned from the query. In this example, emp_name_var will be updated by SQL*Plus to contain the most recently retrieved employee name. Likewise, the emp_name_id variable will be updated with the corresponding employee ID. Declaring these variables is unnecessary. Choose some names that make sense and use them. The NOPRINT clause tells SQL*Plus not to print the employee name and ID columns as part of the report detail.

Modify the page heading to print the employee name and ID

Next, modify the page header to include the employee information. This can be done using the following, updated TTITLE command:

```
TTITLE CENTER "The Fictional Company" SKIP 3 -
       LEFT "I.S. Department" -
       RIGHT "Project Hours and Dollars Detail" SKIP 1 -
       LEFT "=============================================================" -
       SKIP 2 "Employee: " FORMAT 9999 emp_id_var " " emp_name_var SKIP 3
```

The only change to the page header is the addition of a fifth line, which is the bold line in the example. Here's how to interpret this line:

SKIP 2

    Tells SQL*Plus to advance two lines after printing the ruling line of equal sign characters. This effectively leaves *one* blank line before the employee ID and name are printed.

"Employee: "

    This is a quoted literal, so SQL*Plus prints it as it is shown. It serves to label the information that follows.

FORMAT 9999

    Tells SQL*Plus to format any subsequent numeric values in a four-digit field with no leading zeros.

emp_id_var

    Tells SQL*Plus to print the contents of this variable, which contains the most recently retrieved employee ID number.

" "

    Causes a space to print between the employee ID and name, so the two fields don't run together.

emp_name_var

    Tells SQL*Plus to print the contents of this variable, which contains the most recently retrieved employee name.

 Formatting a character field such as the employee name is unnecessary when it appears in a TTITLE, but you do have that option. Specifying FORMAT A20 TRUNCATED, for example, will cause the employee name to print in a 20-character-wide field with any names longer than 20 characters being truncated.

Revisit the report width and the width of the remaining fields

The employee_name and employee_id columns used a total of 22 characters. Because each column was followed by one blank space, eliminating the columns from the detail section of the report frees up 24 characters that may be usable elsewhere.

The one column that can benefit from a longer length is the project_name column. This column prints 12 characters wide on the report but is defined in the database to hold up to 40. A quick look at the actual data shows that all but two project names are 26 characters or less, so let's increase the width of that field to 26 by changing its COLUMN command:

```
COLUMN project_name HEADING 'Project Name' FORMAT A26 WORD_WRAPPED
```

The remaining 10 characters can be taken out of the linesize, which is currently 76, so the new linesize command becomes this:

```
SET LINESIZE 66
```

By adjusting the linesize, you ensure that the right-justified portions of the page title line up with the right edge of the report. Remember to adjust the number of equal signs in the TTITLE and BTITLE commands to match the linesize. Example 5-8 shows the final version of the script, incorporating all the changes described in this section. Example 5-8 incorporates the use of SET RECSEP OFF to eliminate those pesky, blank lines that otherwise print following any detail row with a wrapped column value.

Example 5-8. Master/detail report showing a breakdown of time billed to projects

```
SET ECHO OFF
SET RECSEP OFF

--Set up pagesize parameters
SET NEWPAGE 0
SET PAGESIZE 55
--Set the linesize, which must match the number of equals sign used
--for the ruling lines in the headers and footers.
SET LINESIZE 66

--Set up page headings and footings
TTITLE CENTER "The Fictional Company" SKIP 3 -
       LEFT "I.S. Department" -
       RIGHT "Project Hours and Dollars Detail" SKIP 1 -
       LEFT "=========================================" -
            "==========================" -
       SKIP 2 "Employee: " FORMAT 9999 emp_id_var " " emp_name_var SKIP 3

BTITLE LEFT "=========================================" -
            "==========================" -
       SKIP 1 -
       RIGHT "Page " FORMAT 999 SQL.PNO

--Format the columns
COLUMN employee_id NEW_VALUE emp_id_var NOPRINT
COLUMN employee_name NEW_VALUE emp_name_var NOPRINT
COLUMN project_id HEADING "Proj ID" FORMAT 9999
COLUMN project_name HEADING "Project Name" FORMAT A26 WORD_WRAPPED
COLUMN time_log_date HEADING "Date" FORMAT A11
COLUMN hours_logged HEADING "Hours" FORMAT 9,999
COLUMN dollars_charged HEADING "Dollars|Charged" FORMAT $999,999.99

--Breaks and computations
BREAK ON employee_id SKIP PAGE NODUPLICATES -
      ON employee_name NODUPLICATES -
      ON project_id SKIP 2 NODUPLICATES -
      ON project_name NODUPLICATES

--Execute the query to generate the report.
SELECT e.employee_id,
       e.employee_name,
       p.project_id,
       p.project_name,
```

Example 5-8. Master/detail report showing a breakdown of time billed to projects (continued)

```
      TO_CHAR(ph.time_log_date,'dd-Mon-yyyy') time_log_date,
      ph.hours_logged,
      ph.dollars_charged
 FROM employee e INNER JOIN project_hours ph
      ON e.employee_id = ph.employee_id
      INNER JOIN project p
      ON p.project_id = ph.project_id
ORDER BY e.employee_id, p.project_id, ph.time_log_date;

EXIT
```

The report output, now in master/detail form, will look like this:

```
                        The Fictional Company


    I.S. Department                 Project Hours and Dollars Detail
    ===================================================================


    Employee:   101 Marusia Churai


                                                          Dollars
    Proj ID Project Name            Date      Hours       Charged
    ------- ------------------------ ----------- ------ ------------
       1001 Corporate Web Site       01-Jan-2004     1      $169.00
                                     01-Mar-2004     3      $507.00
                                     01-May-2004     5      $845.00
                                     01-Jul-2004     7    $1,183.00
                                     01-Sep-2004     1      $169.00
                                     01-Nov-2004     3      $507.00


       1002 Enterprise Resource      01-Feb-2004     7    $1,183.00
            Planning System
                                     01-Apr-2004     1      $169.00
```

Printing data in a page footer

You can print data as part of the page footer using the same method shown for the page header. The only difference is that you would normally use the OLD_VALUE clause with the COLUMN command instead of the NEW_VALUE clause shown in the example. That's because when SQL*Plus prints the footer, it has read the next detail record from the database. Using NEW_VALUE for data in the footer would cause the footer to display information pertaining to the next page in the report, not something you normally want to happen.

Settings That Hang Around

Have you been working through the examples in this chapter? If you ignored my advice (see the earlier sidebar "Executing the Example Reports") by executing reports interactively from the SQL*Plus prompt, and if you happened to go back to re-execute a previously run report, you may have generated results that don't match those shown in this book. Formatting commands such as TTITLE and BREAK and COLUMN "stick" for the duration of your SQL*Plus session. For example, if you run *ex5-1.sql* after executing *ex5-2.sql*, while working in the same SQL*Plus session, you'll see that all the COLUMN headings defined in Example 5-2 show up when you execute Example 5-1 even though *ex5-1.sql* contains no COLUMN commands whatsoever.

If you feel that you must run a series of SQL*Plus scripts one after another in a single SQL*Plus session, begin each script with a set of commands to clear existing settings or create a separate, *reset_state.sql* script to run between reports. You can use the STORE command, described in Appendix A, to generate a file of SET commands for such a script, which might look like this:

```
CLEAR COLUMNS
CLEAR BREAKS
TTITLE OFF
BTITLE OFF
SET PAGESIZE 14
SET NEWPAGE 1
SET LINESIZE 80
...
```

Substitution variables, such as those set using NEW_VALUE, must be individually undefined. You can perhaps begin to see why it's safest to run each of your scripts under separate invocations of SQL*Plus. Too much can go wrong. Perhaps someday Oracle will introduce a RESET command to allow you to switch SQL*Plus back to its initial state.

CHAPTER 6

Creating HTML Reports

Beginning with Oracle8*i* Database Release 2 (Version 8.1.6), you can use SQL*Plus to generate HTML pages. Instead of spooling a report to a printer, you can write it to an HTML file for viewing on your corporate intranet. With a bit of creativity and some cascading style sheet (CSS) skills, you can generate some good-looking web pages. In this chapter, I'll revisit some of the character-based reports from Chapter 5 and show some ways to render those same reports as HTML pages.

 CSS is a mechanism for specifying the format of an HTML document. One reason CSS works well for SQL*Plus-generated HTML is because your CSS styles can reside in a file separate from the spool file generated by SQL*Plus, greatly reducing the likelihood that you will need to modify your SQL*Plus script to effect formatting changes. To learn more about CSS, read Eric Meyer's *Cascading Style Sheets: The Definitive Guide* (O'Reilly) and *Eric Meyer on CSS* (New Riders).

Getting the Data into an HTML Table

SQL*Plus doesn't offer much in the way of formatting HTML output, and what little capability SQL*Plus does offer in this area, you're better off avoiding in favor of CSS. When writing a report as HTML, SQL*Plus places all the detail rows, and their column headings, into an HTML table. One approach to generating an HTML page with such data is to capture only that table and concatenate it with other HTML that you write yourself to generate a complete web page.

When generating HTML from SQL*Plus, keep things simple:

* Pagination doesn't apply. All "pages" are written to one HTML file. Thus, you're better off thinking in terms of one, large page. To that end, set PAGESIZE to its maximum value of 50,000.

- Line size is irrelevant. Each column value will be in its own table cell. Your browser, together with any CSS styles and/or table markup that you supply, will control the width of that table and its columns.

- Don't worry about word-wrapping. Your browser will wrap table cell values as needed depending on how the table and its columns are sized. The COLUMN command's WORD_WRAPPED is meaningless in the context of generating HTML.

Example 6-1 shows a stripped-down version of the Project Hours and Dollars Report that you saw in Examples 5-1 through 5-5. This time, the report is output in HTML form. PAGESIZE is 50000 to ensure that only one set of column headings is generated.

Example 6-1. SQL*Plus script to generate an HTML table of report data

```
SET ECHO OFF
SET PAGESIZE 50000
SET MARKUP HTML ON TABLE ""

--Format the columns
COLUMN employee_name HEADING "Employee Name"
COLUMN project_name HEADING "Project Name"
COLUMN hours_logged HEADING "Hours" FORMAT 9,999
COLUMN dollars_charged HEADING "Dollars|Charged" FORMAT $999,999.99

--Turn off feedback and set TERMOUT off to prevent the
--report being scrolled to the screen.
SET FEEDBACK OFF
SET TERMOUT OFF

--Execute the query to generate the report.
SPOOL middle.html
SELECT e.employee_name,
       p.project_name,
       SUM(ph.hours_logged) hours_logged,
       SUM(ph.dollars_charged) dollars_charged
FROM employee e INNER JOIN project_hours ph
     ON e.employee_id = ph.employee_id
     INNER JOIN project p
     ON p.project_id = ph.project_id
GROUP BY e.employee_id, e.employee_name,
         p.project_id, p.project_name;
SPOOL OFF
```

 Remember that these report scripts are designed to be invoked from the operating system command prompt, as in:

```
sqlplus username/password @ex6-1.sql
```

Avoid invoking them interactively from the SQL*Plus prompt, as you won't be starting with a clean slate each time with respect to the various SET, COLUMN, and TTITLE commands.

The key command in Example 6-1 is the SET MARKUP command:

```
SET MARKUP HTML ON TABLE ""
```

You can break down this command as follows:

SET MARKUP HTML ON

    Causes SQL*Plus to write report output into an HTML table. All output is written in HTML, but the table is all we care about for this example.

TABLE ""

    Specifies that no attributes are to be written into the opening table tag. If you don't specify otherwise, SQL*Plus writes some default attributes, such as width="90%", but I recommend avoiding those in favor of using CSS to format your table.

Output from the script in Example 6-1 will be written to a file named *middle.html*. The file begins with a stray <p> tag, which SQL*Plus perhaps generates as a crude way of putting some space before the table. Whatever the reason for the tag, it's a bit of an annoyance when using CSS to format your output. The <p> tag is followed by an HTML table containing report data. Column headings are wrapped in <th> tags in the first row of that table. The *middle.html* file then, begins as follows:

```
<p>
<table>
<tr>
<th scope="col">
Employee Name
</th>
<th scope="col">
Project Name
</th>
<th scope="col">
Hours
</th>
<th scope="col">
Dollars
<br>
Charged
</th>
</tr>
...
```

Each row of report data is written as a row in the HTML table. For example, here is the markup written to *middle.html* for the first data row:

```
...
<tr>
<td>
Marusia Churai
</td>
<td>
Corporate Web Site
```

```
</td>
<td align="right">
   20
</td>
<td align="right">
   $3,380.00
</td>
</tr>
...
```

The *middle.html* file is not a complete HTML page. Examples 6-2 and 6-3 show two additional files containing HTML markup, *first.html* and *last.html*. By wrapping the contents of *middle.html* within the contents of those other two files, you can produce a valid HTML page. On Linux/Unix systems, you can put all the pieces together with a *cat* command:

```
cat first.html middle.html last.html > proj_hours_dollars.html
```

On Windows systems, use the *type* command:

```
type first.html, middle.html, last.html > proj_hours_dollars.html
```

Example 6-2. The first.html file with markup to begin a page

```
<html>
<head>
<meta http-equiv="Content-Type" content="text/html; charset=WINDOWS-1252">
<title>Project Hours and Dollars Report</title>
<style type="text/css">
   table {border-collapse: collapse; width: 100%;}
   td {border: 2 solid black;}
   th {border: 2 solid black;}
</style>
<body>
<h1>Project Hours and Dollars Report</h1>
```

Example 6-3. The last.html file with markup to end a page

```
</body>
</html>
```

 If you download the example scripts for this book, *first.html* and *last. html* are named *ex6-2.html* and *ex6-3.html* respectively. This is so they conform to the same naming convention as all other examples.

Figure 6-1 shows the resulting page as rendered in a browser. It's not a fancy-looking page. I'm focusing on functionality in this first example and don't want to clutter it with all sorts of HTML and CSS markup. I hope you can see, however, the potential for creativity from your ability to control the content of *first.html* and *last.html*.

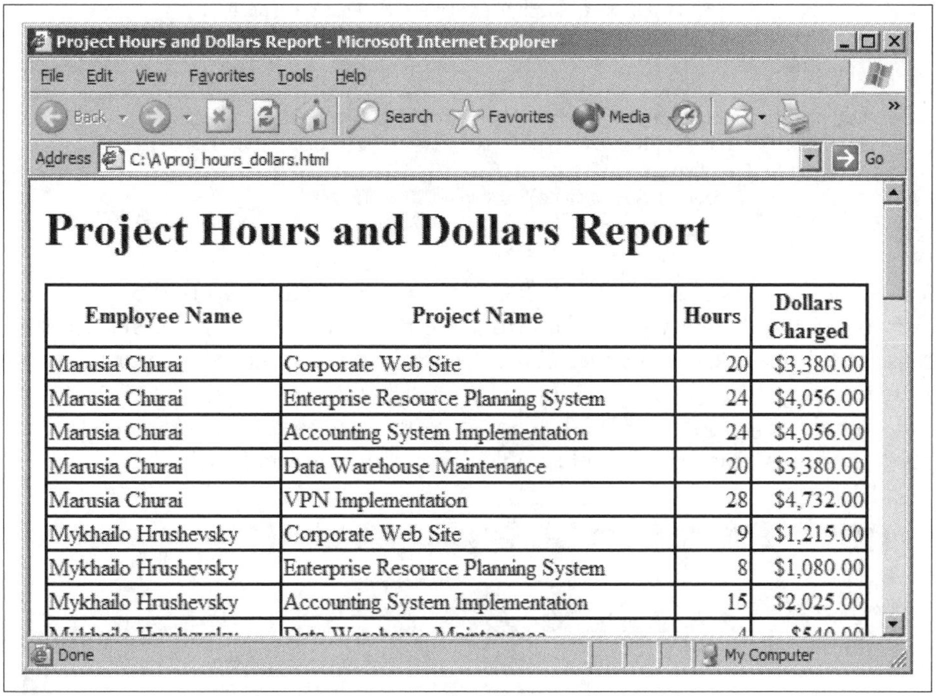

Project Hours and Dollars Report

Employee Name	Project Name	Hours	Dollars Charged
Marusia Churai	Corporate Web Site	20	$3,380.00
Marusia Churai	Enterprise Resource Planning System	24	$4,056.00
Marusia Churai	Accounting System Implementation	24	$4,056.00
Marusia Churai	Data Warehouse Maintenance	20	$3,380.00
Marusia Churai	VPN Implementation	28	$4,732.00
Mykhailo Hrushevsky	Corporate Web Site	9	$1,215.00
Mykhailo Hrushevsky	Enterprise Resource Planning System	8	$1,080.00
Mykhailo Hrushevsky	Accounting System Implementation	15	$2,025.00

*Figure 6-1. An HTML page with report content generated from SQL*Plus*

Generating the Entire Page

Having SQL*Plus generate the entire HTML page is possible. SQL*Plus generates a fairly decent-looking page by default, at least in Oracle Database 10*g*. The one problem you'll likely encounter is that the kinds of page headings you may be used to generating for plain-text reports do not always translate well into headings for HTML reports.

Using SQL*Plus's Default Formatting

To generate a report as a complete HTML page using SQL*Plus's default HTML formatting, add the command SET MARKUP HTML ON SPOOL ON near the beginning of any report script. Following is the beginning of Example 5-5 (in the file *ex5-5.sql*), with the SET MARKUP command added as the second line:

```
SET ECHO OFF
SET MARKUP HTML ON SPOOL ON

--Setup pagesize parameters
SET NEWPAGE 0
SET PAGESIZE 55
```

```
--Set the linesize, which must match the number of equal signs used
--for the ruling lines in the headers and footers.
SET LINESIZE 61

--Setup page headings and footings
TTITLE CENTER "The Fictional Company" SKIP 3 -
      LEFT "I.S. Department" -
      RIGHT "Project Hours and Dollars Report" SKIP 1 -
      LEFT "============================================================="
...
```

The SPOOL ON option to SET MARKUP causes SQL*Plus to write <html>, <head>, and <body> tags before writing data from the query to the spool file, and to close those tags before closing the file. Thus, the result from running the script is a complete web page that you can load into a browser. SQL*Plus will write a series of CSS-style definitions into the HTML heading between the <head> and </head> tags. The result, assuming you began with Example 5-5, is shown in Figure 6-2.

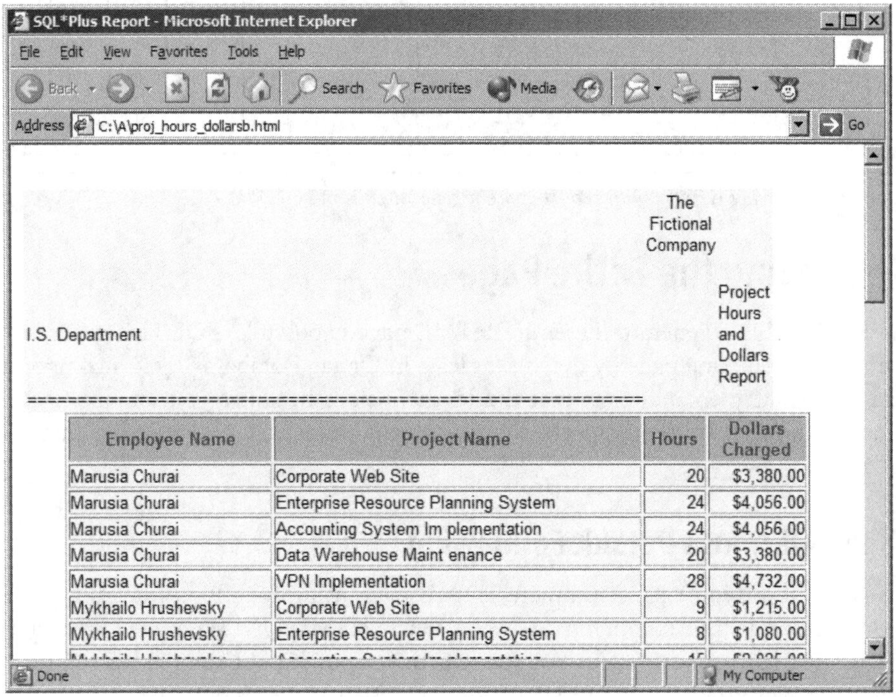

Figure 6-2. Page headers in HTML tables don't work well

The page heading in Figure 6-2 looks ugly, doesn't it? To understand why that is, you need to understand a bit about how SQL*Plus writes HTML page headings. Such headings are written to a table separate from the table used for data from the SELECT statement. This table has three columns: one for the TTITLE content following the

LEFT keyword; another for content following the CENTER keyword; and the third column for content following the RIGHT keyword.

This use of a table for page headings doesn't work as well as you might think. That long, horizontal line of equal sign (=) characters that you see in the figure is specified to be LEFT in the TTITLE command. In a plain-text report, the line extends out under the CENTER and RIGHT content. In an HTML report, however, the line can't undercut the other content because it is restricted to the leftmost column in the heading table. All those characters must display, though, and the line ends up shoving the CENTER and RIGHT content way off to the extreme right-hand side of your browser window.

When generating reports for HTML, it's best to stick with simple, uncomplicated page headings. In fact, I recommend keeping everything LEFT. Use CSS to center any heading lines that you wish centered. Don't mix alignments on the same heading line. For example, avoid using LEFT and CENTER on the same line. If you must mix two alignments, keep the different parts of your heading text short, so text from one HTML table column doesn't push other columns out of their proper alignment.

 Take care to follow any SKIP directive in a TTITLE immediately with an alignment directive such as LEFT. If you fail to do that, SQL*Plus seems to lose track of which cell subsequent text should fall into, and that text will be lost.

Avoid SKIPping more than one line in a TTITLE. When you skip multiple lines, SQL*Plus inserts blank rows into the table. This is a poor way to generate vertical space in your output. Use CSS instead.

Taking Control of the Page Format

You don't have to rely on SQL*Plus's default styles to format your HTML reports. You hold the reins of power and can take almost complete control. The script in Example 6-4 generates a complete web page. Figure 6-3 shows that page as rendered using the CSS styles in Example 6-5. There's a lot to explain in this script and in the accompanying CSS stylesheet. I'll begin by explaining the SET MARKUP command:

SET MARKUP -
> Begins the command.

HTML ON -
> Enables HTML output.

HEAD '<title>Project Hours and Dollars Report</title> -

<link href="ex6-5.css" rel="stylesheet" type="text/css"/>' -
> Specifies content to be written between <head> and </head>. This content replaces the default set of CSS styles that SQL*Plus otherwise writes. I've

wrapped this content within single quotes, so I can write double quotes into the HTML file. The `<title>` tag specifies a page title that most browsers will display on their titlebar. The `<link>` tag causes the browser displaying the HTML page to format the page using the CSS styles defined in *ex6-5.css*.

 I prefer external stylesheets. However, you can take all the styles from Example 6-5 and add them to the HEAD parameter to have them written inline in the HTML document's header.

BODY "" –

Eliminates default attributes that SQL*Plus otherwise writes into the `<body>` tag. Use CSS to format your HTML body.

TABLE 'class="detail"' –

Gives a class name to the HTML table created by SQL*Plus to hold the rows of data in the report. This eliminates the default attributes that SQL*Plus would otherwise write.

ENTMAP OFF –

Prevents SQL*Plus from translating `<` and `>` characters in the script's output stream to the HTML named character entities < and >. My approach here may be somewhat controversial, but it allows you to place HTML tags into the page title and column headings, and to good effect as you'll soon see.

SPOOL ON

Causes SQL*Plus to write `<html>`, `<head>`, and `<body>` tags before writing data from a query to a spool file and to close those tags before closing the file.

I realize that all this advice is a lot to absorb. The key here is to realize that I've specified a link to an external stylesheet, and that I've enabled the script to write HTML tags directly to the spool file. If you look at the stylesheet in Example 6-5, you'll see that the body margin is zero and that I've specified the *comic sans ms* font (not a business-like font, but I like it). The zero margin eliminates any white border that would otherwise surround my content.

Next, take a look at the page heading as specified by TTITLE:

```
TTITLE LEFT "<h1>The Fictional Company</h1>" SKIP 1 -
       LEFT "<h2>Project Hours and Dollars Report</h2>"
```

Only one "page" should be in this report because PAGESIZE is set to 50000 and I know there are fewer than 50,000 rows to be returned by the report's query. The following two lines will be written to the top of the HTML page, prior to the table containing the report data:

```
<h1>The Fictional Company</h1>
<h2>Project Hours and Dollars Report</h2>
```

This is elementary HTML markup: a top-level heading followed by one subheading. By being able to place HTML tags into a page heading, you gain the ability to format that heading to use CSS styles. The stylesheet in Example 6-5 specifies a zero top margin for h1 and h2 to keep them close together.

 In an adventurous mood? Remove the second LEFT directive from the TTITLE command and execute the script. In Oracle Database 10g Release 1 at least, the resulting report will be missing the h2 subhead. Always begin each heading line in a TTITLE with an alignment directive.

To format column headings, I place HTML markup into the HEADING text in my COLUMN commands:

```
COLUMN employee_name HEADING "<p class=left>Employee Name</p>" FORMAT A40
```

All I do here is to wrap each heading in a paragraph tag (<p>) and assign it a class. In this case, my classes are left and right, and I use those styles to align text headings to the left and numeric headings to the right. Otherwise, all headings end up centered over their columns, which doesn't always look good.

When you place HTML markup in text column headings, take care to format each column wide enough to accommodate its markup. I specified FORMAT A40 for employee_name to allow for up to 40 characters in the <p> tag. Were I to specify FORMAT A9, my heading text would be truncated to nine characters, with the result that the incomplete tag <p class= would be written to my HTML file. When generating HTML reports, don't worry about using FORMAT to control the width of a column. Instead, use FORMAT to ensure enough width for your entire heading, including any HTML markup that you add.

 I have not experienced truncation problems with headings of numeric columns. Thus, I can use FORMAT 9,999 for hours_logged without fear that my heading markup, which is much longer than just five characters, will be truncated.

The script in Example 6-4 writes two tables into the HTML file, one for the headings and the other for the data. Example 6-5 specifies the following two styles for these tables:

```
table {background: black; color: white; width: 100%;}
table.detail {background: #eeeeee; color: black}
```

Example 6-4. SQL*Plus script to generate a complete web page

```
SET ECHO OFF
SET PAGESIZE 50000
SET MARKUP -
    HTML ON -
    HEAD '<title>Project Hours and Dollars Report</title> -
        <link href="ex6-5.css" rel="stylesheet" type="text/css"/>' -
    BODY "" -
    TABLE 'class="detail"' -
```

Example 6-4. SQL*Plus script to generate a complete web page (continued)

```
    ENTMAP OFF -
    SPOOL ON

--Set-up page headings and footings
TTITLE LEFT "<h1>The Fictional Company</h1>" SKIP 1 -
       LEFT "<h2>Project Hours and Dollars Report</h2>"

--Format the columns
COLUMN employee_name HEADING "<p class=left>Employee Name</p>" FORMAT A40
COLUMN project_name HEADING "<p class=left>Project Name</p>" FORMAT A40
COLUMN hours_logged HEADING "<p class=right>Hours</p>" FORMAT 9,999
COLUMN dollars_charged HEADING "<p class=right>Dollars|Charged</p>" -
       FORMAT $999,999.99

--Turn off feedback and set TERMOUT off to prevent the
--report being scrolled to the screen.
SET FEEDBACK OFF
SET TERMOUT OFF

--Execute the query to generate the report.
SPOOL proj_hours_dollars.html
SELECT e.employee_name,
       p.project_name,
       SUM(ph.hours_logged) hours_logged,
       SUM(ph.dollars_charged) dollars_charged
FROM employee e INNER JOIN project_hours ph
    ON e.employee_id = ph.employee_id
    INNER JOIN project p
    ON p.project_id = ph.project_id
GROUP BY e.employee_id, e.employee_name,
         p.project_id, p.project_name;
SPOOL OFF
EXIT
```

Example 6-5. CSS styles to format the output from Example 6-4

```
body {margin: 0; font-family: comic sans ms;
      background: black;}
table {background: black; color: white; width: 100%;}
table.detail {background: #eeeeee; color: black}
p.left {text-align: left}
p.right {text-align: right}
th {padding-left: 5px; padding-right: 5px; text-decoration: underline}
td {padding-left: 5px; padding-right: 5px;}
h1 {margin-bottom: 0;}
h2 {margin-top: 0}
```

There is no way to specify a class for the heading table, so I control that table's format through the table style, which sets the background and margin such that the top of the page is white text on a black background that fills the width of the browser window. There is only one other table in the document, the table that holds the data, and for that table I can specify a class, which gives me a way to distinguish between the two tables. The `table.detail` style inherits the 100% width from `table`, and further specifies that the detail area of the page is to be black on a light-gray background.

And there you have it: a credible-looking web page in Figure 6-3 that is generated entirely via SQL*Plus.

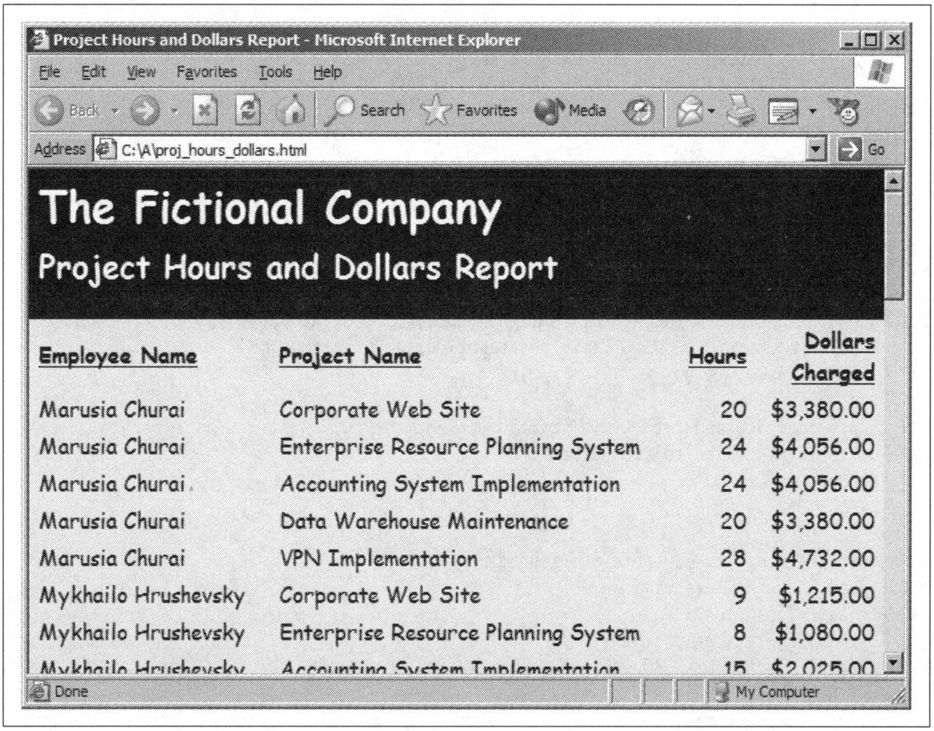

Figure 6-3. Output from Example 6-4 rendered using styles from Example 6-5

Another Approach to Headers

That SQL*Plus writes all page headers into an HTML table bothers me. In the previous section's example, that table represents unwanted markup. The associated `<table>` tag also includes some unwanted attribute settings. One of those, `width="90%"`, can cause you some grief depending on what it is that you want to accomplish in the way of formatting. An alternative, helpful approach is to dispense with using TTITLE altogether and use the PROMPT command to write page headings directly into the HTML output stream.

Example 6-6 shows a new version of the Project Hours and Dollars Report that uses PROMPT to write page headings to the HTML stream. Figure 6-4 shows the result as rendered using the stylesheet in Example 6-7. This example introduces the concept of using <div> tags to format different sections of your HTML page.

Example 6-6. A script that uses PROMPT to write HTML page headings

```
SET ECHO OFF
SET PAGESIZE 50000
SET MARKUP -
   HTML ON -
   HEAD '<title>Project Hours and Dollars Report</title> -
       <link href="ex6-7.css" rel="stylesheet" type="text/css"/>' -
   BODY "" -
   TABLE 'class="detail"' -
   ENTMAP OFF -
   SPOOL ON

--Format the columns
COLUMN employee_name HEADING "<p class=left>Employee Name</p>" FORMAT A40
COLUMN project_name HEADING "<p class=left>Project Name</p>" FORMAT A40
COLUMN hours_logged HEADING "<p class=right>Hours</p>" FORMAT 9,999
COLUMN dollars_charged HEADING "<p class=right>Dollars Charged</p>" -
       FORMAT $999,999.99

--Turn off feedback and set TERMOUT off to prevent the
--report being scrolled to the screen.
SET FEEDBACK OFF
SET TERMOUT OFF

--Execute the query to generate the report.
SPOOL proj_hours_dollars.html
PROMPT <div class="top"> -
       <h1>The Fictional Company</h1> -
       <h2>Project Hours and Dollars Report</h2> -
       </div> -
       <div class="bottom">
SELECT e.employee_name,
       p.project_name,
       SUM(ph.hours_logged) hours_logged,
       SUM(ph.dollars_charged) dollars_charged
FROM employee e INNER JOIN project_hours ph
    ON e.employee_id = ph.employee_id
    INNER JOIN project p
    ON p.project_id = ph.project_id
GROUP BY e.employee_id, e.employee_name,
         p.project_id, p.project_name;
PROMPT </div>
SPOOL OFF
END
```

Example 6-7. CSS styles to format the output from Example 6-6

```
body {margin: 0; font-family: comic sans ms; background: black;}
div {margin-left: 5px; margin-top: 5px; margin-right: 5px;}
div.top {background: white; color: black;
```

```
        padding-bottom: 5px; text-align: center;}
div.bottom {background: #eeeeee; color: black;}
table.detail {position: relative; top: -1.5em;}
p.left {text-align: left;}
p.right {text-align: right;}
th {padding-left: 5px; padding-right: 5px; text-decoration: underline;}
td {padding-left: 5px; padding-right: 5px;
    padding-top: 0; padding-bottom: 0;}
h1 {margin-bottom: 0;}
h2 {margin-top: 0; margin-bottom: 0;}
```

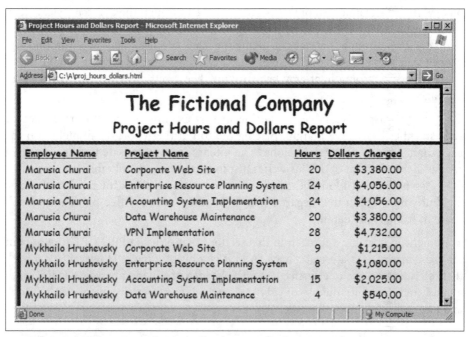

Figure 6-4. Output from Example 6-6 rendered using styles from Example 6-7

 Getting consistently sized black borders around and between the page heading and report content is something I was unable to accomplish when those page headings were embedded within an HTML table. Your mileage may vary, but I found that the table and its 90% width got in the way of what I wanted to do.

Example 6-6 uses the following PROMPT command to write a good bit of markup to the HTML file:

```
PROMPT <div class="top"> -
        <h1>The Fictional Company</h1> -
```

```
<h2>Project Hours and Dollars Report</h2> -
</div> -
```

```
<div class="bottom">
```

I use one PROMPT command because the output from each PROMPT is followed by a `<br>` tag. One unwanted `<br>` is more than sufficient. The markup here writes out a header (h1) and subheader (h2), wraps those in a `<div>` classified as "top," and begins a new `<div>` for the report detail. The detail `<div>` is closed by another PROMPT command that immediately follows the SELECT statement.

The stylesheet in Example 6-7 centers the h1 and h2 content and makes it black text on a white background. All of this is accomplished through the `div.top` style. A five-pixel margin is set for the left, top, and right side of each `<div>`. The black page background shows through that margin, giving the black borders that you see around and between the two sections of the page. The `<div>` containing the report detail is set to display black text on a light-gray background. These settings give the basic form to the page.

One unusual aspect of table formatting in this example is that the `table.detail` style specifies a negative margin, placing the top of the report detail higher on the page than it would otherwise belong. The intent is to compensate for the unwanted `<br>` and `<p>` tags that SQL*Plus writes just in front of the detail table, and the value of −1.5em is one that I found through experimentation. I think the results are pleasing, but you can omit that negative margin setting and live with a bit of extra blank space in front of the detail.

You might look at my approach in this section, that of using PROMPT to write out arbitrary markup, as a bit of a hack. And it is a bit of a hack. However, it's a hack that offends my sense of elegance less than the idea of placing my page headings into a table, and it enables the use of `<div>` tags, which gives better control over the look and feel of the resulting web page.

Master/Detail Reports in HTML

The last HTML reporting challenge that I want to talk about is that of generating master/detail reports such as the Project Hours and Dollars Detail report generated by Example 5-8. For these reports, you cannot avoid the use of TTITLE. You do want to define a header that repeats throughout the report because you need a way to indicate when the master record changes.

Example 6-8 recreates the Project Hours and Dollars Detail report in HTML form. Figure 6-5 shows the result, and as you probably expect by now, Example 6-9 shows the CSS stylesheet used to produce the layout that you see in the figure. Pay particular attention to the following aspects of this report example:

- The page heading, the one that occurs once at the top of the HTML page, is written to the HTML stream using PROMPT commands, just as in Example 6-6. PROMPT commands also write the <div> tags.

- TTITLE is used to specify the line that prints for each new master record. This line is written out as a level-3 heading using the <h3> tag. (Unfortunately, it's written into the leftmost cell of a three-column table.)

- Similar to what was done in the previous section, the <div> containing the page title is formatted as white text on black, while the <div> containing the report detail is formatted as black text on light gray.

- To distinguish the detail lines from the master lines, the detail table has been indented a bit and it has been given a white background. See the table.detail style in Example 6-9.

- The detail table has been given a slight, negative top margin to position each set of detail rows close to their respective master heading. This is optional, but the results are pleasing when rendered in Microsoft Internet Explorer.

This report certainly isn't the last word in the HTML formatting of master/detail reports. It's a good example, though, along with the other reports in this chapter, of how creative you can get using the combination of SQL*Plus, HTML, and CSS. (See Figure 6-5.)

*Example 6-8. SQL*Plus script to write a master/detail report in HTML*

```
SET ECHO OFF
SET PAGESIZE 50000
SET NEWPAGE 1
SET MARKUP -
   HTML ON -
   HEAD '<title>Project Hours and Dollars Detail</title> -
       <link href="ex6-9.css" rel="stylesheet" type="text/css"/>' -
   BODY "" -
   TABLE 'class="detail"' -
   ENTMAP OFF -
   SPOOL ON

--Set up the heading to use for each new employee
TTITLE LEFT "<h3>Employee: " FORMAT 9999 emp_id_var " " emp_name_var</h3>"

--Format the columns
COLUMN employee_id NEW_VALUE emp_id_var NOPRINT
COLUMN employee_name NEW_VALUE emp_name_var NOPRINT
COLUMN project_id HEADING "<p class=right>Proj ID</p>" FORMAT 9999
COLUMN project_name HEADING "<p class=left>Project Name</p>" -
       FORMAT A26
COLUMN time_log_date HEADING "<p class=left>Date</p>" FORMAT A30
COLUMN hours_logged HEADING "<p class=right>Hours</p>" FORMAT 9,999
```

Example 6-8. SQL*Plus script to write a master/detail report in HTML (continued)

```
COLUMN dollars_charged HEADING "<p class=right>Dollars|Charged</p>" -
      FORMAT $999,999.99

--Breaks and computations
BREAK ON employee_id SKIP PAGE NODUPLICATES -
     ON employee_name NODUPLICATES -
     ON project_id SKIP 2 NODUPLICATES -
     ON project_name NODUPLICATES

--Turn off feedback and set TERMOUT off to prevent the
--report being scrolled to the screen.
SET FEEDBACK OFF
SET TERMOUT OFF

--Execute the query to generate the report.
SPOOL hours_detail.html
PROMPT <div class="top"> -
      <h1>The Fictional Company</h2> -
      <h2>Project Hours and Dollars Detail</h2> -
      </div><div class="bottom">
SELECT e.employee_id,
       e.employee_name,
       p.project_id,
       p.project_name,
       TO_CHAR(ph.time_log_date,'dd-Mon-yyyy') time_log_date,
       ph.hours_logged,
       ph.dollars_charged
  FROM employee e INNER JOIN project_hours ph
       ON e.employee_id = ph.employee_id
       INNER JOIN project p
       ON p.project_id = ph.project_id
ORDER BY e.employee_id, p.project_id, ph.time_log_date;
SPOOL OFF
EXIT
```

Example 6-9. CSS styles to format the output from Example 6-8

```
body {margin: 0; font-family: comic sans ms; background: white;}
div {margin: 10px;}
div.top {background: black; color: white;
        padding-bottom: 5px; text-align: center;}
div.bottom {background: silver; color: black;}
table.detail {position: relative; top: -1em;
              margin-left: 2em; background-color: white;}
p.left {text-align: left;}
p.right {text-align: right;}
th {padding-left: 5px; padding-right: 5px;
    text-decoration: underline;}
td {padding-left: 5px; padding-right: 5px;
    padding-top: 0; padding-bottom: 0;}
h1 {margin-bottom: 0;}
```

Example 6-9. CSS styles to format the output from Example 6-8 (continued)

```
h2 {margin-top: 0; margin-bottom: 0;}
h3 {margin-top: 0; margin-bottom: 1.25em;}
```

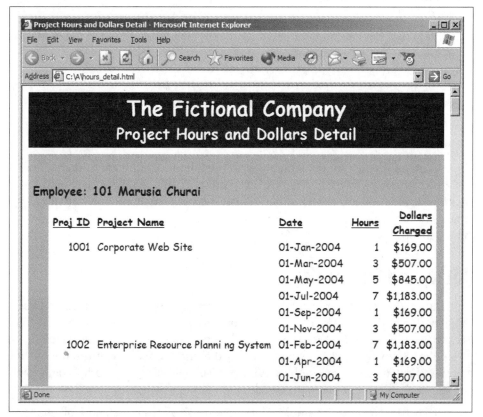

Figure 6-5. Example 6-8's master/detail report rendered using styles from Example 6-9

Advanced Reports

Beyond master/detail reports, which you learned about in Chapter 5, there are several other advanced and less often used reporting techniques that you should know about to exploit the full power of SQL*Plus. This chapter shows you how to design totals and subtotals into a report. You'll also learn some other useful tricks and techniques involving SQL*Plus and SQL.

Totals and Subtotals

SQL*Plus allows you to print totals and subtotals in a report. To do this, you use a combination of the BREAK command and one or more COMPUTE commands. This section continues with the master/detail report last shown in Chapter 5, in Example 5-8. It will show you how to modify that master/detail report so it totals the hours and dollars by project and by employee. You will see how to print grand totals for these columns at the end of the report.

To refresh your memory, Example 7-1 repeats the Project Hours and Dollars Detail report from Example 5-8.

Example 7-1. Master/detail report showing a breakdown of time billed to projects

```
SET ECHO OFF
SET RECSEP OFF

--Set up pagesize parameters
SET NEWPAGE 0
SET PAGESIZE 55
--Set the linesize, which must match the number of equals signs used
--for the ruling lines in the headers and footers.
SET LINESIZE 66

--Set up page headings and footings
TTITLE CENTER "The Fictional Company" SKIP 3 -
       LEFT "I.S. Department" -
       RIGHT "Project Hours and Dollars Detail" SKIP 1 -
```

Example 7-1. Master/detail report showing a breakdown of time billed to projects (continued)

```
        LEFT "=========================================" -
             "==========================" -
        SKIP 2 "Employee: " FORMAT 9999 emp_id_var " " emp_name_var SKIP 3

BTITLE LEFT "=========================================" -
            "==========================" -
       SKIP 1 -
       RIGHT "Page " FORMAT 999 SQL.PNO

--Format the columns
COLUMN employee_id NEW_VALUE emp_id_var NOPRINT
COLUMN employee_name NEW_VALUE emp_name_var NOPRINT
COLUMN project_id HEADING "Proj ID" FORMAT 9999
COLUMN project_name HEADING "Project Name" FORMAT A26 WORD_WRAPPED
COLUMN time_log_date HEADING "Date" FORMAT A11
COLUMN hours_logged HEADING "Hours" FORMAT 9,999
COLUMN dollars_charged HEADING "Dollars|Charged" FORMAT $999,999.99

--Breaks and computations
BREAK ON employee_id SKIP PAGE NODUPLICATES -
      ON employee_name NODUPLICATES -
      ON project_id SKIP 2 NODUPLICATES -
      ON project_name NODUPLICATES

--Execute the query to generate the report.
SELECT e.employee_id,
       e.employee_name,
       p.project_id,
       p.project_name,
       TO_CHAR(ph.time_log_date,'dd-Mon-yyyy') time_log_date,
       ph.hours_logged,
       ph.dollars_charged
  FROM employee e INNER JOIN project_hours ph
       ON e.employee_id = ph.employee_id
       INNER JOIN project p
       ON p.project_id = ph.project_id
ORDER BY e.employee_id, p.project_id, ph.time_log_date;

EXIT
```

The output from Example 7-1 looks like this:

```
                    The Fictional Company


    I.S. Department                  Project Hours and Dollars Detail
    ====================================================================

    Employee:   101 Marusia Churai


                                                        Dollars
    Proj ID Project Name               Date      Hours  Charged
    ------- -------------------------- ----------- ------ ------------
```

```
1001  Corporate Web Site          01-Jan-2004        1       $169.00
                                   01-Mar-2004        3       $507.00
                                   01-May-2004        5       $845.00
                                   01-Jul-2004        7     $1,183.00
                                   01-Sep-2004        1       $169.00
                                   01-Nov-2004        3       $507.00


1002  Enterprise Resource         01-Feb-2004        7     $1,183.00
      Planning System
                                   01-Apr-2004        1       $169.00
```

Printing Subtotals

The Project Hours and Dollars Detail report has two numeric columns showing the hours logged to a project together with the resulting dollar amount that was charged. To total these for each project and employee would be desirable. To accomplish that goal, you can use the COMPUTE command, which is a SQL*Plus command to define summary calculations in a report. The following four commands generate subtotals for hours and dollars, by project and employee:

```
COMPUTE SUM LABEL 'Totals' OF hours_logged ON project_id
COMPUTE SUM LABEL 'Totals' OF dollars_charged ON project_id
COMPUTE SUM LABEL 'Totals' OF hours_logged ON employee_id
COMPUTE SUM LABEL 'Totals' OF dollars_charged ON employee_id
```

The first two COMPUTE commands summarize the hours and dollars by project. Those project totals print whenever the project_id value changes. To help you understand this, let me break the first COMPUTE command down into more digestible pieces:

COMPUTE SUM
> Generate a running total incremented for each detail row that SQL*Plus outputs as part of the report. The OF clause specifies the source of the values to be totaled.

LABEL 'Totals'
> Use this text to identify that total when it prints on the report.

OF hours_logged
> Take values from this column.

ON project_id
> Reset the accumulated total to zero whenever the project_id changes.

The COMPUTE command controls the accumulation of running totals, but if you read this detailed breakdown carefully, you'll see no mention of COMPUTE causing anything to print. It is the BREAK command that causes the accumulated values to print. You have to interpret COMPUTE commands in the context of the BREAK setting for the report in question. That BREAK setting for the Project Hours and Dollars Detail report is as follows:

```
BREAK ON employee_id SKIP PAGE NODUPLICATES -
     ON employee_name NODUPLICATES -
     ON project_id SKIP 2 NODUPLICATES -
     ON project_name NODUPLICATES
```

The report breaks once for each employee. For each employee, the report breaks once per project. The first two COMPUTE commands are ON project_id, and a change in project_id corresponds to a new project. At the end of each project, then, SQL*Plus does the following:

1. Displays the accumulated totals from hours_logged and dollars_charged
2. Resets those accumulators to zero in preparation for the next project

The last two COMPUTE commands accumulate hours_logged and dollars_charged, not for each project but for each employee. Those COMPUTEs are ON employee_id, which means the accumulators will be reset to zero each time the employee changes. The BREAK ON employee_id causes the just finished employee's totals to print before the accumulators are reset.

Example 7-2 shows the Project Hours and Dollars Detail report with the COMPUTE commands added.

Example 7-2. Master/detail report with totals and subtotals

```
SET ECHO OFF
SET RECSEP OFF

--Set up pagesize parameters
SET NEWPAGE 0
SET PAGESIZE 55
--Set the linesize, which must match the number of equals signs used
--for the ruling lines in the headers and footers.
SET LINESIZE 66

--Set up page headings and footings
TTITLE CENTER "The Fictional Company" SKIP 3 -
     LEFT "I.S. Department" -
     RIGHT "Project Hours and Dollars Detail" SKIP 1 -
     LEFT "=========================================" -
          "==========================" -
     SKIP 2 "Employee: " FORMAT 9999 emp_id_var " " emp_name_var SKIP 3

BTITLE LEFT "=========================================" -
          "==========================" -
     SKIP 1 -
     RIGHT "Page " FORMAT 999 SQL.PNO

--Format the columns
COLUMN employee_id NEW_VALUE emp_id_var NOPRINT
```

Example 7-2. Master/detail report with totals and subtotals (continued)

```
COLUMN employee_name NEW_VALUE emp_name_var NOPRINT
COLUMN project_id HEADING "Proj ID" FORMAT 9999
COLUMN project_name HEADING "Project Name" FORMAT A26 WORD_WRAPPED
COLUMN time_log_date HEADING "Date" FORMAT A11
COLUMN hours_logged HEADING "Hours" FORMAT 9,999
COLUMN dollars_charged HEADING "Dollars|Charged" FORMAT $999,999.99

--Breaks and computations
BREAK ON employee_id SKIP PAGE NODUPLICATES -
     ON employee_name NODUPLICATES -
     ON project_id SKIP 2 NODUPLICATES -
     ON project_name NODUPLICATES

COMPUTE SUM LABEL 'Totals' OF hours_logged ON project_id
COMPUTE SUM LABEL 'Totals' OF dollars_charged ON project_id
COMPUTE SUM LABEL 'Totals' OF hours_logged ON employee_id
COMPUTE SUM LABEL 'Totals' OF dollars_charged ON employee_id

--Execute the query to generate the report.
SELECT e.employee_id,
       e.employee_name,
       p.project_id,
       p.project_name,
       TO_CHAR(ph.time_log_date,'dd-Mon-yyyy') time_log_date,
       ph.hours_logged,
       ph.dollars_charged
  FROM employee e INNER JOIN project_hours ph
       ON e.employee_id = ph.employee_id
       INNER JOIN project p
       ON p.project_id = ph.project_id
ORDER BY e.employee_id, p.project_id, ph.time_log_date;

EXIT
```

Here's how the output from Example 7-2 looks:

```
                    The Fictional Company


  I.S. Department                 Project Hours and Dollars Detail
  =================================================================

  Employee:   101 Marusia Churai


                                                         Dollars
  Proj ID Project Name            Date         Hours     Charged
  ------- -------------------------- ----------- ------ -----------
     1001 Corporate Web Site        01-Jan-2004     1      $169.00
                                     01-Mar-2004     3      $507.00
                                     01-May-2004     5      $845.00
                                     01-Jul-2004     7    $1,183.00
                                     01-Sep-2004     1      $169.00
```

```
                                      01-Nov-2004        3       $507.00
****** *************************                     ------  ------------
Totals                                                  20     $3,380.00


...


    1005 VPN Implementation           01-Jan-2004        5       $845.00
                                      01-Mar-2004        7     $1,183.00
                                      01-May-2004        1       $169.00
                                      01-Jul-2004        3       $507.00
                                      01-Sep-2004        5       $845.00
                                      01-Nov-2004        7     $1,183.00
****** *************************                     ------  ------------
Totals                                                  28     $4,732.00


                                                     ------  ------------
                                                       116    $19,604.00
```

Notice that the label "Totals" appears in the project_id column. SQL*Plus places the label you specify into the ON column of the associated COMPUTE command. The label is formatted according to the rules specified in that column's COLUMN command.

 Only one label can be printed for project totals though two COMPUTE commands exist. Had you specified two different labels, the first one would have taken precedence.

Why no label for the employee totals? Because this is a master/detail report, and the NOPRINT option has been used to suppress printing of the employee_name and employee_id columns. Normally, SQL*Plus would print the COMPUTE label in the employee_id column, but that can't be done if the column is not being printed. You can do nothing if you aren't happy with this behavior. You have to live with it or avoid master/detail reports.

The width of the label identifying the project totals is limited by the width of the project_id column, which won't hold a longer, more descriptive label such as "Project Totals". However, you can do a couple of things to make room for a longer label. The first and most obvious thing is to make the project_id column wider. Change the COLUMN command to widen the field from 7 to 14 digits:

```
COLUMN project_id HEADING 'Proj ID' FORMAT 99999999999999
```

Just be sure to bump up the linesize setting by the same amount and the page headers and footers.

A less obvious approach would be to change the computations so the project totals are summarized for each project name rather than for each project ID. This, of course, presumes that no two projects share the same name. The necessary COLUMN commands would be the following:

```
COMPUTE SUM LABEL 'Project Totals' OF hours_logged ON project_name
COMPUTE SUM LABEL 'Project Totals' OF dollars_charged ON project_name
```

The output would then look like:

```
    Proj ID Project Name              Date        Hours      Charged
    ------- -------------------------- ----------- ------ ------------
       1001 Corporate Web Site         01-Jan-2004      1      $169.00
                                       01-Mar-2004      3      $507.00
                                       01-May-2004      5      $845.00
                                       01-Jul-2004      7    $1,183.00
                                       01-Sep-2004      1      $169.00
                                       01-Nov-2004      3      $507.00
    ****** **************************               ------ ------------
            Project Totals                              20    $3,380.00
```

You now have room for a more descriptive label, and the added benefit is that the report looks better with the label indented closer to the printed totals.

COMPUTEs Are Cumulative

The COMPUTE and BREAK commands are closely linked because, although it is COMPUTE that defines summary calculations, it is BREAK that causes those calculations to display. It may seem a bit odd, then, that these two related commands work in a dissimilar manner. You are allowed to have only one BREAK setting in a report. If you want to break on multiple columns, you must list all those columns in the same BREAK command. That syntax helps make the break order clear. COMPUTE is just the opposite. If you wish to compute summary values for multiple columns, you must issue several COMPUTE commands, one for each of those columns. Summary calculations are not relative to each other as breaks are, so there is no need to define them all in a single command.

Printing Grand Totals

Use the REPORT keyword in the ON clause of a COMPUTE statement to define report-level computations. For example, you might wish to generate a grand total for hours and dollars columns in the Project Hours and Dollars Detail report. For report-level computations to print, you need to generate a report-level break, which you do using the REPORT keyword in the BREAK command.

To print grand totals for the project_hours and dollars_charged columns, add the following two lines to the script shown in Example 7-2:

```
COMPUTE SUM LABEL 'Grand Totals' OF hours_logged ON REPORT
COMPUTE SUM LABEL 'Grand Totals' OF dollars_charged ON REPORT
```

Instead of specifying a column in the ON clause, I've used the keyword REPORT. This tells SQL*Plus to sum the data over the entire report. Notice the use of the LABEL clause. Normally, the label would print in the column specified in the ON clause. In cases like this where no ON column exists, SQL*Plus will place the labels in the first column of the report.

The next thing to do is to modify the BREAK command by adding a report break. Forget to do this and the report totals will not print. The final version of the BREAK command looks like this:

```
BREAK ON REPORT -
      ON employee_id SKIP PAGE NODUPLICATES -
      ON employee_name NODUPLICATES -
      ON project_id SKIP 2 NODUPLICATES -
      ON project_name NODUPLICATES
```

The REPORT break was added to the beginning of the BREAK command because it is the outermost break. The position doesn't really matter because SQL*Plus always makes the report break outermost, but I like to put it first anyway for the sake of clarity.

Example 7-3 shows the report as it stands now.

Example 7-3. The report script modified to generate grand totals

```
SET ECHO OFF
SET RECSEP OFF

--Set up pagesize parameters
SET NEWPAGE 1
SET PAGESIZE 55
--Set the linesize, which must match the number of equals signs used
--for the ruling lines in the headers and footers.
SET LINESIZE 66

--Set up page headings and footings
TTITLE CENTER "The Fictional Company" SKIP 3 -
      LEFT "I.S. Department" -
      RIGHT "Project Hours and Dollars Detail" SKIP 1 -
      LEFT "======================================" -
           "==========================" -
      SKIP 2 "Employee: " FORMAT 9999 emp_id_var " " emp_name_var SKIP 3

BTITLE LEFT "======================================" -
            "==========================" -
      SKIP 1 -
      RIGHT "Page " FORMAT 999 SQL.PNO

--Format the columns
COLUMN employee_id NEW_VALUE emp_id_var NOPRINT
COLUMN employee_name NEW_VALUE emp_name_var NOPRINT
COLUMN project_id HEADING "Proj ID" FORMAT 9999
COLUMN project_name HEADING "Project Name" FORMAT A26 WORD_WRAPPED
```

Example 7-3. The report script modified to generate grand totals (continued)

```
COLUMN time_log_date HEADING "Date" FORMAT A11
COLUMN hours_logged HEADING "Hours" FORMAT 9,999
COLUMN dollars_charged HEADING "Dollars|Charged" FORMAT $999,999.99

--Breaks and computations
BREAK ON REPORT -
     ON employee_id SKIP PAGE NODUPLICATES -
     ON employee_name NODUPLICATES -
     ON project_id SKIP 2 NODUPLICATES -
     ON project_name NODUPLICATES

COMPUTE SUM LABEL 'Totals' OF hours_logged ON project_id
COMPUTE SUM LABEL 'Totals' OF dollars_charged ON project_id
COMPUTE SUM LABEL 'Totals' OF hours_logged ON employee_id
COMPUTE SUM LABEL 'Totals' OF dollars_charged ON employee_id
COMPUTE SUM LABEL 'Grand Totals' OF hours_logged ON REPORT
COMPUTE SUM LABEL 'Grand Totals' OF dollars_charged ON REPORT

--Execute the query to generate the report.
SELECT e.employee_id,
       e.employee_name,
       p.project_id,
       p.project_name,
       TO_CHAR(ph.time_log_date,'dd-Mon-yyyy') time_log_date,
       ph.hours_logged,
       ph.dollars_charged
  FROM employee e INNER JOIN project_hours ph
       ON e.employee_id = ph.employee_id
       INNER JOIN project p
       ON p.project_id = ph.project_id
ORDER BY e.employee_id, p.project_id, ph.time_log_date;

EXIT
```

Run the report in Example 7-3, and the grand totals will be printed on a page by themselves at the end of the report. Here's how that output will look:

```
                      The Fictional Company


   I.S. Department                    Project Hours and Dollars Detail
   =================================================================

   Employee:   113 Mykhailo Verbytsky


                                                          Dollars
   Proj ID Project Name            Date        Hours      Charged
   ------- ------------------------ ----------- ------ ------------
                                                ------ ------------
                                                786    $110,779.00
```

Notice three things about how the report totals are printed. First, they print on a page by themselves. Next, the page with the grand totals still shows an employee name in the page header. Finally, the "Grand Totals" label does not print as expected in the first column. I'll explain all of these oddities next.

Grand totals and pagination

First, the pagination issue. Before SQL*Plus executes a report break, it first executes all the other breaks. Execution begins with the innermost break and proceeds outwards until the report break actions are executed. In this example, SQL*Plus will skip two lines for the project break and will skip to a new page for the employee break. Then SQL*Plus prints the report totals. This is usually the behavior you want when printing a master/detail report. You may intend to give each employee his own section of the report so he can check his hours. Because the grand total doesn't "belong" with any one employee, you don't want it on the pages you are giving out.

Grand totals and the final detail record

The last employee's name printed on the page header because it was the last value retrieved from the database. It would be nice if SQL*Plus were smart enough to make this value null or blank, but it isn't. The value in the header is refreshed only when a new value is read from the database, and in the case of a report break, that doesn't happen. This is an issue on master/detail reports only when you use variables to include report data in the header.

One possible solution to this problem of the last set of detail values being carried forward into the grand total row is to use UNION ALL to forcibly add a row of nulls to the end of your result set. For example, you can replace the query in Example 7-3 with the following:

```
SELECT e.employee_id,
       e.employee_name,
       p.project_id,
       p.project_name,
       TO_CHAR(ph.time_log_date,'dd-Mon-yyyy') time_log_date,
       ph.hours_logged,
       ph.dollars_charged
  FROM employee e INNER JOIN project_hours ph
       ON e.employee_id = ph.employee_id
       INNER JOIN project p
       ON p.project_id = ph.project_id
UNION ALL
SELECT NULL, 'Grand Totals', NULL, NULL, NULL, NULL, NULL
FROM dual
ORDER BY employee_id NULLS LAST, project_id, time_log_date;
```

If you have downloaded the example scripts for this book, you'll find this solution in
ex7-3b.sql. The result of executing that script is shown in the following two pages at
the end of the report:

```
                        The Fictional Company


    I.S. Department                  Project Hours and Dollars Detail
    ==================================================================

    Employee:      Grand Totals


                                                              Dollars
    Proj ID Project Name             Date         Hours       Charged
    ------- ------------------------ ----------- ------ ------------

    ****** ************************              ------ ------------
    Totals


                                                 ------ ------------


    ...

                        The Fictional Company


    I.S. Department                  Project Hours and Dollars Detail
    ==================================================================

    Employee:      Grand Totals


                                                              Dollars
    Proj ID Project Name             Date         Hours       Charged
    ------- ------------------------ ----------- ------ ------------
                                                 ------ ------------
                                                  786   $110,779.00
```

This solution is a bit of a hack. It does work, but it generates one extra page of output. The use of NULLS LAST in the query's ORDER BY clause will force the null
record to the end of the result set. The second-to-last page of the report represents
that record as SQL*Plus attempts to report the hours and dollars for the nonexistent
employee named "Grand Totals". Of course, there is no detail for that employee, so
that page is blank except for the page and column titles and some horizontal rules
related to the COLUMN command.

As before, the final page of the report displays a grand total. The employee name is
still carried forward from the final record in the result set, but that final record is the
one manufactured by the UNION ALL query. Just to add clarity to the report, I gave
that null record one non-null column; I specified the employee_name as 'Grand Totals'

because I knew it would print on this final page where it helps identify the final totals as two grand totals.

> The section "Taking Advantage of Unions" shows an alternative to NULLS LAST that forces the order of results from a UNION ALL query.

Grand totals and the lack of a label

The final item to notice about the output from Example 7-3 is the lack of a label for the grand total values. I did say that SQL*Plus puts the label for report-level calculations in the first column of the report. Contrary to what you might intuitively expect, SQL*Plus bases the first column on the SELECT statement, not on what is printed. When this report was converted to a master/detail report, printing the first two columns was suppressed using the NOPRINT clause of the COLUMN command. No employee_id column, no "Grand Totals" label.

> My solution to the problem of the final employee name record carrying over to the grand total page addresses, to some extent at least, the lack of a label for the grand totals. The solution described in this section manages to place the label on the same line as the totals.

Because the employee_id and employee_name columns are not being printed, their position in the SELECT statement is irrelevant. You can move them to the end (making project_id the first column) and widen the project_id column to hold 12 characters instead of 7, and the "Grand Totals" label will now print in the first column of the report.

Example 7-4 shows the final listing, complete with the changes that allow the "Grand Totals" label to print. The listing incorporates the solution described in the preceding section, so the final employee's name doesn't carry over to the grand total page. To widen the project_id column to accommodate 12 characters, five extra leading spaces were inserted into the project_id column title. The linesize was adjusted from 66 to 71, and five equal sign characters were added to the ruling lines in the header and footer.

Example 7-4. A grand total solution that labels the grand totals

```
SET ECHO OFF
SET RECSEP OFF

--Set up pagesize parameters
SET NEWPAGE 1
SET PAGESIZE 55
--Set the linesize, which must match the number of equals signs used
--for the ruling lines in the headers and footers.
SET LINESIZE 71
```

Example 7-4. A grand total solution that labels the grand totals (continued)

```
--Set up page headings and footings
TTITLE CENTER "The Fictional Company" SKIP 3 -
       LEFT "I.S. Department" -
       RIGHT "Project Hours and Dollars Detail" SKIP 1 -
       LEFT "=======================================" -
            "==============================" -
       SKIP 2 "Employee: " FORMAT 9999 emp_id_var " " emp_name_var SKIP 3

BTITLE LEFT "=======================================" -
            "==============================" -
       SKIP 1 -
       RIGHT "Page " FORMAT 999 SQL.PNO

--Format the columns
COLUMN employee_id NEW_VALUE emp_id_var NOPRINT
COLUMN employee_name NEW_VALUE emp_name_var NOPRINT
COLUMN project_id HEADING "     Proj ID" FORMAT 9999
COLUMN project_name HEADING "Project Name" FORMAT A26 WORD_WRAPPED
COLUMN time_log_date HEADING "Date" FORMAT A11
COLUMN hours_logged HEADING "Hours" FORMAT 9,999
COLUMN dollars_charged HEADING "Dollars|Charged" FORMAT $999,999.99

--Breaks and computations
BREAK ON REPORT -
      ON employee_id SKIP PAGE NODUPLICATES -
      ON employee_name NODUPLICATES -
      ON project_id SKIP 2 NODUPLICATES -
      ON project_name NODUPLICATES

COMPUTE SUM LABEL 'Totals' OF hours_logged ON project_id
COMPUTE SUM LABEL 'Totals' OF dollars_charged ON project_id
COMPUTE SUM LABEL 'Totals' OF hours_logged ON employee_id
COMPUTE SUM LABEL 'Totals' OF dollars_charged ON employee_id
COMPUTE SUM LABEL 'Grand Totals' OF hours_logged ON REPORT
COMPUTE SUM LABEL 'Grand Totals' OF dollars_charged ON REPORT

--Execute the query to generate the report.
SELECT p.project_id,
       p.project_name,
       TO_CHAR(ph.time_log_date,'dd-Mon-yyyy') time_log_date,
       ph.hours_logged,
       ph.dollars_charged,
       e.employee_id,
       e.employee_name
  FROM employee e INNER JOIN project_hours ph
       ON e.employee_id = ph.employee_id
       INNER JOIN project p
       ON p.project_id = ph.project_id
UNION ALL
SELECT NULL, NULL, NULL, NULL, NULL, NULL, 'Grand Totals'
```

Example 7-4. A grand total solution that labels the grand totals (continued)

```
FROM dual
ORDER BY employee_id NULLS LAST, project_id, time_log_date;

EXIT
```

Following is the final page of output produced by Example 7-4. The "Grand Totals" label does indeed appear in the project_id column when the grand totals print. The employee name is listed as "Grand Totals", which is the result of the UNION ALL solution described in the previous section.

```
                          The Fictional Company


   I.S. Department                      Project Hours and Dollars Detail
   ======================================================================

   Employee:      Grand Totals


                                                            Dollars
      Proj ID Project Name              Date       Hours    Charged
   ------------ ------------------------- ----------- ------ ------------
                                                     ------ ------------
   Grand Totals                                        786  $110,779.00
```

When printing totals and grand totals, be sure the summarized columns are wide enough to accommodate the final totals. None of the individual "Dollars Charged" values in this report required more than four digits to the left of the decimal, but the final total required six.

Getting the Current Date into a Header

You saw how to display the contents of a substitution variable in the header back in Chapter 5 when the Project Hours and Dollars Detail report was converted to a master/detail style. You saw how to use the COLUMN command to tell SQL*Plus to continuously update the contents of a substitution variable with the value of a column in the query. Getting the system date to display in the header involves a little trick that takes advantage of this use of the COLUMN command. The trick is to execute a query that returns the current date and use the NEW_VALUE clause of the COLUMN command to get that date into a substitution variable. That substitution variable sticks around for the duration of the session and can be used in subsequent reports.

Getting the Date from Oracle

I use the built-in SYSDATE function in the following example to return the current date from the database. Notice that the NEW_VALUE option of the COLUMN command is used to update the user variable report_date with the current value of SYSDATE as returned from the database.

```
COLUMN SYSDATE NEW_VALUE report_date
SELECT SYSDATE FROM DUAL;
```

SYSDATE is an Oracle built-in function that returns the current date and time. DUAL is a special Oracle table that always exists, always contains exactly one row, and always contains exactly one column. You can select SYSDATE from any other table, but DUAL works well because it returns only one row, which is all you need to return the date.

 The date and time returned by SYSDATE reflect the location of the database server, not the client. If you are using a PC to access data on a remote database in a different time zone, you may want to investigate the use of CURRENT_DATE, which was introduced in Oracle9*i* Database and which returns the date and time in the session time zone.

Formatting the Date

You may find that the date format returned by SYSDATE is not what you would prefer. It depends on the setting of the NLS_DATE_FORMAT parameter, which can vary from one database to the next. You can use the ALTER SESSION statement to specify a different format:

```
ALTER SESSION SET NLS_DATE_FORMAT = 'DD-Mon-YYYY';
```

ALTER SESSION changes the format for the duration of the SQL*Plus session. Make sure you execute it prior to selecting SYSDATE from DUAL. Another alternative is to use the built-in TO_CHAR function to specify a format.

```
COLUMN current_date NEW_VALUE report_date
SELECT TO_CHAR(SYSDATE,'DD-Mon-YYYY') current_date FROM DUAL;
```

I specify a column alias of current_date in this example to give a usable name to the date column, one that could be used easily with the COLUMN command.

 Consider using ALTER SESSION to format all dates in your report rather than using TO_CHAR to format each date column separately. This makes your SELECT statements easier to write, gives you one point at which to make changes, and helps to ensure consistency.

Table 7-1 shows some typical date format strings that may be used with Oracle's built-in TO_CHAR function or with the ALTER SESSION statement.

Table 7-1. Date format strings

Date format string	Output
mm/dd/yy	11/15/61
dd-Mon-yyyy	15-Nov-1961
dd-mon-yyyy	15-nov-1961
Mon dd, yyyy hh:mm am	Nov 15, 1961 10:15 AM (or PM, depending on the time of day)
Month dd, yyyy	November 15, 1961

You may or may not care whether the output of the SELECT SYSDATE statement appears on the display, but you can suppress it by using the SET TERMOUT command to toggle the display output off and then back on again. Here's how to do that:

```
SET TERMOUT OFF
ALTER SESSION SET NLS_DATE_FORMAT = 'DD-Mon-YYYY';
COLUMN SYSDATE NEW_VALUE report_date
SELECT SYSDATE FROM DUAL;
SET TERMOUT ON
```

Finally, you need to add the date to the report header or the report footer. Here's an example of how to do that using the BTITLE command from the Project Hours and Dollars Detail report:

```
BTITLE LEFT '=============================================================' -
       SKIP 1 -
       LEFT report_date -
       RIGHT 'Page ' FORMAT 999 SQL.PNO
```

The addition of LEFT report_date to this BTITLE command causes the date to print left-justified on the same line as the page number. When you execute the report, the page footer will look like this:

```
=======================================================================
22-Feb-1998                                                     Page    1
```

In addition to using this technique with the system date, you can use it to retrieve any other value from the database for inclusion in a report.

Report Headers and Footers

Report headers and footers work much like page headers and footers, except that they print only once in a report. A report header prints at the beginning of the report, after the first page title and before the first detail line. A report footer prints at the end of a report, after the last detail line and before the final page footer. Figure 7-1 illustrates this by showing how the different types of headers and footers print relative to each other in a three-page report.

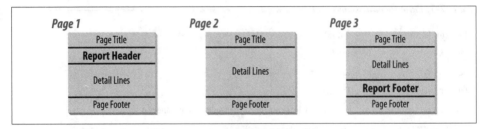

Figure 7-1. Report headers and footers versus page headers and footers

You define a report header using the REPHEADER command. The REPFOOTER command defines a report footer. The parameters you can use with REPHEADER and REPFOOTER are the same as, and work the same way as, those used with the TTITLE command.

One use for a report header is to define a report title that prints only on the first page of a report, leaving only column titles at the top of all subsequent pages. You can use a report footer to mark the end of a report, so you know for sure whether you have all the pages. Here is an example showing how these things can be done.

Recall that the Project Hours and Dollars Report from Example 5-5 used the following commands to define page headers and footers:

```
TTITLE CENTER 'The Fictional Company' SKIP 3 -
       LEFT 'I.S. Department' -
       RIGHT 'Project Hours and Dollars Report' SKIP 1 -
       LEFT '============================================================'

BTITLE LEFT '============================================================' -
       SKIP 1 -
       RIGHT 'Page ' FORMAT 999 SQL.PNO
```

The TTITLE command defined a title containing the name of the report, which in this case was printed on each page of the report. By replacing TTITLE with REP-HEADER and adding a command to turn TTITLE off, you will cause the title containing the report name to print only once. The following example shows how this is done and also defines a report footer:

```
TTITLE OFF
REPFOOTER CENTER '*** End of Hours and Dollars Report ***'
REPHEADER CENTER 'The Fictional Company' SKIP 3 -
       LEFT 'I.S. Department' -
       RIGHT 'Project Hours and Dollars Report' SKIP 1 -
       LEFT '============================================================'

BTITLE LEFT '============================================================' -
       SKIP 1 -
       RIGHT 'Page ' FORMAT 999 SQL.PNO
```

The report footer, defined with the REPFOOTER command, will print on the last page, after the last detail record, to mark the end of the report. Example 7-5 shows this new incarnation of the Project Hours and Dollars Report.

Example 7-5. Project Hours and Dollars Report formatted using report headers and footers

```
SET ECHO OFF

--Set up pagesize parameters
SET NEWPAGE 1
SET PAGESIZE 55

--Set the linesize, which must match the number of equal signs used
--for the ruling lines in the headers and footers.
SET LINESIZE 61

--Set up page headings and footings
TTITLE OFF
REPFOOTER CENTER '***End of Hours and Dollars Report ***'
REPHEADER CENTER "The Fictional Company" SKIP 3 -
      LEFT "I.S. Department" -
      RIGHT "Project Hours and Dollars Report" SKIP 1 -
      LEFT "============================================================="
```

Example 7-5. Project Hours and Dollars Report formatted using report headers and footers (continued)

```
BTITLE LEFT "==============================================================" -
      SKIP 1 -
      RIGHT "Page " FORMAT 999 SQL.PNO

--Format the columns
COLUMN employee_name HEADING "Employee Name" FORMAT A20 WORD_WRAPPED
COLUMN project_name HEADING "Project Name" FORMAT A20 WORD_WRAPPED
COLUMN hours_logged HEADING "Hours" FORMAT 9,999
COLUMN dollars_charged HEADING "Dollars|Charged" FORMAT $999,999.99

--Turn off feedback and set TERMOUT off to prevent the
--report being scrolled to the screen.
SET FEEDBACK OFF
SET TERMOUT OFF

--Execute the query to generate the report.
SELECT e.employee_name,
       p.project_name,
       SUM(ph.hours_logged) hours_logged,
       SUM(ph.dollars_charged) dollars_charged
  FROM employee e INNER JOIN project_hours ph
       ON e.employee_id = ph.employee_id
       INNER JOIN project p
       ON p.project_id = ph.project_id
GROUP BY E.EMPLOYEE_ID, E.EMPLOYEE_NAME,
         P.PROJECT_ID, P.PROJECT_NAME;
EXIT
```

When you run the script in Example 7-5, your results will be as follows:

```
                      The Fictional Company


I.S. Department               Project Hours and Dollars Report
==============================================================
                                                       Dollars
Employee Name        Project Name          Hours       Charged
-------------------- -------------------- ------ ------------

Marusia Churai       Corporate Web Site       20    $3,380.00
Marusia Churai       Enterprise Resource      24    $4,056.00
                     Planning System
...
Mykola Leontovych    Data Warehouse            9    $1,089.00
                     Maintenance

Mykola Leontovych    VPN Implementation       16    $1,936.00
==============================================================
                                                   Page    1
...
                                                       Dollars
Employee Name        Project Name          Hours       Charged
```

```
--------------------    --------------------   ------  -----------
                    Implementation

Igor Sikorsky         Data Warehouse               4    $280.00
                      Maintenance
...
Mykhailo Verbytsky    Data Warehouse              16    $4,800.00
                      Maintenance

Mykhailo Verbytsky    VPN Implementation          16    $4,800.00
                  ***End of Hours and Dollars Report ***
....

============================================================
                                            Page    3
```

As you can see, the report title printed only on the first page of the report. Subsequent pages began with the column titles. The report footer printed on the last page following the last detail line. When you are working with report headers and footers, keep in mind that these report elements still print within the context of a page. Page titles and footers print on each page regardless of whether a report header or footer prints on that page. Had the above report included a page title (TTITLE), the page title would have printed on the first page prior to the report header.

Formatting Object Columns

Oracle8 introduced objects to Oracle's relational database world. You can define object types that you can then use as datatypes for columns in a relational table. The following example shows an object type named employee_type, as well as an employees table that contains an object column named employee. The employee column stores employee_type objects.

```
SQL> DESCRIBE employee_type
 Name                             Null?     Type
 -------------------------------- --------  ----
 EMPLOYEE_NAME                              VARCHAR2(40)
 EMPLOYEE_HIRE_DATE                         DATE
 EMPLOYEE_SALARY                            NUMBER(9,2)

SQL> DESCRIBE employees
 Name                             Null?     Type
 -------------------------------- --------  ----
 EMPLOYEE_ID                                NUMBER
 EMPLOYEE                                   EMPLOYEE_TYPE
```

When you select from this table using SQL*Plus, the employee object is treated as one database column, which in fact it is. The attributes of the employee object are displayed in parentheses:

```
SQL> select * from employees;

EMPLOYEE_ID
-----------
EMPLOYEE(EMPLOYEE_NAME, EMPLOYEE_HIRE_DATE, EMPLOYEE_SALARY)
--------------------------------------------------------------------------------
        111
EMPLOYEE_TYPE('Taras Shevchenko', '23-AUG-76', 57000)

        110
EMPLOYEE_TYPE('Ivan Mazepa', '04-APR-04', 67000)

        112
EMPLOYEE_TYPE('Igor Sikorsky', '15-NOV-61', 77000)
```

This output looks messy. You can tidy it up a bit by formatting the two columns so both fit on one line. As far as SQL*Plus is concerned, only two columns exist: employee_id and employee. Here's an example that formats the columns somewhat better:

```
SQL> COLUMN employee FORMAT A60 HEADING 'Employee Data'
SQL> COLUMN employee_id HEADING 'Employee ID'
SQL> SELECT * FROM employees;

Employee ID Employee Data
----------- ------------------------------------------------------------
        111 EMPLOYEE_TYPE('Taras Shevchenko', '23-AUG-76', 57000)
        110 EMPLOYEE_TYPE('Ivan Mazepa', '04-APR-04', 67000)
        112 EMPLOYEE_TYPE('Igor Sikorsky', '15-NOV-61', 77000)
```

This is an improvement. However, you can do a bit more. SQL*Plus Version 8 introduced a new command called ATTRIBUTE, which allows you to format the individual attributes of an object column. In this case, you can use ATTRIBUTE to format the employee salary so it prints as a dollar value. The following commands do this:

```
ATTRIBUTE employee_type.employee_salary ALIAS emp_sal
ATTRIBUTE emp_sal FORMAT $999,999.99
```

The ATTRIBUTE command references the object column's type and not the object column's name. In other words, employee_type is used, not employee. This is important and is easily overlooked.

When you format an attribute for an object type, that format applies any time an object of that type is displayed. This is true even when the same object type is used in more than one column of a table or in more than one table. If you were to have two tables, each with an employee_type object column, the ATTRIBUTE commands just shown would affect the display format of data from both columns in both tables.

Having used the ATTRIBUTE command to format the employee salary attribute, you can reissue the SELECT to get the following results, which have the salary figures formatted as dollar amounts:

```
SQL> select * from employees;

Employee ID Employee Data
----------- --------------------------------------------------------------
        111 EMPLOYEE_TYPE('Taras Shevchenko', '23-AUG-76', $57,000.00)
        110 EMPLOYEE_TYPE('Ivan Mazepa', '04-APR-04', $67,000.00)
        112 EMPLOYEE_TYPE('Igor Sikorsky', '15-NOV-61', $77,000.00)
```

Look again at the ATTRIBUTE commands shown earlier. You will see that two commands were used instead of one. The first command defined an alias for the attribute. An alias is another name you can use in subsequent ATTRIBUTE commands to save yourself the trouble of typing in the entire object type and attribute name again. The second ATTRIBUTE command referred to the alias. If you have deeply nested objects, the dot notation for an attribute can be long, so this aliasing ability can come in handy.

The only format element that can be used with a text attribute is A. For example, you might specify A10 as the format for the employee object's employee name attribute. When used with the ATTRIBUTE command, a text format such as A10 serves to specify a maximum display length for the attribute. Any characters beyond that length are truncated and consequently not displayed. Notice the full name in the line below:

```
    111 EMPLOYEE_TYPE('Taras Shevchenko', '23-AUG-76', 57000)
```

Applying a format of A10 to the employee name field results in the name being truncated to 10 characters in length, as shown here:

```
    111 EMPLOYEE_TYPE('Taras Shev', '23-AUG-76', 57000)
```

Text attributes are never expanded to their maximum length. Such values are delimited by quotes. Adding extra space inside the quotes would be tantamount to changing the values, and there would be little point putting the extra space outside the quotes.

Attributes of type DATE seem unaffected by any format settings you specify even though they, like text fields, are displayed within quotes.

As with the COLUMN command, the effects of ATTRIBUTE commands are cumulative. That's why two commands are able to be used for the previous example in place of one. In contrast to COLUMN, there is no CLEAR ATTRIBUTES command. However, the CLEAR COLUMNS command will erase any attribute settings you have defined.

Appendix B describes the format specifiers that you can use with the ATTRIBUTE command.

Summary Reports

Sometimes you are interested only in summarized information. Maybe you only need to know the total hours each employee has spent on each project, and you don't care about the detail of each day's charges. Whenever that's the case, you should write your SQL query to return summarized data from Oracle.

Here is the query used in the master/detail report shown in Example 7-4:

```
SELECT p.project_id,
       p.project_name,
       TO_CHAR(ph.time_log_date,'dd-Mon-yyyy') time_log_date,
       ph.hours_logged,
       ph.dollars_charged,
       e.employee_id,
       e.employee_name
  FROM employee e INNER JOIN project_hours ph
       ON e.employee_id = ph.employee_id
       INNER JOIN project p
       ON p.project_id = ph.project_id
UNION ALL
SELECT NULL, NULL, NULL, NULL, NULL, NULL, 'Grand Totals'
FROM dual
ORDER BY employee_id NULLS LAST, project_id, time_log_date;
```

This query brings down all the detail information from the project_hours table, and is fine if you need that level of detail. However, if all you are interested in are the totals by employee and project, you can use the following query instead:

```
SELECT p.project_id,
       p.project_name,
       TO_CHAR(MAX(ph.time_log_date),'dd-Mon-yyyy') time_log_date,
       SUM(ph.hours_logged) hours_logged,
       SUM(ph.dollars_charged) dollars_charged,
       e.employee_id,
```

```
        e.employee_name
    FROM employee e INNER JOIN project_hours ph
        ON e.employee_id = ph.employee_id
        INNER JOIN project p
        ON p.project_id = ph.project_id
    GROUP BY e.employee_id, e.employee_name, p.project_id, p.project_name
    UNION ALL
    SELECT NULL, NULL, NULL, NULL, NULL, NULL, 'Grand Totals'
    FROM dual
    ORDER BY employee_id NULLS LAST, project_id, time_log_date;
```

You can practically plug this second query into Example 7-4 in place of the first. You would need to make only two other changes. First, you would eliminate the project breaks and computations, changing the BREAK and COLUMN commands:

```
BREAK ON REPORT -
        ON employee_id SKIP PAGE NODUPLICATES -
        ON employee_name NODUPLICATES

COMPUTE SUM LABEL 'Totals' OF hours_logged ON employee_id
COMPUTE SUM LABEL 'Totals' OF dollars_charged ON employee_id
COMPUTE SUM LABEL 'Grand Totals' OF hours_logged ON REPORT
COMPUTE SUM LABEL 'Grand Totals' OF dollars_charged ON REPORT
```

Then you might change the title of the date field, which represents the most recent date an employee worked on a project, to something more descriptive:

```
COLUMN time_log_date HEADING 'Last Date|Worked' FORMAT A11
```

Finally, you might change the title from Project Hours and Dollars *Detail* to Project Hours and Dollars *Summary*. Example 7-6 shows the resulting script.

Example 7-6. A summary report

```
SET ECHO OFF
SET RECSEP OFF

--Set up pagesize parameters
SET NEWPAGE 1
SET PAGESIZE 55
--Set the linesize, which must match the number of equals signs used
--for the ruling lines in the headers and footers.
SET LINESIZE 71

--Set up page headings and footings
TTITLE CENTER "The Fictional Company" SKIP 3 -
        LEFT "I.S. Department" -
        RIGHT "Project Hours and Dollars Detail" SKIP 1 -
        LEFT "=======================================" -
            "==============================" -
        SKIP 2 "Employee: " FORMAT 9999 emp_id_var " " emp_name_var SKIP 3

BTITLE LEFT "=======================================" -
            "==============================" -
        SKIP 1 -
        RIGHT "Page " FORMAT 999 SQL.PNO
```

Example 7-6. A summary report (continued)

```
--Format the columns
COLUMN employee_id NEW_VALUE emp_id_var NOPRINT
COLUMN employee_name NEW_VALUE emp_name_var NOPRINT
COLUMN project_id HEADING "     Proj ID" FORMAT 9999
COLUMN project_name HEADING "Project Name" FORMAT A26 WORD_WRAPPED
COLUMN time_log_date HEADING "Last Date|Worked" FORMAT A11
COLUMN hours_logged HEADING "Hours" FORMAT 9,999
COLUMN dollars_charged HEADING "Dollars|Charged" FORMAT $999,999.99

--Breaks and computations
BREAK ON REPORT -
     ON employee_id SKIP PAGE NODUPLICATES -
     ON employee_name NODUPLICATES

COMPUTE SUM LABEL 'Totals' OF hours_logged ON employee_id
COMPUTE SUM LABEL 'Totals' OF dollars_charged ON employee_id
SET ECHO OFF
SET RECSEP OFF

--Set up pagesize parameters
SET NEWPAGE 1
SET PAGESIZE 55
--Set the linesize, which must match the number of equals signs used
--for the ruling lines in the headers and footers.
SET LINESIZE 71

--Set up page headings and footings
TTITLE CENTER "The Fictional Company" SKIP 3 -
     LEFT "I.S. Department" -
     RIGHT "Project Hours and Dollars Summary" SKIP 1 -
     LEFT "=========================================" -
          "===============================" -
     SKIP 2 "Employee: " FORMAT 9999 emp_id_var " " emp_name_var SKIP 3

BTITLE LEFT "=========================================" -
          "===============================" -
     SKIP 1 -
     RIGHT "Page " FORMAT 999 SQL.PNO

oracle@gennick02:~/sqlplus/ExampleScripts>
oracle@gennick02:~/sqlplus/ExampleScripts> cat ex7-6.sql
SET ECHO OFF
SET RECSEP OFF

--Set up pagesize parameters
SET NEWPAGE 1
SET PAGESIZE 55
--Set the linesize, which must match the number of equals signs used
--for the ruling lines in the headers and footers.
SET LINESIZE 71

--Set up page headings and footings
TTITLE CENTER "The Fictional Company" SKIP 3 -
```

Example 7-6. A summary report (continued)

```
      LEFT "I.S. Department" -
      RIGHT "Project Hours and Dollars Summary" SKIP 1 -
      LEFT "=========================================" -
           "=============================" -
      SKIP 2 "Employee: " FORMAT 9999 emp_id_var " " emp_name_var SKIP 3

BTITLE LEFT "=========================================" -
            "=============================" -
       SKIP 1 -
       RIGHT "Page " FORMAT 999 SQL.PNO

--Format the columns
COLUMN employee_id NEW_VALUE emp_id_var NOPRINT
COLUMN employee_name NEW_VALUE emp_name_var NOPRINT
COLUMN project_id HEADING "    Proj ID" FORMAT 9999
COLUMN project_name HEADING "Project Name" FORMAT A26 WORD_WRAPPED
COLUMN time_log_date HEADING "Last Date|Worked" FORMAT A11
COLUMN hours_logged HEADING "Hours" FORMAT 9,999
COLUMN dollars_charged HEADING "Dollars|Charged" FORMAT $999,999.99

--Breaks and computations
BREAK ON REPORT -
      ON employee_id SKIP PAGE NODUPLICATES -
      ON employee_name NODUPLICATES

COMPUTE SUM LABEL 'Totals' OF hours_logged ON employee_id
COMPUTE SUM LABEL 'Totals' OF dollars_charged ON employee_id
COMPUTE SUM LABEL 'Grand Totals' OF hours_logged ON REPORT
COMPUTE SUM LABEL 'Grand Totals' OF dollars_charged ON REPORT

--Execute the query to generate the report.
SELECT p.project_id,
       p.project_name,
       TO_CHAR(MAX(ph.time_log_date),'dd-Mon-yyyy') time_log_date,
       SUM(ph.hours_logged) hours_logged,
       SUM(ph.dollars_charged) dollars_charged,
       e.employee_id,
       e.employee_name
  FROM employee e INNER JOIN project_hours ph
       ON e.employee_id = ph.employee_id
       INNER JOIN project p
       ON p.project_id = ph.project_id
GROUP BY e.employee_id, e.employee_name, p.project_id, p.project_name
UNION ALL
SELECT NULL, NULL, NULL, NULL, NULL, NULL, 'Grand Totals'
FROM dual
ORDER BY employee_id NULLS LAST, project_id, time_log_date;

EXIT
```

The resulting output would look like this:

```
                        The Fictional Company


I.S. Department                         Project Hours and Dollars Summary
=========================================================================

Employee:   101 Marusia Churai


                                Last Date                     Dollars
        Proj ID Project Name    Worked        Hours           Charged
    ------------ ------------------------- ----------- ------ ------------
        1001 Corporate Web Site      01-Nov-2004    20      $3,380.00
        1002 Enterprise Resource     01-Dec-2004    24      $4,056.00
             Planning System

    ...

                        The Fictional Company


I.S. Department                         Project Hours and Dollars Summary
=========================================================================

Employee:       Grand Totals


                                Last Date                     Dollars
        Proj ID Project Name    Worked        Hours           Charged
    ------------ ------------------------- ----------- ------ ------------
                                                       ------ ------------
    Grand Totals                                       786   $110,779.00
```

By letting the database handle the project-level summarization, you save time and paper. You save time because SQL*Plus doesn't need to pull all that data down from the database, and you save paper because you don't print all the unneeded detail.

Taking Advantage of Unions

As I described in Chapter 4, a *union* is an SQL construct that allows you to knit together the results of several SQL queries and treat those results as if they had been returned by just one query. I find them invaluable when writing queries. One of the more creative uses I've discovered involves using unions to produce reports that need to show data grouped by categories and that may need to show the same records in more than one of those categories.

A Typical Union Example

A good example of this type of report would be one that fulfills the following request:

> Produce an employee turnover report that lists everyone employed at the beginning of the year, everyone hired during the year, everyone terminated during the year, and everyone employed at the end of the year. The report should be divided into four sections, one for each of those categories.

This is a common kind of request, for me at least. The interesting thing about this request, though, is that every employee will need to be listed in two categories. That means you would need to write a query that returned each employee record twice in the correct categories.

When you are faced with this type of query, it can be helpful to simplify the problem by thinking in terms of separate queries, one for each category. It's fairly easy to conceive of a query to bring back a list of employees that were on board at the beginning of the year. You need to make sure the first of the year is between the hire date and the termination date, and account for the termination date possibly being null. Here's the query to return a list of people employed as of January 1, 2004:

```
SELECT employee_id,
       employee_name,
       employee_hire_date,
       employee_termination_date
  FROM employee
 WHERE employee_hire_date < TO_DATE('1-Jan-2004','dd-mon-yyyy')
   AND (employee_termination_date IS NULL
        OR employee_termination_date >= TO_DATE('1-Jan-2004','dd-mon-yyyy'))
```

This gives you the first section of the report, which is those employed at the beginning of the year. Retrieving the data for the remaining sections is a matter of using a different WHERE clause for each section. Table 7-2 shows the selection criteria for each section of the report.

Table 7-2. Union query selection criteria

Report section	WHERE clause

Employed at beginning of year	WHERE employee_hire_date < TO_DATE('1-Jan-2004','dd-mon-yyyy')
	    AND (employee_termination_date IS NULL
	        OR employee_termination_date >= TO_DATE('1-Jan-2004',
	        'dd-mon-yyyy'))

Hired during year	WHERE employee_hire_date >= TO_DATE('1-Jan-2004','dd-mon-yyyy') AND (employee_hire_date < TO_DATE('1-Jan-2005','dd-mon-yyyy'))

Terminated during year	WHERE employee_termination_date >= TO_DATE('1-Jan-2004','dd-mon-yyyy')
	    AND (employee_termination_date < TO_DATE('1-Jan-2005',
	        'dd-mon-yyyy'))

Employed at end of year	WHERE employee_hire_date < TO_DATE('1-Jan-2005','dd-mon-yyyy')
	    AND (employee_termination_date IS NULL
	        OR employee_termination_date >= TO_DATE('1-Jan-2005',
	        'dd-mon-yyyy'))

The UNION Query

After separately developing the four queries, one for each section of the report, you can use SQL's UNION operator to link those four queries together into one large query. There are four things to consider when doing this:

- You need to return all the records retrieved by all four queries.
- You need to be able to group the retrieved records by category.
- You need to be able to control which category prints first.
- You need to identify each category on the printed report so the person reading the report knows what's what.

To be certain of getting all the records back from the query, use the UNION ALL operator to tie the queries together. Using UNION by itself causes SQL to filter out any duplicate rows in the result set. That unwanted filtering is done (usually) by a sorting operation, which consumes disk and CPU resources. Use UNION ALL to ensure that you get back all rows in each result set and without any unwanted sorts.

In order to properly group the records, you can add a numeric constant to each of the four queries. For example, the query to return the list of those employed at the beginning of the year could return an arbitrary value of 1:

```
SELECT 1 sort_column,
       employee_id,
       employee_name,
   ...
```

The other queries would return values of 2, 3, and 4 in the sort column. Sorting the query results on these arbitrary numeric values serves two purposes. First, the records for each section of the report will be grouped together because they will all have the same constant. Second, the value of the sort column controls the order in which the sections print. Use a value of 1 for the section to be printed first, a value of 2 for the second section, and so on.

The final thing to worry about is identifying the results to the reader of the report. The values used in the sort column won't mean anything to the reader, so you need to add a column with some descriptive text. Here's how the final query for people employed at the beginning of the year looks with that text added:

```
SELECT 1 sort_column,
       'Employed at Beginning of Year' employee_status_text,
       employee_id,
       employee_name,
       employee_hire_date,
       employee_termination_date
  FROM employee
 WHERE employee_hire_date < TO_DATE('1-Jan-2004','dd-mon-yyyy')
   AND (employee_termination_date IS NULL
        OR employee_termination_date >= TO_DATE('1-Jan-2004','dd-mon-yyyy'))
```

The first column returned by this query is used to sort these records to the top of the report, and the second column serves to identify those records for the reader. Example 7-7 shows the full-blown UNION query to produce all four sections of the report.

Example 7-7. A UNION query to generate a four-section report

```
SELECT 1 sort_column,
       'Employed at Beginning of Year' employee_status_text,
       employee_id,
       employee_name,
       employee_hire_date,
       employee_termination_date
  FROM employee
 WHERE employee_hire_date < TO_DATE('1-Jan-2004','dd-mon-yyyy')
   AND (employee_termination_date IS NULL
        OR employee_termination_date >= TO_DATE('1-Jan-2004','dd-mon-yyyy'))
UNION ALL
SELECT 2 as sort_column,
       'Hired During Year' as employee_status_text,
       employee_id,
       employee_name,
       employee_hire_date,
       employee_termination_date
  FROM employee
 WHERE employee_hire_date >= TO_DATE('1-Jan-2004','dd-mon-yyyy')
   AND (employee_hire_date < TO_DATE('1-Jan-2005','dd-mon-yyyy'))
UNION ALL
SELECT 3 as sort_column,
       'Terminated During Year' as employee_status_text,
       employee_id,
       employee_name,
       employee_hire_date,
       employee_termination_date
  FROM employee
 WHERE employee_termination_date >= TO_DATE('1-Jan-2004','dd-mon-yyyy')
   AND (employee_termination_date < TO_DATE('1-Jan-2005','dd-mon-yyyy'))
UNION ALL
SELECT 4 as sort_column,
       'Employed at End of Year' as employee_status_text,
       employee_id,
       employee_name,
       employee_hire_date,
       employee_termination_date
  FROM employee
 WHERE employee_hire_date < TO_DATE('1-Jan-2005','dd-mon-yyyy')
   AND (employee_termination_date IS NULL
        OR employee_termination_date >= TO_DATE('1-Jan-2005','dd-mon-yyyy'))
ORDER BY sort_column, employee_id, employee_hire_date;
```

The four queries have been unioned together in the same order in which the report is to be printed. That's done for readability though. It's the ORDER BY clause at the bottom that ensures that the records are returned in the proper order.

The Final Report

Now that you've worked out the query, you only have to follow the remaining steps in the report development methodology to format and print the report. Example 7-8 shows a script to produce a reasonably formatted report. I have elided the SELECT statement to save space, but it's the same as in Example 7-7.

Example 7-8. A UNION report with four sections

```
--Set up pagesize parameters
SET NEWPAGE 1
SET PAGESIZE 55

--Set the linesize, which must match the number of equal signs used
--for the ruling lines in the headers and footers.
SET LINESIZE 75

TTITLE CENTER 'The Fictional Company' SKIP 2 -
       CENTER 'Employee Turnover Report' SKIP 1 -
       LEFT '===================================' -
            '===================================' -
       SKIP 3

--Format the columns
CLEAR COLUMNS
COLUMN sort_column NOPRINT
COLUMN employee_id NOPRINT
COLUMN employee_status_text HEADING 'Status' FORMAT A29
COLUMN employee_name HEADING 'Employee Name' FORMAT A20
COLUMN employee_hire_date HEADING 'Hire Date' FORMAT A11
COLUMN employee_termination_date HEADING 'Term Date' FORMAT A11

--Breaks and computations
BREAK ON employee_status_text SKIP 2 NODUPLICATES
CLEAR COMPUTES
COMPUTE NUMBER LABEL 'Total Count' OF employee_name ON employee_status_text

--Set the date format to use
ALTER SESSION SET NLS_DATE_FORMAT = 'dd-Mon-yyyy';

SELECT 1 sort_column,
       'Employed at Beginning of Year' employee_status_text,
       employee_id,
...
EXIT
```

The output from Example 7-8 will look like this:

```
                                The Fictional Company

                             Employee Turnover Report
==============================================================================


Status                          Employee Name         Hire Date    Term Date
------------------------------  --------------------  -----------  -----------
Employed at Beginning of Year   Marusia Churai        15-Nov-1961
                                Mykhailo Hrushevsky   16-Sep-1964  05-May-2004
                                Pavlo Virsky          29-Dec-1987  01-Apr-2004
                                Pavlo Chubynsky       01-Mar-1994  15-Nov-2004
                                Taras Shevchenko      23-Aug-1976
                                Igor Sikorsky         15-Nov-1961  04-Apr-2004
****************************     --------------------
Total Count                                   6


Hired During Year               Mykola Leontovych     15-Jun-2004
                                Lesia Ukrainka        02-Jan-2004
                                Ivan Mazepa           04-Apr-2004  30-Sep-2004
                                Mykhailo Verbytsky    03-Mar-2004  31-Oct-2004
                                Roxolana Lisovsky     03-Jun-2004
****************************     --------------------
Total Count                                   5


Terminated During Year          Mykhailo Hrushevsky   16-Sep-1964  05-May-2004
                                Pavlo Virsky          29-Dec-1987  01-Apr-2004
                                Pavlo Chubynsky       01-Mar-1994  15-Nov-2004
                                Ivan Mazepa           04-Apr-2004  30-Sep-2004
                                Igor Sikorsky         15-Nov-1961  04-Apr-2004
                                Mykhailo Verbytsky    03-Mar-2004  31-Oct-2004
****************************     --------------------
Total Count                                   6


Employed at End of Year         Marusia Churai        15-Nov-1961
                                Mykola Leontovych     15-Jun-2004
                                Lesia Ukrainka        02-Jan-2004
                                Taras Shevchenko      23-Aug-1976
                                Roxolana Lisovsky     03-Jun-2004
****************************     --------------------
Total Count                                   5
```

That's all there is to it. It wouldn't be a big leap to turn this report into a master/detail report with each section starting on a new page. Using this technique, you can develop similar reports with any number of sections you need.

CHAPTER 8
Writing SQL*Plus Scripts

In the previous chapter, you saw how to write a script to produce a report. This chapter delves more deeply into the subject of scripting, and shows you how to write interactive scripts. You will learn how to use *substitution variables*, which allow you to supply values dynamically to a script at runtime. You will learn how to prompt the user for those values and how to display other messages for the user to see. Finally, you will learn how to package your script for easy access when you need it.

Why Write Scripts?

The most compelling reason to write scripts, in my mind, is to encapsulate knowledge. Suppose, for example, that you have developed a query that returns index definitions for a table. You certainly don't want to have to think through the entire process of developing that query each time you need to see an index. If you have a good script available, you just run it. Likewise, if someone asks you how to see index definitions for a table, you can give them a copy of the script.

Another reason for developing scripts is that they save time and effort, making it easy to run a series of commands repeatedly. Look at the script in Example 5-5 used to produce the Project Hours and Dollars Report. It contains 16 commands, some quite long. Who wants to retype all that each time they generate a report? I sure don't, do you?

Finally, scripts can simplify tasks for you and others. When you know you have a good, reliable script, you can run it, answer the questions, and sit back while it does all the work. You don't need to worry, thinking "Did I enter the correct command?" "Did I log on as the correct user?" "Did I get that query just right?"

Any time you find yourself performing a task repeatedly, think about writing a script to do it for you. You'll save yourself time. You'll save yourself stress. You'll be able to share your knowledge more easily.

Using Substitution Variables

Substitution variables allow you to write generic SQL*Plus scripts. They let you mark places in a script where you want to substitute values at runtime.

What Is a Substitution Variable?

A substitution variable is not like a true variable used in a programming language. Instead, substitution variables mark places in the text where SQL*Plus does the equivalent of search and replace at runtime, replacing the reference to a substitution variable with its value.

Substitution variables are set off in the text of a script by preceding them with one or two ampersand characters. Say, for example, you had this query to list all projects to which employee 107 had charged time:

```
SELECT DISTINCT p.project_id, p.project_name
FROM project p INNER JOIN project_hours ph
    ON p.project_id = ph.project_id
WHERE ph.employee_id = 107;
```

This query is specific to employee number 107. To run the query for a different employee, you would need to edit your script file, change the ID number, save the file, and then execute it. That's a pain. You don't want to do that. Instead, you can generalize the script by rewriting the SELECT statement with a substitution variable in place of the employee ID number. That script might look like this:

```
SELECT DISTINCT p.project_id, p.project_name
FROM project p INNER JOIN project_hours ph
    ON p.project_id = ph.project_id
WHERE ph.employee_id = &employee_id;
```

The ampersand in front of &employee_id marks it as a variable. At runtime, when it reads the statement, SQL*Plus sees the substitution variable and replaces it with the current value of that variable. If employee_id contains a value of 104, then &employee_id is replaced by "104", and the resulting line looks like this:

```
WHERE ph.employee_id = 104
```

As I said earlier, and as you can see, SQL*Plus does a search-and-replace operation. The Oracle database doesn't know that a variable has been used. Nor does SQL*Plus compare the contents of the employee_id column against the value of the variable. SQL*Plus does the equivalent of a search-and-replace operation on each statement before that statement is executed. As far as the Oracle database is concerned, you might as well have included constants in your script.

Substitution variables are the workhorse of SQL*Plus scripts. They give you a place to store user input, and they give you a way to use that input in SQL queries, PL/SQL code blocks, and other SQL*Plus commands.

Using Single-Ampersand Variables

The easiest way to generalize a script is to take one you have working for a specific case and modify it by replacing specific values with substitution variables. In this section, we will revisit the Project Hours and Dollars Detail report shown in Example 7-2. You will see how you can modify the script to print the report for one employee, and you will see how you can use a substitution variable to generalize that script by making it prompt for the employee ID number at runtime.

 When SQL*Plus encounters a variable with a single leading ampersand, it always prompts you for a value. This is true even when you use the same variable multiple times in your script. If you use it twice, you will be prompted twice. Double-ampersand variables allow you to prompt a user only once for a given value and are explained later in this chapter.

The report for one specific employee

The report from Example 7-2 produced detailed hours and dollars information for all employees. To reduce the scope to one employee (e.g., employee 107), you can add this line as the WHERE clause in the report's underlying query:

```
WHERE e.employee_id = 107
```

Example 8-1 shows the resulting script, to which I've added a SPOOL command to write the report output to a file.

Example 8-1. Using a substitution variable to mark a user-supplied value

```
SET ECHO OFF
SET RECSEP OFF
```

Example 8-1. Using a substitution variable to mark a user-supplied value (continued)

```
--Set up pagesize parameters
SET NEWPAGE 1
SET PAGESIZE 55
--Set the linesize, which must match the number of equals signs used
--for the ruling lines in the headers and footers.
SET LINESIZE 66

--Set up page headings and footings
TTITLE CENTER "The Fictional Company" SKIP 3 -
       LEFT "I.S. Department" -
       RIGHT "Project Hours and Dollars Detail" SKIP 1 -
       LEFT "========================================" -
            "=========================" -
       SKIP 2 "Employee: " FORMAT 9999 emp_id_var " " emp_name_var SKIP 3

BTITLE LEFT "========================================" -
            "=========================" -
       SKIP 1 -
       RIGHT "Page " FORMAT 999 SQL.PNO

--Format the columns
COLUMN employee_id NEW_VALUE emp_id_var NOPRINT
COLUMN employee_name NEW_VALUE emp_name_var NOPRINT
COLUMN project_id HEADING "Proj ID" FORMAT 9999
COLUMN project_name HEADING "Project Name" FORMAT A26 WORD_WRAPPED
COLUMN time_log_date HEADING "Date" FORMAT A11
COLUMN hours_logged HEADING "Hours" FORMAT 9,999
COLUMN dollars_charged HEADING "Dollars|Charged" FORMAT $999,999.99

--Breaks and computations
BREAK ON employee_id SKIP PAGE NODUPLICATES -
      ON employee_name NODUPLICATES -
      ON project_id SKIP 2 NODUPLICATES -
      ON project_name NODUPLICATES

COMPUTE SUM LABEL 'Totals' OF hours_logged ON project_id
COMPUTE SUM LABEL 'Totals' OF dollars_charged ON project_id
COMPUTE SUM LABEL 'Totals' OF hours_logged ON employee_id
COMPUTE SUM LABEL 'Totals' OF dollars_charged ON employee_id

--Execute the query to generate the report.
SPOOL ex8-1.lst
SELECT e.employee_id,
       e.employee_name,
       p.project_id,
       p.project_name,
       TO_CHAR(ph.time_log_date,'dd-Mon-yyyy') time_log_date,
       ph.hours_logged,
       ph.dollars_charged
  FROM employee e INNER JOIN project_hours ph
       ON e.employee_id = ph.employee_id
       INNER JOIN project p
```

Example 8-1. Using a substitution variable to mark a user-supplied value (continued)

```
       ON p.project_id = ph.project_id
WHERE e.employee_id = 107
ORDER BY e.employee_id, p.project_id, ph.time_log_date;
SPOOL OFF
EXIT
```

Running the script in Example 8-1 will produce a report specifically for employee 107:

```
                        The Fictional Company


I.S. Department                     Project Hours and Dollars Detail
===================================================================

Employee:   107 Lesia Ukrainka


                                                         Dollars
Proj ID Project Name               Date         Hours    Charged
------- -------------------------- -----------  ------  -----------
   1001 Corporate Web Site         02-Jan-2004      1       $45.00
                                   02-Mar-2004      3      $135.00
                                   02-May-2004      5      $225.00
...
```

The next step is to generalize the script to make it usable for any employee.

Generalizing the report with substitution variables

You don't want to modify your script every time you need to produce a report for a different employee, and you don't have to. Instead, you can replace the reference to a specific employee number with a substitution variable and let SQL*Plus prompt you for a value at runtime. Here's how the affected line of script looks with a substitution variable instead of a hardcoded value:

```
WHERE e.employee_id = &employee_id
```

The variable name should be descriptive, and it needs to serve two purposes. It needs to inform the user and you. First and foremost, the variable name is used in the prompt and must convey to the user the specific information needed. In this case, using &id for the variable would leave the user wondering whether to enter an employee ID or a project ID. The use of &employee_id clarifies the answer. The second thing to keep in mind is that you will need to look at the script again someday, so make sure the name is something that will jog your memory as well.

Running the report

In the examples for this book, the modified report script can be found in *ex8-1b.sql*. When you run the report, SQL*Plus will prompt you to provide a value for the

&employee_id substitution variable. Here's how the script execution and prompt will look:

```
oracle@gennick02:~/sqlplus/ExampleScripts> sqlplus gennick/secret @ex8-1b

SQL*Plus: Release 10.1.0.2.0 - Production on Sun Jun 27 22:53:12 2004

Copyright (c) 1982, 2004, Oracle.  All rights reserved.


Connected to:
Oracle Database 10g Enterprise Edition Release 10.1.0.2.0 - Production
With the Partitioning, OLAP and Data Mining options

Enter value for employee_id: 108
```

As commands are executed, SQL*Plus constantly looks for the ampersand character, indicating a substitution variable. When an ampersand is encountered, the next token in the command is treated as a variable. SQL*Plus first looks to see if that variable has been previously defined. In this example it hasn't, so SQL*Plus automatically prompts for the value.

> Be sure to run the examples in this chapter using command-line SQL*Plus. Many commands, notably SPOOL and SET NEWPAGE, are not available in iSQL*Plus, so these scripts that function perfectly well in the command-line environment will fail in the web environment.

After prompting for a value and substituting it into the script in place of the corresponding variable, SQL*Plus displays the old and the new versions of the particular line of script involved. During development, this aids you in verifying that your script is executing correctly. Here are the before and after versions of the line containing the &employee_id variable from the current example:

```
old  12: WHERE e.employee_id = &employee_id
new  12: WHERE e.employee_id = 108
```

Next, SQL*Plus goes on to read the remaining lines from the script, producing the following hours and dollars report for Pavlo Chubynsky.

```
                 The Fictional Company



I.S. Department                     Project Hours and Dollars Detail
====================================================================

Employee:   108 Pavlo Chubynsky


                                                       Dollars
Proj ID Project Name              Date       Hours     Charged
------- ------------------------- ----------- ------ ------------
```

```
1001 Corporate Web Site          01-Jan-2004     1       $220.00
                                 01-Mar-2004     3       $660.00
                                 01-May-2004     5     $1,100.00
                                 01-Jul-2004     7     $1,540.00
                                 01-Sep-2004     1       $220.00
                                 01-Nov-2004     3       $660.00
   ****** *************************           ------  ------------
   Totals                                       20     $4,400.00
   ...
```

In addition to being displayed on the screen, the report is spooled to the *ex8-1b.lst* file, as specified in the script.

When TERMOUT is off

In the example just shown, the report was displayed on the screen and spooled to a file. In Chapter 5 you saw how the SET TERMOUT OFF command could be used to suppress output to the display while allowing it to be spooled, thus making a report run much faster. Doing the same thing in this case presents a special problem. The problem is that the command SET TERMOUT OFF must precede the SELECT statement that generates the report, so terminal output is off by the time SQL*Plus reads the line containing the substitution variable. SQL*Plus does not handle this situation well. You won't see a prompt for the substitution variable because terminal output is off, but SQL*Plus will still be waiting for you to type in a value. Your session will appear to be hung.

Using the example scripts, you can demonstrate the problem of an apparent hung session by executing script *ex8-1c.sql*:

    sqlplus *username*/*password* @ex8-1c

SQL*Plus will display the normal messages about the release of SQL*Plus and the release of the database to which you are connected. And that's it. SQL*Plus will be awaiting your input, but you'll never see a prompt.

There is a solution to this problem. The solution is to use the ACCEPT command to explicitly prompt the user for the employee ID prior to issuing the SET TERMOUT OFF command. You will see how to do this later in the section titled "Prompting for Values."

Using Double-Ampersand Variables

Using a double ampersand in front of a substitution variable tells SQL*Plus to define that variable for the duration of the session. This is useful when you need to reference a variable several times in one script because you usually don't want to prompt the user separately for each occurrence.

An example that prompts twice for the same value

Take a look at the script in Example 8-2, which displays information about a table followed by a list of all indexes defined on the table.

Example 8-2. Prompting twice for the same substitution variable

```
SET HEADING OFF
SET RECSEP OFF
SET NEWPAGE 1

COLUMN index_name FORMAT A30 NEW_VALUE index_name_var NOPRINT
COLUMN uniqueness FORMAT A6 NEW_VALUE uniqueness_var NOPRINT
COLUMN tablespace_name FORMAT A30 NEW_VALUE tablespace_name_var NOPRINT
COLUMN column_name FORMAT A30

BREAK ON index_name SKIP PAGE on column_header NODUPLICATES

TTITLE uniqueness_var ' INDEX: ' index_name_var -
       SKIP 1 '  TABLESPACE: ' tablespace_name_var -
       SKIP 1

DESCRIBE &table_name
SELECT ui.index_name,
       ui.tablespace_name,
       DECODE(ui.uniqueness,'UNIQUE','UNIQUE','       ') uniqueness,
       '    COLUMNS:' column_header,
       uic.column_name
  FROM user_indexes ui,
       user_ind_columns uic
 WHERE ui.index_name = uic.index_name
   AND ui.table_name = UPPER('&table_name')
ORDER BY ui.index_name, uic.column_position;

TTITLE OFF
SET HEADING ON
SET RECSEP WRAPPED
CLEAR BREAKS
CLEAR COLUMNS
```

Example 8-2 uses &table_name twice, once in the DESCRIBE command that lists the columns for the table and once in the SELECT statement that returns information about the table's indexes. When you run this script, SQL*Plus will issue separate prompts for each occurrence of &table_name. The first prompt will occur when SQL*Plus hits the DESCRIBE command:

```
SQL> @ex8-2
Enter value for table_name: project_hours
 Name                                      Null?    Type
 ----------------------------------------- -------- ------------------
 PROJECT_ID                                NOT NULL NUMBER(4)
 EMPLOYEE_ID                               NOT NULL NUMBER
 TIME_LOG_DATE                             NOT NULL DATE
```

```
HOURS_LOGGED                                  NUMBER(5,2)
DOLLARS_CHARGED                               NUMBER(8,2)
```

Because only a single ampersand was used in the script, the value entered is used for that one specific instance. It is not saved for future reference. The result is that next time SQL*Plus encounters &table_name, it must prompt again, this time for the table name to use in the SELECT statement:

```
Enter value for table_name: project_hours
old   9:    AND ui.table_name = UPPER('&table_name')
new   9:    AND ui.table_name = UPPER('project_hours')
```

Notice that SQL*Plus only displays before and after images of a line containing substitution variables when that line is part of an SQL statement. When the DESCRIBE command was read, the script prompted for a table name, and the substitution was made, but the old and new versions of the command were not shown.

The remaining output from the script, showing the index defined on the project_hours table, looks like this:

```
UNIQUE INDEX: PROJECT_HOURS_PK
  TABLESPACE: USERS
     COLUMNS: PROJECT_ID
              EMPLOYEE_ID
              TIME_LOG_DATE
```

A modified example that prompts once

Obviously there's room for improvement here. You don't want to type in the same value over and over just because it's used more than once in a script. Aside from being inconvenient, doing so introduces the real possibility that you won't get it the same each time. One way to approach this problem is to use a double ampersand the first time you reference the table_name variable in the script. Thus, the DESCRIBE command becomes:

```
DESCRIBE &&table_name
```

The only difference between using a double ampersand rather than a single ampersand is that when a double ampersand is used, SQL*Plus saves the value. All subsequent references to the same variable use that same value. It doesn't matter if subsequent references use a double ampersand or a single ampersand. Once the table_name variable has been defined this way, any other reference to &table_name or &&table_name will be replaced with the defined value.

 Execute *ex8-2b.sql* to see the behavior when using a double ampersand. Otherwise, the script is the same as *ex8-2.sql*.

You will be prompted only once for the table name, as the following output shows:

```
SQL> @ex8-2b
Enter value for table_name: project_hours
```

```
Name                                    Null?     Type
------------------------------------    --------  ----------------------------
PROJECT_ID                              NOT NULL  NUMBER(4)
EMPLOYEE_ID                             NOT NULL  NUMBER
TIME_LOG_DATE                           NOT NULL  DATE
HOURS_LOGGED                                      NUMBER(5,2)
DOLLARS_CHARGED                                   NUMBER(8,2)

old   9:    AND ui.table_name = UPPER('&table_name')
new   9:    AND ui.table_name = UPPER('project_hours')

UNIQUE INDEX: PROJECT_HOURS_PK
   TABLESPACE: USERS
      COLUMNS: PROJECT_ID
               EMPLOYEE_ID
               TIME_LOG_DATE
```

A final caveat

If you run the *ex8-2b.sql* script again, you won't be prompted for a table name at all.
Instead, the value entered earlier will be reused, and you will again see information
about the project_hours table and its indexes. The reason for this is that once you
define a variable, that definition sticks around until you exit SQL*Plus or explicitly
undefine the variable.

 You can undefine the table_name variable by placing the following
command at the end of the script:

```
UNDEFINE table_name
```

The version of the script in *ex8-2c.sql* has this command.

Because variable definitions persist after a script has ended, it's usually best to explicitly prompt a user for input rather than depend on SQL*Plus to do it for you. The
ACCEPT command is used for this purpose and is described in the next section. At
the very least, you should UNDEFINE variables at the end of a script so they won't
inadvertently be reused later.

Prompting for Values

The most reliable and robust method for getting input from the user is to prompt for
values using the ACCEPT and PROMPT commands. The ACCEPT command takes
input from the user and stores it in a user variable and allows you some control over
what the user enters. The PROMPT command may be used to display messages to the
user, perhaps supplying a short summary of what your script is going to accomplish.

Several potential problems arise when you place substitution variables in your scripts
and rely on SQL*Plus's default prompting mechanisms. All of these problems can be
avoided through the use of the ACCEPT command. Table 8-1 provides a list of these

Numeric Substitution Variables

SQL*Plus supports four datatypes for substitution variables: CHAR, NUMBER, BINARY_FLOAT, and BINARY_DOUBLE. You can enter only character or CHAR values. You can't use any commands to create a substitution variable of the other types However, you can create one indirectly by using NEW_VALUE to capture a numeric value returned by a query:

```
SQL> COLUMN x NEW_VALUE my_age
SQL> SELECT 42 x FROM dual;

         X
----------
        42

SQL> DEFINE my_age

DEFINE MY_AGE          =          42 (NUMBER)
```

Because numeric values are captured as NUMBERs, you can format those values using SQL*Plus's number-formatting features. You aren't limited by any kind of number-to-character conversion done by the database. The following TTITLE example formats the same value two different ways:

```
ttitle LEFT FORMAT 99 my_age FORMAT 99.99 my_age
```

This page title will contain the string "42" followed by "42.00".

problems, along with a description of how the ACCEPT and PROMPT commands can be used to overcome them.

*Table 8-1. Potential problems with SQL*Plus's default prompting*

Potential problem	Solution
Using double ampersands to define a variable in a script results in your not being prompted for a value the second time you run the script.	Use the ACCEPT command to prompt for a value. This works regardless of whether the variable has previously been defined.
Setting terminal output off, such as when spooling a report to a file, prevents you from seeing the prompts for substitution variables used in the query.	Use the ACCEPT command to prompt for these values earlier in the script, before the SET TERMOUT OFF command is executed.
The default prompt provided by SQL*Plus consists of little more than the variable name.	Use the ACCEPT command to specify your own prompt. For longer explanations, the PROMPT command may be used.

This section shows how to enhance the index listing script in Example 8-2 by using the PROMPT and ACCEPT commands. Use the PROMPT command to better explain what the script is doing and the ACCEPT command to prompt the user for the table name.

The ACCEPT Command

The ACCEPT command allows you to obtain input from the user. With it, you specify a user variable and text for a prompt. ACCEPT displays the prompt for the user, waits for the user to respond, and assigns the user's response to the variable.

 The syntax for the ACCEPT command has evolved significantly from the early days of SQL*Plus. The syntax shown in this chapter is valid for Version 8.1 and higher. Not all of the clauses are available when using prior versions. Check your documentation if you are writing scripts that need to work under earlier versions of SQL*Plus.

You can make Example 8-2's script more reliable by using ACCEPT to get the table name from the user. This ensures that the user is prompted for a table name each time the script is run. The following ACCEPT command should do the trick:

```
ACCEPT table_name CHAR PROMPT 'Enter the table name >'
```

A good place to add the command would be prior to the COLUMN commands, resulting in the new script shown in Example 8-3.

Example 8-3. Using ACCEPT to receive user input

```
SET HEADING OFF
SET RECSEP OFF
SET NEWPAGE 1

ACCEPT table_name CHAR PROMPT 'Enter the table name >'

COLUMN index_name FORMAT A30 NEW_VALUE index_name_var NOPRINT
COLUMN uniqueness FORMAT A6 NEW_VALUE uniqueness_var NOPRINT
COLUMN tablespace_name FORMAT A30 NEW_VALUE tablespace_name_var NOPRINT
COLUMN column_name FORMAT A30

BREAK ON index_name SKIP PAGE on column_header NODUPLICATES

TTITLE uniqueness_var ' INDEX: ' index_name_var -
    SKIP 1 '  TABLESPACE: ' tablespace_name_var -
    SKIP 1

DESCRIBE &&table_name
SELECT ui.index_name,
    ui.tablespace_name,
    DECODE(ui.uniqueness,'UNIQUE','UNIQUE','       ') uniqueness,
    '     COLUMNS:' column_header,
    uic.column_name
  FROM user_indexes ui,
    user_ind_columns uic
 WHERE ui.index_name = uic.index_name
   AND ui.table_name = UPPER('&table_name')
ORDER BY ui.index_name, uic.column_position;
```

Example 8-3. Using ACCEPT to receive user input (continued)

```
TTITLE OFF
SET HEADING ON
SET RECSEP WRAPPED
CLEAR BREAKS
CLEAR COLUMNS
```

It doesn't really matter now whether the script uses &table_name or &&table_name for the substitution variable. Either will work well, and the script in Example 8-3 uses both. When you run the script, here's how the prompt will look:

```
SQL> @ex8-3
Enter the table name >
```

You can run this script many times in succession, and you will be prompted for a different table name each time. In addition, the prompt is a bit more user-friendly than the default prompt generated by SQL*Plus.

The PROMPT Command

The PROMPT command allows you to print text on the display for the user to read. PROMPT lets you provide informative descriptions of what a script is about to do. Use it to provide long and detailed prompts for information or add blank lines to the output to space things out a bit better. Any substitution variables in the prompt text are replaced by their respective values before the text is displayed.

> If you are spooling output to a file when a PROMPT command is executed, the prompt text will be written to the file.

Using PROMPT to summarize the script

It would be nice to add some messages to Example 8-3 to make the script more self-explanatory to the user. You can do that by adding the following PROMPT commands to the beginning of the script:

```
PROMPT
PROMPT This script will first DESCRIBE a table. Then
PROMPT it will list the definitions for all indexes
PROMPT on that table.
PROMPT
```

The first and last PROMPT commands space the output better by adding a blank line above and below the description.

Using PROMPT to explain the output

You can use the PROMPT command to explain the output of a script better. Appropriate messages can be added prior to the DESCRIBE command and the SELECT statement. The relevant part of the resulting script is shown in Example 8-4.

Example 8-4. Using PROMPT to better explain a script

```
...
PROMPT
PROMPT &table_name table definition:
PROMPT
DESCRIBE &&table_name

PROMPT
PROMPT Indexes defined on the &table_name table:
PROMPT
SELECT ui.index_name,
...
```

Following is the result of executing the script with all the PROMPT commands added. The messages not only make the output more clear, but they space it out better as well.

```
SQL> @ex8-4

This script will first DESCRIBE a table. Then
it will list the definitions for all indexes
on that table.

Enter the table name >project_hours

project_hours table definition:

Name                                    Null?    Type
--------------------------------------- -------- ---------------------------
PROJECT_ID                              NOT NULL NUMBER(4)
EMPLOYEE_ID                             NOT NULL NUMBER
TIME_LOG_DATE                           NOT NULL DATE
HOURS_LOGGED                                     NUMBER(5,2)
DOLLARS_CHARGED                                  NUMBER(8,2)


Indexes defined on the project_hours table:

old   9:    AND ui.table_name = UPPER('&table_name')
new   9:    AND ui.table_name = UPPER('project_hours')

UNIQUE INDEX: PROJECT_HOURS_PK
   TABLESPACE: USERS
      COLUMNS: PROJECT_ID
               EMPLOYEE_ID
               TIME_LOG_DATE
```

Cleaning Up the Display

As you've followed the development of the index listing script, you no doubt saw the following lines interspersed in the output:

```
old   9:    AND ui.table_name = UPPER('&table_name')
new   9:    AND ui.table_name = UPPER('project_hours')
```

If you happened to execute the script against a table with more than a few indexed columns, you would have seen a message such as the following:

```
...
6 rows selected.
```

These lines add no value to running the script and serve only to clutter the output. It would be nice to get rid of them, and it is possible to do that by turning verification and feedback off. The commands to do that are described next.

Turning Off Verification

Verification refers to what SQL*Plus does when it encounters a line of script containing substitution variables. By default, SQL*Plus enables you to verify the substitution by displaying the old and the new versions of the line involved. The output from verification looks like this:

```
old   9:    AND ui.table_name = UPPER('&table_name')
new   9:    AND ui.table_name = UPPER('project_hours')
```

Sometimes it's useful to see these before and after images, especially when you are first developing a script, because they let you verify if your substitutions are being made correctly. Once you've developed a script, it's nice to be able to turn this output off, and you can do that by adding the following command to your script:

```
SET VERIFY OFF
```

Turning verification off makes your output a lot cleaner and is helpful if the script is a report that may be run by an end user.

Turning Off Feedback

Feedback refers to the short messages that SQL*Plus displays after executing a SQL statement such as SELECT or COMMIT. Feedback looks like this:

```
6 rows selected.
```

Or, in the case of a COMMIT, it looks like this:

```
Commit complete.
```

As with verification, feedback can clutter the output from a script. The extra lines added by feedback are sometimes enough to scroll output that you want to see off the top of the display, which can be a bit annoying.

You can turn feedback off by adding the following line to your scripts:

```
SET FEEDBACK OFF
```

You may want to turn feedback back on at the end of the script. Use SET FEEDBACK ON for this purpose, so that you get the normal feedback messages when executing interactive commands.

 You'll find a modified version of Example 8-4 in the file *ex8-4b.sql*. This modified version has the additional commands SET VERIFY OFF and SET FEEDBACK OFF.

Turning Off Command Echoing

The echo setting controls whether commands from script files are displayed to the screen as they are executed. Normally off by default, command echoing can be a useful debugging tool. To turn echo on, use the following command:

```
SET ECHO ON
```

Now, when you execute a script, such as *ex8-4b.sql*, all the commands are echoed to the display as they are executed. Here's how that would look:

```
SQL> set echo on
SQL> @ex8-4b
SQL> PROMPT

SQL> PROMPT This script will first DESCRIBE a table. Then
This script will first DESCRIBE a table. Then
SQL> PROMPT it will list the definitions for all indexes
it will list the definitions for all indexes
SQL> PROMPT on that table.
on that table.
SQL> PROMPT

SQL>
SQL> SET HEADING OFF
SQL> SET RECSEP OFF
SQL> SET NEWPAGE 1
SQL> SET VERIFY OFF
SQL> SET FEEDBACK OFF
SQL>
SQL> ACCEPT table_name CHAR PROMPT 'Enter the table name >'
Enter the table name >
...
```

As you can see, echoing is something you usually want turned off. As a safety measure, I often include SET ECHO OFF in my script files to avoid accidentally being deluged by output. The one case where I always turn on echoing is when I build a script file containing DDL commands. If I run a script to create tables, indexes, or some other object, I generally like to see what is happening when I run it.

When running a script to create or otherwise manage database objects such as tables and indexes, it's helpful to SET ECHO ON and spool the resulting output to a file. Then you can review the output later to check for problems.

Turning Off All Terminal Output

Turning off the display output completely is helpful sometimes. You've seen this done in Chapter 5; there, I modified the script to produce the Project Hours and Dollars Report so it would spool the output to a file. Usually, you want to turn off the display when you are spooling a report to a file, or when you are extracting data to a file. You may not want to look at all the data scrolling by on the screen, and turning off the display can accelerate things. The command to turn off terminal output is SET TERMOUT OFF. To turn output back on again, use SET TERMOUT ON. When using these commands, you usually want to bracket the SQL query that produces the report, as shown here:

```
SET TERMOUT OFF
SELECT P.PROJECT_ID,
       P.PROJECT_NAME
       FROM PROJECT P;
SET TERMOUT ON
```

When using the Windows GUI version of SQL*Plus, disabling the display can make a dramatic difference in report performance. The difference is less pronounced in command-line SQL*Plus.

 Any attempt to SET TERMOUT OFF is ignored when you issue the command from the interactive SQL*Plus prompt. You can only disable terminal output from within a script.

Executing a Script

Once you've written a script, you can invoke it in different ways. One option is to invoke it interactively from the SQL*Plus prompt, a technique you've already seen used in previous examples. You do this using the @ command. To run the script *ex8-4b.sql*, you write an @ symbol followed immediately by the filename of the script you wish to execute:

```
SQL> @ex8-4b
```

The *.sql* extension is optional and is assumed unless you specify otherwise.

Usually, you write scripts so you can invoke them automatically. To that end, you should know how to invoke them from your operating system command line. In addition, under Windows, you can package a script in a way that lets you easily

---

invoke it by double-clicking an icon. Finally, *i*SQL*Plus enables you to invoke scripts via the Internet.

Invoking a Script from the Command Line

To execute a script from your operating system command line, use the following syntax:

```
sqlplus username/password @script_name
```

To pass arguments to your script, include them after the script name. Enclose parameters containing whitespace within quotes. If you have any doubts as to whether to use quotes, then use them:

```
sqlplus username/password @script_name arg "arg" ...
```

If you are connecting to a remote database, you must also specify the net service name for that database:

```
sqlplus username/password@service_name script_name
```

Net service names are often defined by your DBA in a file named *tnsnames.ora* but may be defined in an LDAP directory. If you have any doubts about what *service_name* to use, ask your DBA. You may also use the easy connection identifier syntax described in Chapter 2.

 Be sure that any script you invoke from the command line ends with an EXIT command. If you omit EXIT, your command-line session will remain in SQL*Plus, at the SQL> prompt.

If you're invoking a SQL*Plus script from within another program, you may wish to use the *silent mode* to prevent any trace of SQL*Plus from showing through to your users. When you run in silent mode, all prompts and startup messages are suppressed, and command echoing does not occur. Invoke SQL*Plus in silent mode by using the *-S* (or *-s*) option:

```
sqlplus -s username...
```

Ideally, you should avoid embedding Oracle passwords within scripts that invoke SQL*Plus. To that end, you can avoid the need to specify an Oracle password on the SQL*Plus command line by taking advantage of Oracle's operating system authentication feature. See the sidebar "Running SQL*Plus Reports from Shell Scripts" in Chapter 5.

Early versions of SQL*Plus on Windows used names other than *sqlplus* for the SQL*Plus executable. For example, in Oracle7 Release 7.3 for Windows, you had *plus23* and *plus23w*, depending on whether you wanted to invoke command-line SQL*Plus or the Windows GUI version. The changing version numbers embedded in these names were a constant source of frustration. Thankfully, Oracle stopped embedding version numbers in their Windows executable names when Oracle8*i* Database was released.

Accessing Command-Line Arguments

You can access command-line arguments using the special substitution variables &1, &2, &3, etc. The first command-line argument is &1, and the rest are numbered in the order they occur. A sometimes useful technique is to issue PROMPT commands to remind the user of the arguments:

```
PROMPT Script arguments:
PROMPT 1 - Schema name
PROMPT 2 - Table name
DESCRIBE &1..&2
```

This script is meant to be run as follows:

```
@describe gennick employee
```

If you omit the arguments, the PROMPTs will remind you of what the arguments should be. Then, SQL*Plus will automatically prompt you for the undefined substitution variables:

```
SQL> @describe
Script arguments:
1 - Schema name
2 - Table name
Enter value for 1:
```

Like any other substitution variable, any values you supply for &1, &2, etc., will linger for the duration of your SQL*Plus session or until you remove them using the UNDEFINE command.

Specifying a Search Path for Scripts

If you have collections of scripts in different directories, you can specify a search path that SQL*Plus will use to find those scripts. This saves you from the bother of having to type a directory path each time you invoke a script.

Use the SQLPATH environment variable to specify a search path. From Unix and Linux shells, you must separate the directory names using colons, and you usually set environment variables using the *export* command:

```
export SQLPATH=$HOME/sqlplus/ExampleData:$HOME/sqlplus/ExampleScripts
```

What Type of Slash?

Unix requires a forward slash in directory paths, while Windows uses a backward slash. What do you do when you want to write a script that runs on both platforms? It turns out that on Windows you can use either type of slash. For example, on Windows you can use either of the following commands to invoke a script within a subdirectory of your current working directory:

```
@@subdir/new_script
```

If you're writing scripts that you may need to run on both platforms, use a forward slash all the time.

On Windows systems, use the SET command and separate paths by semicolons:

```
set SQLPATH=c:\sqlplus\ExampleData;c:\sqlplus\ExampleScripts
```

When you execute a script using the @ command, SQL*Plus will always look for that script in your current working directory first. Then, it will search the directories specified by SQLPATH, in the order in which they occur.

SQL*Plus on Unix and Linux systems will also search any directories specified by the ORACLE_PATH environment variable. However, SQLPATH directories will be searched first. On VMS systems, you specify the SQL*Plus search path using the ORA_PATH logical name.

Placing SQL*Plus Commands into a Shell Script

On Unix and Linux systems, it's unnecessary to run all scripts from *.sql* files. You can invoke SQL*Plus from within a shell script and redirect standard input to that same script, which will cause SQL*Plus to read subsequent lines in the shell script as if they were typed in from the command line. Example 8-5 illustrates this, showing a shell script that invokes SQL*Plus to execute a MERGE statement that loads new and updated project data from an external table named project_external.

*Example 8-5. SQL*Plus commands embedded directly in a Linux shell script*

```
sqlplus gennick/secret << EOF
SET VERIFY OFF

MERGE INTO project p
USING (SELECT * FROM project_external) pe
ON (p.project_id = pe.project_id)
WHEN MATCHED THEN UPDATE
   /* update budget in an existing project record */
   SET p.project_budget = pe.project_budget
WHEN NOT MATCHED THEN INSERT
   /* insert a new project record */
```

Example 8-5. SQL*Plus commands embedded directly in a Linux shell script (continued)

```
(project_id, project_name, project_budget)
VALUES (pe.project_id, pe.project_name, pe.project_budget);

COMMIT;
EOF
```

There are several important aspects of this script:

`sqlplus gennick/secret << EOF`

The `<< EOF` causes the Unix (or Linux) shell to pass subsequent lines in the shell script to SQL*Plus as input. As far as SQL*Plus is concerned, it's as if you typed those lines yourself interactively from a `SQL>` prompt.

`MERGE INTO project p`

MERGE is a SQL statement that will do an INSERT or an UPDATE depending upon whether a condition that you specify is true.

`ON (p.project_id = pe.project_id)`

This is the condition. When the value of `project_id` from the external table matches an existing `project_id` in the `project` table, the existing row will be updated with (potentially) new information. Otherwise, if no match occurs, a new row will be inserted into `project`.

`WHEN MATCHED THEN UPDATE`

You don't need to update all columns. Example 8-5 updates only the project budget.

`WHEN NOT MATCHED THEN INSERT`

However, if a new project is loaded, then all three values are inserted.

`EOF`

This EOF marker in the shell script has meaning to the shell, not to SQL*Plus. When the shell sees this, it stops passing lines of input to SQL*Plus. This marker must match that used following the `<<` on the line originally invoking SQL*Plus.

 Depending on the shell you are using, you may be able to use arbitrary markers, such as JGG instead of EOF, as long as you are consistent and use the same marker in both places.

The ability to embed SQL*Plus commands within a shell script can sometimes save you from having to create two files. Rather than write a shell script for the sole purpose of running a separate SQL*Plus script, you can combine both into one. Be aware though, that reading SQL*Plus commands that are embedded within a shell script is semantically not quite the same as executing a separate *.sql* file. SQL*Plus sees those lines as interactive input, and in at least one situation the difference is significant: You can't, for example, SET TERMOUT OFF in a shell script because

SQL*Plus refuses to disable terminal output when it's executing interactively. A SET TERMOUT OFF command in Example 8-5 would be ignored.

Creating a Windows Shortcut

Under Windows, it's possible to create an icon or a shortcut that can be used to invoke a SQL*Plus script. Add to that some good prompting and a bit of error checking, and you can write SQL*Plus scripts that are accessible to end users or at least to your more technically inclined end users.

You need to make two decisions if you are going to create an icon or shortcut to execute a script. One is whether to embed the Oracle username and password into the shortcut or to prompt the user for this information. The second is which version of SQL*Plus you want to use: the GUI version or the DOS version.

Both of these decisions affect the command used by the shortcut to invoke SQL*Plus and start the script. Your job is easiest if you can embed an Oracle username and password into the shortcut. However, it's far safer to prompt for at least the password. You want to avoid embedding a password in a Windows shortcut definition where any user of the system can see it.

For purposes of example, let's assume you are going to create a Windows shortcut to run the Project Hours and Dollars Report shown earlier in Example 8-1.

Starting the SQL*Plus executable

The Windows version of Oracle contains two SQL*Plus executables. Use *sqlplus* to start the command-line version. Use *sqlplusw* to start the GUI version. Before you can create the shortcut, you need to decide on the exact command you will use to start SQL*Plus. Here are two possibilities to consider:

```
sqlplus username@service_name @c:\a\ex8-2
```

```
sqlplus /nolog @c:\a\ex8-2
```

The first option provides SQL*Plus with a username but not a password. Consequently, SQL*Plus will prompt the user for a password. This option works well if you know the username up front and if your users will only log in with that one username. To provide more flexibility, use the second option, which requires that your script prompts for username and password. The second option is the one I'll use in this chapter's example.

When you start up SQL*Plus with the /NOLOG option, your script must log into a database before it executes any SQL statements. Use the CONNECT command to do this, and use substitution variables to allow the user to enter her username and password at runtime. Example 8-6 shows a new version of the script from Example 8-1. This script uses two ACCEPT commands and one CONNECT command to prompt for a username and password and then to log the user into Oracle. The script executes

SET TERMOUT OFF to save the user from having to watch the output scroll by on the screen. Finally, report output is spooled to a file named *ex8-6.lst* in the *c:\a* directory (one I commonly use for scratch files on Windows systems).

Example 8-6. A script that explicitly prompts for username and password

```
SET ECHO OFF
SET RECSEP OFF

ACCEPT username CHAR PROMPT 'Enter your Oracle username >'
ACCEPT password CHAR PROMPT 'Enter your password >'
CONNECT &username/&password@db01

--Set up pagesize parameters
SET NEWPAGE 1
SET PAGESIZE 55
--Set the linesize, which must match the number of equals signs used
--for the ruling lines in the headers and footers.
SET LINESIZE 66

--Set up page headings and footings
TTITLE CENTER "The Fictional Company" SKIP 3 -
       LEFT "I.S. Department" -
       RIGHT "Project Hours and Dollars Detail" SKIP 1 -
       LEFT "=======================================" -
            "===========================" -
       SKIP 2 "Employee: " FORMAT 9999 emp_id_var " " emp_name_var SKIP 3

BTITLE LEFT "=======================================" -
            "===========================" -
       SKIP 1 -
       RIGHT "Page " FORMAT 999 SQL.PNO

--Format the columns
COLUMN employee_id NEW_VALUE emp_id_var NOPRINT
COLUMN employee_name NEW_VALUE emp_name_var NOPRINT
COLUMN project_id HEADING "Proj ID" FORMAT 9999
COLUMN project_name HEADING "Project Name" FORMAT A26 WORD_WRAPPED
COLUMN time_log_date HEADING "Date" FORMAT A11
COLUMN hours_logged HEADING "Hours" FORMAT 9,999
COLUMN dollars_charged HEADING "Dollars|Charged" FORMAT $999,999.99

--Breaks and computations
BREAK ON employee_id SKIP PAGE NODUPLICATES -
      ON employee_name NODUPLICATES -
      ON project_id SKIP 2 NODUPLICATES -
      ON project_name NODUPLICATES

COMPUTE SUM LABEL 'Totals' OF hours_logged ON project_id
COMPUTE SUM LABEL 'Totals' OF dollars_charged ON project_id
COMPUTE SUM LABEL 'Totals' OF hours_logged ON employee_id
COMPUTE SUM LABEL 'Totals' OF dollars_charged ON employee_id
```

Example 8-6. A script that explicitly prompts for username and password (continued)

```
--Execute the query to generate the report.
SET TERMOUT OFF
SPOOL c:\a\ex8-6.lst
SELECT e.employee_id,
       e.employee_name,
       p.project_id,
       p.project_name,
       TO_CHAR(ph.time_log_date,'dd-Mon-yyyy') time_log_date,
       ph.hours_logged,
       ph.dollars_charged
  FROM employee e INNER JOIN project_hours ph
       ON e.employee_id = ph.employee_id
       INNER JOIN project p
       ON p.project_id = ph.project_id
WHERE e.employee_id = 107
ORDER BY e.employee_id, p.project_id, ph.time_log_date;
SPOOL OFF
EXIT
```

Once you have decided how to start SQL*Plus and which version to run, you are ready to create a Windows shortcut to run your script.

Creating the shortcut

To create a Windows shortcut, right-click on the Windows desktop and select New → Shortcut from the pop-up menu. Type the command to start SQL*Plus and execute your script in the location (or command) field. For example, if your command is `sqlplusw /nolog @c:\a\ex8-6`, the resulting screen should look like that shown in Figure 8-1.

Press the Next button to advance to the next step in which you select a name for the shortcut. Be sure to pick a name that makes sense, one that will remind you later of what the script does. For this example, use the name "Project Hours and Dollars Report." Figure 8-2 shows this screen after the name has been entered.

Finally, press the Finish button. The shortcut will be created and will appear on your desktop. If you've specified command-line SQL*Plus (*sqlplus*), the icon will be a generic application icon. If you've specified Windows GUI SQL*Plus (*sqlplusw*), the icon will be drawn from the associated executable and will be the familiar disk platter with a plus on top. Both icons are shown in Figure 8-3.

Now you can run the script. Double-click the icon and try it.

Executing a Script Over the Internet

Oracle9i Database introduced the exciting capability of invoking SQL*Plus scripts over the Internet. Rather than specifying the name of a script file on your local filesystem, you can specify the name of a script file accessible via a web server. Oracle9i Database

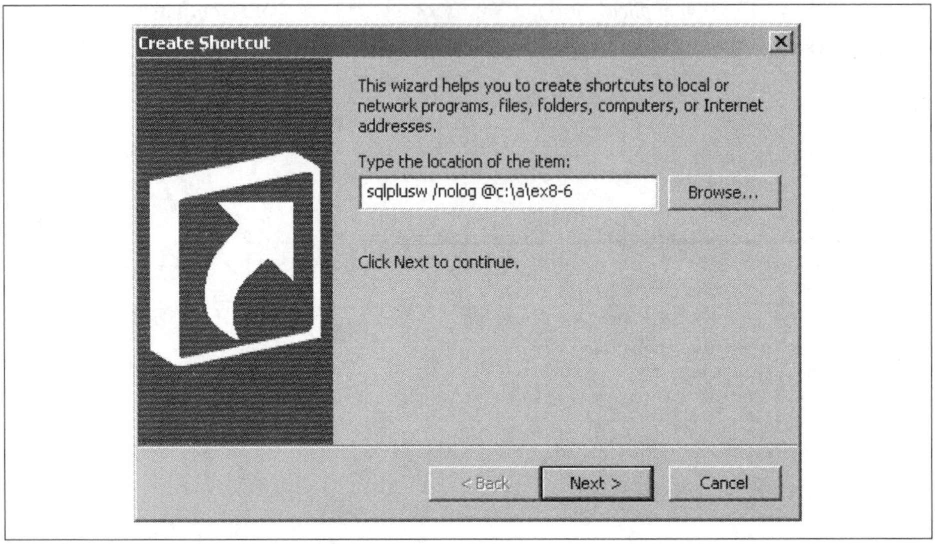

Figure 8-1. The Windows shortcut wizard

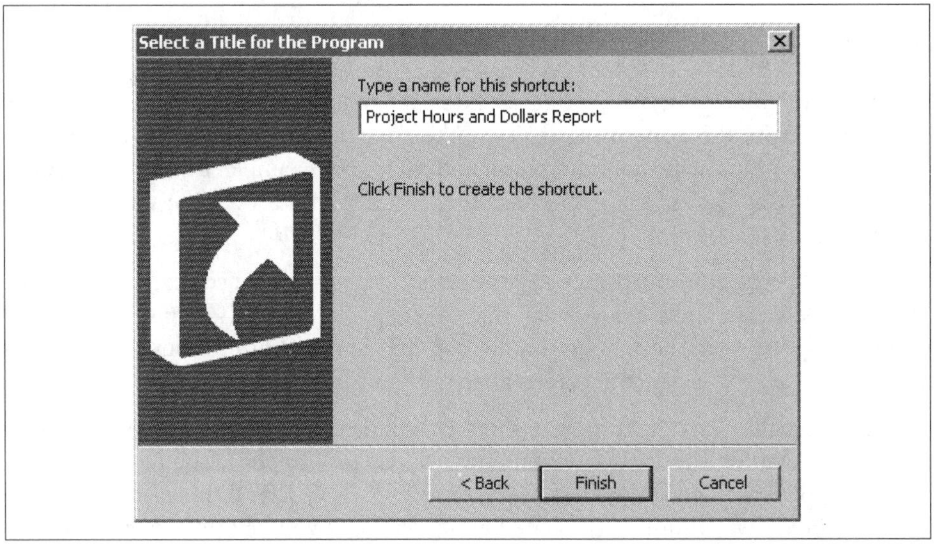

Figure 8-2. Naming the shortcut

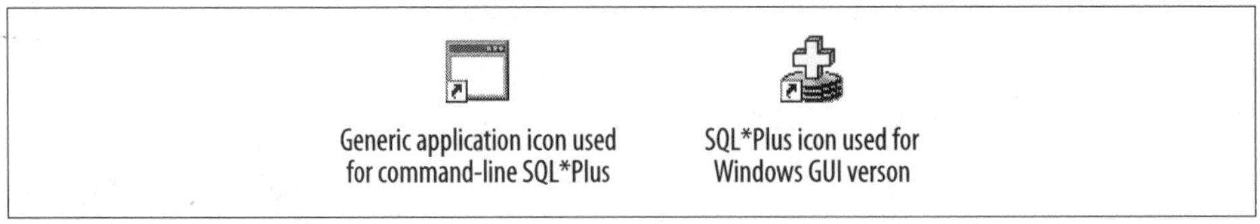

Generic application icon used
for command-line SQL*Plus

SQL*Plus icon used for
Windows GUI verson

Figure 8-3. The shortcut icon

Release 1 introduced this functionality to SQL*Plus on Windows. Release 2 brought the capability to all platforms.

To invoke a script over the Internet, simply specify a URL following the @ command. The following example invokes a version of Example 8-4 from my own web site:

```
SQL> @http://gennick.com/sqlplus/ex8-4b

This script will first DESCRIBE a table. Then
it will list the definitions for all indexes
on that table.

Enter the table name >
```

This is an incredible boon. No longer must you manually cart your library of scripts from server to server, trying vainly to keep all copies of a script in sync. Place your utility scripts on a web server, and you can easily access them from any Oracle server or client connected to the Internet.

Controlling Variable Substitution

As you use SQL*Plus, two problems may arise concerning the use of substitution variables. The first problem you are likely to encounter is that you will need to use an ampersand somewhere in your script, and you won't mean for it to be part of a substitution variable name. This common problem happens most often when you're using an ampersand in a quoted string or as part of a comment.

The second problem, which you may never encounter, is that you may want to place a substitution variable smack in the middle of a word. This is a less common problem.

SQL*Plus provides several ways to deal with these problems. A special escape character can be used whenever you need to place an ampersand in your script and have it stay there. A concatenation character is provided for those unusual cases where you want to place a substitution variable at the beginning or middle of a word. You can change the substitution character entirely if you don't like using the ampersand and want to use some other character instead. Finally, if you aren't really into writing scripts, you can turn the substitution feature completely off. Then you won't have to worry about it at all.

The Escape Character

The escape character preceding an ampersand tells SQL*Plus to leave it alone and that it is not part of a substitution variable. Consider the following DEFINE command:

```
DEFINE friends = "Joe & Matt"
```

If you executed that command, SQL*Plus would interpret "& Matt" as a substitution variable and would prompt you to supply a value. The result would look like this:

```
SQL> DEFINE friends = "Joe & Matt"
Enter value for matt:
```

That's not the behavior you want, yet the ampersand is legitimately part of the string, so what do you do? One solution is to precede the ampersand character with a backslash, which is the default SQL*Plus escape character, like this:

```
DEFINE friends = "Joe \& Matt"
```

However, the escape feature is not on by default. In order for this approach to work, you must enable the escape feature.

Enabling the escape feature

By default, SQL*Plus doesn't check for escape characters when looking for substitution variables. You must turn on this feature before you use it. The command to do that is:

```
SET ESCAPE ON
```

Once turned on, this setting remains in effect until you turn it off again, or until you exit SQL*Plus.

Escaping an ampersand

Now that the escape feature has been turned on, you can place a backslash in front of any ampersand characters you need to embed in your script. The following is a modified version of the previous example that correctly assigns the text "Joe & Matt" to the friends variable:

```
SQL> SET ESCAPE ON
SQL> DEFINE friends = "Joe \& Matt"
```

You can see the current value of the variable by issuing the DEFINE command followed by the variable name:

```
SQL> DEFINE friends
DEFINE FRIENDS         = "Joe & Matt" (CHAR)
```

Because of the preceding backslash, SQL*Plus leaves the ampersand alone, and the friends variable is created containing the desired text.

One thing to keep in mind when you have the escape feature turned on is that you must escape the escape character itself when you need to use it as part of your script. For example, to define a string containing one backslash, you must double the backslash character as shown in the following code:

```
SQL> DEFINE backslash = "\\"
SQL> DEFINE backslash
DEFINE BACKSLASH       = "\" (CHAR)
```

If you are using the backslash a lot, and this causes you problems or becomes cumbersome, you can change the escape character to something else.

Changing the escape character

If you don't like using the backslash as the escape character, you can use the SET ESCAPE command to specify a different character more to your liking. The following command changes the escape character to be a forward slash:

```
SET ESCAPE /
```

Changing the escape character also turns the escape feature on. There is no need to subsequently issue a SET ESCAPE ON command.

 Any time you issue the SET ESCAPE ON command, the escape character is reset to the default backslash. This is true even if the escape feature was on to begin with.

The Concatenation Character

There may come a time when you want to use a substitution variable in a situation where the end of the variable name is not clear. Consider the following code example:

```
DEFINE sql_type = "PL/"
PROMPT &sql_typeSQL
```

The intent is to have SQL*Plus print the text "PL/SQL", but SQL*Plus won't substitute "PL/" in place of "&sql_type". Instead, it will interpret the entire string of "&sql_typeSQL" as a variable.

You can get around this problem by using the SQL*Plus concatenation character. The period is the default concatenation character, and it explicitly tells SQL*Plus where a variable name ends. The following code example shows the concatenation character being used to make the substitution work as intended:

```
SQL> DEFINE sql_type = "PL/"
SQL> PROMPT &sql_type.SQL
PL/SQL
```

Turning off the concatenation feature

By default, the concatenation feature is always on. SQL*Plus looks for the period immediately following any substitution variables encountered in the script. If you need to, you can turn this feature off with the following command:

```
SET CONCAT OFF
```

It's usually not necessary to turn this feature off. You would only need to do it if you were using periods after your substitution variables and you didn't want those periods to disappear from your script.

Changing the concatenation character

The default concatenation character can cause a problem if you intend to use a substitution variable at the end of a sentence. The problem is that the period at the end of the sentence will go away because SQL*Plus sees it as the concatenation character ending the variable name. Here's an example:

```
SQL> DEFINE last_word = 'period'
SQL> PROMPT This sentence has no &last_word.
This sentence has no period
```

There are only three ways to deal with this problem. One is to turn the concatenation feature off. Another is to change it to something other than a period. The following command changes the concatenation character to an exclamation point:

```
SET CONCAT !
```

Now you can execute the example again, and the period at the end of the sentence shows up as expected:

```
SQL> DEFINE last_word = 'period'
SQL> PROMPT This sentence has no &last_word.
This sentence has no period.
```

As with the SET ESCAPE command, using SET CONCAT to change the concatenation character turns the feature on.

You can also put two periods at the end of the line, one to end the substitution variable and one to end the sentence:

```
SQL> PROMPT This sentence has no &last_word..
```

So long as concatenation is enabled, only one period will actually display.

Enabling and Disabling Substitution

Sometimes it's easier to turn substitution completely off rather than worry about how you use ampersand and escape characters in your scripts. You can turn variable substitution completely off with this command:

```
SET DEFINE OFF
```

To reenable substitution, simply issue:

```
SET DEFINE ON
```

If you have a large block of script that doesn't reference any variables, you can toggle substitution off just for that block and turn it on again afterward:

```
...
SET DEFINE OFF              Toggle substitution off for the next few commands.
...
Portion of script that doesn't reference
substitution variables goes here.
...
```

```
SET DEFINE ON          Toggle substitution back on when needed again.
...
```

Changing the Substitution Variable Prefix Character

If you don't like prefixing your substitution variables with an ampersand, or if you need to use ampersands in your script, you can tell SQL*Plus to use a different character for substitution. You can pick any character you like, but it should be something that stands out.

The following command changes the substitution variable prefix character to a caret:

```
SET DEFINE "^"
```

Changing the substitution character can be a handy thing to do if you need to use ampersands in a lot of text constants or if, like me, you tend to use them often in comments. The following code illustrates how to change from an ampersand to a caret and back again:

```
SQL> DEFINE message = "Brighten the corner where you are."
SQL> SET DEFINE ^
SQL> PROMPT &message
&message
SQL> PROMPT ^message
Brighten the corner where you are.
SQL> SET DEFINE &
SQL> PROMPT &message
Brighten the corner where you are.
SQL> PROMPT ^message
^message
```

Another way to reset the substitution character back to the default ampersand is to issue the SET DEFINE ON command. A side effect of issuing SET DEFINE ON is that the substitution character resets to the default. This is true regardless of whether substitution is currently on or off.

Commenting Your Scripts

If you write extensive scripts, you should write extensive comments. In fact, any time you write a script, no matter how short, consider including a few comments to explain the purpose of the script.

Comments may be placed in a script using any of the following three methods:

- By using the REMARK command
- By using double-hyphen characters
- By delimiting the comment by /* and */

Each method works a bit differently from the others. You will probably find yourself gravitating toward the /*...*/ and -- delimiters. I find typing REMARK to be a bit cumbersome.

The REMARK Command

The REMARK command may be used to place comments in a SQL script. Any text on the same line following the REMARK command is considered a comment. The REMARK command may be abbreviated to REM as the following example shows:

```
REMARK This is a comment.
REM This is a comment too.
```

SQL*Plus doesn't look for substitution variables in the text following a REMARK command, so you are free to use ampersands and any other characters you like in your comments.

The /* and */ Delimiters

The /* and */ delimiters are familiar to many programmers and may be used to delimit comments in SQL*Plus. Comments created using this method may span multiple lines:

```
/*
This is the second line of a comment.
This is the third line.
*/
```

You can use /* and */ to add comments to SQL statements or to PL/SQL blocks. When you do this, such comments are not recognized by SQL*Plus, but rather by the database engine. Such comments may appear anywhere within a SQL statement:

```
SELECT *
  FROM employee
 WHERE /* employees are current */
       SYSDATE BETWEEN employee_hire_date
                   AND nvl(employee_termination_date,SYSDATE);
```

SQL*Plus objects to comments that appear following the beginning of a SQL*Plus command:

```
SQL> DESCRIBE /* Is this a comment? */ employee
SP2-0565: Illegal identifier.
```

When commenting SQL*Plus commands, be sure to comment entire commands. Don't add trailing comments to a command, and don't add comments in the middle of a command.

Double Hyphens (- -)

Double hyphens may be used to delimit comments in much the same manner as the REMARK command. Anything following the double hyphen is considered a comment. Here are some examples:

```
--Describe the employee table
DESCRIBE employee
--Select all currently employed people.
SELECT *
  FROM employee
 WHERE -- employees are current
       SYSDATE BETWEEN employee_hire_date
                  AND NVL(employee_termination_date,SYSDATE);
```

Don't use double hyphens to place comments at the end of a SQL*Plus command. For example, the following command fails:

```
SQL> DESCRIBE employee --Is this a comment?
Usage: DESCRIBE [schema.]object[@db_link]
```

As with /*...*/, the double hyphen may be used to embed comments within SQL statements and PL/SQL blocks. The only difference is that double hyphen comments cannot span lines. Within SQL and PL/SQL, you may use -- to place comments at the end of a statement.

Substitution Within Comments

SQL*Plus doesn't normally check comments for substitution variables, but the rules change when comments are embedded in a SQL query or a PL/SQL block. Thus, you can enter the following comment, and SQL*Plus won't treat &var as a substitution variable:

```
--In this comment, &var is not a substition variable.
```

However, if you enter a similar comment as part of a SQL statement, SQL*Plus will see &var as a substitution variable:

```
SQL> SELECT *
  2 FROM employee
  3      --Now, &var is treated as a substitution variable.
  4 WHERE employee_termination_date IS NULL;
Enter value for var:
```

The reason for this seemingly inconsistent behavior is that SQL*Plus doesn't parse your SQL statements; instead, SQL statements are sent to the database engine. As soon as SQL*Plus sees that you have begun to type in a SQL statement or a PL/SQL block, it stops parsing and accepts whatever text you enter into the buffer. Before the contents of the buffer are sent to Oracle, SQL*Plus must replace any substitution variables with their contents. In doing this, it simply scans the entire buffer, including any comments it contains.

Substitution is never an issue with the REMARK command because REMARK is a SQL*Plus command and can never be used in a SQL query.

Resetting Your SQL*Plus Environment

If you are running scripts interactively, the SET commands that you execute in one script can adversely affect the operation of subsequent scripts. For example, you might SET PAGESIZE 0 to disable pagination, only to execute a report script later for which you *want* pagination.

Example 8-7 shows a simple, data-extraction script that sets PAGESIZE to zero in order to avoid writing column headings to the output file. Example 8-8 shows an even simpler report generation script. Example 8-9 shows the results of running these scripts interactively, from one session of SQL*Plus. The first time the report is run, the page title prints. But not the second time. Why not? It's because the effects of the SET PAGESIZE 0 command executed by *ex8-7.sql* linger on for the duration of the session. The effects of SET FEEDBACK OFF linger, too.

Example 8-7. A script that disables pagination as a side effect

```
SET PAGESIZE 0
SET FEEDBACK OFF

SPOOL ex8-7.lst
SELECT project_name
FROM project;
SPOOL OFF
```

Example 8-8. A report generation script that requires pagination

```
TTITLE LEFT "Corporate Project Listing" SKIP 2

SELECT * FROM project;
```

Example 8-9. A demonstration of SET command side effects

```
SQL> @ex8-8

Corporate Project Listing

PROJECT_ID PROJECT_NAME                                    PROJECT_BUDGET
---------- ------------------------------------------- --------------
      1001 Corporate Web Site                                  1912000
      1002 Enterprise Resource Planning System                 9999999
      1003 Accounting System Implementation                     897000
      1004 Data Warehouse Maintenance                           290000
      1005 VPN Implementation                                   415000
      1006 Security Audit                                        99.95
```

Example 8-9. A demonstration of SET command side effects (continued)

```
6 rows selected.

SQL> @ex8-7
Corporate Web Site
Enterprise Resource Planning System
Accounting System Implementation
Data Warehouse Maintenance
VPN Implementation
Security Audit
SQL> @ex8-8
        1001 Corporate Web Site                          1912000
        1002 Enterprise Resource Planning System         9999999
        1003 Accounting System Implementation             897000
        1004 Data Warehouse Maintenance                   290000
        1005 VPN Implementation                           415000
        1006 Security Audit                                99.95
```

One solution to this problem of SET commands from one script interfering with another is to use the STORE SET command to save your current settings at the beginning of a script so you can restore them later. Example 8-10 is a revamped version of Example 8-7 that does just that.

Example 8-10. A script that resets all SET options to their original state

```
STORE SET original_settings REPLACE
SET PAGESIZE 0
SET FEEDBACK OFF

SPOOL ex8-10.lst
SELECT project_name
FROM project;
SPOOL OFF
@original_settings
```

The STORE SET command in Example 8-10 generates a file of SET commands reflecting all current settings. Those SET commands are written to the file *original_settings.sql*. If the file exists, it is replaced. Settings can be freely changed, and the last thing the script does before it ends is to restore the original settings by executing *original_settings.sql*.

I don't much like the STORE SET approach. It's a bit of a hack, and if concurrent users are executing the same script in the same working directory, they will overwrite each other's STORE SET files. On Windows, your current working directory when running the Windows GUI version of SQL*Plus will likely be *$ORACLE_HOME/bin*, and who wants to clutter up that critical directory with such files? I'd prefer some sort of stack mechanism, whereby you could push and pop your settings (to and from memory, not disk) at the beginning and ending of a script. Even better would be if that pushing and popping could be done automatically, perhaps via a new variation on the @ command. For now though, if you need to save and restore settings from a script, STORE SET is your only choice.

Scripting Issues with iSQL*Plus

Using *iSQL*Plus, you can execute your scripts via its browser interface. However, there are differences between command-line SQL*Plus and browser-based SQL*Plus, and not all scripts can be made to execute in both environments.

One issue that you encounter is spool files. Browser-based SQL*Plus runs on an application server. For reasons of security, *iSQL*Plus doesn't allow you to write files to that server. Thus, you cannot spool output. After all, *iSQL*Plus can hardly spool output through your browser to a file on your PC. The only way to capture output is to copy and paste it from your browser window to a file, and that's only feasible for small amounts of data.

Copying *iSQL*Plus output from a browser window and pasting it into another application works best after you issue SET MARKUP HTML ON PREFORMAT ON. Otherwise, you'll be trying to copy an HTML table rather than the output that you desire.

Another problem you'll encounter when executing scripts from *iSQL*Plus is that many SQL*Plus commands are not supported by *iSQL*Plus. These include commands such as HOST that would present a security risk by letting you access the application server at the operating system level, and commands such as EDIT that don't apply in a browser-based environment.

The EDIT command isn't implemented in *iSQL*Plus because your script is sitting in an easily edited text box on your browser page.

Figure 8-4 shows the prompt that you'll receive when you execute *ex8-4b.sql* from *iSQL*Plus (by issuing the command @http://gennick.com/sqlplus/ex8-4b). The prompt is the result of the same ACCEPT command that you saw in Example 8-4. Each ACCEPT command, and each prompt that SQL*Plus generates automatically in response to a script's use of a substitution variable, results in a separate HTML form to which you must respond by typing in a value and clicking Continue.

Figure 8-5 shows a portion of the output after I supplied "employee" as the table name and clicked Continue. Even this relatively benign script has a problem with a command not supported by *iSQL*Plus. You can see the error message resulting from my use of SET NEWPAGE 1. Fortunately, the script continues to execute despite the one, invalid command, and you can see the description of the employee table, formatted into an HTML table, following the error message.

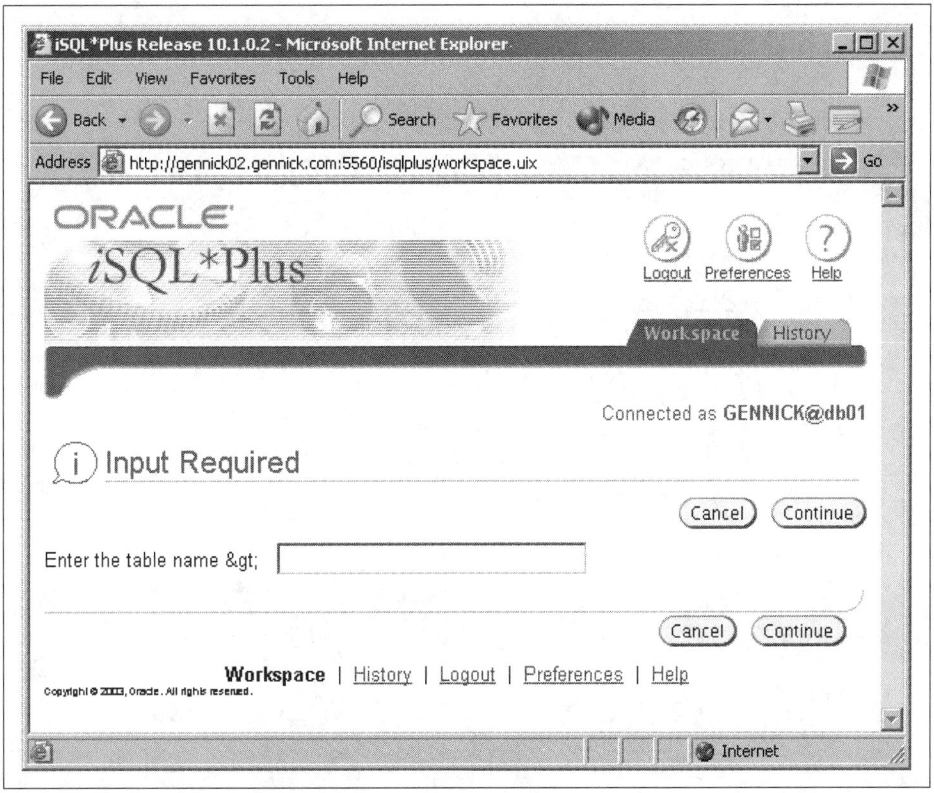

![iSQL*Plus Release 10.1.0.2 - Microsoft Internet Explorer browser window showing the iSQL*Plus workspace with an "Input Required" prompt. Address bar reads http://gennick02.gennick.com:5560/isqlplus/workspace.uix. Connected as GENNICK@db01. The prompt reads "Enter the table name >" with a text input field and Cancel/Continue buttons.]

*Figure 8-4. An iSQL*Plus prompt in response to an ACCEPT command*

> The command reference in Appendix A indicates which commands are not allowed in *i*SQL*Plus.

*i*SQL*Plus is a wonderful thing, but its browser-based interface seems better suited to running interactive commands. If you need to run scripts, and especially when you wish to schedule those scripts using *cron* or some other scheduling software, stick to command-line SQL*Plus.

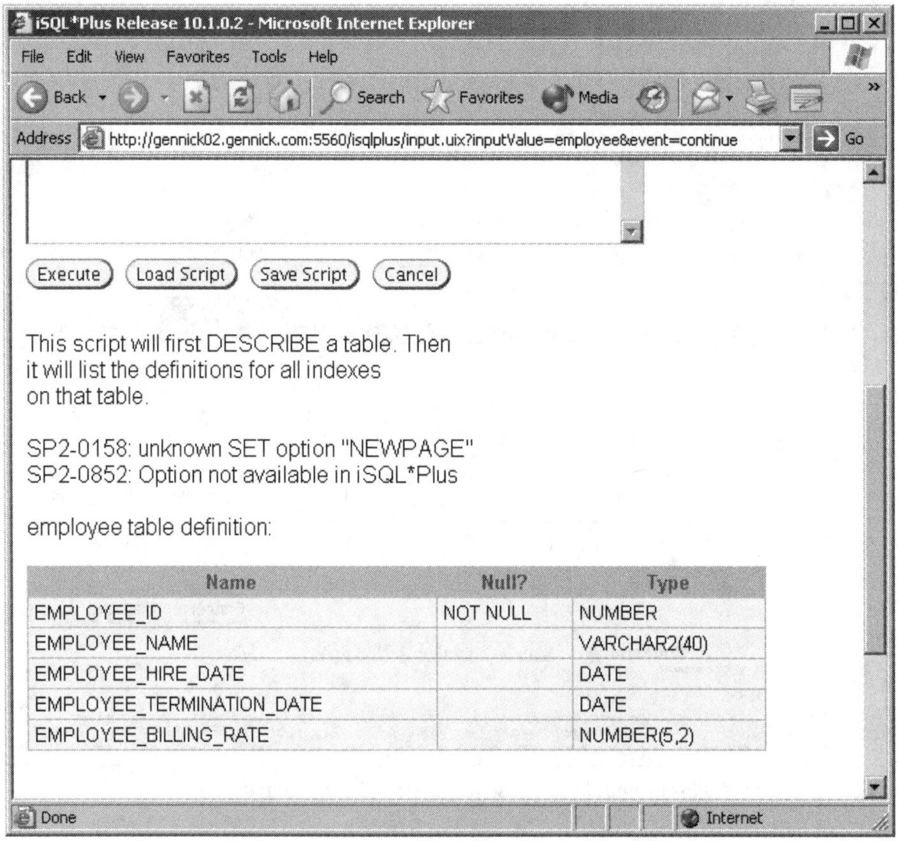

Figure 8-5. An error from executing a command not supported by iSQL*Plus

The window shows the iSQL*Plus browser interface with the following content:

Title bar: iSQL*Plus Release 10.1.0.2 - Microsoft Internet Explorer

Address: http://gennick02.gennick.com:5560/isqlplus/input.uix?inputValue=employee&event=continue

Buttons: Execute Load Script Save Script Cancel

This script will first DESCRIBE a table. Then
it will list the definitions for all indexes
on that table.

SP2-0158: unknown SET option "NEWPAGE"
SP2-0852: Option not available in iSQL*Plus

employee table definition:

Name	Null?	Type
EMPLOYEE_ID	NOT NULL	NUMBER
EMPLOYEE_NAME		VARCHAR2(40)
EMPLOYEE_HIRE_DATE		DATE
EMPLOYEE_TERMINATION_DATE		DATE
EMPLOYEE_BILLING_RATE		NUMBER(5,2)

Extracting and Loading Data

You can use SQL*Plus to extract data from Oracle for use in a spreadsheet or some other application. The need to do this is so common that it's a wonder Oracle doesn't supply an application specifically for that purpose. Unfortunately, the company doesn't. Oracle does provide SQL*Loader, a utility that can load data into Oracle from almost any form of flat file, but there is no corresponding SQL*Unloader.

> Oracle's new, built-in, web development environment, HTML DB, does have some built-in data-unloading capabilities that may be worth investigating if you need that sort of thing.

Oracle does, however, provide SQL*Plus. Even though SQL*Plus is not a generic data extraction utility, you can extract numeric, date, and text data to a flat file through the creative use of SQL and SQL*Plus's formatting options. Depending on your needs, you can format the file as a comma-delimited file or a tab-delimited file, or you can format the data in fixed-width columns. Comma-delimited files are most useful if you are transferring data to a spreadsheet such as Lotus 1-2-3 or a desktop database such Microsoft Access. Fixed-width, columnar datafiles are often used to transfer data to legacy applications.

In addition to extracting data, you can get more creative and use SQL*Plus to generate a script file containing SQL statements. This is referred to as "using SQL to write SQL." You can do something as simple as generating a flat file of INSERT statements to be used in recreating the data at another site, or you can generate a file of data definition language (DDL) statements to modify your own database. I've even seen people use SQL*Plus to generate operating system shell scripts to use in modifying and maintaining their database.

In this chapter, I will walk you through the process of writing a script to extract data from the sample database into a flat file. You will see how SQL can be written to produce a comma-delimited text file, a fixed-width text file, or a file of INSERT statements. Once this is done, you will see how that same data can be loaded back into Oracle.

Types of Output Files

Generally speaking, you can produce four types of output files when extracting data with SQL*Plus:

- Delimited columns
- Fixed-width columns
- Data manipulation language (DML)
- Data definition language (DDL)

There may be variations on these types—delimited files, for example, can be tab-delimited or comma-delimited, and you may be able to dream up some novel format—but, generally speaking, these are the most useful.

Delimited Files

Delimited files use a special text character to separate each data value in a record. Typically, the delimiter is a tab or a comma, but any character may be used. Here's an example of a comma-delimited file containing employee information (ID, rate, hire date, and name):

```
101,169,"15-NOV-1961","Marusia Churai"
105,121,"15-JUN-2004","Mykola Leontovych"
107,45,"02-JAN-2004","Lesia Ukrainka"
```

This example illustrates a commonly used format called the Comma Separated Values (CSV) format. CSV-formatted files use commas to delimit the values, and they enclose text fields within quotes. The CSV format is recognized by most spreadsheets and desktop databases.

Fixed-Width Files

A fixed-width file contains data in columns, where each column is a certain width, and all values in that column are the same width. Here's an example of the same employee data shown earlier, but formatted into fixed-width columns:

```
10116915-NOV-1961Marusia Churai
10512115-JUN-2004Mykola Leontovych
10704502-JAN-2004Lesia Ukrainka
```

In this example, the columns abut each other with no space in between. If you don't want to match an existing file layout, you may prefer to allow at least one space between columns to aid readability.

DML Files

A DML file contains DML statements, such as INSERT, DELETE, UPDATE, and SELECT. This type of file can be used as a quick and dirty way of extracting data from one database for insertion into another. If you want to transfer data for the three employees from the preceding examples, your DML file would contain the following INSERTs:

```
INSERT INTO employee
    (employee_ID,employee_billing_rate,employee_hire_date,employee_name)
    VALUES (101,169,TO_DATE('15-Nov-1961','DD-MON-YYYY'),'Marusia Churai');
INSERT INTO employee
    (employee_ID,employee_billing_rate,employee_hire_date,employee_name)
    VALUES (105,121,TO_DATE('15-Jun-2004','DD-MON-YYYY'),'Mykola Leontovych');
INSERT INTO employee
    (employee_ID,employee_billing_rate,employee_hire_date,employee_name)
    VALUES (107,45,TO_DATE('02-Jan-2004','DD-MON-YYYY'),'Lesia Ukrainka');
```

You can generate these INSERT statements, based on existing data, using SQL*Plus and SQL. Then you can apply those inserts to another database. This may not seem to be the most efficient way of moving data around, but if you have low data volume, such as a few dozen records that you want to send off to a client, it works well.

DDL Files

A DDL file contains DDL statements. It's not much different from a DML file, except that the goal is to modify your database rather than to extract data for another application. Suppose, for example, that you need to create public synonyms for all your tables. You can use an SQL query to generate the needed CREATE PUBLIC SYNONYM statements, spool those to a file, and then execute that file. You will find a brief example showing how to do this later in this chapter. Chapter 10 explores this subject in greater depth.

Limitations of SQL*Plus

When using SQL*Plus to extract data, keep in mind some limitations. Because SQL*Plus was designed as a reporting tool and not a data extraction tool, the output must be text. If you need to write a file containing packed-decimal or binary data, SQL*Plus is not the tool to use.

A second SQL*Plus limitation you may encounter (but you probably won't) when extracting data is the line size. On many platforms, the upper limit for the SET LINE-SIZE command is 32,767 characters. Unless you want to deal with spreading data from one logical record over multiple, physical records, you'll need to keep your output line size at or under the maximum line size for your platform.

Finally, SQL*Plus was designed to work with traditional, scalar datatypes. If you're going to use SQL*Plus as an unloader, you'll find it works best for the following types of data:

- VARCHAR2
- NVARCHAR2
- NUMBER
- DATE
- ROWID
- CHAR
- NCHAR

These types can be converted to character strings, and you can concatenate those strings together to produce whatever output format you want, whether comma-delimited, tab-delimited, or fixed-width. Text is the key to extracting data with SQL*Plus. Think text. If you have nonalphanumeric data to extract, you should use a different tool.

Extracting the Data

To write a script to extract data from Oracle and place it in a flat file, follow these steps:

1. Formulate the query.
2. Format the data.
3. Spool the extract to a file.
4. Make the script user-friendly.

The last step, making the script user-friendly, isn't necessary for a one-off effort. However, if it's an extraction you are going to perform often, it's worth taking a bit of time to make it easy and convenient to use.

Formulate the Query

The first step in extracting data is to figure out what data you need to extract. You need to develop a SQL query that will return the data you need. To extract data for current employees, you could use a query such as in Example 9-1.

Example 9-1. A query to extract current employee data

```
SELECT employee_id,
       employee_billing_rate
       employee_hire_date,
       employee_name
```

Example 9-1. A query to extract current employee data (continued)

```
FROM employee
WHERE employee_termination_date IS NULL;
```

You can write queries that are more complicated than shown here. If necessary, you can join several tables together, or you can UNION several SELECT statements together.

Format the Data

The next step, once you have your query worked out, is to format the data to be extracted. The best way I've found to do this is to modify your query so it returns a single, long expression that combines the columns together in the format that you want in your output file. It's often necessary to include text literals in the SELECT statement as part of this expression. For example, if you want to produce a comma-delimited file, you will need to include those commas in your SELECT statement.

Be sure to keep in mind the ultimate destination of the data. If your purpose is to pull data for someone to load into a spreadsheet, you will probably want to use a comma-delimited format. If you are passing data to another application, you may find it easier to format the data in fixed-width columns. Dates require some extra thought. With Oracle's built-in TO_CHAR function, you can format a date any way you want. Be sure, however, to use a format easily recognized by the application that needs to read that date.

Comma-delimited

To produce a comma-delimited text file, you need to do two things. First, you need to add commas between each field. Second, you need to enclose text fields within quotes. Example 9-2 does both of these things, returning a single column of data that is derived from an expression combining the four columns being extracted.

Example 9-2. A SELECT statement that creates comma-delimited data

```
SELECT    TO_CHAR(employee_id) || ','
       || TO_CHAR(employee_billing_rate) || ','
       || TO_CHAR(employee_hire_date,'MM/DD/YYYY') || ','
       || '"' || employee_name || '"'
FROM employee
WHERE employee_termination_date IS NULL;
```

Here I use Oracle's TO_CHAR function to explicitly convert numeric fields to text strings. I also use TO_CHAR to convert date fields to text and include a date format string to get the dates into MM/DD/YYYY format. SQL's concatenation operator

(||) concatenates all the fields together into one long string, and you can see that commas are included between fields. The output from Example 9-2 looks like this:

```
101,169,11/15/1961,"Marusia Churai"
105,121,06/15/2004,"Mykola Leontovych"
107,45,01/02/2004,"Lesia Ukrainka"
111,100,08/23/1976,"Taras Shevchenko"
114,,07/05/2004,"Marusia Bohuslavka"
116,,07/05/2004,"Roxolana Lisovsky"
```

In addition to the commas, the employee_name field has been enclosed in quotes. This is done to accommodate the possibility that someone's name will contain a comma. Most commercial programs that load comma-delimited data will allow text strings to be optionally enclosed in quotes.

You can use the same technique to generate tab-delimited data. Instead of a comma, use CHR(9) to put a tab character between fields. CHR is an Oracle SQL function that converts an ASCII code into a character. ASCII uses the value 9 to represent a tab character.

Fixed-width

The easiest way to produce an output file with fixed-width columns is to use the SQL*Plus COLUMN command to format the output from a standard SQL query. Example 9-3 shows one way to dump the employee data in a fixed-width column format.

Example 9-3. A fixed-width data extract formatted via COLUMN commands

```
COLUMN employee_id FORMAT 099 HEADING ''
COLUMN employee_billing_rate FORMAT 099.99 HEADING ''
COLUMN employee_hire_date FORMAT A10 HEADING ''
COLUMN employee_name FORMAT A20 HEADING '' TRUNCATED
SELECT employee_id,
       employee_billing_rate,
       TO_CHAR(employee_hire_date, 'MM/DD/YYYY'),
       employee_name
FROM employee
WHERE employee_termination_date IS NULL;
```

Notice some things about the example:

- The heading for each column is explicitly set to a null string. This is important in the case of numeric columns because SQL*Plus implicitly makes the column wide enough to accommodate their heading. You don't want that behavior when unloading data. You want the format specification to control the column width.

- Both numeric fields have been formatted to show leading zeros. Most programs that read fixed-width data, such as COBOL programs, will expect this.

- The TRUNCATED option is used to format the employee_name field because employee_name can be up to 40 characters long in the database. If TRUNCATED were not specified, any names that happened to be longer than 20 characters would wrap to a second line, which is not what you want to happen in a flat file.

 Of course, you may prefer to allow for the entire 40 characters of the employee_name in your extract file. However, you won't always have control over the format of your extract files. Sometimes you'll be trying to match an existing format expected by some other system. If that's the case, you'll have to make compromises.

Here's how the output from Example 9-3 will look:

```
101  169.00 11/15/1961 Marusia Churai
105  121.00 06/15/2004 Mykola Leontovych
107  045.00 01/02/2004 Lesia Ukrainka
111  100.00 08/23/1976 Taras Shevchenko
114         07/05/2004 Marusia Bohuslavka
116         07/05/2004 Roxolana Lisovsky
```

Each column in the output is separated by one space because that's the SQL*Plus default. If you like, you can use the SET COLSEP command to change the number of spaces or eliminate them entirely. To run the columns together, you can eliminate the space between columns by setting the column separator to a null string:

```
SET COLSEP ""
```

Now the output will look like this:

```
101 169.0011/15/1961Marusia Churai
105 121.0006/15/2004Mykola Leontovych
107 045.0001/02/2004Lesia Ukrainka
111 100.0008/23/1976Taras Shevchenko
114         07/05/2004Marusia Bohuslavka
116         07/05/2004Roxolana Lisovsky
```

You can use any column separation string that you like, and you aren't limited to one character.

 Why are there still spaces in the output? They are there because SQL*Plus reserves one space for a potential negative sign at the beginning of any numeric column. Such spaces can be a problem when you're trying to match an existing format.

Example 9-4 dodges around the leading-space-for-a-sign problem by converting numbers to character strings in the SELECT statement (using TO_CHAR), and then by trimming any leading or trailing spaces (using TRIM). Column aliases in the SELECT statement specify names for the computed columns, which are seen by SQL*Plus as text columns. Thus, the corresponding COLUMN commands use the A format element.

Example 9-4. TO_CHAR and TRIM being used to generate "numbers" with no leading or trailing spaces

```
COLUMN employee_id FORMAT A3 HEADING ''
COLUMN employee_billing_rate FORMAT A6 HEADING ''
COLUMN employee_hire_date FORMAT A10 HEADING ''
COLUMN employee_name FORMAT A20 HEADING '' TRUNCATED
SELECT TRIM(TO_CHAR(employee_id,'099')) employee_id,
       TRIM(TO_CHAR(employee_billing_rate,'099.99')) employee_billing_rate,
       TO_CHAR(employee_hire_date, 'MM/DD/YYYY'),
       employee_name
FROM employee
WHERE employee_termination_date IS NULL;
```

Using SQL*Plus to format fixed-width output works best when you have some control over the format expected by the destination of those data. If you are writing the program to load the data somewhere else, of course you can code the data to match what you can produce with SQL*Plus. Sometimes, though, you need to match an existing format required by the destination, which is one you cannot change. Depending on your exact requirements, it may be easier to code one large expression in your SQL statement and use Oracle's built-in functions to gain more control over the output. Example 9-5 produces the same output as Example 9-4 through an expression that returns each line as a single, large text value.

Example 9-5. A single expression to return a line of columnar data

```
SELECT    TRIM(TO_CHAR(employee_id,'099'))
       || NVL(TRIM(TO_CHAR(employee_billing_rate,'099.99')),'       ')
       || NVL(TO_CHAR(employee_hire_date, 'MM/DD/YYYY'),'       ')
       || NVL(SUBSTR(RPAD(employee_name,20,' '),1,20),'                    ')
FROM employee
WHERE employee_termination_date IS NULL;
```

The output from Examples 9-4 and 9-5 appears as follows:

```
101169.0011/15/1961Marusia Churai
105121.0006/15/2004Mykola Leontovych
107045.0001/02/2004Lesia Ukrainka
111100.0008/23/1976Taras Shevchenko
114      07/05/2004Marusia Bohuslavka
116      07/05/2004Roxolana Lisovsky
```

Following are some key points about the SELECT statement in Example 9-5:

- The employee_billing_rate can be null, which would be treated as a zero-length string. When that's the case, NVL supplies an alternative value consisting of six spaces. This keeps the columns in proper alignment. Otherwise a null billing rate would cause the hire date to immediately follow the employee ID.

- Employee hire dates should never be null, but the table definition does allow them to be, so the same NVL technique is applied to the employee_hire_date column.

- To ensure a constant 20-character-wide `employee_name` column, a three-step process is used. Employee names are first right-padded (using RPAD) with enough spaces to create a 20-character-wide column. At that point, any name longer than 20 characters to begin with will still be longer than 20 characters. The SUBSTR function then returns only the first 20 characters of the padded name. Finally, the same NVL technique used for other columns protects against null employee names.
- A combination of TO_CHAR and TRIM is used to eliminate spaces on either side of numeric values, even those spaces reserved for negative signs. TO_CHAR converts numbers to strings, and TRIM removes any unwanted spaces.
- The format strings 099 and 099.99 are used to convert `employee_id` and `employee_billing_rate` to ensure that the resulting values are three and six characters wide respectively.

Many built-in Oracle functions are available. Add to that the ability to write your own, and you should be able to generate output in any conceivable format.

DML

If you are extracting data from Oracle to move it to another database, and if the volume of data isn't too high, you can use SQL*Plus to generate a file of INSERT statements. Example 9-6 shows a query to generate INSERT statements to recreate the same data you've seen extracted by Examples 9-1 through 9-5.

Example 9-6. A query to generate INSERT statements to recreate existing data

```
SELECT 'INSERT INTO employee' || chr(10)
    || '  (employee_id, employee_billing_rate,' || chr(10)
    || '   employee_hire_date, employee_name)' || chr(10)
    || 'VALUES (' || TO_CHAR(employee_id) || ',' || chr(10)
    || '        ' || NVL(TO_CHAR(employee_billing_rate),'NULL')
                  || ',' || chr(10)
    || CASE WHEN employee_hire_date IS NOT NULL then
            '        TO_DATE(''' || TO_CHAR(employee_hire_date,'MM/DD/YYYY')
            || ', ''MM/DD/YYYY'')' || chr(10)
       ELSE
            '        NULL' || chr(10)
       END
    || '        ''' || employee_name || ''');'
FROM employee
WHERE employee_termination_date IS NULL;
```

As you can see, this type of query can get a bit hairy. You have to deal with nested, quoted strings; you have to concatenate everything together; and you have to place line breaks so the output at least looks decent. The doubled-up quotation marks you see in the previous statement are there because single quotes are required in the final output. So, for example, the string `''MM/DD/YYYY''` resolves to `'MM/DD/YYYY'` when the SELECT statement is executed.

The SELECT statement from Example 9-6 produces INSERT statements such as the following:

```
...
INSERT INTO employee
  (employee_id, employee_billing_rate,
   employee_hire_date, employee_name)
VALUES (114,
        NULL,
        TO_DATE('07/05/2004, 'MM/DD/YYYY')
        'Marusia Bohuslavka');

INSERT INTO employee
  (employee_id, employee_billing_rate,
   employee_hire_date, employee_name)
VALUES (116,
        NULL,
        TO_DATE('07/05/2004, 'MM/DD/YYYY')
        'Roxolana Lisovsky');
```

Example 9-6 is further complicated by the need to deal with potential nulls. The example generates an NVL expression to deal with the potential null employee_billing_rate column. The employee_name column is easy because a null employee name will result in an empty string (i.e., '') in the resulting INSERT, and Oracle SQL treats an empty string as a null. Hardest to deal with is the employee_hire_date. For that column, Example 9-6 uses a CASE expression to detect whether the hire date is null and to write out a TO_DATE expression or the keyword NULL.

The technique in Example 9-6 is not one I use often because it can be frustrating to get the SQL just right. I use it most often on code tables and other small tables with two or three columns. I use it sometimes when I'm sending data to a client. That way I send only one file, and my client doesn't have to mess with SQL*Loader or Oracle's Import utility.

DDL

Another twist on using SQL to write SQL is to generate DDL statements that help you maintain your database. Using SQL*Plus to generate DDL scripts can help in automating many database administration tasks and is often well worth the effort. Example 9-7 shows a SELECT statement to generate CREATE PUBLIC SYNONYM statements for each table in the GENNICK schema.

Example 9-7. A script to query the data dictionary and generate DDL statements

```
SELECT 'CREATE PUBLIC SYNONYM ' || table_name
       || ' for ' || user || '.' || table_name || ';'
FROM DBA_TABLES
WHERE owner = 'GENNICK'
AND dropped = 'NO';
```

The two WHERE conditions in Example 9-7 have the following purposes:

WHERE owner = 'GENNICK'

Historically, Oracle has treated schemas and users synonymously. In many, if not in all, data dictionary views, the owner column indicates the schema in which an object resides.

AND dropped = 'NO'

Oracle Database 10g introduces a *recycle bin* feature. The recycle bin holds the definitions and data for dropped tables in case you later want to undrop them. It's the same concept as the recycle bin in Windows. This condition excludes recycle bin tables.

> Omit the AND dropped = 'NO' condition, and you may see table names such as BIN$3oJlQsAVRUfgMKjAAgAV7g==$0 in the output from Example 9-7's query. Such names are from tables that you've dropped and are being held in the recycle bin for you to undrop.

Needing public synonyms is common, and if you have a large number of tables, you can save yourself a lot of typing by letting SQL*Plus do the work for you. The output from the previous statement looks like this:

```
CREATE PUBLIC SYNONYM EMPLOYEE for GENNICK.EMPLOYEE;
CREATE PUBLIC SYNONYM PROJECT for GENNICK.PROJECT;
CREATE PUBLIC SYNONYM PROJECT_HOURS for GENNICK.PROJECT_HOURS;
```

Once you have spooled these statements to a file, you can execute that file to create the synonyms. In addition to one-off tasks like creating synonyms, you can use SQL*Plus to generate DDL statements for use by ongoing maintenance tasks. Going beyond that, you can even use SQL*Plus to generate operating system script files.

Spool the Extract to a File

Once you have your query worked out and the data formatted as you require, it's time to spool your output to a file. To get a clean file, you must do four things.

1. Set the line size large enough to accommodate the longest possible line. Pay close attention to this if you are generating comma-delimited data. You need to allow for the case where each field is at its maximum size. Use the SET LINESIZE command for this.

2. Turn off all pagination features. You can use SET PAGESIZE 0 for this purpose. It turns off all column headings, page headings, page footers, page breaks, and so on.

3. Turn feedback off with the SET FEEDBACK OFF command.

4. Use the SET TRIMSPOOL ON command to eliminate trailing spaces in the output datafile. Use this for comma-delimited output and when you generate a file

of SQL statements. Don't use this command if you are generating a file with fixed-width columns.

The script in Example 9-8 generates a clean, comma-delimited file containing employee information. You'll see two SELECT statements. The first generates a line of comma-delimited column headings, and the second produces the comma-delimited data that follows.

Example 9-8. A script to generate a comma-separated-values file

```
--
--This script extracts data from the employee
--table and writes it to a text file in
--a comma-delimited format.
--

--Set the linesize large enough to accommodate the longest possible line.
SET LINESIZE 80

--Turn off all page headings, column headings, etc.
SET PAGESIZE 0

--Turn off feedback
SET FEEDBACK OFF

--Eliminate trailing blanks at the end of a line.
SET TRIMSPOOL ON

SET TERMOUT OFF
SPOOL current_employees.csv
SELECT '"ID","Billing Rate","Hire Date","Name"'
FROM dual;

SELECT    TO_CHAR(employee_id) || ','
       || TO_CHAR(employee_billing_rate) || ','
       || TO_CHAR(employee_hire_date,'MM/DD/YYYY') || ','
       || '"' || employee_name || '"'
FROM employee
WHERE employee_termination_date IS NULL;
SPOOL OFF

EXIT
```

The SPOOL command in Example 9-8 sends the output to *current_employees.csv*, and SET TERMOUT OFF disables the display while the data are being written to the file. Run the script as follows:

```
SQL> @ex9-8
```

Following is an example of the comma-delimited output:

```
"ID","Billing Rate","Hire Date","Name"
101,169,11/15/1961,"Marusia Churai"
105,121,06/15/2004,"Mykola Leontovych"
```

```
107,45,01/02/2004,"Lesia Ukrainka"
111,100,08/23/1976,"Taras Shevchenko"
114,,07/05/2004,"Marusia Bohuslavka"
116,,07/05/2004,"Roxolana Lisovsky"
```

The initial row of column headings that you see in these data comes in handy if your ultimate target is a spreadsheet. Open *current_employees.csv* in Microsoft Excel, adjust the column widths a bit, and you'll see results resembling Figure 9-1.

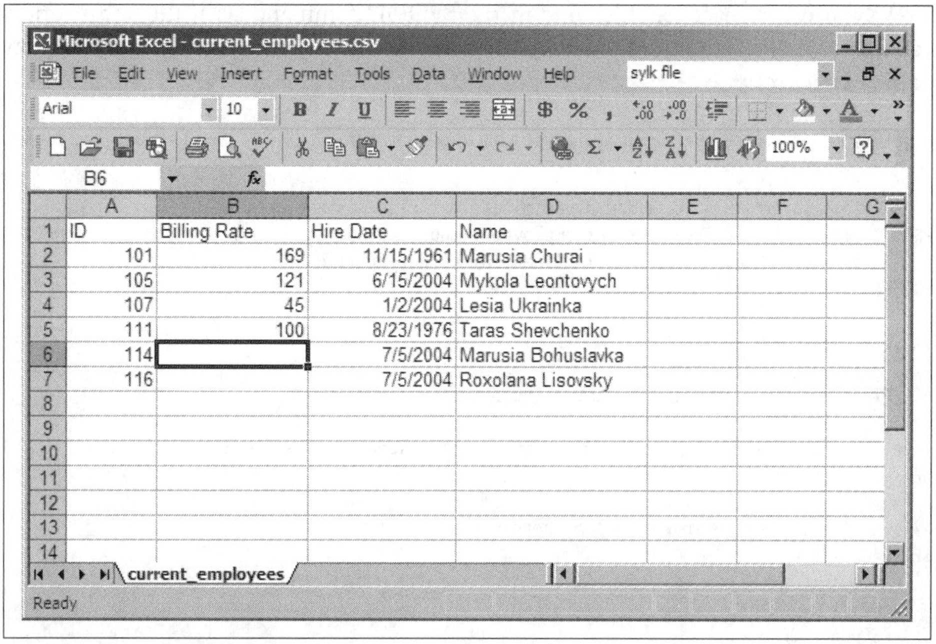

Figure 9-1. A CSV file opened in Microsoft Excel

Of course, if your target is not a spreadsheet program, you may prefer to omit the first SELECT from Example 9-8 to write only the data to the *current_employees.csv* file.

Make Your Extract Script User-Friendly

You can do at least two things to improve the extract script shown in the previous section. First, it might be nice to display a brief message to remind the user of what the script does. This will serve to give the user confidence that he has indeed started the correct script. The following PROMPT commands, added at the beginning of the script, should serve the purpose:

```
PROMPT
PROMPT This script creates a comma-delimited text file containing
PROMPT employee data. Only current employees, those without a
PROMPT termination date, will be included in the output file.
PROMPT
```

It may not be much, but it always makes me feel better to have some indication that the script I am executing does what I believe it to do. For scripts that change data or do something difficult to reverse, you might include a PAUSE command:

```
PAUSE Press ENTER to continue, or ctrl-C to abort.
```

You can even prompt for the output filename rather than hardcoding it:

```
ACCEPT output_file CHAR PROMPT 'Enter the output filename >'
```

Now, you can replace the filename in the SPOOL command with the substitution variable &output_file. Example 9-9 shows the modified, more user-friendly version of the extract script.

Example 9-9. A more user-friendly version of the extract script

```
PROMPT
PROMPT This script creates a comma-delimited text file containing
PROMPT employee data. Only current employees, those without a
PROMPT termination date, will be included in the output file.
PROMPT

PAUSE Press ENTER to continue, or ctrl-C to abort.

ACCEPT output_file CHAR PROMPT 'Enter the output filename >'

--Set the linesize large enough to accommodate the longest possible line.
SET LINESIZE 80

--Turn off all page headings, column headings, etc.
SET PAGESIZE 0

--Turn off feedback
SET FEEDBACK OFF

--Eliminate trailing blanks at the end of a line.
SET TRIMSPOOL ON

SET TERMOUT OFF
SPOOL &output_file
SELECT '"ID","Billing Rate","Hire Date","Name"'
FROM dual;

SELECT    TO_CHAR(employee_id) || ','
       || TO_CHAR(employee_billing_rate) || ','
       || TO_CHAR(employee_hire_date,'MM/DD/YYYY') || ','
       || '"' || employee_name || '"'
FROM employee
WHERE employee_termination_date IS NULL;
SPOOL OFF

EXIT
```

When you run the modified script in Example 9-9, it's much more obvious what is going to happen; you have a chance to abort, and you can specify whatever filename you like for the output:

```
oracle@gennick02:~/sqlplus/ExampleScripts> sqlplus gennick/secret @ex9-9

SQL*Plus: Release 10.1.0.2.0 - Production on Tue Jul 6 20:54:13 2004

Copyright (c) 1982, 2004, Oracle.  All rights reserved.


Connected to:
Oracle Database 10g Enterprise Edition Release 10.1.0.2.0 - Production
With the Partitioning, OLAP and Data Mining options


This script creates a comma-delimited text file containing
employee data. Only current employees, those without a
termination date, will be included in the output file.

Press ENTER to continue, or ctrl-C to abort.

Enter the output filename >current_employees.csv
Disconnected from Oracle Database 10g Enterprise Edition Release 10.1.0.2.0 -
Production
With the Partitioning, OLAP and Data Mining options
oracle@gennick02:~/sqlplus/ExampleScripts>
```

Depending on your needs, you can go further and allow the user to enter some selection criteria to specify which employee records to extract. But validating such input is difficult, so a mistake on the part of the person running the script may well result in a syntactically incorrect SELECT statement.

An Excel-Specific HTML Hack

If you're extracting data for someone to load into Microsoft Excel, you can apply an interesting technique whereby you take advantage of Excel's ability to read from an HTML table. The gist of this technique is as follows:

1. Enable HTML output using the SET MARKUP command.
2. Spool the output to a file with the extension *.xls*. It doesn't matter that the file contains HTML markup.
3. Double-click the file. This launches Excel because of the *.xls* extension, and Excel in turn converts the HTML table into a spreadsheet.

Example 9-10 presents a simple script to implement this technique. The output file is *current_employees.xls*. Double-clicking that file on a Windows system with Microsoft Excel installed produces the spreadsheet that you see in Figure 9-2. You don't need to adjust column widths. Cell titles are bold and nicely centered.

Generating CSV Data Using SET COLSEP

If you don't mind having some extraneous spaces in your output file, you can generate comma-delimited data using the SET COLSEP command:

```
SET COLSEP ","
COLUMN id FORMAT A5
COLUMN rate FORMAT A9
COLUMN hire FORMAT A12
COLUMN name FORMAT A30
SELECT '"' || employee_id || '"' id,
       '"' || employee_billing_rate || '"' rate,
       '"' || employee_hire_date || '"' hire,
       '"' || employee_name || '"' name
FROM employee
WHERE employee_termination_date IS NULL;
```

SET COLSEP changes the column-separator character to a comma; the default is a space. Data are now output in four separate columns, with each value enclosed within double quotation marks. The four COLUMN commands set the maximum width for each column, taking into account the opening and closing quote characters. The results are as follows:

```
"101","169"     ,"15-NOV-61" ,"Marusia Churai"
"105","121"     ,"15-JUN-04" ,"Mykola Leontovych"
"107","45"      ,"02-JAN-04" ,"Lesia Ukrainka"
"111","100"     ,"23-AUG-76" ,"Taras Shevchenko"
"114",""        ,"05-JUL-04" ,"Marusia Bohuslavka"
"116",""        ,"05-JUL-04" ,"Roxolana Lisovsky"
```

A potential drawback of this approach is the columnar nature of these delimited data. However, programs such as Microsoft Excel that read CSV data should ignore the extra spaces between the closing quotes and the commas that follow. If you're manually reading the output file, the columnar nature helps.

Another drawback of this approach is that it places a burden on you to set a proper width for each column. The id column in this example is formatted as A5, allowing for three digits plus two quote characters. If an employee_id happens to require more than three digits, SQL*Plus will wrap the value, and the result will no longer be a properly formatted CSV file.

Ultimately, you must decide whether you prefer to write long expressions to concatenate data together in comma-delimited format, as in Example 9-2, or whether you prefer to use the SET COLSEP approach described here. You must also take into account your target application.

Example 9-10. Generating an HTML table that can be loaded into Microsoft Excel simply by double-clicking on the resulting file

```
SET MARKUP HTML ON
SET TERMOUT OFF
SET FEEDBACK OFF
```

Example 9-10. Generating an HTML table that can be loaded into Microsoft Excel simply by double-clicking on the resulting file (continued)

```
SPOOL current_employees.xls
SELECT employee_id,
       employee_billing_rate
       employee_hire_date,
       employee_name
FROM employee
WHERE employee_termination_date IS NULL;
SPOOL OFF
EXIT
```

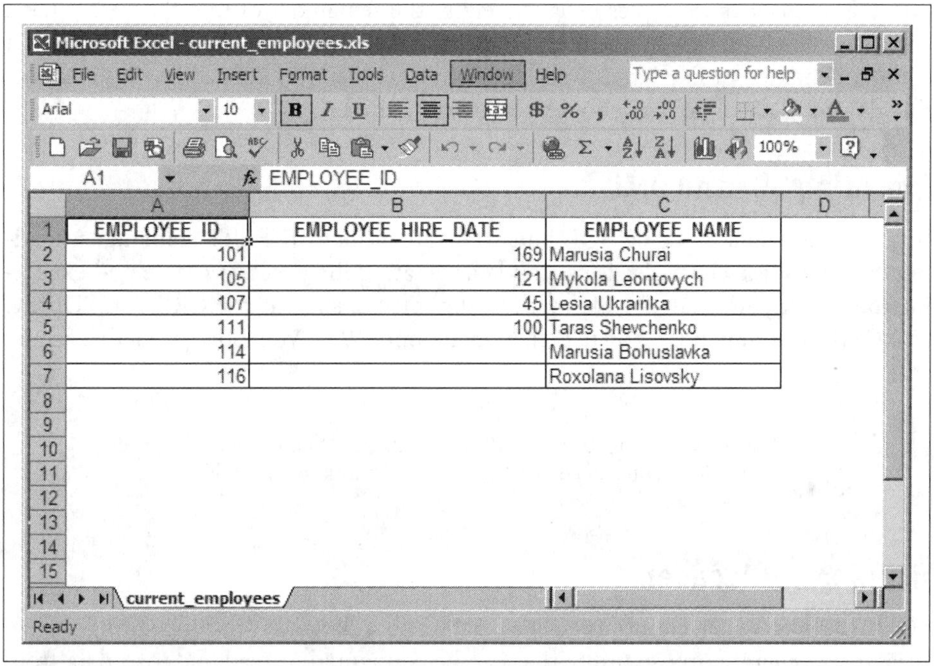

Figure 9-2. An HTML table converted by Microsoft Excel into a spreadsheet

If you're generating pages for a web site, you can serve up a file such as that generated by Example 9-10, and Microsoft Internet Explorer will recognize it as an Excel file. Users will see a spreadsheet in their browser and can save the file to their local disk using File → Save As. They may never even realize they aren't dealing with a true, native Excel file.

Reloading the Data

Now that you know how to extract data from Oracle, you need to know how to load it back in again. This is easy if you have generated a file of SQL statements; you execute that file from within SQL*Plus. Loading data is a little tougher, however, if you have a file of comma-delimited or fixed-width data.

One way to load data into Oracle from a flat file is to use a tool called SQL*Loader, which is a generic utility provided by Oracle for the express purpose of loading data into the database from a file. Another approach is to use the new, external table feature introduced in Oracle9i Database. SQL*Loader is convenient for loading from a relatively small file residing on your client PC, and it's a utility you can use without DBA support, which is a consideration if you don't happen to be the DBA.

An entire book could be written about SQL*Loader and external tables, so it's not possible to cover those topics exhaustively in the remainder of this chapter. What I can do is show you how to use the two methods to reload the employee table from a comma-delimited or fixed-width text file, the same files you learned how to create in this chapter. That should be enough to get you started.

Executing DDL and DML

If you extract data by using SQL*Plus to create a file of INSERT statements, loading the data somewhere else is as simple as creating the necessary table and executing the file. If you created a file of DDL statements, such as the CREATE PUBLIC SYNONYM commands shown earlier in Example 9-7, you only need to execute that file.

 You may want to turn ECHO on, and spool the output of any files that you execute, so you can go back and check for errors later.

Running SQL*Loader

SQL*Loader is an Oracle utility to load data into a database from operating-system files. It's a general-purpose utility that can be configured to read and load data from various record formats. SQL*Loader is a powerful and versatile utility, and possibly because of that, it can be frustrating to learn. Certainly the manual can be a bit overwhelming the first time you look at it.

If you're loading data from a file residing on a client PC, SQL*Loader is the way to go. The other option, that of using an external table, requires that your datafile reside on the database server. SQL*Loader is a good option for one-off, ad hoc loads, even from files that are on the server. External table loads require a bit of upfront setup, which can be a bother to do for a load you want to run only one time.

The control file

To load data from a flat file into a database, you need to provide several types of information to SQL*Loader. First of all, SQL*Loader needs to know what database to connect to, how to connect to it, and what table to load. Then SQL*Loader needs to know the format of the input file. It needs to know where the fields are, how long they are, and how they are represented. If, for example, your input file has date fields, SQL*Loader needs to know whether they are in MM/DD/YYYY format, MM/DD/YY format, or some other format.

The database connection and login information are usually passed to SQL*Loader as command-line arguments. The remaining information, describing the input file, needs to be placed in a text file called the *control file*. When you run SQL*Loader, you tell it where the control file is. Then SQL*Loader reads the control file and uses that information to interpret the data in the flat file you are loading. Figure 9-3 illustrates this, and shows the information flow into and out of SQL*Loader.

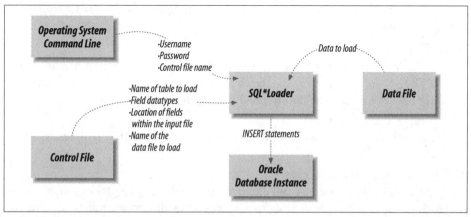

*Figure 9-3. SQL*Loader and the control file*

In addition to describing the input file, the control file can be used to tell SQL*Loader what to do with badly formatted data records, and it can be used to specify conditions limiting the data that are loaded. You can read more about SQL*Loader in the *Oracle Database Utilities* manual.

Building a control file for comma-delimited data

Example 9-8 produced comma-delimited output that looks like this:

```
"ID","Billing Rate","Hire Date","Name"
101,169,11/15/1961,"Marusia Churai"
105,121,06/15/2004,"Mykola Leontovych"
107,45,01/02/2004,"Lesia Ukrainka"
111,100,08/23/1976,"Taras Shevchenko"
114,,07/05/2004,"Marusia Bohuslavka"
116,,07/05/2004,"Roxolana Lisovsky"
```

To load this same data back into the employee table or into another copy of the employee table, you need the control file shown in Example 9-11.

Example 9-11. Control file to load comma-delimited data produced by Example 9-8

```
OPTIONS (SKIP=1)
LOAD DATA
INFILE 'ex9-11.csv'
APPEND INTO TABLE employee_copy
(
 employee_id           INTEGER EXTERNAL TERMINATED BY ',',
 employee_billing_rate DECIMAL EXTERNAL TERMINATED BY ','
 employee_hire_date    DATE "MM/DD/YYYY" TERMINATED BY ',',
 employee_name         CHAR TERMINATED BY ',' OPTIONALLY ENCLOSED BY '"',
)
```

You can think of the above as one long SQL*Loader command. The keywords LOAD DATA tell SQL*Loader to load data, and the rest of the command tells SQL*Loader where to get the data and how the data are formatted. The clauses are interpreted as described below:

OPTIONS (SKIP=1)

> Causes SQL*Loader to skip over the first line containing column headings. The OPTIONS command embeds command-line options in the control file. The SKIP option specifies the number of input records to skip.

INFILE current_employees.csv

> Tells SQL*Loader to read data from the file named *current_employees.csv* in the current working directory.

APPEND INTO TABLE employee_copy

> Tells SQL*Loader to insert the data into the employee_copy table owned by the current user. SQL*Loader queries Oracle's data dictionary tables for the columns and datatypes used in this table. The keyword APPEND specifies that SQL*Loader should load the data even if the target table is not empty, and that SQL*Loader should preserve rows already in the target table.

 Before running the load in Example 9-11, create the target table by executing the following SQL statement:

```
CREATE TABLE employee_copy AS
SELECT * FROM employee
WHERE 1=2;
```

No rows, of course, will satisfy the WHERE clause. The result will be an empty table having the same column structure as the original.

(...column_specifications...)

> Is a comma-delimited list of column specifications. Each column specification consists of the column name, followed by the representation (in the flat file) of the column, followed by the delimiter information.

The column names in the control file must correspond to the column names used in the database table you are loading, and they control the destination of each data element.

For a delimited file, the order in which the column specifications appear in the control file must match the field order in the record.

The four elements of the column specifications used in this example are described in the following list. Table 9-1 describes the datatypes that are used.

column_name
    Must be a column name in the destination table.

datatype
    A SQL*Loader datatype. (See Table 9-1.)

TERMINATED BY ','
    Tells SQL*Loader that a comma marks the end of the value for the data element.

OPTIONALLY ENCLOSED BY '"'
    Tells SQL*Loader that the data element may optionally be enclosed in quotes. If quotes are present, they are stripped off before the value is loaded.

*Table 9-1. SQL*Loader data elements*

Datatype	Description
CHAR	Used for character data.
DATE *"format_string"*	The data is a date, and the date is in the format specified by the format string. See Appendix B for information on writing such format strings.
DECIMAL EXTERNAL	Similar to INTEGER EXTERNAL, except that the number may contain a decimal point. This type is used for the employee_billing_rate field because the billing rate is a dollar and cent value.
FLOAT EXTERNAL	Enables loading of floating-point data, including that formatted using the E notation, as in 1.2345E+4.
INTEGER EXTERNAL	The data is numeric integer data stored as a character string. The character string must consist of the digits 0 through 9. Leading or trailing spaces are OK. Leading positive or negative signs (+ or -) are also OK.

SQL*Loader has its own set of datatypes, and they aren't the same as the ones used by the database. The most common datatypes used for loading data from text files are the numeric EXTERNAL types, CHAR, and DATE. These are described in Table 9-1.

Building a control file for fixed-width data

The control file used to load fixed-width employee data is similar to that used for delimited data. The only difference is that instead of specifying a delimiter for each field, you specify the starting and ending columns. Earlier in this chapter, in Example 9-3, you saw how to create a fixed-width file of employee data that looked like this:

```
101  169.00 11/15/1961 Marusia Churai
105  121.00 06/15/2004 Mykola Leontovych
```

```
107  045.00 01/02/2004 Lesia Ukrainka
111  100.00 08/23/1976 Taras Shevchenko
114         07/05/2004 Marusia Bohuslavka
116         07/05/2004 Roxolana Lisovsky
```

Example 9-12 specifies a control file that will load this fixed-width data into the employee_copy table.

Example 9-12. Control file to load fixed-width data generated by Example 9-3

```
LOAD DATA
INFILE 'ex9-12.dat'
APPEND INTO TABLE employee_copy
(
  employee_id             POSITION (2:4) INTEGER EXTERNAL,
  employee_billing_rate   POSITION (7:12) DECIMAL EXTERNAL
                          NULLIF employee_billing_rate=BLANKS
  employee_hire_date      POSITION (14:23) DATE "MM/DD/YYYY",
  employee_name           POSITION (25:44) CHAR
)
```

Each column in this control file contains a position specification that tells SQL*Loader where each field begins and ends. For some reason I have never been able to fathom, the position specification must precede the datatype, whereas a delimiter specification must follow the datatype. The position specification takes the following form:

```
POSITION (starting_column : ending_column)
```

The starting and ending column numbers tell SQL*Loader where in the record to find the data, and the first character of a record is considered position 1. Unlike the case with delimited files, you do not have to list the column specifications for a fixed-width datafile in any particular order.

The employee_billing_rate column in this control file contains an extra element, a NULLIF clause. The NULLIF clause (the way it is written in the example) tells SQL*Loader to set the employee_billing_rate column to null when the input data record contains spaces instead of a rate. This clause isn't necessary in Example 9-11, which loads the comma-delimited file, because a null rate in that file is represented by an empty string between two adjacent commas. In the case of this fixed-width data, a null rate is represented as a string of spaces, or blanks. Hence, the use of NULLIF to specify that an all-blank field be treated as a null.

Loading the data

Once you have the control file written, you can invoke SQL*Loader to load the data into the database. You can pass the following three items as command-line parameters:

- A login string
- The control file name
- A log file name

The last item, the log file name, is optional. If you include a log file name, SQL*Loader will generate a log of its activity and write it to that file. Among other things, any bad data records will result in log entries being made. At the end of the log file, SQL*Loader will print a summary showing how many records were loaded successfully and how many were rejected because of data errors. You won't get this information without a log file, so it's a good idea to generate one.

SQL*Loader is implemented as a command-line utility. From Oracle8*i* onward, the command to run SQL*Loader is *sqlldr*. In a Windows environment, and prior to Oracle8*i* Database, the command has the Oracle version number appended to it. If you have Oracle8 installed on Windows, the command is *sqlldr80*.

Example 9-13 shows a run of SQL*Loader using the control file from Example 9-11. The comma-delimited data from *ex9-11.csv* is loaded into employee_copy, as per the control file's specifications. A log of the load operation is written to *ex9-11.log*, and Example 9-14 shows the contents of that log file. To load fixed-width data instead, substitute *ex9-12.ctl* and *ex9-12.log* for the control and log file names respectively.

*Example 9-13. SQL*Loader being used to load comma-delimited data*

```
oracle@gennick02:~/sqlplus> sqlldr gennick/secret control=ex9-11.ctl log=ex9-11.log

SQL*Loader: Release 10.1.0.2.0 - Production on Wed Jul 7 21:16:21 2004

Copyright (c) 1982, 2004, Oracle.  All rights reserved.

Commit point reached - logical record count 6
```

Example 9-14. The log from Example 9-13's load

```
SQL*Loader: Release 10.1.0.2.0 - Production on Wed Jul 7 21:16:21 2004

Copyright (c) 1982, 2004, Oracle.  All rights reserved.

Control File:   ex9-11.ctl
Data File:      ex9-11.csv
  Bad File:     ex9-11.bad
  Discard File: none specified

 (Allow all discards)

Number to load: ALL
Number to skip: 1
Errors allowed: 50
Bind array:     64 rows, maximum of 256000 bytes
Continuation:    none specified
Path used:      Conventional

Table EMPLOYEE_COPY, loaded from every logical record.
Insert option in effect for this table: APPEND
```

Example 9-14. The log from Example 9-13's load (continued)

```
     Column Name                     Position  Len  Term Encl Datatype
------------------------------       --------- ----- ---- ---- --------------------
EMPLOYEE_ID                           FIRST     *   ,         CHARACTER
EMPLOYEE_BILLING_RATE                 NEXT      *   ,         CHARACTER
EMPLOYEE_HIRE_DATE                    NEXT      *   ,         DATE MM/DD/YYYY
EMPLOYEE_NAME                         NEXT      *   ,   O(")  CHARACTER


Table EMPLOYEE_COPY:
  6 Rows successfully loaded.
  0 Rows not loaded due to data errors.
  0 Rows not loaded because all WHEN clauses were failed.
  0 Rows not loaded because all fields were null.


Space allocated for bind array:              66048 bytes(64 rows)
Read   buffer bytes: 1048576

Total logical records skipped:          1
Total logical records read:             6
Total logical records rejected:         0
Total logical records discarded:        0

Run began on Wed Jul 07 21:16:21 2004
Run ended on Wed Jul 07 21:16:22 2004

Elapsed time was:      00:00:00.14
CPU time was:          00:00:00.05
```

The most important part of the log file to look at is the summary near the bottom, where SQL*Loader tells you how many rows were successfully loaded. In this case, one row was skipped, and six were successfully loaded. The skipped row was the first row with the column headings. If any records were rejected because of bad data, there would be an entry for each in the log file telling you which record was rejected and why.

There is a lot more to SQL*Loader than what you have seen in this chapter. Here are some of the other things you can do with SQL*Loader:

Bad data detection

> You can specify a *bad file*, which is where SQL*Loader places records that are rejected because of bad data. After a load, you can review the bad file, fix the records, and attempt to load them again.

Record restriction

> You can use a WHEN clause to place a restriction on the records to be loaded. Only those records that match the criteria in the WHEN clause will be loaded. Other records are ignored or may optionally be placed in a *discard file*.

Data manipulation

You can build expressions, using any of Oracle's built-in SQL functions, to manipulate the data in the input file before they are loaded into Oracle.

To learn more about SQL*Loader, consult the *Oracle Database Utilities* manual, which presents several case studies showing you how to use SQL*Loader's various features. You might also look at the book *SQL*Loader: The Definitive Guide* (O'Reilly), which is a joint effort between Sanjay Mishra and myself.

Using an External Table

Oracle9*i* Database introduced a powerful new mechanism for loading data from operating system files. Using a new type of table known as the *external table*, you can retrieve data by issuing a SELECT statement; you can bring the full power of SQL to bear on filtering and transforming the data you are loading. A load then, becomes as simple and as powerful as issuing a CREATE TABLE...AS SELECT FROM or an INSERT INTO...SELECT FROM statement.

Learn more about external tables by reading the online *Oracle Magazine* article "Load Up with the Latest," which you can find at *http://www.oracle.com/oramag/oracle/01-sep/index.html?o51o9i.html*.

Creating a directory

The external table mechanism requires that the file to be loaded reside on the database server because it's the database instance rather than a client utility that reads the file. The file must reside in a directory accessible via an Oracle directory object. Your DBA (or you if you are the DBA) can create such a directory object as follows:

```
CREATE DIRECTORY loads AS '/home/oracle/sqlplus/ExampleScripts';
```

The command in this example creates an Oracle directory object named loads that points to the operating system directory */home/oracle/sqlplus/ExampleScripts*. To issue the CREATE DIRECTORY statement, you must hold the CREATE ANY DIRECTORY system privilege. If you aren't the DBA, you'll need to get together with your DBA, to decide on an operating-system directory to use for loads, and then your DBA can issue the necessary CREATE DIRECTORY statement. The Oracle software owner will need read access to that directory and to any files in it that you wish to load via the external table mechanism. If you plan to write log files to that directory, the Oracle software will also need write access.

You need create a directory object only once. Once it has been created, you can use that directory repeatedly for any loads that you do. Avoid creating a new directory for each new load.

Creating an external table

Your next step is to create an external table. The statement to create such a table looks like a cross between a traditional CREATE TABLE statement and a SQL*Loader control file. Example 9-15 creates an external table to read the same comma-delimited data as loaded earlier by Example 9-11. Likewise, Example 9-16 creates an external table to access the fixed-width data loaded by Example 9-12.

Example 9-15. An external table to read comma-delimited data generated by Example 9-11

```
CREATE TABLE employee_comma (
  employee_id NUMBER,
  employee_billing_rate NUMBER(5,2),
  employee_hire_date DATE,
  employee_name VARCHAR2(40)
)
ORGANIZATION EXTERNAL (
   TYPE oracle_loader
   DEFAULT DIRECTORY loads
   ACCESS PARAMETERS (
      RECORDS DELIMITED BY NEWLINE CHARACTERSET US7ASCII
      BADFILE 'employee_comma.bad'
      LOGFILE 'employee_comma.log'
      FIELDS (
         employee_id CHAR(255) TERMINATED BY ",",
         employee_billing_rate CHAR(255) TERMINATED BY ",",
         employee_hire_date CHAR(255) TERMINATED BY ","
            DATE_FORMAT DATE MASK "MM/DD/YYYY",
         employee_name CHAR(255) TERMINATED BY "," OPTIONALLY ENCLOSED BY '"'
      )
   )
   LOCATION ('ex9-11.csv')
) REJECT LIMIT UNLIMITED;
```

Example 9-16. An external table to read fixed-width data generated by Example 9-12

```
CREATE TABLE employee_fixed (
   employee_id NUMBER,
   employee_billing_rate NUMBER(5,2),
   employee_hire_date DATE,
   employee_name VARCHAR2(40)
)
ORGANIZATION external (
   TYPE oracle_loader
   DEFAULT DIRECTORY loads
   ACCESS PARAMETERS (
      RECORDS DELIMITED BY NEWLINE CHARACTERSET US7ASCII
      BADFILE 'employee_fixed.bad'
      LOGFILE 'employee_fixed.log'
      FIELDS (
         employee_id (2:4) CHAR(3),
         employee_billing_rate (7:12) CHAR(6)
            NULLIF (employee_billing_rate = BLANKS),
```

```
        employee_hire_date (14:23) CHAR(10)
            DATE_FORMAT DATE MASK "MM/DD/YYYY",
        employee_name (25:44) CHAR(20)
    )
    )
    LOCATION ('ex9-12.dat')
) REJECT LIMIT UNLIMITED;
```

Several things are worth noticing about Example 9-15. The ORGANIZATION EXTERNAL clause identifies the table as one that is mapped to an external datafile. TYPE oracle_loader specifies the SQL*Loader-like access driver. The DEFAULT DIRECTORY clause identifies loads as the Oracle directory object pointing to the operating system directory in which the datafile resides, and in which the log file will be created.

The definitions in the FIELDS clause are similar to those used for SQL*Loader in Example 9-11, but they are not quite the same. All the field types are CHAR, because all the values in the input file are in character form. Unlike the case with SQL*Loader, when using the external table oracle_loader access driver, you do need to specify a length, even for delimited columns. Example 9-15 specifies a length of 255 characters. This is a maximum length; no values in the external file even come close to approaching that many characters.

 The oracle_loader access driver does support types such as INTEGER EXTERNAL and DECIMAL EXTERNAL. INTEGER EXTERNAL seems to work like its SQL*Loader namesake, but DECIMAL EXTERNAL does not. The oracle_loader driver does not support DATE as a datatype. It's easiest to use CHAR across the board.

Example 9-15 includes a BADFILE clause, specifying a file to which records that can't be loaded will be written. The file being loaded includes one such record, the one at the beginning with the column headings. There is no provision for skipping records during an external table load. However, the column headings record will always fail to load because it won't contain a valid number for the employee_id column.

Each time you SELECT data from the employee_comma table, a log of the load will be generated and *appended* to the log file. Thus, the *employee_comma.log* file will grow in size over time, and you'll need to delete it periodically. Oddly, the bad file is *overwritten* in each new load and, thus, does not grow in size.

One final thing to notice about Example 9-15 is the optional REJECT LIMIT UNLIMITED clause at the end of the statement. That clause allows for an unlimited number of bad records in the external datafile. The default is to abort an external table load in the event that any bad record is encountered.

Example 9-16 is similar to Example 9-15. The only differences are that each field definition specifies an explicit beginning and ending character position, and the field lengths are calculated to correspond to those character positions. employee_id, for example, runs from position 2 through 4, for a total of three characters.

Migrating to External Tables

If you happen to have a SQL*Loader control file for a particular load, you can migrate that load to the external table mechanism by having SQL*Loader generate all the necessary SQL statements for you. For example, to migrate the load in Example 9-11 to external tables, issue this command:

```
sqlldr gennick/secret control=ex9-11.ctl log=ex9-11.log external_
table=generate_only
```

The external_table=generate_only option causes SQL*Loader not to do the load; instead, it tells it to write the following SQL statements into the log file:

- A CREATE DIRECTORY statement, unless an existing directory can be found that refers to the directory containing your target datafile
- A CREATE TABLE statement with a list of field definitions corresponding to those in your SQL*Loader control file
- An INSERT statement that you can use to load the data from the external datafile, through the external table mechanism, and into your target database table

You may want to tweak SQL*Loader's CREATE TABLE statement to specify your own name for the external table rather than the one SQL*Loader generated for you. Not all SQL*Loader features translate directly to the external table mechanism. For example, there seems to be no external table equivalent of the SKIP parameter. If you run into a feature that doesn't translate, you may need to do some tweaking somewhere to make your load work, but you've still saved yourself plenty of drudgery by having SQL*Loader do so much of the work.

Loading the data

Once you have an external table in place, accessing the data from the external datafile to which the external table points is simply a matter of issuing a SELECT statement, as in Example 9-17.

Example 9-17. SELECTing from an external table

```
SQL> SELECT * FROM employee_comma;

EMPLOYEE_ID EMPLOYEE_BILLING_RATE EMPLOYEE_ EMPLOYEE_NAME
----------- --------------------- --------- --------------------
        101                   169 15-NOV-61 Marusia Churai
        105                   121 15-JUN-04 Mykola Leontovych
        107                    45 02-JAN-04 Lesia Ukrainka
```

Example 9-17. SELECTing from an external table (continued)

```
       111               100 23-AUG-76 Taras Shevchenko
       114                   05-JUL-04 Marusia Bohuslavka
       116                   05-JUL-04 Roxolana Lisovsky

6 rows selected.
```

You can just imagine the possibilities here. You can bring the full power of Oracle SQL, and of Oracle PL/SQL (via stored functions), to bear on transforming the data that you are loading. Example 9-18 demonstrates a load, giving you just a taste of the power that external tables place in your hands.

Example 9-18. Loading from an external table

```
SQL> COLUMN employee_name FORMAT A20
SQL>
SQL> DELETE FROM employee_copy;

4 rows deleted.

SQL>
SQL> SELECT * FROM employee_copy;

no rows selected

SQL>
SQL> INSERT /*+ APPEND */ INTO employee_copy ecc
  2  (employee_id, employee_billing_rate, employee_hire_date, employee_name)
  3  SELECT employee_id,
  4         employee_billing_rate,
  5         employee_hire_date,
  6         UPPER(employee_name)
  7  FROM employee_comma ec
  8  WHERE EXISTS (SELECT * FROM project_hours ph
  9                WHERE ph.employee_id = ec.employee_id);

4 rows created.

SQL> SELECT * FROM employee_copy;
SELECT * FROM employee_copy
*
ERROR at line 1:
ORA-12838: cannot read/modify an object after modifying it in parallel

SQL> COMMIT;

Commit complete.

SQL> SELECT * FROM employee_copy;

EMPLOYEE_ID EMPLOYEE_NAME       EMPLOYEE_ EMPLOYEE_ EMPLOYEE_BILLING_RATE
----------- ------------------- --------- --------- ---------------------
        101 MARUSIA CHURAI      15-NOV-61                             169
```

Example 9-18. Loading from an external table (continued)

```
105 MYKOLA LEONTOVYCH    15-JUN-04                    121
107 LESIA UKRAINKA       02-JAN-04                     45
111 TARAS SHEVCHENKO     23-AUG-76                    100
```

The INSERT statement in Example 9-18 performs the actual load. It uses the APPEND hint to cause the database to insert the loaded data, via the so-called *direct path*, into new blocks above the table's current highwater mark. Using APPEND is optional, but you'll get your best performance on large loads by using it. The APPEND hint is the reason why the first SELECT failed. You have to COMMIT before you can access a table that you've modified via the direct path.

The INSERT...SELECT FROM statement transforms the load in two ways. It applies the built-in UPPER function to the external table's employee_name column to convert all employee names to uppercase. It incorporates an EXISTS predicate that restricts the load to only those employees who have logged time to a project. Uppercasing a name is something you can do easily using SQL*Loader. Filtering records to be loaded based on other data in the database is something you can't do at all using SQL*Loader.

The SELECT statement at the end of the example shows the results of the load. Compare this to the output in Example 9-17, and you will see that two employees were omitted because they haven't charged any time to a project. All the names are uppercase.

External tables give you a great deal more power and flexibility when you are filtering and transforming data to be loaded. Moreover, you may also be able to use such tables to load data faster and more efficiently than with SQL*Loader. One reason for this is because the external table mechanism access driver can parallelize a load with practically no effort on your part. (Read the *Oracle Database Utilities* manual to learn how.) Another reason is that external tables may eliminate the need for temporary staging tables that consume disk space and require CPU and I/O to create. I still find SQL*Loader convenient for one-off, ad hoc loads, but for any load that you perform on a regular basis you should first think of using an external table.

Exploring Your Database

You can create various objects in an Oracle database. You can create tables, indexes on those tables, object types, constraints, and various other objects. It's important to be able to get information about the objects you have created. After a while you are going to find yourself asking questions such as, "What tables do I have defined?" and "What do they look like?" You may have an application fail because of a constraint violation. To understand why the error occurred, you need to know what the definition is for that constraint. Unless you have a good memory, you will need to go to the database for this information.

Using SQL*Plus, you have two ways to display information about objects within your database. The easiest way is to use the DESCRIBE command. DESCRIBE will tell you about columns in a table or view. DESCRIBE will also show you the definition of an object type or of a PL/SQL package. The second method for getting information about objects in your database is to query the Oracle data dictionary. The *data dictionary* is a set of tables Oracle uses to keep track of object definitions. To facilitate your use of the data dictionary, Oracle provides a set of views known as *data dictionary views*. This chapter shows you how some of these views work and how you can write scripts to query them.

The DESCRIBE Command

You may be familiar with the SQL*Plus DESCRIBE command. You can use DESCRIBE to get a list of columns in a table or view, along with its datatypes. Beginning with Oracle8, DESCRIBE may be used to see the definition of an Oracle object type or to list definitions for all the functions and procedures in a stored PL/SQL package.

Describing a Table

DESCRIBE is most often used to view the definition of a table or a view. Enter the command DESCRIBE followed by the name of the table or view you are interested in, as the following example shows:

```
DESCRIBE employee
```

```
Name                               Null?     Type
-----------------------------------  --------  ------------------
EMPLOYEE_ID                        NOT NULL  NUMBER
EMPLOYEE_NAME                                VARCHAR2(40)
EMPLOYEE_HIRE_DATE                           DATE
EMPLOYEE_TERMINATION_DATE                    DATE
EMPLOYEE_BILLING_RATE                        NUMBER(5,2)
```

If you aren't the owner of the table, you can qualify the table or view name using the standard *owner.table_name* dot notation. This next example describes the all_users view, which is owned by the user SYS:

```
DESCRIBE sys.all_users
```

```
Name                          Null?     Type
------------------------------  --------  ------------
USERNAME                      NOT NULL  VARCHAR2(30)
USER_ID                       NOT NULL  NUMBER
CREATED                       NOT NULL  DATE
...
```

DESCRIBE gives you a list of columns in the table or view, along with its resulting datatypes, lengths, and nullability. If you need to know more, such as whether a column has a default value, you will need to query the data dictionary directly. You will see how to do that later in this chapter.

Describing Stored Functions and Procedures

DESCRIBE may be used on stored procedures and functions. When used on a stored function, the DESCRIBE command returns the datatype of the return value and gives you a list of arguments that the function expects:

```
DESCRIBE terminate_employee
```

```
FUNCTION terminate_employee RETURNS NUMBER(38)
 Argument Name                 Type                     In/Out Default?
------------------------------  -----------------------  ------ --------
 EMP_ID                        NUMBER                   IN
 EMP_HIRE_DATE                 DATE                     OUT
 EMP_TERM_DATE                 DATE                     IN
```

DESCRIBE returns the following information for each argument:

- The datatype
- Whether it is an input, output, or both
- The default value if there is one

The order in which the arguments are listed is the order in which they should be passed into the function when you call it. The DESCRIBE command doesn't show you the source code for a function. To see that, you need to query the all_source data dictionary view. Example 10-1 shows how to get the source for the terminate_employee function.

Example 10-1. Getting the source code for a PL/SQL function

```
SELECT text
FROM all_source
WHERE owner = USER
  AND name = 'TERMINATE_EMPLOYEE'
ORDER BY LINE;

TEXT
--------------------------------------------------------------------
FUNCTION terminate_employee
    (emp_id IN employee.employee_id%TYPE,
     emp_hire_date OUT employee.employee_hire_date%TYPE,
     emp_term_date IN employee.employee_termination_date%TYPE)
RETURN INTEGER AS
BEGIN
  UPDATE employee
    SET employee_termination_date = emp_term_date
  WHERE employee_id = emp_id;

  SELECT employee_hire_date INTO emp_hire_date
    FROM employee
  WHERE employee_id = emp_id;

  RETURN 1;
EXCEPTION
WHEN OTHERS THEN
  RETURN 0;
END;
```

Describing a procedure works the same way as describing a function. The only difference is that procedures do not have a return type.

Describing Packages and Object Types

With the release of Oracle8, the SQL*Plus DESCRIBE command was enhanced to return information about Oracle8 object types. The following example shows how this works:

```
DESCRIBE employee_type
```

Name	Null?	Type
EMPLOYEE_NAME		VARCHAR2(40)
EMPLOYEE_HIRE_DATE		DATE
EMPLOYEE_SALARY		NUMBER(9,2)

Another Oracle8 enhancement provides the ability to describe a stored package and get back a list of all functions and procedures that make up the package. This is not surprising because objects and packages are very similar in nature. For example, you can get a list of all the entry points in the DBMS_OUTPUT package by using DESCRIBE, as shown here:

```
DESCRIBE sys.dbms_output
```

```
PROCEDURE DISABLE
PROCEDURE ENABLE
```

Argument Name	Type	In/Out	Default?
BUFFER_SIZE	NUMBER(38)	IN	DEFAULT

```
PROCEDURE GET_LINE
```

Argument Name	Type	In/Out	Default?
LINE	VARCHAR2	OUT	
STATUS	NUMBER(38)	OUT	

```
PROCEDURE GET_LINES
```

Argument Name	Type	In/Out	Default?
LINES	TABLE OF VARCHAR2(255)	OUT	
NUMLINES	NUMBER(38)	IN/OUT	

```
PROCEDURE NEW_LINE
...
```

As with functions and procedures, you can get at the source for a package, or for an Oracle8 object type, by querying the all_source view. For example, to see the detailed comments that Oracle includes in the source to the DBMS_OUTPUT package, you can query all_source as follows:

```
SELECT text
FROM all_source
WHERE name = 'DBMS_OUTPUT'
AND type = 'PACKAGE'
ORDER BY line;
```

```
TEXT
--------------------------------------------------------------------------------
package dbms_output as

-- DE-HEAD      <- tell SED where to cut when generating fixed package


    ------------
    --  OVERVIEW
    --
    --  These procedures accumulate information in a buffer (via "put" and
    --  "put_line") so that it can be retrieved out later (via "get_line" or
    --  "get_lines").  If this package is disabled then all
    --  calls to this package are simply ignored.  This way, these routines
--------------------------------------------------------------------------------
    --  are only active when the client is one that is able to deal with the
    --  information.  This is good for debugging, or SP's that want to want
    --  to display messages or reports to sql*dba or plus (like 'describing
    --  procedures', etc.).  The default buffer size is 20000 bytes.  The
    --  minimum is 2000 and the maximum is 1,000,000.


    -----------
    --  EXAMPLE
    --
    --  A trigger might want to print out some debugging information.  To do
    --  do this the trigger would do
    ...
```

Queries such as this can be handy when you don't otherwise have any documentation at hand. Think of such queries as instant, online documentation.

Why DESCRIBE Is Not Enough

Handy as DESCRIBE is, it doesn't return enough information. While it shows you all
the columns in a table, it leaves out many important details. If you need to know the
primary key for a table, DESCRIBE won't tell you. If you need to know the foreign
key constraints defined on a table, DESCRIBE won't tell you that either. DESCRIBE
won't show you the indexes, won't show you the default values, won't show you the
triggers, and won't tell you anything about the table's security.

How then do you get at this other information? One way is to install the Oracle
Enterprise Manager software. For Oracle Database 10g, you can use Oracle Grid
Control or Oracle Database Control, depending on whether you're running a grid.
Oracle Enterprise Manager implements a GUI-based schema browser that will show
you everything there is to see about tables, indexes, views, triggers, and other
objects. Several third-party software packages on the market provide similar functionality. However, for many people, SQL*Plus is the only option available or at least

the only one conveniently available. If this is the case for you, you can still get the information you need by querying Oracle's data dictionary.

Oracle's Data Dictionary Views

Oracle has to keep track of all the tables, views, constraints, indexes, triggers, and other objects you create. To do that, Oracle needs a place to store the information. This repository of information about your database is referred to as the *data dictionary*. Whenever you create a new object, such as a table, Oracle stores all the information about that object in the data dictionary. Modify the object, and Oracle modifies the data dictionary. It follows, then, that if you want to know anything about your database, the data dictionary is the place to go.

What Is the Data Dictionary?

The data dictionary is a set of tables owned by the user SYS. The structure of these tables ends up being fairly complex, and much of the information isn't stored in a user-friendly form. You probably do not want to query these tables directly, and unless you have been given access to log in as user SYS, you won't be able to see them anyway. To help you out, Oracle provides a set of data dictionary views. These views have names that are easy to remember. The column names used in the views are also easy to remember and use a consistent naming convention. Data dictionary views exist for each different type of schema object, and they present information in an easy-to-understand form. For example, if you are looking at a date column, the dba_tab_columns view will tell you it is of type DATE. The underlying data dictionary table, which happens to be sys.col$, will tell you the type is 12.

Oracle has a large number of data dictionary views. This chapter concentrates on the views used to return information about the structure of a table, its constraints, indexes, columns, triggers, and security. This is the most common type of information needed by application developers and other database users. I encourage you to dig deeper. If you want, or need, to know more, then the *Oracle Database Reference* manual is a good place to start. Look for the section titled "Static Data Dictionary Views," which gives a definitive description of all the views available, and their columns. Another, perhaps handier reference is Dave Kreines's *Oracle Data Dictionary Pocket Reference* (O'Reilly).

The View Types: user, all, and dba

You need to be aware of three different types of data dictionary views. These control the scope of the information you can look at:

user

> The user views show you information only about objects that you own. There is a user_tables view, for example, that lists only your tables.

all

> The all views show you information about all objects you are able to access. Anything you own is included in an all view, as well as anything owned by other users but to which you have been granted access.

dba

> The dba views show you information about all objects. Usually, only DBAs have access to these views, and they can be considered a superset of the all views. dba_tables, for example, will list every single table that exists.

Generally, for any given object type, one view of each type will exist. It's up to you to choose the view you want to look at. Table 10-1 shows how this works in terms of the views discussed in this chapter.

Table 10-1. Correspondence between user, all, and dba views

user view name	all view name	dba view name
n/a	all_scheduler_windows	dba_scheduler_windows
n/a	all_users	dba_users
user_all_tables	all_all_tables	dba_all_tables
user_cons_columns	all_cons_columns	dba_cons_columns
user_constraints	all_constraints	dba_constraints
user_external_tables	all_external_tables	dba_external_tables
user_ind_columns	all_ind_columns	dba_ind_columns
user_indexes	all_indexes	dba_indexes
user_source	all_source	dba_source
user_synonyms	all_synonyms	dba_synonyms
user_tab_columns	all_tab_columns	dba_tab_columns
user_tab_privs	all_tab_privs	dba_tab_privs
user_tables	all_tables	dba_tables
user_triggers	all_triggers	dba_triggers
user_views	all_views	dba_views

As you delve more deeply into Oracle's data dictionary, you will occasionally find instances when corresponding views don't exist in all three categories. When a view is omitted, it's for security reasons, because it doesn't make sense in the context of a particular object, or because it would be redundant. The dba_scheduler_windows and all_scheduler_windows (new in Oracle Database 10g) views provide a good example of this. DBMS_SCHEDULER windows aren't "owned" by users, so a user view doesn't apply in that context.

Which view should you use? The user views limit you to seeing information about objects that you own. If I'm working interactively, I'll frequently use the user views to save myself some typing because I don't need to enter a WHERE clause to restrict the results to my own objects. When writing scripts, I want to use the all views to make the scripts more flexible. It's common, for example, to need to see the definition for a table owned by another user. The all views allow this. I save the DBA views for DBA-related tasks.

The following sections show you how to get information about various types of schema objects. First, I'll show how to list the tables you own and how to look at the column definitions for those tables. Next, you will see how to look at the constraints, indexes, triggers, synonyms, and security for a table. You'll learn how to leverage the data dictionary to automate DBA tasks. Finally, I'll hand you the data dictionary's master key.

Tables

When it comes to looking at a table and its column definitions, you need to be concerned with two data dictionary views:

- all_tables
- all_tab_columns

The all_tables view contains one row for each table. You can use this view to get a quick list of tables you own or to which you have been granted some type of access. all_tables has a one-to-many relationship to all_tab_columns, which contains one record for each column in a table. all_tab_columns is the source for information on column names, datatypes, default values, etc.

Listing Tables You Own

To get a quick list of tables you own, it's easier to use the user_tables view than all_tables. Remember that user_tables shows you only the tables you own. To see a list of your tables, simply select the table_name column and any other columns containing information of interest:

```
SELECT table_name, tablespace_name
FROM user_tables;

TABLE_NAME                      TABLESPACE_NAME
------------------------------  ------------------------------
EMPLOYEE_COPY                   USERS
```

```
PROJECT_HOURS                   USERS
BIN$3oJlQsAlRUfgMKjAAgAV7g==$0  USERS
...
```

The recycle bin

Oops! What's that BIN$3oJlQsAlRUfgMKjAAgAV7g==$0 business all about? Did I give a table a mixed up name like that? No, I didn't. The BIN$3oJlQsAlRUfgMKjAAgAV7g==$0 table that you see represents a table I deleted. Oracle Database 10g introduced a recycle bin for deleted database objects, which somewhat complicates the task of querying the data dictionary views. Filter out any recycle bin objects by adding WHERE dropped = 'NO' to the query:

```
SELECT table_name, tablespace_name
FROM user_tables
WHERE dropped = 'NO';

TABLE_NAME                      TABLESPACE_NAME
------------------------------  ------------------------------
EMPLOYEE_COPY                   USERS
PROJECT_HOURS                   USERS
PROJECT                         USERS
...
```

Tables owned by other users

To see tables owned by other users, you need to query the all_tables view. Be sure to qualify your query by specifying the owner's username in the WHERE clause.

```
SELECT table_name
  FROM all_tables
 WHERE owner = 'SYSTEM'
   AND dropped = 'NO';
```

External tables

External tables, which I described near the end of the previous chapter, are exposed through user/all/dba_tables, as most other tables are. However, if you wish to access attributes specific to external tables, such as the field definitions within their access parameters, you'll need to query user/all/dba_external_tables:

```
COLUMN reject_limit FORMAT A10
COLUMN access_parameters FORMAT A60 WORD_WRAPPED

SELECT reject_limit, access_parameters
FROM user_external_tables
WHERE table_name = 'EMPLOYEE_COMMA';

REJECT_LIM ACCESS_PARAMETERS
---------- ------------------------------------------------------------
UNLIMITED  RECORDS DELIMITED BY NEWLINE CHARACTERSET US7ASCII
           BADFILE        'employee_comma.bad'
```

```
LOGFILE 'employee_comma.log'
FIELDS (
employee_id CHAR(255) TERMINATED BY ",",
employee_billing_rate CHAR(255) TERMINATED BY ",",
employee_hire_date CHAR(255) TERMINATED BY ","
DATE_FORMAT DATE MASK "MM/DD/YYYY",
employee_name CHAR(255) TERMINATED BY "," OPTIONALLY
ENCLOSED BY '"'
)
```

Object tables

Object tables are exposed through their own set of views and aren't included in user/all/dba_tables. To learn about object tables in your database, query all_object_tables:

```
SELECT owner, table_name, tablespace_name
FROM all_object_tables
WHERE dropped = 'NO';

OWNER        TABLE_NAME                       TABLESPACE_NAME
----------   ------------------------------   ------------------------------
SYS          KOTTD$                           SYSTEM
SYS          KOTTB$                           SYSTEM
SYS          KOTAD$                           SYSTEM
...
```

A combined list of tables

Sometimes it can be inconvenient to have database tables split across two views, all_tables and all_object_tables. When that's the case, you can generate a list of all tables you're interested in, regardless of type, querying the rather oddly named all_all_tables view:

```
SELECT owner, table_name, tablespace_name
FROM all_all_tables
WHERE owner = 'GENNICK'
  AND dropped = 'NO';

OWNER       TABLE_NAME                       TABLESPACE_NAME
----------  ------------------------------   ------------------------------
GENNICK     EMPLOYEE_COMMA
GENNICK     EMPLOYEE_FIXED
GENNICK     TEST2                            USERS
GENNICK     ODD_NUMS                         USERS
```

Don't confuse the two alls in all_all_tables. The first all indicates that the view is from the all family. There are also user_all_tables and dba_all_tables. The second all indicates that the view returns a combined list of all table types.

You can query all_views to see the underlying SELECT statement for all_all_tables:

```
SET LONG 6000
SELECT text
FROM all_views
WHERE view_name = 'ALL_ALL_TABLES'
   AND owner = 'SYS';
```

If you issue this query, you'll see that all_all_tables is the UNION of two SELECTs, one against all_tables and the other against all_object_tables. The text column is of type LONG, and the SET LONG command causes SQL*Plus to show more than the default, first 80 bytes.

Listing Column Definitions for a Table

Query the all_tab_columns view to see detailed information about the columns in a table. Table 10-2 describes some of the key columns in this view, explaining how you might use them in a query.

Table 10-2. Key columns in the all_tab_columns view

Column	Description
table_name	Name of the table containing the column. You'll usually want to use this in your WHERE clause to restrict your output to only those columns from a table of interest.
column_id	Sequence number, beginning from 1 for a table's first column. You can use column_id in an ORDER BY clause to report columns in the same order as the DESCRIBE command.
column_name	Name of each column.
data_type	Datatype of each column.
data_length	Column length, in bytes, for columns having datatypes constrained by length. These datatypes include VARCHAR2, CHAR, NVARCHAR2, NCHAR, and RAW.
data_precision	Precision for NUMBER columns.
data_scale	Scale for NUMBER columns.
nullable	Whether a column is nullable. This will be either Y or N.

Example 10-2 shows a simple script that queries all_tab_columns for a table you specify. The COLUMN commands set column widths short enough so the report will fit within 80 characters. Substitution variables in the WHERE clause cause SQL*Plus to prompt you for owner and table names.

Example 10-2. A script to list column definitions for a table

```
COLUMN column_name FORMAT A30 HEADING 'Column Name'
COLUMN data_type FORMAT A17 HEADING 'Data Type'
COLUMN not_null FORMAT A9 HEADING 'Nullable?'
```

Example 10-2. A script to list column definitions for a table (continued)

```
SELECT column_name,
       DECODE (data_type,
          'VARCHAR2','VARCHAR2 (' || TO_CHAR(data_length) || ')',
          'NVARCHAR2','NVARCHAR2 (' || TO_CHAR(data_length) || ')',
          'CHAR','CHAR (' || TO_CHAR(data_length) || ')',
          'NCHAR','NCHAR (' || TO_CHAR(data_length) || ')',
          'NUMBER',
             DECODE (data_precision,
                NULL, 'NUMBER',
                'NUMBER (' || TO_CHAR(data_precision)
                           || ',' || TO_CHAR(data_scale) || ')'),
          'FLOAT',
             DECODE (data_precision,
                NULL, 'FLOAT',
                'FLOAT (' || TO_CHAR(data_precision) || ')'),
          'DATE','DATE',
          'LONG','LONG',
          'LONG RAW','LONG RAW',
          'RAW','RAW (' || TO_CHAR(data_length) || ')',
          'MLSLABEL','MLSLABEL',
          'ROWID','ROWID',
          'CLOB','CLOB',
          'NCLOB','NCLOB',
          'BLOB','BLOB',
          'BFILE','BFILE',
          data_type || ' ???') data_type,
       DECODE (nullable, 'N','NOT NULL') not_null
  FROM all_tab_columns
 WHERE owner = UPPER('&owner_name')
   AND table_name = UPPER('&table_name')
 ORDER BY column_id;
```

No ACCEPT commands are in Example 10-2. Instead, the script relies on SQL*Plus's default behavior when it encounters the two substitution variables in the WHERE clause:

```
WHERE owner = UPPER('&owner_name')
  AND table_name = UPPER('&table_name')
```

As each variable is encountered, SQL*Plus prompts you to supply a value. The value you supply is used once. Because only one ampersand is used in front of each variable name, values are not preserved for use beyond the single substitution.

The results of running Example 10-2 are as follows:

```
SQL> @ex10-2
Enter value for owner_name: gennick
old  29: WHERE owner = UPPER('&owner_name')
new  29: WHERE owner = UPPER('gennick')
Enter value for table_name: employee
old  30:   AND table_name = UPPER('&table_name')
new  30:   AND table_name = UPPER('employee')
```

Case-Sensitivity in the Data Dictionary

Oracle's default behavior is to uppercase the names of any objects that you create. For example, you may create a table giving the lowercase name employee:

```
create table employee (...)
```

Oracle will uppercase this table name, converting it to EMPLOYEE before creating the table, and thereafter you'll need to use the uppercase version of the table name when querying the data dictionary. Because it's so common to type in lowercase, many of the scripts in this chapter use the UPPER function in the WHERE clause to relieve you of the burden of remembering to hit Caps Lock before you type.

```
WHERE owner = UPPER('&owner_name')
  AND table_name = UPPER('&table_name')
```

This WHERE clause, taken from Example 10-2, automatically uppercases any owner and table names that you provide. Bear in mind though, that it is possible, using double quotation marks, to prevent object names from being translated to uppercase. For example, the quotation marks around the identifier in the following statement cause Oracle to leave the name in lowercase as it is specified:

```
CREATE TABLE "employee" (...)
```

If your scripts automatically uppercase the owner and table names that you supply, which is usually a convenience, you'll have a difficult time working with tables having lowercase or mixed-case names. If you were determined enough, you could write a script that would leave names alone when you quoted them, possibly via CASE expressions, thus mimicking the behavior of Oracle. Most DBAs though, myself included, prefer working with identifiers that are all uppercase and don't need to be quoted.

Column Name	Data Type	Nullable?
EMPLOYEE_ID	NUMBER	NOT NULL
EMPLOYEE_NAME	VARCHAR2 (40)	
EMPLOYEE_HIRE_DATE	DATE	
EMPLOYEE_TERMINATION_DATE	DATE	
EMPLOYEE_BILLING_RATE	NUMBER (5,2)	

The SELECT statement in the script looks complex, but that's because the statement must accommodate different column data types. The complication comes from the DECODE statement that starts out like this:

```
DECODE (data_type,
        'VARCHAR2','VARCHAR2 (' || TO_CHAR(data_length) || ')',
        'NVARCHAR2','NVARCHAR2 (' || TO_CHAR(data_length) || ')',
        'CHAR','CHAR (' || TO_CHAR(data_length) || ')',
        'NCHAR','NCHAR (' || TO_CHAR(data_length) || ')',
        'NUMBER',
          DECODE (data_precision,
            NULL, 'NUMBER',
```

```
              'NUMBER (' || TO_CHAR(data_precision)
                      || ',' || TO_CHAR(data_scale) || ')'),
   ...
```

This long DECODE expression exists because some datatypes have a length associated with them, some have a precision and scale, and some have neither. The DECODE function call contains one expression for each possible datatype, and that expression returns the appropriate information for that datatype. Consider the VARCHAR2 datatype, for example. All VARCHAR2 columns have a length associated with them. To display that length, the following two expressions (separated by commas) are included in the DECODE call:

```
   'VARCHAR2','VARCHAR2 (' || TO_CHAR(data_length) || ')'
```

The first expression is the string VARCHAR2. When DECODE is evaluating a datatype that matches that string, it will return the value of the second expression in the pair. In the case of VARCHAR2, here is the second expression:

```
   'VARCHAR2 (' || TO_CHAR(data_length) || ')'
```

This second expression concatenates the string 'VARCHAR2 (' with the length, then follows that with a closing parentheses. The result will be a string resembling the one shown here:

```
   VARCHAR2 (40)
```

The NUMBER and FLOAT datatypes add a bit more complexity. A NUMBER, for example, can be defined as floating-point or fixed-point. Floating-point numbers have null values for data_precision and data_scale. If a NUMBER field is floating-point, the data_precision is null, and the nested DECODE returns just NUMBER as the datatype. Otherwise, the nested DECODE returns NUMBER (*precision, scale*).

Table Constraints

Four different types of constraints can be created on a table:

- Check
- Primary key
- Unique
- Foreign key

These types are different enough that, with the exception of the Primary key and Unique constraints, you need a slightly different query for each to properly see the definitions.

Check Constraints

A *check constraint* is an expression that must be true for each row in a table. This is the simplest of the constraint types when it comes to querying the data dictionary tables. The check expression is stored in the search_condition column of the all_ constraints table. The query in Example 10-3 will get you the definition of all check constraints on a particular table.

Example 10-3. A query to list check constraints on a table

```
COLUMN constraint_name FORMAT A20
COLUMN status FORMAT A8
COLUMN search_condition FORMAT A50 WORD_WRAPPED

SELECT constraint_name, status, search_condition
FROM all_constraints
WHERE owner = UPPER('&owner')
  AND table_name = UPPER('&table_name')
  AND constraint_type ='C';
```

The simple query in Example 10-3 is a matter of finding all constraints of type C for the specified table. You don't even have to join any tables. With the other constraint types, the query gets more complex. Following is an example run to see what check constraints exist on the employee table:

```
SQL> @ex10-3
Enter value for owner: gennick
old    3:   WHERE owner = UPPER('&owner')
new    3:   WHERE owner = UPPER('gennick')
Enter value for table_name: employee
old    4:     AND table_name = UPPER('&table_name')
new    4:     AND table_name = UPPER('employee')


CONSTRAINT_NAME      STATUS   SEARCH_CONDITION
-------------------- -------- --------------------------------------------------
SILLY_CHECK          DISABLED employee_id = employee_id
```

The status column from all_constraints indicates whether a constraint is active. A status of ENABLED means that a constraint is actively being enforced. A status of DISABLED means that the DBA has disabled the constraint, possibly to make it easier to perform maintenance. The SILLY_CHECK constraint is indeed silly. It's probably good that it's disabled.

 The search_condition column is of type LONG. To see check constraint definitions more than 80 bytes in length, you'll need to issue a SET LONG command. Just pick a really high value, such as SET LONG 2000.

Primary Key and Unique Constraints

Primary key and *unique constraints* are similar in that they force each row in a table to have a unique value in one column or combination of columns. They are semantically different but are close enough in structure, concept, and syntax that one query suffices for both. When looking at constraints of these two types, you need to include the all_cons_columns view in your query in order to get a list of the columns involved. Query for constraint types P and U. Example 10-4 shows how to do this.

Example 10-4. A query to list primary key and unique key constraints

```
COLUMN constraint_name FORMAT A30
COLUMN constraint_type FORMAT A1
COLUMN column_name FORMAT A30
COLUMN status FORMAT A8

SELECT ac.constraint_name, ac.constraint_type,
       acc.column_name, ac.status
FROM all_constraints ac INNER JOIN all_cons_columns acc
    ON ac.constraint_name = acc.constraint_name
       AND ac.owner = acc.owner
WHERE ac.owner = UPPER('&owner')
  AND ac.table_name = UPPER('&table_name')
  AND ac.constraint_type in ('P','U')
ORDER BY ac.constraint_name, acc.position;
```

Ordering the columns in the constraint definition by the position column is done so the output matches the column order used when originally defining a constraint. Here's an example run:

```
SQL> @ex10-4
Enter value for owner: gennick
old    5:   WHERE ac.owner = UPPER('&owner')
new    5:   WHERE ac.owner = UPPER('gennick')
Enter value for table_name: employee
old    6:      AND ac.table_name = UPPER('&table_name')
new    6:      AND ac.table_name = UPPER('employee')

CONSTRAINT_NAME                      C COLUMN_NAME                       STATUS
------------------------------ - ------------------------------ --------
EMPLOYEE_PK                          P EMPLOYEE_ID                      ENABLED
```

Oracle generally enforces unique and primary key constraints by creating unique indexes. The column order used when creating the indexes will match that used in defining the constraints and can affect the performance of queries issued against the table.

Foreign Key Constraints

Foreign key constraints are the most complex. A foreign key defines a list of columns in one table, called the *child table*, that correlates to a primary key or a unique constraint on a *parent table*. When a row is inserted into the child table, Oracle checks to be sure that a corresponding parent record exists. Foreign key constraints involve two lists of columns, one in the child table on which the constraint is defined, and another in the parent table.

The trick with foreign key constraints is to find the name of the parent table, then find the names of the columns in the parent table that correspond to the columns in the child table. The key to doing this is to use the r_owner and r_constraint_name columns in the all_constraints view. The constraint type code for foreign key constraints is R. A foreign key always relates to a primary key constraint or a unique constraint on the parent table. The name of this related constraint is in the r_constraint_name column. Usually, the r_owner column matches the owner column, but don't assume that will be the case.

To see the definition of all the foreign key constraints for a given table, you can start with the query used for primary key constraints and modify the WHERE clause to look only at constraint type R. You can get rid of the constraint type columns. Example 10-5 shows the resulting query.

Example 10-5. A script to list foreign key columns

```
COLUMN constraint_name FORMAT A30
COLUMN column_name FORMAT A15

SELECT ac.constraint_name, acc.column_name
FROM all_constraints ac INNER JOIN all_cons_columns acc
    ON ac.constraint_name = acc.constraint_name
        AND ac.owner = acc.owner
WHERE ac.owner = UPPER('&owner')
  AND ac.table_name = UPPER('&table_name')
  AND ac.constraint_type = 'R'
ORDER BY ac.constraint_name, acc.position;
```

This query will give you constraint names and a list of column names. The following are the results showing foreign key constraints defined on project_hours:

```
SQL> @ex10-5
Enter value for owner: gennick
old    5: WHERE ac.owner = UPPER('&owner')
new    5: WHERE ac.owner = UPPER('gennick')
Enter value for table_name: project_hours
old    6:   AND ac.table_name = UPPER('&table_name')
new    6:   AND ac.table_name = UPPER('project_hours')

CONSTRAINT_NAME                     COLUMN_NAME
------------------------------      ---------------
PROJ_HOURS_FKTO_EMPLOYEE            EMPLOYEE_ID
PROJ_HOURS_FKTO_PROJECT            PROJECT_ID
```

Two foreign key constraints each involve one column that relates to a second parent table. However, the query as it stands won't tell you the name of those parent tables, nor the names of the corresponding columns in those tables. For those, you need to join all_constraints to itself via the r_constraint_name and r_owner columns. This will give you access to the parent table's name. Example 10-6 shows this version of the query.

Example 10-6. A script to list foreign key constraints with their target tables

```
COLUMN constraint_name FORMAT A30
COLUMN column_name FORMAT A15
COLUMN owner FORMAT A10
COLUMN table_name FORMAT A15

SELECT ac.constraint_name, acc.column_name,
       r_ac.owner, r_ac.table_name
FROM all_constraints ac INNER JOIN all_cons_columns acc
    ON ac.constraint_name = acc.constraint_name
       AND ac.owner = acc.owner
    INNER JOIN all_constraints r_ac
    ON ac.r_owner = r_ac.owner
       AND ac.r_constraint_name = r_ac.constraint_name
WHERE ac.owner = UPPER('&owner')
  AND ac.table_name = UPPER('&table_name')
  AND ac.constraint_type = 'R'
ORDER BY ac.constraint_name, acc.position;
```

The following are the results from a run of Example 10-6:

```
SQL> @ex10-6
Enter value for owner: gennick
old    9: WHERE ac.owner = UPPER('&owner')
new    9: WHERE ac.owner = UPPER('gennick')
Enter value for table_name: project_hours
old   10:   AND ac.table_name = UPPER('&table_name')
new   10:   AND ac.table_name = UPPER('project_hours')

CONSTRAINT_NAME                COLUMN_NAME     OWNER      TABLE_NAME
------------------------------ --------------- ---------- ---------------
PROJ_HOURS_FKTO_EMPLOYEE       EMPLOYEE_ID     GENNICK    EMPLOYEE
PROJ_HOURS_FKTO_PROJECT        PROJECT_ID      GENNICK    PROJECT
```

Because most foreign key constraints relate to the parent table's primary key, you may want to stop here. However, as it is possible to relate a foreign key to a unique key on the parent table, you may want see the corresponding list of parent table columns to understand the constraint. To do this, you must join with all_cons_columns once again and pick up the columns that go with the related parent table constraint.

> This final join to all_cons_columns can cause quite a performance hit, enough for you to notice. For that reason, you may prefer to remain with the query version in Example 10-6, and simply infer the parent column names based on the foreign key column names that Example 10-6 provides.

Example 10-7 shows a final version of the query to list foreign key constraints. This version joins a second time to all_cons_columns to display the foreign key columns side by side with their respective parent table columns.

Example 10-7. A script to list foreign key constraints together with their target columns

```
COLUMN constraint_name FORMAT A30
COLUMN column_name FORMAT A15
COLUMN target_column FORMAT A20

SELECT ac.constraint_name, acc.column_name,
       r_ac.owner || '.' || r_ac.table_name
       || '.' || r_acc.column_name target_column
FROM all_constraints ac INNER JOIN all_cons_columns acc
    ON ac.constraint_name = acc.constraint_name
       AND ac.owner = acc.owner
    INNER JOIN all_constraints r_ac
    ON ac.r_owner = r_ac.owner
       AND ac.r_constraint_name = r_ac.constraint_name
    INNER JOIN all_cons_columns r_acc
    ON  r_ac.owner = r_acc.owner
        AND r_ac.constraint_name = r_acc.constraint_name
        AND acc.position = r_acc.position
WHERE ac.owner = UPPER('&owner')
  AND ac.table_name = UPPER('&table_name')
  AND ac.constraint_type = 'R'
ORDER BY ac.constraint_name, acc.position;
```

The all_cons_columns table's position column forms part of the join criteria. This ensures that matching columns are output together, on the same line. The results from the script are as follows:

```
SQL> @ex10-7
Enter value for owner: gennick
old  14: WHERE ac.owner = UPPER('&owner')
new  14: WHERE ac.owner = UPPER('gennick')
Enter value for table_name: project_hours
old  15:   AND ac.table_name = UPPER('&table_name')
new  15:   AND ac.table_name = UPPER('project_hours')


CONSTRAINT_NAME                 COLUMN_NAME      TARGET_COLUMN
------------------------------- ---------------- -----------------------------
PROJ_HOURS_FKTO_EMPLOYEE        EMPLOYEE_ID      GENNICK.EMPLOYEE.EMPLOYEE_ID
PROJ_HOURS_FKTO_PROJECT         PROJECT_ID       GENNICK.PROJECT.PROJECT_ID
```

To conserve horizontal space, Example 10-7 combines the target owner, table, and column names into a single, period-delimited string. Thus, GENNICK.EMPLOYEE. EMPLOYEE_ID refers to the EMPLOYEE_ID column of the EMPLOYEE table owned by the user GENNICK.

> The COLUMN definitions in Example 10-7 don't allow for the maximum length of constraint and column names. One of the problems you run into when querying the data dictionary tables is you often end up wanting to display more columns than will fit on your screen.

Indexes

The problem of listing indexes for a table is much the same as that of listing constraints on a table. You have a master-detail relationship between the index and its columns, and you may have multiple indexes on one table.

To list only the indexes on a table, query the all_indexes view:

```
SELECT index_name, index_type, uniqueness
FROM all_indexes
WHERE owner = UPPER('&owner')
  AND table_name = UPPER('&table_name');
```

Listing the indexes alone is seldom enough. You need to know at least the columns involved in each index. To that end, join with all_ind_columns. Example 10-8 shows the query.

Example 10-8. A script to list all indexes on a table

```
COLUMN index_name FORMAT A20
COLUMN index_type FORMAT A10
COLUMN UNIQUENESS FORMAT A10
COLUMN column_name FORMAT A15

SELECT ai.index_name, ai.index_type, ai.uniqueness, aic.column_name
FROM all_indexes ai INNER JOIN all_ind_columns aic
    ON ai.owner = aic.index_owner
    AND ai.index_name = aic.index_name
WHERE ai.owner = UPPER('&owner')
  AND ai.table_name = UPPER('&table_name')
ORDER BY aic.column_position;
```

Here's a run of Example 10-8 showing the two indexes on the employee table:

```
SQL> @ex10-8
Enter value for owner: gennick
old   5: WHERE ai.owner = UPPER('&owner')
new   5: WHERE ai.owner = UPPER('gennick')
Enter value for table_name: employee
old   6:   AND ai.table_name = UPPER('&table_name')
new   6:   AND ai.table_name = UPPER('employee')

INDEX_NAME           INDEX_TYPE UNIQUENESS COLUMN_NAME
-------------------- ---------- ---------- ---------------
EMPLOYEE_PK          NORMAL     UNIQUE     EMPLOYEE_ID
EMPLOYEE_BY_NAME     NORMAL     NONUNIQUE  EMPLOYEE_NAME
```

One thing to keep in mind when working with unique indexes is that Oracle will report a unique index violation as if it were a constraint violation. The error message you get is the same as the one used when you violate a unique constraint, and it looks like this:

```
ORA-00001: unique constraint (GENNICK.UNIQUE_BILLING_RATE) violated
```

The reason for this is no doubt because Oracle enforces unique and primary key constraints by creating indexes on the constrained fields. If you do get the error message just shown, you might want to check two things. First, list the constraints on the table you are updating. Second, if you don't find one with a name that matches the one in the error message, check to see whether there happens to be a unique index with that same name.

 Beginning with Oracle8*i* Database, defining a unique or primary key constraint without having a corresponding index created is possible.

Triggers

Information about triggers can be retrieved from two views, the all_triggers view and the all_trigger_cols view. Most of the time you will find all the information you need in all_triggers. The all_trigger_cols view contains a list of all database columns referenced in the trigger. This view is sometimes useful when you are troubleshooting because it can show you which triggers reference or modify any given database column.

To find out whether any triggers have been defined on a table, query all_triggers as shown in Example 10-9.

Example 10-9. Listing the names of triggers on a table

```
SET VERIFY OFF
COLUMN description FORMAT A40 WORD_WRAPPED
COLUMN status FORMAT A10

SELECT description, status
FROM all_triggers
WHERE table_owner = UPPER('&owner')
  AND table_name = UPPER('&table_name');
```

The following run of Example 10-9 lists the triggers defined on the employee table:

```
SQL> @ex10-9
Enter value for owner: gennick
Enter value for table_name: employee

DESCRIPTION                              STATUS
---------------------------------------- ----------
emp_hire_date_check                      ENABLED
BEFORE INSERT OR UPDATE ON employee
FOR EACH ROW

emp_delete_check                         ENABLED
BEFORE DELETE ON employee
FOR EACH ROW
```

Table 10-3 describes the columns returned by the query in Example 10-9, as well as other important columns you can look at to understand a given trigger more fully.

Table 10-3. The key columns in the view

Column	Description
description	Combination of `trigger_name` (e.g., `emp_hire_date_check`), `trigger_type` (e.g., BEFORE EACH ROW), `triggering_event` (e.g., INSERT OR UPDATE), and `table_name` (e.g., `employee`).
trigger_body	Code that executes when the trigger is fired.
when_clause	Any WHEN clause that restricts the conditions on which the trigger executes.
owner	Owner of the trigger. Triggers are usually owned by their table's owners but that doesn't have to be the case.
trigger_name	Name of the trigger.
referencing_names	Alias names through which the trigger body references old and new columns.

Example 10-10 shows a script that will describe a single trigger in detail. The script's output is a CREATE TRIGGER statement that may be used to re-create the trigger. The FOLD_AFTER option is used in the COLUMN commands to force each column to begin a new line of output. SET PAGESIZE 0 gets rid of any page titles and column headings that would otherwise clutter the output. The `trigger_body` column is of type LONG, so SET LONG 5000 ensures that you'll see at least the first 5000 bytes of a trigger body. Use a higher value if your triggers are longer than that.

Example 10-10. A script to generate a CREATE TRIGGER statement

```
SET VERIFY OFF
SET LONG 5000
SET PAGESIZE 0
COLUMN create_stmt FOLD_AFTER
COLUMN description FOLD_AFTER
COLUMN when_clause FOLD_AFTER

SELECT 'CREATE OR REPLACE TRIGGER ' create_stmt,
       description,
       CASE WHEN when_clause IS NOT NULL THEN
          'WHEN (' || when_clause || ')'
       ELSE
          ''
       END when_clause,
       trigger_body
FROM all_triggers
WHERE owner = UPPER('&owner')
  AND trigger_name = UPPER('&trigger_name');

SET PAGESIZE 14
```

The following invocation of Example 10-10 shows the definition for the trigger emp_delete_check:

```
SQL> @ex10-10
Enter value for owner: gennick
Enter value for trigger_name: emp_delete_check
CREATE OR REPLACE TRIGGER
emp_delete_check
BEFORE DELETE ON employee
FOR EACH ROW

BEGIN
  IF (:OLD.employee_termination_date IS NULL)
     OR (:OLD.employee_termination_date >= TRUNC(SYSDATE)+1) THEN
        RAISE_APPLICATION_ERROR (-20001,
           'You must terminate an employee before deleting his record.');
  END IF;
END;
```

This output contains a blank line in front of the BEGIN keyword. That blank line is where the WHEN clause would go, if one had been defined when the trigger was created. You can execute this output to re-create the trigger. To do that, you could simply copy and paste the output into SQL*Plus, taking care to terminate the block (a trigger is a PL/SQL block) with a forward slash (/) on a line by itself. (Chapter 2 shows examples of PL/SQL block execution.)

Synonyms

A *synonym* is an alternate name for a table. By coding your programs to use synonyms instead of table names, you insulate yourself from any changes in the name, ownership, or table location. All of the scripts in this chapter have used synonyms instead of table names. all_tables, for example, is actually a public synonym for the sys.all_tables table.

To find out about synonyms, you can query the all_synonyms view. Example 10-11 queries all_synonyms to find any synonyms that point to the all_tables system view.

Example 10-11. Listing synonyms referring to all_tables

```
SELECT owner, synonym_name
FROM all_synonyms
WHERE table_owner = 'SYS' AND table_name = 'ALL_TABLES';

OWNER                           SYNONYM_NAME
------------------------------- -------------------------------
PUBLIC                          ALL_TABLES
GENNICK                         ALL_TABLES
```

There are two types of synonyms. Synonyms owned by a user are *private synonyms* and affect only that user. *Public synonyms* are owned by PUBLIC and affect all database users. Example 10-11 shows one synonym of each type. For whatever reason, the user GENNICK has created his own, private synonym pointing to all_tables. He may have done that to illustrate a point for a book.

Private synonyms override public synonym definitions, so it's important to know when both types exist. Change GENNICK's all_tables synonym to point to sys.all_object_tables, and he'd no doubt be one confused DBA the next time he went to look at his table definitions.

One thing you should be aware of when looking at synonyms is that unless you are the DBA, you won't be able to look at all synonyms owned by other users. The all_synonyms view shows you three synonyms:

- Public synonyms (owned by PUBLIC)
- Synonyms you own
- Synonyms owned by other users that reference tables and other objects to which you have access

The only time the all_synonyms view would show you all the synonyms in the database would be if you had access to all the objects in the database.

Table Security

Information about who has been granted access to a particular table can be found in two views, the all_tab_privs view and the all_col_privs view. These views show you information about privileges granted on tables you own or privileges you have been granted on tables owned by other users. Unless you are the DBA or otherwise have access to the dba_tab_privs_made and dba_col_privs_made views, you cannot fully see the security for tables you do not own.

The all_tab_privs view gives you information about table-level grants. For example, if you issue the following statement, it will be reflected in all_tab_privs:

```
GRANT SELECT, DELETE ON employee TO jeff;
```

Some privileges, UPDATE and INSERT, for example, may be restricted to certain columns of a table. For example, the following grant allows jeff to change just the employee's name:

```
GRANT UPDATE (employee_name) ON employee TO jeff;
```

Grants such as this, which are restricted to certain columns, are reflected in the all_col_privs view. To get a complete picture of the privileges you have granted on any particular table, you need to query both of these views. The query against all_tab_privs will look something like that in Example 10-12.

Example 10-12. A query to list privileges granted on a table

```
SELECT grantee, privilege, grantable
  FROM all_tab_privs
 WHERE table_schema = 'GENNICK'
   AND table_name = 'EMPLOYEE';
```

```
GRANTEE                          PRIVILEGE                              GRA
-------------------------------- -------------------------------------- ---
JEFF                             DELETE                                 NO
JEFF                             SELECT                                 NO
```

This query will give you a list of all privileges that have been granted without any column restrictions. The grantable column will tell you whether the privilege was granted using the WITH GRANT OPTION keywords. Granting a privilege WITH GRANT OPTION allows the grantee to pass that privilege on to others.

You will need to know about any column-level privileges that have been granted. These will be reflected in all_col_privs, so you must query that as well. The query in Example 10-13 shows any column-level privileges that have been granted on employee.

Example 10-13. A query to list privileges granted on columns of a table

```
COLUMN grantee FORMAT A12
COLUMN privilege FORMAT A12
COLUMN column_name FORMAT A15

SELECT grantee, privilege, column_name, grantable
  FROM all_col_privs
 WHERE table_schema = 'GENNICK'
   AND table_name = 'EMPLOYEE';
```

```
GRANTEE      PRIVILEGE    COLUMN_NAME      GRA
------------ ------------ ---------------- ---
JEFF         UPDATE       EMPLOYEE_NAME    NO
```

Scripting the Data Dictionary

You can write scripts to remove some of the burden of writing queries against the data dictionary. Example 10-14 shows one way you might go about writing such a script, by presenting one that lists all the indexes on a table. Don't take in the entire script now. Glance over it to get the gist of how it's put together. Then read the sections that follow; they explain the more significant parts of the script in detail.

Example 10-14. A script to list all indexes on a given table

```
SET ECHO OFF

--DESCRIPTION
--Displays information about an index. The index name
--is passed as a parameter to this script.

--Remind the user of what the first argument should be.
--If the user forgot to specify the argument, he/she will
--be prompted for it when the first occurrence of &&1 is encountered.
PROMPT Argument 1 - Table name in [owner.]table_name format
PROMPT Describing indexes on table &&1

SET RECSEP OFF
SET NEWPAGE NONE
SET VERIFY OFF
SET PAGESIZE 9999
SET HEADING OFF
SET LINESIZE 80
SET FEEDBACK OFF
CLEAR COMPUTES
CLEAR COLUMNS
CLEAR BREAKS

--Turn off terminal output to avoid spurious blank lines
--caused by the SELECT that is done only to load the
--substitution variables.
SET TERMOUT OFF

--Dissect the input argument, and get the owner name and
--table name into two, separate substitution variables.
--The owner name defaults to the current user.
DEFINE s_owner_name = ' '
DEFINE s_table_name = ' '
COLUMN owner_name NOPRINT NEW_VALUE s_owner_name
COLUMN table_name NOPRINT NEW_VALUE s_table_name
SELECT
  DECODE(INSTR('&&1','.'),
         0,USER,  /*Default to current user.*/
         UPPER(SUBSTR('&&1',1,INSTR('&&1','.')-1))) owner_name,
  DECODE(INSTR('&&1','.'),
         0,UPPER('&&1'),  /*Only the table name was passed in.*/
         UPPER(SUBSTR('&&1',INSTR('&&1','.')+1))) table_name
  FROM dual;

SET TERMOUT ON

--The following variables receive information about each index
DEFINE s_index_owner = ' '
DEFINE s_index_name = ' '
DEFINE s_index_type = ' '
DEFINE s_uniqueness = ' '
DEFINE s_tablespace_name = ' '
```

Example 10-14. A script to list all indexes on a given table (continued)

```
--Place new, index-related values into the above substitution variables
COLUMN owner NOPRINT NEW_VALUE s_index_owner
COLUMN table_name NOPRINT NEW_VALUE s_table_name
COLUMN index_name NOPRINT NEW_VALUE s_index_name
COLUMN index_type NOPRINT NEW_VALUE s_index_type
COLUMN uniqueness NOPRINT NEW_VALUE s_uniqueness
COLUMN tablespace_name NOPRINT NEW_VALUE s_tablespace_name

--Format the two columns that we'll actually display from the query
COLUMN indent FORMAT A19
COLUMN column_name FORMAT A30

--Skip a page for each new index
BREAK ON owner ON index_name SKIP PAGE

--Information about the index as a whole is printed in
--the page title.
TTITLE SKIP 1 LEFT 'INDEX ' s_index_owner "." s_index_name -
       ' ' s_index_type ' ' s_uniqueness SKIP 1 -
       'DEFINED ON TABLE ' s_owner_name "." s_table_name SKIP 1 -
       'STORED IN TABLESPACE ' s_tablespace_name SKIP 1 -
       'CONTAINING COLUMNS: '

--List the columns that make up the index.
--The indent column moves the column list over to the
--right so that it comes after the 'CONTAINING COLUMNS:'
--portion of the header.
SELECT ai.owner, ai.index_name, ai.index_type,
       ai.uniqueness, ai.tablespace_name,
       ' ' indent,
       aic.column_name
  FROM all_indexes ai JOIN all_ind_columns aic
       ON ai.owner = aic.index_owner
       AND ai.index_name = aic.index_name
 WHERE ai.table_owner = '&&s_owner_name'
   AND ai.table_name = '&&s_table_name'
ORDER BY ai.owner, ai.index_name, aic.column_position;

--Change all settings back to defaults
CLEAR COLUMNS
CLEAR BREAKS
SET PAGESIZE 14
SET HEADING ON
SET NEWPAGE 1
SET FEEDBACK ON
UNDEFINE 1
```

Running the Script

Run the script in Example 10-14 as follows, by passing a table name as a command-line argument:

```
SQL> @ex10-14 employee
Argument 1 - Table name in [owner.]table_name format
Describing indexes on table gennick.employee

INDEX GENNICK.EMPLOYEE_PK NORMAL UNIQUE
DEFINED ON TABLE GENNICK.EMPLOYEE
STORED IN TABLESPACE USERS
CONTAINING COLUMNS:
                EMPLOYEE_ID

INDEX GENNICK.EMPLOYEE_BY_NAME NORMAL NONUNIQUE
DEFINED ON TABLE GENNICK.EMPLOYEE
STORED IN TABLESPACE USERS
CONTAINING COLUMNS:
                EMPLOYEE_NAME
```

As you can see, the script displays information about the two indexes on employee. Both indexes consist of a single column each. The unique index happens to be the primary key index, on the employee_id column. The other index is on employee_name.

When the Parameter Is Omitted

Example 10-14 begins with an interesting bit of script that serves to remind you of what the command-line parameter should be:

```
--Remind the user of what the first argument should be.
--If the user forgot to specify the argument, he/she will
--be prompted for it when the first occurrence of &&1 is encountered.
PROMPT Argument 1 - Table name in [owner.]table_name format
```

This reminder prompt is useful because if you forget to pass the table name as a parameter, SQL*Plus will prompt you when the parameter reference is first encountered in the script. However, parameters are referenced by numerical position, using substitution variable names such as 1, 2, etc. SQL*Plus's default prompt, when you omit the command-line argument, will ask you to enter a value for 1, which doesn't help:

```
SQL> @ex10-14
Argument 1 - Table name in [owner.]table_name format
Enter value for 1: employee
Describing indexes on table employee
...
```

Although the default prompt isn't helpful in this case, the output from the PROMPT command will serve to remind you of what 1 is supposed to be. This is a handy technique to use in scripts that accept parameters, especially when you plan to run those scripts interactively from the SQL*Plus command line.

My thanks to K. Vainstein for suggesting this technique of using PROMPT to remind script users of a script's arguments.

Separating Owner and Table Names

The next significant part of Example 10-14 is a set of COLUMN commands along with a SELECT statement that serve to separate a parameter in *owner.table_name* format into two separate values:

```
COLUMN owner_name NOPRINT NEW_VALUE s_owner_name
COLUMN table_name NOPRINT NEW_VALUE s_table_name
SELECT
  DECODE(INSTR('&&1','.'),
         0,USER,  /*Default to current user.*/
         UPPER(SUBSTR('&&1',1,INSTR('&&1','.')-1))) owner_name,
  DECODE(INSTR('&&1','.'),
         0,UPPER('&&1'),  /*Only the table name was passed in.*/
         UPPER(SUBSTR('&&1',INSTR('&&1','.')+1))) table_name
  FROM dual;
```

The DECODE function calls are what makes this SELECT flexible enough to deal with whether you choose to specify a username in response to the prompt. The first DECODE function call returns the appropriate owner name. You can interpret the arguments to this DECODE call as follows:

INSTR('&&1','.')
> Looks for the character position of the period in the parameter passed to the script. If there is no period, INSTR returns zero. The result of INSTR is argument #1 to the DECODE function.

0,USER
> If argument #1 is zero, meaning that no owner name was given, default to the currently logged in user's name.

UPPER(SUBSTR('&&1',1,INSTR('&&1','.')-1))
> Otherwise, return everything up to, but not including, the period as the owner name.

The second DECODE function implements similar logic, but this time to return the table name:

INSTR('&&1','.')
> Again, looks for the period in the parameter, returning zero if one is not found.

0,UPPER('&&1'), /*Only the table name was passed in.*/
> If argument #1 is zero, return the entire command-line parameter as the table name.

UPPER(SUBSTR('&&1',INSTR('&&1','.')+1))
> Otherwise, return the characters following the period as the table name.

The SELECT described in this section is done with TERMOUT off so you aren't bothered by the output from this SELECT against dual when you run the script.

Generating the Index Headings

Example 10-14 describes each index using a two-part structure. The first part, the *index header*, displays information about each index as a whole. The second part lists the columns in the index. The following are the header and column for employee's primary key index:

```
INDEX GENNICK.EMPLOYEE_PK NORMAL UNIQUE
DEFINED ON TABLE GENNICK.EMPLOYEE
STORED IN TABLESPACE USERS
CONTAINING COLUMNS:
                    EMPLOYEE_ID
```

The reason for this two-part approach is that all the information couldn't possibly fit on a single line. To generate a header for each index, Example 10-14 takes advantage of SQL*Plus's pagination capabilities.

The SELECT statement joins all_indexes with all_ind_columns, and retrieves columns from both views. The following COLUMN commands cause SQL*Plus to continually (for each row retrieved) update a set of substitution variables with information from all_indexes.

```
COLUMN owner NOPRINT NEW_VALUE s_index_owner
COLUMN table_name NOPRINT NEW_VALUE s_table_name
COLUMN index_name NOPRINT NEW_VALUE s_index_name
COLUMN index_type NOPRINT NEW_VALUE s_index_type
COLUMN uniqueness NOPRINT NEW_VALUE s_uniqueness
COLUMN tablespace_name NOPRINT NEW_VALUE s_tablespace_name
```

This information from all_indexes needs to be displayed only once. To that end, Example 10-14's TTITLE command references the substitution variables:

```
TTITLE SKIP 1 LEFT 'INDEX ' s_index_owner "." s_index_name -
       ' ' s_index_type ' ' s_uniqueness SKIP 1 -
       'DEFINED ON TABLE ' s_owner_name "." s_table_name SKIP 1 -
       'STORED IN TABLESPACE ' s_tablespace_name SKIP 1 -
       'CONTAINING COLUMNS: '
```

The following BREAK command generates a page break each time a new index is encountered in the query's result set:

```
BREAK ON owner ON index_name SKIP PAGE
```

The result set is sorted by index and within index by column. The column name is the only value that SQL*Plus displays for each row (aside from some spaces for indention). As SQL*Plus lists the column names, every new combination of owner and index name forces a page break. For each new page, the page title prints, displaying the current values of the s_ substitution variables. SET HEADING OFF prevents any column headings from displaying.

Starting with a Clean Slate

Many settings affect SQL*Plus's operation. It's difficult to write a script that doesn't have any side effects and also difficult to ensure that a script is immune to some setting that you assume will be at its default. It would be nice if you could push the current state of SQL*Plus to a stack at the beginning of a script, issue a RESET command to place SQL*Plus in a known starting state, and then pop the original state back off the stack before exiting the script. Perhaps someday Oracle will provide this functionality.

Example 10-1 executes many SET and other commands to configure SQL*Plus to display information about the tables owned by a given user. The intent is to make every required setting explicit, i.e., to avoid any implicit reliance on a default setting that might not be in effect. The script attempts to undo all that work at the end, restoring the various settings back to their defaults. These two practices help minimize unwanted interactions between scripts run in the same interactive session.

Using SQL to Write SQL

One of the most interesting and useful things you can do using the data dictionary is to automate the generation of SQL statements in a technique often referred to as *using SQL to write SQL*. (We looked briefly at this technique in Chapter 9.) The gist of this technique is to use expressions involving data dictionary columns to build syntactically valid SQL statements that you can, in turn, execute to perform various database maintenance tasks.

A common problem that I encountered on one particular project I worked on was the need to move schemas from one database to another. Moving an actual schema is easy enough. You can do it by exporting that schema from your source database and then importing it into your target database. This is easy to do using Oracle's export and import utilities. What made this simple task into a challenge was that I needed to re-create, on the target database, any public synonyms that referred to objects in the schema I was moving. Because they were public, these synonyms were, of course, not part of the schema and were not exported along with all the objects that were part of the schema.

After scratching my head for a bit, I came up with a script similar to the one in Example 10-15. This script prompts for a schema name and queries dba_synonyms for a list of synonyms referencing objects in that schema. Rather than return a simple list, the script uses the following expression to return a list of CREATE PUBLIC SYNONYM commands:

```
'CREATE PUBLIC SYNONYM '
|| synonym_name
|| ' FOR '
|| table_owner || '.' || table_name
|| ';'
```

Example 10-15. A script to export public synonyms

```
SET ECHO OFF
--
--Creates a file of "create synonym" commands for each
--synonym referencing a table
--in the schema specified by the user running this script.
--
SET VERIFY OFF

--so user doesn't see feedback about the number of rows selected.
SET FEEDBACK OFF

--Tell the user what we are going to do, and prompt for
--the necessary values.
PROMPT
PROMPT
PROMPT This script allows you to build a SQL*Plus script file
PROMPT which will recreate all PUBLIC synonyms referencing
PROMPT objects in a specified schema.
PROMPT
PROMPT To abort execution, press ctrl-C.
PROMPT
ACCEPT SynRefsOwner CHAR PROMPT 'Schema >'
ACCEPT SynScriptFileName CHAR PROMPT 'Output File >'

--Build the script file with the requested "create synonym" commands.
--First set session settings so the output looks nice.
SET LINESIZE 132
SET PAGESIZE 0
SET TERMOUT OFF
SET TRIMSPOOL ON
SET TRIMOUT ON

--Spool the output the file requested by the user.
SPOOL &SynScriptFileName

SELECT 'CREATE PUBLIC SYNONYM '
       || synonym_name
       || ' FOR '
       || table_owner || '.' || table_name
       || ';'
FROM dba_synonyms
WHERE table_owner = UPPER('&SynRefsOwner')
  AND owner = 'PUBLIC'
UNION
SELECT '--No public synonyms were found referencing the schema '''
       || UPPER('&SynRefsOwner')
       || '''.'
FROM dual
WHERE NOT EXISTS (
       SELECT *
       FROM dba_synonyms
       WHERE table_owner = UPPER('&SynRefsOwner')
```

Example 10-15. A script to export public synonyms (continued)

```
        AND owner = 'PUBLIC'
    );

--Turn spooling off to close the file.
SPOOL OFF

--Reset session settings back to their defaults.
SET VERIFY ON
SET FEEDBACK 6
SET LINESIZE 80
SET TERMOUT ON
SET PAGESIZE 24
SET TRIMSPOOL OFF
SET TRIMOUT ON
```

Rather than display these commands on the screen where they will do you no good, the script spools them to a file of your choice. You can take that file to another database, execute using the @ command, and re-create all the synonyms.

The following example runs the script from Example 10-15 to export public synonyms referring to objects owned by SYSTEM:

```
SQL> @ex10-15

This script allows you to build a SQL*Plus script file
which will recreate all PUBLIC synonyms referencing
objects in a specified schema.

To abort execution, press ctrl-C.

Schema >system
Output File >syn.sql
SQL>
```

And here's the resulting file:

```
oracle@gennick02:~/sqlplus/ExampleScripts> cat syn.sql
CREATE PUBLIC SYNONYM OL$ FOR SYSTEM.OL$;

CREATE PUBLIC SYNONYM OL$HINTS FOR SYSTEM.OL$HINTS;

CREATE PUBLIC SYNONYM OL$NODES FOR SYSTEM.OL$NODES;

...
```

Most of the SET commands in Example 10-15 are there to prevent any extraneous information, such as column headings or page titles, from being written to the spool file. The real work is done by the SPOOL and SELECT commands. PAGESIZE is set to zero to inhibit pagination, and LINESIZE is made wide enough to accommodate long synonym names. SET TRIMSPOOL and SET TRIMOUT prevent trailing spaces from being written to the lines in the spool files.

For another look at how you can leverage the data dictionary to manage database objects, read *Managing Database Objects in Groups* at *http://gennick.com/rebuild_indexes_article.html*.

Using SQL to write SQL is handy. It provides a tremendous amount of leverage because rather than work with database objects one at a time, you can manipulate whole classes, or sets, of database objects at once.

The Master Key

It turns out that Oracle's data dictionary is self-documenting. When working with a properly created Oracle database, you can query the dictionary and dict_columns views for descriptions of the data dictionary views and their columns, a sort of meta-metadata. I refer to these two views as the *master key* to Oracle's data dictionary. To find the views giving information about a particular class of database object, I find it helpful to perform a wild-card search on the dictionary view's table_name column. Example 10-16 shows this approach being used to list views having to do with stored sequence generators.

Example 10-16. Looking for data dictionary views describing sequences

```
COLUMN table_name FORMAT A20
COLUMN comments FORMAT A50 WORD_WRAPPED

SELECT table_name, comments
FROM dictionary
WHERE table_name LIKE '%SEQUENCE%';

TABLE_NAME           COMMENTS
-------------------- --------------------------------------------------
USER_SEQUENCES       Description of the user's own SEQUENCEs
ALL_SEQUENCES        Description of SEQUENCEs accessible to the user
DBA_SEQUENCES        Description of all SEQUENCEs in the database
```

The technique used in Example 10-16 is to search for view names containing the word "SEQUENCE".

 Views aren't always named the way you think. The view describing a table's columns is dba_tab_columns; the word table has been abbreviated to tab. If you're interested in information on Oracle object types, you'll find that many views with names containing the word object have nothing whatsoever to do with object types.

Once you've isolated a view of interest, you can query the dict_columns view for a description of the data returned by the columns that make up the view. Example 10-17 retrieves descriptions for the columns in All_sequences.

Example 10-17. Describing the columns in the all_sequences data dictionary view

```
COLUMN column_name FORMAT A30
COLUMN comments FORMAT A40 WORD_WRAP

SELECT column_name, comments
FROM dict_columns
WHERE table_name = 'ALL_SEQUENCES';

COLUMN_NAME                       COMMENTS
------------------------------    ----------------------------------------
SEQUENCE_OWNER                    Name of the owner of the sequence
SEQUENCE_NAME                     SEQUENCE name
MIN_VALUE                         Minimum value of the sequence
MAX_VALUE                         Maximum value of the sequence
INCREMENT_BY                      Value by which sequence is incremented
CYCLE_FLAG                        Does sequence wrap around on reaching
                                  limit?

ORDER_FLAG                        Are sequence numbers generated in order?
CACHE_SIZE                        Number of sequence numbers to cache
LAST_NUMBER                       Last sequence number written to disk
```

Data dictionary views are often interrelated, and these relationships are generally quite apparent from the column names. Look at all_tables and all_tab_columns, and you'll see that you can join those two views on owner and table_name. Some relationships are hard to spot. Sometimes it takes a bit of experimentation and research to be certain you have correctly identified the relationship between two views. The recursive relationship from all_constraints to itself is a good example of the kind of relationship that might not be obvious when you first look at the view.

CHAPTER 11

Advanced Scripting

SQL*Plus was not designed to be a tool used for writing complex scripts. Its capabilities can't compare to those of your typical Unix shell, such as the Korn shell or the Bourne shell. Nor does it have anywhere near the capabilities of an advanced scripting tool such as Perl. Most noticeably, SQL*Plus suffers from the following limitations:

- It lacks an IF statement.
- There are no looping constructs.
- It has limited error handling.
- There is only marginal support for validating user input.

Because of these limitations, SQL*Plus is best suited to executing top-down scripts that don't require any branching, looping, or error handling. Most of the scripts you have seen so far in this book fall into this category. Many are reports that set up some column and page formatting and then execute a query. If something goes wrong, you may not see any data in the report, or you may see some SQL or SQL*Plus error messages.

This limited scripting support is fine when it comes to producing a report. After all, if a report fails, you can fix the problem and rerun the report. But what if you are performing a more complex and critical task? What if you are summarizing some data, posting the summary results to a summary table, and then deleting the underlying detail? In that case, you certainly don't want to delete the data if the summarization failed. You need some kind of error-handling mechanism.

 If you need to write scripts of any significant complexity, I strongly encourage you to investigate the use of PL/SQL in your script. PL/SQL is a powerful programming language in its own right and includes support for error handling, branching, and looping, which are important features that SQL*Plus lacks. Steven Feuerstein's and Bill Pribyl's book, *Oracle PL/SQL Programming*, Third Edition (O'Reilly), is an excellent resource.

This chapter describes some specific ways to work around these limitations of SQL*Plus. Believe it or not, it is possible, using only SQL*Plus, to implement branching and to validate user input. There are even ways to deal with repetitive tasks without resorting to a loop. You will learn about bind variables and see how they better enable you to mix PL/SQL code into your SQL*Plus scripts. You will see how bind variables can make the job of developing queries for application programs easier.

Bind Variables

Back in Chapter 8, you learned about substitution variables. SQL*Plus supports another type of variable called a *bind variable*. Unlike substitution variables, bind variables are real variables, having a datatype and a size.

Bind variables were created to support the use of PL/SQL in a SQL*Plus script. They provide a mechanism for returning data from a PL/SQL block back to SQL*Plus, where that data can be used in subsequent queries or by other PL/SQL blocks. Example 11-1 provides a simple script showing how a bind variable can be used.

Example 11-1. Bind variables can be used to transfer data among PL/SQL blocks and SQL queries

```
--Bind variables can be declared in your SQL*Plus script.
VARIABLE  s_table_name  varchar2(30)

--Preface a bind variable with a colon to reference it
--in a PL/SQL block.
BEGIN
  :s_table_name := 'EMPLOYEE';
END;
/

--Bind variables can even be referenced by SQL queries.
SELECT index_name
  FROM user_indexes
 WHERE table_name = :s_table_name;

--Bind variables persist until you exit SQL*Plus, so
--they can be referenced by more than one PL/SQL block.
SET SERVEROUTPUT ON
BEGIN
  DBMS_OUTPUT.PUT_LINE(:s_table_name);
END;
/
```

The scope of a bind variable is the SQL*Plus session in which it is defined. Variables defined within a PL/SQL block, on the other hand, cease to exist once that block has finished executing. Bind variables are defined one level higher (at the SQL*Plus level), so they can be referenced by many PL/SQL blocks and queries.

Declaring Bind Variables

You use the SQL*Plus VARIABLE command to declare bind variables. The syntax looks like this:

```
VAR[IABLE] var_name data_type
```

Bind variable datatypes correspond to database datatypes. Not all datatypes are supported, but the most commonly used ones are. Example 11-1 has shown one way to declare character variables:

```
VARIABLE s_table_name VARCHAR2(30)
```

You can declare numeric variables using the NUMBER datatype:

```
VAR billing_rate NUMBER
```

When declaring NUMBER bind variables, you can't specify precision and scale. However, a variable of type NUMBER can accommodate values of any precision and scale, so the inability to specify a specific precision and scale presents no problem in practice.

Other datatypes are supported. REFCURSOR is a useful bind variable type that you'll read more about later in this chapter. The new, numeric types (BINARY_FLOAT and BINARY_DOUBLE) are supported if you are running a version of SQL*Plus corresponding to a release of the database software that supports those types.

> For a complete list of supported, bind variable datatypes, see the section on the VARIABLE command in Appendix A.

In addition to declaring variables, you can use the VARIABLE command to list all of the variables you have defined. To do that, issue the command VARIABLE (which may be abbreviated VAR), with no arguments, as shown in the following example:

```
SQL> VAR
variable    s_table_name
datatype    VARCHAR2(30)

variable    billing_rate
datatype    NUMBER
```

If you are interested in one specific variable, you can specify that variable's name as an argument to the VARIABLE command:

```
SQL> VAR billing_rate
variable    billing_rate
datatype    NUMBER
```

There is no way to get rid of a variable once you have defined it.

Using Bind Variables and Substitution Variables Together

Bind variables and substitution variables don't mesh together well in SQL*Plus. Each was created for a different purpose, and the two types can't be used interchangeably. For example, bind variables can't be used with the ACCEPT command, but substitution variables can. Substitution variables can be used with the TTITLE and BTITLE commands that set up page headers and footers, but bind variables cannot. Bind variables are true variables and can be passed as arguments to PL/SQL functions and procedures, but substitution variables cannot. Table 11-1 summarizes the best uses and capabilities of each type of variable.

Table 11-1. Bind variables versus substitution variables

Task	Bind variable	Substitution variable	Comments
Display information to the user—the PROMPT command.		✓	
Accept input from the user—the ACCEPT command.			
Place information from a query into page headers and footers—the TTITLE and BTITLE commands.		✓	
Run a query with user-specified criteria in the WHERE clause.	✓	✓	User input must come through a substitution variable, but you can store the resulting value in a bind variable.
Pass values to a PL/SQL function or procedure.	✓	✓	Substitution variables may be used to pass input arguments as literals.
Return information back from a PL/SQL function or procedure.	✓		Bind variables must be used for OUT and IN OUT arguments.

Each variable type, bind and substitution, exists in its own world, separate from the other. In fact, you can't even directly assign values from a bind variable to a substitution variable, or vice versa. The lines of script shown in Example 11-2, although appearing perfectly reasonable on the surface, will not work.

Example 11-2. You cannot directly place a bind variable value into a substitution variable

```
DEFINE my_sub_var = ' '
VARIABLE my_bind_var VARCHAR2(30)
EXECUTE :my_bind_var := 'Donna Gennick'
my_sub_var = my_bind_var
```

This lack of interoperability between variable types can be a source of frustration when writing scripts. As Table 11-1 shows, you can only use a bind variable for some tasks; for others, you can only use a substitution variable. Yet SQL*Plus doesn't let you move values between the two types. Fortunately, some relatively straightforward incantations let you work around this problem.

From substitution to bind

Putting the value of a substitution variable into a bind variable is the easier of the two tasks. Remember that as SQL*Plus executes your script, any substitution variables are simply replaced by their contents as each line of code is executed. You can take advantage of this to place a value into a bind variable. Take a look at the short script in Example 11-3.

Example 11-3. Assigning a substitution variable value to a bind variable

```
DEFINE my_sub_var = 'Mykola Leontovych'
VARIABLE my_bind_var VARCHAR2(30)
EXECUTE :my_bind_var := '&my_sub_var';
```

EXECUTE is a command that executes one line of PL/SQL code. When SQL*Plus encounters the EXECUTE command in Example 11-3, it replaces the reference to the substitution variable with the value of that variable. The command after substitution, the one that is executed, looks like this:

```
EXECUTE :my_bind_var := 'Mykola Leontovych';
```

The EXECUTE command is a SQL*Plus command. What gets sent to the database is a PL/SQL block:

```
BEGIN
    :my_bind_var := 'Mykola Leontovych';
END;
```

Because the assignment involves a character string, the substitution variable must be contained in quotes; otherwise, you would not have a valid string. If you are working with numeric values, you shouldn't quote them. Example 11-4 declares a variable of type NUMBER and assigns a value to it.

Example 11-4. Assigning a "numeric" value from a substitution variable to a bind variable

```
DEFINE my_sub_num = 9
VARIABLE my_bind_num NUMBER
EXECUTE :my_bind_num := &my_sub_num;
```

The EXECUTE command that SQL*Plus executes from Example 11-4 looks like this:

```
EXECUTE :my_bind_num := 9;
```

So, quote your strings, don't quote your numbers, and remember that substitution is occurring.

The value in the substitution my_sub_num in Example 11-4 is a character string. Substitution variables that you create using the DEFINE command are always character strings. That character string is converted to a true NUMBER when it is assigned to :my_bind_num.

From bind to substitution

Taking a value from a bind variable and placing it into a substitution variable is a more difficult task. What you need to do is take advantage of SQL*Plus's ability to store the result of a SELECT statement into a substitution variable. Let's say you have the following in your script:

```
DEFINE my_sub_var = ' '
VARIABLE my_bind_var VARCHAR2(35)
EXECUTE :my_bind_var := 'Brighten the corner where you are';
```

To get the value of the bind variable into the substitution variable, you need to follow these steps:

1. Think up a column name.
2. Execute a COLUMN command for the column name you thought up. Use the NEW_VALUE clause and specify the substitution variable as the target.
3. Turn off terminal output by executing a SET TERMOUT OFF command. This is optional.
4. Issue a SELECT statement that selects the bind variable from Oracle's dual table. Use the column name you thought up in step 1 as the column alias.
5. Turn terminal output back on.

The SELECT statement will return only one value, but that value will be a new value for the column in question. The COLUMN command, with its NEW_VALUE clause, causes this value to be stored in the specified substitution variable. It's a roundabout solution to the problem, but when it's all over, the substitution variable will contain the value from the bind variable. The important thing is to be sure that the column alias matches the column name used in the COLUMN command. Example 11-5 demonstrates the technique.

Example 11-5. Assigning a bind variable value to a substitution variable

```
--Declare one bind variable and one substitution variable.
--Initialize the bind variable to a value.
DEFINE my_sub_var = ' '
VARIABLE my_bind_var VARCHAR2(35)
EXECUTE :my_bind_var := 'Brighten the corner where you are';

--Store the new value of the my_alias column in my_sub_var.
COLUMN my_alias NEW_VALUE my_sub_var
```

Example 11-5. Assigning a bind variable value to a substitution variable (continued)

```
--SELECT the value of the bind variable. SQL*Plus
--will store that value in my_sub_var because of the
--previous COLUMN command.
SET TERMOUT OFF
SELECT :my_bind_var my_alias
  FROM dual;
SET TERMOUT ON

--Display the new value of the substitution variable
DEFINE my_sub_var
```

Notice in Example 11-5 that a column alias is used in the SELECT statement to give the column a name. This same name must be used in the COLUMN command issued prior to the SELECT. If these two don't match, then the assignment won't be made and my_sub_var will remain blank.

Strictly speaking, it's not necessary to turn the terminal output off for the SELECT statement. The variable assignment will still be made, even with the output on. However, if you are writing a script, you probably won't want the results of this SELECT to clutter up the display.

Displaying the Contents of a Bind Variable

You can display the contents of a bind variable to a user by using the PRINT command, or by listing the variable in a SELECT statement.

Using the PRINT command

The PRINT command takes a bind variable name as a parameter and displays the value of that variable. The results look much like the results you get from a SELECT. Example 11-6 demonstrates.

Example 11-6. PRINTing the value of a bind variable

```
SQL> VAR my_bind_var VARCHAR2(35)
SQL> EXECUTE :my_bind_var := 'Brighten the corner where you are';

PL/SQL procedure successfully completed.

SQL> PRINT my_bind_var

MY_BIND_VAR
--------------------------------------------------------------------------------
Brighten the corner where you are
```

The bind variable is treated like a database column, with the variable name being the default column heading. If you have page titles defined, they will print as well. You can even use the COLUMN command to format the output. Example 11-7 shows how this works.

Example 11-7. Using the COLUMN command to format bind variable output

```
SQL> VAR my_bind_var VARCHAR2(35)
SQL> EXECUTE :my_bind_var := 'Brighten the corner where you are';

PL/SQL procedure successfully completed.

SQL> TTITLE LEFT '*********************' SKIP 1 -
>             'A Song by Ina D. Ogdon' SKIP 1 -
>             '*********************' SKIP 2
SQL> COLUMN my_bind_var FORMAT A35 HEADING 'My Motto'
SQL> PRINT my_bind_var

*********************
A Song by Ina D. Ogdon
*********************

My Motto
-----------------------------------
Brighten the corner where you are
```

All other formatting options, such as PAGESIZE and LINESIZE, apply when printing bind variables. You can use the COLUMN command's NEW_VALUE clause to store the value of a bind variable into a substitution variable, as Example 11-8 shows.

Example 11-8. Using PRINT and NEW_VALUE to store a bind variable value into a substitution variable

```
SQL> TTITLE OFF
SQL> DEFINE my_sub_var = ' '
SQL> VAR my_bind_var VARCHAR2(35)
SQL> EXECUTE :my_bind_var := 'Brighten the corner where you are';

PL/SQL procedure successfully completed.

SQL> COLUMN my_bind_var NEW_VALUE my_sub_var
SQL> PRINT my_bind_var

MY_BIND_VAR
----------------------------------------------------------------------------
Brighten the corner where you are

SQL> PROMPT &my_sub_var
Brighten the corner where you are
```

Issuing the PRINT command by itself causes the contents of all bind variables to be displayed. Here's an example:

```
SQL> PRINT

S_TABLE_NAME
--------------------------------------------------------------------------------
EMPLOYEE


My Motto
-----------------------------------
Brighten the corner where you are


MY_BIND_NUM
-----------
          9
```

Some special considerations apply when printing bind variables of type CLOB and of type REFCURSOR. These are described in the following sections.

PRINTing CLOB variables

CLOB stands for character large object, and variables of this type can hold up to two gigabytes of text data (even more in Oracle Database 10*g*). When printing variables of type CLOB or NCLOB, you can use three SQL*Plus settings to control what you see and how the retrieval of the CLOB data is done, as in Table 11-2.

Table 11-2. Settings that affect the printing of CLOBs

Setting	Default	Description
SET LONG	80	Controls the number of characters that are displayed from a CLOB variable. By default, only the first 80 characters will print. The rest are ignored.
SET LONGCHUNKSIZE	80	CLOB variables are retrieved from the database a piece at a time. This setting controls the size of that piece.
SET LOBOFFSET	1	An offset you can use to start printing with the nth character in the CLOB variable. By default, SQL*Plus will begin printing with the first character. A LOBOFFSET of 80, for example, skips the first 79 characters of the string.

By default, SQL*Plus displays only the first 80 characters of a CLOB value. This is rarely enough characters. After all, if you needed only 80 characters you wouldn't have used a CLOB datatype in the first place. On the other hand, you may not want to risk printing two gigabytes of data either.

Example 11-9 shows the result of displaying a CLOB value using the default settings for the values in Table 11-2.

Example 11-9. PRINTing a CLOB bind variable using default settings

```
SQL> VARIABLE clob_bind CLOB
SQL>
SQL> BEGIN
  2      SELECT clob_value INTO :clob_bind
  3      FROM clob_example;
  4  END;
  5  /

PL/SQL procedure successfully completed.

SQL> SET LINESIZE 60
SQL> PRINT clob_bind

CLOB_BIND
------------------------------------------------------------
By default, SQL*Plus will only display the first 80 characte
rs of a CLOB value.
```

As you can see, only 80 characters of the value were displayed. Annoyingly, although you can use the COLUMN command to set the heading over a bind variable's value, any attempt to use WORD_WRAPPED to enable word wrapping is ignored. You can change the LONG setting to see more of the value, as Example 11-10 shows.

Example 11-10. Example 11-9 rerun with a longer LONG setting

```
SQL> SET LONG 500
SQL> @ex11-9
SQL> SET ECHO ON
SQL>
SQL> VARIABLE clob_bind CLOB
SQL>
SQL> BEGIN
  2      SELECT clob_value INTO :clob_bind
  3      FROM clob_example;
  4  END;
  5  /

PL/SQL procedure successfully completed.

SQL> SET LINESIZE 60
SQL> PRINT clob_bind

CLOB_BIND
------------------------------------------------------------
By default, SQL*Plus will only display the first 80 characte
rs of a CLOB value. This is rarely enough. After all, if you
 only needed 80 characters, you wouldn't have used a CLOB da
tatype in the first place. On the other hand, you may not wa
nt to risk printing 2 gigabytes of data either.
```

By combining the LOBOFFSET and LONG settings, you can print any arbitrary substring of a CLOB variable. Example 11-11 displays characters 81 through 102, which make up the second sentence of the CLOB value shown in the previous two examples.

Example 11-11. Using SET LONG and SET LOBOFFSET to display a substring of a CLOB value

```
SQL> SET LONG 22
SQL> SET LOBOFFSET 81
SQL> @ex11-9
SQL> SET ECHO ON
SQL>
SQL> VARIABLE clob_bind CLOB
SQL>
SQL> BEGIN
  2     SELECT clob_value INTO :clob_bind
  3     FROM clob_example;
  4  END;
  5  /

PL/SQL procedure successfully completed.

SQL> SET LINESIZE 60
SQL> PRINT clob_bind

CLOB_BIND
--------------------
This is rarely enough.
```

Finally, the LONGCHUNKSIZE setting controls the amount of the CLOB fetched from the database at one time. If you have the memory available, you may want to set this to match the LONG setting. That way, SQL*Plus retrieves all that you wish to display with one fetch from the database, possibly improving performance.

PRINTing REFCURSOR variables

SQL*Plus allows you to create bind variables of the type REFCURSOR. A REFCURSOR variable is a pointer to a cursor that returns a result set. Using PL/SQL, you can assign any SELECT query to a variable of this type and then use the SQL*Plus PRINT command to format and display the results of that query. The script shown in Example 11-12 makes use of this capability by using a REFCURSOR to display a list of tables owned by the current user.

Example 11-12. PRINTing a REFCURSOR variable

```
SET ECHO OFF

VARIABLE l_table_list REFCURSOR

-- Set the REFCURSOR variable to the results of
-- a SELECT statement returning a list of tables
-- owned by the user.
```

Example 11-12. PRINTing a REFCURSOR variable (continued)

```
BEGIN
  OPEN :l_table_list FOR
     SELECT table_name
     FROM user_tables;
END;
/

--Print the list of tables the user wants to see.
PRINT l_table_list
```

The script in Example 11-12 defines a SQL*Plus REFCURSOR variable. The cursor is opened and a query is assigned by code within a PL/SQL block. Then the SQL*Plus PRINT command is used to display the results of that query. Following is an example run of the script:

```
SQL> @ex11-12

PL/SQL procedure successfully completed.


TABLE_NAME
------------------------------
CLOB_EXAMPLE
SUBTEST
NBR_CC
BILL_OF_MATERIALS
PART
...
```

The output you get when PRINTing a REFCURSOR variable is identical to the output you would get if you executed the same query directly from SQL*Plus.

SELECTing a bind variable

The SQL*Plus manual, at least the one for Versions 8.0.3 and before, tells you that bind variables can't be used in SQL statements. Don't believe it! Bind variables can be used in SELECT statements, in the column list and in the WHERE clause. You will see this done in scripts where getting the contents of a bind variable into a substitution variable is important. (See the section "Using Bind Variables and Substitution Variables Together.") Example 11-13 shows a SELECT statement being used to display the contents of a bind variable.

Example 11-13. SELECTing the contents of a bind variable

```
SQL> VARIABLE employee_name VARCHAR2(30)
SQL> EXECUTE :employee_name := 'Mykola Leontovych';

PL/SQL procedure successfully completed.

SQL> SELECT :employee_name FROM dual;
```

Example 11-13. SELECTing the contents of a bind variable (continued)

```
:EMPLOYEE_NAME
------------------------------------------------------------
Mykola Leontovych
```

Using SELECT in this way offers no real advantage over the use of the PRINT command. If you need to display one variable, you might as well PRINT it. Being able to use bind variables in a SELECT statement becomes more of an advantage when you need to display information from more than one column, when you want to use the bind variable in an expression for a computed column, or when you want to use it in the WHERE clause. Example 11-14 combines all three of these situations.

Example 11-14. A more extensive use of bind variables in a SQL statement

```
UNDEFINE user_name
VARIABLE l_user VARCHAR2(30)
EXECUTE :l_user := '&user_name';

SELECT 'User ' || :l_user || ' has '
       || TO_CHAR(COUNT(*)) || ' tables.'
FROM all_tables
WHERE owner = UPPER(:l_user);
```

You run Example 11-14 as follows:

```
SQL> @ex11-14
Enter value for user_name: gennick

PL/SQL procedure successfully completed.


'USER'||:L_USER||'HAS'||TO_CHAR(COUNT(*))||'TABLES.'
------------------------------------------------------------
User gennick has 60 tables.
```

Two types of bind variables can't be used in a SQL statement: REFCURSOR and CLOB types. You must use the PRINT command with these bind variables.

When and How to Use Bind Variables

You have three primary reasons for using bind variables in SQL*Plus:

- You need to call PL/SQL procedures or functions that return a value or that use IN OUT parameters.
- You need to execute one of several possible SELECT statements conditionally depending on user input or other circumstances.
- You want to test a query for use in an application, and that query uses colons to mark parameters.

The next few sections briefly describe each of these uses.

Calling PL/SQL procedures and functions from SQL*Plus

Oracle provides a number of useful, built-in PL/SQL packages. Some of the procedures and functions in these packages return values that you may wish to capture and return to SQL*Plus. Capturing the return value from a function is usually easy because you can SELECT that function from the dual table. Example 11-15 generates a random string of alphanumerics (the "X" option) by making a call to DBMS_RANDOM.STRING from within a SELECT statement. The string is returned to SQL*Plus via the COLUMN command's NEW_VALUE mechanism.

Example 11-15. Capturing the return value of a PL/SQL function

```
COLUMN mixed_up NEW_VALUE mixed_up_sub_var
SELECT dbms_random.string('X',30) mixed_up
FROM dual;

DEFINE mixed_up_sub_var
```

Life becomes more difficult, though, if you wish to invoke a procedure or function with an OUT or an IN OUT parameter. DBMS_UTILITY.CANONICALIZE is one such procedure:

```
DBMS_UTILITY.CANONICALIZE(
    name        IN    VARCHAR2,
    canon_name  OUT   VARCHAR2,
    canon_len   IN    BINARY_INTEGER);
```

This procedure takes an identifier, such as a table reference, and returns that identifier in canonical form. For example, pass the table name gennick."Mixed_Case_Table" and you'll get back GENNICK."mixed_case_table". What's interesting about this procedure, and it is a procedure, is that it returns the canonical name via an OUT variable. To execute this procedure, you must send that OUT variable somewhere, and a bind variable provides a convenient destination. Example 11-16 presents a brief SQL*Plus script to invoke DBMS_UTILITY.CANONICALIZE on a string that you supply and then display the result.

Example 11-16. Capturing an OUT value into a bind variable

```
ACCEPT not_can CHAR PROMPT 'Enter a table reference >'
VARIABLE can VARCHAR2(60)
EXECUTE DBMS_UTILITY.CANONICALIZE('&not_can',:can, 60);
COLUMN can HEADING 'Canonicalized Reference IS:'
PRINT can
```

The following is a run of Example 11-16:

```
SQL> @ex11-16
Enter a table reference >gennick."Mixed-Case-Table"

PL/SQL procedure successfully completed.
```

```
Canonicalized Reference IS:
------------------------------------------------------------
"GENNICK"."Mixed-Case-Table"
```

Were it not for the SQL*Plus bind variable (named :can in Example 11-16), you wouldn't be able to capture the canonicalized string for later use in your SQL*Plus script.

Displaying Output Variables

Example 11-16 shows a bind variable being used to capture and display a value returned through a procedure's OUT parameter. If your need is to display such a value, you may execute the procedure from within a PL/SQL block and use DBMS_OUTPUT.PUT_LINE to display the output value, thus avoiding the need to create a SQL*Plus bind variable. You can find the following example in the script file named *ex11-16b.sql*:

```
ACCEPT not_can CHAR PROMPT 'Enter a table reference >'
SET SERVEROUTPUT ON
DEFINE
    can VARCHAR2(60);
BEGIN
    DBMS_UTILITY.CANONICALIZE('&not_can',can, 60);
    DBMS_OUTPUT.PUT_LINE(can);
END;
/
```

The results from running this script are as follows:

```
SQL> @ex11-16b
Enter a table reference >gennick."Mixed-Case-Table"
"GENNICK"."Mixed-Case-Table"

PL/SQL procedure successfully completed.
```

The difference between this method and that shown in Example 11-16 is that, in Example 11-16, you can use the :can bind variable later in your script; thus, you can do something with the value that is returned from the procedure other than displaying it.

Using REFCURSOR variables

As mentioned earlier, the REFCURSOR datatype holds a pointer to a cursor. Using REFCURSOR variables, you can open a cursor for a SELECT statement in PL/SQL and print the results from SQL*Plus. One practical use for this is to write PL/SQL code that selects one query from many possibilities, based on user input or some other factor.

Earlier, in the section on "Printing REFCURSOR variables," Example 11-12 showed the use of a REFCURSOR variable to display a list of tables owned by the current user. Example 11-17 is an enhanced version of that script that allows you to enter a pattern match string to narrow the list of table names to be displayed. The script executes one of two possible queries depending on whether or not a string was supplied.

Example 11-17. Setting a REFCURSOR to return results from one of two possible SELECT statements

```
SET ECHO OFF
SET VERIFY OFF
--Find out what tables the user wants to see.
--A null response results in seeing all the tables.
ACCEPT s_table_like PROMPT 'List tables LIKE > '

VARIABLE l_table_list REFCURSOR

--This PL/SQL block sets the l_table_list variable
--to the correct query, depending on whether or
--not the user specified all or part of a table_name.
BEGIN
  IF '&s_table_like' IS NULL THEN
    OPEN :l_table_list FOR
      SELECT table_name
        FROM user_tables;
  ELSE
    OPEN :l_table_list FOR
      SELECT table_name
        FROM user_tables
       WHERE table_name LIKE UPPER('&s_table_like');
  END IF;
END;
/

--Print the list of tables the user wants to see.
PRINT l_table_list
```

This script first asks the user for a search string to be used with the LIKE operator. Entering this is optional. If a pattern match string is specified, then only table names that match that string are displayed; otherwise, all table names are listed. This conditional logic is implemented by the PL/SQL block, which checks the value of the substitution variable and opens the REFCURSOR variable using the appropriate SELECT statement. Here's how it looks to run the script:

```
SQL> @ex11-17
List tables LIKE > %emp%

PL/SQL procedure successfully completed.


TABLE_NAME
------------------------------
EMPLOYEE
EMPLOYEES
EMPLOYEE_COMMENT
```

```
EMPLOYEE_COPY
EMPLOYEE_EXPENSE
EMPLOYEE_COMMA
EMPLOYEE_FIXED
```

Using REFCURSOR variables is one way to add conditional logic to your SQL*Plus scripts. You'll see another example of this in the section "Simulate Branching by Using REFCURSOR Variables."

> You might be thinking about using REFCURSOR variables with the DBMS_SQL package to return the results of dynamically generated SQL queries back to SQL*Plus. Unfortunately, that can't be done. DBMS_SQL returns integer values that reference cursors held internally, but there is no way to get a REFCURSOR value pointing to one of those cursors.

Testing application queries

Bind variables can make it more convenient to take a query from an application development environment and debug it using SQL*Plus. Such queries often contain parameters to be supplied at runtime, and those parameters are preceded by colons, which is the syntax SQL*Plus uses for bind variables. Example 11-18 shows a query containing a bind variable in the WHERE clause.

Example 11-18. A query using a bind variable

```
SELECT employee.employee_id,
       employee.employee_name,
       employee.employee_hire_date,
       employee.employee_termination_date,
       employee.employee_billing_rate
  FROM employee
 WHERE employee.employee_id = :emp_id
```

If you want to test the query in Example 11-18 and you run it as it is, you will get the following results:

```
SQL> @ex11-18
SQL> SET ECHO ON
SQL> SELECT employee.employee_id,
  2            employee.employee_name,
  3            employee.employee_hire_date,
  4            employee.employee_termination_date,
  5            employee.employee_billing_rate
  6    FROM employee
  7   WHERE employee.employee_id = :emp_id;
SP2-0552: Bind variable "EMP_ID" not declared.
```

At this point, you have two choices. You can change the query and replace the parameter :emp_id with an employee number you know exists. You can test the query, and when you are satisfied the query works, you can replace the hardcoded value with the parameter reference. Woe be unto you, however, if there are several parameters and you forget to change one back. A second and safer approach is to declare bind variables to match the parameters in the query. In this case, there is just one to declare:

```
SQL> VARIABLE emp_id NUMBER
```

Once the variable has been declared, it is a simple matter to initialize it to a known good value:

```
SQL> EXECUTE :emp_id := 101;

PL/SQL procedure successfully completed.
```

Now that you have declared and initialized the variable, it's easy to execute the query, bind variable and all:

```
SQL> @ex11-18
SQL> SET ECHO ON
SQL> SELECT employee.employee_id,
  2         employee.employee_name,
  3         employee.employee_hire_date,
  4         employee.employee_termination_date,
  5         employee.employee_billing_rate
  6    FROM employee
  7   WHERE employee.employee_id = :emp_id;

EMPLOYEE_ID EMPLOYEE_NAME        EMPLOYEE_ EMPLOYEE_ EMPLOYEE_BILLING_RATE
----------- -------------------- --------- --------- ---------------------
        101 Marusia Churai       15-NOV-61                             169
```

Once you are satisfied that everything is correct, you can paste the query directly back into your application without the risk that you might forget to change a hard-coded value back into a bind variable.

Branching in SQL*Plus

SQL*Plus has no IF statement, which is vexing. Script writing is similar to programming. It's natural to want to take different actions depending on user input or some other condition. Imagine how frustrated you would be if your favorite programming language suddenly lost its IF statement. Despite the lack of an IF statement in SQL*Plus, you can take some approaches to get equivalent results. Some are more straightforward than others. All involve some compromises.

You can take at least six approaches to the problem of conditional execution:

- Simulate branching by adjusting the WHERE clause in a query.
- Use REFCUSOR variables.
- Use a multilevel file structure.
- Use SQL to write SQL.

- Use PL/SQL for conditional logic.
- Use an operating-system scripting language.

Some of these approaches are specific to certain types of problems. Using REFCUR-SOR variables, for example, is a good solution when you need to choose which query to run based on user input or some other condition. Other approaches, such as the use of a multilevel file structure for your script, are more general in nature and can be used for any type of branching.

Simulating Branching by Adjusting the WHERE Clause

Suppose you are writing a script to delete all data from the project_hours table. Before you delete the data, you want to ask the user to confirm the operation. You want to write something like the following:

```
ACCEPT s_delete_confirm PROMPT 'Delete project hours data (Y/N)?'

IF s_delete_confirm = 'Y' THEN
   DELETE
      FROM project_hours;
   END IF
```

You can't do that! SQL*Plus has no IF statement, remember? However, you can add a WHERE clause to the DELETE statement that will have the same effect, as shown in Example 11-19.

Example 11-19. Embedding conditional logic into a WHERE clause

```
SET ECHO OFF
SET VERIFY OFF

ACCEPT s_delete_confirm PROMPT 'Delete project hours data (Y/N)?'

DELETE
  FROM project_hours
 WHERE UPPER('&&s_delete_confirm') = 'Y';
```

When you execute the script, the DELETE will be executed. However, if the user answers with anything but Y, the WHERE clause will evaluate to FALSE and no rows will be deleted. Verification is set off to prevent SQL*Plus from echoing the line of the WHERE clause that references the substitution variable. The UPPER function is used in this case to allow the user's response to be case-insensitive.

> There may be performance implications to this technique, as the query optimizer may scan the entire table, evaluating UPPER('&&s_delete_confirm') = 'Y' for each row. Thus, the technique is best confined to use on smaller tables.

Here's how it looks when a user runs this script and doesn't confirm the delete:

```
SQL> @delete_hours
Delete project hours data (Y/N)?n

0 rows deleted.
```

If you want to, you can write an additional query to give the user an error message if the response to the prompt was not Y or N. Example 11-20 shows a version of the script that does this.

Example 11-20. Adding an error message

```
SET HEADING OFF
SET PAGESIZE 0
SET FEEDBACK OFF
SELECT 'You must answer with a Y or N.'
  FROM DUAL
 WHERE UPPER('&&s_delete_confirm') NOT IN ('Y','N')
    OR '&&s_delete_confirm' IS NULL;
SET FEEDBACK ON
SET PAGESIZE 1
SET HEADING ON
```

To make the results of the query in Example 11-20 look like an error message, the headings and pagination are turned off. Feedback is turned off to avoid giving the "1 row selected" message to the user. After the SELECT executes, these settings are returned to their defaults. Here is what happens when you run the modified script and don't answer with Y or N:

```
SQL> @ex11-20
SQL> SET ECHO OFF
Delete project hours data (Y/N)?bad
You must answer with a Y or N.

0 rows deleted.
```

This technique has the advantage of keeping your entire script in one file, but it's limited to handling the case where you have several possible queries to execute and must choose the correct one based on input from the user. You must think about the performance implications from the full tablescans that this technique is likely to unleash.

Simulate Branching by Using REFCURSOR Variables

If you want to present the user with a choice of reports to run, you can place the conditional logic within PL/SQL and use a REFCURSOR variable to return the selected query to SQL*Plus, where the results can be formatted and printed. Example 11-21 gives the user a choice of three different reports. The conditional logic is implemented in a PL/SQL block, and the results are returned to SQL*Plus via bind variables. A

REFCURSOR bind variable is used to return a query that generates the report requested by the user.

Example 11-21. Implementing a choice of reports via REFCURSOR variables

```
--DESCRIPTION
--Print one of three user security reports

SET FEEDBACK OFF
SET PAGESIZE 20
SET LINESIZE 77
SET HEADING ON

--Ask the user what report to print
PROMPT
PROMPT 1 - List users
PROMPT 2 - List users and table privileges
PROMPT 3 - List users and system privileges
PROMPT
ACCEPT s_report_choice PROMPT 'Enter your choice (1,2,3) >'

--A PL/SQL block will set the b_report bind variable
--to a query based on the user's response. Text for the
--report title will be returned in b_report_type.
VARIABLE b_report REFCURSOR
VARIABLE b_report_type VARCHAR2(30)

--Interpret the user's choice.
BEGIN
  IF '&&s_report_choice' = '1' THEN
    --Return some text for the title to identify this report.
    :b_report_type := 'User Listing';

    --Return a query that will list all users.
    OPEN :b_report FOR
      SELECT username
        FROM dba_users
      ORDER BY username;
  ELSIF '&&s_report_choice' = '2' THEN
    --Return some text for the title to identify this report.
    :b_report_type := 'User Table Privileges';

    --Return a query that will list users and any
    --privileges they have on tables in the database.
    OPEN :b_report FOR
      SELECT username, privilege, owner, table_name
        FROM dba_users, dba_tab_privs
       WHERE username = grantee
      ORDER BY username, owner, table_name, privilege;
  ELSIF '&&s_report_choice' = '3' THEN
    --Return some text for the title to identify this report.
    :b_report_type := 'User System Privileges';
```

Example 11-21. Implementing a choice of reports via REFCURSOR variables (continued)

```
    --Return a query that lists users and any system
    --privileges they have been granted.
    OPEN :b_report FOR
      SELECT username, privilege
        FROM dba_users, dba_sys_privs
       WHERE username = grantee
      ORDER BY username, privilege;
  ELSE
    --Return some text for the title to identify this report.
    :b_report_type := 'Invalid Report Choice';

    --The user made an invalid choice, so
    --return a query that will display an error message.
    OPEN :b_report FOR
      SELECT 'You must choose either 1, 2, or 3' error_message
        FROM dual;
  END IF;
END;
/

--Specify formats for all possible report columns.
COLUMN username FORMAT A12 HEADING 'User'
COLUMN privilege FORMAT A20 HEADING 'Privilege'
COLUMN owner FORMAT A12 HEADING 'Table Owner'
COLUMN table_name FORMAT A30 HEADING 'Table Name'
COLUMN error_message FORMAT A40 HEADING 'Error Message'

--Set up the page title. First we have to get the contents of
--b_report_type into a substition variable.
set termout off
COLUMN b_report_type FORMAT A30 NOPRINT NEW_VALUE s_report_type
SELECT :b_report_type b_report_type FROM dual;
set termout on

TTITLE LEFT s_report_type RIGHT 'Page ' FORMAT 999 SQL.PNO SKIP 2

--Run the report requested by the user
PRINT b_report
```

The script contains COLUMN commands for all possible columns from the three different queries. These don't need to be conditionally executed because format definitions for columns not used in the final query are ignored by SQL*Plus. The PL/SQL code does return a query even for the case where the user's input is invalid; this query simply selects an error message from the dual table.

> To run Example 11-21, you will need to be the DBA or at least have access to the DBA data dictionary views.

The following is the output from running this script, first showing the results of an invalid input, then showing the output from one of the reports:

```
SQL> @ex11-21

1 - List users
2 - List users and table privileges
3 - List users and system privileges

Enter your choice (1,2,3) >4


Invalid Report Choice                                          Page     1

Error Message
----------------------------------------
You must choose either 1, 2, or 3

SQL> @ex11-21

1 - List users
2 - List users and table privileges
3 - List users and system privileges

Enter your choice (1,2,3) >2


User Table Privileges                                          Page     1

User         Privilege            Table Owner  Table Name
-----------  -------------------- ------------ ------------------------------
BI           SELECT               OE           BOMBAY_INVENTORY
BI           SELECT               OE           CUSTOMERS
BI           SELECT               OE           INVENTORIES
BI           SELECT               OE           ORDERS
B
```

In this example, the query output is displayed only on the screen. If you want to print it, you need to add a SPOOL command to send the output to a file, which you could later send to a printer.

Branching Using a Multilevel File Structure

The most generic and flexible approach to branching that you can implement using SQL*Plus is to write your script to execute one of several alternative files based on user input or other criteria. This is best explained by example, so Example 11-22 shows a simplified version of the security reports menu shown previously in Example 11-21.

Example 11-22. Branching via a multilevel file structure

```
PROMPT
PROMPT 1 - List users
PROMPT 2 - List users and table privileges
PROMPT 3 - List users and system privileges
PROMPT
ACCEPT s_report_choice PROMPT 'Enter your choice (1,2,3) >'

--Execute the appropriate report
@ex11-22_&&s_report_choice
```

The key to this approach is in the last line, where the user's response is used to form the name of another SQL file to execute. If the user chooses option 1, for example, the last line in the above script will be translated to this:

```
@ex11-22_1
```

You have to make sure that a file named *ex11-22_1.sql* exists and that it will generate the correct report. When you use this approach to branching, you will end up with a set of script files that form an inverted tree structure. The tree diagram in Figure 11-1 shows the relationship between the menu script and the scripts that run the individual reports.

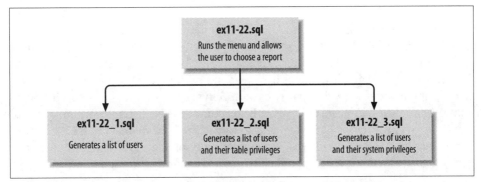

Figure 11-1. Structure for the security reports menu, using a multilevel file structure

Because this branching technique executes another SQL*Plus script, you can continue to ask the user questions and branch again depending on the user's response. The one thing you have to watch for is that SQL*Plus can't nest scripts indefinitely. SQL*Plus can currently nest scripts only 20 levels deep, and some older versions allow only five levels of nesting.

A useful variation on this technique is to code it using a SELECT statement to analyze the user's input and derive the name of the next script to call. You get two benefits from this: the script names are not directly linked to the user's input, and designating one script to be called when the user makes an invalid choice is easier. The penalty is a small amount of added complexity in your script. Example 11-23 shows this technique.

Example 11-23. Using a SELECT statement to get user input

```
SET ECHO OFF

--Ask the user what report to print
PROMPT
PROMPT A - List users
PROMPT B - List users and table privileges
PROMPT C - List users and system privileges
PROMPT
ACCEPT s_report_choice PROMPT 'Enter your choice (A,B,C) >'

--DECODE the user's input.
SET TERMOUT OFF
COLUMN user_choice NOPRINT NEW_VALUE s_next_script
SELECT DECODE (UPPER('&s_report_choice'),
                'A','ex11-22_1.sql',
                'B','ex11-22_2.sql',
                'C','ex11-22_3.sql',
                'ex11-23_bad.sql') user_choice
  FROM DUAL;
SET TERMOUT ON

--Execute the appropriate report
@@&s_next_script
```

The key to this script is the call to DECODE in the SELECT statement. DECODE is a SQL function that allows you to arbitrarily specify an output value for any given input value. In this case, the input value is UPPER('&s_report_choice'). By using the UPPER function, you allow the user to respond in uppercase or lowercase. Following the input are three value pairs, each specifying the output for a specific input value. An input of "A" causes DECODE to return "ex11-22_1.sql," an input of "B" causes it to return "ex11-22_2.sql," and so forth. The final value, "ex11-23_bad.sql," is returned if the user's choice doesn't match any of the others. In this case, that script displays an error message, telling the user what he did wrong.

If you decide to develop a set of scripts like this, it's best to spend some time up front working out the structure before you begin scripting. Making changes after you've written a set of nested scripts can become cumbersome because so many files are involved. Keep things as modular as possible. In this example, any of the reports can be run as standalone scripts without going through the menu.

Using SQL to Write SQL

Another way to branch that also involves a multilevel file structure is to spool some output to a new SQL file and execute that file. To implement the security report menu using this technique, you can spool one of three SELECT statements to a file based on the user's report choice. Example 11-24 presents a version of the script that does that.

Example 11-24. Implementing conditional logic by writing, then executing, a new script

```
--DESCRIPTION
--Print one of three user security reports

SET FEEDBACK OFF
SET PAGESIZE 20
SET LINESIZE 77
SET HEADING ON

--Ask the user what report to print
PROMPT
PROMPT 1 - List users
PROMPT 2 - List users and table privileges
PROMPT 3 - List users and system privileges
PROMPT
ACCEPT s_report_choice PROMPT 'Enter your choice (1,2,3) >'

--Specify formats for all possible report columns.
COLUMN username FORMAT A12 HEADING 'User'
COLUMN privilege FORMAT A20 HEADING 'Privilege'
COLUMN owner FORMAT A12 HEADING 'Table Owner'
COLUMN table_name FORMAT A30 HEADING 'Table Name'
COLUMN error_message FORMAT A40 HEADING 'Error Message'

--Set up the page title. First we have to get the contents of
--b_report_type into a substition variable.
set termout off
COLUMN b_report_type FORMAT A30 NOPRINT NEW_VALUE s_report_type
SELECT DECODE ('&&s_report_choice',
               '1','User List',
               '2','User Table Privileges',
               '3','User System Privileges',
               'Invalid Choice') b_report_type
   FROM dual;
set termout on

TTITLE LEFT s_report_type RIGHT 'Page ' FORMAT 999 SQL.PNO SKIP 2

--Generate the query for the report requested by the user.
--Spool that query to a file.
SET TERMOUT OFF
SET PAGESIZE 0
SET HEADING OFF
SET VERIFY OFF
SET FEEDBACK OFF
COLUMN next_query FORMAT A60
SPOOL user_security_choice.sql

--This query will be successful if the user chooses 1
SELECT 'SELECT username ' || CHR(10) ||
       '  FROM dba_users ' || CHR(10) ||
       'ORDER BY username;' || CHR(10) next_query
   FROM dual
```

```
  WHERE '&&s_report_choice' = '1';

--This query will be successful if the user chooses 2
SELECT 'SELECT username, privilege, owner, table_name' || CHR(10) ||
       '  FROM dba_users, dba_tab_privs' || CHR(10) ||
       ' WHERE username = grantee' || CHR(10) ||
       'ORDER BY username, owner, table_name, privilege;'
  FROM dual
  WHERE '&&s_report_choice' = '2';

SELECT 'SELECT username, privilege' || CHR(10) ||
       '  FROM dba_users, dba_sys_privs' || CHR(10) ||
       ' WHERE username = grantee' || CHR(10) ||
       'ORDER BY username, privilege;'
  FROM dual
  WHERE '&&s_report_choice' = '3';

SELECT 'PROMPT You must choose either 1, 2, or 3'
  FROM dual
  WHERE '&&s_report_choice' NOT IN ('1','2','3')
     OR '&&s_report_choice' IS NULL;

SPOOL OFF
SET TERMOUT ON
SET PAGESIZE 20
SET HEADING ON
SET VERIFY ON

--Now execute the query that we just spooled.
@user_security_choice

--Reset all the settings back to their defaults
SET FEEDBACK ON
CLEAR COLUMNS
TTITLE OFF
```

You have to be careful when using this technique to turn off anything that could cause extraneous text to be written to the temporary command file. This includes page headings, column headings, and verification. You'll want to turn off terminal output to prevent the user from seeing the results of the SELECT on the display. This is why the script in Example 11-24 includes these commands:

```
SET TERMOUT OFF
SET PAGESIZE 0
SET HEADING OFF
SET VERIFY OFF
```

One last thing you have to worry about is the filename itself. In Example 11-24, the filename is hardwired into the script and doesn't include a path. Because no path is specified, the file will be written to the current directory. That's why @, a single at sign, was used to run the intermediate file. Using @ causes SQL*Plus to look in the current directory for the script.

However, having the filename hardwired into the script can cause problems if multiple users execute the script simultaneously and from the same directory. If you are concerned about this, you can write some SQL or PL/SQL code to generate a unique filename based on the Oracle username or perhaps the session identifier (SID) from the V$SESSION data dictionary view.

 Be creative with the technique shown in Example 11-24. You don't need to limit yourself to writing SQL*Plus scripts. You can use SQL*Plus to generate shell script files, SQL*Loader files, DOS batch files, or any other type of text file.

Using PL/SQL

Consider the possibility of using PL/SQL to implement any type of complex procedural logic. After all, that's the reason PL/SQL was invented. If you can manage to prompt the user up front for any needed information and if you don't need to interact with the user during the operation, PL/SQL is the way to go.

 The reports menu can't be implemented in PL/SQL because the menu needs to run another SQL*Plus script corresponding to the user's choice. PL/SQL runs inside the database and can't invoke a SQL*Plus script.

Example 11-19 presents an ideal candidate for the use of PL/SQL because that script asks the user a simple yes/no question and proceeds to delete or not delete data from the project_hours table. One problem with that approach is the potential performance impact from a needless, full table scan. Another problem is that the predicate to implement the conditional logic can be hard to spot in a complex WHERE clause, making such queries difficult to fathom, at least at first glance. PL/SQL avoids these issues. Example 11-25 shows a PL/SQL approach to the script from Example 11-19.

Example 11-25. Using PL/SQL to implement conditional logic
```
SET VERIFY OFF

ACCEPT s_delete_confirm PROMPT 'Delete project hours data (Y/N)?'

SET SERVEROUTPUT ON

DECLARE
  users_yn_response CHAR := UPPER('&&s_delete_confirm');
BEGIN
  IF users_yn_response = 'Y' THEN
```

Example 11-25. Using PL/SQL to implement conditional logic (continued)

```
    DELETE
    FROM project_hours;

    COMMIT;

    DBMS_OUTPUT.PUT_LINE('All PROJECT_HOURS data has been deleted.');
  ELSIF users_yn_response = 'N' THEN
    DBMS_OUTPUT.PUT_LINE('No data was deleted.');
  ELSE
    DBMS_OUTPUT.PUT_LINE('You must answer with a Y or N.');
  END IF;
EXCEPTION
  WHEN OTHERS THEN
    DBMS_OUTPUT.PUT_LINE('The PROJECT_HOURS data could not be deleted. '
                          || SQLERRM);
    ROLLBACK;
END;
/
```

Example 11-25 is a bit longer than Example 11-19, but it's a more robust script. Example 11-25 rolls back the operation if the DELETE fails for any reason, and the DELETE statement is executed only when really necessary.

Using an Operating-System Scripting Language

Don't overlook the possibility that you can use your operating system's scripting language to good advantage. Any Unix shell allows you to write more complex scripts than you can using SQL*Plus alone. Example 11-26 provides an implementation of the user security report menu using the Unix Bash shell.

Example 11-26. User security report implemented as a Unix Bash shell script

```
#!/bin/bash
while :
        do
        echo " "
        echo "1 - List users"
        echo "2 - List users and table privileges"
        echo "3 - List users and system privileges"
        echo "4 - Quit"
        echo
        echo -n "Enter your choice (1,2,3,4) > "

        read

        case $REPLY in
                1 )
                        sqlplus -s gennick/secret @ex11-26_1
                        ;;
                2 )
```

```
                        sqlplus -s gennick/secret @ex11-26_2
                        ;;
        3 )
                        sqlplus -s gennick/secret @ex11-26_3
                        ;;
        4 )
                        break
                        ;;
        * )
                        echo "Please enter 1, 2, 3, or 4"
                        ;;
    esac
done
```

Perl, Python, and other scripting languages are worth considering. The Perl and Python scripting languages are available for Unix and Windows. Both have the advantage of being widely used and of not tying you to one specific operating system.

Looping in SQL*Plus

There is no way to write a real loop using SQL*Plus. Your best option, if you need to do something iteratively, is to use PL/SQL. PL/SQL, however, doesn't allow you any interaction with the user, so it's not always suitable for the task at hand. Your next bet is to look into using your operating system's scripting language, if there is one.

This said, you can do a couple of things in SQL*Plus that might get you the same result as writing a loop:

- Using recursive execution
- Generating a file of commands, and then executing it

The first option has some severe limitations, and I don't recommend it. The second option I use all the time, especially when performing database maintenance tasks.

Recursive Execution

You can't loop, but you can execute the same script recursively. Suppose you have a script that displays some useful information, and you want to give the user the option of running it again. You can do that by recursively executing the script. Take a look at the following interaction, in which the user is looking at indexes for various tables. It looks like a loop. Each time through, the user is prompted for another table name, and the indexes on that table are displayed.

```
SQL> @ex11-27 employee

INDEX_NAME                      COLUMN_NAME
------------------------------- -------------------------------
```

```
EMPLOYEE_PK                  EMPLOYEE_ID
EMPLOYEE_BY_NAME             EMPLOYEE_NAME

Next table >project

INDEX_NAME                   COLUMN_NAME
----------------------------  ------------------------------
PROJECT_PK                   PROJECT_ID

Next table >project_hours

INDEX_NAME                   COLUMN_NAME
----------------------------  ------------------------------
PROJECT_HOURS_PK             PROJECT_ID
                             EMPLOYEE_ID
                             TIME_LOG_DATE

Next table >

Goodbye!
```

It sure does look like a loop, but it's not. Example 11-27 shows the script that is being run.

Example 11-27. Using recursion to simulate a loop

```
SET ECHO OFF
SET VERIFY OFF

COLUMN index_name FORMAT A30
COLUMN column_name FORMAT A30
BREAK ON index_name NODUPLICATES

SELECT index_name, column_name
  FROM user_ind_columns
 WHERE table_name = UPPER('&1');

--Ask the user if he wants to do this again.
PROMPT
ACCEPT s_next_table PROMPT 'Next table >'

--Execute either list_indexes.sql or empty.sql,
--depending on the user's response.
COLUMN next_script NOPRINT NEW_VALUE s_next_script
SET TERMOUT OFF
SELECT DECODE ('&&s_next_table',
               '','ex11-27_empty.sql',
               'ex11-27.sql ' || UPPER('&&s_next_table')) next_script
  FROM dual;
SET TERMOUT ON

@&&s_next_script
```

The key to the looping is in the last part of the script, following the ACCEPT statement. If you enter another table name, the SELECT statement will return another call to the *ex11-27.sql* script. So, when you type "project" in response to the prompt, the s_next_script substitution variable ends up being this:

```
ex11-27.sql PROJECT
```

The only thing missing is the at sign, and that is supplied by the command at the bottom of Example 11-27. In this case, the command:

```
@&&s_next_script
```

will be translated to:

```
@ex11-27.sql PROJECT
```

If you don't enter a table name at the prompt, the s_next_table variable will be null, and the DECODE statement will return "ex11-27_empty.sql". The *ex11-27_empty. sql* script is necessary because the @ command must be executed. *ex11-27_empty.sql* gives you a clean way out of the recursion. In this case, *ex11-27_empty.sql* displays a goodbye message:

```
PROMPT
PROMPT Goodbye!
PROMPT
```

Recursive execution is a limited technique. You can't nest scripts forever. You can only go 20 levels deep, and on some older versions of SQL*Plus the limit may be as low as 5. Exceed that limit, and you will get the following message:

```
SQL*Plus command procedures may only be nested to a depth of 20.
```

Still, recursion can be useful. What are the odds that you will want to type in 20 table names in one sitting? In this case, the convenience may outweigh any chance of exceeding that limit on nesting scripts. And if you do exceed the limit, so what? You can rerun the script.

Looping Within PL/SQL

You should consider PL/SQL when you need to implement any type of complex procedural logic, and that includes looping. Because PL/SQL executes in the database, you can't use it for any loop that requires user interaction. Example 11-27, which repeatedly prompts for another table name, could never be implemented in PL/SQL. It's also impossible to call another SQL*Plus script from PL/SQL. However, if you can get around those two limitations, PL/SQL may be the best choice for the task. Example 11-28 shows a script that uses a PL/SQL block to display indexes on all tables that you own, having names matching a pattern that you specify.

Example 11-28. Looping is often best done in PL/SQL

```
SET ECHO OFF
SET VERIFY OFF
SET SERVEROUTPUT ON

ACCEPT table_name PROMPT 'Show indexes on what table >'

DECLARE

BEGIN
   IF '&table_name' IS NOT NULL THEN
      --Loop for each table and index selected by the user
      FOR xtable IN (
      SELECT table_owner, table_name, index_name
      FROM user_indexes
      WHERE table_name LIKE UPPER('&table_name')
      ORDER BY table_owner, table_name, index_name) LOOP
         --Display the table and index names
         DBMS_OUTPUT.PUT_LINE(CHR(9));
         DBMS_OUTPUT.PUT_LINE('Index ' || xtable.index_name || ' on '
                              || xtable.table_owner || '.' || xtable.table_name);

         --Loop through each column in the index
         FOR xcolumn IN (
         SELECT column_name
         FROM user_ind_columns
         WHERE index_name = xtable.index_name
         ORDER BY column_position) LOOP
            DBMS_OUTPUT.PUT_LINE('      ' || xcolumn.column_name);
         END LOOP;
      END LOOP;
   END IF;
END;
/
```

Output from Example 11-28 looks like this:

```
SQL> @ex11-28
Show indexes on what table >employee

Index EMPLOYEE_BY_NAME on GENNICK.EMPLOYEE
EMPLOYEE_NAME

Index EMPLOYEE_PK on GENNICK.EMPLOYEE
EMPLOYEE_ID
```

Example 11-28 prompts once at the beginning of the script. Then control falls into a PL/SQL block that uses an outer loop to go through each matching table and index, and an inner loop to display each column from each index. PL/SQL can't write to your display. Instead, Example 11-28 uses the DBMS_OUTPUT package to write output to an in-memory buffer on the database server. When the block completes, SQL*Plus reads and displays the contents of that buffer.

SQL*Plus will not display the contents of the DBMS_OUTPUT buffer unless you have first issued the command SET SERVEROUTPUT ON. If you expect to need more than the default 2000-character buffer, use SET SERVEROUTPUT ON SIZE *xxx*, in which *xxx* is the number of bytes to allocate, up to 1,000,000.

DBMS_OUTPUT and Blank Lines

Using DBMS_OUTPUT.PUT_LINE, you can't normally generate blank lines in your output stream. None of the following invocations will result in any output:

```
DBMS_OUTPUT.PUT_LINE('');
DBMS_OUTPUT.PUT_LINE(' ');
DBMS_OUTPUT.PUT_LINE('                    ');
```

Yet Example 11-28 manages to generate blank lines using the DBMS_OUTPUT package. How is that done? Example 11-28 accomplishes the effect of blank lines by sending tab characters, which are CHR(9), to the output stream. A tab character isn't a blank, so it isn't ignored. However, the effect on most displays is to move the cursor to the right, an effect that is, ultimately, is invisible. The net effect is a blank line.

You can issue the command SET SERVEROUTPUT ON FORMAT WRAPPED, which preserves any blank lines in the output stream but at the cost of potentially wrapping a line in the middle of a word (the default FORMAT is WORD_WRAPPED).

Validating and Parsing User Input

Whenever you ask a user for input, you run the risk that it won't make sense. Maybe you are asking for a number, and the user types in some letters. Maybe you are asking for a date, and the user enters a bad value for the month. The SQL*Plus ACCEPT command offers some support for dealing with these situations. You can do more, if you need to, with some creative use of SQL.

Validating Input with ACCEPT

The ACCEPT command implements several options to help you validate user input. Throughout most of this book, the ACCEPT commands have been mostly written like this:

```
ACCEPT my_variable PROMPT 'Enter a value >'
```

This is a least-common-denominator version of the ACCEPT command that should work with any release of SQL*Plus. It takes whatever string the user types in and assigns it to the variable. If you need to go beyond this, ACCEPT allows you to specify a datatype and does not accept input that doesn't convert to the type you specify.

ACCEPT also allows you to specify a format string that the input data must match. You can take good advantage of these options to make your scripts more bulletproof.

The ACCEPT command options illustrated in the following subsections apply to SQL*Plus Versions 8.0.3 and above. Not all options will be available under previous releases. The ACCEPT command is one that has changed a lot over the years. Check the documentation for the release you are using to see which options are available to you.

ACCEPTing numeric values

If you are prompting the user for a number, the first and easiest thing to do is to use the NUMBER keyword with the ACCEPT command:

```
ACCEPT my_variable NUMBER PROMPT 'Enter a number >'
```

When NUMBER is specified, SQL*Plus will accept any input that can be converted to a number. Instead, it will keep repeating the prompt until the user gets it right:

```
SQL> ACCEPT my_variable NUMBER PROMPT 'Enter a number >'
Enter a number >two
"two" is not a valid number
Enter a number >2.2.2
"2.2.2" is not a valid number
Enter a number >
```

SQL*Plus accepts a null input as a valid number, so if the user presses Enter, a "0" is stored in the variable. Spaces, on the other hand, do not constitute numeric input. Using a FORMAT clause for a number prevents null input from being accepted.

You can gain more control over numeric input by taking advantage of the ACCEPT command's FORMAT clause. With it, you can specify a numeric format string, and ACCEPT accepts only input that matches that format. Supposedly, any format string valid for use with the COLUMN command is valid for use with the ACCEPT command. In practice, though, "9," "0," and "." are the most useful as input format specifiers.

Use "9"s when you want to limit the user to entering a certain number of digits:

```
SQL> ACCEPT my_variable NUMBER FORMAT 999 PROMPT 'Enter a number >'
Enter a number >1234
"1234" does not match input format "999"
Enter a number >123
SQL>
```

However, the user is not forced to enter the maximum number of digits allowed by the format string. The user may enter fewer digits, so long as the result is a valid number:

```
SQL> ACCEPT my_variable NUMBER FORMAT 999 PROMPT 'Enter a number >'
Enter a number >12
SQL>
```

One advantage of the FORMAT clause is the user can't get away without entering something. He must enter a valid number, even if it is zero:

```
SQL> ACCEPT my_variable NUMBER FORMAT 999 PROMPT 'Enter a number >'
Enter a number >
"" does not match input format "999"
Enter a number >0
SQL>
```

If you want to allow a decimal value to be entered, then you must include a decimal point in the format string. The user will be limited to the number of decimal places you specify:

```
SQL> ACCEPT my_variable NUMBER FORMAT 999.99 PROMPT 'Enter a number >'
Enter a number >19.76
SQL> ACCEPT my_variable NUMBER FORMAT 999.99 PROMPT 'Enter a number >'
Enter a number >19.763
"19.763" does not match input format "999.99"
Enter a number >19.8
SQL>
```

You can use a leading zero in a format string to force the user to enter a specific number of digits:

```
SQL> ACCEPT my_variable NUMBER FORMAT 099 PROMPT 'Enter a number >'
Enter a number >1
"1" does not match input format "099"
Enter a number >12
"12" does not match input format "099"
Enter a number >123
SQL>
```

However, you can't use the zero after the decimal point to force the user to enter a specific number of decimal digits. The user may always enter fewer digits after the decimal than you specify in the format string. For example, the following statement accepts an input with a single decimal digit even though two are specified in the format string:

```
SQL> ACCEPT my_variable NUMBER FORMAT 099.90 PROMPT 'Enter a number >'
Enter a number >123.1
SQL>
```

Negative values are allowed, regardless of whether the format string specifies a sign. The following example uses a format string of 999 but still accepts a negative value:

```
SQL> ACCEPT my_variable NUMBER FORMAT 999 PROMPT 'Enter a number >'
Enter a number >-123
SQL>
```

SQL*Plus allows you to use other characters with the FORMAT clause (see the COL-UMN command for a complete list), but they may not work as you would expect, and some don't work at all. The "S" character, for example, indicates a leading sign, but rather than being an optional sign it is mandatory, so users must enter positive numbers with a leading "+." That behavior may make sense based on a strict interpretation of the manual, but it's unlikely to be what you want. In some older releases of SQL*Plus, I've had trouble using the $ as a number format specifier.

ACCEPTing date values

You can deal with date values in much the same way as numeric values. The first thing to do is to tell SQL*Plus you want a date. Use the DATE keyword with the ACCEPT command like this:

```
ACCEPT my_variable DATE PROMPT 'Give me a date >'
```

The date format accepted by SQL*Plus depends on your NLS_DATE_FORMAT setting. Often this is DD-MON-YY, but it could be something different depending on how Oracle is configured at your site. When the DATE option is specified, ACCEPT rejects any input that doesn't evaluate to a valid date:

```
SQL> ACCEPT my_variable DATE PROMPT 'Give me a date >'
Give me a date >11/15/61
"11/15/61" does not match input format "DD-MON-YY"
Give me a date >November 15, 1961
"November 15, 1961" does not match input format "DD-MON-YY"
Give me a date >15-Nov-61
SQL>
```

If you enter an invalid date, ACCEPT shows you the format it's expecting. As with numbers, you can specify a format string for dates. Any format string you can use with Oracle's TO_DATE function may be used with the ACCEPT command. Here are a couple of typical examples:

```
SQL> ACCEPT my_variable DATE FORMAT 'MM/DD/YY' PROMPT 'Give me a date >'
Give me a date >15-Nov-1961
"15-Nov-1961" does not match input format "MM/DD/YY"
Give me a date >11/15/61
SQL> ACCEPT my_variable DATE FORMAT 'DD-MON-YYYY' PROMPT 'Give me a date >'
Give me a date >11/15/61
"11/15/61" does not match input format "DD-MON-YYYY"
Give me a date >15-Nov-1961
SQL>
```

Remember that the result of an ACCEPT command is still a character string. The user may enter a date, but it is stored as a character string and will need to be converted again when your script next references that substitution variable.

ACCEPT is somewhat liberal when it comes to checking the date a user enters against the specified format. ACCEPT allows a two- or four-digit year, regardless of what you specify in the format string. ACCEPT isn't too picky about separators and allows hyphens even if your format string specifies slashes. The following examples illustrate this behavior:

```
SQL> ACCEPT my_variable DATE FORMAT 'DD-MON-YYYY' PROMPT 'Give me a date >'
Give me a date >15-Nov-61
SQL> ACCEPT my_variable DATE FORMAT 'MM/DD/YY' PROMPT 'Give me a date >'
Give me a date >11-15-1961
```

Time of day is not treated with much respect by ACCEPT. You may ask for it in your format string, but ACCEPT will take it or leave it. As long as the user enters a date, ACCEPT doesn't care about the rest:

```
SQL> ACCEPT my_variable DATE FORMAT 'MM/DD/YYYY HH:MI AM' PROMPT 'Give me a date>'
Give me a date >11/15/1961
SQL>
```

The user input in response to an ACCEPT command is placed into a substitution variable and those substitution variables are always text. This is true with numbers and is true with dates. Look at the following example:

```
SQL> ACCEPT my_variable DATE FORMAT 'MM/DD/YY' PROMPT 'Give me a date >'
Give me a date >7/4/98
SQL> DEFINE my_variable
DEFINE MY_VARIABLE     = "7/4/98" (CHAR)
```

The date entered was July 4, 1998. It is stored as the character string "7/4/98," which matches the input format used with the ACCEPT command. To reference the date later in your script, you must use the TO_DATE function to convert it again, and you must use the same format string you used to ACCEPT the date. Failure to do this can result in the date's being misinterpreted. The following SELECT, for example, interprets the date entered in the preceding example using the European convention of having the day first, followed by the month and year:

```
SQL> select to_date('&&my_variable','dd/mm/yyyy') from dual;
old    1: select to_date('&&my_variable','dd/mm/yyyy') from dual
new    1: select to_date('7/4/98','dd/mm/yyyy') from dual

TO_DATE('
---------
07-APR-98

SQL>
```

Suddenly, July 4, 1998 has become April 7, 1998. I can't imagine wanting that type of behavior in a script. To avoid problems, use the same date format consistently every time you reference a substitution variable, whether it's in an ACCEPT command or somewhere else in your script.

Validating Input with SQL

The validation you get with the ACCEPT command is limited. You can do more, if you need to, with the creative use of SQL (or PL/SQL) together with the branching techniques discussed earlier in this chapter. With a little thought and effort, you can:

- Code more specific validations than you get with ACCEPT.
- Accept more complicated input from the user.

You can, for example, write a script that asks the user for a date and that requires all four digits of the year to be entered. You can write a script that accepts several values in one string and then pulls apart that string to get at each value. An example of this would be allowing the user to specify a table using the standard *owner.tablename* dot notation syntax and defaulting the owner to the currently logged-on user.

If you are going to code a complex edit check using SQL*Plus, you need to do the following:

- Decide whether the user's input is valid.
- Take different actions depending on the result of that decision.

The first thing you need to decide is which branching technique you are going to use because that tends to drive how you structure the query you use for validation. Usually, if I'm in this deep, I will branch using a multilevel file structure. To facilitate this, I'll write the validation query to return all or part of the filename to run next. If the input is bad, the next script file will display an error message and quit.

The second thing to do is to write the SQL query to perform the validation. Implementing the validation requires four steps:

1. ACCEPT input from the user.
2. Issue a COLUMN command to capture the value returned from the validation query.
3. Execute the validation query.
4. Execute the script file returned by the query, which you captured with the COLUMN command.

The short script in Example 11-29 illustrates how SQL can be used to validate input by determining whether a date was entered using a four-digit year, a two-digit year, or some other quantity of digits.

Example 11-29. Using a SELECT and multilevel file structure to validate input

```
SET ECHO OFF

--Get a date from the user
ACCEPT start_date DATE FORMAT 'DD-MON-YYYY' PROMPT 'Start Date >'
```

Example 11-29. Using a SELECT and multilevel file structure to validate input (continued)

```
--Get the next file to run, based on whether the date
--has a four-digit or a two-digit year.
SET TERMOUT OFF
COLUMN next_script_file NEW_VALUE next_script_file
SELECT DECODE (LENGTH(SUBSTR('&&start_date',
                     INSTR(TRANSLATE('&&start_date','/','-'),'-',-1)+1,
                     LENGTH('&&start_date')-
                     INSTR(TRANSLATE('&&start_date','/','-'),'-',-1))),
            4,'ex11-29_four.sql &&start_date',
            2,'ex11-29_two.sql &&start_date',
              'ex11-29_bad.sql') next_script_file
FROM dual;
SET TERMOUT ON

--Execute the appropriate script
@&&next_script_file
```

The three scripts referenced by Example 11-29 are shown next:

```
oracle@gennick02:~/sqlplus/ExampleScripts> cat ex11-29_four.sql
PROMPT Four digit year: &1
oracle@gennick02:~/sqlplus/ExampleScripts> cat ex11-29_two.sql
PROMPT Two-digit year: &1
oracle@gennick02:~/sqlplus/ExampleScripts> cat ex11-29_bad.sql
PROMPT Year must be either two or four digits!
oracle@gennick02:~/sqlplus/ExampleScripts>
```

The following are several runs to test the functionality of Example 11-29:

```
SQL> @ex11-29
Start Date >15-Nov-1961
Four digit year: 15-Nov-1961
SQL> @ex11-29
Start Date >15-Nov-61
Two-digit year: 15-Nov-61
SQL> @ex11-29
Start Date >15-Nov-961
Year must be either two or four digits!
```

Admittedly, the DECODE expression in Example 11-29 is complex, but it serves to illustrate how much you can accomplish with Oracle's built-in functions.

Parsing Input with SQL

In addition to validating input, you can use SQL and PL/SQL to parse it. Imagine for a moment that you are writing a script to display information about the physical implementation of a table. The script has to know which table you want to look at, and one way to accomplish that is to pass the table name as an argument like this:

```
@show_physical project_hours
```

That's fine if you want to run the script on tables you own. But what if you are the DBA and you want to examine tables owned by other users? As with the DESCRIBE command, you may want to allow for an optional owner name. Then you could also run the script like this:

```
@show_physical jeff.project_hours
```

The first problem you'll encounter in doing this is that the argument jeff.project_hours is one string and not two. The second problem is that you can't depend on the owner to be always specified, and when it's not specified you want it to default to the currently logged-in user. One solution to these problems is to use SQL to parse the input. One way to do that is to extend the WHERE clauses of whatever queries are run by your script. Here's a query to return the amount of space used by a particular table:

```
SELECT SUM(bytes)
  FROM dba_extents
 WHERE segment_name = DECODE(INSTR('&&1','.'),
        0,UPPER('&&1'),
        UPPER(SUBSTR('&&1',INSTR('&&1','.')+1)))
   AND owner = DECODE(INSTR('&&1','.'),
        0,USER,
        UPPER(SUBSTR('&&1',1,INSTR('&&1','.')-1)));
```

This solution works, but it can be cumbersome and error-prone because the parsing logic has to be replicated in each query your script executes. A better solution is to write some SQL at the beginning of your script specifically to parse the input. That way, you end up with two distinct substitution variables, one for the owner and one for the table name, to use in the rest of your script. To do this requires two steps. First, set up some COLUMN commands with NEW_VALUE clauses. You need one of these COLUMN commands for each distinct value in your input string. In keeping with the owner.tablename example, the following two commands could be used:

```
COLUMN owner_name NOPRINT NEW_VALUE s_owner_name
COLUMN table_name NOPRINT NEW_VALUE s_table_name
```

Second, you need to execute a query that returns the results you want. In this case, the query needs to return the owner name and table name as separate columns. Be sure to use column aliases to name these columns, and be sure those aliases match the names used in the COLUMN commands. The following SELECT takes a string in the form owner.tablename and returns two separate values. If the owner is not specified, the name of the current user is returned instead:

```
SELECT
  DECODE(INSTR('&&1','.'),
        0,USER,  /*Default to current user.*/
        UPPER(SUBSTR('&&1',1,INSTR('&&1','.')-1))) owner_name,
  DECODE(INSTR('&&1','.'),
        0,UPPER('&&1'),  /*Only the table name was passed in.*/
        UPPER(SUBSTR('&&1',INSTR('&&1','.')+1))) table_name
FROM dual;
```

Once the query has been executed, the substitution variables named in the COL-UMN commands will hold the values returned by the SELECT. These substitution variables may be used in the remainder of the script. The following is a rewrite of the previous SELECT using these variables:

```
SELECT SUM(bytes)
FROM dba_extents
WHERE segment_name '&&s_table_name'
  AND owner = '&&s_owner_name';
```

By using this technique, you have one point of change that controls how the input is parsed. If there's a bug in your logic, you need to fix it in only one place. The readability of your script is greatly increased, too. You and others will understand your scripts more clearly.

 Example 10-14 implements the parsing technique shown in this section. Following that example is a detailed breakdown of the DECODE function that separates owner and table name.

Error Handling

SQL*Plus doesn't offer too much in the way of error handling. By default, SQL*Plus simply ignores errors and goes on to execute the next command you type in or the next command in the script you are running. For interactive use, this is good enough. If an error occurs, you will see the message and take appropriate action. However, the situation is different when you are running a script. Depending on what the script is doing, you may not want SQL*Plus to blindly proceed to the next command when an error occurs. Consider the following script, which creates a new table, copies data to it, then deletes the original table:

```
CREATE TABLE employee_copy AS
    SELECT * FROM employee;
DROP TABLE employee;
```

If the CREATE TABLE command failed, you certainly wouldn't want the script to continue because you would lose all your data. To help with this type of situation, SQL*Plus provides the WHENEVER command.

The WHENEVER Command

With the WHENEVER command, you can give SQL*Plus instructions on what to do when an error occurs. Your choices are limited: You can continue when an error occurs or exit SQL*Plus entirely, possibly returning an error code. Returning an error code is useful if you are calling SQL*Plus from a Unix shell script or a DOS batch file.

You can handle two types of errors with WHENEVER. Each has its own variation of the command.

WHENEVER SQLERROR
    Used to handle SQL errors and errors raised from PL/SQL blocks

WHENEVER OSERROR
    Used to handle operating system errors, such as those you might get when you
    run out of disk space while spooling a large data extract

You cannot detect an error involving a SQL*Plus command. An example would be if
you were to misspell a command, such as COLUMN. If your script contained the
following command,

```
COLUM employee_name HEADEEN 'Employee Name' FLOORMAT A40
```

SQL*Plus would generate an error and continue on with the script as if nothing had
happened. This isn't usually much of a problem. You should test your scripts to be
sure your SQL*Plus commands are correct, which is easy to do. The consequences of
a failed SQL*Plus command are usually no worse than some messy formatting of the
output. SQL statements, on the other hand, can fail for various reasons that don't
involve simple misspellings. A simple database change can cause a SQL statement
that worked one day to fail the next. Similarly, with operating system errors, you
don't know in advance, for example, when you will run out of disk space.

WHENEVER SQLERROR

The WHENEVER SQLERROR command tells SQL*Plus what to do when a SQL
statement or PL/SQL block fails to execute properly. To use it, issue the command as
shown in the following example, telling SQL*Plus to abort the script when an error
occurs:

```
SQL> WHENEVER SQLERROR EXIT
SQL> SELECT emp_id FROM dual;
SELECT emp_id FROM dual
       *
ERROR at line 1:
ORA-00904: invalid column name


Disconnected from Oracle7 Server Release 7.3.3.0.0 - Production Release
PL/SQL Release 2.3.3.0.0 - Production
$
```

When SQL*Plus exits like this, the default behavior is to commit any transaction that
might be open. For a SELECT statement as shown in the previous example, this is
not a problem. When you are changing records, it might be. If your script executes
several SQL statements that change data, you may not want to commit unless all the
changes can be made. In this situation, use the ROLLBACK option to tell SQL*Plus
to roll back when an error occurs like this:

```
WHENEVER SQLERROR EXIT ROLLBACK
```

If you're calling SQL*Plus from a Unix shell script, DOS batch file, VMS command file, or an equivalent, you can have it pass back a return code so your shell script can tell whether your script executed successfully. The following command tells SQL*Plus to pass back a standard failure code when an error occurs:

```
WHENEVER SQLERROR EXIT FAILURE ROLLBACK
```

The precise code that gets passed back varies from one operating system to the next. If a simple success/fail indication is not enough, you can have SQL*Plus pass back the specific Oracle error code or any other value you want. The following example shows how to pass back the Oracle error code when a SQL error occurs:

```
WHENEVER SQLERROR EXIT SQL.SQLCODE
```

You could choose to return any arbitrary number, the value of a numeric bind variable, or the value of a substitution variable.

> The default behavior of WHENEVER SQLERROR EXIT is to COMMIT any pending transaction. You may want to use the ROLLBACK option to change that behavior.
>
> Using WHENEVER SQLERROR EXIT with the GUI version of SQL*Plus can be annoying at times. Any error results in SQL*Plus terminating, causing the GUI window to close. Usually this happens before you realize an error occurred, making you miss any displayed error message.
>
> Do not use the keyword THEN in your statement. It's WHENEVER SQLERROR EXIT, not WHENEVER SQLERROR THEN EXIT. I often tend to get mixed up on this point.

Capturing SQL*Plus return codes

You can capture the error code returned by SQL*Plus when a script fails. This is handy when writing shell scripts because you can have a shell script take different courses of action depending on whether a SQL*Plus script succeeds. Example 11-30 shows a script that is guaranteed to fail. The script attempts to create a table but uses invalid syntax. The WHENEVER SQLERROR command ensures that the script then exits with a failure status.

Example 11-30. A script demonstrating WHENEVER's error handling

```
WHENEVER SQLERROR EXIT FAILURE
CREATE TABLE pay_raises WITH COLUMNS (
   employee_id NUMBER,
   raise NUMBER
);
EXIT
```

On Unix and Linux systems, you can capture the status of the most recently executed command through the $? shell variable:

```
oracle@gennick02:~/sqlplus/ExampleScripts> sqlplus -s gennick/bramell @ex11-30
CREATE TABLE pay_raises WITH COLUMNS (
                                 *
ERROR at line 1:
ORA-00922: missing or invalid option


oracle@gennick02:~/sqlplus/ExampleScripts> echo $?
1
```

The exact values that SQL*Plus returns on success and failure depend upon your operating system. On Unix and Linux systems, SQL*Plus typically returns 0 for success and 1 for failure. The preceding run of SQL*Plus returned a 1, indicating an error.

Example 11-31 shows a script that traps an error from a SQL*Plus script. SQL*Plus is invoked from the if shell command. That invocation of SQL*Plus, in turn, invokes the script in *ex11-30.sql*. The if statement treats 0 as true and any other value as false. A successful execution of *ex11-30.sql* is followed by an execution of *ex11-31_insert_raises*. Otherwise, an error message is displayed through the standard output device.

*Example 11-31. Capturing the SQL*Plus return status from Unix*

```
#!/bin/bash
if sqlplus -s gennick/secret @ex11-30
then
    sqlplus gennick/secret @ex11-31_insert_raises
else
    echo Unable to create raise table.
fi
```

The following is a run showing how Example 11-31 successfully captures and then acts upon the failure status from Example 11-30:

```
oracle@gennick02:~/sqlplus/ExampleScripts> . ex11-31.sh
CREATE TABLE pay_raises WITH COLUMNS (
                                 *
ERROR at line 1:
ORA-00922: missing or invalid option


Unable to create raise table.
```

Be aware that the range of return codes you can pass back from SQL*Plus varies from one operating system to the next. Under Unix, return codes are limited to one byte, giving you a range of 0 to 255 to work with. Any failure codes in excess of 255 are returned modulo 256, which means that 256 is returned as 0, 257 as 1, and so forth.

VMS, on the other hand, allows much larger values to be returned. Keep this in mind if you are writing a script that needs to be portable across different operating systems.

> You can use the BITAND function to predict the actual, modulo 256 value that will be returned for a given error code:
>
> ```
> SQL> SELECT BITAND(1555, 255)
>   2  FROM dual;
>
> BITAND(1555,255)
> ----------------
>               19
> ```
>
> This output tells you that an ORA-01555 error would be passed back to Unix as a 19, which is helpful to know if you want your shell script to take action on that specific error.

PL/SQL errors and WHENEVER

The WHENEVER SQLERROR EXIT command catches any errors in a PL/SQL block, but only if those errors are raised back to the SQL*Plus level. PL/SQL has its own error-handling mechanism, and using it can prevent SQL*Plus from knowing that an error occurred.

The PL/SQL block in Example 11-32 doesn't contain an error handler, so any SQL errors are raised to the calling routine, which in this case is SQL*Plus.

*Example 11-32. Without an error handler in a block, PL/SQL errors are raised to SQL*Plus, and trigger the WHENEVER logic*

```
BEGIN
  UPDATE employee
    SET employee_billing_rate = employee_billing_rate * 1.10;
  COMMIT;
END;
/
```

However, you can rewrite the block in Example 11-32 so it includes an error handler. In that case, the PL/SQL error handler would get the error, and SQL*Plus wouldn't know about it. Example 11-33 shows the rewritten block.

*Example 11-33. An error handler in a PL/SQL block "hides" errors from SQL*Plus*

```
DECLARE
  success_flag BOOLEAN;
BEGIN
  BEGIN
    UPDATE employee
      SET employee_billing_rate = employee_billing_rate * 1.10;
    success_flag := TRUE;
  EXCEPTION
    WHEN OTHERS THEN
```

```
      success_flag := false;
  END;

  IF success_flag THEN
    COMMIT;
  ELSE
    ROLLBACK;
    DBMS_OUTPUT.PUT_LINE('The UPDATE failed.');
  END IF;
END;
/
```

In this example, the UPDATE statement is contained in its own PL/SQL block, and any error related to that statement is trapped by the exception handler for that block. Even if an error occurs, as far as SQL*Plus is concerned, this block will have executed successfully. If you want to handle an error within PL/SQL but still abort the SQL*Plus script, you can use the RAISE_APPLICATION_ERROR procedure. This procedure is part of a PL/SQL package named DBMS_STANDARD and should be available in all installations. You call it like this:

```
    RAISE_APPLICATION_ERROR (error_code, error_message);
```

in which:

error_code
> Is a negative number. The range from −20000 to −20999 is reserved for user-defined errors.

error_message
> Is a text message of up to 2048 characters.

When you call RAISE_APPLICATION_ERROR from a PL/SQL block, control immediately returns to the calling block. You must call the procedure from the outermost PL/SQL block to return the error to SQL*Plus. When that happens, SQL*Plus prints the error message and takes whatever action you specified in the most recent WHENEVER SQLERROR command. The PL/SQL block in Example 11-34 is the same as in Example 11-33, except for the addition of the RAISE_APPLICATION_ERROR procedure call, which is used to notify SQL*Plus of an error.

Example 11-34. However, you can use RAISE_APPLICATION_ERROR to pass an error up the line to SQL*Plus

```
DECLARE
  success_flag BOOLEAN;
BEGIN
  BEGIN
    UPDATE employee
      SET employee_billing_rate = employee_billing_rate * 1.10;
    success_flag := TRUE;
  EXCEPTION
```

Example 11-34. However, you can use RAISE_APPLICATION_ERROR to pass an error up the line to SQL*Plus (continued)

```
  WHEN OTHERS THEN
    success_flag := false;
  END;

  IF success_flag THEN
    COMMIT;
  ELSE
    ROLLBACK;
    DBMS_OUTPUT.PUT_LINE('The UPDATE failed.');
    RAISE_APPLICATION_ERROR (-20000,
    'The UPDATE of employee billing rates failed.');
  END IF;
END;
/
```

If an error occurs, SQL*Plus will know about it and can abort the script.

WHENEVER OSERROR

The WHENEVER OSERROR command tells SQL*Plus what to do when an operating system error occurs. Running out of disk space would be a likely operating system error, one that you might encounter when spooling large amounts of output from a SQL query.

WHENEVER OSERROR works similarly to the WHENEVER SQLERROR command. The simple version, which causes SQL*Plus to exit when an error occurs, looks like this:

```
WHENEVER OSERROR EXIT
```

By default, any changes are committed when SQL*Plus exits. You can change that behavior using the ROLLBACK keyword as follows:

```
WHENEVER OSERROR EXIT ROLLBACK
```

As with WHENEVER SQLERROR, you can pass a return code back to a shell script to allow it to detect the error:

```
WHENEVER OSERROR EXIT FAILURE
```

Unlike the SQLERROR version of the command, there is no equivalent to SQL. SQLCODE for operating system errors. The other options apply, however, and you can return an arbitrary value, the value from a bind variable, or the value of a substitution variable.

Returning Values to Unix

When writing shell scripts, you can use SQL*Plus as a mechanism for getting information from your database into shell script variables. You can do this in several ways. If you need to return a small numeric value, you can use the EXIT command. Example 11-35 uses the EXIT command to return a count of tables to a shell script variable.

Example 11-35. Returning a value through the EXIT command

```
#!/bin/bash
sqlplus -s gennick/secret << EOF
COLUMN tab_count NEW_VALUE table_count
SELECT COUNT(*) tab_count FROM user_all_tables;
EXIT table_count
EOF

let "tabcount = $?"
echo You have $tabcount tables.
```

Passing data back through the EXIT command is of limited usefulness. The technique is good only for numeric values between 0 and 255 (on Unix/Linux systems), and it precludes access to success or failure status.

Another approach to placing a value into a shell script variable is to write a value to a file and use the Unix *cat* command to place the contents of that file into a variable. Examples 11-36 and 11-37 show two different variations on this theme.

Example 11-36. Redirecting standard output to a file

```
#!/bin/bash
sqlplus -s gennick/secret > tabs << EOF
SET SERVEROUTPUT ON
SET FEEDBACK OFF
DECLARE
   tab_count NUMBER;
BEGIN
   SELECT COUNT(*) INTO tab_count
   FROM user_all_tables;

   DBMS_OUTPUT.PUT_LINE(tab_count);
END;
/
EXIT
EOF

tabcount=`cat tabs`
echo You have $tabcount tables.
```

Example 11-37 redirects standard output to a file named *tabs*. To control the output better, the SQL statement to count tables is embedded into a PL/SQL script. A call to DBMS_OUTPUT.PUT_LINE writes the count to standard output, which in turn redirects to the *tabs* file. The SET SERVEROUTPUT ON command is critical here because it causes SQL*Plus to actually process output generated using the DBMS_OUTPUT package. SET FEEDBACK OFF prevents the message "PL/SQL procedure successfully completed." from being included in *tabs*. After SQL*Plus exits, the contents of *tabs* is placed into the shell variable tabcount.

Example 11-37. Spooling to a file

```
sqlplus -s gennick/secret << EOF
SET PAGESIZE 0
SPOOL tabs
SELECT COUNT(*) FROM user_all_tables;
EXIT
EOF

tabcount=`cat tabs`
echo You have $tabcount tables.
```

Example 11-37 functions on lines similar to Example 11-36. This time, rather than being redirected through standard output, the table count is spooled to the *tabs* file. SET PAGESIZE 0 ensures that *tabs* remains free of column headings, page headings, and the like. The remainder of the script is identical to Example 11-36.

Example 11-38 shows an approach that avoids the need to write anything to a file.

Example 11-38. Capturing standard output directly to a shell variable

```
#!/bin/bash
tabcount=`sqlplus -s gennick/secret << EOF
SET PAGESIZE 0
SELECT COUNT(*) FROM user_all_tables;
EXIT
EOF`

echo You have $tabcount tables.
```

Example 11-38 treats the entire SQL*Plus session as if it were a file. The backticks (`) enclosing the command cause all of SQL*Plus's standard output to be captured and placed into the tabcount shell variable. SET PAGESIZE 0 ensures that the only output to be captured is the table count.

The methods in Examples 11-36 through 11-38 are all good for getting database data into shell script variables. Don't get too fancy with any of these methods. They are all suited for scalar data. Unix and Linux shell script variables aren't designed to handle esoteric datatypes such as Oracle's object types, arrays, etc.

CHAPTER 12
Tuning and Timing

Oracle offers two features you can invoke from SQL*Plus to monitor and improve the performance of your scripts and SQL statements: SQL*Plus timers and the EXPLAIN PLAN command.

SQL*Plus has a built-in timing feature that can be used to monitor the length of time it takes to execute a SQL statement, a PL/SQL block, or any other part of a script. To measure the time it takes to execute a SQL statement, you start a timer prior to executing the statement and display the value of the timer immediately after the statement is executed.

EXPLAIN PLAN, although it is a SQL statement and not a SQL*Plus command, is often issued from SQL*Plus. EXPLAIN PLAN can be used to find out how Oracle intends to execute any given SQL query. It will tell you, for example, whether an index will be used, and what the name of that index will be. Once you know how Oracle intends to execute the query, you can use *hints* to influence or alter Oracle's default plan based on your knowledge of the data. A hint is a command to the optimizer that is embedded in a comment within a SQL query. The optimizer is the part of Oracle that determines how best to retrieve the data required by a SQL statement.

This chapter is not intended to be an exhaustive reference for tuning SQL statements. Several good books have been written on this subject. This chapter provides a quick overview for SQL*Plus users of the mechanics of tuning and a convenient summary of the hints available to you.

Using SQL*Plus Timers

SQL*Plus comes with a crude, built-in timing facility that allows you to measure the elapsed time of a script or any portion of a script. You can even have SQL*Plus report the elapsed execution time of every SQL query and PL/SQL block automatically after each statement has executed. Timers can be nested so you can time the overall execution of a script, as well as the execution time of each individual statement.

Timings can be useful in spotting trends. It may be helpful to know, for example, if a script is taking longer to run. Timings can help compare the relative efficiency of two SQL statements. If you have two statements that return equivalent results and one consistently runs faster than the other, that's the one you probably want to go with.

Take timing with a grain of salt, however. The timer measures elapsed time, sometimes called wall-clock time, not CPU time, and many factors can throw it off. The network throughput might vary between the execution of two queries. The load on the server might vary as well. For example, one query might run more slowly than another because many other users simultaneously happened to hit the database. Be skeptical of one-time results. Look for consistency over several timings.

The SET TIMING Command

You can have SQL*Plus automatically report the elapsed time it takes to execute every query by issuing the SET TIMING ON command:

```
SET TIMING ON
```

Now, whenever you execute a query, SQL*Plus will report the elapsed time. With older Windows versions of SQL*Plus, this time will be reported in milliseconds. The following example shows that it took two hundredths of a second for a query on dba_views to complete:

```
SELECT view_name
FROM dba_views
WHERE view_name = 'DBA_TABLES';

VIEW_NAME
------------------------------
DBA_TABLES

Elapsed: 00:00:00.02
```

When timing is on, SQL*Plus reports the time it takes to execute a PL/SQL block:

```
BEGIN
    DBMS_OUTPUT.PUT_LINE('How long does this take?');
END;
/
How long does this take?

PL/SQL procedure successfully completed.

Elapsed: 00:00:00.04
```

To turn timing off, simply issue the SET TIMING OFF command as follows:

```
SET TIMING OFF
```

When you have timing turned on, SQL*Plus displays elapsed time only for statements executed by the database server. This includes SQL statements and PL/SQL blocks. Elapsed time for SQL*Plus commands, such as ACCEPT and DEFINE, is not reported.

In Oracle Database 10*g*, timings are reported using an hour, minute, second, and hundredth format:

```
Elapsed: 00:00:00.04
```

Older releases of SQL*Plus running under Windows reported elapsed time in milliseconds:

```
real: 90500
```

In all cases, even today, timer resolution varies with the hardware platform. For example, a time interval reported in milliseconds doesn't mean that the underlying hardware can accurately track one-millisecond intervals.

The TIMING Command

The SQL*Plus TIMING command gives you complete control over when timing starts and stops and what is measured. With it, you can turn on a timer at any point in your script. You can display the elapsed time at any point after a timer is turned on, and you can nest timers. Nesting timers gives you a way to time a set of operations, maybe an entire script, while still allowing you to time each individual operation separately.

The TIMING command is useful only in scripts. You can use it interactively, but then the elapsed time will include your "think" time and the time it takes you to type commands.

Think of timers as being implemented on a stack. Each time you issue a TIMING START command, you push a new timer onto the stack. The TIMING SHOW and TIMING STOP commands each operate on whatever timer is currently at the top of the stack. To find out how many timers you have currently running, enter the TIMING command with no arguments.

Starting and stopping a timer

Use the TIMING START command to start a timer. If you like, you can give the timer a name. Timing starts the moment the command is executed. The following example starts a new timer, and gives it a name of for_testing:

```
TIMING START for_testing
```

You stop the timer and display its final value by issuing the TIMING STOP command as follows:

```
SQL> TIMING STOP
timing for: for_testing
Elapsed: 00:00:07.72
```

In this case, the timer ran for a total elapsed time of 7.72 seconds.

Displaying the value of a timer

You can display the value of a timer without stopping it. This is useful if your script is executing several SQL queries and you want to see the cumulative elapsed time after each one:

```
SQL> TIMING START for_show
SQL> TIMING SHOW
timing for: for_show
Elapsed: 00:00:02.61
SQL> TIMING SHOW
timing for: for_show
Elapsed: 00:00:04.97
SQL> TIMING SHOW
timing for: for_show
Elapsed: 00:00:06.33
```

You can see from this example that once I got going, it took me in the neighborhood of two seconds, give or take, to type each TIMING SHOW command.

Nesting timers

Timers can be nested, allowing you to time a group of operations while simultaneously timing each individual operation within the larger group. The following example shows a timer being started, and while that's running, two more timers are started and stopped. Finally, the first timer is stopped.

```
SQL> TIMING START first
SQL> TIMING START second
SQL> TIMING STOP
timing for: second
Elapsed: 00:00:03.66
SQL> TIMING START third
SQL> TIMING STOP
timing for: third
Elapsed: 00:00:02.21
SQL> TIMING STOP
timing for: first
Elapsed: 00:00:17.14
```

The important thing to notice here is that the first timer kept running during this entire example. The total elapsed time was a bit over 17 seconds, while the two intermediate operations took 3.66 and 2.21 seconds respectively.

Example 12-1 shows how this nesting feature can be used. It creates a copy of each example table used for this book and reports the time needed for each copy, as well as the total elapsed time to run the entire script.

Example 12-1. Using nested timers to time a script and its operations

```
TIMING START entire_script

--Drop old versions of the copies, if any exist
DROP TABLE employee_copy;
DROP TABLE project_copy;
DROP TABLE project_hours_copy;

--Copy the employee table
TIMING START copy_employees
CREATE TABLE employee_copy AS
    SELECT * FROM employee;
TIMING STOP

--Copy the project table
TIMING START copy_project
CREATE TABLE project_copy AS
    SELECT * FROM project;
TIMING STOP

--Copy the project_hours
TIMING START copy_project_hours
CREATE TABLE project_hours_copy AS
    SELECT * FROM project_hours;
TIMING STOP

TIMING STOP
```

Here is the output from running Example 12-1:

```
@ex12-1

Table dropped.

Table dropped.

Table dropped.

Table created.

timing for: copy_employees
Elapsed: 00:00:00.07

Table created.

timing for: copy_project
Elapsed: 00:00:00.37

Table created.

timing for: copy_project_hours
Elapsed: 00:00:00.08
timing for: entire_script
Elapsed: 00:00:00.73
```

You can see that the elapsed time was displayed for each table copy and for the script as a whole.

Finding out how many timers you have going

The TIMER command will cause SQL*Plus to report the number of active timers. The following example shows how the count goes up each time you start a timer and goes back down each time you stop one:

```
TIMING START
TIMING
1 timing element in use
TIMING START
TIMING
2 timing elements in use
TIMING STOP
Elapsed: 00:00:00.05
TIMING
1 timing element in use
TIMING STOP
Elapsed: 00:00:00.14
TIMING
no timing elements in use
```

Stopping all timers

You can stop and delete all timers with the CLEAR TIMING command. As each timer is stopped, its final value is displayed:

```
TIMING START first
TIMING START second
TIMING START third
CLEAR TIMING
timing for: third
Elapsed: 00:00:00.02
timing for: second
Elapsed: 00:00:00.06
timing for: first
Elapsed: 00:00:00.10
```

Using EXPLAIN PLAN

EXPLAIN PLAN is a SQL statement that causes Oracle to report the execution plan it would choose for any SELECT, INSERT, UPDATE, DELETE, or MERGE statement. An *execution plans* refers to the approach Oracle will take to retrieve the necessary data for a statement. One example of a plan would be to use an index to find the required rows. Another example of an execution plan would be to sequentially read all rows in the table. If you have a poorly performing SQL statement, you can use EXPLAIN PLAN to find out how Oracle is processing it. With that information, you may be able to take some corrective action to improve performance.

When you use EXPLAIN PLAN, Oracle doesn't display its execution strategy on the screen; instead, it inserts rows into a table. This table is referred to as the *plan table*, and you must query it properly to see the results. The plan table must exist; if you've never used EXPLAIN PLAN before, you may need to create the plan table first.

 Oracle occasionally adds columns to the plan table. If you have a plan table created using a previous version of Oracle, you may want to drop and re-create it to be sure you have the most recent version.

Creating the Plan Table

If you're running Oracle Database 10g, the good news is you don't need to create a plan table. Instead, you can let the EXPLAIN PLAN statement create the table for you. If no plan table exists, EXPLAIN PLAN will create a global temporary plan table. The EXPLAIN PLAN results in such a table will remain for the duration of your session. The temporary table definition will be permanent.

If you're not running Oracle Database 10*g*, or if you prefer working with a plan table that will hold results across more than one session until you delete them, you'll need to create a permanent plan table. For that, Oracle provides a script named *utlxplan.sql*, which resides in the *$ORACLE_HOME/rdbms/admin* directory for your database. You can run the script from SQL*Plus like this:

```
SQL> @$ORACLE_HOME/rdbms/admin/utlxplan
```

```
Table created.
```

 Windows users, refer to the Oracle home directory as follows:

```
@%ORACLE_HOME%/rdbms/admin/utlxplan
```

In particular, note the bracketing of ORACLE_HOME by percent-signs (%).

The columns in the plan table vary from release to release, as Oracle has tended to add columns over the years. Here is what the Oracle Database 10*g* plan table looks like:

```
SQL> DESCRIBE plan_table
```

Name	Null?	Type
STATEMENT_ID		VARCHAR2(30)
PLAN_ID		NUMBER
TIMESTAMP		DATE
REMARKS		VARCHAR2(4000)
OPERATION		VARCHAR2(30)
OPTIONS		VARCHAR2(255)
OBJECT_NODE		VARCHAR2(128)
OBJECT_OWNER		VARCHAR2(30)
OBJECT_NAME		VARCHAR2(30)
OBJECT_ALIAS		VARCHAR2(65)
OBJECT_INSTANCE		NUMBER(38)
OBJECT_TYPE		VARCHAR2(30)
OPTIMIZER		VARCHAR2(255)
SEARCH_COLUMNS		NUMBER
ID		NUMBER(38)
PARENT_ID		NUMBER(38)
DEPTH		NUMBER(38)
POSITION		NUMBER(38)
COST		NUMBER(38)
CARDINALITY		NUMBER(38)
BYTES		NUMBER(38)
OTHER_TAG		VARCHAR2(255)
PARTITION_START		VARCHAR2(255)
PARTITION_STOP		VARCHAR2(255)
PARTITION_ID		NUMBER(38)

```
OTHER                          LONG
DISTRIBUTION                   VARCHAR2(30)
CPU_COST                       NUMBER(38)
IO_COST                        NUMBER(38)
TEMP_SPACE                     NUMBER(38)
ACCESS_PREDICATES              VARCHAR2(4000)
FILTER_PREDICATES              VARCHAR2(4000)
PROJECTION                     VARCHAR2(4000)
TIME                           NUMBER(38)
QBLOCK_NAME                    VARCHAR2(30)
```

The name of the table doesn't have to be plan_table, but that's the default and it's usually easiest to leave it that way. If for some reason you don't have access to the *utlxplan.sql* script, you can create the table manually. Be sure that the column names and datatypes match those shown here.

Explaining a Query

Once you have a plan table, getting Oracle to tell you the execution plan for any given query is an easy task. You need to prepend the EXPLAIN PLAN statement to the front of your query. The syntax for EXPLAIN PLAN looks like this:

```
EXPLAIN PLAN
        [SET STATEMENT_ID = 'statement_id']
        [INTO table_name]
        FOR statement;
```

in which:

statement_id

Can be anything you like, and is stored in the STATEMENT_ID field of all plan table records related to the query you are explaining. It defaults to null.

table_name

Is the name of the plan table, and defaults to PLAN_TABLE. You need to supply this value if you have created your plan table with some name other than the default.

statement

Is the DML statement to be "explained." This can be an INSERT, UPDATE, DELETE, SELECT, or MERGE statement, but it must not reference any data dictionary views or dynamic performance tables.

Consider the following query, which returns the total number of hours worked by each employee on each project:

```
SELECT employee_name, project_name, sum(hours_logged)
  FROM employee, project, project_hours
 WHERE employee.employee_id = project_hours.employee_id
   AND project.project_id = project_hours.project_id
 GROUP BY employee_name, project_name;
```

This query can be explained using the two statements shown in Example 12-2.

Example 12-2. Explaining a query

```
DELETE FROM plan_table WHERE statement_id = 'HOURS_BY_PROJECT';

EXPLAIN PLAN
SET STATEMENT_ID = 'HOURS_BY_PROJECT'
FOR
SELECT employee_name, project_name, sum(hours_logged)
  FROM employee, project, project_hours
 WHERE employee.employee_id = project_hours.employee_id
   AND project.project_id = project_hours.project_id
GROUP BY employee_name, project_name;
```

When you execute this EXPLAIN PLAN statement, you won't see any output because Oracle stores the query plan in the plan table. Retrieving and interpreting the results is your next task.

You should include a DELETE statement prior to the EXPLAIN PLAN statement. When you explain a statement, Oracle doesn't clear the plan table of any previous rows with the same statement ID. If rows with the same statement ID exist from previous executions of EXPLAIN PLAN, you will get strange results.

If you're the only person using the plan table, you can save yourself some typing by omitting the WHERE clause in the DELETE statement, thereby deleting all the records in the plan table. In that case, you don't need to bother with the SET STATEMENT_ID clause.

Interpreting the Results

Having issued an EXPLAIN PLAN, you retrieve and view the results by querying the plan table. The statement ID is the key to doing this. The plan table can contain execution plans for any number of queries. The rows for each query contain the statement ID you specified in your EXPLAIN PLAN statement, so you must use this same ID when querying the plan table to select the plan you are interested in seeing.

Using DBMS_XPLAN to display an execution plan

Beginning in Oracle9i Database Release 2, you can display an execution plan with a call to DBMS_XPLAN.DISPLAY, which is a table function. Example 12-3 shows how to use that function to display the plan generated in Example 12-2. The SET LINESIZE 132 command is there because the results require a bit more than 80 characters per line. Figure 12-1 shows the resulting plan output.

Example 12-3. Invoking DBMS_XPLAN.DISPLAY to show an execution plan

```
SET LINESIZE 132

SELECT *
FROM TABLE(DBMS_XPLAN.DISPLAY(
```

Example 12-3. Invoking DBMS_XPLAN.DISPLAY to show an execution plan (continued)

```
        'PLAN_TABLE','HOURS_BY_PROJECT','TYPICAL')
    );
```

```
Oracle SQL*Plus                                                          _|□|X|
File  Edit  Search  Options  Help
SQL> SET LINESIZE 132
SQL>
SQL> SELECT *
  2  FROM TABLE(DBMS_XPLAN.DISPLAY(
  3              'PLAN_TABLE','HOURS_BY_PROJECT','TYPICAL')
  4          );

PLAN_TABLE_OUTPUT
---------------------------------------------------------------------------
Plan hash value: 3447427452

---------------------------------------------------------------------------
| Id | Operation                    | Name         | Rows | Bytes | Cost (%CPU)| Time     |

|  0 | SELECT STATEMENT             |              |   51 |  4598 | 11  (28)| 00:00:01 |
|  1 |  SORT GROUP BY               |              |   51 |  4598 | 11  (28)| 00:00:01 |
|* 2 |   HASH JOIN                  |              |  279 | 25110 | 10  (20)| 00:00:01 |
|  3 |    TABLE ACCESS FULL         | EMPLOYEE     |   12 |   252 |  3   (0)| 00:00:01 |
|  4 |    MERGE JOIN                |              |  279 | 19251 |  6  (17)| 00:00:01 |
|  5 |     TABLE ACCESS BY INDEX ROWID| PROJECT    |    6 |   180 |  2   (0)| 00:00:01 |

PLAN_TABLE_OUTPUT
---------------------------------------------------------------------------

|  6 |      INDEX FULL SCAN        | PROJECT_PK   |    6 |       |  1   (0)| 00:00:01 |
|* 7 |     SORT JOIN               |              |  279 | 10881 |  4  (25)| 00:00:01 |
|  8 |      TABLE ACCESS FULL      | PROJECT_HOURS|  279 | 10881 |  3   (0)| 00:00:01 |
---------------------------------------------------------------------------

Predicate Information (identified by operation id):

   2 - access("EMPLOYEE"."EMPLOYEE_ID"="PROJECT_HOURS"."EMPLOYEE_ID")
   7 - access("PROJECT"."PROJECT_ID"="PROJECT_HOURS"."PROJECT_ID")
       filter("PROJECT"."PROJECT_ID"="PROJECT_HOURS"."PROJECT_ID")

PLAN_TABLE_OUTPUT
---------------------------------------------------------------------------

Note
-----
  - dynamic sampling used for this statement

26 rows selected.

SQL> |
```

Figure 12-1. Execution plan generated by Example 12-2, as displayed by Example 12-3

This is by far the easiest way to display execution plan details. It would be nice if the TYPICAL display fit within 80 columns, but it doesn't. You may wish to SET LINE-SIZE 132 prior to displaying a plan.

The three arguments to the DBMS_XPLAN.DISPLAY function are:

table_name
> Don't forget to specify your plan table's name as uppercase unless you have a mixed- or lowercase plan table name.

statement_ID
> This is the ID you gave in your EXPLAIN PLAN statement. Use NULL if you did not specify a statement ID.

format
> The format keyword describes how much detail you wish to see. It will ordinarily be one of the following, in increasing order of detail: BASIC, TYPICAL,

ALL. TYPICAL is the default. You may use SERIAL in cases in which you want TYPICAL output but without any information about parallel operations.

Oracle breaks query execution down into a series of nested steps, each of which feeds data to a parent step. The ultimate parent is the query itself, the output of which is returned to the application. You can see this nesting reflected in Figure 12-1.

 When using DBMS_XPLAN to display execution plans, and when leaving statement_id NULL, I haven't had to worry about deleting rows from the plan table prior to re-explaining a plan. See my note at the end of the preceding section.

Using a SELECT statement to display an execution plan

If you're running Oracle9i Database Release 1 or earlier, you'll need to use the traditional way to look at an execution plan, which is to display it using a hierarchical query. Example 12-4 shows a typical query used to display plan output.

Example 12-4. A query to display an execution plan

```
COLUMN id FORMAT 9999
COLUMN parent_id FORMAT 9999 HEADING "PID"
COLUMN "Query Plan" FORMAT A50

UNDEFINE s_statement_id

SELECT id, parent_id,
       LPAD(' ', 2*(level-1)) || operation || ' ' || options
       || ' ' || object_name || ' ' ||
       DECODE(id, 0, 'Cost = ' || position) "Query Plan"
FROM plan_table
START WITH id = 0 AND statement_id = '&&s_statement_id'
CONNECT BY prior id = parent_id AND statement_id = '&&s_statement_id';
```

The result of this query will be a report showing the steps in the execution plan, with each child step indented underneath its parent:

```
SQL> @ex12-3
Enter value for s_statement_id: HOURS_BY_PROJECT
old   6: START WITH id = 0 AND statement_id = '&&s_statement_id'
new   6: START WITH id = 0 AND statement_id = 'HOURS_BY_PROJECT'
old   7: CONNECT BY prior id = parent_id AND statement_id = '&&s_statement_id'
new   7: CONNECT BY prior id = parent_id AND statement_id = 'HOURS_BY_PROJECT'

   ID   PID Query Plan
----- ----- --------------------------------------------------
    0       SELECT STATEMENT    Cost = 11
    1     0   SORT GROUP BY
    2     1     HASH JOIN
    3     2       TABLE ACCESS FULL EMPLOYEE
    4     2       MERGE JOIN
    5     4         TABLE ACCESS BY INDEX ROWID PROJECT
```

```
6    5              INDEX FULL SCAN PROJECT_PK
7    4          SORT JOIN
8    7              TABLE ACCESS FULL PROJECT_HOURS
```

Depending on your needs, you can include additional columns besides those shown here. Table 12-1 describes each of the plan table columns. Be aware that many columns, especially those involving cost, are not filled in by the rule-based optimizer.

 You don't need to write your own plan table script if you don't want to. Oracle distributes two scripts in the *$ORACLE_HOME/rdbms/ admin* directory: *utlxplp.sql* to explain parrallel plans, and *utlxpls.sql* to explain serial plans.

Table 12-1. Plan table columns

Column	Description
STATEMENT_ID	ID you gave the statement when you executed EXPLAIN PLAN.
PLAN_ID	Unique identifier that is automatically generated by the database each time you explain a plan.
TIMESTAMP	Date and time at which you executed the EXPLAIN PLAN statement.
REMARKS	Free-form comments inserted by the database.
OPERATION	Name of an operation to be performed.
OPTIONS	Variations on the OPERATION to be performed.
OBJECT_NODE	Name of a database link used to reference an object, or, for parallel queries, describes the order in which output from parallel operations is consumed.
OBJECT_OWNER	Owner of a table, index, or other object.
OBJECT_NAME	Name of a table, index, or other object on which an OPERATION is to be performed.
OBJECT_ALIAS	Alias associated with a table, view, or index in a SQL statement. This allows you to distinguish between multiple occurrences of the same object in a statement. For example, you can distinguish between multiple occurrences of the same table.
OBJECT_INSTANCE	Ordinal position of an object's name in the original statement.
OBJECT_TYPE	Additional information about an object.
OPTIMIZER	Current optimizer mode.
SEARCH_COLUMNS	Not currently used.
ID	Number assigned to each step in an execution plan.
PARENT_ID	ID of the parent step, which is the step that will consume the output from the current step.
DEPTH	Current depth of an operation in the hierarchical execution plan.

Table 12-1. Plan table columns (continued)

Column	Description
POSITION	Position of one operation with respect to other operations under the same parent. In the ultimate parent operation, the one with ID=0, this column provides the optimizer's estimated cost estimate for the statement as a whole.
COST	Optimizer's cost estimate for an operation.
CARDINALITY	Optimizer's estimate as to the number of rows to be accessed by an operation.
BYTES	Optimizer's estimate as to the number of bytes to be accessed by an operation.

OTHER_TAG	Contents of the OTHER column; will be one of the following values:
	
	SERIAL
	    Serial execution.
	SERIAL_FROM_REMOTE
	    Serial execution at a remote site.
	PARALLEL_FROM_SERIAL
	    Serial execution, but the output will be distributed for parallel execution.
	PARALLEL_TO_SERIAL
	    Parallel execution, but the output will be combined for serial execution.
	PARALLEL_TO_PARALLEL
	    Parallel execution, and the output will be redistributed to a new set of parallel processes.
	PARALLEL_COMBINED_WITH_PARENT
	    Parallel execution, and each parallel process will continue on to the next step in the plan, processing its own output.
	PARALLEL_COMBINED_WITH_CHILD
	    Parallel execution in which the input comes from the same process.

PARTITION_START	First partition in a range of partitions. A numeric value *n* indicates a starting partition identified at compile time. A value of "KEY" indicates that the starting partition will be identified at runtime based on partition key values. The value "ROW REMOVE_LOCATION" indicates that the starting partition will be determined at runtime based on each row to be retrieved. "INVALID" indicates that no range of partitions applies.
PARTITION_STOP	Last partition in a range of partitions. Takes on the forms *n*, "KEY," and "ROW REMOVE_LOCATION," as described for PARTITION_START.
PARTITION_ID	Step in the plan that will compute PARTITION_START and PARTITION_STOP.
OTHER	Other potentially useful information. See OTHER_TAG.

Table 12-1. Plan table columns (continued)

Column	Description

DISTRIBUTION	Method used to distribute rows from producer query servers to consumer query servers; value will be one of the following:
	
	PARTITION (ROWID)
	   Rows are mapped to parallel servers based on table/index partitioning, using ROWID.
	
	PARTITION (KEY)
	   Rows are mapped to parallel servers based on table/index partitioning, using a set of columns.
	
	HASH
	   Rows are mapped to parallel servers using a hash function on a join key.
	
	RANGE
	   Rows are mapped to parallel servers via sort-key ranges.
	
	ROUND-ROBIN
	   Rows are mapped randomly to parallel servers.
	
	BROADCAST
	   All rows in the table are sent to each parallel query server.
	
	QC (ORDER)
	   Rows are sent, in order, to the query coordinator.
	
	QC (RANDOM)
	   Rows are sent randomly to the query coordinator.

CPU_COST	CPU cost estimate that is proportional to the number of machine cycles required for an operation.
IO_COST	I/O cost estimate that is proportional to the number of data blocks read by an operation.
TEMP_SPACE	Estimate, in bytes, of the temporary disk space needed by an operation.
ACCESS_PREDICATES	Predicates used to identify rows required for a step.
FILTER_PREDICATES	Predicates used to filter rows from a step.
PROJECTION	Expressions generated by an operation.
TIME	Elapsed-time estimate for an operation, in seconds.
QBLOCK_NAME	Name of the query block, which you can specify yourself using the QB_NAME hint.

Making sense of the results

The key to interpreting an execution plan is to understand that the display is hierarchical. A step may consist of one or more child steps, and these child steps are shown indented underneath their parent. Executing any given step involves executing all its children, so to understand the plan, you pretty much have to work your way out from the innermost step. For each step in the plan, you'll at least want to look at the operation name, at any options that apply, and at the object of the operation. You may also want to look at the optimizer's cost estimate. All of these are shown in Figure 12-1.

 If you are using the rule-based optimizer, the cost will be null. Oracle will use the rule-based optimizer, even if your database is set to CHOOSE the cost-based optimizer, if you haven't used SQL's ANALYZE TABLE statement to gather statistics for any of the tables involved in the query.

If you're using the cost-based optimizer, it will compute an estimated cost for each operation and for the statement as a whole. In Figure 12-1, the estimate cost for the SELECT STATEMENT operation is 11. This cost means nothing by itself, but the optimizer uses it to compare alternative plans resulting from the query. If you add a hint to the query that changes the cost estimate from 11 to 22, you've probably made your query's performance worse. If you make a change that drives your query's cost from 11 to 5, you've likely made an improvement. Don't fall into the trap, though, of comparing cost estimates from two, unrelated queries.

 For Oracle to compute an accurate cost, you must have up-to-date statistics on the tables involved in the query. Use the ANALYZE TABLE statement to gather these statistics. If your statistics are old, the optimizer may come up with an execution plan that won't be efficient for the data you have now.

Table 12-2 provides a brief description of the various operations, together with their options, that you may see when querying the plan table. For more detailed information about any of these operations, refer to the *Oracle Database Performance Tuning Guide* (Oracle Corporation).

Table 12-2. EXPLAIN PLAN operations

Operation	Description	Option
AND-EQUAL	This step will have two or more child steps, each of which returns a set of ROWIDs. The AND-EQUAL operation selects only those ROWIDs that are returned by all the child operations.	None
BITMAP	Performs an operation involving one or more bitmaps, as described in the accompanying option.	**CONVERSION TO ROWIDS** Converts a bitmap from a bitmap index to a set of ROWIDs that can be used to retrieve the actual data. **CONVERSION FROM ROWIDS** Converts a set of ROWIDs into a bitmapped representation. **CONVERSION COUNT** Counts the number of rows represented by a bitmap. **INDEX SINGLE VALUE** Retrieves the bitmap for a single key value. For example, if the field was a YES/NO field, and your query wanted only rows with a value of "YES," then this operation would be used. **INDEX RANGE SCAN** Similar to BITMAP INDEX SINGLE VALUE, but bitmaps are returned for a range of key values. **INDEX FULL SCAN** The entire bitmap index will be scanned. **MERGE** Merges two or more bitmaps together, and returns one bitmap as a result. This is an OR operation between two bitmaps. The resulting bitmap will select all rows from the first bitmap plus all rows from the second bitmap. **MINUS** Opposite of a MERGE, and may have two or three child operations that return bitmaps. The bitmap returned by the first child operation is used as a starting point. All rows represented by the second bitmap are subtracted from the first. If the column is nullable, then all rows with null values are also subtracted. **OR** Takes two bitmaps as input, ORs them together, and returns one bitmap as a result. The returned bitmap will select all rows from the first plus all rows from the second. **AND** Takes two bitmaps as input, ANDs them together, and returns one bitmap as a result. The returned bitmap will select all rows represented in *both* of the input bitmaps. **KEY ITERATION** Takes each row and finds that row's corresponding bitmap in a bitmap index.

Table 12-2. EXPLAIN PLAN operations (continued)

Operation	Description	Option
CONNECT BY	Rows are being retrieved hierarchically because the query was written with a CONNECT BY clause.	None
CONCATENATION	Multiple sets of rows are combined into one set, essentially a UNION ALL.	None
COUNT	Counts the number of rows that have been selected from a table.	STOPKEY The number of rows to be counted is limited by the use of ROWNUM in the query's WHERE clause.
DOMAIN INDEX	Retrieves ROWIDs from a domain index.	None
FILTER	Takes a set of rows as input, and eliminates some of them based on a condition from the query's WHERE clause.	None
FIRST ROW	Retrieves only the first row of a query's result set.	None
FOR UPDATE	Locks rows that are retrieved. This would be the result of specifying FOR UPDATE in the original query.	None
HASH JOIN	Joins two tables using a hash join method.	ANTI Performs a hash anti-join (e.g., NOT EXISTS). SEMI Performs a hash semi-join (e.g., EXISTS). RIGHT ANTI Performs a hash right outer anti-join. RIGHT SEMI Performs a hash right outer semi-join. OUTER Performs a hash left outer join. RIGHT OUTER Performs a hash right outer join.

Table 12-2. EXPLAIN PLAN operations (continued)

Operation	Description	Option
INDEX	Performs one of the index-related operations described in the Option column.	**UNIQUE SCAN** The lookup of a unique value from an index. You will see this only when the index is unique; for example, an index used to enforce a primary key or a unique key. **RANGE SCAN** An index is being scanned for rows that fall into a range of values. The index is scanned in ascending order. **RANGE SCAN DESCENDING** Same as RANGE SCAN, but the index is scanned in descending order. **FULL SCAN** Scans all ROWIDs in an index, in ascending order. **FULL SCAN DESCENDING** Scans all ROWIDs in an index, in descending order. **SKIP SCAN** Retrieves ROWIDs from an index without using the leading column. Processing skips from one leading column to the next. **FAST FULL SCAN** Scans all ROWIDs in an index in whatever order they can be most efficiently read from the disk. No attempt is made to read in ascending or descending order.
INLIST ITERATOR	One or more operations are to be performed once for each value in an IN predicate.	None
INTERSECTION	Two rowsets are taken as input, and only rows that appear in both sets are returned.	None
MERGE JOIN	Joins two rowsets based on some common value. Both rowsets will first have been sorted by this value. This is an inner join.	**OUTER** Similar to a MERGE JOIN, but an outer join is performed. **ANTI** Indicates that an anti-join is being performed. **SEMI** Indicates that a semi-join is being performed. **CARTESIAN** Indicates that the merge-join technique is being used to generate a Cartesian product.
MINUS	This is the result of the MINUS operator. Two rowsets are taken as inputs. The resulting rowset contains all rows from the first input that do not appear in the second input.	None

Table 12-2. EXPLAIN PLAN operations (continued)

Operation	Description	Option
NESTED LOOPS	This operation will have two children, each returning a rowset. For every row returned by the first child, the second child operation will be executed.	OUTER Represents a nested loop used to perform an outer join.

PARTITION	Executes an operation for one or more partitions. The PARTITION_START and PARTITION_STOP columns show the range of partitions over which the operation is performed.	SINGLE
		  The operation will be performed on a single partition.
		ITERATOR
		  The operation will be performed on several partitions.
		ALL
		  The operation will be performed on all partitions.
		INLIST
		  The operation will be performed on the partitions, and is being driven by an IN predicate.
		INVALID
		  Indicates no partitions are to be operated upon.

PROJECTION	Takes multiple queries as input and returns a single set of records. This is used with INTERSECTION, MINUS, and UNION operations.	None
PX ITERATOR	Is a parallel query operation involving the division of work among multiple, query slave processes that run in parallel.	BLOCK, CHUNK An object is divided into chunks that are then distributed to query slaves.
PX COORDINATOR	Represents a query coordinator, which controls all operations below it in the execution plan.	None
PX PARTITION	Same as the PARTITION operation, but the work is spread over multiple, parallel processes.	None
PX RECEIVE	Represents the receiving of data as it is being repartitioned among parallel processes.	None
PX SEND	Represents the transmission of data as it is being repartitioned among parallel processes.	None
REMOTE	Indicates that a rowset is being returned from a remote database.	None
SEQUENCE	An Oracle sequence is being accessed.	None

Table 12-2. EXPLAIN PLAN operations (continued)

Operation	Description	Option
SORT	Sorts the result set or an intermediate result set. The sort may be either parallel or full. The purpose of the sort is described by the option that is given.	**AGGREGATE** Applies a group function, such as COUNT, to a rowset, and returns only one row as the result. **UNIQUE** Sorts a rowset and eliminates duplicates. **GROUP BY** Sorts a rowset into groups. This is the result of a GROUP BY clause. **JOIN** Sorts a rowset in preparation for a join. See MERGE JOIN. **ORDER BY** Sorts a rowset in accordance with the ORDER BY clause specified in the query.
TABLE ACCESS	Data is read from a table, using the method indicated by the option that is always given for this operation.	**FULL** Oracle will read all rows in the specified table. **CLUSTER** Oracle will read all rows in a table that match a specified index cluster key. **HASH** Oracle will read all rows in a table that match a specified hash cluster key. **BY ROWID** Oracle will retrieve a row from a table based on its ROWID. **BY ROWID RANGE** Rows will be retrieved corresponding to a range of ROWIDs. **SAMPLE BY ROWID RANGE** A sample of rows will be retrieved from a ROWID range. **BY USER ROWID** Rows are retrieved using ROWIDs supplied by the user (i.e., by the SQL statement). **BY INDEX ROWID** Rows are retrieved using ROWIDs returned by index searches. **BY GLOBAL INDEX ROWID** Rows are returned from a partitioned table using ROWIDs from global indexes. **BY LOCAL INDEX ROWID** Rows are returned from a partitioned table using ROWIDs from a combination of global and local indexes or from only local indexes.

Table 12-2. EXPLAIN PLAN operations (continued)

Operation	Description	Option
UNION	Takes two rowsets, eliminates duplicates, and returns the result as one set.	None
VIEW	Executes the query behind a view and returns the resulting rowset.	Nonestatements

Using AUTOTRACE

Oracle SQL*Plus provides an AUTOTRACE setting that automatically displays the execution plan for any query you execute. You can turn AUTOTRACE off and on with the SET command. There is one big catch: the query must be executed before you can see the results. The problem with this is that if you are contemplating a query against a large table, it might take all day for a poorly tuned query to execute. In that case, you might want to see the execution plan before you run the query and not afterward. You also may not want this behavior if you are writing a DELETE or an UPDATE statement because you would need to delete or update some data to see the execution plan.

> Before you can use AUTOTRACE to display execution plans, you must have created a plan table. AUTOTRACE uses this table, and expects the name to be plan_table, which is the default name if you use the *utlxplan.sql* script to create it.

Granting Access to the Performance Views

AUTOTRACE does more than display the execution plan for a query. It displays statistics that show you how much disk I/O and network traffic occurred during a query's execution. Other information, such as the number of sorts performed on the data, is shown as well. With older releases of SQL*Plus, to see the statistical data AUTOTRACE returns, you must have SELECT access to certain of Oracle's *dynamic performance views*. Dynamic performance views, whose names usually begin with V$ or V_$, are pseudoviews maintained by Oracle that contain real-time performance information.

Older releases of Oracle provided a script for DBAs to run, to simplify the process of granting the needed access to users of AUTOTRACE. The script name is *plustrce.sql*, and, in Oracle Database 10g, the script may be found in the *$ORACLE_HOME/ sqlplus/admin* directory. The script must be executed while logged in as user SYS, and it creates a role named PLUSTRACE that has the needed privileges to use AUTOTRACE from SQL*Plus. Usually, only DBAs can log in as SYS. Here's how to run the script:

```
SQL> connect sys/secret as sysdba
Connected.
```

```
SQL>
SQL> @$ORACLE_HOME/sqlplus/admin/plustrce
SQL>
SQL> drop role plustrace;
drop role plustrace
        *
ERROR at line 1:
ORA-01919: role 'PLUSTRACE' does not exist


SQL> create role plustrace;

Role created.

SQL>
SQL> grant select on v_$sesstat to plustrace;

Grant succeeded.

SQL> grant select on v_$statname to plustrace;

Grant succeeded.

SQL> grant select on v_$mystat to plustrace;

Grant succeeded.

SQL> grant plustrace to dba with admin option;

Grant succeeded.
```

Once the script has been run, the PLUSTRACE role will exist. PLUSTRACE should be granted to any user who needs to use AUTOTRACE:

```
SQL> GRANT plustrace TO gennick;

Grant succeeded.
```

The user gennick will now be able to execute the SET AUTOTRACE ON command from SQL*Plus.

Executing a Query with AUTOTRACE On

You can use several options with SET AUTOTRACE. By default, when you turn AUTOTRACE on, SQL*Plus shows the execution plan and some execution statistics for any query you execute. If you wish, you can limit AUTOTRACE to showing only the execution plan or the execution statistics.

If you don't have the PLUSTRACE role, or don't otherwise have access to the required dynamic performance tables, you can issue the command SET AUTOTRACE ON EXPLAIN, discussed later in this section. This command limits the display to the execution plan and doesn't require access to the performance tables.

You have the option of suppressing the output from the query you are executing. This is helpful if the query returns a large amount of data because you aren't forced to watch all the results scroll by before the execution plan is displayed. You'll see how to do this later in this section.

Showing statistics and the plan

To enable AUTOTRACE and set it to show the execution plan and the execution statistics, execute the following command from SQL*Plus:

```
SET AUTOTRACE ON
```

Now execute any query, as shown in Example 12-5. You will see the query results, followed by the execution plan and the execution statistics.

Example 12-5. Using AUTOTRACE to show an execution plan

```
SET AUTOTRACE ON

SELECT employee_name, SUM(hours_logged)
FROM employee, project_hours
WHERE employee.employee_id = project_hours.employee_id
GROUP BY employee_name;
```

EMPLOYEE_NAME	SUM(HOURS_LOGGED)
Igor Sikorsky	48
Ivan Mazepa	68
Lesia Ukrainka	144
Marusia Bohuslavka	68
Marusia Churai	144
Mykhailo Hrushevsky	57
Mykhailo Verbytsky	96
Mykola Leontovych	81
Pavlo Chubynsky	129
Pavlo Virsky	48
Roxolana Lisovsky	68
Taras Shevchenko	144

```
12 rows selected.


Execution Plan
-----------------------------------------------------------
   0      SELECT STATEMENT Optimizer=ALL_ROWS (Cost=7 Card=12 Bytes=288)
```

Example 12-5. Using AUTOTRACE to show an execution plan (continued)

```
   1    0    SORT (GROUP BY) (Cost=7 Card=12 Bytes=288)
   2    1      MERGE JOIN (Cost=6 Card=279 Bytes=6696)
   3    2        TABLE ACCESS (BY INDEX ROWID) OF 'EMPLOYEE' (TABLE) (C
          ost=2 Card=12 Bytes=228)

   4    3          INDEX (FULL SCAN) OF 'EMPLOYEE_PK' (INDEX (UNIQUE))
          (Cost=1 Card=12)

   5    2        SORT (JOIN) (Cost=4 Card=279 Bytes=1395)
   6    5          TABLE ACCESS (FULL) OF 'PROJECT_HOURS' (TABLE) (Cost
          =3 Card=279 Bytes=1395)


Statistics
----------------------------------------------------------
          0  recursive calls
          0  db block gets
          9  consistent gets
          0  physical reads
          0  redo size
        780  bytes sent via SQL*Net to client
        511  bytes received via SQL*Net from client
          2  SQL*Net roundtrips to/from client
          2  sorts (memory)
          0  sorts (disk)
         12  rows processed
```

The execution plan displayed by AUTOTRACE is formatted a bit differently from previous plans shown in this chapter. The two leading numeric columns are the id (of the step) and the parent_id (ID of the parent step) columns.

One key statistic to look at is the number of logical reads, as indicated by "consistent gets," particularly in relation to the number of rows processed. The fewer logical reads per row processed, the better.

When looking at statistics via AUTOTRACE, run any given query at least twice. Statistics from the first run will reflect the overhead of initially parsing the statement. Unless you intend to parse the statement each time you execute it (which is bad), you should pay attention to the statistics from the second run.

Showing only the plan

SQL*Plus allows you to turn AUTOTRACE on with an option to show only the execution plan. This is handy if you do not happen to have the needed privileges to access the execution statistics. Issue the following command from SQL*Plus:

```
SET AUTOTRACE ON EXPLAIN
```

Now, when you issue an SQL statement, only the execution plan is displayed, not the statistics, as Example 12-6 demonstrates.

Example 12-6. AUTOTRACE without the statistics

SET AUTOTRACE ON EXPLAIN

```
SELECT employee_name, SUM(hours_logged)
FROM employee, project_hours
WHERE employee.employee_id = project_hours.employee_id
GROUP BY employee_name;
```

EMPLOYEE_NAME	SUM(HOURS_LOGGED)
Igor Sikorsky	48
Ivan Mazepa	68
Lesia Ukrainka	144
Marusia Bohuslavka	68
Marusia Churai	144
Mykhailo Hrushevsky	57
Mykhailo Verbytsky	96
Mykola Leontovych	81
Pavlo Chubynsky	129
Pavlo Virsky	48
Roxolana Lisovsky	68
Taras Shevchenko	144

12 rows selected.


```
Execution Plan
----------------------------------------------------------
   0      SELECT STATEMENT Optimizer=ALL_ROWS (Cost=7 Card=12 Bytes=564)

   1    0   SORT (GROUP BY) (Cost=7 Card=12 Bytes=564)
   2    1     MERGE JOIN (Cost=6 Card=279 Bytes=13113)
   3    2       TABLE ACCESS (BY INDEX ROWID) OF 'EMPLOYEE' (TABLE) (C
          ost=2 Card=12 Bytes=252)

   4    3         INDEX (FULL SCAN) OF 'EMPLOYEE_PK' (INDEX (UNIQUE))
          (Cost=1 Card=12)

   5    2       SORT (JOIN) (Cost=4 Card=279 Bytes=7254)
   6    5         TABLE ACCESS (FULL) OF 'PROJECT_HOURS' (TABLE) (Cost
          =3 Card=279 Bytes=7254)
```

Suppressing the query output

With AUTOTRACE, you have the option of suppressing the output from any queries you run. This saves you from having to wait for the results to scroll by before you see the execution plan and statistics. To turn AUTOTRACE on and suppress any query output, issue the following command:

```
SET AUTOTRACE TRACEONLY
```

The EXPLAIN option remains valid, so if you want to see only the execution plan, issue the command like this:

```
SET AUTOTRACE TRACEONLY EXPLAIN
```

Execute a query and you will see only the execution plan, not the data, as in Example 12-7.

Example 12-7. AUTOTRACE without the output

```
SET AUTOTRACE TRACEONLY EXPLAIN

SELECT employee_name, SUM(hours_logged)
FROM employee, project_hours
WHERE employee.employee_id = project_hours.employee_id
GROUP BY employee_name;

Execution Plan
----------------------------------------------------------
   0      SELECT STATEMENT Optimizer=ALL_ROWS (Cost=7 Card=12 Bytes=564)

   1    0   SORT (GROUP BY) (Cost=7 Card=12 Bytes=564)
   2    1     MERGE JOIN (Cost=6 Card=279 Bytes=13113)
   3    2       TABLE ACCESS (BY INDEX ROWID) OF 'EMPLOYEE' (TABLE) (C
          ost=2 Card=12 Bytes=252)

   4    3         INDEX (FULL SCAN) OF 'EMPLOYEE_PK' (INDEX (UNIQUE))
          (Cost=1 Card=12)

   5    2       SORT (JOIN) (Cost=4 Card=279 Bytes=7254)
   6    5         TABLE ACCESS (FULL) OF 'PROJECT_HOURS' (TABLE) (Cost
          =3 Card=279 Bytes=7254)
```

When the TRACEONLY option is used, SELECT statements are not executed. However, INSERT, UPDATE, DELETE, and MERGE statements are executed.

 If you enable AUTOTRACE's STATISTICS option, then any statement will be executed because it's only by executing statements that the required statistics can be gathered.

Turning AUTOTRACE off

When you are done using AUTOTRACE, you can turn it off with the following command:

```
SET AUTOTRACE OFF
```

Improving on EXPLAIN PLAN Results

If you don't like the results you get from EXPLAIN PLAN, you can change how Oracle executes your query. Generally speaking, these things fall into the following three categories:

- Restating the query
- Creating or modifying indexes
- Using hints

First, however, you have to be sure the default execution path is a bad one. This isn't as easy as you may think.

Knowing Good Results from Bad

Knowing a good execution plan from a bad one requires some degree of experience and judgment. It helps to understand your data. In many cases, it may not be enough to look at the plan. You may have to do some benchmarking as well.

Consider the issue of doing a full table scan, reading all the rows in the table, to find rows for a query. On the surface, reading the entire table to find the desired rows seems like an inefficient approach. Many people avoid it, thinking that an indexed retrieval is better. But this isn't necessarily the case. If you have a reasonably large table and are searching for one or two rows, then a full table scan is an inefficient approach. However, if you are retrieving or summarizing a large percentage of the rows in the table, then a full table scan will likely outperform an indexed retrieval. The problem is that somewhere between these two extremes lies a large gray area. That's where you have to do some benchmarking and use some judgment based on your expectations of what the query will be asked to do when it is in production.

Here are some questions to ask yourself as you look at an execution plan:

- Is a table scan being used to retrieve only a small percentage of rows from a large table? If so, you may want to create an index.

- Is an index scan being used when you are retrieving, or summarizing, a large percentage of a table's rows? If so, you may be better off forcing a full table scan.

- Is Oracle using the most selective index? An index on a YES/NO field would typically be much less selective than an index on last name, for example.

- Is Oracle joining the largest table last, and the most selective table first? It's generally better to eliminate as many rows as possible prior to any joins.

Determining an execution plan to use for a statement that isn't performing well is perhaps the most crucial step in any tuning exercise. The only author I've ever seen address this problem by providing any kind of repeatable and deterministic methodology is Dan Tow in his book *SQL Tuning* (O'Reilly). If you are tuning SQL statements and require a reliable method for determining the optimal execution plan for a statement, I recommend that you read Dan's book.

Creating Indexes

Creating indexes is an easy way to affect a query. If, for example, you have a large employee table (much larger than the one used in this book), keyed on employee_id, and your query is searching for employees by name, then Oracle will do a full table scan for each name lookup. The response time will be poor, and your users will be unhappy. Creating an index on the employee_name column would improve your results a great deal.

Don't overlook the possibility of creating a multicolumn index even if you don't use all the index columns in your query's WHERE clause. Suppose that you frequently execute the following query, which searches for an employee by name and displays that employee's current billing rate:

```
SELECT employee_name, employee_billing_rate
FROM employee
WHERE employee_name = :emp_name;
```

If you index the employee table by name, Oracle will look up the name in the index, get the ROWID, read the correct employee row, and return the billing rate. However, it takes an extra read to fetch the employee record. You can eliminate that extra read by creating an index such as this one:

```
CREATE INDEX employee_by_name ON employee
  (employee_name, employee_billing_rate);
```

Because the index contains the employee_billing_rate column, Oracle doesn't need to read the actual employee record to retrieve it. Oracle recognizes that all the columns needed to satisfy the query are in the index, and it will take advantage of that fact.

Rewriting the Query

Sometimes you can restate a query, get the results that you want, and have it run much more efficiently. Example 12-8 shows a query listing all employees who have ever charged time to project 1001. To generate that listing, the query joins employee and project_hours.

Example 12-8. The join approach to listing employees who have charged time to a project

```
SET AUTOTRACE ON

SELECT DISTINCT employee.employee_id, employee.employee_name
FROM employee, project_hours
WHERE employee.employee_id = project_hours.employee_id
AND project_hours.project_id = 1001;
```

Example 12-8. The join approach to listing employees who have charged time to a project (continued)

```
EMPLOYEE_ID EMPLOYEE_NAME
----------- ----------------------------------------
        101 Marusia Churai
        102 Mykhailo Hrushevsky
        104 Pavlo Virsky
        105 Mykola Leontovych
        107 Lesia Ukrainka
        108 Pavlo Chubynsky
        110 Ivan Mazepa
        111 Taras Shevchenko
        112 Igor Sikorsky
        113 Mykhailo Verbytsky
        114 Marusia Bohuslavka
        116 Roxolana Lisovsky

12 rows selected.


Execution Plan
-----------------------------------------------------------
   0      SELECT STATEMENT Optimizer=ALL_ROWS (Cost=5 Card=93 Bytes=23
          25)

   1    0   SORT (UNIQUE) (Cost=5 Card=93 Bytes=2325)
   2    1     MERGE JOIN (Cost=4 Card=93 Bytes=2325)
   3    2       TABLE ACCESS (BY INDEX ROWID) OF 'EMPLOYEE' (TABLE) (C
          ost=2 Card=12 Bytes=228)

   4    3         INDEX (FULL SCAN) OF 'EMPLOYEE_PK' (INDEX (UNIQUE))
          (Cost=1 Card=12)

   5    2       SORT (JOIN) (Cost=2 Card=93 Bytes=558)
   6    5         INDEX (RANGE SCAN) OF 'PROJECT_HOURS_PK' (INDEX (UNI
          QUE)) (Cost=1 Card=93 Bytes=558)

Statistics
-----------------------------------------------------------
          0  recursive calls
          0  db block gets
          3  consistent gets
          0  physical reads
          0  redo size
        782  bytes sent via SQL*Net to client
        511  bytes received via SQL*Net from client
          2  SQL*Net roundtrips to/from client
          2  sorts (memory)
          0  sorts (disk)
         12  rows processed
```

The query in Example 12-8 can be restated using an EXISTS predicate instead of joining the employee and project_hours tables together. Example 12-9 shows that version.

Example 12-9. The EXISTS approach to listing employees who have charged time to projects 1001 or 1002

```
SET AUTOTRACE ON

SELECT employee_id, employee_name
FROM employee
WHERE EXISTS (SELECT *
             FROM project_hours
             WHERE project_hours.project_id = 1001
               AND project_hours.employee_id = employee.employee_id);
```

```
EMPLOYEE_ID EMPLOYEE_NAME
----------- ----------------------------------------
        101 Marusia Churai
        102 Mykhailo Hrushevsky
        104 Pavlo Virsky
        105 Mykola Leontovych
        107 Lesia Ukrainka
        108 Pavlo Chubynsky
        110 Ivan Mazepa
        111 Taras Shevchenko
        112 Igor Sikorsky
        113 Mykhailo Verbytsky
        114 Marusia Bohuslavka
        116 Roxolana Lisovsky

12 rows selected.


Execution Plan
----------------------------------------------------------
   0      SELECT STATEMENT Optimizer=ALL_ROWS (Cost=4 Card=12 Bytes=30
          0)

   1    0   MERGE JOIN (SEMI) (Cost=4 Card=12 Bytes=300)
   2    1     TABLE ACCESS (BY INDEX ROWID) OF 'EMPLOYEE' (TABLE) (Cos
          t=2 Card=12 Bytes=228)

   3    2       INDEX (FULL SCAN) OF 'EMPLOYEE_PK' (INDEX (UNIQUE)) (C
          ost=1 Card=12)

   4    1     SORT (UNIQUE) (Cost=2 Card=93 Bytes=558)
   5    4       INDEX (RANGE SCAN) OF 'PROJECT_HOURS_PK' (INDEX (UNIQU
          E)) (Cost=1 Card=93 Bytes=558)

Statistics
----------------------------------------------------------
          0  recursive calls
```

Example 12-9. The EXISTS approach to listing employees who have charged time to projects 1001 or 1002 (continued)

```
    0  db block gets
    5  consistent gets
    0  physical reads
    0  redo size
  782  bytes sent via SQL*Net to client
  511  bytes received via SQL*Net from client
    2  SQL*Net roundtrips to/from client
    1  sorts (memory)
    0  sorts (disk)
   12  rows processed
```

The performance results from Examples 12-8 and 12-9 are a bit inconclusive. When you compare estimated costs, you'll see a cost of 5 for Example 12-8 and a cost of 4 for Example 12-9. Look further at the execution plans, and you'll see that Example 12-9 avoids the sort triggered in Example 12-8 by the use of DISTINCT. Interestingly, the number of logical reads (consistent gets) is lower in the plan with the higher estimated cost, potentially leaving you in a quandary as to which choice to make here. My own feeling is to go with Example 12-9, which avoids the sort because the number of rows to be sorted will only grow as the project_hours table grows.

> The cost of the sort in Example 12-9 doesn't come through in the AUTOTRACE statistics. One approach to getting a better handle on such costs is to generate the kind of SQL trace data that Cary Millsap and Jeff Holt talk about in their book, *Optimizing Oracle Performance* (O'Reilly).

Using Hints

Rather than allowing Oracle to have total control over how a query is executed, you can provide specific directions to the optimizer through the use of hints. A *hint*, in Oracle, is an optimizer directive embedded in a SQL statement in the form of a comment. Here is a query with an optimizer hint telling Oracle to do a full table scan:

```
SELECT /*+ FULL(employee) */
employee_id, employee_name, employee_billing_rate
FROM employee
WHERE employee_name = 'Igor Sikorsky';
```

The hint in this case is FULL(employee), which tells Oracle to do a full table scan of the employee table. Oracle will honor this hint and perform a full table scan even if there happens to be an index on the employee_name field.

Syntax for a hint

A hint applies to a single SQL statement, and hints may be specified only for SELECT, INSERT, UPDATE, DELETE, and MERGE statements. A hint takes the form of a specially formatted comment and must appear immediately following the keyword that begins the statement:

```
keyword /*+ [hint [hint...]] */
```

in which:

keyword

> Is the keyword that begins the statement. This will be one of the keywords SELECT, INSERT, UPDATE, DELETE, or MERGE.

hint

> Is the hint, sometimes with one or more arguments enclosed in parentheses. Tables 12-3 through 12-10 provide a list of the hints available in Oracle Database 10*g*, Release 1. Hints aren't case-sensitive. A single comment may contain more than one hint, as long as the hints are separated by at least one space.

 Oracle allows you to intersperse comments with your hints.

Here are some examples of how hints may be specified:

```
SELECT /*+ FULL(employee) */ employee_id, employee_name
FROM employee
WHERE employee_billing_rate > 100;

SELECT /*+ FULL(e) do a full table scan on the employee table, because
               most employees do have billing rates > 100. */
      employee_id, employee_name
FROM employee e
WHERE employee_billing_rate > 100;
```

In the second example, the table name is employee, but an alias of e has been given. The hint for the table uses the same alias and is specified as FULL(e). Whenever an alias is used, you must use the alias name in any hints for the table. Be careful about this because hints are specially formatted comments, and you won't get any error messages as the result of a malformed hint.

If you want to supply multiple hints for a statement, they must all appear in the same comment:

```
SELECT /*+ FULL(employee) first_rows */
      employee_id, employee_name
FROM employee
WHERE employee_billing_rate > 100;
```

When subqueries are used, they are allowed to have their own hints. The hint for a subquery follows immediately after the keyword that starts the subquery:

```
SELECT /*+ FIRST_ROWS */ employee_id, employee_name
FROM employee
WHERE exists (SELECT /*+ FULL(project_hours) */*
                FROM project_hours
                WHERE project_hours.project_id = 1001
                  AND project_hours.employee_id = employee.employee_id);
```

When using hints, be very careful to get the syntax right. Because hints are embedded in statements as comments, Oracle can't do any syntax checking. Oracle treats any incorrectly specified hint as a comment. In addition, you should do an EXPLAIN PLAN after you code your hints to be sure that the optimizer is really doing what you think you told it to do.

Specifying table and index names

Many hints take one or more table names as arguments. The FULL hint, for example, takes one table name as an argument.

```
/*+ FULL(employee) */
```

Some access method hints are index-related and allow you to specify one or more indexes to be used. In many cases, as with the INDEX hint, you have the choice of specifying an index name or not. The following hint, for example, tells Oracle that you want to do an index scan on the employee table, but it's up to Oracle to pick the index:

```
/*+ INDEX(employee) */
```

This is useful if you think Oracle will make the correct choice, or if you don't want to hardcode an index name into the hint. You have the option, however, of specifying the exact index to use. Here's an example:

```
/*+ INDEX(employee employee_by_name) */
```

You may specify a list of indexes, and Oracle will choose from the indexes in that list. If, for example, you had seven indexes on the employee table but you believed that only two would be useful for the query in question, you could specify a hint like this:

```
/*+ INDEX(employee employee_by_name, employee_by_billing_rate) */
```

This tells Oracle that you want to use an index scan to access the employee table, and that you want to use either the name index or the billing rate index.

Hint conflicts and applicability

Whenever two hints are in conflict, Oracle will ignore at least one of them. Oracle ignores hints that can't be followed. For example, take a look at the following query:

```
SELECT /*+ USE_CONCAT */
       employee_id, employee_name
```

```
FROM employee
WHERE employee_name = 'Jeff Gennick';
```

The USE_CONCAT hint makes no sense here because the query doesn't contain an OR condition. You can't break this into two queries and then UNION the results together, so Oracle will ignore the hint.

A bad hint will be honored, however, whenever it is implementable. The following query contains a hint to do an index scan on the primary key index for the employee table:

```
SELECT /*+ INDEX(employee employee_pk) */
       employee_name
FROM employee
WHERE employee_name = 'Jeff Gennick';
```

The primary key for employee is the employee_id field. An index on employee_name does exist. The query seeks one record based on the employee name. Even though it makes perfect sense to look up the name in the name index, Oracle will honor the request to use the primary key index. Here is the execution plan for this statement:

```
0 SELECT STATEMENT   Cost = 2
1    TABLE ACCESS BY INDEX ROWID EMPLOYEE
2       INDEX FULL SCAN EMPLOYEE_PK
```

Oracle is going to read every entry in the primary key index, retrieve the associated row from the employee table, and check the name to see if it has a match. This is worse than a full table scan. Oracle does this because the hint requested it and because it physically can be done; so be careful what you ask for, and check the results.

Hint query blocks

Oracle Database 10g introduces a new, *query block* syntax to hints. When you have a statement, such as a SELECT, that consists of a main statement and one or more subqueries, each statement and subquery is a query block. The new query block syntax lets you refer to those query blocks by name from a hint.

You can name the query blocks in a statement using the QB_NAME hint. The statement in Example 12-10 contains two query blocks that are given the names main and sub respectively. The two FULL hints use query block names to fully qualify their respective table references, with the end result that both instances of employee are accessed via a full table scan.

Example 12-10. A statement with named query blocks

```
SELECT /*+ QB_NAME(main) FULL(@main e1) FULL(@sub e2) */
       e1.employee_name, employee_hire_Date
FROM employee e1
WHERE EXISTS (SELECT /*+ QB_NAME(sub) */ e2.employee_id
               FROM employee e2
```

Example 12-10. A statement with named query blocks (continued)

```
        WHERE employee_hire_date >=
              TO_DATE('1-Jan-2000','dd-mon-yyyy')
          AND e1.employee_id = e2.employee_id);
```

If you don't name the query blocks in a statement, Oracle will generate query block names for you. To see those names automatically, run an EXPLAIN PLAN on your statement followed by a query using the ALL option of DBMS_XPLAN.DISPLAY:

```
SELECT PLAN_TABLE_OUTPUT
FROM TABLE(DBMS_XPLAN.DISPLAY(NULL, NULL, 'ALL'));
```

Oracle's Hint Syntax

The following subsections categorize the various hints available in Oracle Database 10*g* and provide a quick summary of the hints.

> The hints in Tables 12-3 through 12-10 are valid for Oracle Database 10*g*. Many, but not all of those hints work in previous releases. Hints from previous releases that are deprecated in Oracle Database 10*g* aren't listed here.

Optimizer goal hints

Optimization goal hints allow you to influence the optimizer's overall goal when formulating an execution plan. You may, for example, specify that you want the plan optimized to return the first record as quickly as possible. Table 12-3 gives a list of these hints.

Table 12-3. Optimizer goal hints

Hint	Description
ALL_ROWS	Tells the optimizer to produce an execution plan that minimizes resource consumption
FIRST_ROWS(*n*)	Tells the optimizer to generate a plan that gets to the first *n* rows as soon as possible

You should avoid the now obsolete RULE hint if at all possible. That hint causes the rule-based optimizer to be used. The rule-based optimizer uses a fixed set of rules when determining the execution plan for a statement and doesn't attempt to factor in the ultimate cost of executing that plan. The cost-based optimizer, on the other hand, bases its decision on the estimated I/O and CPU overhead required by various alternative plans. Although Oracle still supports the rule-based optimizer, it hasn't been enhanced in years, won't be enhanced in the future, and will be de-supported at some point. Oracle is putting its development effort into the cost-based optimizer.

Access method hints

Access method hints allow you to control the way data are accessed. For example, you can tell Oracle to do a full table scan or to use an index when accessing a table. You can name the specific index to be used. Table 12-4 provides a list of these hints.

Table 12-4. Access method hints

Hint	Description
FULL(*table*) FULL(*@block table*)	Requests a full table scan of the specified table, regardless of any indexes that may exist.
CLUSTER(*table*) CLUSTER(*@block table*)	Tells Oracle to do a cluster scan of the specified table. This hint is ignored if the table is not clustered.
HASH(*table*) HASH(*@block table*)	Tells Oracle to do a hash scan of the specified table. This hint is ignored if the table is not clustered.
INDEX(*table* [*index*...]) INDEX(*@block table* [*index*...])	Tells Oracle to access the specified table via an index scan. Optionally, you may specify the index to use; otherwise, Oracle chooses the index. You may also specify a list of indexes to choose from, and Oracle will choose from that list.
NO_INDEX(*table*[*index*...]) NO_INDEX(*@block table*[*index*...])	Prevents Oracle from using indexes on a table. Optionally, you may specify a list of indexes to avoid, thus allowing all others.
INDEX_ASC(*table* [*index*...]) INDEX_ASC(*@block table* [*index*...])	Similar to the INDEX hint but tells Oracle to scan the index in ascending order.
INDEX_COMBINE(*table* [*index*...]) INDEX_COMBINE(*@block table* [*index*...])	Tells Oracle to use some combination of two indexes. You may specify the indexes to choose from, or let Oracle make the choice.
INDEX_JOIN(*table* [*index*...]) INDEX_JOIN(*@block table* [*index*...])	Instructs the optimizer to resolve conditions on two or more columns by joining indexes containing those columns.
INDEX_DESC(*table* [*index*...]) INDEX_DESC(*@block table* [*index*...])	Similar to INDEX_ASC, but forces Oracle to scan the index in descending order.
INDEX_FFS(*table* [*index*...]) INDEX_FFS(*@block table* [*index*...])	Tells Oracle to do a fast full index scan.
NO_INDEX_FFS(*table* [*index*...]) NO_INDEX_FFS(*@block table* [*index*...])	Inhibits the use of a fast full index scan. New in Oracle Database 10*g*.
INDEX_SS(*table* [*index*...]) INDEX_SS(*@block table* [*index*...])	Chooses an index skip scan. New in Oracle Database 10*g*.
INDEX_SS_ASC(*table* [*index*...]) INDEX_SS_ASC(*@block table* [*index*...])	Chooses an index skip scan in ascending order. New in Oracle Database 10*g*.
INDEX_SS_DESC(*table* [*index*...]) INDEX_SS_DESC(*@block table* [*index*...])	Chooses an index skip scan in descending order. New in Oracle Database 10*g*.
NO_INDEX_SS(*table* [*index*...]) NO_INDEX_SS(*@block table* [*index*...])	Inhibits the use of an index skip scan. New in Oracle Database 10*g*.

Query transformation hints

Sometimes Oracle's query optimizer will rewrite a query in a different form, from which it is possible to generate a more efficient (you hope) execution plan. The query transformation hints in Table 12-5 provide some control over whether and how your queries get rewritten.

Table 12-5. Query transformation hints

Hint	Description
NO_QUERY_TRANSFORMATION	Prevents any transformation at all. New in Oracle Database 10*g*.
NO_EXPAND NO_EXPAND(*@block*)	Prevents the optimizer from expanding IN predicates into a series of OR predicates.
REWRITE REWRITE(*view* [*view...*]) REWRITE(*@block view* [*view...*]])	Specifies that a query be rewritten in terms of materialized views whenever possible, without regard to the cost.
NO_REWRITE(*@block*)	Disallows materialized view rewrites. New in Oracle Database 10*g* (renamed from Oracle9*i* Database NOREWRITE).
MERGE MERGE(*view*) MERGE(*@block*) MERGE(*@block view*)	Merges a view into a query.
NO_MERGE NO_MERGE(*view*) NO_MERGE(*@block*) NO_MERGE(*@block view*)	Prevents views from being merged into a query.
STAR_TRANSFORMATION STAR_TRANSFORMATION(*@block*)	Tells Oracle to transform the query into a star query if possible and uses the best plan for such a query.
NO_STAR_TRANSFORMATION NO_STAR_TRANSFORMATION(*@block*)	Prevents transformation into a star query. New in Oracle Database 10*g*.
FACT(*table*) FACT(*@block view*)	Indicates that a table should be considered as a fact table in a star query.
NO_FACT(*@block*) NO_FACT(*@block table*)	Indicates that a table is not a fact table.
USE_CONCAT USE_CONCAT(*@block*)	Turns a query with OR conditions into two or more queries unioned together with a UNION ALL.
UNNEST UNNEST(*@block*)	Specifies that subqueries be merged into the body of the main query, when possible.
NO_UNNEST NO_UNNEST(*@block*)	Prevents subqueries from being merged into the main query.

Join order hints

Join order hints allow you to exercise some control over the order in which Oracle joins tables. Only three of them exist, and they are listed in Table 12-6.

Table 12-6. Join order hints

Hint	Description
ORDERED	Tells Oracle to join tables left to right, in the same order in which they are listed in the FROM clause.
LEADING(`table` [`table`...]) LEADING(`@block table` [`table`...])	Specifies one or more leading tables for a join query. Tables are joined in the order listed, if possible; otherwise, the hint is ignored.

Join operation hints

Join operation hints allow you to control the manner in which two tables are joined. Oracle uses three basic methods whenever two tables are joined: the merge join, the nested loops join, and the hash join.

Merge join

This type of join is done by sorting the rows from each table by the join columns. Once the two rowsets have been sorted, Oracle reads through both and joins any matching rows together. A merge may use fewer resources than the other options, but you have to wait for all the records to be sorted before you get the first one back. You have to have enough memory and temporary disk space to handle the sort.

Nested loops join

The method used for a nested loops join corresponds to the mental image most people have in mind when they think of joining tables. Oracle picks one table as the driving table and reads through that table row by row. For each row read from the driving table, Oracle looks up the corresponding rows in the secondary table and joins them together. Because no sort is involved, a nested loops join will get you the first record back more quickly than a merge join. For the same reason, a nested loops join doesn't require large amounts of disk space and memory. However, a nested loops join may result in a considerably greater number of disk reads than a merge join.

Hash join

A hash join is similar to a merge join, but a sort is not required. A hash table is built in memory to allow quick access to the rows from one of the tables to be joined. Then rows are read from the other table. As each row is read from the second table, the hash function is applied to the join columns, and the result is used to find the corresponding rows from the first table.

Table 12-7 lists the join operation hints.

Table 12-7. Join operation hints

Hint	Description
USE_NL(*table* [*table*...]) USE_NL(*@block table* [*table*...])	Tells Oracle to use a nested loop when joining the specified table(s). The table(s) specified by this hint will be the one(s) accessed by the innermost loop(s). New in Oracle Database 10*g*.
USE_MERGE(*table* [*table*...]) USE_MERGE(*@block table*[*table*...])	Tells Oracle to use the sort merge method when joining the listed table(s).
USE_HASH(*table* [*table*...]) USE_HASH(*@block table*[*table*...])	Tells Oracle to use a hash join for the specified table(s).
NO_USE_NL(*table* [*table*...]) NO_USE_NL(*@block table* [*table*...])	Prevents the use of nested loops when joining the specified table(s). New in Oracle Database 10*g*.
USE_NL_WITH_INDEX(*table* [*index* [*index*...]]) USE_NL_WITH_INDEX(*@block table* [*index* [*index*...]])	Specifies a nested loops join in a manner similar to USE_NL, but requires the use of at least one index having columns corresponding to those in the join predicates. New in Oracle Database 10*g*.
NO_USE_MERGE(*table* [*table*...]) NO_USE_MERGE(*@block table* [*table*...])	Prevents the use of merge joins to the listed table(s). New in Oracle Database 10*g*.
NO_USE_HASH(*table* [*table*...]) NO_USE_HASH(*@block table*[*table*...])	Prevents the use of hash joins to the listed table(s). New in Oracle Database 10*g*.

Parallel execution hints

The hints shown in Table 12-8 allow you to influence the way Oracle executes a query in a parallel processing environment. In an environment with a single CPU, parallel processing is not possible, and these hints are ignored.

Table 12-8. Parallel execution hints

Hint	Description
PARALLEL(*table*) PARALLEL(*table degree*) PARALLEL(*table* DEFAULT) PARALLEL(*@block table*) PARALLEL(*@block table degree*) PARALLEL(*@block table* DEFAULT)	Specifies that data from *table* be processed in parallel, and optionally allows you to specify the *degree* of parallelism. Use DEFAULT to request the instance-wide default degree of parallelism.
NO_PARALLEL(*table*) NO_PARALLEL(*@block table*)	Tells Oracle not to access the specified table in parallel. New in Oracle Database 10*g* (renamed from Oracle9*i* Database NOPARALLEL).
PARALLEL_INDEX(*table* [*index* [*index*...]] *degree*) PARALLEL_INDEX(*table* [*index* [*index*...]] DEFAULT) PARALLEL_INDEX(*@block table* [*index* [*index*...]] *degree*) PARALLEL_INDEX(*@block table* [*index* [*index*...]] DEFAULT)	Similar to PARALLEL, but specifies that indexes are to be range-scanned in parallel.

Table 12-8. Parallel execution hints (continued)

Hint	Description
PQ_DISTRIBUTE(*table outer inner*) PQ_DISTRIBUTE(*@block table outer inner*)	Specifies how rows from joined tables should be distributed among producer and consumer query servers. See Table 12-9 for a list of valid values for *outer* and *inner*.
NO_PARALLEL_INDEX(*table [index [index...]]*) NO_PARALLEL_INDEX(*@block table [index [index...]]*)	Prevents parallel index scans. New in Oracle 10*g* (renamed from Oracle9*i* Database NOPARALLEL_INDEX).

Table 12-9. Outer and inner distribution values for PQ hints

Outer	Inner	Description
HASH	HASH	Rows from each table are mapped to query servers using a hash function on the join keys.
BROADCAST	NONE	All rows from the outer table are sent to each of the query servers while inner rows are randomly distributed to the query servers.
NONE	BROADCAST	The reverse of BROADCAST, NONE.
PARTITION	NONE	Rows from the outer table are mapped to query servers based on the partitioning of the inner table, which must itself be partitioned on the join keys.
NONE	PARTITION	The reverse of PARTITION, NONE.
NONE	NONE	Each query server handles a corresponding pair of partitions from the outer and inner tables, both of which must be partitioned on the join key.

Other hints

A few hints don't fit neatly into one of the other categories. These are listed in Table 12-10.

Table 12-10. Other hints

Hint	Description
CACHE(*table*) CACHE(*@block table*)	Applies only when a full table scan is being performed on the specified table. It tells Oracle to place blocks for that table at the most recently used end of the buffer cache, so they will remain in memory as long as possible. This can be useful for small lookup tables that you expect to access repeatedly.
NOCACHE(*table*) NOCACHE(*@block table*)	This is the opposite of CACHE, and tells Oracle to place blocks at the least recently used end of the buffer cache, where they will be cleared out as soon as possible.
PUSH_SUBQ PUSH_SUBQ(*@block*)	Tells Oracle to evaluate non-merged subqueries as soon as possible during query execution. If you expect a subquery to eliminate a large number of rows, this can result in a performance improvement.

Table 12-10. Other hints (continued)

Hint	Description
DRIVING_SITE(*table*) DRIVING_SITE(*@block table*)	This hint applies when you are executing a distributed join, one that joins tables from two or more databases. Without a hint, Oracle will choose which database collects the tables and does the join. By using the hint, you are telling Oracle that you want the join performed by the database containing the specified table.
APPEND	Enables direct-path INSERT.
NOAPPEND	Explicitly requests conventional INSERT, and disables parallelism.
PUSH_PRED PUSH_PRED(*table*) PUSH_PRED(*@block*) PUSH_PRED(*@block table*)	Pushes a join predicate into the specified view.
NO_PUSH_PRED NO_PUSH_PRED(*table*) NO_PUSH_PRED(*@block*) NO_PUSH_PRED(*@block table*)	Prevents join predicates from being pushed into views.
NO_PUSH_SUBQ NO_PUSH_SUBQ(*@block*)	Relegates non-merged subqueries to the final steps in the execution plan.
QB_NAME(*block*)	Defines a name for a query block. New in Oracle Database 10*g*.
CURSOR_SHARING_EXACT	Prevents the optimizer from replacing literals in a SQL statement with bind variables.
DYNAMIC_SAMPLING(*effort*) DYNAMIC_SAMPLING(*table effort*) DYNAMIC_SAMPLING(*@block effort*) DYNAMIC_SAMPLING(*@block table effort*)	Specifies, on a scale from 0 to 10, the amount of effort put into dynamic sampling to determine more accurate predicate selectivity and statistics for tables and indexes involved in a query.
SPREAD_MIN_ANALYSIS	Reduces compile time by omitting some compile-time optimizations of MODEL clause rules. New in Oracle Database 10*g*.

Where to Find More Tuning Information

Tuning Oracle SQL is a complex subject. The information in this chapter provides only a brief overview of some of Oracle's features to help you during the tuning process.

To start with, read the manual. The *Oracle Database Performance Tuning* manual contains much tuning information although some of it is more oriented toward tuning the database server rather than tuning individual SQL statements. You'll find detailed information and examples on Oracle hints, the use of EXPLAIN PLAN, and the use of the TKPROF utility. TKPROF is difficult to use but can provide a great deal more information about the cost of a query than you will get from EXPLAIN PLAN.

I can recommend two good O'Reilly books on tuning.

Optimizing Oracle Performance
    By Cary Millsap and Jeff Holt. Cary and Jeff's book gives you the tools you need to find and diagnose performance problems in your database. Often, those

performance problems are related to poorly performing SQL statements, and that's where the next book comes into play.

SQL Tuning

By Dan Tow. This is the only book I've seen that presents a reliable and methodical approach that you can use to determine the optimal (or near-optimal) execution plan for a query. This book will help you determine which hints to apply, if any, to improve the performance of a SQL statement.

The Product User Profile

In addition to the standard database security Oracle provides and enforces for all database objects—tables, views, and the like—Oracle provides an application security scheme for SQL*Plus. This allows you to control the specific commands a SQL*Plus user is allowed to execute. At the core of the SQL*Plus application security scheme is the product user profile.

What Is the Product User Profile?

The *product user profile* is an Oracle table, owned by the SYSTEM user, that contains a list of SQL*Plus command restrictions by user. The table may contain role restrictions as well. The name of this table used to be product_user_profile. Now it is product_profile, but a synonym named product_user_profile exists to ensure backward compatibility.

Why Does the Product User Profile Exist?

Primarily, the aproduct user profile enables you to give end users access to SQL*Plus for reporting and ad hoc query purposes, yet restrict them from using SQL statements such as INSERT and DELETE that might damage production data.

Real-world applications typically implement many business rules, edit checks, and security at the application level rather than within the database. Modifying the data using an ad hoc tool, such as SQL*Plus, bypasses the rules and risks data integrity. Because of this, it's usually important to ensure that data are modified through the application, where the rules can be enforced.

If you give people an application that requires a database username and password, and those people have access to SQL*Plus, it won't be too long before some curious and adventurous soul will figure out that the same username and password that works for the application will work for SQL*Plus. Next thing you know, you will have someone running ad hoc queries that haven't been tuned, or, worse yet, you may have someone issuing ad hoc INSERT, UPDATE, or DELETE statements. The product user profile allows you to defend against this risk.

The product_profile Table

The product_profile table is owned by SYSTEM and has the following structure:

```
Name                            Null?     Type
------------------------------- --------  ----
PRODUCT                         NOT NULL  VARCHAR2(30)
USERID                                    VARCHAR2(30)
ATTRIBUTE                                 VARCHAR2(240)
SCOPE                                     VARCHAR2(240)
NUMERIC_VALUE                             NUMBER(15,2)
CHAR_VALUE                                VARCHAR2(240)
DATE_VALUE                                DATE
LONG_VALUE                                LONG
```

Most users won't have SELECT access on the table itself, so if you aren't logged in as SYSTEM, you may not be able to DESCRIBE the table. Instead, you should have access to a view on the table named product_privs. This view returns all the records from the product_profile table that apply to the currently logged-on user—you. Figure 13-1 shows the table, the view, the synonyms that normally exist, and the relationships among them.

Table 13-1 summarizes the purpose of each of the elements shown in Figure 13-1.

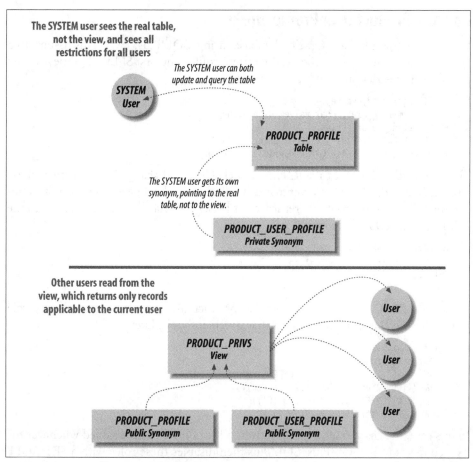

Figure 13-1. The product user profile table, view, and synonyms

Table 13-1. Product user profile elements

Element	Who sees it?	Purpose
product_profile table	SYSTEM	This is the product user profile table itself
product_user_profile private synonym	SYSTEM	Provides backward compatibility, because the table name used to be product_user_profile
product_privs view	All users	A view that shows each user the restrictions that apply to him
product_user_profile public synonym	All users	A public synonym pointing to the view
product_profile public synonym	All users	A public synonym pointing to the view

How the Product User Profile Works

When you log into an Oracle database using SQL*Plus, SQL*Plus issues two SELECT statements against the product user profile. The first SELECT retrieves a list of command restrictions and looks like this:

```
SELECT attribute, scope,
       numeric_value, char_value, date_value
FROM system.product_privs
WHERE (UPPER('SQL*Plus') LIKE UPPER(product))
  AND (UPPER(user) LIKE UPPER(userid))
```

The two fields of interest to SQL*Plus are attribute and char_value. Together, these columns tell SQL*Plus which commands to disable for the logged-on user. For example, the following two rows are returned for a user who has been denied access to the DELETE and HOST statements:

```
ATTRIBUTE   CHAR_VALUE
----------  ----------------------
DELETE      DISABLED
HOST        DISABLED
```

A second SELECT is issued against the product user profile to retrieve any role restrictions for the user. Here's what that statement looks like:

```
SELECT char_value
FROM system.product_privs
WHERE (UPPER('SQL*Plus') LIKE UPPER(product))
  AND ( (UPPER(user) LIKE UPPER(userid))
        OR (UPPER(userid) = 'PUBLIC'))
  AND (UPPER(attribute) = 'ROLES')
```

In this case, the char_value column returns a list of roles to be disabled whenever the user connects using SQL*Plus. SQL*Plus then disables these roles with a SET ROLE command. By way of example, assume that the following data were returned:

```
CHAR_VALUE
----------------------
PAYROLL_ADMINISTRATOR
HR_ADMINISTRATOR
```

There are two roles to be disabled. SQL*Plus turns them off by issuing the following command to Oracle:

```
SET ROLE ALL EXCEPT payroll_administrator, hr_administrator
```

This establishes the default condition for the user of having those roles turned off. The user may be able to issue another SET ROLE command to turn them back on again, but the starting condition is that the roles are off.

If SQL*Plus's attempt to query the product user profile results in an error, perhaps because the table doesn't exist, you will see the following message from SQL*Plus:

```
Error accessing PRODUCT_USER_PROFILE
Warning:  Product user profile information not loaded!
```

```
You may need to run PUPBLD.SQL as SYSTEM
Connected.
```

If you do happen to get this error message, see the section "Creating the Profile Table" later in this chapter, or notify your DBA.

 The SYSTEM user presents a special case. If you log into Oracle as SYSTEM, SQL*Plus detects this and does not query the product user profile. Therefore, you can never restrict what the SYSTEM user is allowed to do.

Product User Profile Limitations

The product user profile is used for application security. The application is SQL*Plus. No other applications respect the limitations set in the profile. In today's world, with Open DataBase Connectivity (ODBC) on every desktop, and every application under the sun capable of connecting to an Oracle database, securing SQL*Plus should be a small part of your overall security plan. Someone with Microsoft Access, for example, can easily connect to an Oracle database. Once that's done, users will be able to edit, insert, and delete any data to which they have access. Guard against this by implementing as much of your security as possible at the database level.

You should be aware of some potential security "holes" when using the product user profile to secure SQL*Plus. Oracle is a complex product, and there is often more than one way to accomplish any given task. You have to be vigilant about the possible use of PL/SQL, for example. The next two sections describe some issues to be aware of when setting limits with the product user profile.

Issues related to PL/SQL

Any SQL statement you can issue from the SQL*Plus prompt can be issued from a PL/SQL block. Using the profile, you can restrict a user's access to an SQL statement, but it may be possible to get around that restriction with PL/SQL. For this reason, you may want to restrict access to PL/SQL as well.

Take the UPDATE statement, for example. Using the profile, you can restrict a SQL*Plus user from issuing the UPDATE statement. Should the user try an update, an error will be returned, as the following example shows:

```
SQL> UPDATE sqlplus.employee
invalid command: update
```

This is all well and good, but the update can easily be coded in PL/SQL. Here's how:

```
SQL> BEGIN
  2  UPDATE sqlplus.employee
  3     SET employee_billing_rate = 300
  4   WHERE employee_id = 101;
```

```
5  END;
6  /
```

    PL/SQL procedure successfully completed.

That was easy enough, wasn't it? So much for your security. If you need to restrict a user from issuing any INSERT, UPDATE, DELETE, or SELECT statements, you should restrict the user from using PL/SQL.

Data definition language (DDL) statements, such as GRANT or CREATE TABLE, are more difficult to code from PL/SQL, but they can be done. As long as a user has EXECUTE access to the DBMS_SQL package, you should consider the possibility that the user may be able to code dynamic SQL statements.

 A new method of issuing dynamic SQL was implemented in the Oracle8*i* Database release. This method allows users to code dynamic SQL by simply embedding the desired statements in a PL/SQL block. Thus, the lack of EXECUTE privileges on the DBMS_SQL package won't necessarily stop the user from being able to issue dynamic SQL.

There are two obvious ways to execute PL/SQL from SQL*Plus. One way is to type a PL/SQL block at the command prompt and execute it. The other way is to use the SQL*Plus EXECUTE command. To restrict a user's access to PL/SQL, you must disable the following three SQL*Plus commands:

- DECLARE
- BEGIN
- EXECUTE

Leave any one of the above commands enabled, and you might as well leave them all enabled; the user will still have full access to PL/SQL. There are even less obvious ways to execute PL/SQL, and you may want to guard against these as well. The user could create a stored function and execute that from a SELECT statement, or the user could create a trigger on a table and then fire that trigger. The easiest way to guard against either of these possibilities is to ensure that the user doesn't have the system privileges required to do these things. An alternative would be to restrict access to the CREATE statement from SQL*Plus.

Issues related to roles

When you disable a role, SQL*Plus turns that role off when the user first connects, but that doesn't prevent the user from turning the role on again. The user can issue a SET ROLE command of his own, as the following example shows, turning the desired role back on:

```
SQL> SELECT employee_name, employee_billing_rate
  2  FROM gennick.employee;
    FROM gennick.employee
```

```
                    *
ERROR at line 2:
ORA-00942: table or view does not exist


SQL> SET ROLE ALL;

Role set.

SQL> SELECT employee_name, employee_billing_rate
  2  FROM gennick.employee;

EMPLOYEE_NAME                            EMPLOYEE_BILLING_RATE
---------------------------------------- ---------------------
Marusia Churai                                             169
Mykhailo Hrushevsky                                        135
Pavlo Virsky                                                99
...
```

In this example, the first SELECT failed because the PAYROLL_ADMINISTRATOR role had been disabled by SQL*Plus, and the user couldn't see the employee table. All the user has to do is issue a SET ROLE ALL command to enable the role, allowing him to see the data. It is not even necessary for the user to know the name of the specific role that needs to be enabled. For this reason, disabling the SET ROLE command should usually go hand in hand with disabling roles.

If you have disabled a role for a user and disabled the SET ROLE command, you should give some thought to disabling PL/SQL as well. You might want to revoke EXECUTE privileges on the DBMS_SQL package. The reason for this is that by using dynamic SQL, the SET ROLE command can be executed from within a PL/SQL block. Admittedly, this would take a knowledgeable and determined user, but it can be done. Here is an example:

```
SQL> SELECT employee_name, employee_billing_rate
  2      FROM gennick.employee;
    FROM gennick.employee
            *
ERROR at line 2:
ORA-00942: table or view does not exist


SQL> SET ROLE ALL;
invalid command: set role
SQL>
SQL> DECLARE
  2      set_role_cursor    INTEGER;
  3      rows_affected      INTEGER;
  4  BEGIN
  5      set_role_cursor := DBMS_SQL.OPEN_CURSOR;
  6      DBMS_SQL.PARSE (set_role_cursor,
  7                      'SET ROLE payroll_administrator',
  8                      DBMS_SQL.NATIVE);
```

```
 9    rows_affected := DBMS_SQL.EXECUTE(set_role_cursor);
10    DBMS_SQL.CLOSE_CURSOR(set_role_cursor);
11 END;
12 /

PL/SQL procedure successfully completed.

SQL> SELECT employee_name, employee_billing_rate
  2     FROM gennick.employee;

EMPLOYEE_NAME                            EMPLOYEE_BILLING_RATE
---------------------------------------- ---------------------
Marusia Churai                                             169
Mykhailo Hrushevsky                                        135
Pavlo Virsky                                                99
...
```

SQL*Plus honors the restriction against using the SET ROLE command from the SQL*Plus prompt, but it has no way of knowing what is going on inside a PL/SQL block. Remember that PL/SQL is sent to the database for execution; SQL*Plus does not look inside a block.

Using the Product User Profile

To use the product user profile, you must create it first. Oracle provides a script for this purpose. Once the product user profile table has been created, you need to know how to do three things:

- Restrict a user, or group of users, from using a specific command.
- Set a role so it will be disabled for a given user or group of users when SQL*Plus first connects.
- Report the restrictions currently in the profile table.

The next few sections show you how to perform each of these tasks.

Creating the Profile Table

Oracle supplies a script named *pupbld.sql* that creates the table, views, and synonyms shown in Figure 13-1. You can generally find the script at the following location:

```
$ORACLE_HOME/sqlplus/admin/pupbld.sql
```

You should execute *pupbld.sql* while logged in as user SYSTEM. Executing it while logged in as some other user will result in the profile table's being created in the wrong schema, and may result in a few privilege violations as the script creates public synonyms. The following example shows the script being executed:

```
SQL> @c:\orant\dbs\pupbld
drop synonym product_user_profile
     *
```

```
ERROR at line 1:
ORA-01434: private synonym to be dropped does not exist


  date_value from product_user_profile
                 *
ERROR at line 3:
ORA-00942: table or view does not exist


drop table product_user_profile
           *
ERROR at line 1:
ORA-00942: table or view does not exist


alter table product_profile add (long_value long)
*
ERROR at line 1:
ORA-00942: table or view does not exist
Table created.
View created.
Grant succeeded.
Synonym created.
Synonym created.
Synonym created.
Table created.
Grant succeeded.
View created.
Grant succeeded.
Synonym created.
0 rows updated.
SQL>
```

Do not be alarmed by the error messages. They are simply the result of the way Oracle wrote the script. If you were to run the script again, you would see a different set of errors. Any errors returned because an object exists does not exist may safely be ignored.

Limiting Access to Commands and Statements

To limit access to a SQL*Plus command or a SQL or PL/SQL statement, you need to insert a row into the product_profile table. This row tells SQL*Plus which command statement to disable and for which user. To re-enable a command or statement, delete the row with the restriction. The following sections show you how to do this.

Commands and statements that can be disabled

A specific list of commands or statements may be disabled using the product user profile.

For SQL*Plus, these are:

ACCEPT	EXECUTE	RUN
APPEND	EXIT	SAVE
ARCHIVE LOG	GET	SET[b]
ATTRIBUTE	HELP and ?	SHOW
BREAK	HOST[a]	SHUTDOWN
CHANGE	INPUT	SPOOL
CLEAR	LIST and ;	START[c]
COLUMN	PASSWORD	STARTUP
COMPUTE	PAUSE	STORE
CONNECT	PRINT	TIMING
COPY	PROMPT	TTITLE
DEFINE	QUIT	UNDEFINE
DEL	RECOVER	VARIABLE
DESCRIBE	REMARK	WHENEVER OSERROR
DISCONNECT	REPFOOTER	
EDIT	REPHEADER	

[a] Disabling HOST also disables $, !, or any other operating-system-specific shortcut for executing a host command.

[b] Disabling the SET command takes SET ROLE and SET TRANSACTION with it. That's because SQL*Plus simply looks at the first word to see if it matches the entry in the profile table.

[c] Disabling the START command also disables @ and @@.

For SQL, these are:

ALTER	RENAME	COMMIT
ANALYZE	REVOKE	DISASSOCIATE
AUDIT	SELECT	EXPLAIN
CREATE	SET ROLE	FLASHBACK
DELETE	SET TRANSACTION	MERGE
DROP	TRUNCATE	PURGE
GRANT	UPDATE	ROLLBACK
INSERT	ASSOCIATE	SAVEPOINT
LOCK	CALL	SET CONSTRAINTS
NOAUDIT	COMMENT	VALIDATE

For PL/SQL, these are:

BEGIN	DECLARE

Disabling a command or statement

To disable a command or statement for a user, insert a row into the product_profile table. You should normally log in as SYSTEM, and your INSERT statement should look like this:

```
INSERT INTO product_profile
    (product, userid, attribute, char_value)
    VALUES ('SQL*Plus','username','command','DISABLED');
```

in which:

'SQL*Plus'
> This is a constant. It identifies the product to which the restriction applies, in this case SQL*Plus. It should always be mixed-case as shown here.

username
> The username of the user you are restricting. It should always be uppercase. You can wildcard this using the wildcard characters used with the LIKE predicate, the percent sign, and the underscore. A value of '%' would make the restriction apply to all users.

command
> This is the name of the command or statement you wish to disable. It should always be uppercase, and it should be one of those listed in the "Commands and statements that can be disabled" section.

'DISABLED'
> The keyword 'DISABLED' must be stored in the CHAR_VALUE field.

Fields in the product_profile table other than the four listed above aren't used by SQL*Plus. They should be left alone and will default to null. The following example disables the DELETE statement for the user named SCOTT:

```
INSERT INTO product_profile
    (product, userid, attribute, char_value)
    VALUES ('SQL*Plus','SCOTT','DELETE','DISABLED');
```

You can wildcard the userid field to disable a command for a number of users at once. You can disable a command or statement across the board for all users. The following statement inserts a row into the product_profile table that will disable the SQL*Plus HOST command for everyone:

```
INSERT INTO product_profile
    (product, userid, attribute, char_value)
    VALUES ('SQL*Plus','%','HOST','DISABLED');
```

Be careful when using wildcards other than %. You have to be sure you know which users you are affecting when you create the restriction, and you have to worry that you might create a new username that inadvertently matches some existing restriction. Wildcards make it difficult to remove a restriction for one of the users who meet the criteria. For example, you might use "J%" to disable DELETE for all usernames starting with "J." If you later decide that "JONES" needs DELETE access, but "JASON" and "JENNIFER" don't, you have to rethink everything.

Re-enabling a command or statement

To remove a restriction you have created, delete that row from the product_profile table. For example, to allow all users to issue the HOST command again, issue the following command:

```
DELETE
   FROM product_profile
 WHERE product='SQL*Plus'
   AND userid='%'
   AND char_value='HOST'
```

Limiting Access to Roles

You disable roles for a user in much the same way that you disable commands and statements. The primary reason to disable a role is that a user might have a role for purposes of running an application, but you don't want the user to have that role when issuing ad hoc commands from SQL*Plus.

Disabling a role

To disable a role for a user, log in as SYSTEM and insert a row into the product_profile table, as follows:

```
INSERT INTO product_profile
    (product, userid, attribute, char_value)
    VALUES ('SQL*Plus','username','ROLES','role_name');
```

in which:

`'SQL*Plus'`
> Is a constant. It identifies the product to which the restriction applies, in this case SQL*Plus. It should always be mixed-case as shown here.

username
> Is the username of the user you are restricting. It must be uppercase. You can wildcard the username when restricting a role, but you must be careful when doing so.

`'ROLES'`
> Instead of a command or statement, the keyword ROLES in this field tells SQL*Plus you are restricting a role.

role_name
> Is the name of the role to disable.

Fields in the `product_profile` table not listed above should be left alone and will default to null. The following example will disable the PAYROLL_ADMINISTRATOR role for the user named SCOTT:

```
INSERT INTO product_profile
    (product, userid, attribute, char_value)
    VALUES ('SQL*Plus','SCOTT','ROLES','PAYROLL_ADMINISTRATOR');
```

You can wildcard the username when disabling a role, but you must be careful when doing this. SQL*Plus translates all the role restrictions for a user into a single SET ROLE command like this:

```
SET ROLE ALL EXCEPT role, role, role...
```

If any one of those roles is not valid for the user in question, the command will fail and none of the roles will be disabled. If you wildcard the username when disabling a role, you must be certain either that each user has been granted the role in question or that the role has been granted to PUBLIC.

Re-enabling a role

The method for removing a role restriction is the same as that used to remove a command restriction: delete the row from the `product_profile` table. For example, to allow SCOTT to be a PAYROLL_ADMINISTRATOR when logged in using SQL*Plus, issue the following DELETE statement:

```
DELETE
   FROM product_profile
  WHERE product='SQL*Plus'
    AND userid='SCOTT'
    AND command='ROLES'
    AND char_value='PAYROLL_ADMINISTRATOR'
```

You normally need to be logged in as SYSTEM to delete from the `product_profile` table.

Reporting on the Product User Profile

The following sections show you two different ways to look at the product user profile. The first section provides a script you can run to generate a report showing all the restrictions defined in the `product_profile` table. The second section provides a script that shows you the restrictions for a particular user, which you can specify.

You should run these scripts while logged in as the SYSTEM user. If you run them while logged in as anyone else, you will see only the restrictions that apply to you.

Listing all restrictions

The script in Example 13-1 generates a report showing all the command and role restrictions defined in the `product_profile` table.

Example 13-1. A script to report on product user profile restrictions

```
SET ECHO OFF
SET PAGESIZE 50
SET LINESIZE 60
SET NEWPAGE 0
SET FEEDBACK OFF
SET TRIMSPOOL ON

TTITLE LEFT 'Product User Profile Report' -
       RIGHT 'Page ' FORMAT 9999 SQL.PNO SKIP 6
BTITLE OFF

COLUMN userid FORMAT A12 HEADING 'User'
COLUMN sort_by NOPRINT
COLUMN command FORMAT A15 HEADING 'Disabled|Commands'
COLUMN role FORMAT A30 HEADING 'Disabled|Roles'

BREAK ON userid SKIP 1

PROMPT You are about to generate a product user profile report.
ACCEPT PUP_REPORT_FILE -
       PROMPT 'Enter the filename for the report output: ' -
       DEFAULT 'PUP_REPORT.LIS'

SPOOL &&PUP_REPORT_FILE
SET TERMOUT OFF

SELECT userid, 1 sort_by, attribute command, '' role
  FROM product_profile
 WHERE product = 'SQL*Plus'
   AND attribute <> 'ROLES'
   AND char_value = 'DISABLED'
UNION
SELECT userid, 2 sort_by, '' command, char_value role
  FROM product_profile
 WHERE product = 'SQL*Plus'
   AND attribute = 'ROLES'
ORDER BY userid, sort_by, command, role
;

SPOOL OFF
SET TERMOUT ON

--Restore these settings to their defaults
TTITLE OFF
CLEAR COLUMNS
SET PAGESIZE 14
SET LINESIZE 80
SET NEWPAGE 1
SET FEEDBACK ON
SET TRIMSPOOL OFF
```

When you run the script, you will be prompted for a filename, and the report output will be sent to that file. Here's an example showing how to run the script:

```
SQL> @ex13-1
You are about to generate a product user profile report.
Enter the filename for the report output: c:\a\profile.lis
SQL>
```

When you look in the file, you will see that the report looks like this:

```
Product User Profile Report                        Page     1


            Disabled        Disabled
User        Commands        Roles
---------   --------------- ------------------------------
GEORGE      BEGIN
            DECLARE
            EXECUTE
                            HR_ADMINISTRATOR
                            PAYROLL_ADMINISTRATOR

JONATHAN    BEGIN
            DECLARE
            DELETE
            EXECUTE
            HOST
            SET ROLE

JEFF        HOST
```

Listing restrictions for a particular user

To find out what restrictions apply to any one user, remember that the userid field in the product_profile table may contain wildcards. The script in Example 13-2 prompts you for a username, and displays a list of all the disabled commands, statements, and roles for that user. The queries involved use the LIKE operator to account for any possible wildcards.

Example 13-2. A script to list product user profile restrictions for a given user

```
SET ECHO OFF
SET FEEDBACK OFF
SET VERIFY OFF

BTITLE OFF
SET HEADING OFF
SET PAGESIZE 9999
SET NEWPAGE 1

ACCEPT user_to_show -
       PROMPT 'Show the product profile for which user? '

TTITLE LEFT restriction_heading SKIP 2
COLUMN restriction_type_heading NOPRINT NEW_VALUE restriction_heading
```

Example 13-2. A script to list product user profile restrictions for a given user (continued)

```
COLUMN sort_by NOPRINT
COLUMN restriction FORMAT A30
BREAK ON restriction_type_heading SKIP PAGE

SELECT 'User ' || UPPER('&&user_to_show')
       || ' is restricted from executing the following commands:'
       restriction_type_heading,
       1 sort_by, '     ', attribute restriction
  FROM product_profile
 WHERE product = 'SQL*Plus'
   AND attribute <> 'ROLES'
   AND char_value = 'DISABLED'
   AND UPPER('&&user_to_show') LIKE userid
UNION
SELECT 'User ' || UPPER('&&user_to_show')
       || ' has the following roles disabled:'
       restriction_type_heading,
       2 sort_by, '     ', char_value restriction
  FROM product_profile
 WHERE product = 'SQL*Plus'
   AND attribute = 'ROLES'
   AND ( UPPER('&&user_to_show') LIKE userid
       OR userid = 'PUBLIC')
UNION
SELECT 'User ' || UPPER('&&user_to_show')
       || ' does not exist.'
       restriction_type_heading,
       3 sort_by, '     ', ' ' restriction
  FROM dual
 WHERE NOT EXISTS (
          SELECT username
            FROM all_users
           WHERE username = UPPER('&&user_to_show'))
ORDER BY sort_by, restriction
;

--Restore these settings to their defaults.
SET HEADING ON
SET PAGESIZE 14
SET FEEDBACK ON
SET VERIFY ON
TTITLE OFF
CLEAR BREAKS
CLEAR COLUMNS
```

The following example shows how to run the script and what the output looks like:

```
SQL> @ex13-2
Show the product profile for which user? george

User GEORGE is restricted from executing the following commands:
```

```
BEGIN
DECLARE
EXECUTE
```

User GEORGE has the following roles disabled:

```
HR_ADMINISTRATOR
PAYROLL_ADMINISTRATOR
```

The script will tell you whether the user exists. It is possible to create entries in the product_profile table for users who do not exist. It is possible to drop a user, leaving orphan entries in the profile. The following example demonstrates this:

```
SQL> @ex13-2
Show the product profile for which user? Jonathan
```

User JONATHAN is restricted from executing the following commands:

```
BEGIN
DECLARE
DELETE
EXECUTE
HOST
SET ROLE
```

User JONATHAN does not exist.

CHAPTER 14

Customizing Your SQL*Plus Environment

This chapter describes how you can modify the SQL*Plus environment to make things more convenient for you or for the users you support. A number of settings can be customized. Some, like the search path used for SQL scripts, are more useful than others. In addition, two SQL scripts are automatically run whenever you start SQL*Plus. These SQL scripts are useful, for example, if you have specific SET commands that you want to execute at the beginning of a session.

SQL*Plus Settings You Can Control

The specific customizations you can make may vary depending on the operating system and the SQL*Plus version. Generally, though, you need to be aware of the login scripts and the environment variable settings.

Two SQL scripts are executed whenever SQL*Plus starts up:

Site profile
> The first script, known as the site profile, is named *glogin.sql*. It applies globally to all users on a particular computer.

User profile
> The second script, known as the user profile (not the same thing as the product user profile discussed in Chapter 13), is named *login.sql*. Each user may have his or her own user profile script.

The most obvious use for these files is to execute SET commands to customize the environment settings to something other than their defaults.

Several operating system environment variables affect how SQL*Plus operates. Some of what these environment variables allow you to specify include:

SQLPATH
> The search path to use for SQL scripts

LOCAL or TWO_TASK
  A default database connection

NLS_LANG
  The language being used

Under Windows, these settings can be made in the registry, but environment variables take precedence over their corresponding registry settings.

The Site and User Profiles

Two script files are executed every time SQL*Plus is started. These scripts define the site profile and the user profile and are named, respectively, *glogin.sql* and *login.sql*. Beginning with Oracle Database 10g, these scripts are executed each time you create a new database connection via the CONNECT command.

The site profile is made up of the commands contained in *glogin.sql*, which is the *global login file*. For all recent releases of Oracle, you'll find *glogin.sql* in the *$ORACLE_HOME/sqlplus/admin* directory.

> An Oracle8 install on a Windows system would place *glogin.sql* in a directory such as *C:\ORAWIN95\PLUS80*. For an Oracle 7.3 install on Windows, you would find *glogin.sql* in *C:\ORAWIN95\PLUS33*, or in a similarly named directory. In those releases, the registry entries PLUS80 and PLUS33 under the Oracle registry tree would point to the respective *glogin.sql* directories.

The user profile is similar to the site profile, except that it is intended to be user-specific. The script name is *login.sql*, and it is executed immediately after *glogin.sql*. SQL*Plus searches for the *login.sql* file in the current directory first, and then searches the directories listed in the SQLPATH environment variable. In a Unix installation and in Windows installations of recent releases, no default *login.sql* file or default SQLPATH variable will exist.

> Windows installs of Oracle8 and Oracle 7.3 typically included default, *login.sql* files in directories named after the specific version of Windows that you were running: *C:\ORAWIN95\DBS* (Windows 95), *C:\ORANT\DBS* (Windows NT), or *C:\ORAWIN\DBS* (Windows 3.1, 3.11).

You can add to the *login.sql* file, entering in whatever commands make your life easier. Make certain that your SQLPATH environment variable points to the directory containing your *login.sql*; otherwise, SQL*Plus won't find it when you are working in another directory.

For a full description of all the many SET commands that you can use to customize your SQL*Plus environment, see Appendix A.

Customizing the SQL*Plus Prompt

It's common to customize the SQL*Plus prompt to provide an indication of the database to which you are connected. This helps when you have multiple SQL*Plus windows open to different databases. Under such circumstances, embedding the database name into your prompt might save you from dropping a table in production when you mean to drop it in test. Example 14-1 shows a *login.sql* script to set your SQL*Plus prompt to a combination of username, net service name, and database name.

*Example 14-1. User profile (login.sql) to embed username, net service name, and database name into the SQL*Plus prompt*

```
SET TERMOUT OFF

--Specify that new values for the database_name column
--go into a substitution variable called databasae_name
COLUMN database_name NEW_VALUE database_name

--Use SYS_CONTEXT  to retrieve the database name. Alias the
--column as database_name to correspond to previous COLUMN
--command
SELECT SYS_CONTEXT('USERENV','DB_NAME') database_name
FROM dual;

--Set the prompt. Use predefined variables to access login
--user name and net service name
SET SQLPROMPT "&_user@&_connect_identifier(&database_name) >"

SET TERMOUT ON
```

The prompt set by the *login.sql* script from Example 14-1 will take the following form:

```
username@net_service_name(database_name) >
```

For example:

```
oracle@gennick02:~/sqlplus/ExampleScripts> sqlplus gennick/secret@prod

SQL*Plus: Release 10.1.0.2.0 - Production on Mon Aug 2 20:58:05 2004

Copyright (c) 1982, 2004, Oracle.  All rights reserved.
```

```
Connected to:
Oracle Database 10g Enterprise Edition Release 10.1.0.2.0 - Production
With the Partitioning, OLAP and Data Mining options

GENNICK@prod(db01) >
```

The SET TERMOUT OFF and SET TERMOUT ON commands bracketing the *login.sql* script prevent showing the output from the script, and especially from the SELECT against dual, thus preserving a clean-looking login.

Table 14-1 lists predefined substitution variables that you may use when customizing your prompt. The variables listed are automatically initialized by SQL*Plus with the values described in the table.

Table 14-1. Predefined substitution variables

Variable	Description
_CONNECT_IDENTIFIER	Net service name used to make the connection. New in Oracle Database 9*i*, Release 2.
_DATE	Current date. New in Oracle Database 10*g*.
_EDITOR	Command used to invoke an external text editor in response to the EDIT command.
_O_VERSION	Text message describing the version of the Oracle database software corresponding to the copy of SQL*Plus that you are running. This is the same message that SQL*Plus displays upon login. For example: "Oracle Database 10g Enterprise Edition Release 10.1.0.2.0 – Production."
_O_RELEASE	Release number, corresponding to _O_VERSION, but in the form of a "number" (a string of digits). For example: "1001000200."
_PRIVILEGE	Whether you have connected AS SYSDBA or AS SYSOPER. Otherwise, this variable will contain an empty string. New in Oracle Database 10*g*.
_SQLPLUS_RELEASE	Release of SQL*Plus that you are running, in the same form as _O_VERSION. For example: "1001000200."
_USER	Your login user name. New in Oracle Database 10*g*.

Choosing an Editor

Another common customization of the SQL*Plus environment is to designate the editor to be invoked in response to the EDIT command. On Linux and Unix systems, the default editor is often a command-line editor named *ed*. Changing your editor setting is as simple as changing the substitution variable named _EDITOR:

```
GENNICK@db01(db01) >define _editor = "vi"
```

You can make this definition in your *login.sql* file, so you don't need to make it repeatedly each time you run SQL*Plus. Whatever value you place in _EDITOR, that is the command that SQL*Plus uses to invoke an external editor in response to an EDIT command. SQL*Plus will pass the name of the file to be edited as the first command-line argument to that command.

Environment Variables That Affect SQL*Plus

A number of environment variable settings affect the behavior of SQL*Plus. The following sections describe some commonly used environment variables. For detailed descriptions of all the environment variables applicable to your version of SQL*Plus, consult your manual.

Specifying a Search Path for Scripts

Use the SQLPATH environment variable to designate one or more directories containing *.sql* files you wish to invoke from the SQL*Plus command prompt. Here are two from Linux:

```
oracle@gennick02:~> SQLPATH=$HOME/sqlplus/ExampleScripts:$HOME/sqlplus/ExampleData
oracle@gennick02:~> export SQLPATH
```

These commands designate a search path consisting of two directories, which are separated by colons. When you execute a script using this SQLPATH setting, SQL*Plus will search the following directories in order:

1. Your *current working directory*, which is the directory you were in when you started SQL*Plus
2. *$HOME/sqlplus/ExampleScripts*
3. *$HOME/sqlplus/ExampleData*

On Windows systems, you set environment variables from the Advanced tab of the System Control Panel, after clicking the Environment Variables button, as illustrated in Figure 14-1.

A Windows install of Oracle Database 10*g* includes a default SQLPATH specified in a registry entry such as the following:

```
My Computer\HKEY_LOCAL_MACHINE\SOFTWARE\ORACLE\KEY_OraDb10g_home1
```

The default path specified in the registry points to the *dbs* directory in your Oracle Home directory:

```
C:\oracle\product\10.1.0\Db_1\dbs
```

When you specify a path via the SQLPATH environment variable, the environment variable overrides the path specified in the registry.

Designating a Default Net Service Name

If you frequently connect to a remote database using a net service name, you can make SQL*Plus use that service name by default by setting the LOCAL environment variable. The following example is taken from Windows and shows how environment variables can be specified at the Windows command prompt:

```
C:\Documents and Settings\JonathanGennick>SET LOCAL=prod
```

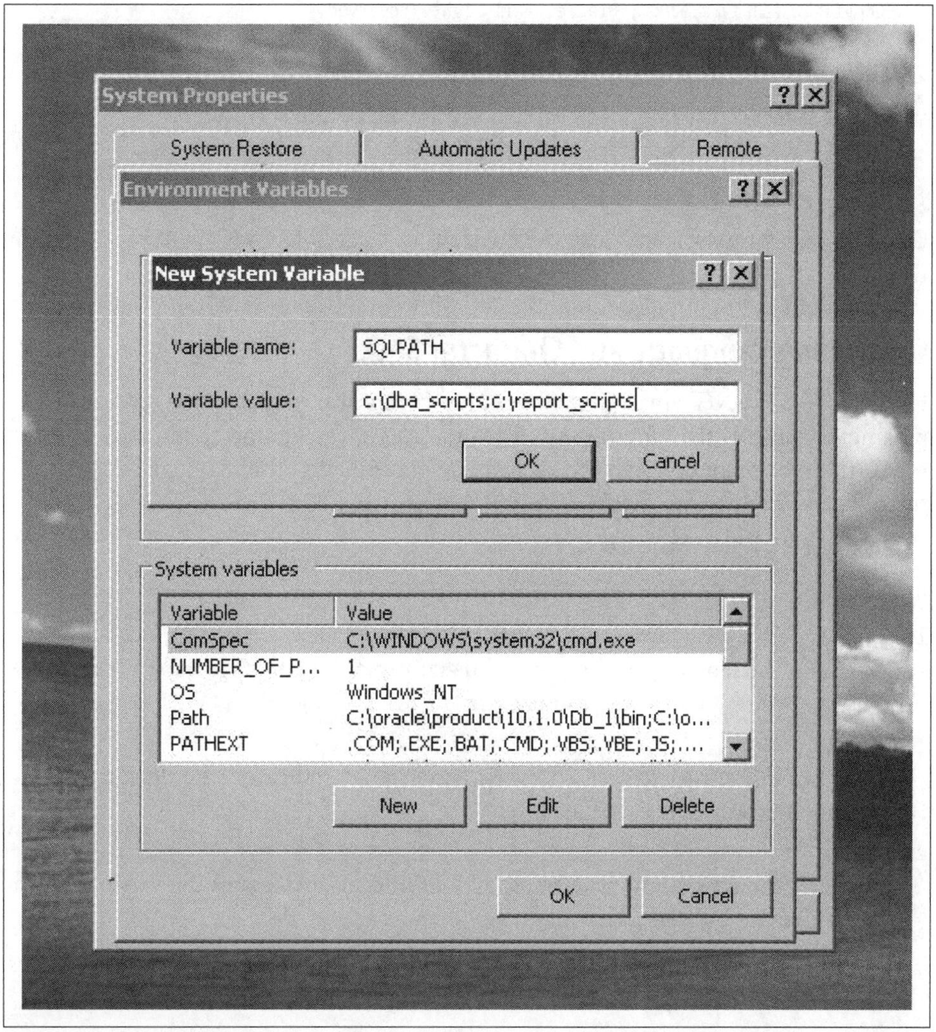

Figure 14-1. Setting SQLPATH on a Windows system

From here on, whenever you connect with a username and password:

```
sqlplus gennick/secret
```

it will be as if you had typed:

```
sqlplus gennick/secret@prod
```

You can see this behavior at work in the following example. Notice the occurrence of the net service name prod in the prompt created by the *login.sql* script:

```
C:\Documents and Settings\JonathanGennick>sqlplus gennick/secret

SQL*Plus: Release 10.1.0.2.0 - Production on Mon Aug 2 21:20:28 2004
```

```
Copyright (c) 1982, 2004, Oracle.  All rights reserved.


Connected to:
Oracle Database 10g Enterprise Edition Release 10.1.0.2.0 - Production
With the Partitioning, OLAP and Data Mining options

GENNICK@prod(db01) >
```

On Unix and Linux systems, use the environment variable TWO_TASK rather than LOCAL.

Controlling Language and Character Set

Use the NLS_LANG environment variable to specify globalization options. This parameter controls the language used for messages, the character set used, the sort order used, the manner in which dates are displayed, and other language-specific settings. The format for this setting is as follows:

```
language_territory.character_set
```

in which:

language
> Specifies the language to be used. This controls the language used for messages and the names of days and months among other things.

territory
> Specifies the territory. This controls the currency indicator, the decimal character, and the way dates are formatted.

character_set
> Specifies the character set to be used. This affects sorting and the way characters are converted between uppercase and lowercase.

The following example requests the French language and France's territory settings. Character set is omitted, so the current, operating system default will be assumed:

```
oracle@gennick02:~> NLS_LANG=french_france
oracle@gennick02:~> export NLS_LANG
oracle@gennick02:~> sqlplus gennick/secret

SQL*Plus: Release 10.1.0.2.0 - Production on Lun. Août 2 21:41:02 2004

Copyright (c) 1982, 2004, Oracle.  All rights reserved.


Connected to:
Oracle Database 10g Enterprise Edition Release 10.1.0.2.0 - Production
With the Partitioning, OLAP and Data Mining options

GENNICK@db01(db01) >
```

Look at the first line that SQL*Plus displays after login. You'll see that the date is displayed as "Lun. Août 2". The remaining messages are in English, likely because the French language files aren't installed on my PC.

The NLS_LANG setting is used by other Oracle products and is not one to toy with lightly. It affects SQL*Plus and SQL*Loader, Export, Import, and any other utility used to pass data between server and client. If you aren't sure what you are doing, it's best to leave this alone. For detailed information on Oracle's language support, see the *Oracle Database Globalization Support Guide* (Oracle Corporation).

Windows GUI SQL*Plus

The Windows GUI version of SQL*Plus implements an Environment dialog from which you can specify values for many of the options you would otherwise control via the SET command. Two environment options are unique to Windows GUI SQL*Plus. To get to this Environment dialog, run the Windows GUI version of SQL*Plus and select the Options → Environment menu option. You'll see the dialog in Figure 14-2.

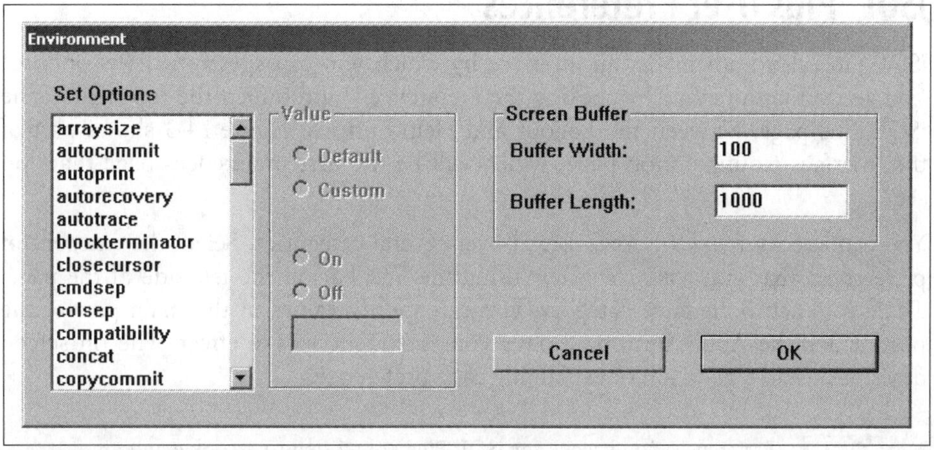

*Figure 14-2. Windows GUI SQL*Plus Environment dialog*

The left half of the dialog in Figure 14-2 provides a cumbersome alternative to using the SET command. For example, rather than issue SET LINESIZE 132, you can open this dialog, scroll down in the list of Set Options to linesize, click the Custom radio-button, and type the value 132 into the text box below the On and Off radio buttons. Believe me, you'll find it easier to use the SET command.

The right half of the dialog however, provides two options unique to the Windows GUI version of SQL*Plus. Buffer Length represents the number of lines of scrollback history that SQL*Plus maintains. If you're bringing back large amounts of query results that you'd like to scroll through, you may find it helpful to bump up the Buffer Length to a higher value. At least, I've often used that ability.

Buffer Width represents the left-to-right width of the SQL*Plus window. If you increase LINESIZE above 100, you'll find that Buffer Width is automatically increased to match, so you don't need to worry about manually specifying a value. The only reason to specify a value manually for Buffer Width is if you want to free up memory by reducing it. Probably due to the generous amounts of memory in most modern computers, I've never found memory consumption by the SQL*Plus screen buffer to be anything worth being concerned about.

Changes to Buffer Width and Buffer Length persist from one run of SQL*Plus to the next. Set the SQL*Plus Buffer Length to, say, 5000, and it will be 5000 each time you run the Windows GUI version. However, Set Options that you specify from the Environment dialog in Figure 14-1 are valid only for the one instance of SQL*Plus that you are running. When you next start SQL*Plus, all *Set Options* will return to their defaults.

iSQL*Plus User Preferences

*i*SQL*Plus also implements an interface by which you can specify various options. You get to that interface by clicking the Preferences button near the top right of the iSQL*Plus page, between the Logout and Help buttons. Figure 14-3 shows part of the Interface Configuration page, which will be the first preferences page that you see.

You can specify many options spread over several categories. Select the category of preferences that you wish to review using the link bar on the left side of the page. Then, for each preference category, you can specify values in the main part of the page. Click the Apply button to have your preferences take effect. The on screen descriptions do a good job of explaining each preference.

Preferences you specify for *i*SQL*Plus are written to a cookie and are used for all subsequent *i*SQL*Plus sessions unless you delete that cookie. If you connect to two different *i*SQL*Plus application servers from the same machine, each will write its own cookie and each will maintain its own set of preference settings.

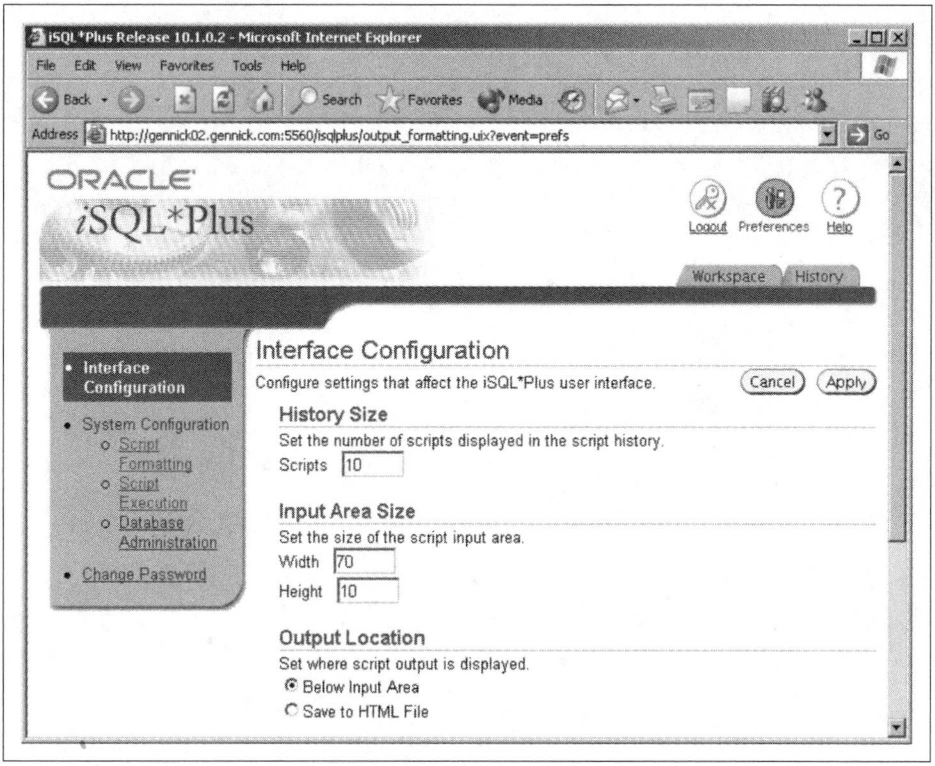

Figure 14-3. iSQL*Plus's Interface Configuration preferences

SQL*Plus Command Reference

The Command to Invoke SQL*Plus

The *sqlplus* command is used from the operating system prompt to start SQL*Plus. Chapter 2 shows various examples of the command being used. The syntax is:

```
sqlplus [options] [logon] [start]

options ::= option [option...]

option ::= {-H[ELP]
          | -V[ERSION]
          | -C[OMPATIBILITY] x.y[.z]
          | -L[OGON]
          | -M[ARKUP]  markup
          | -R[ESTRICT] {1 | 2 | 3}
          | -S[ILENT]}

markup ::= HTML [ON | OFF] [HEAD text] [BODY text] [TABLE text]
          [ENTMAP {ON | OFF}] [PREFORMAT {ON | OFF}]

logon ::= {typical | os_authenticated | administrative | /NOLOG}

typical ::= username[/password][@net_service_name]

os_authenticated ::= /

administrative ::= typical AS {SYSDBA | SYSOPER}

start ::= @{url | file_path} [param [param...]]
```

Command-line options are case-insensitive. The command itself may or may not be case-sensitive, depending on the underlying operating system. Parameters of a textual nature that include spaces or other non-alpha characters should be enclosed within double-quotation marks, as in HEAD "<title>My Page</title>".

The parameters are as follows:

-H[HELP]

Displays the syntax for the *sqlplus* command and then exits.

-V[ERSION]

Displays the current SQL*Plus version number and related information and then exits.

-C[OMPATIBILITY]*x.y[.z]*

Specifies a prior version (*x*), a release (*y*), and optionally an update (*z*) of SQL*Plus with which you wish to be compatible.

-L[OGON]

Inhibits reprompting for a username and password should the initial login credentials prove invalid. Use this option when invoking SQL*Plus from, say, a *cron* job, where reprompting makes no sense because there is no interactive user to see and respond to the prompt.

-M[ARKUP] *markup*

Controls whether SQL*Plus output is given in plain text or HTML, and, if in HTML, further specifies various options.

-R[ESTRICT] {1 | 2 | 3}

Disables commands that interact with the operating system. You may choose from one of three restriction levels:

1. Disable the EDIT and HOST commands

2. Disable EDIT, HOST, SAVE, SPOOL, and STORE

3. Disable EDIT, GET, HOST, SAVE, SPOOL, START, @, @@, and STORE

In addition, level 3 prevents the execution of the user profile script in *login.sql*.

-S[ILENT]

Tells SQL*Plus to run in silent mode. No startup messages, such as the copyright message, are displayed. No command prompt is displayed, and no commands are echoed to the screen. This is useful if you are invoking SQL*Plus from within some other program and you want to do it transparently. Normally, you would use this option in conjunction with invoking a script file.

HTML [ON | OFF]

Enables or disables HTML output. The default is HTML OFF.

[HEAD *text*]

Specifies content for the HEAD tag, which ends up as <HEAD>*text*</HEAD>.

[BODY *text*]

Specifies attributes for the BODY tag, which ends up as <BODY *text*>.

[TABLE *text*]

Specifies attributes for the TABLE tag used to define tables holding query output, which ends up as <TABLE *text*>. Tables used to hold page headers and footers aren't affected by this parameter.

[ENTMAP {ON | OFF}]

Specifies whether SQL*Plus replaces special characters such as "<" and ">" with their corresponding HTML entities (e.g., "<" and ">"). The default is ENTMAP ON.

[PREFORMAT {ON | OFF}]

Matters only when HTML output is enabled and specifies whether SQL*Plus writes query output as an HTML table or as a preformatted text block (using <pre>...</pre>). The default is PREFORMAT OFF.

/NOLOG

Starts SQL*Plus without a database connection.

typical ::= username[/*password*][@*net_service_name*]

Authenticates you using the given username, password, and net service name. Net service names are often defined in a file known as *tnsnames.ora*.

os_authenticated ::= /

Authenticates you by virtue of the fact that you have logged into the operating system. Your Oracle username must be specifically configured to support this type of authentication.

administrative ::= typical AS {SYSDBA | SYSOPER}

Authenticates you as a system database administrator (SYSDBA) or system operator (SYSOPER).

@{*url* | *file_path*}

Invokes a SQL*Plus script via a URL or a path and filename. URLs may be either *http://* or *ftp://*. filenames may include paths and extensions. The default file extension is *.sql*.

[*param* [*param...*]]

Are one or more parameters to pass to a script that you are invoking.

Commands You Can Issue Within SQL*Plus

The following sections describe in detail all the many commands that you can issue from within SQL*Plus. These are SQL*Plus commands only. For information on SQL statements or PL/SQL syntax, see Oracle's documentation, or a book such as *Oracle in a Nutshell* by Rick Greenwald and David C. Kreines (O'Reilly).

Comment Delimiters (/*…*/)

The /* and */ delimiters set off a comment in SQL*Plus. Comments entered this way may span multiple lines. If you use /*…*/ in a script file, the comments are displayed on the screen when the script is executed.

Syntax

```
/*
comment_text
comment_text
comment_text
*/
```

Parameters

/*   Marks the beginning of the comment

comment_text
   Is the text making up the comment

*/   Marks the end of the comment

Double Hyphen (- -)

The double hyphen places a single-line comment in a SQL*Plus script. The double hyphen works the same way as REMARK, except that it may be used in SQL statements and PL/SQL blocks. When used in a SQL statement or PL/SQL block, the double hyphen may be used to add trailing comments to a line.

Syntax

```
--comment_text
```

Parameters

- -   Is a double hyphen and tells SQL*Plus that the line in question is a comment line

comment_text
   Is the comment

At Sign (@)

The at sign executes a SQL*Plus script file. A script file is a text file containing SQL*Plus commands. The commands appear in the file just as you would enter them from the keyboard. See Chapters 2 and 8 for an introduction to this command. Also see the @@ and START commands.

From *i*SQL*Plus, you can only run scripts via *http* or *ftp*.

Syntax

@{*url* | *file*} [*argument* [*argument*...]]

Parameters

url

> Is a URL, either *http* or *ftp*, pointing to a script that you wish to execute. Oracle9*i* Database Release 1 brought this option to SQL*Plus on Windows; Oracle9*i* Database Release 2 brought it to SQL*Plus on all platforms.

file

> Is the name of the file you want to execute, which may include the path and extension. The default extension is *.sql*. If you don't specify a path, SQL*Plus looks for the file first in the current working directory and then searches each directory listed in the SQLPATH environment variable. See Chapter 14 for information about customizing the search path.

argument

> Is an argument you wish to pass to the script. You may pass as many arguments as you like. Arguments must be separated from each other by at least one space. Arguments may be enclosed in quotes, and should be if they contain spaces. Either single or double quotation marks may be used, at your discretion. Your script may reference the first argument as &1, the second as &2, and so forth.

Double At Sign (@@)

The double at sign is used within a script file to execute another script file contained in the same directory as the first. This is convenient if you have two scripts, one that calls the other. Use the @@ command in the first script file to call the second. Then put both files in the same directory. Now, regardless of whether that directory is in the search path, SQL*Plus will find the second file whenever the first calls for it. If used interactively, @@ functions exactly the same as @.

From *i*SQL*Plus, you can only run scripts via *http* or *ftp*.

Syntax

@{*url* | *file*} [*argument* [*argument*...]]

Parameters

Are the same as for the @ command.

Forward Slash (/)

A forward slash (/) executes the SQL statement or PL/SQL block that is in the buffer. See Chapter 2 for more information and for examples.

ACCEPT

The ACCEPT command gets input from a user. It causes SQL*Plus to display a prompt and wait for the user to type something in response. You can read about ACCEPT in Chapter 8 and in Chapter 11.

Syntax

```
ACC[EPT] variable [NUM[BER] | CHAR | DATE | BINARY_FLOAT | BINARY_DOUBLE]
         [FOR[MAT] format_specification]
         [DEF[AULT] default_value]
         [PROMPT prompt_text | NOPR[OMPT]]
         [HIDE]
```

Parameters

ACC[EPT]

Is the command, which may be abbreviated ACC.

variable

Is the variable you want to define. Don't include leading ampersands. If your script uses &*table_name* for a substitution variable, you should use *table_name* here.

NUM[BER] | CHAR | DATE | BINARY_FLOAT | BINARY_DOUBLE

Is the type of data you are after. The default is CHAR, which allows the user to type in anything as a response. Use NUMBER, BINARY_FLOAT, or BINARY_DOUBLE to force the user to enter a number. Use DATE when you want a date.

FOR[MAT] *format_specification*

Is a format specification, which may optionally be enclosed in quotation marks. ACCEPT rejects any input that doesn't conform to the specification. An error message is displayed and the prompt is reissued. Specifying a format makes the most sense when dealing with numeric and date data, and SQL*Plus is somewhat loose in enforcing the format. Chapter 11 delves into this aspect of the ACCEPT command in detail. Format elements are described in Appendix B.

DEF[AULT] *default_value*

Specifies a default value to assign to the variable. This is used if the user bypasses the prompt by pressing ENTER without entering a response. The default value should be enclosed within quotes.

PROMPT *prompt_text*

This is the prompt text displayed to the user before waiting for input. Enclose it within quotes.

NOPR[OMPT]

Indicates that you don't want the user to see a visible prompt. *i*SQL*Plus, because it is not a traditional command-line application, ignores NOPROMPT and prompts anyway.

HIDE

Causes SQL*Plus not to echo the user's response back to the display. This is useful if you are prompting for a password.

The syntax shown here for ACCEPT is valid for SQL*Plus in Oracle8*i* Database onward. Not all of the clauses are available when using prior versions. Check your documentation if you are writing scripts that need to work under earlier versions of SQL*Plus.

APPEND

Not available in *i*SQL*Plus

APPEND, an editing command, lets you add text onto the end of the current line in the SQL buffer.

Syntax

A[PPEND] *text*

Parameters

A[PPEND]
    Is the command, which may be abbreviated A

text
    Is the text you want appended to the current line

APPEND, and all other editing commands, are described in Chapter 2.

ARCHIVE LOG

The ARCHIVE LOG command controls or displays information about archive logging. You must be connected as SYSDBA or SYSOPER to use this command.

Syntax

```
ARCHIVE LOG { LIST
            | STOP
            | START [TO destination]
            | NEXT [TO destination]
            | ALL [TO destination]
            | log_sequence_number [TO destination]}
```

Parameters

LIST
    Causes SQL*Plus to display information about the current state of archiving. This includes the current destination, an indication of whether automatic archiving is enabled (the ARCH process), the oldest online log sequence number, the sequence number of the next log to be archived, and the current log sequence number.

STOP
    Stops log files from being automatically archived. You must manually archive redo log files as they fill; otherwise, you run the risk of the instance suspending operation because the log files have run out of space.

START
Turns on automatic archiving of redo log files.

NEXT
Manually archives the next log file group in the sequence provided that it is filled. Use ARCHIVE LOG LIST to see the sequence number of this file.

ALL
Manually archives all log file groups that have been filled but not previously archived.

log_sequence_number
Manually archives a specific log file group, provided that group is still online. Use ARCHIVE LOG LIST to find the sequence number of the oldest remaining log file group.

TO destination
Specifies a destination for archived log files. If used with ARCHIVE LOG START, this becomes the destination for all log files as they are archived. If used with NEXT, ALL, or a specific sequence number, this becomes the destination for files archived by that one command. If you don't specify a destination when using ARCHIVE LOG START, the value from the LOG_ARCHIVE_DEST initialization parameter is used.

ATTRIBUTE

The ATTRIBUTE command formats attributes of an Oracle object type. It functions like the COLUMN command but with fewer parameters. Chapter 7 shows examples of this command. Issuing the ATTRIBUTE command with no parameters gives you a list of all current attribute settings.

Syntax

```
ATTRIBUTE [object_type.attribute | attribute_alias [option [option...]]]

option ::= {ALI[AS] alias |
            CLE[AR] |
            FOR[MAT] format_spec |
            LIKE source_attribute |
            ON |
            OFF}
```

Parameters

object_type
Is the name of an Oracle object type.

attribute
Is the name of an attribute of the specified object type and is the attribute you are formatting. If you stop here and don't supply any other parameters, the current display settings for this attribute are shown.

attribute_alias
Is an alias that you have previously given to an attribute via an ATTRIBUTE ALIAS command.

ALI[AS]

> May be abbreviated ALI. ALIAS allows you to specify an alternate name for this attribute that is meaningful to SQL*Plus.

alias

> Is an alternate name for the attribute that may be used in other ATTRIBUTE commands, in place of having to spell out the full object type and attribute name again.

CLE[AR]

> May be abbreviated CLE. CLEAR erases any format settings for the attribute in question. This puts things back the way they were before any ATTRIBUTE commands were issued for the attribute.

FOR[MAT]

> May be abbreviated FOR. Allows you to control how the data for the attribute are displayed. For text fields, the format controls the maximum display length. For numeric fields, you can control the width, placement of commas, placement of the dollar sign, etc.

format_spec

> Is a string that specifies the display format for the attribute. Appendix B describes the format specification elements that may be used with the ATTRIBUTE command.

LIKE

> Causes the attribute to be defined with the same format attributes as another attribute.

source_column

> Is the name of the source attribute used with the LIKE parameter. This may be an alias or a complete attribute reference using the standard dot notation.

ON

> Causes SQL*Plus to print the attribute using the format you have specified. This is the default behavior. You don't need to use ON unless you have previously used OFF.

OFF

> Disables the format settings for the attribute. SQL*Plus acts as if you had never issued any ATTRIBUTE commands for the attribute in question.

When used with text attributes, formats such as A10 specify a maximum length to be displayed. Longer values are truncated to match the length specified, and shorter values are left alone.

BREAK

The BREAK command defines page breaks and line breaks based on changing column values in a report. It controls whether or not duplicate values print in a column, and it controls the printing of computed values such as totals and subtotals. Chapter 5 demonstrates the use of this command.

BREAK

Syntax

```
BRE[AK] [ON element_actiON [ON element_action...]]

element_action ::= {element [action_1 [action_2]]
                    | element [ action_2 [ action_1]]}


element ::= {column_name | ROW | REPORT}

action_1 ::= SKI[P] {lines_to_skip | PAGE}

action_2 ::= {NODUP[LICATES] | DUP[LICATES]}
```

Parameters

BRE[AK]

Is the command, which may be abbreviated BRE. Issuing the BREAK command with no parameters causes SQL*Plus to display the current break setting.

column_name

Specifies a report column to watch. When the value in the column changes, SQL*Plus skips lines or pages as specified. SQL*Plus inhibits repeating, or duplicate, values from printing more than once unless the DUPLICATES keyword is used.

ROW

Causes SQL*Plus to break on each row. You could double space a report by using BREAK ON ROW SKIP 1.

REPORT

Specifies a report-level break and is used to cause SQL*Plus to print grand totals at the end of the report. SKIP PAGE is ignored if it is specified as a report break action, but, strangely enough, the other form of the SKIP parameter will work. You can skip lines on a report break.

SKI[P] *lines_to_skip*

Tells SQL*Plus to skip the specified number of lines when a break occurs. SKIP may be abbreviated SKI. Line skipping does not apply to HTML output, whether from *i*SQL*Plus or not, unless you have also requested such output to be preformatted within <pre>...</pre> tags.

SKI[P] PAGE

Tells SQL*Plus to advance to a new page when a break occurs.

NODUP[LICATES]

Tells SQL*Plus to print a column's value only when it changes. By default, whenever you put a break on a column, you get this behavior. May be abbreviated NODUP.

DUP[LICATES]

Forces SQL*Plus to print a column's value in every line on the report, regardless of whether or not the value is the same as that printed for the previous record. May be abbreviated DUP.

BTITLE

The BTITLE command defines page footers for a report. Chapter 5 discusses BTITLE and contains several examples. Also see the TTITLE command. BTITLE and TTITLE work the same way.

Syntax

```
BTITLE [OFF | ON] | option [option...]

option ::=  [COL x |
             S[KIP] x |
             TAB x |
             LE[FT] |
             CE[NTER] |
             R[IGHT] |
             BOLD |
             FOR[MAT] format_spec | text | variable]
```

Parameters

BTI[TLE]

Is the command, which may be abbreviated BTI. Issuing the BTITLE command with no parameters causes SQL*Plus to display the current bottom title setting.

OFF

Turns the page footer off but does not erase its definition. You can turn it back on with ON.

ON

Turns on printing of page footers. The default footer, if you do not specify another, will be the first part of the SELECT statement.

COL x

Causes any footer text following this parameter to print at the specified column position.

S[KIP] x

May be abbreviated S. Inserts the specified number of line breaks before printing any subsequent footer text.

TAB x

TAB is similar to COL but moves you the specified number of columns relative to the current position. Negative numbers move you backward. TAB has nothing whatsoever to do with tab characters.

LE[FT]

May be abbreviated LE. Causes subsequent footer text to be printed beginning at the leftmost column of the current footer line.

CE[NTER]

May be abbreviated CE. Causes subsequent footer text to be centered within the current line. The LINESIZE setting controls the line width.

R[IGHT]

May be abbreviated R. Causes subsequent footer text to be printed flush right. The LINESIZE setting controls where SQL*Plus thinks the right end of the line is.

BOLD

Makes your footer "bold" by printing it three times. Only title text following the BOLD command is repeated on each line. There is no NOBOLD parameter.

FOR[MAT]

May be abbreviated FOR. Allows you to control how subsequent numeric data in the footer is displayed.

format_spec

Is a string that specifies the display format to use for subsequent numeric data in the footer. The format elements you can use here are the same as for the COLUMN command, and are described in Appendix B. It is possible to specify a character format, such as A20, but that has no effect on subsequent character strings.

text

Is any text you want to have in the footer. To be safe, enclose this in quotes, but you don't have to as long as your title text doesn't include any keywords like BOLD or TAB that have meaning to BTITLE. Either single or double quotes may be used. If you need to include a quote as part of your text, use two quote characters back to back.

variable

May be one of the variables shown in Table A-1.

*Table A-1. SQL*Plus system variables*

System variable	Value
SQL.PNO	Current page number
SQL.LNO	Current line number
SQL.RELEASE	Current Oracle release
SQL.SQLCODE	Error code returned by the most recent SQL query
SQL.USER	Oracle username of the user running the report

When using BTITLE, you should start off with one of the keywords such as LEFT, RIGHT, or CENTER. Otherwise, if the first parameter after the command is text, SQL*Plus will assume you have used an obsolete syntax for this command, and you won't get the results you want.

CHANGE   Not available in *i*SQL*Plus

CHANGE, an editing command, allows you to search and replace on a line in the SQL buffer. The CHANGE command also deletes text.

Syntax

C[HANGE] */old_text[/[new_text[/]]*

Parameters

C[HANGE]
> Is the command, which may be abbreviated C.

old_text
> Is the text you want to change or delete.

new_text
> Is the replacement text.

/ The forward slash character is commonly used to delimit the old and new text strings, but any other character may be used as long as it is not a number or a letter, and as long as it is used consistently throughout the command.

CHANGE and all the other editing commands are described in Chapter 2.

CLEAR

The CLEAR command deletes all column definitions, break settings, compute definitions, etc.

Syntax

CL[EAR] {BRE[AKS] | BUFF[ER] | COL[UMNS] | COMP[UTES] | SCR[EEN] | SQL | TIMI[NG]}

Parameters

CL[EAR]
> Is the command, which may be abbreviated CL.

BRE[AKS]
> Deletes any break setting you may have defined using the BREAK command.

BUFF[ER]
> Erases the contents of the buffer.

COL[UMNS]
> Deletes any column definitions you may have made using the COLUMN command.

COMP[UTES]
> Deletes any computations you may have defined using the COMPUTE command.

SCR[EEN]
> Clears the screen. Does not apply to *i*SQL*Plus.

SQL
> Erases the contents of the SQL buffer.

TIMI[NG]
> Deletes any timers you may have created using the TIMING command.

COLUMN

The COLUMN command formats report output for columnar reports. Using this command, you can control column width, the column title, the way numbers are displayed, whether or not long values wrap to a new line, and a host of other things. Chapter 5 discusses this command.

Syntax

```
COL[UMN] [column_name [ALI[AS] alias |
                       CLE[AR] |
                       ENTMAP {ON | OFF} |
                       FOLD_A[FTER] |
                       FOLD_B[EFORE] |
                       FOR[MAT] format_spec |
                       HEA[DING] heading_text |
                       JUS[TIFY] {LEFT | CENTER | CENTRE | RIGHT} |
                       LIKE source_column_name |
                       NEWL[INE] |
                       NEW_V[ALUE] variable |
                       NOPRI[NT] |
                       PRI[NT] |
                       NUL[L] null_text |
                       OLD_V[ALUE] variable |
                       ON |
                       OFF |
                       TRU[NCATED] |
                       WOR[D_WRAPPED] |
                       WRA[PPED]...]]
```

Parameters

COL[UMN]

> May be abbreviated COL. Issuing the COLUMN command with no parameters gets you a list of all current column formats.

column_name

> Is the name of the column you are formating. If it is a computed column, the expression is the name. If your SELECT statement aliases the column, you must use that alias name here. Issuing the command COLUMN with no further parameters causes SQL*Plus to display the current format for that column.

ALI[AS]

> May be abbreviated ALI. ALIAS allows you to specify an alternate name for this column that is meaningful to SQL*Plus. Do not confuse this with the column alias in a SELECT statement.

alias

> Is an alternate name for the column that may be used in BREAK commands, COMPUTE commands, and other COLUMN commands.

CLE[AR]

> May be abbreviated CLE. CLEAR erases any format settings for the column in question. This puts you back to the way things were before any COLUMN commands were issued for the column.

ENTMAP {ON | OFF}

Enables or disables HTML entity mapping for the column. When enabled, characters such as "<" are replaced by their corresponding HTML entity names, as in "<". The default is to follow the ENTMAP setting from the SET MARKUP options current in force.

FOLD_A[FTER]

May be abbreviated FOLD_A. Causes SQL*Plus to advance to a new line before displaying the next column. In other words, the output is wrapped after this column prints.

> FOLD_AFTER and FOLD_BEFORE are ignored when generating HTML output unless PREFORMAT has been set to ON.

FOLD_B[EFORE]

May be abbreviated FOLD_B. This is the opposite of FOLD_AFTER and causes SQL*Plus to wrap to a new line before this column is printed.

FOR[MAT]

May be abbreviated FOR, and allows you to control how the data for the column are displayed. For text fields, you can control the width. For numeric fields, you can control the width, placement of commas, placement of the dollar sign, etc.

format_spec

Is a string that specifies the display format for the column. Appendix B describes the format specification elements that may be used with the COLUMN command.

HEA[DING]

May be abbreviated HEA. Allows you to define a heading for the column. The heading text displays at the top of each column and is redisplayed every time a page break occurs.

heading_text

Is the text you want for the column heading. You should enclose this in quotation marks, but you don't have to if the heading is a single word. Single or double quotation marks may be used. If you need to include a quotation mark as part of your heading, use two quote characters back to back.

JUS[TIFY]

May be abbreviated JUS. Controls where the heading text prints relative to the column width. By default, headings for numeric fields print flush right, and headings for text fields print flush left. This parameter allows you to change that behavior. You must follow this keyword with one of the following: LEFT, RIGHT, CENTER, or CENTRE. LEFT causes the heading to print flush left. RIGHT causes the heading to print flush right. CENTER and CENTRE cause the heading to print centered over the top of the column. Note that this parameter has no effect whatsoever on how the data for the column is displayed.

LIKE

> Causes the column to be defined with the same format attributes as another column. LIKE must be followed by a column name, and that column becomes the source column.

source_column_name

> Is the name of the source column used with the LIKE parameter.

NEWL[INE]

> May be abbreviated NEWL. This is the same as FOLD_BEFORE and causes SQL*Plus to wrap to a new line before the column is printed.

> NEWLINE is ignored when generating HTML output unless PREFORMAT has been set to ON.

NEW_V[ALUE]

> May be abbreviated NEW_V. Causes SQL*Plus to keep a user variable updated with the current value of the column. The user variable is updated whenever the column value changes.

variable

> Is the name of a user variable for use with the NEW_VALUE and OLD_VALUE parameters.

NOPRI[NT]

> May be abbreviated NOPRI. Tells SQL*Plus not to print the column. NOPRINT is sometimes used when you want to get a column value into a user variable (see NEW_VALUE), but you don't want it displayed. This is often done when generating master/detail reports, as shown in Chapter 5.

PRI[NT]

> May be abbreviated PRI. Is the opposite of NOPRINT. Use PRINT when you want to turn printing back on for a column.

NUL[L]

> May be abbreviated NUL. Allows you to specify text to be displayed when the column value is null.

null_text

> Is the text you want displayed when the column in question is null. As with the heading text, this may be optionally enclosed in quotes.

OLD_V[ALUE]

> May be abbreviated OLD_V. Must be followed by a user variable name. OLD_VALUE works like NEW_VALUE, except that when the column changes, the previous value is stored in a user variable. This is useful when you need to print a value in the page footer of a master/detail report, as shown in Chapter 5.

ON

> Causes SQL*Plus to print the column using the format you have specified. This is the default behavior. You don't need to use ON unless you have previously used OFF.

OFF

> Disables the format settings for the column. SQL*Plus acts as if you had never issued any COLUMN commands for the column in question.

TRU[NCATED]

> May be abbreviated TRU. Causes the column text to be truncated to the width of the column. Longer values are not wrapped.

WOR[D_WRAPPED]

> May be abbreviated WOR. WORD_WRAPPED is similar to WRAPPED, but line breaks occur at word boundaries. Words that are longer than the column is wide will still be broken at the column boundary.

WRA[PPED]

> May be abbreviated WRA. WRAPPED affects the printing of values that are longer than the column is wide and causes SQL*Plus to wrap those values to a new line as many times as necessary to print the entire value. Line breaks will occur exactly at the column boundary, even in the middle of a word.

COMPUTE

The COMPUTE command defines summary calculations needed in a report. You can use COMPUTE in conjunction with BREAK to calculate and print column totals, averages, minimum and maximum values, etc. These calculations are performed by SQL*Plus as the report runs. COMPUTE is a complex command, and must be used in conjunction with the BREAK command to get results. See the section "Totals and Subtotals" in Chapter 7 for help with this command.

Syntax

```
COMP[UTE] [functions OF column_names ON breaks]

function ::= function [function...]

function ::= {AVG | COU[NT] | MAX[IMUM] | MIN[IMUM] |
              NUM[BER] | STD | SUM | VAR[IANCE]} [LABEL label_text]

column_names ::= column_name [column_name...]

break ::= break [break...]

break ::= group_column_name | ROW | REPORT}...]
```

You must have the same number of *functions*, *column_names*, and *breaks*.

Parameters

COMP[UTE]

> Is the command, which may be abbreviated COMP. Entering COMPUTE with no parameters causes SQL*Plus to list all currently defined computations.

AVG

> Computes the average of all non-null values for a column. AVG applies only to columns of type NUMBER.

COU[NT]
> Computes the total number of non-null values for a column. COUNT may be used with columns of any datatype and may be abbreviated COU.

MAX[IMUM]
> Computes the maximum value returned for a column. MAXIMUM may be abbreviated MAX, and applies to columns of type NUMBER, CHAR, VARCHAR2, NCHAR, and NVARCHAR2.

MIN[IMUM]
> Computes the minimum value returned for a column. MINIMUM may be abbreviated MIN, and applies to columns of type NUMBER, CHAR, VARCHAR2, NCHAR, and NVARCHAR2.

NUM[BER]
> Similar to COUNT, but computes the number of all values, including nulls. This applies to columns of any datatype and may be abbreviated NUM.

STD
> Computes the standard deviation of all non-null values for a column. STD applies only to columns of type NUMBER.

SUM
> Computes the sum of all non-null values for a column. SUM applies only to columns of type NUMBER.

VAR[IANCE]
> Computes the variance of all non-null values for a column. VARIANCE applies only to columns of type NUMBER and may be abbreviated VAR.

LABEL
> Allows you to specify a label for the computed value. If possible, this label will be printed to the left of the computed value.

label_text
> Is the text you want to use as a label when the computed value is printed. This may be enclosed in single or double quotation marks. To embed a quotation mark within the label when that label has been quoted, place two quote characters back to back.

column_name
> Is the name of the column you are summarizing. If the column is a computed column, the expression is the name. If your SELECT statement aliases the column, you must use that alias name here.

group_column_name
> Causes SQL*Plus to restart the calculation every time this column changes. Typically, the report is sorted or grouped by this column, and the computed value is printed once for each distinct value of the group column.

ROW
> Causes the computation to be performed once for each row returned by the query.

REPORT
> Causes the computation to be performed at the end of the report and to include values from all rows. REPORT is used for grand totals.

CONNECT

The CONNECT command changes your database connection, logs in as a different user, or connects you to the database in an administrative mode. Chapter 2 provides examples of CONNECT.

Syntax

CONN[ECT] [*username*[*/password*][*@connect*] | /] [AS {SYSOPER | SYSDBA}]

Parameters

CONN[ECT]
:   Is the command, which may be abbreviated CONN.

username
:   Is your database username.

password
:   Is your database password.

connect
:   Is the connect string, or host string, telling SQL*Plus the database to which you want to connect.

/
:   Use a forward slash instead of your username, password, and connect string when you want to connect to a local database using operating system authentication or when you want to connect as SYSDBA or SYSOPER while logged in as the Oracle software owner.

AS {SYSOPER | SYSDBA}
:   Tells SQL*Plus you are connecting in an administrative role.

COPY

The COPY command uses SQL*Plus as a conduit for transferring data between two Oracle databases.

COPY is not being enhanced to handle datatypes and features introduced with or after Oracle8*i* Database. COPY is a deprecated command and may be removed in a future release of SQL*Plus.

Syntax

```
COPY [FROM connection] [TO connection]
    {APPEND | CREATE | INSERT | REPLACE}
    destination_table [(column_list)]
    USING select_statement
```

Parameters

[FROM *connection*] [TO *connection*]
:   Specifies the source and target databases for the copy. The database to which you are connected is the default in both cases and will be used as both source and destination unless you specify otherwise.

connection
> Is the login information to use when connecting to the other database. This must be in the typical *username/password@connect_string* format.

APP[END]
> Causes SQL*Plus to insert the copied rows into the destination table, creating it first if necessary.

CRE[ATE]
> Causes SQL*Plus to copy the data only if the destination table is a new table. If the destination table exists, the COPY command will abort.

INSERT
> Causes SQL*Plus to insert the copied rows into the destination table only if it exists. If the destination table is a new table, the COPY command will abort.

REP[LACE]
> Causes SQL*Plus to drop the destination table if it currently exists. A new table is created, and the data are copied.

destination_table
> Is the name of the table to which you want to copy the data.

column_list
> Specifies column names to use when the COPY command creates a new destination table. This is a comma-delimited list, and the number of column names must match the number of columns in the SELECT statement.

select_statement
> Specifies a SELECT statement that returns the data you want to COPY.

DEFINE

The DEFINE command creates a user variable (or substitution variable) and may assign it a value. DEFINE may be used to list the value of a particular variable, or of all variables. DEFINE is discussed in Chapter 8.

Syntax

```
DEF[INE] [variable_name [= text]]
```

Parameters

DEF[INE]
> Is the command, which may be abbreviated DEF. Entering DEFINE by itself causes SQL*Plus to display a list of all currently defined user variables.

variable_name
> Is the name of the variable you want to create. Issue the command with only a variable name, and SQL*Plus will display the current contents of that variable if it exists.

text
> Is the text you want to assign to that variable. This may be optionally enclosed by single or double quotes, which you should use any time the value contains spaces or any other nonalphabetic character.

DEL

The DEL command, an editing command, deletes the current line from the buffer.

Syntax

```
DEL [{b | * | L}[ {e | * | L}]]
```

Parameters

b   Is a line number representing the beginning of a range of lines to delete. If no ending line number is specified, then only this one line will be deleted.

*   The asterisk refers to the current line number. It may be used in place of a line number to mark either the beginning or the end (or both) of a range of lines to be deleted.

L   L functions similarly to *, but refers to the last line in the buffer.

e   Is a line number representing the end of a range of lines to delete.

DEL, and all the other editing commands, are described in Chapter 2.

DESCRIBE

The DESCRIBE command displays information about a table, a view, an Oracle object type, a stored package, a stored procedure, or a stored function. When used against a table or view, DESCRIBE returns a list of columns, including datatypes and lengths. When used against an Oracle object type or a stored package, DESCRIBE returns a list of procedures, functions, and variables accessible from outside the package or type. Parameters for each function, procedure, and method are listed as well. When used against a stored procedure or function, DESCRIBE returns a list of parameters. In the case of a function, DESCRIBE displays the return type as well. DESCRIBE is discussed in Chapter 10.

Syntax

```
DESC[RIBE] [schema.]object_name[@database_link_name]
```

Parameters

DESC[RIBE]
   Is the command, which may be abbreviated DESC.

schema
   Is the name of the object's owner. This defaults to your username.

object_name
   Is the name of the object, often a table or a view, that you want to describe. You can describe any of the following: a table, a view, a stored procedure, a stored function, a stored package, or an Oracle object type.

database_link_name
   Is the name of a database link pointing to the database where the object exists. You need to specify this only if the object you want to describe exists in a database other than the one to which you are currently connected. Your DBA can help create a database link if you need one.

DISCONNECT

The DISCONNECT command closes your database connection without terminating SQL*Plus. DISCONNECT is discussed in Chapter 2.

Syntax

DISC[ONNECT]

Parameters

DISC[ONNECT]
> Is the command, which may be abbreviated DISC.

EDIT

Not available in *i*SQL*Plus

The EDIT command invokes an external editor to edit the contents of the buffer or to edit the contents of an operating system file.

Syntax

ED[IT] [*filename*]

Parameters

ED[IT]
> Is the command, which may be abbreviated ED. The EDIT command with no parameters allows you to edit the current contents of the buffer.

filename
> Specifies an external file to edit instead of the buffer. The filename may include a path and an extension.

EDIT, and all the other editing commands, are described in Chapter 2.

EXECUTE

The EXECUTE command allows you to execute a single PL/SQL statement and is discussed in Chapter 2.

Syntax

EXEC[UTE] *statement*

Parameters

EXEC[UTE]
> Is the command, which may be abbreviated EXEC.

statement
> Is the PL/SQL statement you want to execute.

EXIT

The EXIT command terminates a SQL*Plus session and returns to the operating system. In *i*SQL*Plus, you are returned to the *i*SQL*Plus input area without being disconnected from your database.

Syntax

```
EXIT [SUCCESS | FAILURE | WARNING | value | sub_variable | :bind_variable]
     [COMMIT | ROLLBACK]
```

Parameters

SUCCESS

Returns a success status. The exact value of the success status is operating system–dependent, but is often 0. SUCCESS is the default setting, and applies if no other return value is specified.

FAILURE

Returns a failure status. The value of the failure status is operating system–dependent, but is often 1.

WARNING

Returns a warning status. The exact value of the warning status is operating system–dependent.

value

Returns an arbitrary value as the status.

sub_variable

Returns the value of the specified substitution variable as the status. You can also specify SQL.SQLCODE here, to return the status of the most recently executed SQL statement.

:bind_variable

Returns the value of the specified bind variable as the status.

COMMIT

Causes SQL*Plus to automatically commit before exiting.

ROLLBACK

Causes SQL*Plus to automatically roll back any open transaction before exiting.

GET   Not available in *i*SQL*Plus

The GET command reads a SQL statement from a file and loads it into the buffer.

Syntax

```
GET filename [LIS[T] | NOL[IST]]
```

Parameters

filename

Is the name of the file containing the SQL statement you want to load. This can be any filename, including path and extension, that your operating system recognizes.

LIST
> Causes SQL*Plus to display the buffer after loading the file. This is the default.

NOL[IST]
> Causes SQL*Plus to load the file without displaying it.

GET, and all the other editing commands, are described in Chapter 2.

HELP

The HELP command gets help on SQL*Plus commands, SQL statements, PL/SQL statements, and other topics. HELP is described in Chapter 2.

Syntax

```
HELP [topic]
```

Parameters

topic
> Is the help topic you want to read about. Most SQL statements, SQL*Plus commands, and PL/SQL statements are valid help topics. There are others as well. Entering HELP INDEX will get you a complete list of valid topics.

Installing the online help

The SQL*Plus HELP command reads from a table named help in the SYSTEM schema of whatever database you are connected to. Thus, the help that you get will be for the version of SQL*Plus that corresponds to your database version and will not necessarily correspond to the version of SQL*Plus you are running.

To load the system help table, do the following:

1. Make your current working directory $ORACLE_HOME/sqlplus/admin/help.
2. Run SQL*Plus and connect to your database as the SYSTEM user.
3. Execute the *hlpbld.sql* script as follows:

   ```
   @hlpbld helpus.sql
   ```

   The *helpus.sql* file loads English language help text. You may need to load help in some other language. Issue an *ls* command to see what other *helpxx.sql* files are available.

To drop the help table (and possibly an associated view), should you ever wish to do that, just log in as SYSTEM and run $ORACLE_HOME/sqlplus/admin/help/helpdrop.sql.

> Older releases of Oracle used SQL*Loader to load the help table. For example, for Oracle8i Database, Release 8.1.5, you needed to connect as SYSTEM and run *helptbl.sql* followed by *helpindx.sql* to create the necessary table and indexes. Then, to load the help text, you would invoke SQL*Loader against the *plushelp.ctl* control file.

HOST

The HOST command executes an operating system command or invokes the command interpreter so you can execute several such commands.

Syntax

HO[ST] [*os_command*]

Parameters

HO[ST]

> Is the command, which may be abbreviated HO. Issuing HOST without specifying a command will get you a command prompt from which you may enter several commands.

os_command

> Is the operating system command you wish to execute. SQL*Plus will execute this one command for you, and then you will be returned to the SQL*Plus prompt.

INPUT

The INPUT command inserts one or more lines of text into the buffer. The lines are inserted after the current line.

Syntax

I[NPUT] [*text*]

Parameters

I[NPUT]

> Is the command, which may be abbreviated I. When you issue the INPUT command with no text after it, SQL*Plus puts you in insert mode, allowing you to type as many lines as you like. These are all inserted into the buffer following the current line. Press ENTER on a blank line to terminate insert mode.

text

> Is the text you want to insert. Use this if you are only inserting one line.

INPUT, and all the other editing commands, are described in Chapter 2.

LIST

The LIST command, an editing command, lists the current line from the buffer.

Syntax

L[IST] [{b | * | L}[{e | * | L}]]

Parameters

L[IST]
> Is the command, which may be abbreviated L. LIST by itself will cause SQL*Plus to display all lines in the buffer.

b
> Is a line number representing the beginning of a range of lines to list. If no ending line number is specified, only this one line will be listed.

*
> The asterisk refers to the current line number. It may be used in place of a line number to mark either the beginning or the end (or both) of a range of lines to be list.

L L functions similarly to * but refers to the last line in the buffer.

e Is a line number representing the end of a range of lines to list.

LIST, and all the other editing commands, are described in Chapter 2.

PASSWORD
Not available in *i*SQL*Plus

The PASSWORD command allows you to change your Oracle password using SQL*Plus and is described in Chapter 2.

Syntax

PASSW[ORD] [*username*]

Parameters

PASSW[ORD]
> Is the command, which may be abbreviated PASSW.

username
> Is the user whose password you want to change. Usually, only DBAs can change passwords for other users. You don't need to supply a username if you are changing your own password.

PAUSE

The PAUSE command, most commonly used from script files, prompts the user to press the ENTER key before the script can continue.

Syntax

PAU[SE] [*pause_message*]

Parameters

PAU[SE]
> Is the command, which may be abbreviated PAU.

pause_message
> Is an optional message you want displayed to the user. It's generally a good idea to include a message telling the users to press ENTER, lest they think the system has locked up on them.

PRINT

The PRINT command displays the value of a bind variable. One of its most useful applications is to retrieve and print data from a REFCURSOR variable that has been opened within a PL/SQL block or returned from a PL/SQL procedure. PRINT is discussed in Chapter 11.

Syntax

```
PRI[NT] [bind_variable_name]
```

Parameters

PRI[NT]
> Is the command, which may be abbreviated PRI. Entering PRINT by itself causes SQL* Plus to print the values of all bind variables.

bind_variable_name
> Is the name of the bind variable you want to print.

PROMPT

The PROMPT command displays a message for the user to see. See Chapter 8 for more information.

Syntax

```
PRO[MPT] text_to_be_displayed
```

Parameters

PRO[MPT]
> Is the command, which may be abbreviated PRO

text_to_be_displayed
> Is whatever text you want displayed to the user. This should not be a quoted string. If you include quotes, they will appear in the output.

QUIT

The QUIT command functions the same way as the EXIT command. It terminates a SQL*Plus session and returns you to the operating system. In *i*SQL*Plus, you are returned to the *i*SQL*Plus input area without being disconnected from your database.

Syntax

```
QUIT [SUCCESS | FAILURE | WARNING | value | sub_variable | :bind_variable]
    [COMMIT | ROLLBACK]
```

Parameters

SUCCESS

> Returns a success status. The exact value of the success status is operating system–dependent, but is often 0. SUCCESS is the default setting, and it applies if no other return value is specified.

FAILURE

> Returns a failure status. The value of the failure status is operating system–dependent but is often 1.

WARNING

> Returns a warning status. The exact value of the warning status is operating system–dependent.

value

> Returns an arbitrary value as the status.

sub_variable

> Returns the value of the specified user variable as the status. You can specify SQL. SQLCODE here, to return the status of the most recently executed SQL statement.

:bind_variable

> Returns the value of the specified bind variable as the status.

COMMIT

> Causes SQL*Plus to automatically commit before exiting.

ROLLBACK

> Causes SQL*Plus to automatically roll back any open transaction before exiting.

RECOVER

The RECOVER command initiates media recovery on a database, a tablespace, or a datafile. You must be connected as SYSDBA or SYSOPER in order to use this command. The syntax shown here is for Oracle Database 10*g*.

Syntax

```
RECOVER {general | managed | bracket}


general ::= [AUTOMATIC] [FROM location]
            {full_recovery | partial_recovery | LOGFILE filename}
            [general_option [general_option...]]

managed ::= MANAGED STANDBY DATABASE {managed_recovery | cancel | finish}

bracket ::= {BEGIN BACKUP | END BACKUP}
```

```
full_recovery ::= [STANDBY]DATABASE [full_option [full_option...]]

partial_recovery ::= {partial_type | STANDBY partial_type}
                     UNTIL [CONSISTENT WITH] CONTROLFILE

general_option ::= {TEST | ALLOW integer CORRUPTION | parallel}

managed_recovery ::= managed_recovery_option [managed recovery option...]

cancel ::= CANCEL [IMMEDIATE] [WAIT | NOWAIT]

finish ::= [DISCONNECT [FROM SESSION]] [parallel]
          FINISH [SKIP [STANDBY LOGFILE]] [WAIT | NOWAIT]


full_option ::= {UNTIL {CANCEL | TIME datetime | CHANGE integer}
                | USING BACKUP CONTROLFILE}

partial_type ::= {TABLESPACE tablespace[, tablespace...]
                | DATAFILE {filename | filenumber}[, filename | filenumber...]}

managed_recovery_option ::=
                  {{DISCONNECT [FROM SESSION] | TIMEOUT integer | NOTIMEOUT}
                  | {NODELAY | DEFAULT DELAY | DELAY integer}
                  | NEXT integer
                  | {EXPIRE integer | NO EXPIRE}
                  | parallel
                  | USING CURRENT LOGFILE
                  | UNTIL CHANGE integer
                  | THROUGH {[THREAD integer] SEQUENCE integer
                            | ALL ARCHIVELOG
                  | {ALL | LAST | NEXT} SWITCHOVER}


parallel ::= {NOPARALLEL | PARALLEL [degree]}
```

Parameters

AUTOMATIC
> Automatically determines the names of the redo log files to apply. The default is to prompt you for each name.

FROM location
> Specifies the directory in which archived redo log files are located. The default is to use the location specified by the LOG_ARCHIVE_DEST or LOG_ARCHIVE_DEST_1 initialization paremeters.

LOGFILE filename
> Begins media recovery with the specified log file.

MANAGED STANDBY DATABASE
> Places a standby database into sustained recovery mode, in which logs from the primary are automatically applied.

BEGIN BACKUP
> Moves all database files into online backup mode.

END BACKUP
> Moves all database files out of online backup mode.

STANDBY DATABASE
> Initiates recovery of the standby database.

UNTIL [CONSISTENT WITH] CONTROLFILE
> Recovers datafiles in the standby database until they are consistent with the standby database's control file.

TEST
> Initiates a trial recovery for the purpose of detecting problems that would occur during a real recovery. Redo is applied in memory, but none of the resulting data blocks are written to disk.

ALLOW *integer* CORRUPTION
> Specifies the number of corrupt blocks to allow before aborting a recovery operation.

CANCEL [IMMEDIATE] [WAIT | NOWAIT]
> Terminates recovery. Specify no options to terminate recovery after the current archived redo log file is applied. Use IMMEDIATE to cancel after the next redo log read, or after the current redo log file is applied, whichever comes first. Use WAIT to have the command wait for the termination. The default is to WAIT. Use NOWAIT if you wish to get back to the SQL*Plus command prompt without waiting for the termination to occur.

DISCONNECT [FROM SESSION]
> Causes recovery to proceed in the background, freeing up your session for other work.

FINISH [SKIP [STANDBY LOGFILE]] [WAIT | NOWAIT]
> Initiates recovery of any remaining, unapplied redo logs against the standby database. Use the SKIP clause to skip the application of standby redo log files. Use NOWAIT to get a command prompt back immediately without waiting for the recovery operation to finish. Use WAIT to specify the default behavior, in which the command waits for the operation to finish.

UNTIL CANCEL
> Performs recovery one log file at a time until you cancel the operation.

UNTIL TIME *datetime*
> Recovers up through a date and time, which you should specify using the format 'YYYY-MM-DD:HH24:MI:SS'.

UNTIL CHANGE *integer*
> Recovers up through a specified System Change Number (SCN).

USING BACKUP CONTROLFILE
> Uses the backup control file as the basis for recovery.

tablespace
> Specifies a tablespace to be recovered.

filename
> Specifies a datafile to be recovered.

filenumber

Specifies the number of a datafile to be recovered.

DISCONNECT [FROM SESSION]

Allows you to do other work in your session while the recovery is running.

TIMEOUT *integer*

Specifies a timeout in minutes, after which, if a requested archive redo log is not made available to the standby database, recovery terminates.

NOTIMEOUT

Explicitly requests the default behavior of sustained recovery with no timeout.

NODELAY

Overrides any DELAY setting in LOG_ARCHIVE_DEST_*n*.

DEFAULT DELAY

Delays application of a redo log file by the number of minutes specified in LOG_ARCHIVE_DEST_*n*.

DELAY *integer*

Overrides the DELAY setting in LOG_ARCHIVE_DEST_*n* with a new timeout, specified in minutes.

NEXT *integer*

Overrides any default DELAY, and applies the next *integer* log files as soon as they can be applied.

EXPIRE *integer*

Sets the number of minutes for which managed recovery will run, after which the operation will terminate.

NOEXPIRE

Removes any expiration time that may have been set for a managed recovery operation.

USING CURRENT *logfile*

Recovers redo from standby online logs, obviating the need to archive them first.

THROUGH [THREAD *integer*] SEQUENCE *integer*

Performs a managed standby recovery up through the specified thread and log sequence number.

THROUGH ALL ARCHIVELOG

Performs a managed standby recovery until all logs have been applied.

THROUGH {ALL | LAST | NEXT} SWITCHOVER

Continues a managed recovery through all switchover operations, through only the next switchover, or through the last switchover.

NOPARALLEL

Specifies that a recovery be done serially.

PARALLEL [degree]

Specifies that recovery be done in parallel and, optionally, the degree of parallelism to use. The default degree of the parallelism is the number of CPUs available on all instances multiplied by the value of the PARALLEL_THREADS_PER_CPU initialization parameter.

REMARK

The REMARK command places comments in a SQL*Plus script. See Chapter 5. In addition to REMARK, comments may set off with /*...*/, or by preceding each comment line with a double hyphen (- -).

Syntax

REM[ARK] *comment_text*

Parameters

REM[ARK]
> Is the command, which may be abbreviated REM.

comment_text
> Is your comment.

REPFOOTER

The REPFOOTER command defines a report footer. Report footers print on the last page of a report, after the last detail line and before the bottom title. See Chapter 7 for more information.

Syntax

REPF[OOTER] [PAGE] [OFF | ON] | *option* [*option*...]

```
option ::=    [COL x |
              S[KIP] x |
              TAB x |
              LE[FT] |
              CE[NTER] |
              R[IGHT] |
              BOLD |
              FOR[MAT] format_spec |
              text |
              variable]
```

Parameters

REPF[OOTER]
> REPFOOTER is the command, which may be abbreviated REPF. Issuing the REPFOOTER command with no parameters causes SQL*Plus to display the current report footer setting.

[PAGE]
> Begins a new page before printing the footer.

OFF
> Turns the report footer off but does not erase its definition. You can turn it back on with ON.

ON
> Turns on printing of report footers.

COL *x*

> Causes any footer text following this parameter to print at the specified column position.

S[KIP] *x*

> May be abbreviated S. Inserts the specified number of line breaks before printing any subsequent footer text.

TAB *x*

> TAB is similar to COL but moves you the specified number of columns relative to the current position. Negative numbers move you backward. TAB has nothing to do with tab characters.

LE[FT]

> May be abbreviated LE. Causes subsequent footer text to be printed beginning at the leftmost column of the current footer line.

CE[NTER]

> May be abbreviated CE. Causes subsequent footer text to be centered within the current line. The LINESIZE setting controls the line width.

R[IGHT]

> May be abbreviated R. Causes subsequent footer text to be printed flush right. The LINESIZE setting controls where SQL*Plus thinks the right end of the line is.

BOLD

> Makes a footer "bold" by printing it three times. Only text following the BOLD command is repeated on each line. There is no NOBOLD parameter.

FOR[MAT]

> May be abbreviated FOR. Allows you to control how subsequent numeric data in the footer is displayed.

format_spec

> Is a string that specifies the display format to use for subsequent numeric data in the footer. The format elements you can use here are the same as for the COLUMN command and are described in Appendix B. It is possible to specify a character format, such as A20, but that has no effect on subsequent character strings.

text

> Is any text you want to have in the footer. To be safe, you should enclose this in quotes, but you don't have to as long as your title text doesn't include any keywords like BOLD or TAB that have meaning to REPFOOTER. Either single or double quotes may be used. If you need to include a quote as part of your text, use two quote characters back to back.

variable

> May be one of the variables shown in Table A-1 (see the BTITLE command).

REPHEADER

The REPHEADER command defines a report header. Report headers print on the first page of a report, after the page title and before the first detail line. See Chapter 7 for more information.

Syntax

```
REPH[EADER] [PAGE] [OFF | ON] | option [option...]

option ::=  [COL x |
             S[KIP] x |
             TAB x |
             LE[FT] |
             CE[NTER] |
             R[IGHT] |
             BOLD |
             FOR[MAT] format_spec |
             text |
             variable]
```

Parameteres

REPH[EADER]
> Is the command, which may be abbreviated REPH. Issuing the REPHEADER command with no parameters causes SQL*Plus to display the current report header setting.

[PAGE]
> Begins a new page after printing the header.

OFF
> Turns the report header off but does not erase its definition. You can turn it back on with ON.

ON
> Turns on printing of report headers.

COL x
> Causes any header text following this parameter to print at the specified column position.

S[KIP] x
> May be abbreviated S. Insert the specified number of line breaks before printing any subsequent header text.

TAB x
> TAB is similar to COL, but moves you the specified number of columns relative to the current position. Negative numbers move you backward. TAB has nothing to do with tab characters.

LE[FT]
> May be abbreviated LE. Causes subsequent footer text to be printed beginning at the leftmost column of the current footer line.

CE[NTER]
> May be abbreviated CE. Causes subsequent header text to be centered within the current line. The LINESIZE setting controls the line width.

R[IGHT]
> May be abbreviated R. Causes subsequent header text to be printed flush right. The LINESIZE setting controls where SQL*Plus thinks the right end of the line is.

BOLD

> Makes a footer "bold" by printing it three times. Only text following the BOLD command is repeated on each line. There is no NOBOLD parameter.

FOR[MAT]

> May be abbreviated FOR. Allows you to control how subsequent numeric data in the header is displayed.

format_spec

> Is a string that specifies the display format to use for subsequent numeric data in the header. The format elements you can use here are the same as for the COLUMN command and are described in Appendix B. It is possible to specify a character format, such as A20, but that has no effect on subsequent character strings.

text

> Is any text you want to have in the header. To be safe, you should enclose this in quotes, but you don't have to as long as your title text doesn't include any keywords like BOLD or TAB that have meaning to REPHEADER. Single or double quotation marks may be used. If you need to include a quotation mark as part of your text, use two quote characters back to back.

variable

> May be one of the variables shown in Table A-1 (see the BTITLE command).

RUN

The RUN command displays and executes the command currently in the SQL buffer.

Syntax

R[UN]

Parameters

R[UN]

> Is the command, which may be abbreviated R. No parameters are necessary.

RUN, and all the other editing commands, are described in Chapter 2.

SAVE   Not available in *i*SQL*Plus

The SAVE command writes the contents of the SQL buffer to an operating system file.

Syntax

SAV[E] *filename* [CRE[ATE] | REP[LACE] | APP[END]]

Parameters

SAV[E]

> Is the command, which may be abbreviated SAV.

filename

> Is the filename, including the path and extension, to which you want to write the buffer contents.

CRE[ATE]
> Causes the operation to succeed only if the file doesn't exist. This is the default setting.

REP[LACE]
> Overwrites any existing file of the same name.

APP[END]
> Appends the contents of the buffer to the file.

SAVE, and all the other editing commands, are described in Chapter 2.

SET APPINFO

The APPINFO setting controls whether or not SQL*Plus automatically registers command files using the DBMS_APPLICATION_INFO package.

Syntax

```
SET APPI[NFO] {OFF | ON | app_text}
```

Paremeters

SET APPI[NFO]
> Is the command, which may be abbreviated SET APPI.

OFF
> Disables the automatic registration of command filenames. With this off, SQL*Plus will make an entry using the current value of *app_text* whenever you execute a command file.

ON
> Enables the automatic registration of command files. This is the default setting.

app_text
> Provides a text string that is used instead of the command filename. The default setting for this is "SQL*Plus".

Examples

The DBMS_APPLICATION_INFO package controls the contents of the module field in both the v$session and v$sqlarea views. Whenever you connect to a database, SQL*Plus registers itself as the active application by making a call to the DBMS_APPLICATION_INFO.SET_MODULE procedure. This sets the module name for your session to "SQL*Plus". This is reflected in the v$session view, as the following example demonstrates:

```
SELECT module FROM v$session WHERE username=USER;

MODULE
------------------------------------------------
SQL*Plus
```

SQL*Plus has the ability to update the module name whenever you execute a command file. The module name can be set to the command filename or to some arbitrary text that you specify. The default setting for APPINFO causes SQL*Plus to register the name of each command file you execute. So, if you execute a command file from one SQL*Plus session and query the v$session view from a second SQL*Plus session, you will get results like the following:

```
SELECT module FROM v$session WHERE username='JEFF';

MODULE
--------------------------------------------------
01@ /home/oracle/sqlplus/ExampleScripts/ex5-3.sql
```

In this example the module column tells you the name of the command file being executed by the user named JEFF. SQL*Plus crams in more information than the filename. You can break down the format of the module field as follows:

NL@tFFFFFFFF

in which:

NL   Is the nesting level. Command files executed from the SQL*Plus prompt will have a 01 in this position. If one command file executes another command file, then the nesting level will be 02, indicating that a second command file was invoked. The deeper the command files are nested, the larger this number becomes.

@   Is a constant.

t   Is a flag indicating whether or not SQL*Plus had to truncate the name of the command file in order for it to fit within the module field. The maximum length of a module is 48 bytes. If the filename was truncated, this value will be a less-than sign (<).

FFFFFFFF
   Is the filename, or as much as will fit within 48 characters.

You may find that you don't care about command filenames but that you want to know when users are using SQL*Plus. You can accomplish that by setting APPINFO to OFF. In that case, SQL*Plus will register itself but will not subsequently change the module name. It will always be "SQL*Plus". For this to apply to all users, you would need to place the setting in each user's global or site profile.

An additional option is to supply a fixed-text string that SQL*Plus can use instead of a filename. This string is passed as the module name whenever a command file is executed. The result is that while you will know that a command file is being executed, you won't know which one.

SET ARRAYSIZE

The ARRAYSIZE setting controls the number of rows SQL*Plus fetches from the database at one time.

Syntax

```
SET ARRAY[SIZE] array_size
```

Parameters

SET ARRAY[SIZE]
   Is the command, which may be abbreviated SET ARRAY.

array_size
> Is the number of rows fetched at one time. The default value is 15. The allowed range is from 1 to 5000.

Increasing the array size allows SQL*Plus to return more rows in one fetch, thus lessening the required number of network round trips between it and the database server. The tradeoff is that larger array size settings require more memory. Using the default value of 15, SQL*Plus would require 10 fetches to return 150 rows from a query. By increasing the array size to 50, you reduce the number of fetches to three.

SET AUTOCOMMIT

The AUTOCOMMIT setting controls whether SQL*Plus automatically commits changes you make to the database, and it controls how often those changes are committed.

Syntax

```
SET AUTO[COMMIT] {OFF | ON | IMMEDIATE | statement_count}
```

Parameters

SET AUTO[COMMIT]
> Is the command, which may be abbreviated SET AUTO.

OFF
> Turns off autocommit and requires you to commit (or roll back) changes manually. This is the default setting.

ON
> Causes SQL*Plus to issue a COMMIT after each successful SQL statement or PL/SQL block you execute.

IMMEDIATE
> Has the same effect as ON.

statement_count
> Causes SQL*Plus to issue a COMMIT after successfully executing the specified number of SQL statements or PL/SQL blocks. This value may range from 1 to 2,000,000.

Examples

When you set autocommit to occur after a specified number of successful SQL statements, be aware that manually executing a COMMIT, a ROLLBACK, or another SET AUTO-COMMIT command will cause the counter to be reset back to zero. Take a look at the following example:

```
SET AUTOCOMMIT 5
DELETE FROM project_hours WHERE employee_id = 101 AND project_id = 1001;
DELETE FROM project_hours WHERE employee_id = 102 AND project_id = 1001;
COMMIT;
DELETE FROM project_hours WHERE employee_id = 103 AND project_id = 1001;
DELETE FROM project_hours WHERE employee_id = 104 AND project_id = 1001;
DELETE FROM project_hours WHERE employee_id = 105 AND project_id = 1001;
```

```
DELETE FROM project_hours WHERE employee_id = 106 AND project_id = 1001;
DELETE FROM project_hours WHERE employee_id = 107 AND project_id = 1001;
```

The COMMIT statement in the fourth line will cause the counter to be reset. Counting will start over again, and five more SQL statements must be executed successfully before an automatic commit occurs.

SET AUTOPRINT

The AUTOPRINT setting controls whether SQL*Plus automatically prints the contents of any bind variables referenced by a PL/SQL block after it executes.

Syntax

```
SET AUTOP[RINT] {OFF | ON}
```

Parameters

SET AUTOP[RINT]
> Is the command, which may be abbreviated SET AUTOP.

OFF
> Keeps bind variables from being automatically printed after being referenced by a PL/SQL block. This is the default setting.

ON
> Causes bind variables to be printed automatically, following the execution of any PL/SQL block or SQL statement that references them.

SET AUTORECOVERY

The AUTORECOVERY setting causes the RECOVER command to run without user intervention, as long as the archived log files are in the destination pointed to by the LOG_ARCHIVE_DEST parameter and the names conform to the LOG_ARCHIVE_FORMAT parameter.

Syntax

```
SET AUTORECOVERY {OFF | ON}
```

Parameters

OFF
> Turns off autorecovery. This is the default setting.

ON
> Turns on autorecovery, causing the RECOVER command to run without user intervention.

SET AUTOTRACE

The AUTOTRACE setting controls whether SQL*Plus displays the execution plan and statistics for each SQL statement as it is executed.

Syntax

SET AUTOT[RACE] {OFF | ON | TRACE[ONLY]} [EXP[LAIN]] [STAT[ISTICS]]

Parameters

SET AUTOT[RACE]
> Is the command, which may be abbreviated SET AUTOT.

OFF
> Disables the autotrace feature. SQL*Plus won't display the execution plan or the statistics for each SQL statement.

ON
> Turns the autotrace feature on. If no other parameters are supplied, SQL*Plus will default to displaying the statistics. SET AUTOTRACE ON is equivalent to SET AUTOTRACE ON STATISTICS.

TRACE[ONLY]
> Inhibits the display of all data returned when the SQL statement in question is a SELECT statement.

EXP[LAIN]
> Causes SQL*Plus to display the execution plan for each SQL statement you execute.

STAT[ISTICS]
> Causes SQL*Plus to display execution statistics for each SQL statement you execute.

See Chapter 12 for comprehensive examples showing how to use the autotrace feature of SQL*Plus. Chapter 12 shows how to interpret the execution plan output and describes the operations that may be used in that plan.

SET BLOCKTERMINATOR

The BLOCKTERMINATOR setting controls the character used to terminate a PL/SQL block being entered into the buffer for editing.

Syntax

SET BLO[CKTERMINATOR] {block_term_char | ON | OFF}

Parameters

SET BLO[CKTERMINATOR]
> Is the command, which may be abbreviated SET BLO.

block_term_char
> Is the new terminator character for use when entering PL/SQL blocks. The default value is a period.

ON
> Enables the use of a block termination character and resets that character to the default of a period.

OFF
> Disables the use of a block termination character, which means that the only way to terminate a block is to execute it using the forward slash (/).

Examples

When you enter a PL/SQL block into the buffer, you need a way to tell SQL*Plus when the block has ended. By default, the period can be used for this purpose, but you can use the SET BLOCKTERMINATOR command to change that. The following example changes the block terminator to a pound sign character:

```
SQL> SET BLOCKTERMINATOR #
SQL> BEGIN
  2    DBMS_OUTPUT.PUT_LINE('PL/SQL is powerful.');
  3  END;
  4  #
SQL>
```

Terminating the block this way leaves it in the buffer for you to edit. Don't confuse this with the use of the slash command, which terminates and executes a block.

 Changing the terminator to a slash character by using SET BLOCK-TERMINATOR / prevents you from subsequently using the / character to execute the contents of the buffer.

SET BUFFER

The SET BUFFER setting switches to another buffer for editing purposes.

Syntax

```
SET BUF[FER] {buffer_name | SQL}
```

Parameters

SET BUF[FER]
> Is the command, which may be abbreviated SET BUF.

buffer_name
> Is the name of the buffer you want to edit. You can create any name you like. If the named buffer doesn't exist, SQL*Plus will create it for you.

SQL
> Switches you to the SQL buffer. This is the default setting. The SQL buffer is the one used when you type in a SQL statement at the command prompt and is the only buffer from which you can execute a SQL statement (or PL/SQL block).

Examples

Changing the buffer has limited use because you can execute a statement only from the SQL buffer. The GET, SAVE, and EDIT commands work, as do all the editing commands. The following example shows a second buffer being used to edit a statement that exists in a text file without disturbing the statement currently in the SQL buffer:

```
SQL> SHOW BUFFER
buffer SQL
SQL> SELECT * FROM employee
  2
SQL> L
  1* SELECT * FROM employee
SQL> SET BUFFER project
SQL> L
No lines in PROJECT buffer.
SQL> GET c:\a\project.sql
  1* SELECT * FROM project
SQL> I
  2  WHERE project_budget > 1000000
  3
SQL> SAVE c:\a\project.sql REPLACE
Wrote file c:\a\project.sql
SQL> SET BUFFER SQL
SQL> L
  1* SELECT * FROM employee
SQL>
```

As you can see, using a second buffer made it possible to edit the SQL statement in the *project.sql* file without disturbing the statement currently in the SQL buffer. You could do the same thing more easily with the EDIT command.

SET CLOSECURSOR

The CLOSECURSOR setting controls whether SQL*Plus closes the cursor used to execute a SQL statement after the statement has executed.

Syntax

```
SET CLOSECUR[SOR] {OFF | ON}
```

Parameters

SET CLOSECUR[SOR]
> Is the command, which may be abbreviated SET CLOSECUR.

OFF
> Causes SQL*Plus to leave the cursor open for use by subsequent SQL statements. This is the default setting.

ON
> Causes SQL*Plus to close the cursor after a SQL statement has been executed.

While you normally think of a cursor only in the context of returning data from a SELECT statement, Oracle also uses cursors to execute other SQL statements, such as DELETE,

INSERT, UPDATE, etc. The same cursor can be used to execute many SQL statements, so SQL*Plus leaves it open all the time by default.

SET CMDSEP

The CMDSEP setting controls whether you can enter multiple commands on one line. Both commands in question must be SQL*Plus commands. SET CMDSEP is used to change the character used to separate these commands.

Syntax

```
SET CMDS[EP] {OFF | ON | separator_char}
```

Parameters

SET CMDS[EP]
: Is the command, which may be abbreviated SET CMDS.

OFF
: Turns off the feature, requiring you to enter each command on a separate line. This is the default setting.

ON
: Allows you to enter multiple SQL*Plus commands on one line and resets the separator character back to the default of a semicolon.

separator_char
: Causes SQL*Plus to recognize the specified character as the command separator. You won't be allowed to make the command separator an alphabetic, numeric, or space character. This character may optionally be enclosed in either single or double quotes. In some cases, such as when you change it to a semicolon, you will need the quotes.

Examples

The following example turns this feature on, sets the separator character to an exclamation point, and shows how two commands may be placed on one line:

```
SQL> SET CMDSEP ON
SQL> SET CMDSEP "!"
SQL> SHOW CMDSEP! SHOW BUFFER!
cmdsep "!" (hex 21)
buffer SQL
SQL>
```

SET COLSEP

The COLSEP setting changes the text that prints between columns of data.

Syntax

```
SET COLSEP column_separator
```

Parameters

column_separator

> Is the text you want to print between columns. You should enclose this text in quotes if it contains any spaces or punctuation.

Examples

The default column separator is a single space. The following example shows how you can change it to a comma:

```
SQL> SET COLSEP ","
SQL> SELECT 'One' one,
  2            'Two' two
  3      FROM dual;

ONE,TWO
---,---
One,Two
```

Like a space, the comma in this example is a single character. You aren't limited to one character though. You could just as easily change the column separator to a string of several characters.

SET COMPATIBILITY

The COMPATIBILITY setting tells SQL*Plus the version of Oracle to which you are connected.

Syntax

```
SET COM[PATIBILITY] {V7 | V8 | NATIVE}
```

Parameters

SET COM[PATIBILITY]

> Is the command, which may be abbreviated SET COM.

V7

> Tells SQL*Plus you are connected to a Version 7 server or that you want SQL*Plus to act as if you were.

V8

> Tells SQL*Plus that you are connected to a Version 8 database.

NATIVE

> Causes SQL*Plus to automatically determine the compatibility setting based on the version of the database to which you are connected. This is the default setting.

This setting controls the way that SQL statements are transmitted to the server and the way that the results are brought back. It's usually best to leave this at the default, which causes

SQL*Plus to choose the correct method automatically based on the database to which you are connected.

SET CONCAT

The CONCAT setting changes the character used to terminate a substitution variable reference. You can use the command to turn the feature off so that SQL*Plus doesn't recognize any character as the terminator.

Syntax

```
SET CON[CAT] {OFF | ON | concat_char}
```

Parameters

SET CON[CAT]
> Is the command, which may be abbreviated SET CON.

OFF
> Turns off this feature completely. SQL*Plus won't recognize any character as the termination character for substitution variable names.

ON
> Turns this feature back on and resets the character back to the default value of a period.

concat_char
> Is the new termination character. The default value is a period.

Examples

This setting is important only when you immediately follow a substitution variable name with characters that SQL*Plus might interpret as part of the name. Consider the following example:

```
DEFINE table="PROJECT"
SELECT &&table._name FROM &&table;
```

The period (or concatenation character) in the SELECT statement is used to terminate the reference to &&table. Without the period, SQL*Plus would see &&table_name as the substitution variable.

> The concatenation character is never left in the line. When SQL*Plus substitutes a value for the variable, the concatenation character goes away along with the variable name.

SET COPYCOMMIT

The COPYCOMMIT setting controls how often SQL*Plus commits during execution of a COPY command.

Syntax

```
SET COPYC[OMMIT] batch_count
```

Parameters

SET COPYC[OMMIT]
> Is the command, which may be abbreviated SET COPYC.

batch_count
> Is the maximum number of uncommitted batches you want to allow during a copy operation. After this many batches are sent to the server, SQL*Plus commits the changes and resets the counter before sending another batch. The default value is 0, which means that SQL*Plus commits changes only when the COPY command is finished. The maximum value for this setting is 5000.

Examples

Normally, when you execute a COPY command, SQL*Plus copies all the rows from the source table to the destination table, then commits those changes. This can make for a rather large transaction if you are copying a large number of records, and your rollback segments may not be big enough to accommodate it. You can use SET COPYCOMMIT to have SQL*Plus periodically commit the changes, thus reducing the transaction size.

The COPYCOMMIT setting works in conjunction with the ARRAYSIZE setting. The ARRAYSIZE setting controls the number of rows in a batch. The COPYCOMMIT setting controls how many batches are copied before committing. The number of rows copied before each commit is equal to ARRAYSIZE * COPYCOMMIT. Take a look at this example:

```
SET ARRAYSIZE 15
SET COPYCOMMIT 10
COPY TO jonathan/secret@jonathan
CREATE employee_copy
USING SELECT * FROM employee;
```

Because the ARRAYSIZE is 15 and the COPYCOMMIT setting is 10, the COPY statement shown here will commit changes after every 150 rows (15 * 10).

SET COPYTYPECHECK

The COPYTYPECHECK setting controls whether SQL*Plus checks the datatypes when you use the COPY command to move data between two databases.

Syntax

```
SET COPYTYPECHECK {OFF | ON}
```

Parameters

OFF
> Turns off type checking.

ON
> Enables type checking. This is the default setting.

This setting was created specifically for use when copying data to a DB2 database.

SET DEFINE

The SET DEFINE command changes the prefix character used to mark substitution variables. You can use SET DEFINE to turn variable substitution off.

Syntax

```
SET DEF[INE] {OFF | ON | prefix_char}
```

Parameters

SET DEF[INE]
> Is the command, which may be abbreviated SET DEF.

OFF
> Disables variable substitution.

ON
> Enables variable substitution, and resets the substitution prefix character back to the default ampersand (&) character. Variable substitution is on by default.

prefix_char
> Is the new substitution prefix character.

When you start SQL*Plus, variable substitution will be on by default, and the default prefix character is an ampersand. If you are running a script that uses ampersands in text strings, you may want to change the prefix character to something else. If your script doesn't use substitution variables, you may find it easiest to turn the feature off.

SET DESCRIBE

The DESCRIBE setting controls the depth to which an object such as an object type or object table is described.

Syntax

```
SET DESCRIBE [DEPTH {levels | ALL}] [LINENUM {ON | OFF}] [INDENT {ON | OFF}]
```

Parameters

DEPTH {levels | ALL}
> Specifies the depth to which to recursively describe an object. The default is to describe only the top level of columns, attributes, or parameters.

LINENUM {ON | OFF}
> Adds or removes line numbers from the object's description. The default is LINENUM OFF.

INDENT {ON | OFF}
> Indents nested descriptions. The default is INDENT ON.

Examples

Suppose you had the following type and table:

```
CREATE OR REPLACE TYPE employee_type AS (
    employee_name VARCHAR2(40),
    employee_hire_date DATE,
    employee_salary NUMBER(9,2));
/

CREATE TABLE employees AS (
    employee_id NUMBER,
    employee_data employee_type);
```

If you describe the table, DESCRIBE's default behavior is to list the datatype for each column in the table, but not to expand any object types:

```
DESCRIBE employees
```

Name	Null?	Type
EMPLOYEE_ID		NUMBER
EMPLOYEE		EMPLOYEE_TYPE

If you want to know what EMPLOYEE_TYPE looks like, you must issue a second DESCRIBE command:

```
DESCRIBE employee_type
```

Name	Null?	Type
EMPLOYEE_NAME		VARCHAR2(40)
EMPLOYEE_HIRE_DATE		DATE
EMPLOYEE_SALARY		NUMBER(9,2)

The SET DESCRIBE command gives you the option of getting all this information with only one DESCRIBE command. The following example requests that all levels of nested object types be expanded. The example requests line numbering to make it easier to refer to specific definitions:

```
SET DESCRIBE DEPTH ALL LINENUM ON
DESCRIBE employees
```

		Name	Null?	Type
1		EMPLOYEE_ID		NUMBER
2		EMPLOYEE		EMPLOYEE_TYPE
3	2	EMPLOYEE_NAME		VARCHAR2(40)
4	2	EMPLOYEE_HIRE_DATE		DATE
5	2	EMPLOYEE_SALARY		NUMBER(9,2)

The first column of numbers in this example shows line numbers. The second column of numbers shows level numbers, indicating the nesting level of the element being described. Both come from using LINENUM ON.

SET DOCUMENT

The DOCUMENT setting controls whether SQL*Plus prints text created with the DOCU-MENT command.

Syntax

```
SET DOC[UMENT] {ON | OFF}
```

Parameters

SET DOC[UMENT]
: Is the command, which may be abbreviated SET DOC.

ON
: Allows DOCUMENT text to be displayed. This is the default setting.

OFF
: Keeps DOCUMENT text from being displayed.

Examples

This setting affects the DOCUMENT command only when it is issued from a script file. Suppose that you had a file with the following lines:

```
DOCUMENT
This is documentation.
#
```

The following example shows the results of executing this file with the DOCUMENT setting on and then with it off.

```
SQL> SET DOCUMENT ON
SQL> @c:\a\doc
DOC>This is documentation.
DOC>#
SQL> SET DOCUMENT OFF
SQL> @c:\a\doc
```

SET ECHO

The ECHO setting tells SQL*Plus whether you want the contents of script files to be echoed to the screen as they are executed.

Syntax

```
SET ECHO {OFF | ON}
```

Parameters

OFF
: Keeps commands from being echoed to the screen while a script file is being executed. This is the default setting.

ON
: Causes commands from a script file to be echoed to the screen as they are being executed.

Examples

SET ECHO is one of the few debugging tools SQL*Plus has. It often helps to turn on command echoing while you are developing and testing a new script file. The following example shows the same script file being executed, once with ECHO on and once with it off:

```
SQL> @c:\a\echo_test

D
-
X

SQL> SET ECHO ON
SQL> @c:\a\echo_test
SQL> SELECT * FROM dual;

D
-
X
```

For the second execution of the script, ECHO had been turned on, so the SELECT statement was displayed on the screen when SQL*Plus executed it.

> If you are writing a script that spools data to a file, you will almost certainly want to leave ECHO off. Otherwise, the commands in your script would be spooled to the file along with the data.

SET EDITFILE   Not available in /SQL*Plus

The EDITFILE setting lets you change the name of the work file that is created when you use the EDIT command to edit the SQL statement in the buffer.

Syntax

```
SET EDITF[ILE] edit_filename
```

Parameters

SET EDITF[ILE]
> Is the command, which may be abbreviated SET EDITF.

edit_filename
> Is the filename you want SQL*Plus to use when you issue an EDIT command. The default value is *afiedt.buf*. The filename you specify may optionally include a path.

If you don't include an extension as part of the filename, the current value of the SUFFIX setting will be used as the extension.

SET EMBEDDED

The EMBEDDED setting command controls the printing of embedded reports. The default setting is OFF, which causes the results of each new query to print on a new page and causes page numbering to start over each time a SELECT statement is executed.

Syntax

```
SET EMB[EDDED] {ON | OFF}
```

Parameters

SET EMB[EDDED]

Is the command, which may be abbreviated SET EMB.

ON

Turns the embedded report feature on. Executing a SELECT statement will not force a page break, nor will it reset the page number.

OFF

Turns the embedded report feature off. Executing a SELECT statement will force a page break, and the page number will be reset to 1.

Examples

An *embedded report* is one that prints as if it were the continuation of a previous report. The following example shows the results of executing two SELECT statements with the default setting. A page title has been created to show the effect on page numbering:

```
SQL> SET EMBEDDED OFF
SQL> SET PAGESIZE 24
SQL> SET NEWPAGE 1
SQL> TTITLE LEFT "Example of SET EMBEDDED, Page " SQL.PNO
SQL> SELECT * FROM dual;

Example of SET EMBEDDED, Page        1
D
-
X

SQL> SELECT * FROM dual;

Example of SET EMBEDDED, Page        1
D
-
X
```

The second SELECT statement generated a page break; you can see the page title printed again. By looking at the titles, the page numbering for each query began with page one. Look at the same example but with SET EMBEDDED ON:

```
SQL> SET EMBEDDED OFF
SQL> SET PAGESIZE 24
SQL> SET NEWPAGE 1
SQL> TTITLE LEFT "Example of SET EMBEDDED, Page " SQL.PNO
SQL> SELECT * FROM dual;
```

```
Example of SET EMBEDDED, Page        1
D
-
X

SQL> SET EMBEDDED ON
SQL> SELECT * FROM dual;
D
-
X
```

This time, the second SELECT statement didn't generate a page break. The second report began printing on the same page on which the first report ended.

> Be sure to execute the first query of a report with SET EMBEDDED OFF. Otherwise, you may find that SQL*Plus continues the page numbering from a query executed earlier during the session.

SET ESCAPE

The ESCAPE setting specifies the character used to escape the substitution variable prefix.

Syntax

SET ESC[APE] {OFF | ON | *escape_char*}

Parameters

SET ESC[APE]
: Is the command, which may be abbreviated SET ESC.

OFF
: Turns the escape feature off completely. SQL*Plus will not recognize any character as an escape character. This is the default setting.

ON
: Enables the escape feature and resets the escape character back to the default value, a backslash (\).

escape_char
: Is the new escape character. By default, this is a backslash.

Examples

You use the escape character when you want to place an ampersand in a command and you don't want that ampersand interpreted as a substitution variable prefix character. The following example shows a case where this can be a problem:

```
SQL> SELECT 'Matt & Joe Williams' FROM dual;
Enter value for joe:
```

The ampersand in front of the word "Joe" causes SQL*Plus to interpret it as a substitution variable name. To work around this behavior, you can turn the escape feature on and precede the ampersand with a backslash. Here's an example:

```
SQL> SET ESCAPE ON
SQL> SELECT 'Matt \& Joe Williams' FROM dual;

'MATT&JOEWILLIAMS'
-------------------
Matt & Joe Williams
```

You can use the SET ESCAPE command to change the escape character to something other than a backslash.

SET FEEDBACK

The FEEDBACK setting controls whether SQL*Plus displays the number of records returned by a SELECT statement, deleted by a DELETE statement, updated by an UPDATE statement, or inserted by an INSERT statement. You can set a threshold, below which you don't get any feedback regardless of whether the setting is on.

Syntax

```
SET FEED[BACK] {OFF | ON | row_threshold}
```

Parameters

SET FEED[BACK]
Is the command, which may be abbreviated SET FEED.

OFF
Turns off feedback completely. SQL*Plus won't tell you how many rows are affected by any SQL statements you issue.

ON
Turns on feedback, and is equivalent to SET FEEDBACK 1. For any SQL statement you issue, SQL*Plus will tell you how many rows were affected. By default, feedback is on with a threshold of 6 rows.

row_threshold
Allows you to specify a row threshold, and also turns feedback on if it is not already on. A row threshold causes SQL*Plus to print the row count returned by a SELECT statement when that row count exceeds the threshold. The row threshold applies only to the SELECT statement. As long as feedback is on, the INSERT, DELETE, and UPDATE statements always return the number of rows affected, regardless of the row threshold.

Examples

The following example shows a feedback message from a SELECT statement:

```
SQL> SET FEEDBACK 1
SQL> SELECT * FROM dual;
```

```
  D
  -
  X
```

1 row selected.

In this example, feedback was set to 1 prior to executing the SELECT statement. That caused a feedback message to be displayed even though the statement returned only one row.

SET FLAGGER

The FLAGGER setting checks your SQL statements for conformance to ANSI/ISO SQL92 syntax. You can choose from three compliance levels: entry, intermediate, and full.

Syntax

```
SET FLAGGER {OFF | ENTRY | INTERMED[IATE] | FULL}
```

Parameters

OFF
    Turns off this feature. This is the default setting.

ENTRY
    Allows SQL statements that use only the entry-level features of the standard.

INTERMED[IATE]
    Allows SQL statements that use the intermediate-level features of the standard.

FULL
    Allows any SQL statement that is defined in the standard.

Using the SET FLAGGER command has the same effect as executing the statement ALTER DATABASE SET FLAGGER. However, SET FLAGGER is a SQL*Plus command, so you can execute it even before connecting to the database. Once you have turned this feature on, any attempt to execute a nonconforming statement will result in an error message such as the following:

```
ERROR:
ORA-00097: Use of Oracle SQL feature not in SQL92 Entry Level
```

This feature is useful if you are writing software for the federal government and are required to deliver an implementation that uses no nonstandard, vendor-specific features.

SET FLUSH

The FLUSH setting indicates whether the host operating system is allowed to buffer output.

Syntax

SET FLU[SH] {OFF | ON}

Paremeters

SET FLU[SH]

Is the command, which may be abbreviated SET FLU.

OFF

Allows output to be buffered.

ON

Causes output to be displayed immediately. This is the default.

If you are running a command file, turning off FLUSH might keep you from seeing any output until SQL*Plus is finished executing that file.

SET HEADING

The HEADING setting controls whether column headings print when you SELECT or PRINT data. The default value for this setting is ON, which allows column headings to print.

Syntax

SET HEA[DING] [ON | OFF]

Parameters

SET HEA[DING]

Is the command, which may be abbreviated SET HEA.

ON

Causes column headings to print when you select data.

OFF

Suppresses column headings.

Examples

This setting is on by default, so you normally get a column heading whenever you select or print data using the SELECT statement or the PRINT command:

```
SQL> SELECT * FROM dual;

D
-
X
```

Change the value to OFF and your column headings go away. The following example shows this:

```
SQL> SET HEADING OFF
SQL> SELECT * FROM dual;

X
```

Issuing a SET PAGESIZE 0 command also turns off headings. If you want to enable headings and SET HEADING ON doesn't appear to be working, you should check the pagesize as well.

SET HEADSEP

The HEADSEP setting changes the character used when defining a two-line column heading.

Syntax

```
SET HEADS[EP] heading_separator
```

Parameters

SET HEADS[EP]
> Is the command, which may be abbreviated SET HEADS.

heading_separator
> Is the new heading separator character, which may be used in subsequent COLUMN commands to mark line breaks in multiline column headings.

Examples

Normally, the heading separator is a vertical bar and marks the place in a column's heading where you want a line break to occur. The following example shows a two-line heading being defined:

```
SQL> COLUMN dummy FORMAT A10 HEADING 'Line 1 | Line 2'
SQL> SELECT * FROM dual;

Line 1
Line 2
----------
X
```

The vertical bar in the column's heading text was replaced by a line break when the column heading was printed. If you need to use the vertical bar as part of a column heading, use SET HEADSEP to choose some other character to act as the line break marker.

The line break in a heading is set when you first define that heading using the COLUMN command. Subsequently changing the heading separator character doesn't affect column headings you have defined.

SET INSTANCE

The INSTANCE setting specifies a default database to which to connect when you use the CONNECT command without specifying a service name. You can't issue the SET INSTANCE command while connected to a database; you must disconnect first. Issuing the command SET INSTANCE with no parameters has the same effect as SET INSTANCE LOCAL.

Syntax

```
SET INSTANCE [service_name | LOCAL]
```

Parameters

service_name
> Is a net service name.

LOCAL
> Sets the default instance to be your local database. This is the default setting. In a Windows environment, the local database is the one specified by the LOCAL registry setting.

SET LINESIZE

The LINESIZE setting controls the number of characters SQL*Plus prints on one physical line. The default setting is 80 (150 in *i*SQL*Plus). The maximum width is system-dependent, though it's often 32,767 characters.

Syntax

```
SET LIN[ESIZE] line_width
```

Parameters

SET LIN[ESIZE]
> Is the command, which may be abbreviated SET LIN.

line_width
> Is the new line width, expressed as a number of characters.

The LINESIZE setting is referenced by SQL*Plus when you define any headers or footers (see TTITLE, BTITLE, REPHEADER, REPFOOTER) that are centered or right-justified.

SET LOBOFFSET

The LOBOFFSET setting represents an index into a LONG column. When SQL*Plus displays a LONG, it begins with the character pointed to by LOBOFFSET.

Syntax

```
SET LOBOF[FSET] offset
```

Parameters

SET LOBOF[FSET]
> Is the command, which may be abbreviated SET LOBOF.

offset
> Is the offset used when retrieving LONG values and represents the first character you want to display.

Using the LOBOFFSET setting in conjunction with the LONG setting allows you to print any arbitrary substring from a LONG column.

SET LOGSOURCE

The LOGSOURCE setting specifies the location of the archive log files and is referenced during recovery.

Syntax

```
SET LOGSOURCE logpath
```

Parameters

logpath
> Is the path to the directory containing the archived redo log files.

SET LONG

The LONG setting controls the number of characters displayed by SQL*Plus from any LONG columns returned by a query.

Syntax

```
SET LONG long_length
```

Parameters

long_length
> Represents the number of characters you want displayed from any LONG columns you select from the database. The default setting is 80 characters.

SET LONGCHUNKSIZE

The LONGCHUNKSIZE setting, a performance-related setting, controls the number of characters retrieved at one time from a LONG column.

Syntax

```
SET LONGC[HUNKSIZE] size
```

Parameters

SET LONGC[HUNKSIZE]
> Is the command, which may be abbreviated SET LONGC.

size
> Is the number of characters you want to retrieve from a LONG column in one fetch. The default value is 80.

With the default setting of 80 characters, SQL*Plus will need 10 round trips to the database to retrieve an 800-character LONG value. These network round trips take time, so you will tend to get better performance by increasing this setting. If you can afford the memory, make LONGCHUNKSIZE equal to the LONG setting. That way, the entire LONG value will be retrieved in one fetch.

SET MARKUP

The MARKUP setting specifies markup options for use in generating HTML output. See Chapter 6 for detailed information on generating HTML reports from SQL*Plus.

Syntax

```
SET MARKUP ::= HTML [ON | OFF] [HEAD text] [BODY text] [TABLE text]
               [ENTMAP {ON | OFF}] [SPOOL {ON | OFF}] [PREFORMAT {ON | OFF}]
```

Parameters

HTML [ON | OFF]
> Enables or disables HTML output. The default is HTML OFF.

[HEAD text]
> Specifies content for the HEAD tag, which ends up as <HEAD>text</HEAD>.

[BODY text]
> Specifies attributes for the BODY tag, which ends up as <BODY text>.

[TABLE text]
> Specifies attributes for the TABLE tag used to define tables holding query output, which ends up as <TABLE text>. Tables used to hold page headers and footers aren't affected by this parameter.

[ENTMAP {ON | OFF}]
> Specifies whether SQL*Plus replaces special characters such as "<" and ">" with their corresponding HTML entities (e.g., "<" and ">"). The default is ENTMAP ON.

[SPOOL {ON | OFF}
> Specifies whether a spooled report is generated as a complete, HTML page (ON) or as an HTML fragment (OFF) suitable for embedding into a page that you create. The default is SPOOL OFF.

[PREFORMAT {ON | OFF}]
> Matters only when HTML output is enabled, and specifies whether SQL*Plus writes query output as an HTML table or as a preformatted text block (using <pre>...</pre>). The default is PREFORMAT OFF.

SET MAXDATA   Obsolete

The MAXDATA setting is an obsolete setting; don't use it. SQL*Plus supports it in order to be backward compatible. MAXDATA controls the maximum row length SQL*Plus can handle.

Syntax

```
SET MAXD[ATA] max_row_width
```

Parameters

SET MAXD[ATA]
> Is the command, which may be abbreviated SET MAXD.

max_row_width
> Is the new setting for the maximum row width you expect to process.

The default setting is usually zero but may vary from one operating system to the next. Under some operating systems and/or versions of SQL*Plus, this setting seems to have no effect on SQL*Plus's behavior.

SET NEWPAGE

The NEWPAGE setting controls the manner in which the transition from one page to the next is marked. You can have SQL*Plus print a formfeed character at the start of each new page, skip a specific number of lines between pages, or do nothing at all when advancing from one page to another.

Syntax

```
SET NEWP[AGE] {lines_to_print | NONE}
```

Parameters

SET NEWP[AGE]
> Is the command, which may be abbreviated SET NEWP.

lines_to_print
> Tells SQL*Plus to print a specific number of blank lines when a page break occurs. These lines will be printed following the footer (BTITLE) of the page just ending, and prior to the header (TTITLE) of the page just starting. If this value is zero, a formfeed character will be printed instead of any blank lines. The default value is 1.

NONE
> Causes SQL*Plus to do nothing at all when a page break occurs. You'll get no blank lines and no formfeed.

 Use SET NEWPAGE 0 if you want a formfeed printed at the start of each new page.

SET NULL

The NULL setting changes the text SQL*Plus prints in a column when the value for that column is null.

Syntax

SET NULL *null_text*

Parameters

null_text
> Is the text you want to print in place of a null value.

Examples

The default null text setting is an empty string, which causes null values to print as blanks. The following example shows this and shows how the null text may be changed:

```
SQL> SELECT employee_termination_date
  2    FROM employee
  3    WHERE employee_id=101;

EMPLOYEE_
---------

SQL> SET NULL "*NULL*"
SQL> SELECT employee_termination_date
  2    FROM employee
  3    WHERE employee_id=101;

EMPLOYEE_
---------
*NULL*
```

If you use the COLUMN command to format a column, the NULL clause of that command will override this setting but only for that one column.

SET NUMFORMAT

The NUMFORMAT setting specifies the default formatting of numeric values returned from a SELECT statement. Any number format usable with the COLUMN command may also be used with SET NUMFORMAT.

Syntax

SET NUMF[ORMAT] *format_spec*

Parameters

SET NUMF[ORMAT]
> Is the command, which may be abbreviated SET NUMF.

format_spec
> Is a numeric format specification, which controls the default manner in which numeric values are displayed. See Appendix B for a list of formats.

Examples

The following example shows the effect of changing the NUMFORMAT setting:

```
SQL> SELECT 123456.7 FROM dual;

 123456.7
---------
 123456.7

SQL> SET NUMFORMAT $999,999.99
SQL> SELECT 123456.7 FROM dual;

   123456.7
------------
 $123,456.70
```

The NUMFORMAT setting controls the default display format for numeric values. You can use the COLUMN command to specify display formats on a column-by-column basis, and those take precedence over the NUMFORMAT setting.

SET NUMWIDTH

The NUMWIDTH setting controls the default width used when displaying numeric values.

Syntax

```
SET NUM[WIDTH] width
```

Paremeters

SET NUM[WIDTH]
> Is the command, which may be abbreviated SET NUM.

width
> Is the default column width used when displaying a numeric value.

Examples

The default NUMWIDTH setting is 10. NUMWIDTH is used only when no other settings apply. The following example shows the effect of setting NUMWIDTH to 5:

```
SQL> SET NUMWIDTH 5
SQL> SELECT 123 FROM dual;

 123
----
 123
```

A numeric format specified by a COLUMN command or by a SET NUMFORMAT command will override NUMWIDTH. The following example shows this:

```
SQL> SET NUMWIDTH 5
SQL> SET NUMFORMAT 999,999.99
SQL> SELECT 123 FROM dual;
```

```
       123
----------
    123.00
```

```
SQL> SHOW NUMWIDTH
numwidth 5
```

NUMWIDTH is still five, but that value is ignored because the NUMFORMAT setting takes precedence. A long column title can cause NUMWIDTH to be ignored:

```
SQL> SET NUMWIDTH 5
SQL> SET NUMFORMAT ""
SQL> COLUMN a HEADING "This is a long column title"
SQL> SELECT 123 a FROM dual;

This is a long column title
---------------------------
                        123
```

The column title takes precedence over NUMWIDTH when it comes to determining the width of the column.

SET PAGESIZE

The PAGESIZE setting tells SQL*Plus the number of printed lines that will fit on one page of output. You can also use this setting to completely turn off all pagination functions.

Syntax

```
SET PAGES[IZE] lines_on_page
```

Parameters

SET PAGES[IZE]
> Is the command, which may be abbreviated SET PAGES.

lines_on_page
> Is the number of lines you want SQL*Plus to print on one page. This includes detail lines, header lines, and footer lines. The default value for PAGESIZE is 14 (24 in *i*SQL*Plus).

The PAGESIZE must be set in conjunction with NEWPAGE. The sum of PAGESIZE and NEWPAGE should equal the number of lines that will physically fit on one page. SQL*Plus will print headers, detail, and footers until PAGESIZE lines have been printed. Then it will print NEWPAGE lines to advance to the next page, where the process starts again. Your page titles will drift up or down with each new page if these settings don't match the page's physical size. The exception to this is when you use SET NEWPAGE 0.

If you use SET NEWPAGE 0 to cause a formfeed to print at the beginning of each page, you should set PAGESIZE to at least one less than the physical number of lines on a page. Failure to do so may result in alternating blank pages in your printed report.

You can turn off all pagination by issuing a SET PAGESIZE 0 command. This will eliminate page titles, page footers, column titles, and any blank lines or formfeeds from the NEWPAGE setting.

SET PAUSE

The PAUSE setting pauses SQL*Plus after each page of output when displaying rows returned by a query.

Syntax

SET PAU[SE] {ON | OFF | *pause_message*}

Parameters

SET PAU[SE]
> Is the command, which may be abbreviated SET PAU.

ON
> Causes SQL*Plus to pause after each page of output. The user must press Enter to continue to the next page.

OFF
> Turns off the pause feature. This is the default setting.

pause_message
> Provides a message for SQL*Plus to display after each page when prompting the user to continue. This doesn't turn on the pause feature. You must issue a separate SET PAUSE ON command to do that.

Examples

The following example shows how the pause feature works:

```
SQL> SET PAGESIZE 10
SQL> SET PAUSE ON
SQL> SET PAUSE "Press ENTER to continue..."
SQL> SELECT view_name FROM all_views;
Press ENTER to continue...

VIEW_NAME
------------------------------
ALL_ALL_TABLES
ALL_ARGUMENTS
ALL_CATALOG
ALL_CLUSTERS
ALL_CLUSTER_HASH_EXPRESSIONS
ALL_COLL_TYPES
ALL_COL_COMMENTS
Press ENTER to continue...
```

The PAGESIZE setting controls the number of lines printed on a page. In this example, PAGESIZE was set to 10, so SQL*Plus paused after every 10 lines of output.

SET RECSEP

The RECSEP setting tells SQL*Plus whether or not to print a record separator between each record displayed as the result of a query. The default setting is not to print anything, except when a long record wraps to a second line. In that case, a blank line is printed as a record separator.

Syntax

```
SET RECSEP {WR[APPED] | EA[CH] | OFF}
```

Parameters

WR[APPED]
> Tells SQL*Plus to print a record separator only when a line wraps. This is the default setting.

EA[CH]
> Tells SQL*Plus to print a record separator after each record.

OFF
> Tells SQL*Plus not to print any record separators at all.

Examples

The default setting is WRAPPED, which is probably a safe choice because it causes a separator to print only in cases where a break between records may not be obvious, that is when each line doesn't necessarily start a new record. Here is an example of a record separator being printed:

```
SQL> COLUMN view_name FORMAT A15
SQL> SELECT view_name FROM all_views;
ALL_ALL_TABLES
ALL_ARGUMENTS
ALL_CATALOG
ALL_CLUSTERS
ALL_CLUSTER_HAS
H_EXPRESSIONS

ALL_COLL_TYPES
...
```

You can see that the record separator, a blank line by default, was printed after the ALL_CLUSTER_HASH_EXPRESSIONS view was listed. This blank line removes any ambiguity about whether H_EXPRESSIONS and ALL_CLUSTER_HAS are two separate views or if a long view name has wrapped to a second line. Setting RECSEP to OFF yields the following results:

```
SQL> SET RECSEP OFF
SQL> SELECT VIEW_NAME from all_views;
ALL_ALL_TABLES
ALL_ARGUMENTS
ALL_CATALOG
ALL_CLUSTERS
ALL_CLUSTER_HAS
H_EXPRESSIONS
ALL_COLL_TYPES
```

Do you see six views listed, or seven? How would you know?

In addition to controlling whether or not the record separator prints, you can control the character used as well. See the SET RECSEPCHAR command.

SET RECSEPCHAR

The RECSEPCHAR setting changes the record separator to something other than a line of space characters.

Syntax

```
SET RECSEPCHAR separator_char
```

Parameters

separator_char
> Is the character you want to use in the record separator line. The default value is a space.

Examples

The default record separator is a blank line. The following example shows how you can change it to be a line of asterisks instead:

```
SQL> SET RECSEPCHAR "*"
SQL> SET RECSEP EACH
SQL> SELECT view_name FROM all_views;
ALL_ALL_TABLES
***********************************************************************
ALL_ARGUMENTS
***********************************************************************
ALL_CATALOG
***********************************************************************
```

This example uses SET RECSEP EACH to cause a separator to print after each record, so you will see something. The separator character was set to an asterisk, causing you to get a full line of asterisks between each record. The length of the separator line will match the LINESIZE setting.

SET SCAN   Obsolete

The SCAN setting, an obsolete setting, allows you to choose whether SQL*Plus scans for substitution variables.

Syntax

```
SET SCAN {OFF | ON}
```

Parameters

OFF
> Disables variable substitution, and has the same effect as SET DEFINE OFF.

ON
> Enables variable substitution, and has the same effect as SET DEFINE ON.

The SET SCAN command duplicates functionality provided by the SET DEFINE command.

SET SERVEROUTPUT

The SERVEROUTPUT setting controls whether SQL*Plus prints the output generated by the DBMS_OUTPUT package from PL/SQL procedures.

Syntax

```
SET SERVEROUT[PUT] {OFF | ON}
                [SIZE buffer_size]
                [FOR[MAT] {WRA[PPED] | WOR[D_WRAPPED] | TRU[NCATED]}]
```

Parameters

SET SERVEROUT[PUT]
> Is the command, which may be abbreviated SET SERVEROUT.

OFF
> Keeps PL/SQL output from being displayed. This is the default setting.

ON
> Causes SQL*Plus to check for and display output generated by the DBMS_OUTPUT package after each PL/SQL block, procedure, or function you execute.

SIZE buffer_size
> Sets the size of the buffer, in bytes, on the server that holds the output. This value can range from 2,000 to 1,000,000, and controls the maximum amount of output that any one PL/SQL routine can produce. The default buffer size is 2,000 bytes.

WRA[PPED]
> Causes the output to be wrapped within the current line size. Line breaks will occur in the middle of words, if necessary.

WOR[D_WRAPPED]
> Causes the output to be word-wrapped within the current line size. Line breaks will occur only at word boundaries.

TRU[NCATED]
> Causes any output longer than the line size to be truncated.

Examples

By default, SQL*Plus doesn't display output from PL/SQL. The following example shows this:

```
SQL> BEGIN
  2    DBMS_OUTPUT.PUT_LINE('Hello World');
  3  END;
  4  /

PL/SQL procedure successfully completed.
```

The same block is executed again after issuing a SET SERVEROUTPUT ON command:

```
SQL> SET SERVEROUTPUT ON
SQL> BEGIN
```

```
  2   DBMS_OUTPUT.PUT_LINE('Hello World');
  3   END;
  4   /
Hello World
```

```
PL/SQL procedure successfully completed.
```

Older versions of SQL*Plus don't support the SIZE and FORMAT clauses of this command.

SET SHIFTINOUT

Not available in iSQL*Plus

The SHIFTINOUT setting controls whether shift characters are displayed as part of the output. It is usable only with IBM 3270 terminals and their equivalent, and only when SQL*Plus is displaying data in a shift-sensitive character set.

Syntax

```
SET SHIFT[INOUT] {VIS[IBLE] | INV[ISIBLE]}
```

Parameters

SET SHIFT[INOUT]
> Is the command, which may be abbreviated SET SHIFT.

VIS[IBLE]
> Enables the display of shift characters.

INV[ISIBLE]
> Keeps shift characters from being displayed. This is the default.

SET SHOWMODE

Not available in iSQL*Plus

The SHOWMODE setting controls the feedback you get when you use the SET command to change a setting.

Syntax

```
SET SHOW[MODE] {ON | OFF | BOTH}
```

Parameters

SET SHOW[MODE]
> Is the command, which may be abbreviated SET SHOW.

ON
> Turns on SHOWMODE, causing SQL*Plus to list the before and after values of each setting you change using the SET command.

OFF
> Turns off SHOWMODE and is the default setting.

BOTH
> Has the same effect as ON.

Examples

The following example shows the results of turning on SHOWMODE:

```
SQL> SET SHOWMODE ON
new: showmode BOTH
SQL> SET LINESIZE 132
old: linesize 80
new: linesize 132
SQL> SET PAGESIZE 60
old: pagesize 10
new: pagesize 60
```

With SHOWMODE on, the old and new values of each setting are displayed when they are changed.

SET SPACE

The SPACE setting, an obsolete setting, is similar to SET COLSEP. It allows you to specify the number of spaces SQL*Plus prints between columns of output.

Syntax

```
SET SPACE num_of_spaces
```

Parameters

num_of_spaces
> Is the new setting for the number of spaces you want to print between columns. The default setting is one space.

Examples

The following example shows how SET SPACE works by changing the spacing between columns from one to five spaces:

```
SQL> SELECT 'A' a, 'B' b FROM dual;

A B
- -
A B

SQL> SET SPACE 5
SQL> SELECT 'A' a, 'B' b FROM dual;

A     B
-     -
A     B
```

Issuing SET SPACE 5 has the exact same effect as issuing SET COLSEP "   " (with five spaces). In fact, the two settings are kept in sync with one another. The SET SPACE command will change the COLSEP setting to match.

SET SQLBLANKLINES

The SQLBLANKLINES setting, a new feature in Version 8.1 of SQL*Plus, allows SQL statements to contain embedded blank lines.

Syntax

```
SET SQLBLANKLINES {OFF | ON}
```

Parameters

OFF
> Turns off this feature. This is the default setting and doesn't allow a SQL statement to have embedded blank lines.

ON
> Turns on the feature and allows you to enter a SQL statement with an embedded blank line.

Examples

Pressing Enter on a blank line while typing a SQL statement into SQL*Plus normally signals the end of the statement. The statement is placed into the buffer, and you have the option of making further edits or of executing the statement. Turning SQLBLANKLINES ON allows you to put a blank line in the middle of your statement, as in the following example:

```
SQL> SET SQLBLANKLINES ON
SQL> SELECT
  2  *
  3
  4  FROM EMPLOYEE
  5
SQL>
```

This feature was added to SQL*Plus to allow it to execute Server Manager scripts, such as *catproc.sql*, without the need to go through and modify all the SQL statements in those scripts. Unlike SQL*Plus, the now defunct Server Manager utility allowed blank lines in a SQL statement.

SQLCASE

The SQLCASE setting controls whether SQL*Plus automatically uppercases or lowercases SQL statements and PL/SQL blocks as they are transmitted to the server for execution.

Syntax

```
SET SQLC[ASE] {MIXED | UPPER | LOWER}
```

Parameters

SET SQLC[ASE]
> Is the command, which may be abbreviated SET SQLC.

MIXED

    Leaves each statement just as you entered it. This is the default setting.

UPPER

    Uppercases each statement, including any quoted text literals.

LOWER

    Lowercases each statement, including any quoted text literals.

Examples

Be careful when changing this setting. Any case conversions that SQL*Plus does will affect your SQL statement keywords and any quoted text literals as well. This is seldom desirable behavior, as in the following example:

```
SQL> SET SQLCASE UPPER
SQL> SELECT * FROM dual WHERE dummy='x';

D
-
X
```

You can see the SELECT statement succeeded even though the lowercase "x" in the WHERE clause doesn't match the uppercase "X" in the dummy column.

Case conversion occurs when the statement is transmitted to the database server. The contents of the buffer always reflect what you typed.

SET SQLCONTINUE   Not available in iSQL*Plus

The SQLCONTINUE setting controls the prompt used when you continue a statement to a second line, using the SQL*Plus continuation character.

Syntax

```
SET SQLCO[NTINUE] continuation_prompt
```

Parameters

SET SQLCO[NTINUE]

    Is the command, which may be abbreviated SET SQLCO.

continuation_prompt

    Is the new continuation prompt. The default value is ">"—the greater-than character. You may optionally enclose the prompt in either single or double quotation marks.

Examples

The following example shows the effect of changing this setting:

```
SQL> SET SQLCONTINUE "Continue > "
SQL> DESCRIBE -
Continue >
```

The SQL*Plus continuation character, a dash, was used following the DESCRIBE command. The continuation prompt is used only when you use the continuation character to continue a command to a new line. It isn't used when you enter a multiline SQL statement.

SET SQLNUMBER

Not available in /SQL*Plus

The SQLNUMBER setting controls whether SQL*Plus uses the line number as a prompt when you enter a multiline SQL statement.

Syntax

```
SET SQLN[UMBER] {OFF | ON}
```

Parameters

SET SQLN[UMBER]
> Is the command, which may be abbreviated SET SQLN.

OFF
> Causes SQL*Plus to use the same prompt for all lines of a SQL statement or PL/SQL block.

ON
> Causes SQL*Plus to use the line number as the prompt for the second and subsequent lines of a SQL statement or PL/SQL block. This is the default setting.

Examples

The following example shows the difference between the ON and OFF settings:

```
SQL> SET SQLNUMBER ON
SQL> SELECT
  2  *
  3  FROM dual
  4
SQL> SET SQLNUMBER OFF
SQL> SELECT
SQL> *
SQL> FROM dual
SQL>
```

I can't imagine any reason to ever turn this setting off. Look at the first and second statements in the example. It's immediately obvious that the three lines of the first query all belong together as one statement. This is not so obvious with the second statement—you have to think about it a bit. The visual cue provided by the line numbers is missing, making you take more time to figure out what you are really looking at.

SET SQLPLUSCOMPATIBILITY

The SQLPLUSCOMPATIBILITY setting requests the behavior of a specific version of SQL*Plus. Its use is much like that of the COMPATIBILITY setting of a database instance.

Syntax

```
SET SQLPLUSCOMPAT[IBILITY] version.release[.update]
```

Parameters

SET SQLPLUSCOMPAT[IBILITY]
  Is the command, which may be abbreviated SET SQLPLUSCOMPAT.
version
  Is a version number, such as the 8 in 8.1.7.
release
  Is a release number, such as the 1 in 8.1.7.
update
  Is an update number, such as the 7 in 8.1.7.

Table A-2 describes those aspects of SQL*Plus behavior controlled by the SQLPLUSCOM-PATIBILITY setting. The threshold in the table represents the point at which the described behavior became available. The earliest acceptable value for SQLPLUSCOMPATIBILITY is 7.3.4.

Table A-2. SQLPLUSCOMPATIBILITY behaviors

Threshold	Behavior
10.1	SHOW ERRORS sorts PL/SQL error messages using some new data dictionary columns from user_errors that are available only beginning in Oracle Database 10*g*.
10.1	The CREATE, REPLACE, and SAVE options become available for the SPOOL command.
10.1	The Windows versions of SQL*Plus allows filenames enclosed in quotes to contain whitespace characters.
10.1	*glogin.sql* and *login.sql* are executed when SQL*Plus is first run and after every successful CONNECT command.
10.1	SQL*Plus stops prefacing lines from /* comments with "DOC>".
9.2	A column defined as FOLD_AFTER may be displayed at the beginning of a new line if that's necessary because of the column's width.
9.0	A slash preceded by whitespace will be treated as a terminator and will execute the statement. See the "Examples" section.
9.	NCHAR and NVARCHAR2 column lengths are consistently treated as numbers of characters. Prior to this release, whether such lengths were byte lengths or character lengths depended on the character set being used.

Examples

The following is an example from a Windows system demonstrating SQL*Plus 10.1's acceptance of filenames containing spaces:

```
SQL> SET SQLPLUSCOMPATIBILITY 9.2
SQL> SPOOL "two words"
SP2-0556: Invalid filename.
SQL> SET SQLPLUSCOMPATIBILITY 10.1
SQL> SPOOL "two words"
SQL> SPOOL OFF
SQL>
```

Similarly, beginning in 9.0, a forward slash (/) can't appear on a line by itself, even when it is preceded by spaces. Prior to 9.0, you could write a division operation that spanned multiple lines:

```
SQL> SET SQLPLUSCOMPAT 7.3.4
SQL> SELECT 1
  2          /
  3          2
  4  FROM dual;

        1/2
----------
        .5
```

However, beginning in 9.0, the forward slash in the second line of the query will trigger the as yet incompletely entered query's execution:

```
SQL> SET SQLPLUSCOMPAT 9.0
SQL> SELECT 1
  2          /
SELECT 1
       *
ERROR at line 1:
ORA-00923: FROM keyword not found where expected
```

Any non-whitespace character on the same line with the forward slash prevents premature statement execution. For example, with respect to the preceding example, had /2 been entered on line 2, the statement would not have executed.

SET SQLPREFIX

Not available in *i*SQL*Plus

The SQLPREFIX setting controls the SQL*Plus prefix character. The prefix character allows you to execute a SQL*Plus command while in the middle of entering an SQL statement (or PL/SQL block).

Syntax

SET SQLPRE[FIX] *prefix_char*

Parameters

SET SQLPRE[FIX]
> Is the command, which may be abbreviated SET SQLPRE.

prefix_char
> Is the new prefix character. The default prefix character is a pound sign. This may optionally be enclosed in single or double quotation marks.

Examples

The following example shows how the prefix character is used by using it to execute a DESCRIBE command while entering a SELECT statement:

```
SQL> SELECT
  2  #DESCRIBE EMPLOYEE
```

```
Name                           Null?    Type
------------------------------ -------- ----
EMPLOYEE_ID                    NOT NULL NUMBER
EMPLOYEE_NAME                           VARCHAR2(40
EMPLOYEE_HIRE_DATE                      DATE
EMPLOYEE_TERMINATION_DATE               DATE
EMPLOYEE_BILLING_RATE                   NUMBER

  2  employee_id, employee_name
  3  FROM employee
  4
```

This ability to execute a SQL*Plus command (and it must be a SQL*Plus command) while entering a SQL statement can come in handy when you need to refresh your memory regarding the column names in the table.

SET SQLPROMPT

Not available in *i*SQL*Plus

The SET SQLPROMPT setting changes the SQL*Plus command prompt.

Syntax

```
SET SQLP[ROMPT] prompt_text
```

Parameters

SET SQLP[ROMPT]
> Is the command, which may be abbreviated SET SQLP.

prompt_text
> Is the new prompt text. The default prompt text is "SQL> ".

Examples

The following example shows the prompt being changed from "SQL> " to "SQL*Plus> ":

```
SQL> SET SQLPROMPT "SQL*Plus> "
SQL*Plus>
```

In Chapter 14, the section "The Site and User Profiles" shows how you can set your prompt to automatically reflect the database to which you are connected.

SET SQLTERMINATOR

The SQLTERMINATOR setting controls whether SQL*Plus allows you to use a semicolon to terminate and execute a SQL statement. This setting controls the specific character used for this purpose.

Syntax

```
SET SQLT[ERMINATOR] {OFF | ON | term_char}
```

Parameters

SET SQLT[ERMINATOR]
> Is the command, which may be abbreviated SET SQLT.

OFF
> Turns off the feature that allows you to terminate and execute a SQL statement using a semicolon or other character.

ON
> Turns on this feature and resets the terminator character to the default value of a semicolon.

term_char
> Is the character you want to use as a statement terminator. This may be optionally enclosed in single or double quotation marks.

Examples

The following example changes the terminator character to a percent sign and uses it to terminate and execute a SELECT statement:

```
SQL> SET SQLTERMINATOR "%"
SQL> SELECT employee_name FROM employee%

EMPLOYEE_NAME
--------------------------------------
Pavlo Chubynsky
Ivan Mazepa
Taras Shevchenko
...
```

SET SUFFIX   Not available in *i*SQL*Plus

The SUFFIX setting controls the default extension used for command files.

Syntax

```
SET SUF[FIX] extension
```

Paremeters

SET SUF[FIX]
> Is the command, which may be abbreviated SET SUF.

extension
> Is the default extension to use when referring to SQL files. The default value for this setting is *sql*.

This setting is used by commands such as START, @, SAVE, and others that refer to SQL files. It doesn't apply to files created with the SPOOL command.

SET TAB

The TAB setting controls whether SQL*Plus uses tab characters when generating whitespace in terminal output. This setting is a throwback to the days when terminal connections ran at slow data rates (e.g., 1200 bits per second).

Syntax

```
SET TAB {OFF | ON}
```

Parameters

OFF

Forces SQL*Plus to use space characters for all whitespace.

ON

Is the default setting, and allows SQL*Plus to insert tabs into the output rather than displaying a large number of space characters.

SET TERMOUT

The TERMOUT setting controls whether SQL*Plus displays output generated by SQL statements, PL/SQL blocks, and SQL*Plus commands. This setting applies only when SQL*Plus is executing a script file. SQL*Plus displays output from commands entered interactively.

Syntax

```
SET TERM[OUT] {OFF | ON}
```

Parameters

SET TERM[OUT]

Is the command, which may be abbreviated SET TERM.

OFF

Turns off terminal output.

ON

Turns on terminal output. This is the default setting.

Terminal output is often turned off while a command file is running to keep the user's screen from becoming cluttered with query output and feedback messages.

SET TIME

The TIME setting controls whether SQL*Plus displays the current time with each command prompt.

SET TIMING

Syntax

SET TI[ME] {OFF | ON}

Parameters

SET TI[ME]
> Is the command, which may be abbreviated SET TI.

OFF
> Keeps the time from being displayed with the prompt. This is the default setting.

ON
> Causes the time to be displayed as part of each prompt.

Examples

The following example shows the effect of issuing a SET TIME ON command:

```
SQL> SET TIME ON
22:44:41 SQL>
```

SET TIMING

The TIMING setting controls whether or not SQL*Plus displays the elapsed time for each SQL statement or PL/SQL block you execute.

Syntax

SET TIMI[NG] {OFF | ON}

Parameters

SET TIMI[NG]
> Is the command, which may be abbreviated SET TIMI.

OFF
> Turns off the timing feature. This is the default setting.

ON
> Enables the display of elapsed execution time for SQL statements and PL/SQL blocks.

See Chapter 12 for examples of this command.

SET TRIMOUT   Not available in iSQL*Plus

The TRIMOUT setting controls whether SQL*Plus displays any trailing spaces that may occur at the end of a line. The default setting is ON, which causes SQL*Plus to display only up to the last nonblank character on a line.

Syntax

```
SET TRIM[OUT] {ON | OFF}
```

Parameters

SET TRIM[OUT]
> Is the command, which may be abbreviated SET TRIM.

ON
> Causes SQL*Plus to trim any trailing spaces from each line before it's displayed. This is the default setting.

OFF
> Causes SQL*Plus to display all characters on a line, even the trailing spaces.

The default setting of ON usually works well when displaying data on a terminal, so there's rarely a reason to turn this setting off. TRIMOUT has no effect on spooled output. If you are spooling output to a file, the TRIMSPOOL setting controls whether trailing spaces are spooled as well.

SET TRIMSPOOL   Not available in iSQL*Plus

The TRIMSPOOL setting controls whether SQL*Plus writes trailing spaces when spooling data to a file. The default setting is OFF, which causes SQL*Plus to write each line to the spool file in its entirety, trailing spaces and all.

Syntax

```
SET TRIMS[POOL] {ON | OFF}
```

Parameters

SET TRIMS[POOL]
> Is the command, which may be abbreviated SET TRIMS.

ON
> Causes SQL*Plus to trim any trailing spaces from each line before it is written to the spool file.

OFF
> Causes SQL*Plus to write all characters of a line to the spool file, even the trailing spaces. This is the default setting.

If you are spooling data to a file to load it into another program, you may want to leave TRIMSPOOL ON. Otherwise, the program reading the spool file might return errors because the records are shorter than expected.

SET TRUNCATE   Obsolete

The obselete TRUNCATE setting gives you the same choice as SET WRAP. You can choose whether to truncate lines longer than the LINESIZE setting.

Syntax

```
SET TRU[NCATE] {OFF | ON}
```

Parameters

SET TRU[NCATE]
> Is the command, which may be abbreviated SET TRU.

OFF
> Is the default setting, and allows long lines to be wrapped.

ON
> Causes long lines of output to be truncated to match the current LINESIZE setting.

Examples

TRUNCATE and WRAP affect the same internal setting. Turning one on results in the other being turned off, and vice versa:

```
SQL> SHOW WRAP
wrap : lines will be wrapped
SQL> SET TRUNCATE ON
SQL> SHOW WRAP
wrap : lines will be truncated
```

 Although you can issue the SHOW WRAP command to see the current value of the WRAP setting, you can't issue SHOW TRUNCATE. The SHOW command doesn't recognize TRUNCATE as a valid SQL*Plus setting.

When you select data longer than the LINESIZE and the WRAP setting is off, some versions of SQL*Plus display a warning message telling you that your rows may be truncated.

SET UNDERLINE

The SET UNDERLINE setting controls the character used to underline column headings. You can also control whether column headings are underlined at all.

Syntax

```
SET UND[ERLINE] {underline_char | {ON | OFF}}
```

Parameters

SET UND[ERLINE]
> Is the command, which may be abbreviated SET UND.

underline_char
> Is the character you want to use when underlining column headings. By default, a dash character (-) is used.

ON

Causes column headings to be underlined and resets the underline character back to the dash.

OFF

Keeps column headings from being underlined.

Examples

The following example shows the underline character being changed to an asterisk:

```
SQL> SET UNDERLINE *
SQL> SELECT USER FROM dual;

USER
*****************************
JEFF
```

You can use SET UNDERLINE to turn off underlining:

```
SQL> SET UNDERLINE OFF
SQL> SELECT USER FROM dual;

USER
JEFF
```

One reason you might turn underlining off would be if you wanted some columns to print without any headings at all. First, you would turn UNDERLINE off. Then you would define column headings for all columns with the COLUMN command. Those headings you did want to print would need to include the underlines as part of the heading definition. Other headings would be defined as empty strings.

SET VERIFY

The VERIFY setting controls whether or not SQL*Plus displays before and after images of each line that contains a substitution variable.

Syntax

```
SET VER[IFY] {OFF | ON}
```

Parameters

SET VER[IFY]

Is the command, which may be abbreviated SET VER.

OFF

Turns off verification.

ON

Turns on verification. Lines containing substitution variables will be displayed before and after the substitution occurs. This is the default setting.

Examples

Verification is done only on lines that are part of a SQL statement or a PL/SQL block. When substitution occurs in a SQL*Plus command, before and after images are never displayed. The following example shows what verification looks like:

```
SQL> DEFINE dummy_char = 'X'
SQL> SELECT * FROM dual
  2    WHERE dummy = '&&dummy_char';
old   2:  where dummy = '&&dummy_char'
new   2:  where dummy = 'X'

D
-
X
```

Notice that line 2, which contained the reference to the &&dummy_char substitution variable, was displayed before and after the reference to the variable was replaced by its value. If you don't like this display, you can turn it off with SET VERIFY OFF.

SET WRAP

The WRAP setting controls how SQL*Plus prints lines that contain more characters than the current LINESIZE setting allows. With WRAP ON, long lines are wrapped around and continued on as many physical lines as necessary. With WRAP OFF, lines are truncated to match the LINESIZE setting.

Syntax

```
SET WRA[P] {ON | OFF}
```

Parameters

SET WRA[P]
> Is the command, which may be abbreviated SET WRA.

ON
> Causes long lines to be wrapped around to two or more physical lines in order to print and still fit within the LINESIZE setting.

OFF
> Causes long records to be truncated to the current LINESIZE setting.

Examples

The following example shows the results of issuing the same SELECT statement, once with WRAP turned on and once with it turned off:

```
SQL> SET WRAP ON
SQL> SELECT * FROM ALL_VIEWS WHERE VIEW_NAME = 'ALL_VIEWS';

OWNER                          VIEW_NAME                      TEXT_LENGTH
------------------------------ ------------------------------ -----------
TEXT
----------------------------------------------------------------------------
```

```
TYPE_TEXT_LENGTH
----------------
TYPE_TEXT
-----------------------------------------------------------------------------
OID_TEXT_LENGTH
---------------
OID_TEXT
-----------------------------------------------------------------------------
VIEW_TYPE_OWNER                    VIEW_TYPE
------------------------------     ------------------------------
SYS                                ALL_VIEWS                              821
select u.name, o.name, v.textlength, v.text, t.typetextlength, t.typetext,


SQL> SET WRAP OFF
SQL> /
rows will be truncated

rows will be truncated

rows will be truncated

rows will be truncated

rows will be truncated

rows will be truncated


OWNER                              VIEW_NAME                     TEXT_LENGTH TEXT
------------------------------     -----------------------------  ----------- ----
SYS                                ALL_VIEWS                              821 select
```

SQL*Plus displays several warning messages telling you that the rows you are about to see displayed may have been truncated.

SHOW

The SHOW command looks at the state of your SQL*Plus environment. You can use it to display the current value of any setting controlled by the SET command. (TRUNCATE is the one exception.) SHOW can look at page titles, page footers, etc.

Syntax

```
SHO[W] {setting
       ALL      |
       BTI[TLE] |
       ERR[ORS] [{FUNCTION | PROCEDURE | PACKAGE | PACKAGE BODY |
                  TRIGGER | TYPE | TYPE BODY | VIEW} [owner.]object_name] |
       LNO |
       PARAMETER[S] [parameter_name] |
       PNO |
```

```
        REL[EASE] |
        REPF[OOTER] |
        REPH[EADER] |
        SGA |
        SPOO[L] |
        SQLCODE |
        TTI[TLE] |
        USER}
```

Parameters

SHO[W]
> Is the command, which may be abbreviated SHO.

setting
> Is any one of the settings you can set using the SET command.

ALL
> Shows everything, except for errors and the System Global Area (SGA).

BTI[TLE]
> Displays the current page footer.

ERR[ORS]
> Displays an error listing for a stored object. The command SHOW ERRORS causes the error listing for the most recently created object to be displayed. You can get the error listing for a specific object by specifying the object type (function, procedure, and so forth) and the object name.

FUNCTION | PROCEDURE | PACKAGE | PACKAGE BODY | TRIGGER | TYPE | TYPE BODY | VIEW
> Used with SHOW ERRORS to specify the object type of interest. This is necessary only if you are specifying the name of the object.

[owner.]object_name
> Used with SHOW ERRORS to name the object for which you want to display an error listing.

LNO
> Displays the current line number.

PARAMETER[S] *[parameter_name]*
> Displays the current value of one or more initialization parameters.

PNO
> Displays the current page number.

REL[EASE]
> Displays the release number (the version) of the Oracle database to which you are connected.

REPF[OOTER]
> Displays the current report footer.

REPH[EADER]
> Displays the current report header.

SGA
> Displays information about the current state of the System Global Area.

SPOO[L]
>   Tells you whether or not output is currently being spooled to a file.

SQLCODE
>   Displays the SQL code returned by the most recent SQL statement.

TTI[TLE]
>   Displays the current page title.

USER
>   Displays the current username.

Examples

The following few examples demonstrate how the SHOW command displays the value of
one item, such as a setting or a page title:

```
SQL> SHOW LINESIZE
linesize 80
SQL> SHOW USER
USER is "JEFF"
SQL> SHOW TTITLE
ttitle OFF and is the 1st few characters of the next SELECT statement
```

The ALL option may be used to display the values of all settings at once:

```
SQL> SHOW ALL
appinfo is ON and set to "SQL*Plus"
arraysize 15
autocommit OFF
autoprint OFF
autotrace OFF
shiftinout INVISIBLE
blockterminator "." (hex 2e)
...
```

When you use SHOW ALL, the settings are displayed in alphabetical order.

The SHOW ERRORS command has more parameters than the other options, so it's more
complex. SHOW ERRORS is used to display error listings for stored procedures, stored
functions, packages, triggers, and other such objects. Typically, you first issue a CREATE
statement, and then, if errors are reported, you follow that with a SHOW ERRORS
command. The following example uses SHOW ERRORS to display an error listing for the
most recent creation attempt:

```
SQL> CREATE OR REPLACE TRIGGER employee_set_key
  2  BEFORE INSERT ON employee
  3  FOR EACH ROW
  4  BEGIN
  5    :new.employee_id := employee_seq.nextval;
  6  END;
  7  /

Warning: Trigger created with compilation errors.

SQL> SHOW ERRORS
Errors for TRIGGER EMPLOYEE_SET_KEY:
```

```
LINE/COL
------------------------------------------------------------------
ERROR
------------------------------------------------------------------
2/3
PL/SQL: Statement ignored

2/23
PLS-00201: identifier 'EMPLOYEE_SEQ.NEXTVAL' must be declared

SQL>
```

You can show errors for a specific object by telling SQL*Plus the object type and the object name:

```
SQL> CREATE OR REPLACE PROCEDURE JEFF.DISABLE_TRIGGER AS
  2  BEGIN
  3    ALTER TABLE EMPLOYEE DISABLE TRIGGER EMPLOYEE_SET_KEY;
  4  END;
  5  /

Warning: Procedure created with compilation errors.

SQL> SHOW ERRORS PROCEDURE JEFF.DISABLE_TRIGGER
Errors for PROCEDURE JEFF.DISABLE_TRIGGER:

LINE/COL
--------------------------------------------------------------------------
ERROR
--------------------------------------------------------------------------
3/3
PLS-00103: Encountered the symbol "ALTER" when expecting one of the following:

    begin declare exit for goto if loop mod null pragma raise
    return select update while <an identifier>
    <a double-quoted delimited-identifier> <a bind variable> <<
    close current delete fetch lock insert open rollback
    savepoint set sql commit <a single-quoted SQL string>
```

The error listings remain even after you end the session in which you tried to create the object. You can come back later, display the errors, and pick up where you left off. But when you do that, you must name the object you are working with.

SHUTDOWN

The SHUTDOWN command closes a database and stops an Oracle instance. Chapter 10 discusses this command. To use SHUTDOWN, you must be connected as SYSDBA, SYSOPER, or INTERNAL.

Syntax

```
SHUTDOWN [NORMAL | IMMEDIATE | TRANSACTIONAL [LOCAL] | ABORT]
```

Parameters

NORMAL

> Causes a normal shutdown to take place. New users are blocked from connecting. The database remains open until all currently connected users voluntarily disconnect. When the last user disconnects, the database files are closed, the database is dismounted, and the instance is stopped.

IMMEDIATE

> Causes users to be summarily disconnected when their current SQL statement completes execution. Users not in the middle of executing a statement are disconnected immediately. As each remaining user's currently executing SQL statement completes, she is forcibly disconnected from the database. Any open transactions are rolled back, the database files are closed, the database is dismounted, and the instance is stopped.

TRANSACTIONAL

> A compromise between NORMAL and IMMEDIATE. Users are allowed to finish their current transactions. As each user completes his current transaction, he is forcibly disconnected. When the last user disconnects, the database is closed and dismounted, and the instance is stopped.

[LOCAL]

> A TRANSACTIONAL LOCAL shutdown waits only for local transactions to finish, and then aborts any distributed transactions in progress.

ABORT

> Is tantamount to pulling the plug on the server. All background processes are immediately aborted. Users are summarily disconnected. No rollback is done on open transactions, and dirty buffers aren't written back to the disk. Crash recovery occurs the next time you start the database. This is the only shutdown option that doesn't leave the database files in a consistent state.

SPOOL   Not available in *i*SQL*Plus

The SPOOL command writes output to a text file. You must use this if you are going to print a report. The only way to print a report is to spool it to a file, then print that file. See Chapter 5 for an example of SPOOL being used to generate a report file. SPOOL may be used to generate a new file of SQL statements to be executed. Chapter 11 shows you how to take advantage of that powerful technique.

Syntax

SP[OOL] *file_name* [*option*] | OFF | OUT

option ::= {CRE[ATE] | REP[LACE] | APP[END]}

Parameters

SP[OOL]
> Is the command, which may be abbreviated SP.

file_name
> Is the name of the file to which you want to write the report. The default extension is usually *.lst*, or sometimes *.lis*, and it's an operating system-specific value.

OFF
> Turns off spooling. You must have turned spooling on before you can turn it off.

OUT
> Turns off spooling and prints the file on the default printer. This option isn't available in the Windows versions of SQL*Plus.

CREATE
> Requires that a new file be created. If the named file exists, then the SPOOL command aborts with an error.

REPLACE
> Replaces an existing file or creates an entirely new file, whichever applies. This represents the default behavior.

APPEND
> Adds subsequent output to the end of an existing spool file.

START

The START command functions the same way as the @ command and is used to execute a SQL*Plus script file. From *iSQL*Plus, you can only run scripts via *http* or *ftp*.

Syntax

STA[RT] {*script_file* | *url*} [*argument* [*argument* . . .]]

Paremeters

STA[RT]
> Is the command, which may be abbreviated STA.

script_file
> Is the name of the file you want to execute and may include the path and the extension. The default extension is *sql*. If you don't specify a path, SQL*Plus will look for the file first in the current working directory and then search each directory listed in the SQLPATH environment variable. See Chapter 14 for information about customizing the search path.

url

> Is an *http* or *ftp* URL pointing to a script that you wish to execute. Oracle9*i* Database Release 1 brought this option to SQL*Plus on Windows; Oracle9*i* Database Release 2 brought it to SQL*Plus on all platforms.

argument

> Is an argument you wish to pass to the script. You may pass as many arguments as you like. Arguments must be separated from each other by at least one space. Arguments may be enclosed in quotation marks, and should be if they contain spaces. Single or double quotation marks may be used at your discretion. Your script may reference the first argument as &1, the second as &2, etc.

STARTUP

The STARTUP command starts an Oracle instance and opens a database. Chapter 10 discusses this command. To use STARTUP, you must be connected as SYSDBA, SYSOPER, or INTERNAL.

Syntax

```
STARTUP {options | upgrade_options}

options ::= [FORCE] [RESTRICT]
            [PFILE= parameter_filename]
            [QUIET] [mount]

mount ::= { MOUNT [database_name]
          | OPEN [ open_options]
          | NOMOUNT}

open_options ::= {READ {ONLY | WRITE [RECOVER]}
                | RECOVER}

upgrade_options ::= [PFILE=parameter_filename]
                    {UPGRADE | DOWNGRADE}
                    [QUIET]
```

Parameters

FORCE

> Forces the instance to start. If the instance is currently running, then FORCE will cause the equivalent of a SHUTDOWN ABORT to be done first; then the instance will be restarted.

RESTRICT

> Opens the database in restricted session mode. Only users with the RESTRICTED SESSION system privilege will be allowed to connect.

PFILE=*parameter_filename*

> Tells SQL*Plus to use the specified parameter file (initialization file) when starting the instance. You may specify a path with the filename.

STORE

 SQL*Plus, not the Oracle instance, reads the parameter file. The path to the parameter file must be relative to the machine running SQL*Plus. This matters, for example, if you are using SQL*Plus on a PC and connecting remotely to an instance on a server to start it.

QUIET
Prevents SQL*Plus from displaying details about the allocation of memory for the instance's SGA.

MOUNT [*database_name*]
Causes the database to be mounted but not opened. The instance will be started, and the control file will be opened, but none of the other database files will be opened. The MOUNT stage is the one between NOMOUNT and OPEN. You may optionally specify a non-default name for the database. Otherwise, the database name is derived from the DB_NAME initialization parameter.

OPEN
Causes the database to be mounted, then opened for normal operation.

NOMOUNT
Starts the instance without opening the control file, nor any other database files.

READ ONLY
Opens the database for reading but disallows any writes.

READ WRITE
Opens the database for normal read/write operation. This is the default.

RECOVER *or* READ WRITE RECOVER
Tells Oracle to perform media recovery if necessary. If no recovery is necessary, the database will open in the usual way. If recovery is necessary, it will proceed automatically. You will be prompted for any needed log files that can't be found. A failed recovery leaves the database mounted but not opened.

UPGRADE
Opens the database in a mode that allows you to run scripts (supplied by Oracle) to upgrade the database to a newer version. See the *Oracle Database Upgrade Guide* (Oracle Corporation) before using this option.

DOWNGRADE
Similar to UPGRADE but enables database downgrade scripts to be run.

STORE   Not available in *i*SQL*Plus

STORE generates a file of SET commands based on the current state of those settings. This file can be used after those settings have been changed to reset everything back to a known state.

Syntax

```
STORE SET filename [CRE[ATE] | REP[LACE] | APP[END]]
```

Parameters

SET

Is an option indicating what you want to store. Currently, the only option available is SET.

filename

Is the name of the file, including the path and extension, to which you want to write the SET commands.

CRE[ATE]

Causes the command to fail if the file already exists.

REP[LACE]

Causes SQL*Plus to overwrite any existing file with the same name.

APP[END]

Causes the SET commands to be appended to an existing file.

TIMING

The TIMING command starts, stops, or displays the value of a timer. Timers let you measure elapsed time and are described in Chapter 12.

Syntax

```
TIMI[NG] [START [timer_name] | SHOW | STOP]
```

Parameters

TIMI[NG]

Is the command, which may be abbreviated TIMI.

START [timer_name]

Starts a new timer and optionally gives it the name you provide.

SHOW

Shows the current value of the most recently started timer.

STOP

Stops the most recently started timer, shows its current value, then deletes it.

TTITLE

Use the TTITLE command to define page titles for a report. Chapter 5 discusses TTITLE and provides several examples. Also see the BTITLE command. TTITLE and BTITLE work the same way.

Syntax

```
TTITLE [OFF | ON] | option [option...]

option ::=  [COL x |
             S[KIP] x |
             TAB x |
             LE[FT] |
             CE[NTER] |
             R[IGHT] |
             BOLD |
             FOR[MAT] format_spec |
             text |
             variable]
```

Parameters

TTI[TLE]

Is the command, which may be abbreviated TTI. Issuing the TTITLE command with no parameters causes SQL*Plus to display the current top title setting.

OFF

Turns the page title off but doesn't erase its definition. You can turn it back on with ON.

ON

Turns on printing of page titles. The default title, if you don't specify another, is the current date, the page number, and all or part of the SELECT statement.

COL x

Causes any title text following this parameter to print at the specified column position.

S[KIP] x

May be abbreviated S. Inserts the specified number of line breaks before printing any subsequent title text.

TAB x

TAB is similar to COL, but moves you the specified number of columns relative to the current position. Negative numbers move you backward. TAB has nothing to do with tab characters.

LE[FT]

May be abbreviated LE. Causes subsequent title text to be printed beginning at the leftmost column of the current title line.

CE[NTER]

May be abbreviated CE. Causes subsequent title text to be centered within the current line. The LINESIZE setting controls the line width.

R[IGHT]

May be abbreviated R. Causes subsequent title text to be printed flush right. The LINESIZE setting controls where SQL*Plus thinks the right end of the line is.

BOLD

Makes your title "bold" by printing it three times. Only title text following the BOLD command is repeated on each line. There is no NOBOLD parameter.

FOR[MAT]

> May be abbreviated FOR. Allows you to control how subsequent numeric data in the title is displayed.

format_spec

> Is a string that specifies the display format to use for subsequent numeric data in the title. The format elements you can use here are the same as for the COLUMN command, and are described in Appendix B. Specifying a character format, such as A20, is possible but that has no effect on subsequent character strings.

text

> Is any text you want to have in the title. To be safe, you should enclose this in quotes, but you need not as long as your title text doesn't include any keywords like BOLD or TAB that have meaning to TTITLE. Single or double quotation marks may be used. If you need to include a quotation mark as part of your text, use two quote characters back to back.

variable

> May be one of the system variables maintained by SQL*Plus and listed in Table A-1 (see the BTITLE command).

When using TTITLE, you should start off with one of the keywords, such as LEFT, RIGHT, or CENTER. Otherwise, if the first parameter after the command is only text, SQL*Plus will assume you have used an obsolete syntax for this command and you won't get the results you want.

UNDEFINE

UNDEFINE, the opposite of DEFINE, erases a user variable definition. UNDEFINE is discussed in Chapter 8.

Syntax

UNDEF[INE] *variable_name* [*variable_name*...]

Parameters

UNDEF[INE]

> Is the command, which may be abbreviated UNDEF.

variable_name

> Is the name of a substitution variable to delete. You can delete several variables with one command by listing them out separated by spaces.

VARIABLE

The VARIABLE command declares bind variables. Bind variables are discussed in Chapter 7. They are real variables that can be used within a PL/SQL block or SQL statement.

Syntax

VAR[IABLE] *variable_name data_type*

Parameters

VAR[IABLE]
>   Is the command, which may be abbreviated VAR.

variable_name
>   Is whatever name you want to give the variable. A variable name must start with a letter, but after that the name may contain any combination of letters, digits, underscores, pound signs, and dollar signs. Thirty characters is the maximum length for a variable name.

data_type
>   Is the datatype of the variable. The following datatypes are allowed:

>   NUMBER
>>   Results in a floating-point number and is the same as a NUMBER variable in PL/SQL or a NUMBER column in a table. Unlike PL/SQL, SQL*Plus doesn't let you specify a length or a precision, so a declaration like NUMBER (9,2) wouldn't be allowed.

>   BINARY_FLOAT
>>   Results in a BINARY_FLOAT value. Not available before Oracle9*i* Database.

>   BINARY_DOUBLE
>>   Results in a BINARY_DOUBLE value. Not available before Oracle9*i* Database.

>   CHAR [(*length*)]
>>   Results in a fixed-length character string. *length* is optional. If it is omitted, you get a one-character string.

>   NCHAR [(*length*)]
>>   Results in a fixed-length character string in the national character set. *Length* is optional. If it is omitted, you get a one-character string.

>   VARCHAR2 (*length*)
>>   Results in a variable-length character string.

>   NVARCHAR2 (*length*)
>>   Results in a variable-length character string using the national language character set.

>   CLOB
>>   Results in a character large object (CLOB) variable.

>   NCLOB
>>   Results in a CLOB variable using the national language character set.

>   REFCURSOR
>>   Gives you a cursor variable you can use to return the results of a SQL query from PL/SQL to SQL*Plus.

WHENEVER

The WHENEVER command controls the behavior of SQL*Plus when an operating system or SQL error occurs and is discussed in Chapter 11. You can choose between having

SQL*Plus exit immediately or continue on whenever an error occurs. You can choose whether to automatically COMMIT or ROLLBACK in the event of an error. If you decide to abort in the event of an error, you can pass a value back to the operating system. If you are calling SQL*Plus from an operating system script, you can use this return value to determine that script's next course of action.

 When used from *i*SQL*Plus, WHENEVER performs the action you specify (e.g., COMMIT or ROLLBACK) and returns you to the *i*SQL*Plus input area. You aren't disconnected from your database session.

Syntax

```
WHENEVER {OSERROR | SQLERROR}
        {EXIT [SUCCESS | FAILURE | value | :bind_variable | sub_variable]
            [COMMIT | ROLLBACK]
        | CONTINUE [COMMIT | ROLLBACK | NONE]}
```

Parameters

WHENEVER OSERROR
> Use this command form to tell SQL*Plus what to do in case an operating system error occurs.

WHENEVER SQLERROR
> Use this command form to tell SQL*Plus what to do in case an error is returned from a SQL statement or PL/SQL block.

EXIT SUCCESS
> Exit with a success status. The exact value of the success status is operating-system-dependent but is often 0. This is the default setting and it applies if the EXIT keyword is used without specifying any return value.

EXIT FAILURE
> Exit with a failure status. The value of the failure status is operating-system-dependent but is often 1.

EXIT *value*
> Exit and return the value specified as the status.

EXIT :*bind_variable*
> Exit and return the value of the specified bind variable as the status.

EXIT *sub_variable*
> Exit and return the contents of the specified substitution variable as the status.

CONTINUE
> Don't exit if an error occurs. This is the default behavior when you first start SQL*Plus.

COMMIT
> This keyword may be used in conjunction with EXIT and CONTINUE. It causes SQL*Plus to COMMIT the current transaction automatically when an error occurs. This is the default behavior when you use the EXIT keyword.

ROLLBACK

May be used in conjunction with EXIT and CONTINUE and causes SQL*Plus to roll back the current transaction when an error occurs.

NONE

May be used only in conjunction with CONTINUE, and causes SQL*Plus neither to COMMIT nor ROLLBACK when an error occurs. This is the default behavior when you use the CONTINUE keyword.

SQL*Plus Format Elements

Several SQL*Plus commands control data formats using what is called a *format specification*. A format specification is a string of characters that tells SQL*Plus exactly how to format a number, date, or text string when it is displayed. The most notable of these commands is the COLUMN command, which is used to format columns of output from a SELECT query. Other commands exist as well. The complete list of SQL*Plus commands that accept format specification strings is shown here:

ACCEPT
>   Prompts the user to enter a value from the keyboard.

COLUMN
>   Controls various aspects of the way a column of data is displayed.

SET NUMBER
>   Defines the default display format for numbers.

TTITTE, BTITLE, REPHEADER, REPFOOTER
>   Allow number format specifications to control the way numbers are formatted in page headers, page footers, report headers, and report footers.

There are three different broad types of values SQL*Plus can format: numbers, character strings, and dates. Not all commands can handle each type. With most commands, you can specify only number and date formats. The COLUMN command is a good example. The ACCEPT command is the only one that allows you to specify a date format string.

Format specification strings are made up of special characters that have meaning to SQL*Plus in the context of formatting a value for display. Numeric format strings, for example, tend to have many 0s, 9s, decimal points, and dollar signs. Date format strings tend to include things like MM, DD, YYYY, etc. Character string formats are the simplest of all because you have only one thing you can influence: length.

Formatting Numbers

SQL*Plus offers the most options when it comes to formatting numbers. Numeric format strings may contain any of the elements shown in Table B-1.

Table B-1. Numeric format elements

Format element	Function
$	Causes a number to be displayed with a leading dollar sign.
,	Places a comma in the output.
.	Marks the location of the decimal point and makes it a period.
B	Forces zero values to be displayed as blanks.
MI	Used at the end of a format string to cause a trailing negative sign to be displayed for negative values.
S	May be used at the beginning or end of a format string, and causes a sign to be displayed. The plus (+) sign is used to mark positive numbers, and the minus (-) sign marks negative numbers. When you use S, a sign is always displayed.
PR	Causes negative values to be displayed within angle brackets. For example, -123.99 is displayed as <123.99>. Positive values are displayed with one leading and one trailing space in place of the angle brackets.
D	Marks the location of the decimal point. The specific character used is derived from your NLS settings.
G	Places a group separator (usually a comma) in the output. The specific character used is derived from your NLS settings.
C	Marks the place where you want the ISO currency indicator to appear. For US dollars, this is USD.
L	Marks the place where you want the local currency indicator to appear. For US dollars, this is the dollar sign character. You can't use L and C in the same format specification.
V	Used to display scaled values. The number of digits to the right of the V indicates how many places to the right the decimal point is shifted before the number is displayed.
EEEE	Causes SQL*Plus to use scientific notation to display a value. You must use exactly four Es, and they must appear at the right end of the format string.
RN	Allows you to display a number using Roman numerals. This is the only numeric format element where case makes a difference. An uppercase "RN" yields uppercase Roman numerals, while a lowercase "rn" yields Roman numerals in lowercase. Numbers displayed as Roman numerals must be integers, and must be between 1 and 3,999, inclusive.
DATE	Causes SQL*Plus to assume that the number represents a Julian date and to display it in MM/DD/YY format.
FM	This prefix removes any leading or trailing blanks from the return value.
TM	This prefix returns a number using the minimum number of characters. TM stands for text minimum. Follow TM with one 9 if you want a regular, decimal notation (the default). Follow TM with one E if you want scientific notation to be used.
U	Results in a Euro symbol being placed at the specified location. The NLS_DUAL_CURRENCY parameter actually controls the character returned by this format element.
X	Returns a number in hexadecimal value. You can precede this element with 0s to return leading zeros, or with FM to trim leading and trailing blanks. X can't be used in combination with any other numeric format elements.

Table B-1. Numeric format elements (continued)

Format element	Function
0	A 0 is used to mark the spot in the result where you want to begin displaying leading zeros. It replaces one of the 9s. The most common location for a 0 is at the extreme left of the format string, but you can place it elsewhere.
9	9s are used to control the number of significant digits to be displayed.

To format a numeric column or other number, simply string together the format elements that yield the result you want. Except for the RN element, none of the numeric format elements are case-sensitive. Table B-2 contains a number of examples showing you how these format elements work.

Table B-2. Numeric format examples

Value	Format	Result	Comments
123	9999	123	A basic number
1234.01	9,999.99	1,234.01	Comma and decimal point
23456	$999,999.99	$23,456.00	Dollar value
1	0999	0001	Leading zeros
1	99099	001	Leading zeros only within the rightmost three digits
23456	9,999.99	########	Overflow condition
0	099B		Display zeros as blanks
1	099B	001	Leading zeros displayed, even with B, when the value is nonzero
−1000.01	9,999.99mi	1,000.01−	Trailing minus sign
1000.01	9,999.99mi	1,000.01	Trailing space
−1001	S9,999	−1,001	Leading sign
−1001	9,999PR	<1,001>	Negative values in angle brackets
1001	9,999PR	1,001	Spaces instead of angle brackets
1001	9.999EEEE	−1.001E+03	Scientific notation
1995	RN	MCMXCV	Roman numerals, uppercase
1988	rn	mcmlxxxviii	Roman numerals, lowercase
1	date	01/01/12	Julian date, day one

The ACCEPT command is unique in that it uses a format string to constrain the user's input. However, in doing so, and especially in older releases of SQL*Plus, it takes a loose interpretation of the format elements shown in Table B-1. You can see several examples of ACCEPT's use in Chapter 11. For the most part, though, only the 9, 0, and period are useful with ACCEPT.

SQL*Plus always allows for a sign somewhere when you display a number. The default is for the sign to be positioned to the left of the number, and the sign is displayed when the number is negative. Positive numbers have a blank space in the leftmost position. Because space is made for a sign character, number columns are typically one space wider than your format specification seems to account for. That's the default behavior. Things change when you use S, MI, or PR. With S, you always get a sign. With MI, you get a trailing sign, or a trailing blank for positive numbers. PR gives you angle brackets or spaces in place of them.

Formatting Character Strings

SQL*Plus offers only one format element when it comes to character strings: A. A is always followed by a number specifying the column width in characters. Character strings shorter than the column width are displayed as left-justified within the column. Character strings that exceed the column width are wrapped or truncated based on the option specified in the COLUMN command. The following example shows a text column formatted wide enough to display the entire character string:

```
SQL> COLUMN a FORMAT A40
SQL> SELECT 'An apple a day keeps the doctor away.' A
  2    FROM dual;

A
----------------------------------------
An apple a day keeps the doctor away.
```

You can format the column so it is 18 characters wide, which results in the text being wrapped within that space:

```
SQL> COLUMN a FORMAT A18
SQL> SELECT 'An apple a day keeps the doctor away.' A
  2    FROM dual;

A
------------------
An apple a day kee
ps the doctor away
.
```

By default, SQL*Plus wraps the text right in the middle of a word if necessary. You can use the WORD_WRAPPED option of the COLUMN command to wrap text only at word boundaries:

```
SQL> COLUMN a FORMAT A18 WORD_WRAPPED
SQL> SELECT 'An apple a day keeps the doctor away.' A
  2    FROM dual;
```

```
A
------------------
An apple a day
keeps the doctor
away.
```

You also have the ability to truncate text at the column boundary:

```
SQL> COLUMN a FORMAT A18 TRUNCATE
SQL> SELECT 'An apple a day keeps the doctor away.' A
  2    FROM dual;

A
------------------
An apple a day kee
```

When used with the ACCEPT command, a character format defines the maximum number of characters SQL*Plus will accept from the user:

```
SQL> ACCEPT some_text CHAR FORMAT A10
thisthatthen
"thisthatthen" does not match input format "A10"

SQL>
```

Although the character format used with ACCEPT specifies a maximum length, it doesn't specify a minimum length. You can enter fewer characters than the format calls for, even to the point of entering nothing at all.

Formatting Dates

SQL*Plus doesn't format dates at all. If you are selecting a date column from the database, you must use Oracle's built-in TO_CHAR function to convert the date to a character string, formatting it the way you want it. As far as SQL*Plus is concerned, that makes it another character column. Table B-3 shows the date format elements that can be used with the TO_CHAR function.

Table B-3. Date format elements

Format element	Function
- / , . ; :	Punctuation may be included anywhere in the date format string, and will be included in the output.
'text'	Quoted text may also be included in the date format string, and will be reproduced in the output.
AD or A.D. BC or B.C.	Includes an AD or BC indicator with the date.
AM or A.M. PM or P.M.	Prints AM or PM, whichever applies, given the time in question.
CC	Century number. This is 20 for years 1900 through 1999.
D	Number of the day of the week. This is 1 through 7.
DAY	Name of the day. This is Saturday, Sunday, Monday, etc.

Table B-3. Date format elements (continued)

Format element	Function
DD	Day of the month.
DDD	Day of the year.
DL	Returns a date in a long-date format, which depends on NLS_TERRITORY and NLS_LANGUAGE. May be combined only with TS.
DS	Returns a date in a short-date format, which depends on NLS_TERRITORY and NLS_LANGUAGE. May be combined only with TS.
DY	Abbreviation for name of the day. This is Sat, Sun, Mon, and so forth.
E	Abbreviation for era name. Valid only for the following calendars: Japanese Imperial, ROC Official, and Thai Buddha. Input only.
EE	Full era name.
FF FF1..FF9	Fractional seconds. Valid only when used with TIMESTAMP values. Prior to Oracle Database 10*g*, use FF (two Fs) regardless of the number of decimal digits you wish to see or use. Any other number of Fs is invalid. Beginning with Oracle Database 10*g*, you may use FF1..FF9 to specify the number of fractional digits you desire.
FM	Element that toggles suppression of blanks in output from conversion. (FM stands for Fill Mode.)
FX	Element that requires exact pattern matching between data and format model. (FX stands for Format eXact.)
HH	Hour of the day. This is 1–12.
HH12	Hour of the day. This is 1–12, the same as HH.
HH24	Hour of the day on a 24-hour clock. This is 0–23.
I	Last digit of the ISO standard year. Output only.
IW	Week in the year, from 1–52 or 1–53, based on the ISO standard. Output-only.
IY	Last two digits of the ISO standard year. Output only.
IYY	Last three digits of the ISO standard year. Output only.
IYYY	Four-digit ISO standard year. Output only.
J	Julian day. Day 1 is equivalent to Jan 1, 4712 BC.
MI	Minute.
MM	Month number.
MON	Three-letter month abbreviation.
MONTH	Month name, fully spelled out.
Q	Quarter of the year. Quarter 1 is Jan-Mar, quarter 2 is Apr-Jun, and so forth.
RM	Month number in Roman numerals.
RR	When used with TO_CHAR, returns the last two digits of the year.
RRRR	When used with TO_CHAR, returns the four-digit year.
SCC	Same as CC, but BC dates will be negative.

Format element	Function
SP	Suffix that converts a number to its spelled format. This element can appear at the end of any element that results in a number. For example, a mask such as "DDth-Mon-Yyyysp" results in output such as "15th-Nov-One Thousand Nine Hundred Sixty-One." The return value is in English, regardless of the date language. (Yyyy resulted in mixed-case words).
SPTH	Suffix that converts a number to its spelled and ordinal format; for example, 4 becomes FOURTH and 1 becomes FIRST. This element can appear at the end of any element that results in a number. For example, a mask such as "Ddth Mon, Yyyysp" results in output such as " Fifteenth Nov, One Thousand Nine Hundred Sixty-One." The return value is in English, regardless of the date language.
SS	Second.
SSSSS	Number of seconds since midnight.
SYEAR	Year spelled out in words, with a leading negative sign when the year is BC.
SYYYY	Four-digit year, with a leading negative sign when the year is BC.
TH	Suffix that converts a number to its ordinal format; for example, 4 becomes 4th and 1 becomes 1st. This element can appear at the end of any element that results in a number. For example, "DDth-Mon-YYYY" results in output such as "15th-Nov-1961." The return value is in English, regardless of the date language.
TS	Returns a time in a short-time format, which depends on NLS_TERRITORY and NLS_LANGUAGE. May be combined with only DL or DS.
TZD	Abbreviated time zone name; for example: EST, PST, etc. This is an input-only format, which may seem odd at first.
TZH	Time zone hour displacement. For example, -5 indicates a time zone five hours earlier than UTC.
TZM	Time zone minute displacement. For example -5:30 indicates a time zone that is five hours, thirty-minutes earlier than UTC. A few such time zones do exist.
TZR	Time zone region. For example, "US/Eastern" is the region in which EST (Eastern Standard Time) and EDT (Eastern Daylight Time) are valid.
W	Week of the month. Week one starts on the first of the month. Week two starts on the 8th of the month, and so forth.
WW	Week of the year.
X	Local radix character. In American-English, this is a period (.). This element can be placed in front of FF, so that fractional seconds are properly interpreted and represented.
Y	Last digit of the year number.
Y,YYY	Four-digit year with a comma after the first digit.
YEAR	Year spelled out in words.
YY	Last two digits of the year number.
YYY	Last three digits of the year number.
YYYY	Four-digit year.

The one SQL*Plus command that does recognize these date format elements is the ACCEPT command. When you ask the user to enter a date, you can provide a date format specification. SQL*Plus rejects any date the user enters that doesn't match that format.

When displaying a date, you can use the TO_CHAR function to specify the format. The following example displays the current value of SYSDATE, including the time:

```
SQL> SELECT TO_CHAR(SYSDATE,'dd-Mon-yyyy hh:mi:ss PM')
  2    FROM dual;

TO_CHAR(SYSDATE,'DD-MON
-----------------------
13-Dec-1998 09:13:59 PM
```

When you use a date format element that displays a text value, such as the name of a month, you need to pay attention to the case. The case of the element displayed follows the case used when you specified the element. Suppose you want to display the three-letter abbreviation for a month. You could place "Mon," "mon," or "MON" in your format string, and you would get back "Dec," "dec," or "DEC," respectively. You will see examples of this in Table B-4, which shows the results of several sample date format specifications.

Table B-4. Date format examples

Value	Format	Result
13-Dec-1998 09:13:59 PM	dd-mon-yyyy	13-dec-1998
13-Dec-1998 09:13:59 PM	dd-Mon-yyyy	13-Dec-1998
13-Dec-1998 09:13:59 PM	DD-MON-YYYY	13-DEC-1998
13-Dec-1998 09:13:59 PM	Month dd, yyyy	December 13, 1998
13-Dec-1998 09:13:59 PM	Month dd, yyyy "at" hh:mi am	December 13, 1998 at 09:13 pm
13-Dec-1998 09:13:59 PM	mm/dd/yy	12/13/98
13-Dec-1998 09:13:59 PM	mm/dd/rr	12/13/98
13-Dec-1998 09:13:59 PM	mm/dd/yyyy	12/13/1998
13-Dec-1998 09:13:59 PM	Day	Sunday
13-Dec-1998 09:13:59 PM	ddd	347
13-Dec-1998 09:13:59 PM	ww	50
13-Dec-1998 09:13:59 PM	q	4
13-Dec-1998 09:13:59 PM	year	nineteen ninety-eight
13-Dec-1998 09:13:59 PM	Year	Nineteen Ninety-Eight
13-Dec-1998 09:13:59 PM	YEAR	NINETEEN NINETY-EIGHT

To find out how to use a date format with the ACCEPT command, consult Chapter 11. ACCEPT uses the date format to validate what the user enters, and there are some limits on how closely the user is forced to follow that format.

Index

Symbols

/* and */ comment delimiters, 236, 432
* (asterisk)
    identifying errors in SQL statements, 55
    line-editing keyword, 51, 449, 454
    in SELECT statement, 91, 92
@ (at sign) command, 67, 432
    disabling, 430
&& (double ampersand)
    in variables, 212–215
    with substitution variables, problems
        with, 216
@@ (double at sign) command, 433
    disabling, 430
-- (double hyphens) for comment
        delimiters, 237, 432
/ (forward slash), executing SQL buffer, 433
. (period), terminating PL/SQL blocks, 42
; (semicolon)
    improper SQL termination, 65
    terminate PL/SQL blocks, 65
    terminate SQL statements, 36, 503
        in SQL*Plus, 36
        SET SQLTERMINATOR, 503
& (single ampersand) command, in
        variables, 208–212

A

ABORT parameter (SHUTDOWN), 515
aborting database instance, 515

ACC[EPT] command, 215, 434
    format specifications with, 525, 527, 529
    validating user input, 341–345
access method hints, 394
administration
    automating routine DBA tasks, 10
    starting/stopping databases, 514, 517
advanced reports
    current date into headers, 187–189
        formatting, 188, 189
        from Oracle, 187
    formatting object columns, 193–196
    headers and footers, 189–193
    summary reports, 196–200
    timestamping spool files, 191
    totals and subtotals, 174–187
        COMP[UTE] and BRE[AK]
            commands, 180
        printing grand totals, 180–187
        printing subtotals, 176–180
    unions, 200–205
        final report, 204–205
        typical example, 201
        UNION query, 202–204
advanced scripting, 308–357
    bind variables, 309–325
    blank lines, generating, 341
    conditional execution, 325–337
        multilevel file structure, using, 330
        OS scripting language for, 336
        PL/SQL for, 335

We'd like to hear your suggestions for improving our indexes. Send email to *index@oreilly.com*.

COUNT function, 115
COUNT operation (EXPLAIN PLAN), 375
COU[NT] parameter (COMPUTE
        command), 446
CRE[ATE] parameter
    COPY command, 448
    SAVE command, 464
    STORE command, 519
CSS (cascading style sheets), 157
CSV (Comma Separated Values)
        format, 244, 247
current line (line editor), 44
CURSOR_SHARING_EXACT hint, 399
customizing environment with startup
        scripts, 419

D

data
    deleting, 96
    detecting bad data, 266
    extracting, 243–259
        Excel-specific hack, 257–259
        files, output types, 244, 245
        formatting the data, 247–253
        formulating the query, 246
        limitations of SQL*Plus, 245
        scripts for, 246–257
        spooling to a file, 253–255
        user-friendly scripts, 255–257
    inserting, 90
    merging, 91
    reloading, 259–272
        DDL and DML, executing, 260
        external tables, using, 267–272
        SQL*Loader utility (see SQL*Loader
            utility)
    retrieving, 91
    sample, 13
    samples, obtaining, xviii
data definition language (see DDL)
data dictionary
    case sensitivity to, 285
    definition of, 278
    master key, 306
    scripts, 297–303
        clean slate for, 303
        index headings, generating, 302
        owner and table name separation, 301
        parameter omitted, 300
        running, 300

self documenting, 306
    views, 278–280
        ALL, 279
        DBA, 279
        naming of, 306
        types, correspondence between, 279
        types of, 279, 280
        USER, 279
data format specifications, 525
data manipulation language (see DML)
database administration, 10
database administrator (see DBA)
database sample for book, 11–19
    data model (ERD), 11
    data of, 13
    loading, 14–19
        privileges needed, 15
    script files, 15, 16
databases
    aborting instance of, 515
    archive and recovery information, 486
    choosing default, 21
    command prompt without disconnect,
            HOST command, 34
    committing changes automatically, 466
    data dictionary
        definition of, 278
        views, 278–280
    disconnecting from, DISCONNECT
            command, 34
    exploring, 273–307
    immediate shutdown, 515
    logging into, 27
        CONN[ECT] command, 33, 34, 447
        default database for, 484
        error accessing PRODUCT_USER_
            PROFILE, 29
        startup scripts, 418
    maintaining with DDL statements, 252
    object information, viewing, 273
    passwords for, changing, 454
    starting and stopping, 514, 517
    tables, listing column definitions, 32
    viewing object information, 449
datatypes
    checking when COPYing, 474
    function return values, viewing, 274
    returning column information, 285
DATE datatype (SQL*Loader), 263
DATE parameter (ACCEPT), 344

environment; variables *(continued)*
  script search path, 422
  service name LOCAL environment
    variable, 422–424
  SQL*Plus, significant, 422–425
  Windows GUI version, 425
ERD (Entity Relationship Diagram) (sample
  database), 11
error codes, capturing, 351–353
error-handling limitations in
  SQL*Plus, 349–355
ERR[ORS] parameter (SHOW), 512, 513
ESC[APE] setting, 232, 480
escaping the substitution variable prefix, 480
Excel-specific hack, extracting data, 257–259
EXEC[UTE] command, 42, 312, 450
executing
  DDL and DML, 260
  / (forward slash) command, 433
  single PL/SQL statement, 450
  SQL, 35, 433
execution plans, 363–379
  creating plan table, 365
  displaying plan, 367–372
  execution statistics. displaying, 380–384
  explaining queries, 366
  improving performance, 385–399
  interpreting results, 367–379
  judging results, 385
  operations, 374–379
  performance views, accessing, 379
  query output, suppressing, 383
  understanding, 367
execution statistics, 381
EXISTS subquery, 121
EXIT clause (WHENEVER), 355, 523
EXIT command, 19, 30, 451
exiting, 451
exiting SQL*Plus, 30, 451
EXP[LAIN] parameter (SET
  AUTOTRACE), 468
EXPLAIN PLAN, 10, 358, 363–379
  creating plan table, 364, 365
  displaying execution plan, 367–372
  interpreting results, 367, 373–379
  syntax for, 366
external text editors, 61
  editing buffers with, 450

F

FACT hint, 395
failure codes, 351
  passing back to shell scripts, 355
FAILURE parameter
  EXIT command, 451
  QUIT command, 456
  WHENEVER SQLERROR
    command, 351, 355, 523
FEED[BACK] setting, 221, 481
  spooling data to file, 253
feedback, turning off, 253
filename extension, default, 504
files
  data output files, types of, 244, 245
    DDL files, 245
    delimited files, 244
    fixed-width files, 244
  default extension for command files, 504
  global login, 419
  glogin.sql script (site profile), 418
  login.sql script, 419
  sending report output to, 142
  spooling data to, 253–255
  spool,timestamping, 191
  SQL*Loader control file, 260
  startup scripts, 418
FILTER operation (EXPLAIN PLAN), 375
FIRST ROW operation (EXPLAIN
  PLAN), 375
FIRST_ROWS hint, 393
FLAGGER setting, 482
FLOAT datatype, 286
FLU[SH] setting, 482
FOLD_A[FTER] parameter (COLUMN
  command), 443
FOLD_B[EFORE] parameter (COLUMN
  command), 443
font size for reports, 140
footers and headers
  bottom title, 136
  HTML reports, 157–170
  report pages, 439, 519
  reports, print once, 189–193
  system variables for defining, 136
  top title, 134
FOR UPDATE operation (EXPLAIN
  PLAN), 375
FORCE parameter (STARTUP), 517
foreign key constraints, 288

NO_QUERY_TRANSFORMATION hint,
395
NO_REWRITE hint, 395
normal database shutdown, 515
NORMAL parameter (SHUTDOWN), 515
NO_STAR_TRANSFORMATION hint, 395
NOT IN predicates, nulls in, 123
NO_UNNEST hint, 395
NO_USE_HASH hint, 397
NO_USE_MERGE hint, 397
NO_USE_NL hint, 397
NUL[L] clause (COLUMN), 444
NULL setting, 488
null string as column separator, 471
NULLIF clause (SQL*Loader), 264
nulls, 102–106
    detecting, 104
    in expressions, 105, 106
    in NOT IN predicates, 123
NUMBER datatype, 286, 522
    column width for displaying, 490
    default formatting, 489
    formatting
        elements, 526
        examples, 527
    validating, 342
NUM[BER] parameter
    ACCEPT command, 434
    COMPUTE command, 446
numeric substitution variables, 216
numbers, formatting, 526
NUMF[ORMAT] setting, 489
NUM[WIDTH] setting, 490
NVARCHAR2 datatype, 522

O

object types, viewing information
    on, 276–277
OLD_V[ALUE] clause (COLUMN
    command), 155, 444
ON clause (COMPUTE), 179, 180
OPEN parameter (STARTUP), 518
operating systems, xvi
    allowing output buffers, 482
    errors, 523
    scripting language, using with, 336
operators, UNION, 202–204
optimizer, 358
    goal hints, 393

OPTIONALLY ENCLOSED BY clause
    (SQL*Loader), 263
options, iSQL*Plus, 426
Oracle BIN directory, 68
Oracle Enterprise Manager software, 277
Oracle home directory, 68
Oracle version, specifying, 472
ORDER clause (SELECT), 113
ORDERED hint, 396
OSERROR parameter (WHENEVER), 350,
    523
OUT parameter, returned values,
    displaying, 322
output from PL/SQL execution, 495
output, scripts
    allowing operating system buffers, 482
    displaying case, 496
    echoing, commands, turning off, 477
    prompt text, customizing, 218
    suppressing from display
        feedback, 253
        prompting for values and, 212, 216
        verification, 509
    trailing spaces, suppressing, 253
    wrapping lines, 510, 528
OWNER column, ALL_CONSTRAINTS
    view, 289

P

packages
    built-in PL/SQL, 321
    describing, 276–277
    error in, showing, 513
    UTL_MAIL or UTL_SMTP, Oracle built
        in, 364
page breaks in reports, 144, 437
page headers and footers (reports), 439, 519
pages, report, 138
PAGES[IZE] setting, 491
    spooling data to files, 253
parallel execution hints, 397, 398
PARALLEL hint, 397
parallel processing hints, 397, 398
PARALLEL_INDEX hint, 397
PARAMETER[S] parameter (SHOW), 512
parsing user input, SQL for, 347
PARTITION operation (EXPLAIN
    PLAN), 377
PASSW[ORD] command, 30, 454
passwords, changing, 454

About the Author

Jonathan Gennick is a writer and editor with more than 10 years of programming and relational database experience. He writes extensively on Oracle and SQL topics, and is well-known for such successful O'Reilly books as *Oracle SQL*Plus: The Definitive Guide*, *Oracle SQL*Plus Pocket Reference*, *Oracle SQL*Loader: The Definitive Guide*, *Oracle Net8 Configuration and Troubleshooting*, and, most recently, *SQL Pocket Guide*.

In addition to writing books, Jonathan is a frequent contributor to *Oracle Magazine*. His articles, often describing new features, have been a fixture in *Oracle Magazine* since mid-2000. Jonathan often likes to delve deeply into aspects of SQL, or of Oracle, and does so in his articles on his own web site, or in articles that run in his Oracle-article email list.

Jonathan holds a Bachelor of Arts degree in Information and Computer Science from Andrews University in Berrien Springs, Michigan. He currently resides in Munising, Michigan, with his wife Donna and their two children: 15-year-old Jenny, who often wishes her father wouldn't spend quite so much time writing, and 8-year-old Jeff, who has never seen it any other way.

Jonathan enjoys hearing from readers and does his best to answer questions about his writing. Contact him through his web site (*http://www.gennick.com*), where interested readers can also subscribe to his Oracle-article list.

Colophon

Our look is the result of reader comments, our own experimentation, and feedback from distribution channels. Distinctive covers complement our distinctive approach to technical topics, breathing personality and life into potentially dry subjects.

The animal on the cover of *Oracle SQL*Plus: The Definitive Guide*, Second Edition is a moving leaf (*Phyllium giganteum*), a large (about 10 cm in length) Malaysian leaf insect related to stick insects; together these constitute the order Phasmatida, derived from the Greek word for "ghost." These stunning insects imitate local foliage with intricate detail, down to the leaf-like veins on their legs and tattered brown edges to mimic dead leaves. Moving leaf insects feed on bramble and other plant material. Kept by many entymologists as exotic pets, they require high temperature and humidity.

Matt Hutchinson was the production editor for *Oracle SQL*Plus: The Definitive Guide*, Second Edition. GEX, Inc. provided production services. Darren Kelly and Marlowe Shaeffer provided quality control.

Edie Freedman designed the cover of this book. The cover image is a 19th-century engraving from the Dover Pictorial Archive. Clay Fernald produced the cover layout with QuarkXPress 4.1 using Adobe's ITC Garamond font.

David Futato designed the interior layout. This book was converted by Julie Hawks to FrameMaker 5.5.6 with a format conversion tool created by Erik Ray, Jason McIntosh, Neil Walls, and Mike Sierra that uses Perl and XML technologies. The text font is Linotype Birka; the heading font is Adobe Myriad Condensed; and the code font is LucasFont's TheSans Mono Condensed. The illustrations that appear in the book were produced by Robert Romano and Jessamyn Read using Macromedia FreeHand MX and Adobe Photoshop CS (except for Figure 4-1, which was provided by Matt Williams). The tip and warning icons were drawn by Christopher Bing. This colophon was written by Nancy Kotary.

Better than e-books

Search
inside electronic versions of thousands of books

Browse
books by category. With Safari researching any topic is a snap

Find
answers in an instant

Read books from cover to cover. Or, simply click to the page you need.

Search Safari! The premier electronic reference library for programmers and IT professionals

Related Titles Available from O'Reilly

Oracle PL/SQL

Learning Oracle PL/SQL

Oracle PL/SQL Best Practices

Oracle PL/SQL Developer's Workbook

Oracle PL/SQL Language Pocket Reference, *3rd Edition*

Oracle PL/SQL Programming, *3nd Edition*

Oracle Books for DBAs

Oracle DBA Checklists Pocket Reference

Oracle RMAN Pocket Reference

Unix for Oracle DBAs Pocket Reference

Oracle SQL and SQL Plus

Mastering Oracle SQL

Oracle SQL Plus: The Definitive Guide

Oracle SQL Tuning Pocket Reference

Oracle SQL*Plus Pocket Reference, *2nd Edition*

Oracle SQL: The Essential Reference

Oracle

Building Oracle XML Applications

Java Programming with Oracle JDBC

Oracle Application Server 10g Essentials

Oracle Essentials: Oracle Database 10g, *3rd Edition*

Oracle in a Nutshell

Perl for Oracle DBAs

TOAD Pocket Reference

Keep in touch with O'Reilly

1. Download examples from our books

To find example files for a book, go to:

www.oreilly.com/catalog

select the book, and follow the "Examples" link.

2. Register your O'Reilly books

Register your book at *register.oreilly.com*

Why register your books?
Once you've registered your O'Reilly books you can:

- Win O'Reilly books, T-shirts or discount coupons in our monthly drawing.
- Get special offers available only to registered O'Reilly customers.
- Get catalogs announcing new books (US and UK only).
- Get email notification of new editions of the O'Reilly books you own.

3. Join our email lists

Sign up to get topic-specific email announcements of new books and conferences, special offers, and O'Reilly Network technology newsletters at:

elists.oreilly.com

It's easy to customize your free elists subscription so you'll get exactly the O'Reilly news you want.

4. Get the latest news, tips, and tools

www.oreilly.com

- "Top 100 Sites on the Web"—PC Magazine
- CIO Magazine's Web Business 50 Awards

Our web site contains a library of comprehensive product information (including book excerpts and tables of contents), downloadable software, background articles, interviews with technology leaders, links to relevant sites, book cover art, and more.

5. Work for O'Reilly

Check out our web site for current employment opportunities:

jobs.oreilly.com

6. Contact us

O'Reilly & Associates
1005 Gravenstein Hwy North
Sebastopol, CA 95472 USA

TEL: 707-827-7000 or 800-998-9938
      (6am to 5pm PST)

FAX: 707-829-0104

order@oreilly.com
For answers to problems regarding your order or our products. To place a book order online, visit:

www.oreilly.com/order_new

catalog@oreilly.com
To request a copy of our latest catalog.

booktech@oreilly.com
For book content technical questions or corrections.

corporate@oreilly.com
For educational, library, government, and corporate sales.

proposals@oreilly.com
To submit new book proposals to our editors and product managers.

international@oreilly.com
For information about our international distributors or translation queries. For a list of our distributors outside of North America check out:

international.oreilly.com/distributors.html

adoption@oreilly.com
For information about academic use of O'Reilly books, visit:

academic.oreilly.com

O'REILLY®

Our books are available at most retail and online bookstores.
To order direct: 1-800-998-9938 • *order@oreilly.com* • *www.oreilly.com*
Online editions of most O'Reilly titles are available by subscription at *safari.oreilly.com*